The Food Lover's Guide to Paris

Fourth Edition

CHOCOLAT
ET
THÉ
CONSOMMATION
DE CHOIX
BIÈRE
BRUNE & BLONDE
TÉLÉPHONE
Sauté
de Veau
Riz
CONCERT
DE
SOUTIEN

FOURTH EDITION

The Food Lover's Guide to Paris

PATRICIA WELLS

Assisted in various editions by

SUSAN HERRMANN LOOMIS

Jane Sigal

Sarah Greenberg

Heather Mallory

Photographs by

Peter Turnley and Steven Rothfeld

Workman Publishing, New York

On the front cover: Ladurée (left), classic Parisian facade (right); on the back cover: La Palette (top), L'Ambroisie (bottom)

 Published simultaneously in Canada by Thomas Allen & Son Limited.

Library of Congress Cataloging-in Publication Data.

Wells, Patricia.
The food lover's guide to Paris / Patricia Wells:
assisted by Susan Herrmann Loomis . . . [et al.] :
photographs by Peter Turnley and Steven Rothfeld. — 4th ed.
p. cm.
Includes index.
ISBN 0-7611-1479-3
1. Restaurants,—France—Paris Guidebooks.
2. Grocery trade—France—Paris Guidebooks. 3. Cookery, French.
4. Hotels—France—Paris Guidebooks.
5. Paris (France)—Guidebooks. I. Title.
TX907.5.F72P3778 1999
647.95443'61—dc21 99-22292
CIP

Workman books are available at special discounts when purchased in bulk for premiums and sales promotions as well as for fund-raising or educational use. Special editions or book excerpts can also be created to specification. For details, contact the Special Sales Director at the address below.

Workman Publishing Company, Inc.
708 Broadway
New York, NY 10003-9555

Manufactured in the United States of America
Fourth edition first printing, April 1999
10 9 8 7 6 5 4 3

To Walter, with gratitude
for his unwavering love,
trust, and support.

Acknowledgments

Thanks to the generosity, enthusiasm, and encouragement of so many fine people over the years, much of the work on this book was transformed into sheer pleasure. I am deeply grateful to Susan Herrmann Loomis, Jane Sigal, Sarah Greenberg, and Heather Mallory, who have assisted me with the four editions.

I was touched by the generosity of the French chefs, bakers, restaurateurs, and shopkeepers who gave so freely of their time and expertise and shared their recipes.

None of this would have been possible without the remarkable confidence of Peter Workman and the expert attention of my editor, Suzanne Rafer, who believed in both me and the book when others remained doubtful. Thanks also go to Kathie Ness for her careful editing and to Paul Hanson for the beautiful design of the book.

Introduction to the Fourth Edition

Paris has been my home for almost twenty years, and not a day passes without a new discovery, disappointment, revelation, elation. I love the city as one loves a human being, filling with joy with the unearthing of a golden, crackling, crusty *baguette,* surging with anticipation at the opening of a bustling new bistro, contented with the satisfaction of a wholesome, gratifying meal at a favorite haunt, frustrated by the internationalization and universality of much of the world's cuisine. Paris is still born anew with each season, and the sighting of the first asparagus, sweet cherry, fragrant morel, briny oyster, golden Vacherin cheese, or earthy wild duck is cause for confident expectation and celebration.

When I moved to this gracious city in the gray days of January 1980, Paris wrapped me in its net. Everything was new, and there was everything to learn about a culture steeped in history, tradition, and excellence. Food, of course, has long been one of its main attractions, with lively open-air markets, cafés for lingering and contemplation, bistros for stellar meals laden with the aura of good times among friends.

I have witnessed the birth, flourishing, and death of *nouvelle cuisine,* shared in the ascendance of many of today's finest chefs (Guy Savoy, Bernard Pacaud, Alain Dutournier, Alain Passard, Michel Rostang, and Jean-Pierre Vigato), watched as bistros and brasseries came in and went out of favor many times over (Allard, L'Ami Louis, Benoit, Chez Georges, Balzar, Bofinger), and witnessed the transformation of many of the city's most historic dining spots (Le Grand Véfour, Le Pré Catelan, Laurent, Les Ambassadeurs, Jules Verne). Good fortune shone upon me as I was able to chart the birth, meteoric rise, and retirement of the century's most influential chef, Joël Robuchon. And now I can bask in the sunshine of his talents as his acolytes—Benoit Guichard at Jamin, Frédéric Anton at Le Pré Catelan, and Eric Lecerf at L'Astor—work their own personal form of magic. Some restaurants—Taillevent, Le Petit Marguery, Au Trou Gascon—never let me down over the years and fueled my conviction that hard work, intelligence, and a willingness to change all make for a fine, successful career in any field. Modern cuisine came in the form of "baby" bistros set up by some of Paris's finest chefs, and once the 1990s rolled around, a whole new crop of chef-owner restaurants fueled our enthusiasm for contemporary fare: restaurants such as Les Olivades, La Bastide d'Odéon, Chez Michel, Eric Frechon, L'Epi Dupin, Bamboche, Au Bon Accueil, all flourish at the hands of young modern chefs with heads on their shoulders.

But perhaps the greatest change for the positive has been the constant multiplication of varieties of fruits and vegetables at our disposal, with dozens of sizes, shapes, and flavors given to the once lowly potato; new colors, flavors, and sweetness to the choice of strawberries; tomatoes that taste of the garden all year round; and markets with no fewer than twenty-five varieties of farm-fresh apples. Organic poultry farms now bring us robust, chewy chickens that would make our grandmothers weep with joy, and constant innovation in the meat world—from succulent and tender lamb to delicate veal—makes cooking and dining a joy. As France takes greater pride in the fish and shellfish from its waters, we find markets laden with glistening swordfish and tuna, plump and briny oysters sold by the names of their growers, excellent farm-raised sea bass and turbot, and plump, rich scallops from Brittany's coast.

Bread went through its awkward stage in Paris during the past twenty years. The fragrant, golden, wheaty, crispy *baguette* became almost a dinosaur, only to be reborn with the passion of such bakers as Eric Kayser, Michel Moisan, Philippe Gosselin, Jean-Noël Julien, and Stéphane Delaunay. Paris pastry shops remain a mystery to me, however, as most remain stuck in a classical fog with minimal creativity on the horizon, save for the innovations of such chefs as Pierre Hermé, Gérard Mulot, and Gérard Beaufort.

While some sectors, such as cheese and *charcuterie,* see little change, I have witnessed an increasing standard of excellence for regional products that find their way to the capital's markets and tables. In recent years the coveted A.O.C. *(appellation d'origine controlée)* has been awarded to olives and oil from Nyons and Mausanne in Provence, honey from the Lorraine, tiny green lentils from the Auvergne, guinea hen from the Drôme. All the while the organic world expands, as special markets and supermarkets make it possible for organic farmers to reach new customers, with a flourish of organic breads, meats, poultry, wines, and dairy products.

On the flip side, a low-quality supermarket blandness seems to blanket the world wherever I go: I cannot imagine *who* would want to be proud of the flabby *baguette* sandwiches, tasteless salads, and oversweetened desserts I find on the trains, in cafés, and at some establishments that dare to call themselves restaurants. More than ever, the slogan is "Buyer (and diner) beware."

But, despite a world of cuisine sameness, French food remains essentially French. Chefs may use a touch of lemongrass, a few more grains of coriander, the spices of Moroccan harissa, and they may borrow from Japanese technique as well as presentation, but at its core French cuisine remains tied to its roots, whether it is the vegetable garden or the olive grove, the vineyard or the barnyard.

Like all of us, the city and its cuisine are pulled in two directions. On the one hand, we all want to be modern, slim, and fit, gliding through our days with delicious food at our fingertips with a minimum of fuss and labor. On the other hand, discipline takes a day off as gourmandise wins out and we weaken against the onslaught of crusty bread, bittersweet chocolates, golden French fries, and hearty stews at our disposal. As I have learned from the French, moderation is the key to life, as is the ability to appreciate and savor life in measured doses. I hope that this new edition of *The Food Lover's Guide* will tempt as well as inspire, excite as well as inform, all the while satisfying our endless craving for all that is Paris.

Paris, 1999

To remain up to date on the food scene in Paris, visit www.patriciawells.com

A Taste for Paris

From the moment I set foot in France one chilly, gray January morning in 1973, I knew that Paris was a city I would love the rest of my life. More than a quarter of a century later, after spending twenty of those years in this gentle city, each day I am moved by Paris's elegance and beauty, its coquettish appeal. The quality of life here is better than in any other place I know, and eating well has much to do with it.

This is the book I came to Paris to write. Equal only to my passion for food is my love for reporting. I have always thought that one of the most enjoyable aspects of journalism is that you get to know people on their own turf, and you get to poke around, asking the questions that any curious person wants answers to. In researching this book, I—along with various companions—walked just about every street in Paris in search of the gastronomic best the city has to offer, talking, chatting, interviewing, meeting with the city's men and women who are responsible for all things great and edible. We set out to find the crispest *baguette,* the thickest cup of steaming hot chocolate; to spot the most romantic site for a warm morning *croissant* or a sun-kissed summer lunch; to track down the trustiest cheese or chocolate shop; to uncover the happiest place to sip wine on a brisk winter's day. We quickly gave up counting the number of times we got lost or rained out as we checked off addresses and discovered back streets and sleepy neighborhoods. We toured the markets and tea salons, sparred with butchers, laughed with the owners of a favorite bistro, and shared the incomparable aroma of a great loaf of bread as it came crackling from the oven. We rose eagerly at dawn to catch a pastry chef as he pulled the first batch of steaming *croissants* from his wood-fired oven; climbed down rickety ladders into warm and cozy baking cellars to discuss the state of the French *baguette* with a skilled baker; shivered as we toured aromatic, humid, spotless rooms stacked with aging Brie and Camembert, Vacherin and Roquefort. Each day we lunched and dined, sometimes at modest neighborhood bistros, sometimes in fine restaurants. We gathered recipes from pastry chefs, cooks, bakers, and tea shop owners, and tested, tested, tested until my apartment took on the same irresistible mixture of aromas as the food streets and shops of Paris. Throughout, it was an exhilarating labor of love, one from which I hope you will profit, the joy of which I hope you will share.

This is a personal guide, and whenever I had to decide whether to include or delete a shop, a restaurant, a market, I asked myself one question: Would I want to go back there again? If the answer was no, the address was tossed into the ever-growing reject file.

In choosing restaurants, I have tried to be comprehensive but selective. I have tried as best I know how to tell you exactly what I think you will want to know about a restaurant: why you should go, where it is, how to get there, what you'll find when you arrive, and what it will cost. I intentionally did not rate restaurants, for I find personal restaurant ratings clumsy, arbitrary, and generally unreliable. Besides, they make a burdensome science out of what should, essentially, be joyful discovery.

No doubt, some places you will love less than I. Some you will love more. I hope this book will stimulate every reader to explore, look around, and ask questions, and will help everyone to understand just a bit more clearly the history, daily customs, and rich texture of Paris, the great gastronomic capital of the world.

How to Use This Book

Alphabetizing

Within each chapter, establishments are grouped by the *arrondissements* in which they are located, then listed in alphabetical order. Following French style, any articles such as *au, la,* or *le* and words such as *bistro, brasserie, café,* or *chez* that appear before the proper name of the establishment are ignored in the alphabetizing. For example, Brasserie de la Poste, Le Petit Marguery, and Au Pied de Cochon are all listed under the letter *P.* Likewise, when the name of a restaurant is also the full name of a person, such as Guy Savoy, the last name (Savoy) is used for purposes of alphabetizing.

What's an arrondissement?

Many major cities are divided into variously named districts for easy identification and organization. Paris is divided into twenty *arrondissements,* within each of which there may be several *quartiers,* or neighborhoods. The *arrondissements* are arranged numerically in a spiral, beginning in the center of the city on the Right Bank (with the 1st *arrondissement* at the Louvre and Les Halles) and moving clockwise, making two complete spirals until reaching the central eastern edge of the city (at the 20th *arrondissement,* at Père Lachaise cemetery).

In organizing the book, we have listed establishments by *arrondissement,* also noting the popular quarters—the Madeleine, Montmartre, Invalides—in which they are located.

Listings

Each listing presented in *The Food Lover's Guide to Paris* includes the following information: the name of the establishment; its address; its phone numbers; the closest Métro stop; when it is open and closed.

If applicable, any or all of the following information is also included: its fax number; its e-mail or Internet address; whether the establishment is air-conditioned; whether it has a terrace, outdoor dining, or private dining facilities; what the specialties include; what you can expect to spend; and what credit cards you can use.

Abbreviations

The following abbreviations are used for credit cards in the listings:

AE: American Express
DC: Diners Club
V: Visa or Carte Bleue

The following abbreviations are used in the recipes to indicate weights and measures:

cm: centimeter	ml: milliliter
g: gram	kg: kilogram
cl: centiliter	

THE EURO ARRIVES . . . GRADUALLY

France and ten other members of the European Union are abandoning their national currencies in favor of a single currency called the *euro*— valued at 6.55 francs, or approximately $1.20 (at 5.5 francs to the dollar), when it was introduced on January 1, 1999.

Although many shops and restaurants, as well as airlines and hotels, have begun posting prices in both euros and francs, the new currency will be used primarily for credit card and bank transactions until January 1, 2002, when coins and bills will be introduced. The euro and the national currency will both be in use until July 2002, when the franc becomes a mere souvenir.

Contents

INTRODUCTION TO THE FOURTH EDITION .... *vi*
A TASTE FOR PARIS .... *ix*
How to Use this Book .... *x*

Restaurants

RESTAURANTS 2

Palais-Royal, Les Halles, Tuileries *11*
1st arrondissement

Opéra, Bourse *27*
2nd arrondissement

Rambuteau, Temple, Arts et Métiers *32*
3rd arrondissement

Le Marais, Hôtel de Ville, Ile Saint-Louis *36*
4th arrondissement

Latin Quarter *45*
5th arrondissement

Saint-Germain des Prés, Luxembourg, Odéon, Montparnasse *50*
6th arrondissement

Faubourg Saint-Germain, Invalides, Ecole Militaire *68*
7th arrondissement

Madeleine, Saint-Lazare, Champs-Elysées, Place des Ternes .. *79*
8th arrondissement

Gare de l'Est, Gare du Nord, République *90*
9th and 10th arrondissements

Bastille, République *95*
11th arrondissement

Gare de Lyon, Bastille, Nation, Place d'Italie *102*
12th and 13th arrondissements

Denfert-Rochereau, Porte d'Orléans, Montparnasse *110*
14th arrondissement

Grenelle, Convention *118*
15th arrondissement

Trocadéro, Victor-Hugo, Bois de Boulogne 121
16th arrondissement

Clichy, Ternes, Wagram, Etoile 130
17th arrondissement and Clichy

Buttes-Chaumont, Nation 136
19th and 20th arrondissements

Restaurants: An Alphabetical Listing (with *arrondissements*) 138

Restaurants Listed by *Arrondissements* 139

Cafés

CAFES 141

Les Halles, Pont Neuf, Tuileries, Louvre 143
1st arrondissement

Châtelet, Marais, Ile Saint-Louis 147
4th arrondissement

Latin Quarter, Luxembourg, Saint-Germain, Sèvres-Babylone, Quai d'Orsay 150
5th, 6th, and 7th arrondissements

Champs-Elysées 155
8th arrondissement

Bastille, Oberkampf 156
11th arrondissement

Montparnasse, Grenelle 158
14th and 15th arrondissements

Victor-Hugo, Arc de Triomphe 160
16th arrondissement

Père Lachaise 163
20th arrondissement

Salons de Thé

TEA SALONS 164

Palais-Royal, Louvre, Tuileries 165
1st arrondissement

Marais 168
4th arrondissement

Luxembourg, Rue du Bac, Assemblée Nationale 169
6th and 7th arrondissements

Concorde, Madeleine, Champs-Elysées, Pigalle 172
8th and 9th arrondissements

Trocadéro, Ternes, Villiers 175
16th and 17th arrondissements

Bistros et Bars à Vin

Wine Bars 176

Les Halles, Palais-Royal 178
1st and 2nd arrondissements

Marais, Ile de la Cité 180
4th arrondissement

Luxembourg, Saint-Michel, Sèvres-Babylone, Ecole Militaire 182
5th, 6th, and 7th arrondissements

Les Grands Boulevards 188
8th arrondissement

Bastille, Nation 189
11th arrondissement

Denfert-Rochereau 191
14th arrondissement

Arc de Triomphe 192
17th arrondissement

Montmartre, Belleville 192
18th and 20th arrondissements

Marchés

Markets 195

Rues Commerçantes 199
Merchant Streets

Marchés Volants 207
Roving Markets

Markets at a Glance 218

Pâtisseries

Pastry Shops 220

Bastille, Ile Saint-Louis, Marais, Les Halles 221
2nd and 4th arrondissements

Latin Quarter, Saint-Germain 223
5th and 6th arrondissements

Sèvres-Babylone, Ecole Militaire, La Tour Maubourg 231
7th arrondissement

Madeleine, Champs-Elysées 233
8th arrondissement

Passy, Auteuil, Ternes 234
16th and 17th arrondissements

Ménilmontant 237
20th arrondissement

Boulangeries

BAKERIES 239

Les Halles, Bourse, Opéra 242
1st and 2nd arrondissements

République, Marais 246
3rd and 4th arrondissements

Latin Quarter 251
5th arrondissement

Saint-Germain, Sèvres-Babylone, La Tour Maubourg 256
6th and 7th arrondissements

Les Grands Boulevards 262
8th arrondissement

Faubourg, Saint-Antoine, Bastille, République, Vincennes 263
11th and 12th arrondissements

Bir Hakeim, Montparnasse, Plaisance 265
14th arrondissement

Convention, Porte de Vanves 268
15th arrondissement

Victor-Hugo, Auteuil, Saint Cloud 268
16th arrondissement

Arc de Triomphe, Porte Maillot, Villiers 270
17th arrondissement

Montmartre, Barbes-Rochechouart 271
18th arrondissement

Ménilmontant 272
20th arrondissement

Fromageries

CHEESE SHOPS 274

Opéra, Palais-Royal *277*
1st arrondissement

Temple *278*
3rd arrondissement

Ile Saint-Louis *278*
4th arrondissement

Bac, Sèvres-Babylone, Ecole Militaire *279*
7th arrondissement

Etoile, Madeleine *285*
8th arrondissement

Denfert-Rochereau, Porte d'Orleans, Porte de Versailles *286*
14th and 15th arrondissements

Courcelles, Villiers *288*
17th arrondissement

Montmartre *291*
18th arrondissement

Charcuteries

PREPARED FOODS TO GO 292

Marais, Bastille *294*
4th arrondissement

Saint-Germain des Prés, Odéon, Sèvres-Babylone *298*
6th arrondissement

Madeleine *299*
9th arrondissement

Victor-Hugo, Etoile, Villiers *302*
16th and 17th arrondissements

Chocolatiers

CHOCOLATE SHOPS 304

Bourse *306*
2nd arrondissement

Saint-Germain des Prés, Sèvres-Babylone, Ecole Militaire *306*
6th and 7th arrondissements

Madeleine, Rond-Point, Arc de Triomphe, Grands Boulevards, Trinité, Le Peletier, Gare Saint-Lazare ... *308*
8th and 9th arrondissements

Bastille ... *313*
11th arrondissement

Spécialités Gastronomiques

Specialty Shops 315

Palais-Royal, Opéra, Tuileries, Les Halles ... *316*
1st and 2nd arrondissements

Temple ... *319*
3rd arrondissement

Marais ... *320*
4th arrondissement

Saint-Germain, Invalides, Eiffel Tower ... *324*
6th and 7th arrondissements

Madeleine, Le Peletier, Gare du Nord ... *328*
8th and 9th arrondissements

Gare de l'Est, Oberkampf ... *333*
10th and 11th arrondissements

Pasteur ... *333*
15th arrondissement

Trocadéro, Ternes ... *334*
16th and 17th arrondissements

Vins et Alcools

Wine and Liquor Shops 336

Concorde, Bourse ... *337*
1st and 2nd arrondissements

Odéon, Saint-Germain des Prés, Rue du Bac ... *339*
6th and 7th arrondissements

Champs-Elysées, Madeleine, Grands Boulevards ... *341*
8th and 17th arrondissements

Librairies Spécialisées: Gastronomie

FOOD AND WINE BOOKSHOPS 345

Les Halles, Concorde, Opéra 345
1st arrondissement

Pyramides 346
2nd arrondissement

Saint-Michel, Monge 347
5th arrondissement

Odéon, Saint-Germain, Duroc 349
6th arrondissement

Musée d'Orsay 350
7th arrondissement

Pour la Maison

KITCHEN AND TABLEWARE SHOPS 351

Les Halles, Châtelet, Palais-Royal, Place des Victoires 352
1st and 2nd arrondissements

Marais, République 355
3rd and 4th arrondissements

Latin Quarter, Saint-Germain, Sèvres-Babylone, Montparnasse 365
5th, 6th, and 7th arrondissements

Madeleine, Courcelles, Franklin Roosevelt 373
8th arrondissement

Bastille 375
12th arrondissement

Montparnasse, Grenelle 376
15th arrondissement

Arc de Triomphe 376
16th arrondissement

FRENCH/ENGLISH FOOD GLOSSARY 377

FOOD LOVER'S READY REFERENCE 416

INDEX 422

RECIPE INDEX 430

Recipe Contents

Restaurants

RESTAURANTS 2

Fenouil Il Cortile, Sauce au Thon 14
Il Cortile's Fresh Fennel with Tuna Sauce

Cannelloni Chez La Vieille 25
Chez La Vieille's Corsican Spinach and Cheese Cannelloni

Côte de Boeuf en Croûte de Sel La Vieille 26
Chez La Vieille's Rib Steak with Salt and Pepper

Chou Farci Ambassade d'Auvergne 35
Ambassade d'Auvergne's Stuffed Cabbage

Saumon Fumé Mariné aux Aromates Benoit 38
Benoit's Marinated Smoked Salmon with Herbs

Salade Verte au Comte Moissonnier 47

Moissonnier's Tossed Green Salad with Gruyère

Scarole à la Julienne de Jambon et aux Pommes 49
Escarole Salad with Ham and Apples

Haricot de Mouton Chez René 51
Chez René's Mutton with White Beans

Fondant aux Poires Le Caméléon 56
Le Caméléon's Golden Pear Cake

Poulette à la Crème Gratinée Chez Maître Paul 64
Chez Maître Paul's Broiled Gratinéed Chicken

Choucroute 71
Sauerkraut, Sausages, and Bacon

Marquise au Chocolat Taillevent 88
Taillevent's Chocolate Cake

Sauce à la Pistache 89
Pistachio Sauce

Pâte de Pistache 89
Pistachio Paste

Saumon en Rillettes Julien 94
Julien's Salmon Pâté

Salade au Lard Cartet 97
Cartet's Salad of Bacon, Greens, Shallots, and Parsley

Salade Verte aux Echalotes et aux Ciboulettes L'Oulette 101
L'Oulette's Field Salad with Shallots and Chives

Lapin à la Moutarde 105
Rabbit with Mustard

Pot-au-Feu 106
Beef Simmered with Vegetables

Soupe de Pèches 108
Summer Peach Soup

Salade de Lardons de Thon La Cagouille 112
La Cagouille's Salad of Tuna and Curly Endive

Saumon Nature Sauce Basilic Le Duc 115
Le Duc's Salmon with Basil Sauce

Marinade de Thon Tiède et Fenouil, Vinaigrette aux Agrumes 120
Warm Fresh Tuna with Fennel and Spicy Citrus Vinaigrette

Paleron Braisé à la Bourgeoise 122
Benoit's Braised Beef Shoulder

Pasta Romantica 133
Claudio's Quick Fresh Tomato and Basil Pasta

Cafés

CAFES 141

Salade Niçoise 159
Summer Salad from Nice

Croque-Monsieur 162
Grilled Ham and Cheese Sandwich

Salons de Thé

TEA SALONS 164

Sablés à la Lavande Tea Follies 166
Tea Follies' Lavender Shortbread Cookies

Tarte Abricot Verlet 170
Verlet's Apricot Tart

Bistros et Bars à Vin

WINE BARS 176

Flognarde aux Framboises Caves Petrissans 184
Caves Petrissan's Raspberry Fruit Flan

Marchés

MARKETS 195

Espadon aux Capres, Citron, et Coriandre 203
Quick Swordfish with Capers, Lemon, and Cilantro

Capres à l'Huile d'Olive 203
Oil-Cured Capers

Pain Pépitas 211
Avenue de Saxe Pumpkin Seed Bread

Pâtisseries

PASTRY SHOPS 220

Madeleines 225
Lemon Tea Cakes

Brioche Mousseline Denis Ruffel 230
Denis Ruffel's Mousseline Brioche

Financiers 232
Almond Cakes

Kougelhoph André Lerch 236
André Lerch's Alsatian Coffee Cake

Boulangeries

BAKERIES 239

Pain de Mie Denis Ruffel 245
Denis Ruffel's Sandwich Loaf

Pissaladière 249
Provencal Onion Tarte

Pain 250
Basic Bread Dough

Pain Poilâne au Levain Naturel 253
Poilâne's Natural Sourdough Bread

Bostock Bernard Ganachaud 269
Bernard Ganachaud's Bostock

Fromageries

CHEESE SHOPS 274

Fontainebleau 284

Crème Fraîche 290

Fromage de Chèvre Mariné à l'Huile d'Herbes 290
Goat Cheese Marinated in Oil with Herbs

Chocolatiers

CHOCOLATE SHOPS 304

Macarons Créoles 312
Chocolate Macaroons

Spécialités Gastronomiques

SPECIALTY SHOPS 315

Cornichons 321
Tiny Tart Pickles

Ligo
Pickled Dill Cucumbers
MAISON

The Food Lover's Guide to Paris

Fourth Edition

Restaurants
RESTAURANTS

Studying the menu in elegant restaurant surroundings.

I am constantly being asked to name my favorite Paris restaurant. For me, that is akin to trying to name my best friend, favorite piece of music, film, or classic novel. The answer depends on the hour, the season, my mood, the company. This is a personal guide representing a cross section of Paris restaurants, including only those I enjoy returning to, those I recommend to others. I hope they will serve simply as a starting point, enabling you to begin exploring and sorting out until you discover the kinds of restaurants you like. You should not have a bad meal at any listed here. But this doesn't mean you can't.

I dine out in Paris four or five times each week. I always make a reservation and always arrive hungry, for that's one of the best compliments one can pay a chef. I dine anonymously and so am known at few of these restaurants. What do I look for? Final judgment rests on the quality of ingredients, the chef's creativity, and overall service. In menus, I look for a healthy balance of dishes. In wine lists, value and variety are essential. A good restaurant is like good theater: One leaves in a good frame of mind, with a feeling that the time and the money have been well spent.

Likewise, your restaurants and meals should be chosen according to your own mood and appetite, the time of year, and of course the time of day.

Where Am I, Anyway?

An American traveler once related this story: She was stopped on a street in Paris by another American visitor, who asked, in a state of sheer frustration, "What I don't understand here is with all these restaurants, how do you tell which ones are French? You know, the ones that serve soufflés." Slightly less complicated, but equally frustrating for visitors, are the distinctions among bistro, brasserie, and restaurant. Although the lines between bistro and restaurant are often blurred, here are a few definitions that should clear the matter.

Bistro

A traditional bistro is a rather small restaurant, traditionally a mom-and-pop establishment with mom at the cash register and pop at the stove. Bistro menus are usually handwritten or mimeographed, and offerings are limited to a small selection of traditional home-style dishes. Wine is generally offered by the *carafe,* while wines available by the bottle are listed on the single-page menu. Bistro décor is usually simple, not fancy (though Paris's Belle Epoque bistros have some of the city's most beautiful interiors), often with a long zinc bar, tile floors, paper tablecloths, and sturdy, serviceable tableware. At some of the most modest establishments, diners may share long tables.

Today the definition of *bistro* has been widely expanded, due to an increasing appetite for restaurants that are casual and less expensive, offering contemporary décor and updated traditional fare. So within the new crop of updated bistros, one might find modern art on the walls, waiters dressed in designer uniforms, and such nontraditional fare as grilled tuna, platters of Japanese-inspired raw fish (sushi), and daily specials influenced only by the chef's inspiration of the morning.

Brasserie

Brasserie is French for brewery, and almost all of Paris's large and lively brasseries have an Alsatian connection: That means lots of beer, Alsatian white wines such as Riesling and Gewürztraminer, and usually *choucroute,* that hearty blend of sauerkraut and assorted sausages. Brasseries tend to be brightly lit and full of the sounds of good times, fine places for going with a large group. Generally, snacks or full meals are available whenever the restaurant is open. Brasseries tend to keep late hours, and while a reservation is recommended, one can often get a table without one.

Restaurants

Beyond bistros and brasseries, Paris offers numerous sorts of full-fledged restaurants, some serving elegant and classic cuisine, some specializing in creative, inventive, modern cooking. As well, there are restaurants that specialize in fish or grilled meats, in the cooking of specific regions of France. Classifications for all restaurants listed in the guide appear on page 416.

Reservations

Almost without exception, reservations are necessary. For the grand restaurants, such as Taillevent, Pierre Gagnaire, Alain Ducasse, and l'Ambroisie, reserve weeks to months in advance. For others, reservations can be made several days ahead for popular weekend dinners, though for a weekday lunch, reserving the same day is often sufficient. If you are unable to keep a reservation, call to cancel. Many restaurants now require that advance reservations be confirmed by telephone the day you plan to dine there. Another good reason for reserving: Restaurants freely, and without warning, change opening and closing times and vacation plans, particularly during summer months and holiday periods. So it is always safest to call to make sure the restaurant will be open when you plan to visit.

Dining Hours

Set aside plenty of time for a Paris restaurant meal. In general, expect to spend anywhere from one and a half to three hours at table for a substantial lunch or dinner. If you want to be in and out within thirty minutes to an hour, visit a café, tea salon, wine bar, or brasserie, but don't attempt to rush through a meal at a serious restaurant. Currently, most Parisians begin lunch at 12:30 or 1:00 P.M. (although one can begin at noon), and most dine starting at 8:30 or 9:00 P.M. (although some restaurants will accept reservations as early as 7:00 P.M.). Despite the later hours, most kitchens close early, so a 2:00 P.M. lunch or 10:00 P.M. dinner reservation would be stretching it. On the other hand, the majority of cafés and brasseries serve at almost any hour. A few restaurants continue taking orders until 11 P.M. or later, and a list of those can be found in the Ready Reference beginning on page 416.

Prices

The price range of restaurants listed here goes from low to high. I have made no attempt to include restaurants serving mediocre food simply because they are inexpensive. Bargains are few and far between, but there are always ways to cut costs, even in the most expensive restaurants. Forgo the before-dinner drink, the after-dinner Cognac or cigar, and if you smoke, buy cigarettes at a neighborhood *tabac,* where they will be cheaper than in the restaurant. Share dishes, if you like. You are not obliged to order either cheese or dessert, and if they do not suit your budget or appetite, forget them. You can often cut costs by ordering from a fixed-price menu (though it is not always cheaper than ordering *à la carte*), or by opting for a *carafe* of wine or an inexpensive house wine. More and more restaurants are offering wine by the glass, generally cheaper than a bottle or half-bottle.

In all cases, the price noted with each restaurant listing represents an average meal for one person, including a first course, main course, and cheese or dessert, as well as the service charge. Generally, a good inexpensive meal can be had for under 200 francs, a good moderately priced meal for 300 francs, while a luxury meal, in a higher class of restaurant with more expensive wines, will range from 800 to 1,000 francs. Almost without exception, prices are the same for lunch and dinner.

Advice on Paying the Bill and Tipping

No subject is more confusing to visitors than French restaurant bills. You need remember only one fact: You are never required to pay more than the final "net" total on the bill. Service, which ranges from twelve to fifteen percent, depending upon the class of the restaurant, must be included in the price of individual dishes, and is part of the final bill. Etiquette does not require you to pay more than the total. If you have particularly enjoyed the meal, if you feel the *maître d'hôtel* or *sommelier* has offered exceptional service, if you are in a particularly generous mood, then you might wish to leave anywhere from a few francs to five percent of the total bill as an additional tip, preferably in cash.

Credit Cards

The majority of Paris restaurants accept credit cards, and almost all will accept traveler's checks in French francs. Although every attempt has been made to ensure the accuracy of credit card information in this guide, policies change rapidly. When reserving, it is a good idea to confirm credit card information. If you are sharing the bill with another person or couple and you both wish to pay by credit card, most restaurants will oblige by dividing the bill between the two or more credit cards. Out of kindness to the waiters and *sommelier,* any tips (beyond the obligatory twelve to fifteen percent service charge) should be left in cash.

A Private Room

Many restaurants, including such establishments as Taillevent, Alain Ducasse and Le Grand Véfour, offer private dining rooms for anywhere from eight to several hundred people. Some rooms, such as those at Taillevent, are particularly elegant and well appointed. Others may be drab, uncomfortable, and less appealing than the restaurant's main dining room, so see the room before making plans.

There are advantages and disadvantages in reserving a private room. One advantage is that it is easier to organize a special feast. The main disadvantage is that you must plan several weeks ahead and in most cases will need a French-speaking person to make arrangements. Also keep in mind that since your group will be set apart from the main dining room, you will miss much of the "theater" and ambience that goes with the dining experience. There is no extra charge for the private rooms, and in many cases the total bill will be less expensive than if the group chose from the regular menu. Where private rooms are available, such facilities are noted with each restaurant description, and a separate listing can be found in the Ready Reference beginning on page 416.

What to Expect at the Table

Suggestions on Ordering

There are four simple things to keep in mind when ordering in a Paris restaurant. First, think about what foods are likely to be fresh and in season. Thank goodness the French are still fanatical about freshness, and about eating only what is naturally in season. When dining out in Paris, I often go on seasonal "binges," eating asparagus, melon, scallops, oysters, or game day after day when they are at their peak. If you see melon on the menu in January, or scallops during July, beware.

Second, take the time to learn about the restaurant's specialties. Every restaurant has at least one or two dishes of which it is particularly proud, and the majority of restaurants either offer a *plat du jour* or underline or boldface their specialties. These dishes, assuming they are to your liking, will usually be a good buy, and generally fresh. Note that the fish is usually freshest on Fridays (when the demand is greatest) and least fresh on Mondays, when the wholesale market is closed.

Third, stick to your guns and order the kind of food you really like to eat. This is a caveat to those diners who will blindly accept a critic's or a waiter's suggestion, then all too late realize that they hate tripe, or duck, or whatever it was that was recommended.

Finally, today many restaurants offer a tasting menu, or *menu dégustation,* which allows diners to sample small portions of from four to eight different dishes. I am generally opposed to such menus, for in the end they are rarely good buys and inevitably provide more food than it is humanly (and healthily) possible to eat. Because a tasting menu offers so many different dishes, it is difficult, if not impossible, to take with you a memorable impression of the meal or the restaurant. While the *menu dégustation* is often easier on the kitchen, you just may get the feeling that the dishes you are eating came off an assembly line.

Butter

Most, but not all, restaurants offer butter at the table. If you don't see butter, just ask for it. Only at the smallest cafés will a supplement be charged.

Since the French do not always butter their bread, restaurants do not systematically offer it, unless you order a dish that generally calls for buttered bread—*charcuterie,* oysters served with rye bread, sardines, or radishes, or the cheese course. Almost all French butter is unsalted.

Coffee

The French have very specific coffee-drinking habits. Many Frenchmen begin their day with a *café au lait*—usually lots of hot milk with a little bit of coffee. During the rest of the day they drink either black coffee or *café crème* (coffee with steamed milk). But in restaurants, the coffee taken after meals is always black coffee, never coffee with added milk. Some restaurants will provide cream or milk if requested, some will not. In France coffee is always taken at the very end of the meal (never with the meal), almost served as a course of its own. In finer restaurants, chocolates and/or *petits fours* might also be served.

Fish, Meat, and Poultry

Almost all fish, meat, and poultry taste better when cooked on the bone. If you have problems boning fish, ask if the dish you are ordering is boned (*sans arêtes*), and if not, ask the waiter to debone it before serving (*enlevez les arêtes*). The French prefer their meat and some poultry (particularly duck) cooked quite rare, or *rose.* But if rare meat or poultry really bothers you, be insistent, and ask for it *bien cuit* (well done). Be prepared for the waiter to wince. (For rare meat, order it *saignant;* for medium, *à point.*)

Salt and Pepper

Some chefs are insulted if diners alter their creations with additional seasonings, and so do not offer salt and pepper at the table. If you don't see any, just ask for them. But do be sure to taste the food before reaching for the mill or shaker.

Water

I am always shocked when, in this day and age, people ask, "Is it safe to drink the water in Paris?" Of course it is. Perhaps visitors assume that because the French are so passionate about bottled water—a table of eight diners might include four different preferred brands of mineral water—the tap water is unsafe. Either tap water (ask for une carafe d'eau) or mineral water (plat is flat bottled water, gazeuse is bubbly mineral water) may be ordered with all meals. If ordering Perrier brand mineral water, don't be surprised if only small bottles are available. The French consider Perrier too gaseous to drink with meals, so most restaurants stock only small bottles, for drinking as an apéritif or with mixed drinks.

Wines and Liquor

This is one area where I firmly advise you to follow the rule "When in Paris, do as the Parisians do." Most French people do not drink hard liquor before meals and few restaurants are equipped with a full bar. If you are accustomed to drinking hard liquor before meals, try to change your habits during a Paris visit. The liquor will numb your palate for the pleasures to follow, and requests for a martini or whiskey before a meal will not put you in good stead with the waiter or the management. Almost all restaurants offer a house cocktail—most often a Kir, a blend of either white wine or Champagne with *crème de Cassis* (black currant liqueur). I personally dislike most of these concoctions (which can be expensive and run up the bill) and always ask for the wine list when requesting the menu. Then I usually order as an *apéritif* a white wine that will be drunk with the meal, or at least with the first course.

Selecting Wines

I have learned almost all I know about wines by tasting, tasting, tasting in restaurants: I study wine lists, keep track of average prices and favorite food and wine combinations, and am always eager to sample a wine that's new or unfamiliar to me.

Although I have found some *sommeliers,* or wine stewards, to be outrageously sexist (I was once refused even a simple glance at a wine list, and a few *sommeliers* still bristle when I insist on ordering the wine), generally I haven't found them to be unfair or unwilling to help when I sought information or assistance. If you don't know a lot about wine, ask the *sommelier*'s advice. Give him a rough idea of your tastes and the price you would like to pay. This

The staff of Julien (see entry, page 92).

assumes, of course, that you share a common language. If you do not, ask simply whether there is a *vin de la maison* (house wine).

If you are knowledgeable about wine, you will want to study the wine list. Don't allow yourself to be pressured or bullied into making a quick decision (this isn't always easy), and if pressed, simply explain that you are fascinated by the restaurant's wonderful selection and would like a few minutes to examine and fully appreciate the list of offerings.

Prices for the same wines vary drastically from restaurant to restaurant: Some have large, long-standing wine cellars, others are just getting started. I love wine, consider it an essential part of any good meal, and probably tend to spend slightly more than the average diner on a good bottle. When dining in a bistro or brasserie, I often order the house wine, either by the *carafe* or by the bottle.

Palais-Royal, Les Halles, Tuileries

1st arrondissement

L'ARDOISE
28, rue du Mont-Thabor,
Paris 1.
Tel: 01.42.96.28.18.
Métro: Tuileries or Concorde.
Service 12:30 to 2 P.M. and 8 to 10:30 P.M.
Closed Monday, one week in May, Christmas week, and the last three weeks of August.
Private dining room for 15 to 17.
Credit card: V.
165-franc menu.

SPECIALTIES:
Modern bistro: tartare de saumon (salmon tartare); jarret d'agneau braisé au jus d'herbes (braised lamb shanks with natural herb juices); turbot rôti galette de pomme de terre (roast turbot with potato cake); clafoutis minute aux abricots (apricot custard tart).

It's many a chef's dream to open a bistro with no printed menu or wine list, simply an *ardoise,* a blackboard, on which one starts anew each day. Pierre Jay is living that dream, hustling at the stove, creating classic, simple, inspired fare in a compact, bare-bones bistro steps from the Tuileries. Do not come here for plush surroundings or efficient service. Come instead for the bargain menu, the well-priced wines, and the sturdy, honest cuisine.

Jay offers a deliciously moist and manly *terrine* of rabbit and hazelnuts that's all but perfect; I missed the crock of *cornichons* and wished he had been a bit more aggressive with his seasoning. A refreshing salad—much like a Parisian *ratatouille*—arrives in the form of a giant tomato stuffed with carrots, leeks, and herbs. A main-course roasted pigeon is sublime: The tiny bird is partially boned, and the innards are cooked to a regal *confit* and spread on toast. A bed of lamb's lettuce and mixed greens serves to soak up the rich, meaty sauce. A crown of crisp, thinly sliced potatoes cooked to an almost-burnt crisp serves as a warm, welcoming counterpoint. You feel that the chef is connected to the food in an intimate way. Classic *terrines* of *foie gras,* a beef fillet with morels, and a lovely lobster stew (with a reasonable 75-franc supplement) take the cuisine beyond the ordinary, day-to-day, serviceable bistro fare.

Dessert fans will love the caramelized *ballon de fraises,* a mix of cream, strawberries, and caramel

Paris bistro conviviality.

layered in a fanciful champagne glass. Treasures from the wine list include the feminine, elegant 1996 Fleurie from the Domaine du Vissoux and the meaty 1995 Côtes-du-Rhône Domaine Gramenon. The bread comes from Kayser on Rue Monge, one of the city's finest *boulangeries*.

CARRE DES FEUILLANTS
(Alain Dutournier)
14, rue de Castiglione,
Paris 1.
Tel: 01.42.86.82.82.
Fax: 01.42.86.07.71.
Métro: Concorde or Tuileries.
Service noon to 2:30 P.M. and 7:30 to 10:30 P.M.
Closed Saturday lunch, Sunday, and the first three weeks of August.
Credit cards: AE, DC, V.
Private dining room for 7 to 35.
Air-conditioned.
295-franc lunch menu; 780-franc tasting menu.
A la carte, 550 to 700 francs.

SPECIALTIES:
Seasonal: velouté de châtaignes à la truffe blanche (creamy chestnut soup with white truffles); langoustines à la nougatines d'ail doux (Dublin Bay prawns with sweet garlic sauce); noisettes de brebis en croûte (tender center cut of mutton chop, roasted in an herb crust).

As history proves, many get to the top but few get to stay there. Staying power, then, is the true professional challenge. Chef Alain Dutournier seems to have made a brilliant career of that special talent. Since he first journeyed from France's southwest more than twenty-five years ago with a dream of making it big in the capital, he's proved that there's more to southwestern cuisine than *foie gras* and Armagnac, and that there's more to grand dining than Champagne and *petits fours*. Dutournier—a cigar lover and a healthy eater—might easily have been taken as one more brash kid. Over the years, however, both at his original Au Trou Gascon (managed by his wife, Nicole) and at the Carré des Feuillants, he has demonstrated his ability to fuse a hearty regional cuisine with grand cuisine, giving us big, satisfying flavors.

While fish and shellfish always shine here, Dutournier's real passions are the big, gutsy, meaty flavors of milk-fed lamb, beef, roast veal knuckle, venison, and such classic dishes as calf's head, or *tête de veau*. And I don't think any restaurant in Paris serves such a satisfying version of *steak frites:* His personally aged Chalosse beef is grilled to rare perfection over a charcoal fire and served with crisp golden potatoes fried in goose fat. The juicy, fragrant, chewy meat is accompanied by a rich, sophisticated sauce of beef juices and mushrooms, ideal for pairing with a vigorous, earthy red Madiran, Cru du Paradis "Réserve Royale." Roasted meats—such as tender, fragrant milk-fed lamb and veal knuckle roasted in a covered copper *cocotte*—also are not to be missed.

Yet Dutournier understands another need of modern diners: a desire to experience new flavors, new combinations, to sample foods they are not going to create at home. So he weaves a complex and elegant "*lasagne,*" layering thin slices of *foie gras,* generous slices of black truffles, and paper-thin slices of *topinambour,* or Jerusalem artichokes. Earlier in the season, he combines thick pillars of potatoes with a touch of *foie gras* and tops them with a halo of thinly sliced white truffles. The combination can be simply brilliant. The potatoes act like a sponge, absorbing the rich *foie gras* juices as well as the elusive essence of the white truffle.

Dutournier even manages to make me fall in love with dishes I don't expect to enjoy. Sea scallops sliced paper-thin have become a cliché, and rarely does a chef succeed at elevating the preparation to memorable heights. But Dutournier weaves pungent leaves of celery with truffles (sometimes black, sometimes white) and scallops and allows each to carry its own character, elegance, and flavor.

Maître d'hôtel Patrick Vuldary and *sommelier* Christophe Serpin work well in tandem, transmitting Dutournier's friendliness, spirit of generosity, and sense of perfection.

Only the desserts leave me less than enthused. A late fall *croustade* of figs was marred by fruit with a flavor so elusive it was invisible. And the mango tart, which should have provided a soft, fragrant close to the meal, was too firm and timidly flavored, the fruit far from ripe.

All this comes at a price, to be sure. Yet even those on a budget are not likely to leave disappointed.

IL CORTILE
Hotel Castille
37, rue Cambon,
Paris 1.
Tel: 01.44.58.45.67.
Fax: 01.40.15.97.64.
Métro: Concorde
or Madeleine.
Service noon to 2:30 P.M.
and 7:30 to 10:30 P.M.
Closed Saturday, Sunday,
and holidays.
Credit cards: AE, DC, V.
Garden terrace.
Air-conditioned.
A la carte, 300 to 350 francs.

Despite a universal love affair with Italian cuisine, gastronomic Paris remains a wasteland for authentic Italian pastas, breads, risottos, and traditional grilled fare. Leave it to Alain Ducasse, lover of all things Mediterranean, to bail us out here. As consultant along with French chef Nicolas Vernier, he is mixing up some very delicious "I'll come back for more" Italian fare. The menu is based on inventive, fresh, and seasonal fare, and every few months the menu changes and showcases a different ingredient, such as artichokes, broccoli, or scallops.

My only regret here is that the breads are so delicious you are likely to leave room for little else. Seconds after you are seated in the tastefully decorated dining room, you are showered with a selection of fresh delights such as an oil-brushed

Fenouil Il Cortile, Sauce au Thon
IL CORTILE'S FRESH FENNEL WITH TUNA SAUCE

Il Cortile is a delightful Michelin-starred Italian restaurant in the center of Paris (see page 13). An elegant spot with a garden for good-weather dining, it serves a generous antipasto platter made up of everything from pissaladière *to deep-fried fresh anchovies. On one visit, they served this zesty tuna sauce over crunchy, paper-thin slices of fresh fennel. It's a delightful warm-weather first course: The saltiness of the anchovies and capers stimulates the appetite and excites the palate for more to come.*

Tonnato sauce:
1 can (6½ ounces; 190 g) imported tuna packed in olive oil (do not drain; see Note)
5 anchovy fillets in oil
4 tablespoons (2 ounces; 60 g) unsalted butter, softened
¼ cup extra-virgin olive oil
2 tablespoons freshly squeezed lemon juice
2 tablespoons capers, rinsed and well drained

Handful arugula or watercress, rinsed and dried
2 large fennel bulbs, trimmed and cleaned

1. Prepare the sauce: With a fork, flake the tuna in the can. Transfer the tuna, oil and all, to a food processor. Add the remaining sauce ingredients and process until smooth and creamy. Taste for seasoning. Transfer to a medium-size bowl. (The sauce can be stored, covered and refrigerated, up to 3 days. Serve at room temperature.)

2. Arrange several leaves of arugula or sprigs of watercress around the edge of six salad plates. Using a mandoline or a very sharp knife, cut the fennel lengthwise into paper-thin slices. Arrange the sliced fennel in the center of the salad plates, allowing the arugula or watercress to serve as a leafy green background. (Slice the fennel at the very last moment. It will quickly turn brown on contact with the air.) Spoon the tuna sauce over the fennel and serve as a first course. (Alternatively, pass the sauce in a bowl, allowing guests to serve themselves.)

Yield: 6 servings.

Note: If tuna packed in olive oil is unavailable, use top-quality white tuna packed in water. Drain the tuna, discard the water, and add an additional tablespoon of extra-virgin olive oil when preparing the sauce.

SPECIALTIES:
Italian: farfalle à l'encre (bow-tie pasta with squid ink); espadon frotté d'agrumes et de poivres, brochette de légumes (swordfish rubbed with citrus and pepper, with grilled skewered vegetables); agneau à la broche (rotisserie-grilled lamb); risotto aux trois tomates, confite, poêlée et en concassé (tomato risotto with tomato confit, sautéed tomatoes, and coarsely chopped tomatoes).

rosemary flatbread, crisp and crunchy; nicely risen little squares of *focaccia;* and firm fresh *grissini* wrapped with prosciutto.

The changing antipasti platter might include a deeply salty *pissaladière;* paper-thin slices of raw fennel bathed in a *tonnato* sauce (for recipe, see this page); sardines marinated with citrus and capers; or a Swiss chard *tourte.* Pasta and rice selections might include an unusual risotto flavored with a trio of tomato flavors—slow-roasted, pan-fried, and freshly chopped; a ravioli filled with ricotta, sage, and ham; or a classic fettuccine with *pistou* and aged Parmigiano-Reggiano. Swordfish arrives perfectly, evenly cooked and so, so moist, with a stock-based sauce so shiny you can almost see your reflection. Vegetables are treated with equal respect; when I was there the swordfish was paired with artichokes, potatoes, mushrooms, apple, and onion, all tasting solely of themselves. Equally triumphant is the evenly, perfectly grilled guinea hen, roasted on a spit and accompanied by full-flavored *caillettes* of guinea hen liver, gizzard, and heart, wrapped in caul fat and pan-fried. The accompanying polenta was a model of its genre—steaming, flavorful, smooth, and rich. On one evening, the open ravioli of artichokes and shrimp proved just too dry and without character; and the rabbit with gnocchi was less than astonishing, with the rabbit just a bit too tough to enjoy.

Service is impeccable, friendly, and discreet, and the wine list a joy. I adore the lightly chilled, easy-drinking Vernaccia di San Gimignano, a distinctive, highly flavored wine from the village north of Siena. In the summertime, Il Cortile has one of the city's loveliest outdoor gardens for open-air dining. But don't wait until temperatures soar to give the spot a try.

LE GRAND VEFOUR
17, rue de Beaujolais,
Paris 1.
Tel: 01.42.96.56.27.
Fax: 01.42.86.80.71.
Métro: Palais Royal–Musée du Louvre.
Service 12:30 to 2:15 P.M. and 7:30 to 10:15 P.M.
Closed Saturday, Sunday, and August.
Credit cards: AE, DC, V.
Private dining room for 8 to 22.
Air-conditioned.
345-franc lunch menu; 780-franc dinner menu.
A la carte, 590 to 850 francs.

It has been a long time since I left a restaurant feeling such excitement about the creativity of a young French chef. Guy Martin has been at the stove at Le Grand Véfour for several years now, and it is clear he has his feet planted solidly on the hallowed ground.

A first glance at the menu makes you wonder if this isn't sheer folly. Or perhaps *nouvelle cuisine* dragged out of the mothbails. Salmon with poppy seeds? Oysters with turnips? Squid with sorrel and orange? Lamb dusted with ground coffee? And then, as a grand finale, an artichoke *tourte* for dessert? Imposing a wildly creative cuisine upon such a landmark as this 18th-century café at the edge of the Palais Royal seems bold, to say the least. Most would say pure insanity, sure to fail. Yet Martin is French and sure of himself. What's more, he has the technical ability and maturity to pull it off. Best of

SPECIALTIES:
Seasonal: ravioles de foie gras à l'imulsion de crème truffée (ravioli filled with foie gras in a sauce of truffled cream); noisettes d'agneau panées au moka (tender center cut of lamb chop dusted with coffee); tourte d'artichauts et légumes confits (artichoke and mixed vegetable pie); sorbet aux amandes amères (bitter-almond sorbet).

all, once his carefully executed creations are on your plate, the presentation, the aromas, the flavors, all transport you to a land of culinary bliss.

Flavors you expect to bop you over the head just caress your palate, blending with whatever ingredient is playing the starring role at the time. Once you're well into the dish, it doesn't seem weird at all, simply surprising and satisfying. Martin's first-course creation of oysters wrapped in thin rounds of turnip—ravioli "lite"—is sublime; a touch of sesame gives the dish a very welcoming Asian flavor. His poached lobster sauced with a blend of chiles, cilantro, and pecans sounds like something from a Wild West cooking competition but, oh, does it do the job. The richness of the lobster meat is met head-on by the bold peppers, the bright flavor of the cilantro, and the crunch of the pecans. Main-course nuggets of lamb dusted with coffee come off as a traditional dish of roasted young lamb with an indescribably delicious sauce. Almost like a trained chemist, Martin has figured just how to heighten, not compete or camouflage, the flavors of the main ingredient.

By all means save room for the cheese tray, which always features some rare entity from the chef's native Savoie, such as the almost extinct fat,

The dining room at Le Grand Véfour.

nutty, and naturally blue Termignon, a rustic, crumbling cheese with Alpine aromas of grass and wildflowers. I do part company with the chef in his use of vegetables for dessert. On one visit, a waiter came over to look at my barely touched artichoke *tourte* flanked by two tiny candied carrots and all I could respond was, "I don't like to see carrots on my plate at midnight." And there are some things at the "new" Grand Véfour that need attention. The breads are uneven, and the vegetables are all but nonexistent (save for dessert) and badly done when they do appear. On the other hand, the dining room staff deserves a round of applause: Rarely does one witness such a graceful shift from the old-fashioned, nose-in-the-air attitude of days past to the friendly, congenial service we have come to expect today. The waiters move about the elegant 18th-century dining room with the grace of dancers, always attentive yet ever discreet.

LESCURE
7, rue de Mondovi,
Paris 1.
Tel: 01.42.60.18.91.
Métro: Concorde.
No reservations. Service noon to 2:15 P.M. and 7 to 10:15 P.M.
Closed Saturday evening, Sunday, and three weeks in August.
Credit card: V.
Sidewalk terrace.
Private dining room for 12.
Air-conditioned.
Nonsmoking area.
100-franc menu.
A la carte, 140 francs.

SPECIALTIES: Traditional bistro: pâté en croûte chaud salad (meat pie in a pastry crust with green salad); maquereaux frais marinés (fresh marinated mackerel); poule au pot farcie Henri IV (poached stuffed chicken); sauté de calamars (sautéed squid); vacherin aux fruits rouges (berries in a meringue shell).

Now into its eightieth year, this traditional Paris standby is still going strong. Even though this tiny spot is just off the Place de la Concorde, its *auberge*-like atmosphere will make you feel as though you are in the country. If you crave snails or a fillet of duck, green apple sorbet sprinkled with Calvados, or any of the traditional specialties, this place is for you. The menu price has risen only 2 francs in the past seven years!

This is a great address to know when visiting the Louvre or shopping along rue Saint-Honoré, when you're in the mood for a quick, inexpensive meal. In good weather, tables tumble out onto the sidewalk (it is an exaggeration to call it a terrace), while inside, diners sit elbow-to-elbow beneath rafters dangling with strings of garlic and country sausage. This is very simple, basic French home cooking, nothing fancy but generally satisfying. I've enjoyed the *poule au pot* and the *travers de porc demi-sel* (meaty salt-cured spareribs on a bed of cabbage). Many ingredients could be fresher here, and some dishes taste as though they've been reheated once too often. But the service is swift, the price is right, and it all comes with a welcoming smile.

MACEO
15, rue des Petits-Champs, Paris 1.
Tel: 01.42.97.53.85.
Fax: 01.47.03.36.93.
Métro: Palais Royal–Musée du Louvre or Bourse.
Service noon to 2:30 P.M. and 7 to 11 P.M.
Closed Sunday.
Credit cards: AE, V.
Private dining rooms for 10 and 50.
185-franc lunch menu; 220-franc dinner menu.
A la carte, 250 francs.

SPECIALTIES: Contemporary: salade de ricotta aux olives écrasées et tomates confites (salad of ricotta, olives, and confit of tomato); poulet fermier sauté au romarin, caviar d'aubergines et tomates confit (sautéed farm chicken with rosemary, eggplant caviar, and confit of tomato); farmhouse Cheddar with a salad of apples, celery, and walnuts.

Mark Williamson has turned into a bit of a Parisian superman. Already the owner of two popular, well-established wine bars—Willi's and Juveniles—he has flown in, cape flapping, to rescue one of the city's prettiest and most neglected restaurants, Le Mercure Galant, next to the Palais Royal. Since the fall of 1997 the restaurant—renamed Maceo, after the saxophonist Maceo Parker—has been playing to a full house, thanks largely to considerable local enthusiasm, overflow from Willi's just a few doors away, and Williamson's impeccable sense of presence. Not to mention that wherever "Willi" can be found, you are certain to discover at least one or two new, spectacular wines.

A fine starter on my last visit was an Asian-inspired trio of fresh giant shrimp on a bed of sautéed bean sprouts, all bathed in a delicate, palate-opening curry cream. Equally fine was the wild-mushroom terrine, a compact vegetable pâté that's carefully seasoned.

Main courses include a pleasurable *canon d'agneau,* or nuggets of lamb wrapped around minced black olives, sautéed to order. The accompanying eggplant "caviar" and *confit* of fresh tomatoes give the dish a proper Provençal accent. Also worth ordering is the beef fillet in a well-spiced red wine sauce.

Two current wines to search out include Weingut Loosen's slightly bubbly German Riesling from the Mosel River valley and the dark, aromatic, peppery purple Jade Mountain "Cote du Soleil" from Sonoma, California. The 1995 vintage, made with a blend of mourvèdre and syrah, popular Rhône Valley grape varieties, is pricey but worth it for those eager to further explore the best wines of California. Some of the better-priced wines on the list include the pleasant Côtes-du-Rhône Seguret from winemaker Jean David; the always dependable Coudelet de Beaucastel; the best of the Beaujolais *cru,* a 1996 Fleurie from the Domaine des Vissoux; and the eternally welcoming Domaine Tempier rosé from Bandol. And if you don't know where to turn when you open the wine list, the young *sommelier* will eagerly assist.

Desserts are included in the well-priced dinner menu. Try the feather-light pear *millefeuille,* perfumed lightly with licorice, or *réglisse.* Only the bread—flabby, antiquated dinner rolls—needs desperate attention.

RESTAURANT DU PALAIS-ROYAL
110, galerie de Valois, Paris 1.
Tel: 01.40.20.00.27.
Fax: 01.40.20.00.82.
Métro: Bourse or Palais Royal–Musée du Louvre.
Service noon to 2 P.M. and 7:30 to 10 P.M.
Open daily in summer. Otherwise closed Saturday lunch and Sunday. Closed Christmas week.
Credit cards: AE, DC, V.
Garden terrace.
Private dining room for 15.
A la carte, 300 to 350 francs.

SPECIALTIES:
Modern bistro: carpaccio de thon (raw marinated tuna); salade de saison aux herbes fraîches (tossed green salad with fresh herbs); thon de Saint-Jean-de-Luz poêlé sauce vierge (pan-seared tuna from Saint Jean de Luz with a sauce of olive oil and tomatoes); petit bar grillé entier (whole grilled baby sea bass).

Historic settings ultimately create their own ambience and turn into romantic stage sets. Such is the case with the Restaurant du Palais-Royal, nestled under the arches of the 17th-century *palais,* originally built as Richelieu's Palais-Cardinal. During the summer months, I have spent many agreeable evenings seated outdoors, at the edge of the refined gardens in the square, watching the play of Parisians as they pass through, pause, and linger here. This is simply one of Paris's best spots for summer terrace dining. Chef Bruno Hess has created a simple, no-nonsense menu for the restaurant, and his food serves as a fine modern backdrop for a square laden with history. In cooler weather, when we are required to dine indoors, the setting is less romantic, less airy, but given the right lighting it could be just as gratifying. With the feel of an elegant 1920s bistro, with crisp ocher linens and mirrors that reflect the stone arches, metal gates, and garden beyond, the restaurant feels like a safe haven. A small spark is still missing here, and it's hard to say what it will take to ignite it: Maybe the ghosts of the past simply need to be hushed away.

If you're in the mood for simple, unfussy fare, go for the *salade de saison aux herbes,* a veritable forest of tiny greens and herbs, served in a copious, well-dressed mound. I often opt for the simple grilled *bar de ligne,* sea bass caught on a line, not in a net. The fish is grilled to perfection, arriving moist, fresh-tasting, sure to satisfy. Daily specials might include a platter of six giant crinkle-shelled *creuses* oysters from Brittany, with their welcome Bordeaux-style accompaniment of small, spicy pork sausages; or a gratin dish overflowing with sautéed wild *cèpe* mushrooms. The main-course *steak tartare* is a rare wonder in a city filled with mush parading as the real thing. Here it's truly cut by hand, so the meat remains chewy, and the seasoning to order is right on the mark. A simple grilled slice of tuna fits the bill for grilled-food lovers, as does the fine grilled chicken.

Desserts are on par with the rest of the fare, and include a soothingly delicious serving of *sorbet au fromage blanc* made of the young fresh cheese, as well as a *fondant au chocolat chaud,* a warm dessert that's neither cake nor soufflé but in some delightful never-never land in between. There's also a classic and still satisfying *crème brûlée,* as well as a model *baba au rhum,* served with a dollop of whipped cream and a homemade syrup of rum, vanilla seeds, and lemon zest. The wine list is spotty but does include some worthy bottles, such as the always reliable Loire Valley Saumur-Champigny from the Domaine Filliatreau, Domaine Tempier's Bandol rosé, and the pricey but delicious Chablis *premier cru* "La Forêt" from Vincent and René Fauvist. Don't miss the excellent *baguettes* from prize-winning baker Jean-Noël Julien (see Bakeries, page 242).

AU PIED DE COCHON
6, rue Coquillière,
Paris 1.
Tel: 01.40.13.77.00.
Fax: 01.40.13.77.09.
Internet: http://www.blanc.net
Métro: Châtelet–Les Halles.
Nonstop service 24 hours a day.
Open daily.
Credit cards: AE, DC, V.
Sidewalk terrace.
Private dining room for 20 to 40.
Air-conditioned.
178-franc menu.
A la carte, 200 to 300 francs.

SPECIALTIES:
Brasserie: banc d'huîtres et de fruits de mer toute l'année (fresh oysters and shellfish, year-round); soupe à l'oignon (onion soup); viandes grillées (grilled meats); choix de Beaujolais (choice of Beaujolais wines).

It is always heartening to see a restaurant keep pace with the times over a long period. When Au Pied de Cochon first opened its doors in the 1940s, Les Halles, the giant wholesale fruit and vegetable market that kept the neighborhood thriving and Parisians well fed, seemed to be the center of the universe, and neighboring restaurants took part. While the market is long gone, Au Pied de Cochon thrives as though nothing has changed. My most recent dinner here was a delight from start to finish. On a summer Sunday evening, the huge multistory restaurant was bulging at the seams, with waiters dashing here and there with professional aplomb. The famous onion soup is satisfying and wholesome—good beef broth laced with bits of browned onions, all topped with toast and a generous sprinkling of cheese. The dish lacked that final touch of seasoning, which was quickly set right with a touch of salt. Their *coeur de filet*—meaty heart of beef fillet—was perfectly rare, served with decent fries (though not quite cooked enough for me) and a touch of watercress. I was elated by the perfect platter of warm pork sausage studded with whole pistachios and with the lovely potato salad prepared

Au Pied de Cochon (see entry, facing page).

with first-of-season tiny potatoes, cooked and served in their skins. This is also the place to go for excellent oysters year-round and for giant seafood platters that might include oysters from Normandy and Brittany, almond-like raw clams, *langoustines,* and Canadian lobster.

There is the entire assortment of Georges Duboeuf Beaujolais (including the oddball white) to lighten up the evening. A good place to know on holidays: The restaurant is open 24 hours a day, 365 days a year. Service is remarkably democratic and careful. The waiter at our table spoke French, English, and Spanish fluently.

PIERRE AU PALAIS ROYAL
10, rue de Richelieu,
Paris 1.
Tel: 01.42.96.09.17
Fax: 01.42.96.09.62.
Métro: Palais Royal–Musée du Louvre.
Service noon to 2 P.M. and 7:15 P.M. to midnight.
Closed Sunday, and Christmas Eve through January 2.
Credit cards: AE, DC, V.
Air-conditioned.
Valet parking.
A la carte, 300 to 350 francs.

Some city restaurants have an uncanny way of allowing themselves to be reinvented for each generation of diners. Pierre au Palais Royal, situated right behind the Comédie Française, is one of those endlessly flexible restaurants. Owners, waiters, and waitresses change, the clientele moves on or passes away, but this longtime beacon of true French bourgeois fare remains steadfast. Well, sort of. Restaurateur Jean-Paul Arabian (formerly of Lille's and Paris's Ledoyen) has taken over, giving the cozy restaurant a new face-lift and wisely altering the menu to please a broader range of palates while remaining true to the cause. Fashions have fads, so why shouldn't food? And since it's not likely that the world will end its love affair with pasta and rice any time soon, Arabian offers a bit of each, along with such tried-and-true Pierre

SPECIALTIES:
Mixed traditional and contemporary bistro: terrine de joues de boeuf au foie gras (terrine of beef cheeks with foie gras); gaspacho, tartare de thon aux herbes (spicy tomato and vegetable soup with tuna tartare and herbs); pâtes, risotto, légumes (daily rice, pasta, and vegetable specials); quenelles de brochet gratinées à la Lyonnaise (gratineed Lyon-style pike dumplings); langue de veau pochée, fricassée de légumes en vinaigrette (poached veal tongue with mixed sautéed garden vegetables); entrecôte poêlée, pommes frites, béarnaise, coeur de laitue (pan-fried beef rib steak with thick French fries, tarragon-flavored sauce, and green salad); éclair au chocolate (chocolate éclair).

favorites as *foie gras,* organ meats, steak, *boeuf à la ficelle,* roast duck with peas, and the extraordinary cheeses of Paris's best cheesemonger, Roger Alléosse.

Dinner here can be close to perfection. My last meal at "Chez Pierre" began with a truly modern and thoroughly refreshing *gaspacho*—lots of minutely chopped vegetables floating in a slightly spicy tomato broth—set off with a sparkling fresh *tartare* of tuna and a flourish of fresh herbs. Less exciting, and an old-fashioned preparation that might as well be scratched from the books, was an overcooked, soggy portion of white asparagus topped with a needless rectangle of puff pastry, all bathed in a buttery *sauce mousseline.* Even at its best, I think this dish speaks of days past, when smothering the regal vegetable was the rage. Today we like our asparagus a bit less gussied up, and certainly less cooked.

The pastas and rice are a revelation, in that they are French versions, not Italian. And once the French learn how to cook pasta and rice, Italy watch out! The spaghetti with *palourdes,* or baby clams, was distinctly French-tasting, with a broth that had a rich, substantive base and flavors that really hung together. The clams could have been cleaned a bit better, but the overall effect was truly satisfying. Ditto for the mushroom risotto that bound delicious fresh *girolles* (chanterelles) and *mousserons* to the firm grains of rice, all bathed in a densely flavored stock.

For culinary classicists, Pierre offers giant portions of veal tongue, or *langue de veau,* poached and served with a brilliant fricassee of seasonal vegetables. Perhaps the dish most often ordered here is the pan-seared *entrecôte,* or beef rib steak. Each steak is beautifully cooked and served with a simple green salad and a gargantuan mound of crisp hand-cut fries.

Desserts are nothing to rave about. The *mille-feuille à la fraise,* thin squares of puff pastry layered with cream and fresh strawberries, was on the bland side, as was the traditional cherry flan, or *clafoutis aux cerises.* The wine list is limited but includes a nice selection of Chinon and the fine light Marsannay red Burgundy from Domaine Bruno Clair. On my last visit, smokers were ubiquitous and annoying, so be forewarned.

LA TOUR DE MONTLHERY
(Chez Denise)
5, rue des Prouvaires, Paris 1.
Tel: 01.42.36.21.82.
Fax: 01.45.08.81.99.
Métro: Louvre-Rivoli or Châtelet–Les Halles.
Service 7 A.M. Monday to 7 A.M. Saturday.
Closed Saturday, Sunday, and mid-July through mid-August.
Credit card: V.
A la carte, 250 to 350 francs.

SPECIALTIES: Traditional bistro: salade frisée aux croûtons ailés (curly endive salad with garlic croutons); saumon cru mariné au citron (fresh raw marinated salmon); saumon braisé à la moutarde de Meaux (salmon braised with coarse-grain mustard); haricot de mouton (mutton and white beans); onglet grillé (grilled hanger or flank steak); tendrons de veau (boned strips of veal breast); pied de porc pané (breaded pig's foot); profiteroles (choux pastry with ice cream and chocolate sauce); pot-au-feu le jeudi (boiled beef with vegetables on Thursday).

Early one morning while I was reserving a table for dinner, the booming voice at the other end of the phone roared, *"La Tour! Je vous écoute!"* ("I'm listening!"). The enthusiasm was enough to force me into a state of alert and to run right over. La Tour de Montlhéry is located on the rue des Prouvaires in Les Halles, a street with one of the most spectacular views of the St. Eustache church, and it is one of the city's more unique restaurants.

La Tour is not for everyone. Don't go if you demand a nonsmoking table; don't like literally rubbing elbows with your neighbor as you tuck into your gargantuan salad of curly endive, eggs, and rustic croutons; don't like noise or crowds; and hate restaurants that are decorated helter-skelter from top to toe with posters, signs, hanging sausages, bric-a-brac, air conditioners, pianos, and whirling ceiling fans. Do go if you are a nostalgia buff in search of an authentic red-and-white-checkered-tablecloth bistro where strangers are greeted like long-lost friends; love single portions that would feed a family of four on a good day; are a meat eater; and just love the scene of a restaurant where tables stay empty for no more than a minute. I am of the latter school. I love digging into La Tour's gigantic endive salad and reach carnivore utopia with their perfectly rare and thoroughly delicious grilled *onglet* (hanger steak), which is delightfully thick, moist, richly flavored, well aged, and properly chewy. Accompanied by a finely accented sauté of mellow shallots, it's a classic bistro dish in a dying breed of old-fashioned restaurants. Washing it down with Beaujolais drawn from the barrel at the front bar merely completes the experience.

CHEZ LA VIEILLE
(Chez Adrienne)
1, rue Bailleul,
Paris 1.
Tel: 01.42.60.15.78.
Fax: 01.42.33.85.71.
Métro: Pont Neuf or Louvre-Rivoli.
Service noon to 2:30 P.M.; open for dinner on Thursday only, 7:30 to 9:30 P.M. (Will open other evenings for groups of ten or more.)
Closed Saturday, Sunday, and three weeks in August.
Credit cards: AE, V.
Private dining room for 28.
150-franc menu.
A la carte, 250 to 350 francs.

SPECIALTIES: Traditional bistro: tous les hors d'oeuvre, terrines et la tomate farcie (procession of salads, terrines, and tomato stuffed with seasoned meat); foie de veau aux échalotes (calf's liver with shallots); aiguillette de boeuf aux carottes (beef with carrots); rognon de veau entier (whole roasted veal kidney); chariot de desserts (dessert trolley).

Marie-Josée Cervoni has just left her accountant's office, and she's ready to celebrate. "Business is great!" she exclaims, aware that she's in that rare minority of French restaurateurs who speak well of their current situation. Ever since this bubbling, outgoing Corsican native took over the direction of the legendary bistro Chez la Vieille in 1994, she and her staff have played to a contented full house. Like most secrets for success, there is no secret. Following in the footsteps of the former owner, Adrienne Biasin, Cervoni has built her reputation on simple, elemental, old-fashioned Parisian bistro fare, and plenty of it. While she still serves the nutritionally incorrect dishes that made the restaurant famous—sautéed calf's liver with shallots and whole roasted veal kidneys—she also adds her own native touch from time to time, featuring recipes learned at the elbow of her Corsican grandmother. So at times she will allow you to dig into platters of delicious Corsican *charcuterie* (fragrant pork sausages, sweet dark ham), an unforgettable cannelloni stuffed with fresh herbs and the rich fresh sheep's milk cheese *brocciu* (see recipe, facing page); beautifully seasoned lamb terrine; and fat slices of herb-rich headcheese. And that's just for starters. Main courses might include roasted *abbacchio,* or leg of baby lamb enlivened by a last-minute sprinkling of garlic, parsley, and bread crumbs; a lovely sauté of veal embellished with a meaty tomato sauce; and a fragrant platter of giant white Soissons beans with lamb meatballs. There is nothing tricky about any of her food; it's all solid, welcoming, grandmotherly fare that's cooked long and slowly and takes well to reheating. Later in the season she is likely to exchange the *pot-au-feu* for a simple *navarin d'agneau* (lamb stew with young vegetables), or an always appreciated roast chicken.

Like the rest of the meal, desserts go on and on until you shout, "Enough." The restaurant's rich chocolate *mousse* is legendary, and at times you will find the smooth Corsican cheesecake known as *fiadone.* The best-buy wines on the brief list include Bernard Grippa's white Saint-Péray and red Saint-Joseph, and André Roméro's rich red Rhône, Rasteau Domaine la Soumade.

Cannelloni Chez La Vieille

CHEZ LA VIEILLE'S CORSICAN SPINACH AND CHEESE CANNELLONI

Marie-Josée Cervoni is the smiling, effervescent hostess at the Parisian landmark Chez la Vieille (see facing page). She often presents dishes from her native Corsica, and this is one of my favorites. Madame Cervoni uses dried lasagne rather than cannelloni shells for this dish.

1 pound (500 g) fresh spinach or Swiss chard
Sea salt and freshly ground black pepper, to taste
4 large eggs
1 pound (500 g) ricotta cheese
Freshly grated nutmeg, to taste
8 sheets dried Italian lasagne (do not use the precooked variety)
2 cups (50 cl) tomato sauce, preferably homemade
About ½ cup (60 g) freshly grated Parmigiano-Reggiano cheese

1. Wash and dry the green leafy portions of the spinach or chard, trimming and discarding the center stems. With a large study knife, finely chop the leaves.

2. Place the greens in a large shallow skillet, and season with salt and pepper. Cover. Over low heat, wilt the greens and cook until most of the exuded liquid has evaporated, 2 to 3 minutes. Drain and set aside.

3. In a large bowl, combine the eggs and cheese and blend with a fork. Incorporate the greens and mix well. Season to taste with salt, pepper, and nutmeg. Set aside.

4. Preheat the oven to 350°F (175°C).

5. In a large pot, bring 6 quarts (6 l) of water to a rolling boil. Add 3 tablespoons salt and the lasagne, stirring to prevent the pasta from sticking. Precook just until the pasta is soft and pliable, about 2 minutes. Drain thoroughly, and place the sheets of pasta on clean cotton towels to absorb the excess liquid. Then, using a sharp knife, cut each sheet of pasta in half crosswise.

6. Pour a thin layer of tomato sauce over the bottom of a rectangular baking pan that is just large enough to hold the cannelloni in a single layer. Lay one square of pasta on a clean work surface. Spread 2 tablespoons of the filling evenly along one edge of the square. Starting at the filled edge, carefully roll the pasta to form a cylinder. Place it in the baking pan, seam side down. Continue filling and rolling the remaining sheets of pasta, placing the cannelloni side by side in a single layer in the baking dish. Spoon the remaining tomato sauce over the finished cannelloni.

7. Sprinkle the Parmesan cheese over the cannelloni, and place the pan in the center of the oven. Bake until bubbling, about 30 minutes. Serve immediately.

Yield: 4 to 6 servings.

Note: The dish can be prepared through step 6 up to 12 hours in advance; cover and refrigerate. Remove from the refrigerator 1 hour before baking. Then sprinkle with the Parmesan cheese and bake.

Variations: *At home in Corsica, Madame Cervoni creates many variations of this dish. Instead of Swiss chard or spinach she may use a variety of salad greens from the garden or market, including arugula, any variety of lettuce, and herbs such as mint, parsley, sage, thyme, or tarragon. Bits of ham or minced leftover veal or lamb may also be added to the verdant filling.*

Cote de Boeuf en Croute de Sel La Vieille
CHEZ LA VIEILLE'S RIB STEAK WITH SALT AND PEPPER

Pan-broiling is a quick and delicious way to prepare thick cuts of meat, such as the popular côte de boeuf, *or beef rib. This version, from the homey bistro Chez la Vieille (see page 24), is coated with crushed black peppercorns and coarse sea salt, and served with a marvelous shallot sauce. The beef is just as tasty the next day, cubed and tossed in a salad. Likewise, any leftover shallot sauce is great spread on toasted homemade bread.*

Shallot sauce:
3 tablespoons (1½ ounces; 45 g) unsalted butter
7 ounces (200 g) shallots, minced
Salt and freshly ground white pepper, to taste
¾ cup (18.5 cl) dry white wine
¾ cup (18.5 cl) beef or chicken stock

2 teaspoons black peppercorns
¼ cup coarse sea salt
1 beef rib steak, bone in, cut 1½ inches (4 cm) thick, about 2 pounds (1 kg), at room temperature
3 tablespoons (1½ ounces; 45 g) unsalted butter
3 tablespoons peanut oil

1. Prepare the shallot sauce: In a medium-size saucepan, heat the butter over medium heat. When the butter begins to foam, add the shallots and cook until softened but not colored, about 5 minutes. Season lightly with salt and pepper. Add the wine and the stock, and cook until most of the liquid is reduced and the sauce is thick and almost jamlike, 30 to 40 minutes. (The sauce may be prepared up to 30 minutes ahead. Keep warm, covered, in the top of a double boiler over simmering water. Just before serving, taste for seasoning.)

2. Meanwhile, on a work surface, crush the peppercorns with a heavy mallet or with the bottom of a heavy skillet. Alternatively, crush the peppercorns in a mortar with a pestle. In a small bowl, combine the crushed peppercorns and the sea salt. Press the mixture onto both sides of the meat. Set aside for about 30 minutes at room temperature.

3. Heat a very large cast-iron or heavy-bottomed skillet over high heat for 5 minutes. Add the 3 tablespoons butter and the oil. When the butter has melted, add the steak and sear for 2 minutes on each side, turning with a two-pronged fork inserted into the side of the meat so that the coating is not disturbed. Reduce the heat to medium and cook, without turning, until the meat is done to taste, about 8 minutes more for rare, 10 minutes more for medium-rare, and 12 minutes more for medium. Transfer the beef to a cutting board, cover loosely with foil, and let rest for at least 10 minutes and up to 25 minutes.

4. To serve, carve the beef into ½-inch-thick (1 cm) slices and arrange them on warmed serving plates. Spoon the shallot sauce alongside.

Yield: 4 servings

Opera, Bourse

2nd arrondissement

CHEZ GEORGES
1, rue de Mail,
Paris 2.
Tel: 01.42.60.07.11.
Métro: Sentier.
Service noon to 2 P.M. and 7:30 to 9:30 P.M.
Closed Sunday, holidays, and three weeks in August.
Credit cards: AE,V.
Air-conditioned.
A la carte, 250 to 300 francs.

SPECIALTIES: Bistro: salade de frisée au lard, oeuf poché (curly endive salad with bacon and a poached egg); escalope de saumon à l'oseille (salmon with sorrel); sole au pouilly (sole baked in Pouilly wine); coeur de filet grillé, sauce béarnaise (grilled steak with béarnaise sauce); steak de canard aux cèpes (pan-fried duck breast with meaty wild mushrooms).

Rare is the Parisian bistro that remains solid, steady, and satisfying year after year. But for twenty years I've made repeated pilgrimages to the classic 1900s neighborhood bistro Chez Georges, off the Places des Victoires, and it remains an inimitable example of the dream Paris bistro: convivial and relaxed amidst a controlled murmur of good times. Every millimeter of the long, narrow dining room, with its mirrored walls and Gothic columns, is packed elbow-to-elbow, filled with a carefree, carnivorous crowd that's here as much for the ambience as for the cuisine, and enjoying the warm welcome of owner Bertrand Brouillet. The weight-obsessed, the impatient, the person who needs a space of his own should go elsewhere. Here coats are hung or draped wherever there is room, perfect strangers chat across tables, baskets of freshly sliced country bread from Poilâne and *baguettes* from the nearby *boulangerie* Lebon need constant refilling, and the chirpy waitresses all but skate across the old tile floors, racing through the room with steaming platters of steak, kidneys, grilled lamb chops, duck, sole, and turbot. (That means service can be slow at times, as your hungry eyes follow a steaming platter from the kitchen. You'll tap your fingers and roll your eyes, waiting for a lull so the waitress can take your order.)

On my last visit, starters were as satisfying as ever: celery root bathed in a mustard-rich mayonnaise; fillets of silken marinated herring floating in oil and herbs; *jambon persillé* as fresh as a day in May; springtime curly endive, or *frisée,* tossed with crisp chunks of hot crusty bacon and topped with a perfect poached egg. We may change but the food does not. The bistro star remains the classic *onglet de boeuf,* pan-seared hanger steak that needs little more than salt, pepper, and shallots to bring out its succulent brilliance. At Chez Georges, this prized morsel arrives chewy, tender, silken in texture, with a rich, meaty flavor. As custom dictates, the meat is showered (a bit too generously for my palate) with finely minced shallots, which serve to sweeten and heighten the flavor of the beef. Alongside come fine traditional French fries, which arrive properly crisp from the kitchen. The *steak de canard* is as juicy and meaty as ever, served with huge portions of equally meaty *cèpe* mushrooms; and the almost sweet, truly tender *coeur de filet*—seared beef fillet—comes with a fine *sauce béarnaise,* where the tang of the vinegar and the tarragon cut right into the richness of the meat.

Desserts follow suit, with a fine *profiteroles* and a golden *tarte Tatin.* And the house Brouilly hits the spot, fitting the mood and the moment. Who can ask for more?

ISSE
56, rue Sainte-Anne,
Paris 2.
Tel: 01.42.96.67.76.
Métro: Pyramides.
Service noon to 2 P.M. and 7 to 9:30 P.M.
Closed Saturday lunch, Sunday, Monday lunch, two weeks in August, and two weeks in January.
Credit card: V.
Private dining room for 8.
150-franc lunch menu.
A la carte, 300 to 500 francs.

SPECIALTIES: Japanese: poissons crus (raw fish); sushi bar; grillades (grilled meats).

Issé—a favorite among the city's Japanese restaurants—offers some of the best sushi, sashimi, and tempura in town. This small, casual two-story restaurant not far from the Paris Opéra has a lovely spark, a certain electricity, even though the brown décor is hopelessly plain. The place bustles at lunch and dinner, as Japanese businessmen fill the upstairs dining room, downing chilled bottles of dry Kirin beer along with their sushi, sashimi, and bowls of cloudlike tofu. Downstairs is more casual, with a sushi bar and a few tables for a quick sushi snack. The atmosphere is not unlike a typical Parisian bistro, with waiters weaving past carrying trays full of steaming tofu, giant boats of fresh multitoned sushi, and tiny bamboo trays stacked with crispy tempura.

Go with at least two other diners and order the giant sushi platter, an impressive selection of neat little rounds and rectangles of raw fish fillets on vinegared rice. The assortment includes chunks of silvery-skinned mackerel, mounds of bright red caviar, and little slabs of chewy snow-white squid. There is also bright red fatty tuna, perfect pink crabmeat, remarkably fresh salmon, as well as giant scallops and shrimp, all set on little beds of rice and served with a dab of the fiery green horseradish called wasabi. The chef, Mitsuro Sudo, is also known for his excellent appetizers, such as a feather-light portion of grilled *aubergines,* soft, moist, warm, and full-flavored. Equally wonderful are the stuffed zucchini blossoms filled with crabmeat. As a close to a Japanese feast, try the delicate passion-fruit *sorbet.*

PILE OU FACE
52 bis, rue Notre-Dame-des-Victoires,
Paris 2.
Tel: 01.42.33.64.33.
Fax: 01.42.36.61.09.
Internet: http://www.pileouface.com
Métro: Bourse.
Service noon to 2:30 P.M. and 7:30 to 10:30 P.M.
Closed Saturday lunch, Sunday, and August.
Credit card: AE, V.
Private dining room for 8 to 20.
Air-conditioned.
245-franc lunch menu;
280-franc dinner menu;
320-franc tasting menu.
A la carte, 300 to 450 francs.

SPECIALTIES: Seasonal: les oeufs brouillés de la ferme et purée de morilles (farm-fresh scrambled eggs with a purée of wild morel mushrooms); les ravioles de volaille aux champignons, sauce au foie gras (chicken and mushroom ravioli with foie gras sauce); la mousse de thé Earl Grey, sorbet menthe fraîche en infusion (mousse of Earl Grey tea with fresh mint sorbet).

Well over a decade ago I fell in love with the Pile ou Face style of cooking. It was a cuisine developed by Claude Udron—who trained as a pastry chef in Normandy—and embellished by his partners, Alain Dumergue and Philippe Marquet. Their approach was simple, yet filled with personality and integrity. They wanted their small two-story restaurant across from the Paris Bourse to be at once classic, elegant, and homey. Their cuisine gradually developed into one devoted to farm products from Normandy, including plump chickens, rabbits, and pigeons. Their wine list favored the best of the Rhône valley. And luscious made-to-order desserts, such as a cross between a warm chocolate soufflé and a chocolate mousse, became their signature.

The Pile ou Face (Heads or Tails) trio sold the restaurant in 1996, and it is now in the hands of the capable Gilles Angoulvent, who served as chef at the Michelin two-star Vieille Fontaine in the Paris suburb of Maisons-Laffitte. After a long absence I returned with trepidation. Would one, and could one, carry on the Udron-Dumergue-Marquet legacy? I shouldn't have worried, and I should have returned even sooner. Angoulvent not only pays his respects to what the trio built over the years but adds his own creativity and style. The trademark *marmelade de lapin* (long-simmered rabbit seasoned with herbs, black peppercorns, and cream) was as moist and flavorful as ever, injected with a vigorous hit of fresh rosemary; the fat free-range roast chicken arrived bathed in rich reduced cooking juices and slices of garlic-infused potatoes; and the warm caramelized pineapple with rich vanilla ice cream managed to mitigate my fears. The menu continues to tempt with its caramelized fresh *foie gras;* scrambled eggs with wild morel mushrooms; and guinea hen stuffed with fresh chervil. Angoulvent's own touch of creativity comes forth in a very cohesive and successful beggar's purse of warm goat cheese—a baked, cheese-filled phyllo packet served with a warm tomato-cream sauce and a dollop of a Provençal purée (the personification of a smooth and enticing ratatouille). Equally professional was his sauté of varied wild mushrooms, rich as a meat *daube* and equally fulfilling.

The plush, dark décor—which some loathe, some adore, and others simply tolerate—remains unchanged, while the service is youthful, good-humored, and nonintrusive. The wine list still offers many worthy selections, including R. and L. Legras's good-value dry Champagne; the strong dry red Collioure 1992 Domaine du Mas Blanc; the simply delicious 1993 Bourgogne from the Potel family's Domaine de la Pousse d'Or in Volnay; and J. Faivelay's tasty white Rully.

CAFE RUNTZ
16, rue Favart,
Paris 2.
Tel: 01.42.96.69.86.
Fax: 01.40.20.92.95.
Métro: Richelieu-Drouot or Opéra.
Service 11:45 A.M. to 2:45 P.M. and 6:00 to 11:30 P.M.
Closed Saturday lunch, Sunday, one week in May, and three weeks in August.
Credit cards: AE, DC, V.
Air-conditioned.
Private dining room for 40.
129-franc menu.
A la carte, 180 to 220 francs.

SPECIALTIES:
Alsatian: salade de cervelas (salad of potatoes and pork sausage); jambonneau grillé (grilled pork knuckle); boudin noir aux pommes (blood sausage with apples); choucroute gourmet (sauerkraut, potatoes, sausages, bacon, and pork knuckle).

The French have a wonderful expression for those days when you can't seem to make any progress, when you feel as though you are permanently stuck: *"pédaler dans le choucroute,"* or pedal in sauerkraut. Well, you won't feel that way after you've had the top-rate *choucroute* platter served at the small, adorable Café Runtz, one of the city's best Alsatian finds, not far from the Paris Opéra. The café itself dates from 1850, when it took its place across the street from the Salle Favart, the former Opéra Comique. Since 1989 Odette and Hubert Leport have pampered and polished this historic café, newly decorated with cheery blue-and-white plaid fabric tablecloths and comfortable upholstered chairs.

Madame Leport will most likely greet you wearing the traditional dress of her native Strasbourg. The aromas, too, are authentic. Nine out of ten diners who pass through the door here order one of the Leport *choucroute* platters. As chef Hubert Leport enjoys adding his own variations, he offers a delicious version that includes a pair of grilled *boudins noirs* (blood sausages), a layer of apples, and grilled bacon set on a mound of well-seasoned *choucroute.* His traditional signature dish, billed as *choucroute paysanne,* includes a top-quality assortment of grilled and poached sausages, beautifully grilled mildly smoked bacon, as well as the traditional steamed potato accompaniment.

Since Madame Leport herself finds Alsatian beer the most digestible accompaniment, Café Runtz offers some of the finest regional beer from the house of Schutzenberger. I also love their house Riesling, a 1992 from the winemaker Gustave Loretniz in Bergheim, a wine with a brilliant balance of sweetness and acidity.

VAUDEVILLE
29, rue Vivienne,
Paris 2.
Tel: 01.40.20.04.62.
Fax: 01.49.27.08.78.
Métro: Bourse.
Service noon to 3:30 P.M. and 7 P.M. to 2 A.M.
Closed Christmas Eve.
Credit cards: AE, DC, V.
Sidewalk terrace.
Air-conditioned.
123-franc lunch menu; 169-franc dinner menu.
A la carte, 220 to 270 francs.

SPECIALTIES:
Brasserie: banc d'huîtres et de fruits de mer toute l'année (fresh oysters and shellfish, year-round); foie gras frais, gelée au Riesling (fresh fatted duck liver in a Riesling wine gelatin); poisson du marché (fresh seasonal fish); grillades (grilled meats).

Vaudeville is a bustling, dependable 1925 brasserie filled with mirrors, marble, and the sounds of good times. This is the sort of place I like to go with a large group, order up some *carafes* of the chilled house Riesling, and feast on oysters, scallops, mussels, or sole. Meatier specialties, such as pork knuckle with lentils, calf's liver, and a duck and white bean *cassoulet,* are also part of the huge menu that changes from day to day. In good weather, reserve a table on the sidewalk terrace, facing the imposing Bourse, or stock exchange.

THAT PARISIAN PALLOR

"City dwellers of long standing and newly arrived rustics were widely different in appearance and manners. The former were large and plump, pink and white, their complexion unspoilt by work in the fields, and their physical ideal was the round-bellied bulk of the self-made bourgeois, accustomed to good food and unwearied by manual labor. The *patronnes* of inns and brothels were always fresh and pale, real Parisians who neither knew nor liked the sun, which scarcely penetrated the narrow streets of the old *quartiers.*"

The People of Paris, An Essay in Popular Culture in the 18th Century, by Daniel Roche

Rambuteau, Temple, Arts et Metiers

3rd arrondissement

AMBASSADE D'AUVERGNE
22, rue du Grenier Saint-Lazare,
Paris 3.
Tel: 01.42.72.31.22.
Fax: 01.42.78.85.47.
Métro: Rambuteau.
Service noon to 2 P.M. and 7:30 to 10:30 P.M.
Open daily.
Credit cards: AE, V.
Private dining rooms for 10 to 40.
Air-conditioned.
150-franc menu.
A la carte, 220 to 250 francs.

SPECIALTIES:
Auvergnat: salade de lentilles vertes du Puy (dark green lentil salad with vinaigrette); soupe au choux (cabbage soup); saucisse aligot (pork sausage with mashed potatoes with tomme, the fresh curds used in making Cantal cheese, and garlic); filet de boeuf de Salers (beef fillet from Salers in the Auvergne).

I would be hard-pressed to name a Parisian restaurant with more regional soul than Ambassade d'Auvergne, a veritable temple devoted to such robust delights as the Auvergne's sturdy pork sausage, beef from Salers, seven-hour leg of lamb, and potatoes and cabbage in many wondrous forms.

For nearly two decades, this large yet quietly familial and casual restaurant just steps from the Beaubourg has been a personal favorite, a place I love to go to when I crave the simple, the rustic, the robust, all at prices that won't break the bank. Their ingredients are top-rate, with prized beef from the village of Salers, Roquefort from the Carles family, mountain cheese from Laguiole, and *cabécou* goat cheese from the Périgord. I always come prepared for portions of hearty, homey fare, sipping the berry-like red Chanturgue, a pinot noir from the vineyards surrounding the town of Clermont-Ferrand. Do try the salad of dark green lentils bathed in a vinegary-pungent vinaigrette; the crowd-pleasing *saucisses d'auvergne* served with generous portions of rich *aligot,* that smooth and unctuous mix of potato purée, garlic, and gentle *tomme fraîche;* and the fabulous selection of regional cheeses.

L'Ami Louis (facing page).

L'AMI LOUIS
32, rue Vertbois,
Paris 3.
Tel: 01.48.87.77.48
Métro: Temple.
Service noon to 2 P.M. and 8 to 11 P.M.
Closed Monday, Tuesday, and July 19 to August 25.
Credit cards: AE, DC, V.
A la carte, 750 to 850 francs.

SPECIALTIES:
Bistro: foie gras (fatted duck liver); coquilles Saint-Jacques (scallops sautéed with garlic and tomatoes); gigot d'agneau (roast leg of lamb); poulet rôti (roast chicken).

L'Ami Louis is a veritable Paris phenomenon. Few restaurants are as dilapidated, quirky, or outrageously priced. Yet people beg, cry, weep, for a table here. I go at least two or three times a year, always with friends who love the place and can't get enough of it. It is always an evening to remember. No one in Paris—not even the top chefs—offers a better roast chicken or tender roast baby leg of lamb. Those two dishes are worth the price of admission all on their own. I always find the *foie gras* overcooked and underseasoned, the *pommes allumettes* (shoestring potatoes) a bit dull, the thick potato cake too harshly showered with raw garlic. However, on a cold winter's night the sea scallops sautéed with garlic can hit the spot, and the recent addition of an excellent *tarte Tatin* for dessert is long overdue. Warning: If you have to ask the prices here, you can't afford to go.

AU BASCOU
38, rue Réamur,
Paris 3.
Tel: 01.42.72.69.25.
Métro: Arts et Métiers.
Service noon to 2 P.M. and 8 to 10:30 P.M.
Closed Saturday lunch, Sunday, three weeks in August, and Christmas week.
Credit cards: AE, V.
A la carte, 180 to 250 francs.

SPECIALTIES:
Modern bistro, with Basque specialties: pimentoes del piquillo farcie (red peppers stuffed with salt cod purée); pipérade basquaise (modern version of scrambled eggs with tomato, ham, onions, and peppers); boudin de pays (fresh blood sausage); axoa de veau comme à Espelette (ground veal, onions, and fresh Basque chiles); chipirons à l'encre (tiny squid in ink).

In cooking, as in many arts, the most obvious rule is all too often ignored: Cook with the freshest of ingredients and you're 90 percent assured of success. The rule has never seemed as self-evident as it did at a recent dinner at Jean-Guy Lousteau's rustic bistro. If anything can save French cuisine from modern-day decline, it is chefs like Lousteau. The key to his success? Deep roots in the French countryside, precise knowledge of the region's ingredients, and a true passion for his work. What's more, he puts a personal imprint on his establishment, setting it apart from the trend toward faceless, run-of-the-mill bistros. Lousteau—who comes from the picturesque Basque village Saint-Jean-Pied-de-Port—opened his quirky little spot (complete with comfortable old movie-theater seats at some tables) after long stints with chef Alain Dutournier at Au Trou Gascon and later at Carré des Feuillants.

Once you sample the luscious, ultra-fresh fare at Au Bascou, you will wonder where the place has been all your life. It's all about earthy food with intense flavors, prepared with ingredients that simply make you stand up and take notice. Even Lousteau's little starters, offered with a glass of chilled fino sherry, are top-of-the-line: green and black olives bathed in herbs and oil and a tiny platter of *cochonnailles,* including glistening sausages and slices of ham that taste fresh, intense, obviously cured with care and attention.

First courses, such as the *gambas grillées à la barigoule* and the *salade de pipérade basquaise,* follow suit. The ultra-fresh giant prawns are grilled in their shells and served with baby mussels set on a bed of artichokes laced with a touch of cream. Each ingredient maintains its own character, yet each seems logically at home with the other. The Basque-style salad updated for the 1990s includes a dense mélange of red and green sweet peppers, onions, and hot peppers bound with a bit of egg and set upon a tossed salad. All is topped with paper-thin slices of full-flavored ham.

Among the main courses, there's a crispy-crunchy sauté of *chipirons,* or baby squid, on a bed of delicious almondy rice—simple yet sublime. But the one dish worth a detour all of its own is the roasted baby lamb, *agneau de lait,* from the Pyrénées. As Lousteau points out, fall is the time of year to eat baby lamb, since the animals were born in the mountains during the summer months while their mothers nibbled wild mountain fare. The chef marinates the super-tender, moist lamb in oil with a touch of mustard, then roasts it at very high heat. Alongside he serves a mixed purée of potatoes and nutty white beans, glazed with a touch of butter and a thin slice of ham and gratinéed ever so carefully. The flavors are explosive, warming, and unforgettable.

After all this, dessert may seem like an afterthought. But it was not: Lousteau suggested a cool and soothing parfait flavored with Basque Izarra liqueur (prepared with an Armagnac base) and set on a bed of cherry preserves. The wine choice is huge and well chosen: Allow Lousteau to guide you, from the heady Madiran to the pleasing Irouléguy.

Chou Farci Ambassade d'Auvergne
Ambassade d'Auvergne's Stuffed Cabbage

This is a "Sunday-night supper" dish; it's easy to make and popular with those who love hearty one-dish meals. I also find it fun to make. The Ambassade d'Auvergne (see page 32) features the cuisine of the Auvergne region in central France, where cabbage, sausage, and smoked bacon are daily fare. The restaurant's version is stuffed with well-seasoned pork sausage, prunes, and Swiss chard, the popular green and white ribbed vegetable known in France as blette. *Chopped fresh spinach can be substituted, but when I could find neither Swiss chard nor spinach in the market, I made the dish anyway, and it was a big hit. Be sure to cook the bacon just before serving so that it offers a crispy contrast in color and texture. Bring the whole cabbage to the table on a platter, and slice it in front of the family or guests, for it forms a pretty mosaic pattern.*

Stuffing:
6 ounces (185 g) fresh Swiss chard or spinach, rinsed, dried, and coarsely chopped
1 large bunch parsley, minced
1 large onion, minced
1 clove garlic, minced
10 ounces (310 g) pork sausage meat
1 egg
1 slice white bread, soaked in 2 tablespoons milk
Salt and freshly ground black pepper, to taste

1 cabbage
Salt and freshly ground black pepper, to taste
6 ounces (185 g) prunes, pitted
1 cup (25 cl) dry white wine
1 quart (1 liter) meat or poultry stock
6 ounces (185 g) slab bacon, rind removed, cut into bite-size pieces

1. Preheat the oven to 475°F (245°C).

2. In a large bowl, combine the stuffing ingredients and mix until well blended. Season to taste.

3. Bring a large pot of water to boil. Separate the leaves of the cabbage and blanch them in the boiling water for 5 minutes. Rinse under cold water until cool, then drain.

4. Lay a dampened 24 × 24-inch (60 × 60-cm) piece of cheesecloth on a work surface. "Reconstruct" the cabbage, beginning with the largest leaves, arranging the leaves so the outer side, where the rib is most prominent, is on the inside. Season each layer with salt and pepper. Continue until all the leaves have been used.

5. Form the stuffing into a ball, pushing 4 pitted prunes into the center. Place the ball of stuffing in the center of the cabbage and bring the leaves up to envelop the stuffing. Bring the cheesecloth up around the rounded cabbage and tie securely. Place the cabbage in a deep baking dish. Add the remaining prunes and the wine, season to taste, and cover with the stock.

6. Bake for 1½ to 2 hours. Just before serving, sauté the slab bacon in a small skillet until very crisp. Unwrap the cabbage and place on a serving platter. Garnish with the prunes and grilled bacon. Cut into wedge-shaped pieces and serve immediately.

Yield: 4 to 6 servings

Le Marais, Hotel de Ville, Ile Saint-Louis

4th arrondissement

L'AMBROISIE
9, place des Vosges,
Paris 4.
Tel: 01.42.78.51.45.
Métro: Saint-Paul.
Service noon to 2:15 P.M. and 8 to 10:15 P.M.
Closed Sunday, Monday, three weeks in August, and during school vacations in February.
Credit cards: AE, V.
Private dining room for 10 to 12.
Air-conditioned.
A la carte, 900 to 1,300 francs.

SPECIALTIES:
Seasonal: feuillantine de queues de langoustines aux graines de sésame, sauce au curry (Dublin Bay prawns with sesame in curry sauce); pigeon confit à l'ail doux (confit of pigeon with sweet garlic); ragoût de févettes à la sarriette (ragoût of baby fava beans with summer savory); tarte fine sablée au chocolat (chocolate tart).

Ever since Bernard and Danielle Pacaud opened their modest little Left Bank bistro in the 1980s, they have followed a clear and steady course. Always discreet, always refined, always eager to communicate their passion for their work, they have also always won. Their elegant, newly redecorated restaurant on the luxurious Place des Vosges is one of the city's most romantic, and also one of the best. It's hard to beat the L'Ambroisie look, with ancient stone floors, glorious tapestries, impeccable lighting, ebullient sprays of flowers, and a myriad of well-considered details that form a perfect backdrop to Pacaud's compact, faithful repertoire of dishes that seamlessly encompass the classic and the modern.

Diners will never go wrong with the signature dishes—feathery *langoustines* in an Asian-inspired curry sauce; densely flavored oxtail stew; and a fortifying chocolate tart—but such contemporary additions as a well-focused and airy lasagne of wild *cèpe* mushrooms will keep us all coming back. Add to this the service of a personable, well-trained staff led by Danielle Pacaud and Pierre Le Moullac, and you have one of Paris's finest examples of a grand French restaurant.

BARACANE–BISTROT DE L'OULETTE
38, rue des Tournelles,
Paris 4.
Tel: 01.42.71.43.33.
Métro: Bastille or Chemin Vert.
Service noon to 2:15 P.M. and 7 P.M. to midnight.
Closed Saturday lunch and Sunday.
Credit card: V.
52- and 85-franc lunch menus; 135- and 215-franc lunch and dinner menus.
A la carte, 200 to 300 francs.

Baracane–Bistrot de l'Oulette, just a few steps from the Place des Vosges in the Marais, remains one of the neighborhood's bargain bistros. Owner Marcel Baudis—who opened the original L'Oulette on this spot several years ago—has moved on to new quarters in the Bercy neighborhood, near the Gare de Lyon. But he still oversees this modest, highly popular spot with a fine eye, and the food served in this narrow dining room is unchanged from its L'Oulette days. Chef Baudis, a native of Montauban in France's southwest, offers solid country fare that's unfussy, ultra-fresh, and intelligently seasoned. Some of the best selections here include the fresh marinated sardines served with a delicious

SPECIALTIES:
Southwestern: salade Quercynoise aux gésiers confits (green salad with preserved duck gizzards); terrine de poireaux, vinaigrette de xères (leek terrine with sherry vinegar vinaigrette); confit de canard aux pommes de terre persillées (preserved duck with parsleyed potatoes); le cabécous de Rocamadour (goat's milk cheese from Rocamadour); clafoutis aux poires (pear flan).

confit of tomatoes; an earthy terrine of chicken livers and *foie gras;* roasted duck breast, or *magret de canard;* and leg of lamb from the Lozère, grilled with a touch of thyme. Not to mention the wonderful bread from a favorite Paris baker, Jean-Luc Poujauran.

BENOIT
20, rue Saint Martin, Paris 4.
Tel: 01.42.72.25.76.
Fax: 01.42.72.45.68.
Métro: Châtelet or Hôtel de Ville.
Service noon to 2 P.M. and 8 to 10 P.M.
Open daily. Closed in August.
Credit card: AE.
Air-conditioned.
200-franc lunch menu.
A la carte, 450 to 500 francs.

SPECIALTIES:
Bistro: filet de saumon fumé mariné (smoked salmon marinated in oil and vegetables); cassoulet maison (casserole of beans and meats); boeuf mode aux carrottes (beef with carrots); coquilles Saint-Jacques en saison (fresh sea scallops from October to May).

Benoit is such a Paris institution that it is hard to picture the city without it. It's the quintessential old-time bistro, founded by Benoit Matray in 1912. Since 1959 this sparkling, romantic, museum-quality bistro has been run by Matray's grandson, Michel Petit. I visit in each season, anticipating such standbys as a well-seasoned *salade de boeuf;* an imaginative mussel soup flavored with smoked bacon; and great roast game or poultry with wild mushrooms.

Monsieur Petit makes sure the menu offers a mix of old and new, and he is always updating (and trying to lighten) the classics, so diners leave hungering to return. Some favorites here include a hearty *jarret de veau,* or veal knuckle, served with a mix of tomatoes and green olives; a soothing chicken in tarragon vinegar and tomato sauce; marinated smoked salmon with potato salad; and a stunning *charlotte aux fruits rouge,* a refreshing dessert of lady fingers filled with raspberries and wild strawberries. On my last visit, the *salade printanière* was fantastic, a blend of white and green asparagus, snow peas, green beans, chives, artichokes, and chervil dressed with a walnut vinaigrette. Also appealing is Monsieur Petit's version of a whole chicken roasted in a crust of sea salt.

The crusty *baguettes* come from prize-winning baker Gosselin and the cheese from master cheesemonger Roger Alléosse. Best bets from the wine list include Charles Jouguet's meaty and memorable Chinon "Clos de la Cure" and Bernard Gripa's white Saint-Péray.

Saumon Fume Marine aux Aromates Benoit
BENOIT'S MARINATED SMOKED SALMON WITH HERBS

Bistro goes modern in this updated version of marinated smoked salmon. At one of my favorite bistros, Benoit (see page 37), they marinate house-smoked salmon as one would smoked herring—that is, smothered in onions, carrots, herbs, and oil. The dish is served as a first course, out of large white terrines, and is accompanied by a vinaigrette-dressed potato salad. It's a wonderful dish to have on hand to serve with a tossed green salad or with sliced potatoes. Any good-quality smoked fish can be used here, including trout, salmon trout, sturgeon, or salmon.

12 ounces (375 g) smoked fish (such as fillets or thin slices of salmon, salmon trout, trout, or sturgeon)
2 shallots, peeled and sliced into thin rounds
2 onions, peeled and sliced into thin rounds
2 carrots, peeled and sliced into thin rounds
2 bay leaves
2 teaspoons fresh thyme leaves
12 black peppercorns
2 to 3 cups (50 to 75 cl) peanut oil

1. In a 1-quart (1-liter) oval or rectangular terrine, layer half of each of the ingredients, except for the oil, in this order: smoked fish, shallots, onions, carrots, bay leaves, thyme, peppercorns. Add a second layer in the same order. Add enough oil to cover. Cover securely and refrigerate for at least 2 days and up to 2 weeks.

2. Remove the terrine from the refrigerator 1 hour before serving. To serve: With a large fork, carefully remove a portion of fish, drain it thoroughly, and place on a small salad plate. Garnish with a few rounds of carrots and onions. Serve with bread, warm potato salad, or a tossed green salad.

Yield: 8 servings

BOFINGER
5, rue de la Bastille,
Paris 4.
Tel: 01.42.72.87.82.
Fax: 01.42.72.97.68.
Métro: Bastille.
Service noon to 3 P.M. and 7 P.M. to 1 A.M.
Open daily.
Credit cards: AE, DC, V.
Private dining rooms for 30 to 80 at lunch, 10 at dinner.
178-franc menu, including service and a half-bottle of wine.
A la carte, 230 to 250 francs, including service.

There are institutions—like Bofinger—that one loves to love. But sometimes love gets in the way. I've stopped counting how many times I've returned to Bofinger, the glistening movie set of a Belle Epoque brasserie imbued with that carefree turn-of-the-century *joie de vivre* and the modern sounds of good times. Too often I have left saying I would never return. No matter how lovely, no matter how historical, the slapdash service and slapdash food were always too much. I don't think this is the way Frédéric Bofinger thought it should be when, as a young refugee from Alsace-Lorraine, he opened Paris's first brasserie on rue de la Bastille in 1864. He was the first to serve freshly brewed beer on tap—*"à la pompe"*—and kept the restaurant open 24

SPECIALTIES:
Brasserie: plateaux de fruits de mer (platters of raw and cooked shellfish); mariné de sardines fraîches aux légumes croquants (marinated fresh sardines with crunchy vegetable salad); choucroute (sauerkraut, sausages, bacon, and pork).

hours a day. City folks came to down bowls of gratinéed onion soup and platters of sausages and sauerkraut, known as *choucroute.* Over the years, the menu remained constant and generations of celebrated diners, from Maurice Chevalier to gastronome Curnonsky, came and went, while a revolving door of owners embellished and enlarged. What we see today—the sparkling glass roof, the voluptuous ceramics, the frivolous tulip-shaped lamps, the undulating wrought-iron staircase—is pure 1919, preserved and restored in 1982.

So enter Jean-Paul Boucher, brasserie king, who took over this venerable institution in 1996, vowing to "change nothing." Change he did. And change he didn't. First for the food: thank goodness it's better. A few recent return visits—one in the company of Monsieur Boucher himself and another as a civilian diner stuffed in an Anglophone corner on a sweltering Paris night—suggest the cuisine is crawling its way out of the slump. Suddenly the food appears clean, sparkling, original (but not too much so), and satisfying. Fresh sardines are marinated ever so lightly, then teamed with a salad of *légumes croquants* (crunchy vegetables), which I would dub a deliciously updated French coleslaw: Minute bits of cabbage and carrots are bathed in light sauce and molded in a very French *timbale.* Daily specials—such as *calmars,* or squid, sautéed with tomatoes and peppers, or cubes of veal sautéed and bathed in a light stock—arrive fresh, well seasoned, and convincing. The menu justifiably keeps such classics as Baltic herring bathed in cream and dill, but also offers a refreshing, richly flavored cold tomato soup dotted with cubes of monkfish and showered with leaves of fresh basil.

The compact wine list offers quite a few worthy selections, including Guigal's red Côtes-du-Rhône, his Tavel, and Faiveley's Montagny, a white Burgundy.

The service is another story. On a given night you may be ushered to your table by one waiter, be handed the menu by another, have your order taken by a third presence, and be served by a fourth. That means that when you wave your hand, put in a second request for an *apéritif,* or simply flail your arms in impatient rage, no one is responsible, no one is in charge. Democracy is also not a word to be found in Bofinger's dictionary. Neighboring diners who arrive after you may be served well before you. Some diners are given olives with their *apéritifs,* some a bowl of pretzels. Some tables are offered *petit fours* with coffee, others are not. Petty details, you say? Restaurateurs think diners don't notice what's going on at the next table. But with so much time on one's hands while waiting for results from the wait staff, you bet they do.

BISTROT DU DOME BASTILLE
2, rue de la Bastille,
Paris 4.
Tel: 01.48.04.88.44.
Fax: 01.48.04.00.59.
Métro: Bastille.
Service 12:30 to 2:30 P.M. and 7:30 to 11:30 P.M.
Open daily.
Credit card: V.
Air-conditioned.
A la carte, 180 to 240 francs.

SPECIALTIES:
Fish and shellfish: friture de céteaux (pan-fried whole baby sole); raie en vinaigrette (poached skate in vinaigrette); turbotin béarnaise (whole turbot with tarragon sauce).

This popular Bastille annex of the famed Le Dôme restaurant in Montparnasse serves the same excellent, well-priced fare as its sister offshoot, the Bistrot du Dôme on rue Delambre in the 14th *arrondissement* (see pages 113 and 114).

There are some welcome givens here: The fish is uniformly fresh. The food is traditional without being trite. The white wine is always good and will never break the bank. And after the meal, you get to stroll through the charming Place des Vosges.

LE GRIZZLI
7, rue Saint-Martin,
Paris 4.
Tel: 01.48.87.77.56.
Métro: Châtelet–Les Halles or Hôtel de Ville.
Service noon to 2:15 P.M. and 7:30 to 10 P.M.
Closed Sunday.
Credit cards: AE, V.
Terrace dining.
Private dining room for 30 to 35.
120-franc lunch menu; 160-franc lunch and dinner menu.
A la carte, 200 to 250 francs.

If you want a spot on a breezy terrace on a fine summer's night, food that is prepared with care, knowledge, and attention, and the fine greeting of owner Bernard Areny, Le Grizzli is for you. There is the bright red exterior, the handsome grizzly greeting you at the door, and broad city views from the pleasant terrace to let you know you are in the center of Paris. If they are on the menu when you visit, do order the platter of perfectly sautéed *girolle* (chanterelle) mushrooms—woodsy fresh, filling, and satisfying. The lamb chops (and other meats and fish) are cooked *"sur l'ardoise,"* over pieces of slate set directly on the flame, the way it's still done in the Auvergne in central France. My lamb (direct from the Auvergne) was deliciously moist and ten-

SPECIALTIES:
Bistro: ratatouille froide l'oeuf poché (cold ratatouille with warm poached egg); pièce de boeuf cuit sur l'ardoise (beef cooked on a slate); fricot de veau aux queues de cèpes sechées (veal shoulder simmered in white wine with vegetables and dried wild mushrooms); cassoulet aux haricots tarbas (casserole of large white beans, including various combinations of sausages, duck, pork, lamb, mutton, and goose).

der, and served with a copious garnish of sautéed potatoes and a fresh green salad.

Le Grizzli offers an extraordinary farm-made and farm-aged Saint-Nectaire cheese (even the best cheese shops in Paris can't compete with this one), earthy rye bread, and a delightful pure syrah from Corbières, a 1994 Délicatesse de Charles Cros.

BRASSERIE DE L'ILE SAINT LOUIS
55, quai de Bourbon, Paris 4.
Tel: 01.43.54.02.59.
Fax: 01.46.33.18.47.
Métro: Pont Marie.
No reservations. Continuous service, noon to 1 A.M.
Closed Wednesday and August.
Credit card: V.
Sidewalk terrace.
A la carte, 150 to 180 francs.

SPECIALTIES:
Alsatian brasserie: choucroute garnie (sauerkraut, pork, and sausages); jarret de porc aux lentilles (pork knuckle with lentils); omelettes (omelets); munster au cumin (Alsatian cow's milk cheese with cumin); tarte à l'oignon (onion and cream tart); sorbets Berthillon (Berthillon sorbets).

Always bustling, noisy, and crowded, this Ile Saint-Louis institution hits the spot when your mood is jovial and social. The price is right, the beer is chilled, and the selections are authentically Alsatian. I love to go with a crowd for Sunday lunch, and order up sauerkraut and sausages, a mug of beer, and a slice of Alsatian Munster, served with a sprinkling of cumin alongside. With its location right across from Notre Dame and in the heart of Ile Saint-Louis, the Brasserie is in a "win-win" situation.

LET THEM EAT PEAS

"Eat peas with the rich and cherries with the poor" is an old French saying. The rich were able to afford the best crop of peas, the very earliest. The finest cherries of the season, however, are the last: They are usually the ripest and most flavorful, also the cheapest and most plentiful. During the seventeenth century, the French became impassioned over the fashionable pea: At court, women would dine with the king, feasting on peas, then return home to eat more before going to bed, even if it meant indigestion. "It is a fashion, a furor," wrote one court chronicler.

OYSTERS

He was, indeed, a brave man who first ate an oyster. But from the moment that intrepid gentleman slid it down his throat, this pale, glistening, meaty shellfish was destined for stardom, and one can be certain that Frenchmen eagerly shouldered their gastronomic responsibilities.

Up until the 1850s oysters were so plentiful in Paris they were considered poor man's food, even though the journey from the Brittany shores to Paris was never a simple one. Oysters traveled in wooden carts laden with ice, and as it melted it was regularly replenished at ice houses set along the route.

During the 18th century, oyster criers filled the streets of Paris, carrying wicker hampers on their backs filled with their inexpensive fare. Although the colorful hawkers are gone, today France remains a major oyster producer—cultivating some 1,400 tons of precious shallow, round, flat-shelled Belon-style *plates* oysters and more than 81,000 tons of deep, elongated, crinkle-shelled *creuses* oysters. From Cherbourg in the north to Toulon along the Mediterranean, French fishermen in high rubber boots and thick jerseys carry out their battle with nature. Each oyster is nursed from infancy to maturity, a labor of three to four years.

Baby oyster larvae begin life floating in the sea with plankton, searching about for something to grip onto. Their survival rate is low: Out of a batch of 100,000 larvae, only a dozen survive.

Six to seven months later the larvae have grown to spats—now about the size of a fingernail—and are detached and moved along to another *parc* (oyster bed) where they remain from 1 to 2½ years.

Then the flat-shelled *plates* are often dispatched to river estuaries, where the shallow, warmish blend of salt and fresh water helps them develop their distinctly sweet, creamy flavor.

The more common, crinkle-shelled *creuses*—which grow twice as fast as the *plates*—might be transferred several times before they swing into their final stage of development. They spend the last few months of their lives in swampy, shallow, slightly alkaline fattening beds known as *claires*, where they pick up their unusual green tinge by feasting on certain flourishing microscopic blue algae. The longer the oysters remain in the fattening beds, the greener, more richly flavored, and more valuable they become.

Just before oysters are ready for the market, they spend a few days being purified in reservoirs. There they are dipped in and out of water so they learn to keep their shells shut. As long as the oyster remains chilled and the shell stays closed during transport, the oyster can survive on its own store of saline solution. Once out of the water, it will easily stay alive for eight days in winter, two days in warmer summer months.

Oysters are generally available in a number of sizes. The larger are more expensive, though not necessarily better. They are best eaten raw, on the half shell from a bed of crushed ice, without lemon or vinegar. They need no further embellishment than a glass of Muscadet or Sancerre and a slice of buttered rye bread.

Plates: The two most popular types of flat French oyster are the prized *Belon*, a small, elegant oyster that is slightly salty, faintly oily, with a hint of hazelnut; and the fringy, green-tinged *Marennes*. *Plates* are calibrated according to their weight; the smallest and least expensive, no. 5, offers about 1 ounce (30 grams) of meat, while the largest and most expensive, no. 0000, called the *pied de cheval*, or horse's hoof, about 3 ounces (100 grams).

Creuses: France's most common oyster—deep, elongated, and crinkle-shelled. The *creuse* is sometimes called the *Portugaise*, even though this variety of oyster was essentially replaced by the *Japonaise* after the Portuguese oyster was struck by a gill disease in 1967.

The three common subcategories of *creuse* relate to the method of final aging, or fattening. The smallest are the *huîtres de parc*; the medium-size are known as *fines de claires*, oysters that have spent about two months aging in the fattening beds, or *claires*, with forty to fifty oysters to the square meter; and the *spéciales*, the largest, are aged in fattening beds for up to six months, just three to five oysters to the square meter.

Creuses are calibrated according to weight, from the smallest and least expensive, *petite*, which weighs a bit over 1 ounce (50 grams), to the largest and most expensive, *très grosse*, which weighs about 3 ounces (100 grams).

MIRAVILE
72, quai de l'Hôtel de Ville, Paris 4.
Tel: 01.42.74.72.22.
Fax: 01.42.74.67.55.
Métro: Pont Marie.
Service noon to 2 P.M. and 7:30 to 10:30 P.M.
Closed Saturday lunch, Sunday, and two weeks in August.
Credit cards: AE, V.
Small terrace.
Private dining room for 10 to 30.
Air-conditioned.
250-franc menu.
A la carte, 350 francs.

SPECIALTIES:
Contemporary: terrine de jarret de veau (veal knuckle terrine); rémoulade de betterave (slivers of beets tossed in mayonnaise with capers and mustard); pintadeau en crapaudine (flattened and grilled guinea hen).

Some addresses seem destined for constant turnover, and 72, Quai de l'Hôtel de Ville is one of them. In the past fifteen years, the spot has hosted a number of successful chefs, at least two of whom (Georges Masraff and Gilles Epie) packed their bags for the United States and never came back. One almost wonders if the newest chef, David Feau, who took over the stoves in the spring of 1998, already has his papers in order for the journey across the Atlantic. For Parisian diners' sake, one hopes that the young and boyish Feau will stay awhile, for his simple, sane, clear food is what we need more of in Paris. When French chefs hit it right, they can make one plus two taste like fifty-five.

Feau's style appeals to jaded palates who want something classic with a modern touch. He might open with a surprise offering of a creamy molded *dariole* of *foie gras* and chicken livers, a silken and not-too-rich starter that is drizzled with a sweet caramel sauce, making your palate wonder whether it's the beginning or the end of the meal. In truth, the sweetness is appealing, and a fine contrast to the rich acidity of the *foie gras.* The 250-franc menu might include a slightly bland first-course *terrine* of *jarret de veau* paired with a wonderful *rémoulade* of red beets, slivers of beets tossed in a mayonnaise enriched with capers and mustard. The same menu offers a delightful *pintadeau en crapaudine,* or farm-fresh guinea hen flattened and grilled and served with an exquisite polenta. From the regular menu, try the tender and delicious roast Bresse chicken and the *tarte Tatin aux poires.*

The bread is pretty dreadful. The homemade olive bread is too soft and without character, and the tough, dry rolls are an embarrassment to an otherwise successful meal.

LATIN QUARTER

5th arrondissement

BALZAR
49, rue des Ecoles,
Paris 5.
Tel: 01.43.54.13.67.
Fax: 01.44.07.14.91.
Métro: Odéon or Cluny–La Sorbonne.
Service noon to midnight.
Open daily.
Credit cards: AE, V.
Sidewalk terrace.
Air-conditioned.
A la carte, 160 to 200 francs.

SPECIALTIES:
Traditional bistro: poireaux vinaigrette (leeks in vinaigrette); foie de veau poêlé (pan-fried calf's liver); raie au beurre fondu (skate sautéed in butter); poulet fermier rôti (roasted farm chicken); soupe à l'oignon gratinée (onion soup, evenings only).

When the Brasserie Flo chain took over the famed Balzar in 1998, it was front-page news in the French press. The vociferous regulars feared this national monument would lose its luster. So far, however, this quintessential lively, noisy, bustling brasserie remains one of the best Left Bank hangouts. I love their crisp roast chicken, simple but fresh *salade de mâche* (lamb's lettuce), extraordinary *tarte Tatin,* and very drinkable Côtes-du-Rhône. The well-seasoned waiters, dressed in black vests and long white aprons, carry on the perfect French bistro banter, teasing and cajoling to gales of laughter and good times. This is a good place to know about during off-hours—when you want a full meal at three in the afternoon, for example.

LES BOUCHONS DE FRANCOIS CLERC
12, rue de l'Hôtel Colbert,
Paris 5.
Tel: 01.43.54.15.34.
Fax: 01.46.34.68.07.
Métro: Maubert-Mutualité.
Service noon to 2 P.M. and 7:30 to 10:30 P.M.
Closed Saturday lunch and Sunday.
Credit cards: AE, V.
117-franc lunch menu.
219-franc universal lunch and dinner menu.

SPECIALTIES:
Contemporary: escabèche de sardines (sardines pan-fried, then marinated in a blend of herbs, wine, and vinegar); tournedos de thon (pan-fried tuna steak); épaule de Pauillac rôtie sur os (lamb from Pauillac roasted on the bone).

Situated in a beautifully restored stone and wood-beamed space around the corner from Notre Dame, Les Bouchons de François Clerc made headlines when it opened in 1995. Owner François Clerc wisely decided to offer all his wines at cost rather than the normal three to four times markup found at most restaurants. The restaurant was an instant success and remains one of the city's best bargains for sampling everything from a simple white Vouvray to the generally expensive Domaine de Trevallon from Provence.

The food is honorable, with a delicious whole duck precisely roasted on the giant rotisserie that juts out into the main-floor dining room. Brushed with a fragrant honey and ginger sauce, the poultry was delicately moist and had been allowed to rest just long enough to allow the juices to settle back into the flesh. Also worth sampling is the thick pan-fried *tournedos de thon* and the seven-hour leg of lamb, or *gigot,* served in a pastry-wrapped crust. And the crusty homemade bread gets a huge *bravo!*

BRASSERIE LES FONTAINES
9, rue Soufflot,
Paris 5.
Tel: 01.43.26.42.80.
Fax: 01.44.07.03.49.
Métro: Maubert-Mutualité or RER Luxembourg.
Service noon to 3 P.M. and 7 to 11 P.M.
Closed Sunday.
Credit card: V.
Sidewalk terrace.
56-franc *plat du jour* at lunch.
A la carte, 150 to 250 francs.

SPECIALTIES:
Bistro: salade d'endives au bleu (Belgian endive salad with blue cheese); fillets de hareng, pommes à l'huile (fillet of herring with potatoes in oil); sole meunière (fillet of sole cooked in butter); crème brûlée à l'ancienne (old-fashioned caramelized custard).

If one ever doubted that there was still good food to be had in simple Paris neighborhood cafés, then one hasn't tried Les Fontaines. It's a very nondescript café on a very well-placed street (rue Soufflot runs from the Panthéon down to the fountain-filled Place Edmond-Rostand and the Luxembourg Gardens). Nothing on the outside or the inside would make you suspect that Les Fontaines is anything more than a spot to play pinball or grab a glass of wine and a *croque-monsieur* in the middle of the day. But don't let the paper tablecloths fool you. Former owner Roger Lacipière has left the restaurant in the hands of a new chef-owner (Jean-Marie Plas-Debecker), but the food remains unchanged. Try the hearty salad of endive and blue cheese, giant and beautifully aged steaks, and well-chosen Alsatian wines from the house of Trimbach. The clientele is very Left Bank intellectual: Everyone looks studious or professorish, and you'll often see men and women dining alone, with their obligatory newspaper, *Le Monde,* to keep them company.

MAVROMMATIS
42, rue Daubenton,
Paris 5.
Tel: 01.43.31.17.17.
Fax: 01.43.36.13.08.
Métro: Censier-Daubenton.
Service noon to 2 P.M. and 7 to 11 P.M.
Closed Monday.
Sidewalk terrace.
Air-conditioned.
120-franc lunch menu; 150- and 160-franc dinner menus.
A la carte, 220 to 280 francs.

SPECIALTIES:
Greek: gratin d'aubergines (egg-plant gratin); agneau de lait à la broche, artichauts confits au citron (spit-roasted leg of lamb with artichokes cooked with lemon); crème de lait à la fleur d'oranger (orange-flower-flavored cream); parfait glacé aux dattes et à la vanille (date and vanilla parfait).

The Mavrommatis family operates this lively, pleasing little establishment right across from the Saint-Médard church. Decorated in sky blue and white, this casual restaurant offers good value for the money. On my last visit I feasted on fabulous crisp roast goat set on a bed of wilted greens and paired with a thin lemony sauce. Equally good was roast lamb with a shower of fresh fava beans. Their Greek salad was on the boring side, and desserts were disappointing.

Salade Verte au Comte Moissonnier
MOISSONNIER'S TOSSED GREEN SALAD WITH GRUYERE

This is one of those make-it-or-break-it recipes: If you can secure the freshest and crispest escarole and top-quality, well-aged Gruyère cheese from France or from Switzerland, you've got it made. It's a thoroughly satisfying Saturday afternoon salad, a winter pick-me-up. This is one of the many salads served at the fine, old-fashioned restaurant Moissonnier (see below), where they prepare it with a fine Comté cheese from the Jura and serve it with a slightly chilled Beaujolais, preferably a light Regnié.

- 2 tablespoons best-quality red wine vinegar
- Salt
- ½ cup (12.5 cl) peanut oil
- Freshly ground black pepper, to taste
- 1 head escarole, rinsed, dried, and torn into bite-size pieces
- 7 ounces (200 g) imported Comté or Gruyère cheese
- Small handful of fresh flat-leaf parsley leaves
- Small handful of fresh chives, minced

In a large salad bowl, whisk together the vinegar and salt. Whisk in the oil, then season to taste with pepper. Add the escarole. Remove the rind from the cheese and cut into matchstick-size pieces. Sprinkle the cheese, parsley, and chives on top of the greens. Toss to coat thoroughly and evenly with the vinaigrette. Season with additional salt and pepper, if desired. Serve.

Yield: 4 servings

MOISSONNIER
28, rue des Fossés-Saint-Bernard,
Paris 5.
Tel: 01.43.29.87.65.
Métro: Jussieu or Cardinal Lemoine.
Service noon to 2 P.M. and 7:30 to 10 P.M.
Closed Sunday dinner, Monday, and August.
Credit card: V.
150-franc menu.
A la carte, 200 to 250 francs.

Who doesn't love abundance? Especially when the abundance has to do with food with a Lyonnais flavor. I'm speaking, in short, about the tradition known as *"les saladiers lyonnais,"* the procession of huge terra-cotta bowls that all but march to your table, bowls filled with wonderfully gelatinous *pieds de veau,* crunchy *grattons,* soothing *filets de hareng,* or hearty chunks of *cervelas* pork sausage. Then maybe some tart red cabbage, a spoonful of soft red beans, a serving of well-seasoned lentils, or thin slices of *museau de boeuf* in vinaigrette. If that's not enough, head for the potatoes bathed in oil, or a green salad tossed with beef. And don't forget to save room for a sparkling fresh salad of *escarole,* julienned strips of ham, and slices of apple, or a simple duet of *escarole* and beef. You'll find all this and

SPECIALTIES:
Cuisine lyonnaise and Franc-Comtoise: les saladiers lyonnais (varied assortment of meat and vegetable salads); boudin campagnard aux pommes fruits (blood sausage with apples); carré d'agneau rôti persillé, pour deux personnes (roast rack of lamb, for two).

more at Moissonnier, now well past its thirty-fifth year as one of Paris's more generous family restaurants, a no-frills two-story affair. I love to go with a large group of friends for a joyous evening of good food and good times.

After more than thirty years at the helm, Monsieur and Madame Louis Moissonnier have retired, leaving the place in the hands of chef-owner Philippe Mayet, and so far so good. Nothing seems to have changed. The Moissonnier menu, with a dual accent of the Jura and the Lyonnais, has changed imperceptibly over the years. There are always salads of crunchy *escarole* tossed with slivers of crisp apple (see recipe, facing page), mackerel marinated in white wine, the standard *frisée aux lardons,* and *breuzi,* the air-dried beef of the Franche-Comté.

Main courses are equally pantagruelian, with a fine version of *petit salé aux lentilles* with huge meaty chunks of well-trimmed pork, meaning you're getting plenty of meat and not all gristle.

AU MOULIN A VENT
(Chez Henri)
20, rue des Fossés Saint-Bernard,
Paris 5.
Tel: 01.43.54.99.37.
Métro: Jussieu or Cardinal Lemoine.
Service 12:30 to 1:45 P.M. and 7:30 to 10:15 P.M.
Closed Sunday, Monday, holidays, and August.
Credit card: V.
A la carte, 200 to 280 francs.

SPECIALTIES:
Traditional bistro: les cochonnailles au poids (varied sausages, sold by weight); boeuf à la ficelle (boiled beef fillet tied with string); coquilles Saint-Jacques fraîches à la provençale (fresh scallops, from October to April); le riz au lait (rice pudding).

French critics like to call this the Left Bank L'Ami Louis, and though there is no lamb or chicken to compare to what one finds on the rue du Vertbois, Chez Henri does the job when you are looking for a busy, old-fashioned, and purely Parisian bistro. This is the place to go to with a crowd when you're in the mood for red meat and Beaujolais. With a barely legible menu in purple ink, a jovial *patron,* and sausages hanging from the ceiling, this is one rare spot to find authentic *boeuf à la ficelle:* top-quality fillet of beef that's tied tightly with a string, then cooked quickly in boiling water. The boiling technique seals the outside, making for meat that's perfectly rare and without a trace of fat. (Don't be turned off by the unappetizing gray appearance of the beef—the inside will be gloriously red and appetizing.) Other dishes worth trying—if they're on the menu that day—include a refreshing salad of mushrooms and green beans, another of perfectly cooked and thinly sliced artichoke bottoms, and a classic *sole meunière.* The *magret de canard,* or fatted duck breast, can be dry and tough. Stay away on a hot day: The ventilation here is almost nonexistent.

Scarole a la Julienne de Jambon et aux Pommes
ESCAROLE SALAD WITH HAM AND APPLES

*The first time I saw this salad at the homey Left Bank restaurant Moissonnier (see page 47), I assumed it was a typical—and ever-pleasing—*salade mixte, *or greens tossed with strips of ham and cheese. My eyes were fooled, for my palate told me otherwise—what I assumed was cheese turned out to be apples. I like the combination because the slight acidity of the apples cuts the fattiness of the ham, making for a fine and filling first-course salad. Use the best-quality ham you can find, preferably a thick slice from a freshly cooked, unsmoked country ham. Serve with an equally acidic wine, such as a Beaujolais.*

2 tablespoons best-quality red wine vinegar
Salt
½ cup (12.5 cl) peanut oil
Freshly ground black pepper, to taste
1 head escarole, rinsed, dried, and torn into bite-size pieces
¼ pound (250 g) thickly sliced unsmoked cooked ham, cut into matchstick-size pieces
2 Golden Delicious apples, peeled, cored, and cut into matchstick-size pieces
Small handful of fresh chives, minced

In a large salad bowl, whisk together the vinegar and salt. Add the oil and season to taste with pepper. Add the escarole. Sprinkle the ham, apples, and chives on top of the greens. Toss to coat thoroughly and evenly with the vinaigrette. Season with additional salt and pepper, if desired. Serve.

Yield: 4 servings

CHEZ RENE
14, boulevard Saint-Germain,
Paris 5.
Tel: 01.43.54.30.23.
Métro: Cardinal Lemoine.
Service 12:15 to 2 P.M. and 7:45 to 10:30 P.M.
Closed Saturday lunch, Sunday, August, and Christmas week.
Credit cards: V.
Sidewalk terrace.
158-franc lunch menu.
A la carte, 200 to 300 francs.

On the right day, in the right mood, Chez René can be a cheery breath of Beaujolais country air right at the end of the Boulevard Saint-Germain. It's the sort of place where the food is plain but not banal, and though the menu may be familiar, it still holds the ability to surprise. Don't come here for garnishes of chervil or *sel fin de Guérande,* fussy presentations, or the wine of the century. Go with an eye toward tradition, and you're sure to have a good time. Tuck into hearty portions of warm poached pork sausage, wintry beef stew, or a hearty beef salad. In good weather there's a nice sidewalk terrace to make you feel as though you're right in the

SPECIALITES:
Bistro: plats du jour (changing daily specials); saucisson chaud (warm poached pork sausage); salade de boeuf (cold beef salad tossed with tomatoes, potatoes, and cornichons); andouillette au pouilly (tripe sausage poached in white wine); coq au vin (chicken in red wine); boeuf bourguignon (beef stewed in red wine, onions, mushrooms, and bacon); plateau de fromages (varied cheese platter).

center of things. The house Beaujolais is more than drinkable, and I highly recommend the cheese tray, particularly the vast selection of goat cheeses from the Beaujolais, offered in multiple stages of *affinage,* from the fresh, white, and moist to the firm, blue-gray, and tangy.

SAINT-GERMAIN DES PRES, LUXEMBOURG, ODEON, MONTPARNASSE

6th arrondissement

ALCAZAR
62, rue Mazarine,
Paris 6.
Tel: 01.53.10.19.99.
Fax: 01.56.24.02.21.
Métro: Odéon.
Service noon to 2 P.M. and 7 P.M. to 1 A.M.
Open daily.
Credit cards: AE, DC, V.
Private dining room for 15 to 30.
Air-conditioned.
A la carte, 300 to 400 francs.

SPECIALTIES:
Brasserie: huîtres et fruits de mer (oysters and shellfish); saumon fumé du Loch Fyne, crème de caviar sur galette (Scottish smoked salmon with caviar cream); entrecôte grillée, béarnaise et grosses frites (grilled beef rib steak with tarragon-flavored sauce, with fried potatoes).

The Parisians have been invaded by the British, and they love it. Sir Terence Conran—of design fame—has expanded his restaurant empire to Paris with the bright, airy, smart, and bustling 200-seat Left Bank brasserie Alcazar. All red, white, black, and modern, this stylish spot is just the sort of injection the Paris restaurant world needs. Conran is not out to lose: He has chosen chef Guillaume Lubard (formerly of Taillevent) to man the stoves of the open kitchen; the bread comes from Boulangerie Kayser, a few blocks away; and Alcazar is open seven days a week, with a special Sunday brunch from noon to 3:30. While the menu breaks no new ground—there are ultra-fresh oysters and seafood platters, *steak frites* and braised sea bass with fennel—the service is exquisite. An upstairs piano bar offers wine by the glass and everything from caviar to oysters, sashimi to tempura.

Haricot de Mouton Chez Rene

CHEZ RENE'S MUTTON WITH WHITE BEANS

This is a regular plat du jour*—daily special—at the popular Left Bank bistro Chez René (see page 49).* Haricot de mouton *is a classic bistro dish, and one that French women prepare often at home, usually with either lamb or mutton shoulder. I prefer it with big, hearty chunks of lamb and lots and lots of white beans. If you have fresh herbs around, all the better.*

Lamb or mutton:

3 tablespoons (1½ oz; 45 g) unsalted butter
3 tablespoons olive oil
3½ pounds (approximately 1.75 kg) lamb or mutton shoulder, cut into 2-inch (5-cm) chunks (a butcher can do this for you)
⅓ cup (45 g) unbleached all-purpose flour
1 cup (25 cl) dry white wine
3 cups (75 cl) water
2 fresh tomatoes, cubed
4 carrots, peeled and cut into 1-inch (2.5-cm) rounds
2 medium onions, peeled and halved
2 teaspoons fresh thyme, or 1 teaspoon dried
3 bay leaves
3 tablespoons chopped fresh parsley
4 whole cloves
Salt and freshly ground black pepper, to taste

Beans:

1 pound (500 g) dried white beans
2 bay leaves
6 whole cloves
2 teaspoons dried thyme
Salt

1. In a large skillet, heat the butter and oil over medium-high heat. When hot, begin browning the lamb. You may want to do this in batches. Do not crowd the pan, and be sure that each piece is thoroughly browned before turning.

2. When all the lamb is browned, sprinkle with the flour and mix well. Leaving the lamb in the skillet, add the white wine, then the water, and deglaze the pan, scraping up any browned bits. Add the tomatoes, vegetables, herbs, and spices, and cook, covered, over medium heat for about 1 hour and 15 minutes. Season to taste with salt and pepper.

3. While the lamb is cooking, prepare the beans: Rinse them well, put them in a large saucepan, and cover with cold water. Over high heat, bring to a boil. Once boiling, remove the pan from the heat, leave covered, and let rest for 40 minutes.

4. Drain the beans, discarding the cooking liquid (to help make the beans more digestible). Rinse the beans and cover again with cold water. Add the bay leaves, cloves, and thyme, and bring to a boil over medium heat. Cook, covered, over medium heat for about 40 minutes. The beans should be cooked through but still firm. Add salt to taste.

5. To serve, check the lamb and beans for seasoning, then arrange the meat on a platter, surrounded by the white beans.

Yield: 6 servings

ALLARD
41, rue Saint André des Arts, Paris 6.
Tel: 01.43.26.48.23.
Métro: Odéon.
Service 12:30 to 2 P.M. and 7:30 to 11 P.M.
Closed Sunday, three weeks in August, and Christmas.
Credit cards: AE, DC, V.
Air-conditioned.
150-franc lunch menu; 200-franc dinner menu.
A la carte, 200 to 280 francs.

SPECIALTIES:
Bistro: frisée au lardons (curly endive with bacon); épaule d'agneau Baronet du Limousin, pour deux (roasted lamb shoulder from the Limousin, for two); tarte fine chaude aux pommes (thin-crusted apple tart).

The word is out: Allard is good again. Oh, maybe not as good as it was back in the 1940s, when André and Fernande Allard held court. But this quintessential bistro—with its great zinc bar, brass coatracks, steaming platters of gigantic portions parading from the kitchen—was taken over by the Layrac group a few years back and they seem to have breathed some new life into this charming spot. This is one place in town where you can find whole roasted lamb shoulder, expertly cooked in a large enameled cast-iron skillet and carved at the table. I always start with a hearty salad, usually a very vinegar-rich curly endive salad showered with chunks of bacon. The restaurant is expensive for what you get, but consider the classic décor—the old tile floors, elbow-to-elbow tables, moleskin banquettes, and chatty waiters—as part of the price of admission.

LA BASTIDE D'ODEON
7, rue Corneille, Paris 6.
Tel: 01.43.26.03.65.
Fax: 01.44.07.28.93.
E-mail: bastide.odeon @wanadoo.fr
Métro: Odéon.
Service noon to 2:30 P.M. and 7:30 to 11 P.M.
Closed Sunday, Monday, the first three weeks of August, and Christmas week.
Credit cards: AE, DC, V.
Private dining for 12 to 15.
Air-conditioned.
150- and 190-franc menus.
A la carte, 250 francs.

SPECIALTIES:
Modern bistro: asperges tièdes à l'oeuf cassé et lard grillé tuile au parmesan (warm asparagus with poached egg, grilled bacon, and Parmesan wafers); cochon de lait farci en porchetta polenta gratinée au parmesan (stuffed suckling pig with Parmesan-gratinéed polenta).

Sometimes it is good to be proven wrong. When Gilles Ajuelos opened his Bastide d'Odéon across from the Odéon theater in 1995, I liked the bistro well enough but wasn't sure it would have staying power. How wrong I was. Today the place is bustling day and night, with hordes of customers being turned away at the door. That's because Ajuelos and his staff know what we want: food that's modern, light, of the moment, and well thought out. On my last visit I loved the bowl of tiny *ravioles de Royans* (the tiny cheese-filled ravioli from Royans, near Valence) floating in a light broth seasoned with tomatoes, a ton of parsley, and lots of Parmesan. Equally excellent was the grilled baby chicken—*coquelet*—served with lemon *confit,* fennel with saffron, and a marvelous sauté of wild mushrooms.

Desserts included an inventive *tarte fine aux rhubarbes,* a *moelleux mi-cuit au chocolat Valrhona, glace vanille* (warm Valrhona chocolate cake with vanilla ice cream), as well as a warm *financier* topped with apricots, and a yogurt *sorbet.* Good wine choices here include the firm and fruity red Corbières Bastide de la Baronne as well as the same wine in white.

AU BON SAINT-POURCAIN
10 bis, rue Servandoni, Paris 6.
Tel: 01.43.54.93.63.
Métro: Saint-Sulpice.
Service 12:30 to 2:30 P.M. and 8 to 10:30 P.M.
Closed Sunday and July 14 to September 1.
No credit cards.
A la carte, 200 to 250 francs.

SPECIALTIES:
Bistro: poireaux vinaigrette (leeks in vinaigrette); terrine de queue de boeuf (oxtail terrine); cassoulet maison (casserole of meat, sausage, and white beans); entrecôte marchand de vin (beef rib steak with sauce of red wine and shallots).

If you are a fan of retro 1930s-style bistros with simple, traditional fare and are looking for something in the heart of Saint-Germain, this place is for you. Don't come for stunning food or service, but for old-time neighborhood ambience. The radio blares. Owner Daniel Pesle alternately cares about his customers not at all or cares very much. As soon as you sit down you're offered a glass of Saint Pourçain, the light wine of Vichy, about the only thing worth drinking in this bare-bones bistro with imitation leather banquettes, Formica tabletops, and paper napkins. On my last visit, I loved the earthy oxtail *terrine,* well seasoned and hearty, as well as the *sauté d'agneau* with a Moroccan accent, highly seasoned and showered with almonds. This is one place where you can still drink wine *"au compteur"*—that is, you pay only for the portion of wine you have drunk.

LES BOOKINISTES
53, quai des Grands-Augustins,
Paris 6.
Tel: 01.43.25.45.94.
Fax: 01.43.25.23.07.
Internet: http://www.guysavoy.com
Métro: RER Saint-Michel.
Service noon to 2:30 P.M. and 7 P.M. to midnight.
Closed Saturday lunch and Sunday lunch.
Credit cards: AE, DC, V.
Air-conditioned.
140-franc vegetarian menu; 160-franc lunch menu; 180-franc Sunday evening menu.
A la carte, 250 francs.

This butter-yellow and bottle-green bistro, open since 1994, is devoted to updated French home cooking. The man behind the stove is William Ledeuil, who won praise for his cooking at Guy Savoy's other satellite bistros. Les Bookinistes—an Anglicized play on the French word for bookseller—was Savoy's first venture across the Seine and an instant hit. The fifty-seat bistro looks out onto the *quai,* and in warm weather tables are placed outside for a view of the Seine. Ledeuil strikes

SPECIALTIES:
Modern bistro: crème de coco en fenouil aux girolles et huile d'amandes (white bean and fennel soup with chanterelle mushrooms and almond oil); tempura de crevettes, salade de fenouil à l'huile et piment doux (shrimp tempura with fennel salad in sweet pepper oil); cuisse de lapin "tandoori" rôtie, polenta à la tomate, jus à la sarriette (roast rabbit thigh in Indian spices with tomato polenta and summer savory).

it right with simple, robust fare in intensely flavored, modern versions of what he was once fed by a doting grandmother in the Loire Valley. He takes fresh cod, or *cabillaud,* crushes and sautés it in virgin olive oil, adds a touch of crushed potatoes and then a bit of cream to create a brilliant, light salad of *brandade.* Huge white mushrooms are stuffed with a Parmesan-laced polenta, then grilled and set in a light mushroom broth. Many classics, such as beef with carrots, arrive unrevised: just moist, chewy chunks of beef topped with an avalanche of carrots. On my last visit, Ledeuil wowed the crowd with a stunning cannelloni of mushrooms served in a full-flavored chicken *bouillon* laced with Parmesan and truffles, and a slow-cooked veal breast flavored with marjoram and flanked by both artichokes and asparagus. My favorite dessert here is the oversized warm madeleines, filled with bittersweet chocolate and served with vanilla-rich ice cream.

BOUILLON RACINE
3, rue Racine,
Paris 6.
Tel: 01.44.32.15.60.
Fax: 01.44.32.15.61.
E-mail: Bouillon.Racine @wanadoo.fr
Métro: Odéon.
Service 11:45 A.M. to 2:45 P.M. and 7 P.M. to midnight.
Open daily.
Credit cards: AE, V.
Private dining room for 22.
Air-conditioned.
75-, 105-, and 169-franc menus.
A la carte, 150 to 200 francs.

SPECIALTIES:
Belgian: croquettes de crevettes grises de la Mer du Nord (batter-fried North Sea shrimp); waterzooi de poulet fermier à la gantoise (poached farm chicken bathed in cream, chicken broth, and vegetables); anguilles au vert (river eels poached in herb sauce).

For years I walked down rue Racine, always lingering to study and admire the fanciful though long-neglected Art Nouveau exterior of the defunct Bouillon Chartier, one of a chain of populist restaurants founded in 1860 by a butcher named Pierre-Louis Duval. His idea was to serve simple meals at a single price, and the specialty was boiled beef (*bouilli*) served with its stock. The menu grew, as did the restaurants' popularity and number, and Duval was quickly imitated. (The Chartier copycat still exists at 7, rue du Faubourg Montmartre.)

Of course there are other romantics in the food world: When Olivier Simon found this glorious two-story restaurant, with its undulating chandeliers, stylized *atelier*-style windows, stained glass, and giant beveled mirrors, he had to have it. He found willing partners in several Belgian breweries, as well as France's Department of Historic Monuments, which oversaw the restoration. Here, beers like Benedictine Mardesous, Broucsella 1900, and Westvleteren Abt lead an extensive hit parade of special brews. With a cuisine devoted to the best of Belgium, the food is hearty and filling even without the help of several thirst-quenching drafts. But even if you are not a beer lover, loosen up a bit here, for what you'll find is Belgium's best artisanal brews, including the Palm Spéciale on tap, a light and golden beer that's honey-like and pleasantly bitter at the same time. Equally satisfying is the house Blonde de Bouillon, a pale golden pilsner that's very, very dry.

All this talk of beer brings on a strong appetite, the better to tuck into chef Simon's ethereal *mousse* prepared from *jambon d'Ardennes* and accompanied by a juniper-berry-flavored gelatin. At once salty, creamy, and pungent, it's an ideal palate waker-upper, accompanied by the excellent bread from Pain Quotidien in Brussels. Equally hearty is the generous casserole of mussels, tiny shrimp, and baby clams (though I wish the chef would try to rid the shellfish of sand with a bit more care). The rabbit braised in beer is fitting and filling, though the accompanying fries can be anemic and undercooked. The classic *waterzooi*—poached chicken bathed in cream and vegetables—is warming and generous, one of the finer versions of the dish I've sampled. The menu, which changes monthly, includes Belgium's greatest hits—such as shrimp *croquettes,* river eel in green sauce, and the brioche-like *cramique* with currants and raisins—but also features a number of attractive-sounding dishes that depend upon beer for their character, including suckling pig roasted with the emphatically bitter Orval beer and rack of lamb roasted in a pale *bière blonde.* The décor—all in celadon green and ocher—puts one in a festive mood, and the service is impersonal but effective.

LE CAMELEON
6, rue de Chevreuse,
Paris 6.
Tel: 01.43.20.63.43.
Métro: Vavin.
Service noon to 2 P.M. and 8 to 10:30 P.M.
Closed Saturday lunch, Sunday, and August.
Credit cards: AE, V.
120-franc lunch menu
A la carte, 180 to 220 francs.

Raymond and Jacqueline Faucher have sold this small, friendly Montparnasse restaurant to new owners, but diners looking for classic bistro fare can still find many of the Le Caméléon classics, such as the excellent *morue provençale,* a rich serving of salt cod in herbed tomato sauce, served with mashed potatoes and a heady garlic mayonnaise; the pleasing salad of green beans teamed up with a small slice of *foie gras;* lemon-marinated zucchini; and a personal favorite, the soft, moist, meltingly tender golden pear cake, *fondant aux poires* (see recipe, page 56). New offerings include delicious, well-seasoned homemade pork sausage served with a moun-

SPECIALTIES:
Bistro: courgettes marinées au citron (lemon-marinated zucchini); morue provençale (salt cod in herbed tomato sauce, with potatoes and garlic mayonnaise); saucisse de campagne maison (homemade country pork sausage); fondant aux poires (golden pear cake).

tain of mashed potatoes; a fine *blanquette de veau;* and a series of changing daily specials. The brief wine list still offers some good values, including Jabouelt's heady 1994 Croze-Hermitage Domaine de Thalabert. The black wallpaper continues to give me a headache, but the friendly service and homey old-fashioned atmosphere keep me coming back.

Fondant aux Poires Le Cameleon

LE CAMELEON'S GOLDEN PEAR CAKE

Each time I dine at the bustling little Montparnasse bistro Le Caméléon (see page 55), I order this simple, satisfying dessert. Here, the slightly cooked pears give off a distinctly "pear" flavor, one that's soothing, gentle, and reassuring. This unusual "double batter" method of constructing the cake makes for a soft and moist dessert. It's really half cake, half tart, and it goes well with a sweet chilled Beaumes-de-Venise from Provence.

- 3 large ripe pears (about 1½ pounds; 750 g), peeled, cored and quartered, with each quarter cut into 4 slices
- 5 large eggs
- 6 tablespoons (10 cl) peanut oil
- 1 tablespoon rum
- 6 tablespoons (55 g) unbleached all-purpose flour
- 1¼ cups (250 g) sugar
- 5 tablespoons (2½ ounces; 75 g) butter, at room temperature
- 1 to 2 tablespoons sugar, for garnish

1. Preheat the oven to 425°F (220°C). Butter a 9-inch (23-cm) round cake pan.

2. Lay the pear slices in the prepared cake pan in concentric circles, starting at the outside and working toward the center.

3. Prepare the first batter: In a medium-size bowl, whisk together 3 of the eggs, the oil, and the rum. In the bowl of a mixer, combine the flour and ½ cup (100 g) of the sugar. Add the liquid ingredients to the dry ingredients and mix until thoroughly blended. Set aside.

4. Prepare the second batter: Slowly cream the butter with the remaining ¾ cup (150 g) sugar until well blended. Add the remaining 2 eggs, one at a time, beating well after each addition, until the batter is thick and smooth.

5. Pour the first batter over the pears. Place the pan in the center of the oven and bake just until the cake has begun to set and is bubbly, about 10 minutes. Remove from the oven and pour the second batter on top. Reduce the oven temperature to 350°F (175°C). Return the cake to the center of the oven and continue baking until firm and golden, about 20 minutes more. Remove to a rack to cool, dusting the top lightly with a few tablespoons of sugar. Serve at room temperature, cut into pie-shaped wedges.

Yield: 8 servings

AUX CHARPENTIERS
10, rue Mabillon,
Paris 6.
Tel: 01.43.26.30.05.
Fax: 01.46.33.07.98.
Métro: Mabillon or Saint-Germain des Prés.
Service noon to 3 P.M. and 7:30 to 11:30 P.M.
Open daily except May 1 and several days at Christmas.
Credit cards: AE, DC, V.
Sidewalk terrace.
120-franc lunch menu; 158-franc dinner menu.
A la carte, 200 to 230 francs.

SPECIALTIES:
Bistro: plats du jour (changing daily specials); fromage de tête à l'ancienne (headcheese); caneton rôti, sauces olives et porto (roast duck with olives and port); selle d'agneau rôti (roasted saddle of lamb).

Few bistros have managed to change with the times and stay the same all the while. Aux Charpentiers always has that right look and buzz: old tile floors, crisp linen napkins, that great zinc bar, waiters scurrying about. Chef and owner Pierre Bardèche does his job to make sure the food is fresh, varied, and authentic: fresh veal, lamb, and beef from the heart of France, changing daily specials with *petit salé aux lentilles* (salted pork with lentils) each Wednesday, roast leg of lamb each Friday.

But while this endearing spot—decorated with models created by master *charpentiers* (carpenters), whose museum is right next door—looks unchanged, Bardèche has been sure to add such modern fare as *ratatouille,* as well as a trio of daily fish specials such as a *fricassée* of monkfish. The restaurant is also now open seven days a week, instead of closed tight much of the summer and on weekends.

My last visit was a delight, with a delicious *salade compagnon,* just soft butter lettuce in a creamy dressing all showered with walnuts, and an inspired rabbit cooked with rosemary and mustard, a marriage made in heaven. The duck terrine was copious and the *petit salé aux lentilles* was fine once we sent it back to be warmed up a bit. Desserts need help: The fillings for both the chocolate and lemon tarts were excellent, but the pastry was heavy, dull, and thuddy. The wine list could also use more attention.

Perhaps it is a pot-au-feu *they are enjoying.*

LA CLOSERIE DES LILAS
171, boulevard du Montparnasse,
Paris 6.
Tel: 01.40.51.34.50.
Fax: 01.43.29.99.94.
E-mail: scretariat@closerie-des.lilas.com.
Internet: http://www.closerie-des-lilas.com
Métro: Vavin or RER Port-Royal.
Café service 8 A.M. to 11 P.M.; restaurant service 12:30 to 3 P.M. and 7:30 to 11 P.M.
Open daily.
Credit cards: AE, DC, V.
Private dining room for 20.
250-franc lunch menu, including wine and coffee.
A la carte, 400 to 450 francs.

SPECIALTIES:
Traditional: huîtres (oysters); foie gras de canard maison, marmelade de figues (homemade preserved duck liver with fig marmalade); quenelles de brochet (pike dumplings); volaille fermière pochée et ses légumes, sauce aux truffes (poached farm chicken with vegetables and truffle sauce).

How can you not love La Closerie des Lilas? The place that Hemingway made so famous has been revived, thanks to new director Jean-Jacques Caimant, last seen managing Joël Robuchon's dining rooms. La Closerie's lovely outdoor terrace beneath the shimmering sycamore trees is more welcoming than it has been for a long time, and the clientele is as chic Left Bank as ever. And now we have the freshest of oysters, excellent whole grilled *bar* (on my last visit just a touch overcooked), and a staff that is willing to help you along with your choices. The wine list is expensive, but count on Monsieur Caimant or *sommelier* Evo Iacobozzi to steer you toward a good-buy find, such as a little-known white from the Gers. The brasserie awaits those who want less fuss and fanfare, and offers the same quality oysters as well as such classics as herring, *steak tartare,* and changing daily specials.

L'EPI DUPIN
11, rue Dupin,
Paris 6.
Tel: 01.42.22.64.56.
Fax: 01.42.22.30.42.
Métro: Sèvres-Babylone.
Service noon to 2:30 P.M. and 7:30 to 11 P.M.
Closed Saturday and Sunday.
Credit cards: AE, V.
Sidewalk terrace at lunch.
110- and 165-franc menus.
A la carte, 200 francs.

The contemporary good-value-bistro trend shows no sign of a slowdown, and L'Epi Dupin is proving itself a model of the genre. With an ambience that's both casual and sophisticated and a rib-sticking bargain menu that's satisfying, creative, and memorable, chef François Pasteau and his staff turn away hordes of eager diners. Choosing from half a dozen entrées, half a dozen main courses, the same number of desserts, and a changing roster of daily specials, diners are almost certain to leave with spirits heightened.

SPECIALTIES:
Modern bistro: effiloché de queue de boeuf et pommes aux herbes (shredded oxtail with potatoes and herbs); éventail de fruits rouges et pistache au coulis de griottes (fan of red fruits with pistachios in a red cherry sauce).

L'Epi Dupin, just steps from the Sèvres-Babylone crossroads, attracts a chic Parisian crowd. The décor is in keeping with the times: bare bones, with taste. Exposed stone walls add warmth, wooden beams add a touch of history, and the bright halogen lighting and sisal carpeting bring it all up-to-date. What a delight to know that most of your dinner check won't be going to pay for the drapery, linen, and flowers.

The menu created by the young chef features all the trendy words of the era: *pissaladière* for a touch of Provence; *tagliatelle* for a hint of Italy; honey and ginger for a bit of contact with Asia; *pastilla* for a glimmer of the Mediterranean. Yet there's substance behind those words, and some mighty good food. And bravo for Pasteau, who bakes his own wonderful bread twice a day.

The best starters include his *charlotte tiède de fenouil aux pommes,* a warm and soothing fennel and fruit creation that benefits from the apple's acidity, and a delightfully fresh green watercress salad paired with just a few meaty bites of rich preserved duck, or *confit de canard,* a warming touch on a cold winter's night. My favorite dish here is his *pintade farcie,* a farm-raised guinea hen stuffed with fennel and served with a thin *tuile,* or wafer, flavored with anise. The poultry was roasted to perfection and served with a welcoming sauté of zucchini. Pasteau takes a classic French *capilotade* (basically any leftover meat or poultry cooked to tenderness in a well-reduced sauce) and weaves some truly magical flavors by combining lamb, eggplant, garlic, tarragon, and potatoes into a sort of stew that sings of the south.

Less successful are his first-course dish of cold *tagliatelle* in pesto sauce, unnecessarily embellished with strips of salmon, and a *roulade* of calf's head and saffron potatoes that went down with a thud and lacked flavor. The menu and the chef's hand could use a bit of lightening: Too many dishes are doused with an excess of cream, and too many dishes are wrapped in thick pastries that hide the finer qualities of the main ingredients.

Desserts are hit-and-miss. Almost everyone orders the lemon-crêpe soufflé, which is flamed tableside with vodka with a good deal of hokey cinematic flourish. The day I sampled the dish, the alcohol had not sufficiently burned off and all one could taste was the flavor of acrid, bitter lemon with alcoholic vapors rising to the nostrils. The *pastilla de mendiant*—a mix of dried fruits and nuts wrapped in pastry—was delightful, as was the warm and creamy chocolate *dariole,* bathed in a pistachio sauce.

CHEZ GRAMOND
5, rue de Fleurus,
Paris 6.
Tel: 01.42.22.28.89.
Métro: Saint-Placide or Notre-Dame des Champs.
Service noon to 2 P.M. and 7 to 10:30 P.M.
Closed Sunday and August.
Credit card: V.
A la carte, 360 to 400 francs.

SPECIALTIES:
Traditional: coquilles Saint-Jacques (sea scallops); terrine de foie gras (homemade duck liver terrine); agneau de lait rôti à l'oseille (roasted milk-fed leg of lamb with sorrel sauce); gibier en saison (wild game in fall and winter); soufflé Grand Marnier (Grand Marnier soufflé).

If the walls at 5, rue de Fleurus could talk, they would speak volumes. Even before 1967—when Jean-Claude and Jeannine Gramond took over this minuscule bistro that might well have served as the setting for A. J. Liebling's gastronomic splurges—the address had flair. Gertrude Stein is said to have lived at some point in the tiny two-story house in the courtyard, now occupied by the Gramonds. Hemingway lived down the street. One can chart the social and cultural changes that have overtaken the neighborhood since the day the couple opened their restaurant with 5 francs in the cash register and nothing more than a desire to serve simple, classic French fare. In the 1960s they often did two services at lunch, sending the overflow for a walk in the Luxembourg Gardens until places were liberated. Before François Mitterrand became president of the French republic, he lived around the corner, on rue Guynemer, and was a frequent diner. The bourgeoisie of the neighborhood, including august members of the Académie Française, politicians from the mayor's office, bishops from Rome, United Nations leaders, and editors from the many publishing houses within a stone's throw of the Luxembourg Gardens, made this their *cantine.* In short, the sort of place Parisians like to call an *"établissement confidentiel."*

Today the lace tablecloths, the bouquets of dried flowers, the fish tank in the tiny glassed-in terrace are all testaments to days long past, another life, another style of cooking. Chef Gramond's cuisine is both earnest and admirable. He makes twice-weekly middle-of-the-night treks to the Rungis wholesale market to shop for fresh produce, meat, and fish. One of a rare breed of chef left in France today, Gramond refuses to alter the classic cuisine he learned more than forty years ago in the hotel school in Toulouse. The menu, still handwritten and mimeographed in purple ink on the machine the Gramonds bought three decades ago, is brief and to the point: If it is spring you will find fresh green asparagus from Provence bathed in a chervil vinaigrette; a commendable terrine of *foie gras;* plump scallops seared in butter and served on a bed of leeks; small and tender baby leg of lamb served with a fine sorrel sauce. Daily specials might include a lamb stew prepared with white beans (*haricots blancs*), grown by Gramond on their farm in the Vosges. And come fall, his game specialties take over, with a delectable wild hare terrine; a *civet de lièvre;* and fresh roasted partridge.

Three bulging cellars beneath the restaurant also harbor treasures from days past: a hoard of sturdy Santenays from the Côte de Beaune, dating back to 1978; a charming 1982 Les-Carmes-Haut-Brion; as well as an exceptional, long-maturing Chasse-Spleen.

BRASSERIE LIPP
151, boulevard Saint-Germain,
Paris 6.
Tel: 01.45.48.53.91.
Fax: 01.45.48.53.91.
Internet: http//www.brasserie-lipp.fr
Métro: Saint-Germain des Prés.
Brasserie service 9 A.M. to 2 A.M.; restaurant service noon to 1 A.M.
Open daily.
Credit cards: AE, DC, V.
Terrace for light snacks.
Private dining room for 45.
Air-conditioned.
196-franc menu, including wine.
A la carte, 200 to 300 francs.

SPECIALTIES:
Brasserie: plats du jour (changing daily specials); choucroute garnie (sausages, pork, and sauerkraut); cassoulet maison (casserole of meat, sausage, and white beans); blanquette de veau (veal stew with vegetables).

Since 1880, when Léonard Lipp left his native Alsace to set up his Brasserie des Bord du Rhin, *choucroute* has been the dish to sample at this world-famous brasserie. With its bright lights, colorful ceramic wall murals of parrots and cranes, and team of waiters parading about in crisp white aprons that nearly touch their toes, Brasserie Lipp is Paris's quintessential brasserie. The home of the chicest Left Bank clientele—artists, intellectuals, and politicians who double-park their luxury cars on the sidewalk—Lipp remains one of the best scenes in Paris. The menu tells you in English, big and bold, NO SALAD AS A MEAL. That should tip you off to the fact that many a diner has come here, appetite-less, looking for a touch of history and a dose of nostalgia. But do come, and bring your hunger with you. And unless you're a Parisian star or a bonafide regular, expect to be sent to the upstairs dining room (the main floor is the choice "see and be seen" spot). But upstairs is not such a bad place after all, for the waiters are jovial and thoroughly professional (they've seen everything, I'm sure), the food can vary from mediocre to hit-the-spot delicious, and if you're counting *centimes* you can have a decent meal for not too much money.

Lipp happens to offer one of the city's best platters of *choucroute,* or sauerkraut and sausages. With sauerkraut that is crisp, oh-so-lightly cooked, and refreshingly acidic, the Lipp platter is laden with crisp-skinned sausages, beautifully braised pork, and a thick layer of ham, all to be downed with plenty of their house Riesling, served from elegant *carafes* and poured into delightful green-stemmed Alsatian wineglasses. The Lipp mustard is sharp enough to blow your head off. The excellent cheese assortment—from Roquefort to Brie to goat cheese—comes from the excellent cheesemonger Quatrehomme (see Cheese Shops, page 285). A sign of the times: While one old sign requests that clients refrain from smoking pipes, a more modern one prohibits using a portable telephone at the table.

CHEZ MAITRE PAUL
12, rue Monsieur-le-Prince, Paris 6.
Tel: 01.43.54.74.59.
Fax: 01.46.34.58.33.
Métro: Odéon or RER Luxembourg.
Service noon to 2:30 P.M. and 7:30 to 10:30 P.M.
Open daily. July and August closed Sunday, and Monday lunch.
Credit cards: AE, DC, V.
Private dining room for 20.
Air-conditioned.
165- and 195-franc menus (including wine).
A la carte, 220 to 260 francs.

SPECIALTIES:
Cuisine of the Jura and Franche-Comté: salade comtoise (curly endive salad with Comté cheese, smoked ham, and walnuts); saucisse de Montbéliard chaude, pommes à l'huile (warm cumin-flecked sausage and potatoes bathed in vinegar and oil); poulet au vin jaune (chicken in sherry-like white wine); foie de veau au vin de paille (calf's liver in sweet white wine).

Nothing makes one feel more secure than returning to an old-time favorite restaurant to find that nothing has changed. My last visit to the small, updated Chez Maître Paul right near the Odéon theater was as good as my first, when I downed with great pleasure plump, cumin-flecked Montbéliard pork sausages paired with a mound of warm potato salad, followed by moist and chewy portions of farm chicken, grilled and then gratinéed with rich cow's milk Comté from the Jura mountains (see recipe, page 64). When owner Jean-François Debert took over this traditional regional bistro several years ago, he enlarged and modernized what was once a minuscule, old-fashioned dining room, but he has retained the charming upstairs *salon* for private affairs. He's also added a list of daily specials that might include a traditional salad of cheese, ham, and walnuts from the Jura along with a tangle of escarole. I also love the *poulet aux morilles,* generous portions of chicken served with wild morel mushrooms in a light cream sauce. The wine list is limited but offers diners a chance to try the unjustly little-known wines of the Jura. If it is on the list, by all means try the welcoming Pinot Noir Vieilles Vignes, a simple but outstanding *vin de pays* of Franche-Comté.

L'O A LA BOUCHE
157, boulevard du Montparnasse,
Paris 6.
Tel: 01.43.26.26.53.
Fax: 01.43.26.43.40.
Métro: Vavin.
Service noon to 2:30 P.M. and 7:30 to 11 P.M.
Closed Sunday, Monday, the first week of January, two weeks in April, and the first three weeks of August.
Credit card: V.
100- and 130-franc weekday lunch menus; 190-franc dinner menu.
A la carte, 180 francs.

SPECIALTIES:
Modern bistro: salade multicolore de gambas croustillantes au sésame (salad of shrimp, beets, greens, and other vegetables with sesame seeds); dorade en écailles (porgy fillet cooked with its scales); ravioles du Royans au basilic et copeaux de parmesan (small cheese-filled raviolis with basil and Parmesan shavings).

Copying, they say, is the greatest form of flattery. If that's the case, then chefs such as Joël Robuchon and Guy Savoy should be very flattered indeed, since their creations show up—in one form or another—on a multitude of tables—and in cookbooks—in France. The multi-talented Savoy has certainly made his mark in Paris, with numerous bistros run by his increasingly mammoth organization. But since the fall of 1996, chef Franck Paquier—a former Savoy chef—has had the audacity to carbon-copy the Savoy formula under his own wings and his own power.

It would be a shame—and a restaurant not worth visiting—if Paquier did not execute Savoy's recipes to a T. But the fact is, he does. As he does the décor, the ambience, the *savoir-faire* that make a modern bistro so welcoming, so easy to enjoy without fanfare or effort. Nothing says "bistro" like the crush of elbows, the pleasing aromas of roasting meat and poultry, the joyful noise of people having a great time at the table. And that's what you'll find here on any given night: a cacophony of good-time sounds and mouthwatering aromas.

Begin, if you will, with the delightful *salade multicolore de gambas croustillantes au sésame,* one of my favorites, first introduced several years ago at Savoy's La Butte Chaillot near Trocadéro. A quartet of ultrafresh giant shrimp are breaded with a touch of sesame seeds and deep-fried, then set atop a matchstick-sliced salad of beets, greens, and varied vegetables. Perfect for the summer, the 1990s. Equally omnipresent at Savoy bistros and less successfully executed is the *tarte* of tomato and mozzarella, a layered affair attempting to capture the fine Italian sun but marred by boring cheese and tomatoes that have a tasteless northern personality. I have always adored Savoy's *dorade en écailles,* literally fillets of fresh fish—skin, scales, and all—dropped into sizzling fat until the scales sort of stand up like the hair on your arms when you have goose bumps. The result is ultra-crispy, crusty, crunchy. All this is set on a bed of crushed cooked potatoes laced with olive oil. *Miam!*

Poulette a la Creme Gratinee Chez Maitre Paul
CHEZ MAITRE PAUL'S BROILED GRATINEED CHICKEN

This is the dish I order whenever I dine at Chez Maître Paul (see page 62), a small Left Bank restaurant that specializes in the foods of the Jura. This dish combines many of the region's specialties, including free-range chicken, fresh cream, and the nutty cow's milk cheese known as Comté. Serve this with plenty of steamed rice and a fruity red wine.

1 free-range roasting chicken (about 3 pounds; 1.25 kg), well rinsed and patted dry
½ cup freshly squeezed lemon juice
3 tablespoons peanut oil
2 pounds (1 kg) mushrooms, rinsed, trimmed, and patted dry
Salt
2 tablespoons (1 ounce; 30 g) unsalted butter, at room temperature
2 tablespoons superfine flour, such as Wondra
2 cups (50 cl) chicken stock, heated
1 cup (25 cl) *crème fraîche* (see recipe, page xxx) or heavy (whipping) cream
Freshly ground black pepper, to taste
Freshly grated nutmeg, to taste
2 cups (about 5 ounces; 160 g) freshly grated imported Comté or Gruyère cheese

1. Prepare the chicken: Place the chicken on a work surface, breast side down. With poultry shears or a sharp knife, split the bird lengthwise along one side of the backbone. Open it flat and press it down with the heel of your hand to flatten completely. With a sharp knife, make slits in the skin near the tail and tuck the wing tips in to secure them. The bird should be as flat as possible to ensure even cooking.

2. Place the chicken in a roasting pan and add 5 tablespoons of the lemon juice and the oil. Marinate at room temperature for 10 minutes, turning the chicken once or twice.

3. Meanwhile, thinly slice the mushrooms. In a large saucepan, combine the mushrooms, the remaining 3 tablespoons lemon juice, a pinch of salt, and water to cover. Cover and cook over medium heat until the mushrooms are tender and most of the liquid has been absorbed, about 25 minutes. Set aside and keep warm.

4. In a medium-size non-aluminum saucepan, melt the butter over low heat. Add the flour and cook gently, whisking constantly, until the mixture separates slightly and takes on a granular look, 2 to 3 minutes. Do not let the mixture brown. Whisking constantly, add the hot chicken stock all at once, whisking to blend the mixture smoothly. Increase the heat to medium, and whisking steadily, bring the mixture to a boil. When the sauce boils, reduce the heat to low and simmer gently, whisking occasionally, until the stock reduces to a scant cup, about 40 minutes. Remove from the heat and let cool slightly. Stir in the *crème fraîche.* Season with salt, pepper, and nutmeg to taste. (The sauce may be prepared up to 1 hour in advance. Keep warm in the top of a covered double boiler, over simmering water.)

5. Preheat the broiler for 15 minutes.

6. Remove the chicken from the marinade and season generously with salt and pepper. Broil the chicken 5 inches (13 cm) from the heat, breast side up, for about 10 minutes. Baste occasionally with the marinade so the

skin gets browned. Using tongs so you do not pierce the meat, turn the chicken over and broil, basting occasionally, about 15 minutes more. The chicken is done when the juices run clear when the thighs are pierced with a skewer. Season again with salt and pepper. Quarter the chicken and set aside.

7. Reheat the oven heat to 475°F (245°C).

8. In a shallow baking dish just slightly larger than the chicken, spread the mushrooms and their liquid in an even layer. Place the quartered chicken on top of the mushrooms and pour the cream sauce over all. Sprinkle with the grated cheese. Place in the center of the oven and bake until the cheese has melted and is lightly browned, about 15 minutes. Serve immediately, from the baking dish, with white or brown rice alongside.

Yield: 4 to 6 servings

LE PALANQUIN
12, rue Princesse,
Paris 6.
Tel: 01.43.29.77.66.
Métro: Mabillon or Saint-Germain des Prés.
Service 12:30 to 2 P.M. and 7:30 to 10 P.M.
Closed Sunday.
Credit card: V.
Private dining room for 16.
75-franc lunch menu; 110-, 128-, and 148-franc dinner menus.
A la carte, 180 to 220 francs.

SPECIALTIES:
Vietnamese: pho (thin soup of rice noodles, mint, cilantro, onions, ginger, beef, and hot chiles); marmite de riz au poulet, gingembre, et champignon parfumé (casserole of rice, chicken, ginger, and mushrooms); crevettes à la canne à sucre (shrimp with sugar cane).

One of the most pleasing and most refined Vietnamese restaurants in town is the Left Bank La Palanquin, where owner Kim Tran prepares one of my favorite dishes, *pho*—the spicy, endless, and satisfying bowl of soup that combines rice noodles, cilantro, mint, onions, ginger, beef, and hot red chiles cooled down with a touch of lime. (I have been known to weep real tears from the heat of those wonderful chiles.) Another extraordinary specialty is the *marmite de riz au poulet,* a fragrant and warming dish served out of a glazed round casserole, a preparation marrying moist nuggets of chicken, richly perfumed wild mushrooms, and a bold touch of ginger. Service is impeccable and the food always up to the same high standards.

A staff luncheon at Chez Maître Paul (see entry, page 62).

LA TABLE D'AUDE
8, rue de Vaugirard, Paris 6.
Tel: 01.43.26.36.36.
Fax: 01.43.26.90.01.
Métro: Odéon or RER Luxembourg.
Service noon to 2 P.M. and 7 to 10 P.M.
Closed Sunday and August.
Credit cards: AE, V.
Private dining rooms for 12 and 50.
Air-conditioned.
99- (wine included) and 109-franc (unlimited wine) lunch menus; 155- (wine included) and 175-franc (unlimited wine) tasting menus.
A la carte, 150 to 200 francs.

SPECIALTIES:
Regional bistro, Languedoc specialties: saladette de Cabardès (green salad with dried pork liver and sliced raw artichokes); poule de l'Alaric façon grand-mère (chicken in white wine sauce with mushrooms and olives); cassoulet de Castelnaudary (white beans, grilled pork sausages, pork skin, and choice of duck or goose confit).

Pure regionalism is all but dead in Paris. Yes, we have *foie gras* from southwestern farmyards, *tapenade* from Provençal olive groves, and *langoustines* that sing of the freshness of Brittany seas. But that's all simple veneer, a tease for the palate. So along comes La Table d'Aude, a tiny rectangle of a restaurant the size of a cozy railroad car, not far from the Luxembourg Gardens. No, this little jewel is not named after a lady chef, but after the Aude, as in the French *département,* that long stretch in the Languedoc-Roussillon beginning in the *massif central* and reaching all the way to the Mediterranean. Both Carcassonne and the Canal du Midi are within its borders. La Table d'Aude serves as a veritable ambassador for the region, offering dishes that are not simply regional but local, and rarely found beyond the confines of a village or of a single farmhouse. Here the food is not just hearty but earthy, the sort you'd expect to find while wandering down a country road searching for a place for an authentic Sunday lunch.

Add to this the warm and chatty welcome of *patron* Bernard Pautou and that of his demure wife, Véronique. And then there's the wine: rich, inky, deep, and delicious—Minervois, Fitou, Corbières, and La Clape. The region produces more than half of France's red table wine and is unquestionably the country's up-and-coming wine region. So come for the rich and earthy *cassoulet de Castelnaudary,* that rich blend of fat white *lingots* beans, grilled Black Mountain pork sausages, pork skin, and a choice of duck or goose *confit.* Tuck into a *saladette du Cabardès,* a unique mixture of wilted greens, crunchy raw artichoke slices, and salty morsels of earthy dried pork liver. Sounds strange, I know, but try it once and you won't be disappointed.

The food is salty, but your palate and your appetite nudge you on to devour a simple platter of *haricots du Père Falcou,* plump white beans cooked to a soft and soothing *confit* in goose fat, then doused with rich olive oil and a shower of raw minced garlic. Your heart is happy. Move on to the simple and satisfying platter of chicken *façon grand-mère,* farm chicken cooked without fanfare but with plenty of flavor, sauced with a blend of white wine, mushrooms, and olives. Or go for the convincing *coq au vin,* properly chewy, marinated and simmered in the red *vin de Limoux,* with a generous dose of white onions, and a touch of herbs. For dessert, don't miss the refreshing thyme *sorbet:* You'll feel as though you just walked in from the thyme-covered hillside. Don't come to this earnest spot for the finishing touch—the napkins and napery are of paper—but for a touch of the genuine. And wash it all down with a 1993 Minervois Fontelier, a pure syrah that's a pure bargain. (Wines may be purchased to take home.)

LA TABLE DE FES
5, rue Saint-Beuve,
Paris 6.
Tel: 01.45.48.07.22.
Métro: Notre-Dame des Champs or Vavin.
Open for dinner only. Service from 8 to 10:30 P.M.
Closed Sunday and three weeks in August.
Credit card: V.
A la carte, 220 to 280 francs.

SPECIALTIES: Moroccan: couscous; pastilla de fès (savory pigeon pastry); tagine d'agneau au pruneau (lamb stew with prunes); poulet citron (chicken with preserved lemon); desserts maison (homemade desserts).

Couscous—which is both the tiny grain of semolina and the national dish of Morocco, prepared in numerous variations—has become an almost integral element in modern French cooking. You'll find couscous salads in the *charcuteries,* in the supermarkets, and on the menu at many a corner café. When I'm in a casual mood and hungry for couscous, I reserve a table at La Table de Fès, a brightly lit and lively Moroccan restaurant near Montparnasse. I like to go with a group so we can sample a wide variety of the highly flavored dishes. The *merguez* is super-spicy, and the *tagines* are moist and filling. Try either the chicken with preserved lemons or the chicken with plump, moist prunes, or either version prepared with tender morsels of lamb. It is impossible not to take seconds of the fine, delicate, buttery, hand-rolled couscous, which is served in traditional fashion, mounded on a large round clay platter. With the couscous comes the delicious broth, which contains chickpeas and raisins, and with it, as much fiery *harissa* red pepper sauce as your palate will endure. This popular restaurant is always lively, crowded, and noisy, with everyone getting just a bit more vocal on the heady Moroccan red wine, Domaine Riad Jamil.

FAUBOURG SAINT-GERMAIN, INVALIDES, ECOLE MILITAIRE

7th arrondissement

L'AFFRIOLE
17, rue Malar,
Paris 7.
Tel: 01.44.18.31.33.
Fax: 01.44.18.91.12.
Métro: Invalides or La Tour-Maubourg.
Service noon to 2:30 P.M. and 7:30 to 11:30 P.M.
Closed Saturday lunch and Sunday.
Credit card: V.
Air-conditioned.
120-franc lunch menu; 190-franc universal dinner menu.

SPECIALTIES:
Modern bistro: tartare de saumon et haddock (salmon and haddock tartare); pièce d'agneau de Pauillac, aubergine confite, jus réduit à l'origan (lamb with eggplant in reduced juices flavored with oregano); carpaccio de Saint Jacques à la rémoulade de céleri (scallop carpaccio with celery root in a sauce of mayonnaise, capers, mustard, herbs, anchovies, and pickles).

The French always have a word for it. To tempt, to seduce, to charm . . . of course, *affrioler.* In the 15th century, the word *friolet* meant gourmand, and today bistro L'Affriolé is seducing gourmands of all ages. In the summer of 1996, Véronique and Alain Atibard opened this jewel of a spot, just steps from the Seine on the tiny Rue Malar. Right from the outset, you know you're in for a treat: The spanking-clean exterior, the 1930s bistro front, the sign advertising *"Cuisine Traditionnelle,"* and the crisp red-and-white-checkered curtains tug at the heart-strings of every romantic Parisian. Once inside, the soft brown moleskin banquettes, Deco chandeliers, straight-backed bistro chairs, and smiling waiter in traditional black vest shout "bistro" with a capital B. Look a little deeper, however, and you spy suggestions of modernity and whimsy: A glass champagne bucket is filled with water and a swimming goldfish. Flowers are replaced by a single pot containing an artichoke plant in full, glorious flower.

A glance at the menu and you know you're straddling the line between classic and modern here as well. Following the formula that has brought success to many contemporary Paris bistros, Alain Atibard keeps the selection short and sweet, with a single changing menu suggesting the day's dozen or so offerings. The bargain 190-franc menu includes first course, main course, cheese, and dessert. With a wine list featuring at least ten decent wines at less than 125 francs a bottle, a couple can have a high old time on less than 500 francs. Not everything this well-trained chef offers is manna from heaven, but several recent meals suggest that he will be heard from in years to come. Atibard's food is varied, generally well seasoned, and original without being far-fetched. He seems determined to please the customer as much as himself, and he has certainly learned with the masters, including Alain Dutournier and Alain Senderens.

The best of several starters include a textbook lobster salad, with the elegant crustacean cooked to moist perfection and paired with a nicely seasoned salad of finely chopped carrots and endive, and a light and flavorful *tartare de dorade*—precise cubes of fresh uncooked porgy tossed with tomatoes, herbs, and an excellent *vinaigrette,* served with a *chiffonnade* of finely chopped cabbage seasoned with a lemony dressing. Equally good are the platter of fresh marinated sardines attentively seasoned with herbs, and a bright and summery gravlax of salmon served with his cabbage *chiffonnade.*

The main-course roast salmon arrived hot and sizzling and flaked into moist chunks, while the accompanying tangle of Swiss chard, or *blette,* was tossed with just the right amount of rich salted butter. Equally satisfying was the simple roast chicken served on a bed of cubed sautéed potatoes. Some of the dishes lack seasoning and purpose, such as a very dry and underseasoned *colin rôti* (roasted hake wrapped in bacon) and a lackluster main course of veal *tendrons,* or ribs, which on one visit arrived barely warm and devoid of seasoning.

Each day L'Affriolé offers two or three different cheeses with a proper accompaniment, such as a slice of rich *brebis de Pyrénées* (firm sheep's milk cheese) with a brilliant and traditional touch of cherry *confiture* alongside. The salty cow's milk blue *forme d'Ambert* is paired with a thin slice of apple, a simple marriage that is made in heaven; and the delicate disc of Rocamadour goat cheese arrives escorted by a finely dressed green salad.

Desserts could use a bit more attention: On one evening the *tarte à la reine claude* (greengage plum tart) arrived dry and without flavor, as did the imaginative but dry *bonbon d'abricots* (fresh apricots wrapped in phyllo dough). A touch of raspberry sauce would have done wonders for both.

Chef Atibard wins my heart with his warm slices of crisp homemade country-style bread, and with such wines as Jean-Maurice Raffault's rich and racy Chinon, the powerful and berry-filled Château Lancyre Pic-Sur-Loup from the Languedoc, and Ludovic Cornillon's bargain Coteaux du Tricastin.

ARPEGE
84, rue de Varenne,
Paris 7.
Tel: 01.45.51.47.33.
Fax: 01.44.18.98.39.
Métro: Varenne.
Service noon to 2:30 P.M. and 7:30 to 11 P.M.
Closed Saturday and Sunday.
Credit cards: AE, DC, V.
Private dining room for 14.
Air-conditioned.
390-franc lunch menu; 960-franc tasting menu.
A la carte, 650 to 900 francs.

SPECIALTIES:
Contemporary: homard et navet à la vinaigrette aigre douce (lobster and turnips in sweet and sour vinaigrette); langoustines rôties aux senteurs de Provence (Dublin Bay prawns roasted with fresh herbs); feuilletage au chocolat (chocolate puff pastry); pain maison (homemade bread).

Dining with Alain Passard can be an epiphany. When he and his staff are in top form, flashes of brilliance pass from the kitchen to the dining room, where copies of Art Deco Lalique glass panels elegantly grace the clean, unfussy paneled walls. Passard is not the kind of chef who will allow you to ignore his food. His standard opener—scrambled eggs spooned back into the shell and topped with a sweet, intense maple syrup sauce—cannot be casually overlooked. It comes on like someone whispering in your ear, reminding you to pay attention to what's on your plate. The starter sets us up for what's to come, with its voluptuous texture and final flavor bang of intensity, of sweetness. The native Breton goes to the limit of simplicity with his platter of six plump warm oysters in salty Breton butter—nothing but oysters and butter, but what flavor, what essence. The simplicity is overwhelming, as the palate focuses on the sensual pleasure of the oyster, its softness, roundness, slipperiness, brininess, its lingering saline aftertaste. Even his crusty, irresistible homemade rolls, so salty they could be pretzels, do not seem out of place here.

But Passard's finest dish is his lobster braised in the sherry-like *vin jaune* of the Jura. Thin strips of lobster cooked in its shell arrive lightly brushed with a rich wine sauce that's at once sweet, nutty, buttery, and not the least bit cloying. Somehow those thin strips of lobster tail (anointed with a single wild horn-of-plenty mushroom) seem lean, dainty, accessible, making other lobster dishes seem fat and richly overwhelming.

I ordered his grilled lamb chops coated with walnuts on a dare: The combination seemed unlikely. I should have known better. Once again, Passard takes two essential ingredients and creates a dish that's far greater than the sum of its parts. By coating the delicate lamb chops with finely chopped walnuts, he manages to coax intense flavors from each. It's as if the walnut draws out the inherent nuttiness of the lamb, prolonging its distinct flavor. The contrast of the warm, bitter endive accompaniment acts as a counterpoint, a dramatic relief.

Passard's wine choices are extensive, and after dining here often, I've concluded he's a chef whose food loves Burgundy: They're both round, without rough edges. Two worthy choices include the red Aloxe-Corton from the house of Tollot-Beaut, a wine that holds its own when matched with many varied flavors, and the white Chassagne-Montrachet of Olivier Leflaive, which seems to flatter everything.

Choucroute

SAUERKRAUT, SAUSAGES, AND BACON

I have loved sauerkraut and sausages all my life. When choucroute *is at its best, the sauerkraut is ultimately digestible (not too bland, acidic, fatty, or greasy) and is neither dried out from overcooking nor swimming in watery juices. You know the platter is just right when it complements, as well as compliments, chilled Alsatian Riesling.*

- 3 pounds (1.5 kg) sauerkraut, preferably fresh bulk sauerkraut, not canned
- 3 tablespoons lard or goose or chicken fat
- 2 onions, peeled and coarsely chopped
- 2 cups (50 cl) Riesling wine
- 1 cup (25 cl) fresh chicken stock or water
- 2 pounds (1 kg) pork chops
- Freshly ground black pepper, to taste
- 2 whole cloves
- 6 juniper berries
- 2 bay leaves
- 2 cloves garlic
- 6 knackwurst
- 6 fresh German frankfurters
- 1 pound (500 g) smoked pork sausage, such as Polish kielbasa
- 2 pounds (1 kg) new potatoes
- 1 pound (500 g) slab bacon, cut into large chunks

1. Preheat the oven to 350°F (175°C).

2. Rinse the sauerkraut in a colander under cold running water. If it is very acidic or very salty, repeat several times. Drain well.

3. In a large flameproof casserole over low heat, melt the fat and add the onions. Sauté until the onions are wilted, 5 minutes. Then add the wine and stock or water.

4. Add the pork chops. Cover with the sauerkraut. Add the pepper, cloves, juniper berries, bay leaves, and garlic. Cover, and bake in the oven for 1 to 1½ hours.

5. In separate saucepans, cook each variety of sausage in gently simmering water for about 20 minutes. Do not allow the water to boil or the sausages will burst. Drain all the sausages, slice the kielbasa, and keep all warm until serving time.

6. Meanwhile, steam or boil the potatoes until tender, about 20 minutes. Allow them to cool just enough to handle, then peel. Keep warm.

7. Just before serving, grill or broil the slab bacon until very crisp.

8. To serve, drain the sauerkraut (removing the herbs and spices) and mound it in the center of a large heated platter. Surround the sauerkraut with the pork chops, the sausages, including the sliced kielbasa, the potatoes, and the bacon. Serve with several kinds of mustard and plenty of chilled white Riesling wine.

Yield: 8 to 10 servings

LE BAR AU SEL
49, quai d'Orsay,
Paris 7.
Tel: 01.45.51.58.58.
Fax: 01.40.62.97.30.
Métro: Invalides.
Service noon to 2:30 P.M. and 7 to 10:30 P.M.
Open daily.
Credit card: V.
Sidewalk terrace.
190-franc menu.
A la carte, 250 to 300 francs.

SPECIALTIES:
Fish: bar et daurade en croûte de sel (sea bass and porgy baked in a salt crust); sardines grillées aux herbes (sardines grilled with herbs); tartare de saumon aux herbes (salmon tartare); poêlée de langoustines de Loctudy (seared Dublin Bay prawns from Brittany's Loctudy).

With its sea blue décor, yellow and blue Basque linens, and black-and-white photos of life at sea, there is no question about the theme of Le Bar au Sel. The specialty of the house is, of course, sea bass cooked in sea salt, my absolute favorite fish cooked in my absolute favorite way. As one would expect, it is very good here, as is the less prized porgy cooked in sea salt. This open, welcoming restaurant along the Quai d'Orsay is honest and well priced, with such specialties as grilled fresh sardines, grilled sea bass with *beurre blanc* (far less successful than the version in salt), and a salmon *tartare* showered with fresh herbs. The bread here is crusty and delicious, the cruet of olive oil at each table is the very finest in France (from the cooperative in Mausanne-les-Alpilles), and the wine list is brief but well priced.

AU BON ACCUEIL
114, rue de Monttessuy,
Paris 7.
Tel: 01.47.05.46.11.
Métro: Alma-Marceau.
Service noon to 2:15 P.M. and 7:30 to 10:15 P.M.
Closed Saturday and Sunday.
Credit card: V.
Sidewalk terrace.
135-franc lunch menu; 155-franc dinner menu.
A la carte, 280 to 350 francs.

SPECIALTIES:
Bistro: escabèche de sardines (sardines browned in oil, then marinated in vinegar and herbs and served very cold); bar de ligne rôti (roasted line-caught sea bass); tarte au citron (lemon tart).

When Jacques Lacipière decided to follow family tradition and open a bistro in Paris, his grandfather gave him a word of advice: "When people walk out of your bistro, they must see the Eiffel Tower. Forever, they will leave with a good memory of your restaurant." He dutifully took the man's advice, and has had little to regret since. Lacipière, a fourth-generation *bistrotier,* found a 130-year-old neighborhood bistro, complete with pink neon sign, a fanciful name (The Welcome), and, as you leave his doorstep, a view of the Eiffel Tower that cannot be ignored. The place is on a block-long Left Bank street, the rather nondescript rue de Monttessuy. Over time Lacipière has built a steady and faithful clientele, and today he turns away sixty to seventy diners a night, serving the simple but uncompromisingly fresh bistro fare on which he has made his reputation. From the age of fifteen, he followed his father around the wholesale food market, learning to purchase meat, fish, poultry, and vegetables. Today he maintains the tradition, setting off for the Rungis wholesale market in the wee hours, returning with sparkling fresh fish (tiny Brittany sardines, plump fresh sea bass, sweet and iodine-rich *langoustines,* sole from the Atlantic port of Royan), game in season, and choice produce. Meats and *charcuterie* come from "down home," the Auvergne, where the family still runs the town bistro.

Most diners here opt for the daily menu, which might include hefty portions of steamed *moules de bouchot,* the small, prized mussel that is cultivated on stakes driven into the sediment of shallow coastal beds; saddle of rabbit roasted with olives; and the ultra-Parisian lemon tart, properly puckery. On my last visit, I opted for the Brittany sardines, which the chef turned into a well-seasoned *escabèche*—the fish are first pan-fried, then marinated in a blend of vinegar, herbs, and spices, and served alongside a well-dressed salad. Main-course options include an unfussy roasted *bar de ligne* (the preferred line-caught sea bass as opposed to those captured in nets) and an equally straightforward yet satisfying roast pheasant, served with a stick-to-your-ribs potato purée.

The only thing I don't like about Au Bon Accueil is the fact that the clientele is made up of diehard smokers, the sort that set their Marlboros on the table even before they sit down, clutching them like a life-support system, puffing between bites and phrases. The simple, unadorned restaurant is, alas, too small to merit a nonsmoking section. Service can also be annoyingly slow.

For wine, try the Domaine Sarda Mallet Côtes-du-Roussillon or Marcel Richaud's dependable Cairanne Côtes-du-Rhône.

LA FONTAINE DE MARS
129, rue Saint-Dominique,
Paris 7.
Tel: 01.47.05.46.44.
Fax: 01.47.05.11.13.
Métro: Ecole Militaire.
Service noon to 2:45 P.M.
and 7:30 to 10:45 P.M.
Open daily.
Credit cards: AE, V.
Terrace.
Private dining room
for 16 to 20.
A la carte, 200 to 300 francs.

If, like me, you are a hopeless romantic who loves those perfectly ironed faded red-checkered tablecloths, lace curtains, sturdy oak bistro doors, and waiters who refuse to pick up a plate until you have finished every last morsel, then La Fontaine de Mars is for you. On a sunny summer's day I know few better spots in Paris for enjoying simple bistro fare such as a *fricassée* of chicken with wild morels in cream or sautéed calf's liver in sherry vinegar sauce, great crispy sautéed potatoes, and an excellent house Beaujolais.

SPECIALTIES:
Bistro: salade quercynoise (tossed green salad with warm sautéed duck gizzards and hearts); pipérade aux oeufs pochées (sauté of peppers, tomatoes, and onions with poached eggs); boudin aux pommes fruits (blood sausage with apples); sole meunière pommes à l'anglaise (pan-fried sole with steamed potatoes).

In warm weather desserts should fit your mood, and La Fontaine de Mars offers a delightful fresh peach soup (*soupe aux pêches*) or a cooling orange and grapefruit soup (*soupe aux agrumes*). Coffee comes with an excellent square of Valrhona bittersweet chocolate. If you get the right table, you will even be able to gaze up at the tip of the Eiffel Tower.

PAUL MINCHELLI
54, boulevard de La Tour-Maubourg,
Paris 7.
Tel: 01.47.05.89.86.
Fax: 01.45.56.03.84.
Métro: La Tour-Maubourg.
Service 12:30 to 2:15 P.M. and 8 to 11 P.M.
Closed Sunday, Monday, holidays, August, and Christmas week.
Credit cards: AE, V.
Private dining room for 8 to 10.
Air-conditioned.
A la carte, 500 to 600 francs.

SPECIALTIES:
Fish and shellfish: tartare de bar (sea bass tartare); sardines crues à l'huile d'olive et basilic (raw sardines marinated in oil and basil); tronçon de turbot grillé (grilled turbot); ailes de raie au vinaigre d'estragon (skate wings in tarragon vinegar); rougets grillés au safran, fenouil, et pommes de terre (grilled red mullet with saffron, fennel, and potatoes).

For many years, Paris's best fish restaurant—and its clubbiest—was Le Duc, the Montparnasse eatery where one endured snobbery and abrupt service for the pleasure of sampling the Minchelli brothers' top-notch fish cuisine. During the summer of 1994, Paul Minchelli—the cooking partner—went off on his own, remodeling the long-established Chez les Anges on boulevard de La Tour-Maubourg.

Much like a fashion designer with a special, unmistakable look, Minchelli imprints fish dishes with his own fine stamp: freshness and purity of flavor. He does little to his fish and shellfish, but what he does is inevitably the right thing. Try a simple lobster salad—lobster, greens, and vegetables—and you'll see. No fancy dancing, no combinations that set you in a spin. Yet you'll swear that it is the most impeccably prepared lobster salad that ever passed your lips. I'd do handstands if I ever achieved a poached *lotte* as perfect as Paul Minchelli's—hyper-fresh monkfish poached ever so gently and served with a garlic-rich *aïoli* lightened with a potato purée. Here, be warned, you do pay the price for quality.

The wine list is extensive and includes some well-priced finds, including an excellent Muscadet-sur-Lie and Lucien Crochet's famed Sancerre, served by Didier Garnier, an enthusiastic, well-versed *sommelier.* The crusty bread is from the fine Moulin de la Vierge (see Bakeries, page 265).

LES OLIVADES
41, avenue de Ségur,
Paris 7.
Tel: 01.47.83.70.09.
Fax: 01.42.73.04.75.
Métro: Ségur.
Service noon to 2 P.M. and 7:30 to 11 P.M.
Closed Saturday lunch, Sunday, Monday lunch, August, and one week in January.
Credit cards: AE, V.
Small interior terrace.
Private dining room for 20.
Air-conditioned.
179- and 230-franc menus.
A la carte, 250 francs.

SPECIALTIES:
Provençale: petits légumes et fleurs de courgettes en beignets (deep-fried baby vegetables and zucchini flowers); carré d'agneau au romarin, risotto d'épeautre (roast rack of lamb with risotto of Provençal wheat); caille confit dans l'huile d'olive (confit of quail cooked in olive oil); rouget barigoule d'artichauts (red mullet with artichokes cooked with vegetables and wine).

Young Flora Mikula seems to have done the right thing. Few chefs at any age have such a pleasingly compact résumé, chockablock with character-building experiences, cooking in restaurants from Montparnasse cafés to Michelin top-starred restaurants. She's done her duty in her native Provence, in London, and even in New York. In early 1996, at the age of twenty-seven, this native of Nîmes struck out on her own with the small, well-appointed Les Olivades, a youthfully romantic and feminine restaurant near the Champ-de-Mars, with two small dining rooms decked out in bright red-and-white Provençal fabric with pale pink napkins. It could easily turn into too much of a cute thing if the service were less attentive and the cuisine less earnest.

Mikula, a sturdy blonde who often leaves the kitchen at the end of the meal to make the rounds, appears to have turned her single-minded passion to good advantage. Cooking with people like the Michelin three-star chef Alain Passard of Arpège and the Michelin two-star chef Jean-Pierre Vigato of Apicius has not seemed to hurt her either. But it's clear that her greatest resource is Provence itself, with its abundance of olives, oil, zucchini blossoms, honey, herbs, eggplant, and robust wines. She hasn't yet reached her destination in the kitchen, with numerous rough edges to round out. But arrive on the right day in the right mood, and you're pretty well assured of a meal that sings of summer and the southern sun.

A typical starter is batter-fried zucchini blossoms, which arrive hot and properly crisp. A drizzle of herb-rich vinaigrette and a mint-infused mayonnaise serve as delicate dipping sauces for the golden *fleurs de courgette.* Equally zesty and welcoming is the layered *terrine* of fried eggplant, soft goat cheese, and finely minced black olives bathed in a simple tomato sauce. The daily bargain menu might include a nicely spiced creation of tiny thick rings of sautéed squid mounded on a bed of tabbouleh, an all-white dish that somehow works visually, thanks to a variety of textures and forms.

At Les Olivades, the plates and food arrive piping hot, a practice I wish more chefs would embrace. The main-course roasted sea bass, or *bar rôti,* was not the freshest fish I have ever sampled, but it was expertly prepared, served with a touch of cilantro and a spirited eggplant caviar spiced with cumin. Desserts include a fruit and ice cream sandwich made of homemade shortbread cookies filled with raspberry *sorbet* and topped with a fresh fruit sauce of cherries and raspberries. The shortbread, alas, suffered from the same fault as Mikula's homemade breads: it was pale and anemic. Service is efficient and helpful, with a brief, honestly priced wine list that includes Bernard Gripa's elegant, lemony white Saint-Péray and Domaine Richaud's dependable red Côtes-du-Rhône "Les Ebrescades," from the village of Cairanne.

TAN DINH
60, rue de Verneuil,
Paris 7.
Tel: 01.45.44.04.84.
Fax: 01.45.44.36.93.
Métro: Rue du Bac or Solférino.
Service noon to 2 P.M. and 7:30 to 11 P.M.
Closed Sunday and August.
No credit cards.
Private dining room for 20 to 30.
A la carte, 350 francs.

SPECIALTIES:
Vietnamese: ravioles vietnamiens à l'oie fumée (ravioli filled with smoked goose); rouleaux de crevettes asam (fried spring rolls filled with fresh shrimp); pâtes fraîches aux crevettes piquantes (pasta with spicy shrimp sauce); émincé de filet de boeuf tan dinh (thin strips of marinated beef).

Walk through the simple red doorway of Tan Dinh and you enter a cozy, welcoming world where strangers are greeted as friends and faithful clients as part of the family. This most Parisian of Vietnamese restaurants serves as a club where everyone becomes an instant member. The real family is named Vifian, with father Robert and sons Robert and Freddy holding court, tending the stove, embellishing the wine cellar, to enhance their customers' enjoyment. It is not too much to say that this bistro-like restaurant is unique in the world, with a compact list of South Vietnamese specialties and a voluminous selection of wines from the around the globe. For those uninitiated in the ways of the Vifians, it may seem sacrilegious to pair a rare Pomerol with deep-fried spring rolls, or a pricey Côte-Rôti with pasta and spicy shrimp. But trust me. Trust Robert and Robert and Freddy.

Like many wonderful things in the world, the food at the red, white, and black Tan Dinh is deceptively simple. Son Robert may work his way through a dozen different versions of the original, using native cooks—from his mother to aunts to total strangers—as resources. And so his much-studied spring rolls come off fresh and refreshing, studded with herbs and chicken and right for pairing with his 1990 Domaine de Chastelet, a stunning and rare Bordeaux rosé made in a Burgundian style. Or with his *brochettes* of veal (delicately perfumed with cardamom), sample a peppy 1993 Savigny-lès-Beaune "Les Serpentiers." Whether his light and easily digestible fare is steamed or sautéed, gently tinged with star anise, ginger, or garlic, it is a cuisine that's studied and then reinvented and refined for today's palates and, most important, designed to go with wines. Instead of ravioli filled with beef, the family from Saigon fills them with smoked goose, the better to pair with a fulfilling white Graves. The ultrafresh whole *bar* (sea bass) is sprinkled with a symphony of Asian spices, and boned Bresse chicken is wok-fried with a light, crunchy mix of red onions, broccoli, and zucchini, all gently spiced with a touch of star anise.

JULES VERNE
Champ de Mars (second floor, Eiffel Tower), Paris 7.
Tel: 01.45.55.61.44.
Fax: 01.47.05.29.41.
Métro: Bir-Hakeim or Ecole Militaire.
Service 12:15 to 2 P.M. and 7:30 to 10 P.M.
Open daily.
Credit cards: AE, DC, V.
Air-conditioned.
Valet parking.
290-franc weekday lunch menu; 680-franc dinner menu.
A la carte, 750 to 800 francs.

SPECIALTIES:
Fish and shellfish: quelques langoustines à la vapeur d'algues, salade de tomates grappes au basilic (Dublin Bay prawns with steamed seaweed, tomatoes, and basil); langoustines marinées et huîtres au caviar sevruga, pommes écrasées (marinated Dublin Bay prawns with oysters, sevruga caviar, and mashed potatoes); filet de bar de ligne en laitue braisée, crème de fèves, jus au Saint-Emilion (line-caught sea bass fillet with braised lettuce and fava bean purée in a red Bordeaux wine sauce).

It is rare that "celebration" restaurants such as the Jules Verne manage to please everyone, but ever since chef Alain Reix took over in 1993, I have had nothing but great meals and wonderful times at this, perhaps the most celebratory restaurant in Paris. But don't wait until your next birthday, anniversary, or special occasion to reserve a table at this modernist black and gray dining room with the most spectacular of city views from its perch on the second floor of the Eiffel Tower. I like it best at lunch (at night the harsh lighting is quite unflattering), when Reix treats your palate to such delights as a *fricassée* of summer vegetables in a faintly creamy sauce; a mound of fresh crabmeat flanked by sautéed *langoustines* and topped with a crisp, wafer-thin potato cake; and a delightful salad of green asparagus topped with a layer of seared truffle slices, a touch of pan-seared *foie gras,* and a salad of wild greens. Dessert-lovers will adore the roasted apricots stuffed with fresh almonds and paired with a sweet almond milk ice cream.

Diners enter from their own "foot" of the tower, where tailcoated gentlemen usher guests into the glass-enclosed elevator to ascend the 123 meters to the second level, where live piano music greets them at the door.

LE VIOLIN D'INGRES
135, rue Saint-Dominique, Paris 7.
Tel: 01.45.55.15.05.
Fax: 01.45.55.48.42.
E-mail: le-violin-d-ingres @horeca.tm.fr.
Métro: Ecole Militaire.
Service 12:30 to 2:30 P.M. and 7:30 to 10:30 P.M.
Closed Sunday, Monday, and August.
Credit cards: AE, V.
Air-conditioned.
240-franc lunch menu; 400-franc tasting menu.
A la carte, around 400 francs.

SPECIALTIES:
Modern: mousseline d'oeufs brouillés (soft scrambled eggs); tatin de pied de porc caramelisé (caramelized pig's feet); carré d'agneau rôti sous la cendre, friture de légumes (roasted rack of lamb with fried vegetables); tarte sablée au chocolat noir, glace vanille (bittersweet chocolate tart with vanilla ice cream).

Since Christian Constant left the Hôtel Crillon to open his own restaurant in early 1997, he's become a favorite of many diners, wooing them with a number of dishes that are models of purity and classicism, such as a moist *poulette de Bresse* as tender as butter, served with giant wands of fried potatoes, as well as textbook-perfect roasted lamb chops that are worth their weight in gold. Equally outstanding are his moist and meaty breast of guinea hen on a brilliantly conceived bed of turnip "sauerkraut," and a grilled prime rib of beef teamed up with a welcoming shallot sauce. Also on the plus side you'll find a soothing and satisfying risotto (one of the better risottos I have sampled at the hands of a French chef) dotted with meaty nuggets of chicken and ringed with a brilliant green herb sauce.

Some other items are either too strange or too boring to place him among the top chefs working in Paris today: The salad of scallops sandwiched with fresh truffles is hardly cutting edge, and there are more imaginative uses for fresh black truffles these days; and I found the braised calf's-head starter interesting, but no more. Fish offerings such as *rouget* with olives and saffron-flavored vegetables are simply ho-hum, and no matter how hard I try, I can't imagine swooning over brill (*barbue*) and chestnuts or pollack (*lieu jaune*) with "scales" of chorizo sausage. I don't love the railroad-car dining room (which was last seen as Jean Delaveyne's Regain) but do love some of the wines on the list, including Robert Jasmin's rich and jammy Côte-Rôtie.

Madeleine, Saint-Lazare, Champs-Elysees, Place des Ternes

8th arrondissement

LES AMBASSADEURS
Hôtel de Crillon
10, place de la Concorde, Paris 8.
Tel: 01.44.71.16.16.
Fax: 01.44.71.15.02.
Métro: Concorde.
Service noon to 2:30 P.M. and 7:30 to 10:30 P.M.
Open daily.
Credit cards: AE, DC, V.
Air-conditioned.
360-franc lunch menu; 650-franc dinner menu.
A la carte, 800 francs.

SPECIALTIES:
Modern: saumon fumé, chantilly au caviar, et croustillant de pommes de terre (smoked salmon with whipped cream and caviar, with crisp potato cake); turbot rôti et poché au lait fumé, confitures d'oignons rouges et céleri rave (roasted turbot poached in smoked milk, with red onions and celery root).

Anyone looking for a road map to some of the most up-to-date French restaurants would do well to bring a generous appetite and a sackful of money to the Crillon to sample the excellent fare of chef Dominique Bouchet. His substantial track record includes stints in the 1970s as assistant to Joël Robuchon and in the 1980s as chef at the then Michelin three-star Tour d'Argent and the then two-star Jamin. He went on to capture two stars at his own Moulin de Marcouze in the Charente. Bouchet is calm, forceful, and direct, characteristics that serve him well at the giant Crillon. His menu offers something for everyone, and the professionalism in the vast Crillon kitchens reveals itself evenly and solidly in the glorious ocher-marbled dining room of Les Ambassadeurs.

Bouchet's straightforward combinations, sublimely prepared, do make a statement: The trendy chicken of the day, Gauloise Blanche from France's southwest, is served with flavorful flat parsley tucked beneath the skin and with tiny, woodsy *girolle* mushrooms. Tender, succulent lobster is flanked by firm green asparagus and delicate, buttery fava beans. The entire eye of the lamb loin is seared to perfection and teamed up, ever so honestly, with flawlessly turned artichokes. Desserts include an ultra-rich Robuchon-style chocolate tart served with vanilla ice cream flavored with a touch of maple syrup and a sprinkling of sweet caramelized walnuts.

An informal formality—attentive tableside service.

L'APPART'
9, rue du Colisée,
Paris 8.
Tel: 01.53.75.16.34.
Fax: 01.53.76.15.39.
Internet: http://www.leschampselysees.com
Métro: Franklin D. Roosevelt.
Service noon to 2:30 P.M. and 7:30 P.M. to midnight
Open daily.
Credit cards: AE, V.
Air-conditioned.
120-franc lunch menu; 175-franc lunch menu, including wine; 175-franc dinner menu.
A la carte, 220 to 280 francs.

SPECIALTIES:
Modern bistro: salade maraîchère au vinaigre de framboises et huile de noisettes (mixed green salad with a dressing of raspberry vinegar and hazelnut oil); fraîcheur de haricots verts, parmesan, et vinaigre balsamic (salad of green beans, Parmesan, and balsamic vinegar); les légumes de saison en font tout un plat (mixed seasonal vegetables as a main course); pavé de morue fraîche, pommes de terre écrasées, et jus de viande (thick cod steak in meat juices with mashed potatoes); onglet de veau poêlé à la graine de moutarde, gratin dauphinois (veal flank steak in mustard sauce with potato gratin).

When you combine a good location, pleasant surroundings, a modern sense of liveliness, and good food with good value, you've got a real winner. L'Appart' (short for apartment) is just that, with its shiny wooden floors, Oriental rugs, walls lined with books, and an unmatched selection of gilt-framed mirrors. Just steps from the Champs-Elysées, the restaurant has a chic, vibrant, spunky air with food that hits the spot. Give me half a kilo of greens and I am happy any day, and L'Appart's *salade maraîchère* satisfies to the core. The classic *ravioles de Royans* have become staples in many of the city's modern bistros, and there's a good reason why. Give people good fresh pasta and a touch of cheese, and you're sure to bring smiles to their faces. At L'Appart', the tiny cheese-filled ravioli arrive steaming hot, bathed in stock. Other worthy offerings include a platter of fresh cod (*morue*) on a bed of creamy mashed potatoes, all served in a pool of rich beef stock; a duck *carpaccio* paired with a green salad; and a four-cornered hot apple tart topped with a huge scoop of vanilla ice cream.

Freshly opened briny oysters.

LE RESTAURANT DE L'ASTOR
Hotel Astor
11, rue d'Astorg,
Paris 8.
Tel: 01.53.05.05.20.
Fax: 01.53.05.05.30.
Métro: Saint-Augustin.
Service noon to 2 P.M. and 7:30 to 10 P.M.
Closed Saturday, Sunday, and August.
Credit cards: AE, DC, V.
Private dining room for 10 to 20.
Air-conditioned.
Valet parking.
298-franc lunch and dinner menus, including wine and coffee; 520-franc tasting menu, including wine and coffee.
A la carte, 350 to 400 francs.

SPECIALTIES:
Modern and seasonal: araignée de mer en gelée anisée à la crème de fenouil (spider crab in anise gelatin with fennel cream); blanc de bar cuit en peau, sauce verjutée (sea bass fillet cooked in its skin, with a sauce of fermented grape juice); suprême de pigeon au chou et au foie gras (pigeon breasts with cabbage and foie gras).

Consider it Robuchon without Robuchon. All the familiar faces in the dining room, the same (or close to the same) flavors from the kitchen, a little trip down memory lane. When Joël Robuchon retired from the day-to-day business of running a restaurant, he never intended to retire his chef's hat or his influence on French cuisine. He wanted out of the business while staying in the business, and he held the joker, all the while managing to deal the first hand. He chose the route of consultant, meaning he got to choose the team, call the plays, and make a living while his legendary cuisine stayed alive. The result is a small and smashingly beautiful dining room in a nondescript part of the 8th *arrondissement,* a hotel restaurant in the newly refurbished Hotel Astor. The gray-and-white-striped dining room is cozy, Art Deco in style, sumptuous and spacious, just right for special meals or doing business. The dining room staff is headed by former *sommelier* Antoine Hernandez, now playing the role of *maître d'hôtel* (which the French have somehow transformed into the modern title of *directeur de salle*). In the kitchen is Eric Lecerf, a longtime Robuchon acolyte who translates Robuchon's food as well as any human might without the benefit of his constant presence or unlimited battery of chefs.

The Astor is as close as anyone will get to Robuchon's cooking today, and that's not half bad. Lecerf manages to deliver on 85 percent of the orders, and considering the challenge, that's pretty wonderful. Many of the Robuchon signatures are here: If you crave (or never had) the famed potato purée, the roasted guinea hen, or the salad of potatoes, black truffles, tomatoes, and Parmesan, then this is your chance. If you want to sample the deep-fried *merlan* (whiting) or the veal sweetbreads and kidneys, they are waiting for you.

And if you have no memories, is there reason to go? Yes. The Astor has been created by some of the best people working in the business today, and if they can't make a go of it, France might as well close up shop. Forget the traditional negative aspects of the hotel dining room and focus on the present. I dare any chef to astonish and please your palate more with the *cannelloni d'aubergines,* a rich and evasively complex cannelloni that rolls sweet eggplant, fresh tuna, olive oil, and tomatoes into a seriously satisfying first course. The *langoustines juste rôties* are sumptuous, and the tiny milk-fed leg of lamb that is braised, then roasted, is delicious in its falling-apart moistness. The roast pigeon, the veal kidneys and sweetbreads, the fried whiting, and the sole cooked in its skin follow suit: They parade around saying, "This is who I am, in all simplicity." This is food cooked by those who understand that the ingredient is master, not the chef. Some wine bargains include J. M. Alquier's rewarding red Faugères from the Languedoc and Corrine Couturier's solid, robust Cairanne. And the "club menu" available at lunch and dinner is one of the city's best buys.

CAP VERNET
82, avenue Marceau,
Paris 8.
Tel: 01.47.20.20.40.
Fax: 01.47.20.95.36.
E-mail: savoy@calvacom.fr
Internet: http://www.calvacom.fr/savoy/
Métro: Charles de Gaulle–Etoile.
Service noon to 2:30 P.M. and 7 P.M. to midnight.
Open daily except Christmas and Christmas Eve dinner.
Credit cards: AE, DC, V.
Private dining room for 20.
Air-conditioned.
Sidewalk terrace.
215-franc lunch menu.
A la carte, 260 to 270 francs.

"Oysters," says Yvon Madec, skillfully forcing a knife between the shells of a tiny mollusk, "are like wine. They owe everything to their *terroir.*" But in this case, it is the sea—its salinity, temperature, and plankton—and not the soil that gives each oyster its special iodine-infused aroma, flavor, texture, and color. Madec is a passionate, successful, and ambitious oyster grower who has made a name for himself in recent years with his tiny crinkle-shelled oyster known as *boudeuse,* from the far north Breton port of Prat-au-Coum, which produces some of brightest, most saline oysters to be found in this land. On certain Saturdays you will find him and other oyster growers holding court in front of the stylish, popular brasserie Cap Vernet, one of chef Guy Savoy's best satellite restaurants. On many weekends through the fall, Cap Vernet hosts various oyster growers from Brittany and Normandy, pairing them with wine growers from throughout France. For oyster- and wine-lovers, there is no better way to understand the products and the marriage of the two than to meet the maker face to face.

On our visit, Madec was teamed up with Alsatian winemaker André Ostertag, whose bone-dry white Sylvaner stood shoulder-to-shoulder with Madec's remarkable oysters. They're called *boudeuses,* or pouters, because their shells will grow only so

SPECIALTIES:
Brasserie: huîtres (oysters); plateau de fruits de mer (platter of raw and cooked shellfish); émincé de thon mi-cuit à l'origan et paprika (lightly cooked tuna with oregano and paprika); filet de dorade poêlé, étuvée de poireaux au beurre citronné (pan-fried porgy fillet with leeks and lemon butter); gigot d'agneau de lait des Pyrénées rôti, coco de Paimpol à la truffe (roasted milk-fed leg of lamb from the Pyrénées with white shell beans from Brittany and a shower of black truffles).

big. The shell of a three-year-old *boudeuse* is about a third the size of any other full-grown oyster, but the meat inside is as plump and generous as its full-size counterpart. But there are more than oysters and platters of fresh fish and shellfish at Cap Vernet, where chef Stéphane Perraud offers an appealing, creative menu that features everything from a snappy modern *millefeuille* of fresh marinated sardines enlivened with a touch of balsamic vinegar and a *confit* of tomatoes, to an earthy casserole of fragrant *lyonnaise* pork sausage, potatoes, and mushrooms. Equally delicious and fresh are the *cappelletti* stuffed with *langoustines* floating in a creamy crabmeat soup, and the ethereal *parfait* of tomato, caviar, and smoked salmon, embellished with a crunchy cabbage salad. Wines to try here include Mardon's pleasing white Quincy and the fine country Côtes-du-Lubéron red Val Joanis.

LES ELYSEES DU VERNET
Hôtel Vernet
25, rue Vernet,
Paris 8.
Tel: 01.44.31.98.98.
Fax: 01.44.31.85.69.
Métro: Charles de Gaulle–Etoile.
Service noon to 2 P.M. and 7:30 to 9 P.M.
Closed Saturday, Sunday, holidays, August, and one week at Christmas.
Credit cards: AE, DC, V.
Private dining room for 2 to 17.
Air-conditioned.
Valet parking.
430-franc lunch menu; 790-franc dinner menu.
A la carte, 700 francs.

It's a little hidden harbor of romance in the heart of Paris. Exquisite piano music from an antique Pleyel piano floats in from the adjacent room. A dozen or so well-appointed tables are discreetly arranged beneath the expansive Belle Epoque skylight. The outgoing staff seems to love being part of the theatrical setting, performing with rare enthusiasm night after night. And chef Alain Solivères lets his imagination run wild—sometimes too much for his own good, but for the most part, the diner wins out. The surprise to all is that the restaurant is in the heart of Paris, and in a hotel. The Elysées du Vernet is a small, charming restaurant tucked away in the Hotel Vernet, just a block off the Etoile. Solivères and the restaurant's staff understand what we want today in terms of dining and cuisine. The accent on the menu and in the wine list is distinctly southern, with Provençal, Basque, and Italian fare leading the way. The bad news is that the chef and his staff are often out of sync with the dining room (odd waits can try one's patience even on the most romantic of occasions), and on several visits the glitches were close to unpardonable. (Once a roasted sea bass was so overcooked and waterlogged it was inedible. Another

SPECIALTIES:
Modern: épeautre du pays de Sault cuisiné comme un risotto à l'encre de seiche (risotto-style spelt with squid ink); turbot doré aux câpres, citron, et truffes écrasées (turbot with capers, lemon, and crushed black truffle); chausson feuilleté au chocolat amer (bitter-sweet chocolate in puff pastry); crème glacée aux fèves torréfiées (roasted-cocoa-bean ice cream).

time the kitchen ran out of pricey turbot and replaced it with inexpensive *pageot* without changing the price, a tactic sure to drive away knowing customers.) Just hope that you go on a day when all systems are go. If they are, you'll be assured of efficient service that is friendly and unstuffy.

Meals always begin with crisp (and sometimes overcooked) yard-long *grissini* bread sticks and various openers that might include a soothing topknot of smoked salmon sprinkled with a few grains of caviar. (This is also the land of huge portions, so go when you're in the mood for serious dining.) The best dish I've sampled here, consistently, is the chef's seasonal variations with *épeautre,* the trendy Provençal "poor-man's wheat," better known as spelt in English. He manages to turn this ricelike grain into marvelously rich and complex risotto concoctions, sometimes paired with frog's legs, other times with wild asparagus and crayfish or with seasonal wild mushrooms. In other hearty starters, he pairs meaty *chipirons* (squid) with fiery Espelette peppers, onions, black olives, and his omnipresent (and delicious) tomato *confit* in portions large enough to feed at least two as a main course. His menus are peppered with the best products that France has to offer, including potatoes from Noirmoutier, baby artichokes from the farmland north of Nice, *foie gras* from Chalosse, and line-caught turbot from Brittany.

The wine list may be pricey, but *sommelier* Thierry Pelven and dining room manager Alain Moser are sure to steer you in the right direction. There's the always dependable Château Simone, from the rare appellation Palette in Provence, as well as Eloi Durbach's ever appealing red Coteaux d'Aix Domaine de Trevallon. Desserts are generally worth the effort here, with a soothing fig tart adorned with an ethereal *fromage blanc* ice cream and a fine cinnamon ice cream designed to escort a seasonal plum tart. And as you leave the dining room, there's always a long-stemmed red rose for the ladies and a little bag of irresistible candied almonds for the men to send you off to dreamland in a very good mood.

PIERRE GAGNAIRE
6, rue Balzac,
Paris 8.
Tel: 01.44.35.18.25.
Fax: 01.44.35.18.37.
Métro: George V or Charles de Gaulle–Etoile.
Service noon to 2:30 P.M. and 8:15 to 10:30 P.M.
Closed Saturday lunch, Sunday, holidays, and July 15 to August 15.
Credit cards: AE, DC, V.
Air-conditioned.
Private dining room for 15.
500- and 900-franc menus.
A la carte, 700 to 850 francs.

SPECIALTIES:
Modern: grosse langoustines en scampi, feuilles croustillantes de légumes (giant Dublin Bay prawns with thin, crunchy vegetables); pièce du turbot de ligne poêlée au vadouvan (pan-fried line-caught turbot with mixed spices); soufflé au chocolat pure Caraïbe (pure Caribbean-chocolate soufflé).

From the very beginning, we should have known that Pierre Gagnaire would be different. During his rise to stardom in a happy, skylit restaurant in the dreary city of Saint Etienne (not far from Lyons) during the early 1980s, he always seemed like the classmate who had the most fun as well as the most trouble sitting still. After just a moment with him you'd find your mind reeling with ideas, your heart pounding with a certain excitement. He never even tried to contain his enthusiasms or energy, and soon his menus were jam-packed with sensory stimulation. It was a style of cooking he called *"cuisine immédiate,"* and we swooned over his tempura of *langoustines,* delicately fried and served with a cinnamon-infused *beurre blanc,* and his astonishing rich chocolate *soufflé,* so creamy he called it a soup. Even then, before his newsmaking 1992 move to a stunning Art Deco mansion in the same town and his subsequent anointing with the coveted triple Michelin crown, you did not go to Pierre Gagnaire's to fuel your body, but to partake in a roller-coaster sort of culinary voyage.

While Gagnaire stayed much the same, the world changed. Saint Etienne was too far to go for lunch or for dinner. The days of wacky gastronomic pilgrimages were over. And Saint Etienne is not Lyons, not the sort of place to applaud a chef who offers a cheese course made up of runny Brie, a cream of Roquefort with aged port, supple Vacherin, and soft white raisins. Just give me a wedge of Camembert, the locals seemed to be saying. Gagnaire got the message and so did his bank, and he became the first Michelin three-star chef in the history of France to go bankrupt.

Feeling a bit like the sacrificial lamb, Gagnaire packed up his staff and his talents and reopened in Paris in 1996, taking over the elegant, modern, bright steel-blue and silver restaurant in the Hotel Balzac, near the Etoile. The tall, lean blond chef has not lost a gram of his energy or excitement, and you still want to spray a dose of Valium on him to reduce his enthusiasm to a more human level. Nor has the experience toned down his cuisine, which is still filled with artistry, poetry, audacity, and rich classic flavors. Here diners feast on not one, but on four or five baby starters, such as single-bite portions of a simple *tartare* of tuna with leeks and mushrooms or cubes of calf's foot bathed in a rich mayonnaise-like *ravigote.*

His menu is vast and complex, mixing unexpected flavors such as *foie gras,* dried figs, and buckwheat *galettes,* or sole, quince juice, and tarragon. The best dish sampled during my last visit was a first-course feast of thinly sliced raw black truffles and baby artichokes bathed in a Jerusalem artichoke cream. The marriage was perfect, with intense, deep, flinty flavors of the winter earth, miraculously echoed by sips of a 1994 white Châteauneuf-du-Pape from Château de Beaucastel. In a close second place, Gagnaire served a *lasagne* of black truffles and buffalo mozzarella, a dish that played up the plainness of the pasta, the rich creaminess of the cheese, and the dominant flavor and texture of the truffle. Less interesting was the braised Saint Pierre, its crisp skin topped with a thin crisp slice of Corsican ham. The dish, though, was saved by a soothing portion of polenta topped with a warm and inviting ricotta cream.

The dessert list is extensive, with *soufflés* flavored with chocolate, honey, or tamarillo, as well as a procession of tiny desserts that are downright explosive, including a trio of tropical fruit *sorbets,* miniature tarts bathed in a puckery *crème de cassis,* and an apple tart with rich vanilla ice cream.

LES GOURMETS DES TERNES
87, boulevard de Courcelles, Paris 8.
Tel: 01.42.27.43.04.
Métro: Ternes.
Service noon to 2 P.M. and 7 to 10 P.M.
Closed Saturday, Sunday, August, and two weeks at Christmas.
Credit card: V.
Sidewalk terrace.
A la carte, 165 francs.

The more Paris changes, the more it stays the same. This tried-and-true establishment in the upscale neighborhood around the Place des Ternes remains a great hangout for those who do not want to admit that modern cuisine is upon us. The menu (and prices) at this small 1892 bistro have barely changed over the years. Some starters begin at 18 francs. The menu still boasts a telephone number from the past—CARnot 43 04—as well as *oeufs mayo* (hard-cooked eggs slathered with mayonnaise), radishes and butter, and a simple beet salad. Come with a big hunger and in the mood for meat, preferably a thick flank steak, or *onglet,* or another version showered with coarsely ground black pepper. I always start with their delicious room-

SPECIALTIES:
Bistro: viandes grilleés et frites (grilled meats and French fries); radis beurre (radishes and butter); filets de harengs à l'huile (herring fillets marinated in oil); escargots (snails); betteraves rouges en salade (beet salad).

temperature *ratatouille Niçoise,* big chunks of tomato and zucchini (no eggplant) bathed in lots of tomato sauce. Like a lot of bistro fare, it needs help from the salt shaker. The wine to have here is Brouilly (drink plenty—it's cheap). The *"Complet"* sign appears in the window around eleven each morning, meaning that tables are already reserved. Although none of the chairs or light fixtures match and the waitresses lost interest a long time ago, the regulars keep returning, enjoying the solid, simple fare. In good weather, you can enjoy your meal on the small sidewalk terrace.

LAURENT
41, avenue Gabriel,
Paris 8.
Tel: 01.42.25.00.39.
Fax: 01.45.62.45.21.
Métro: Champs Elysées–Clemenceau.
Service 12:30 to 2 P.M. and 8 to 10 P.M.
Open daily.
Credit cards: AE, DC, V.
Terrace dining.
Private dining rooms for 4 to 70.
390- to 960-franc menus.
A la carte, 700 to 800 francs.

SPECIALTIES:
Modern and seasonal: langoustines croustillantes au basilic (deep-fried Dublin Bay prawns wrapped in basil and thin pastry); quasi de veau poêlé aux girolles (rump of milk-fed veal with chanterelle mushrooms); crêpes Suzettes (hot crêpe dessert flamed with orange liqueur).

Some places are worth the splurge—especially on a warm summer's night when you are seated on the terrace with those you love, sipping Champagne selected by *sommelier* Philippe Bourgignon, perusing the careful menu created by Philippe Braun with the help of the restaurant's consultant, Joël Robuchon. The pianist is here to add just one more touch of romance. Laurent is yet another of those rejuvenated restaurants that had fallen on hard times and was taken out of the slump by those who care. Next to Le Pré Catelan, it offers one of the city's most romantic and sophisticated outdoor dining experiences. At this pastel-pink 19th-century hunting lodge set in the gardens of the Champs-Elysées, one dines in the shade of enormous chestnut trees as waiters in crisp white jackets all but waltz about the terrace. A tall hedge of shrubbery surrounds the twenty or so well-separated tables, providing a fine buffer from urban clamor.

The menu changes with the seasons. One of my favorite dishes is the *langoustines croustillantes,* tender cloudlets of Dublin Bay prawns wrapped in a basil leaf, then in the phyllo-like pastry known as brick, and delicately deep-fried. Or try a thick slice of line-caught turbot, cooked on the bone for flavor, then delicately pan-fried. Bathed in a touch of veal roasting juices and paired with a mound of fresh fava beans, it's a heavenly dish. A wonderful dessert that pairs cold raspberry soufflé with warm lemon soufflé will send you to dreamland. And should the weather turn less than perfect, the plush indoor dining room offers the same opportunity for romance.

MARQUISE AU CHOCOLAT TAILLEVENT
TAILLEVENT'S CHOCOLATE CAKE

This is the dessert I order almost every time I dine at Taillevent (see page 90), the finest restaurant in Paris. The cake is rich and classic, rather like a ripened chocolate mousse. A marquise *is easy to make and requires no baking. Taillevent adds its signature by serving it with a rich pistachio sauce, actually a* crème anglaise *flavored with ground pistachio nuts. The sauce is a bit time-consuming but not difficult. The cake may, of course, be served without a sauce or with a plain* crème anglaise. *Both the cake and the sauce should be made twenty-four hours before serving.*

- 9 ounces (280 g) bittersweet chocolate (preferably Lindt or Tobler brand), broken into pieces
- ¾ cup (100 g) confectioners' sugar
- ¾ cup (6 ounces; 185 g) unsalted butter, at room temperature
- 5 eggs, separated
- Pinch of salt
- Pistachio Sauce, optional (recipe follows)

1. Make the chocolate batter: Place the chocolate in the top of a double boiler, and melt over simmering water. Add these ingredients in the following order, mixing well after each addition: ½ cup (70 g) confectioners' sugar, all the butter, and the egg yolks.

2. In a small mixing bowl, beat the egg whites with a pinch of salt until stiff; then add the remaining ¼ cup (30 g) sugar and beat another 20 seconds, or until glossy.

3. Remove the chocolate batter from the heat, and add one-third of the egg white mixture, folding it in gently but thoroughly. Then gently fold in the remaining whites. Don't overmix, but be sure that the mixture is well blended.

4. Rinse an 8½-inch (22-cm) springform pan with water. Leave the pan wet and fill it with the mixture. Refrigerate for 24 hours. Remove from the refrigerator about 30 minutes before serving. To serve, pour several tablespoons of the pistachio sauce onto each dessert plate. Place a thin slice of the *marquise* in the center of the plate, and serve.

Yield: One 8½-inch (22-cm) cake; 8 to 10 servings

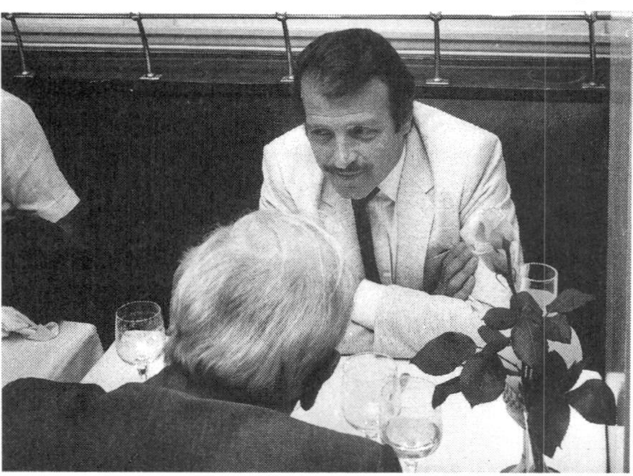

The business lunch, a Paris tradition.

Sauce a la Pistache
PISTACHIO SAUCE

⅓ cup (100 g) pistachio paste (see recipe below)
1 quart (1 liter) milk
8 egg yolks
1¼ cups (250 g) sugar

1. Prepare the pistachio paste.

2. In a medium-size saucepan, combine the pistachio paste with the milk and bring the mixture to a boil over medium heat. Remove from the heat, cover, and allow it to steep for 5 minutes. Then strain through cheesecloth or a fine-mesh sieve into another medium-size saucepan. Set aside.

3. In a medium-size mixing bowl, combine the egg yolks and sugar, and beat until thick and light. Whisk in half the warm strained milk, then whisk the mixture back into the remaining milk.

4. Warm the sauce gently over medium heat, stirring constantly, until it thickens, about 20 minutes. Do not allow the sauce to boil or it will curdle. You can prepare this 24 hours in advance and refrigerate, removing it from the refrigerator 1 hour before using.

Yield: 1 quart (1 liter)

Pate de Pistache
PISTACHIO PASTE

Generous ½ cup (60 g) shelled pistachio nuts, preferably raw unsalted
⅓ cup (65 g) sugar
White of 1 small egg

1. Preheat the oven to 300°F (150°C).

2. Toast the nuts on a baking sheet in the oven for 5 minutes. Allow them to cool. Then, squeezing them between your thumb and forefinger, remove as much skin as possible from the nuts. (If using already roasted, salted nuts, remove as much skin as possible from the shelled nuts, then rinse quickly under boiling water. Drain, then remove as much remaining skin as possible.)

3. Place the nuts in a food processor or nut grinder, and grind the nuts to a paste.

4. In a small bowl, mix the nut paste with the sugar; then add the egg white to give it a sticky quality. The pistachio paste will keep in a tightly sealed container in the refrigerator for a week.

Yield: ½ cup (150 g)

TAILLEVENT
15, rue Lamennais,
Paris 8.
Tel: 01.44.95.15.01.
Fax: 01.42.25.95.18.
Métro: Charles de Gaulle–Etoile or George V.
Service 12:30 to 2:30 P.M. and 7 to 10:30 P.M.
Closed Saturday, Sunday, and from the last week of July to the last week of August.
Credit cards: AE, DC, V.
Private dining rooms for 12 and 32.
Air-conditioned.
Valet parking.
A la carte, 800 to 900 francs.

SPECIALTIES:
Classic, seasonal: crème de cresson au caviar sévruga (cream of watercress soup with sevruga caviar); cannelloni de tourteau (crab cannelloni); pigeon rôti en bécasse (long-cooked pigeon); marquise au chocolat à la pistache (chocolate cake with pistachio sauce; see recipe, page 88); glace au lait d'amandes (almond milk ice cream).

If Taillevent did not exist, someone would have to invent it: the pillar of French cuisine, the ideal of what can and should be done in running a restaurant, in treating each guest with honor and dignity. With Jean-Claude Vrinat at the helm, this grown-up, intimate club is in fact open to all. Taillevent is a sober (but never somber) Napoléon III *hôtel particulier* rich with wood, decorated in deep tones of blue and red. With the newly transformed kitchen in the hands of Philippe Legendre, the cuisine shines with offerings that are both classic and modern. On my last visit, he wooed us all with a memorable hot cream of watercress soup served with a dollop of *crème fraîche* and generous spoonfuls of sevruga caviar. He took us to Provence with a sparkling fresh fillet of *daurade,* or porgy, sprinkled with coarse sea salt and served with a vibrant-flavored *tapenade* (black olive purée). We were whisked north to Brittany with a scrumptious preparation of *langoustines* (Dublin Bay prawns) served in a fetching orange butter. Vrinat's flawless choice of wines—from a soft and fragrant Domaine Muliter Condrieu Château du Rozy to nutty, mellow Domaine Michelot-Buisson Meursault Narvaux and on to a distinguished Domain J. Arbon Pommard Rugiens—will ensure a memorable experience.

Gare de l'Est, Gare du Nord, Republique

9th and 10th arrondissements

L'ALSACO
10, rue Condorcet,
Paris 9.
Tel: 01.45.26.44.31.
Métro: Poissonière.
Service noon to 2 P.M. and 7 to 11 P.M.
Closed Saturday lunch, Sunday, and August.
Credit cards: AE, V.
89- and 170-franc menus.
A la carte, 130 to 200 francs.

In winter, the gray northern skies over Paris cry out for hearty, restorative fare, and nothing fills the bill like a heaping, steaming platter of *choucroute,* a mound of braised sauerkraut teamed with a parade of sausages and meats. It's generally one of those "safe" dishes that has to be pretty bad to be awful, and so it's the dish I order on almost every visit to such popular brasseries as La Coupole and Lipp, both of which offer excellent versions of this Alsatian specialty. But if average or even excellent isn't good enough for you, if what you crave is a *choucroute* platter that's truly fragrant, with a mild hint of smokiness, a gentle scent of cumin, the pun-

SPECIALTIES: Alsatian: choucroute (sauerkraut, sausages, bacon, and pork with potatoes); flammekuchen (thin-crusted savory tart covered with cream, onions, and bacon); backofa ("baker's oven" stew of beef, lamb, pork, potatoes, onions, and wine).

gency of purplish-black juniper berries, and the mildly acidic aroma of freshly cured cabbage, then reserve a table at the city's best *winstub,* Claude Steger's Alsaco, near the Gare du Nord. Here, in a tiny, cramped wine bar with a few tables stuck in the back of the narrow dining room, you can feast on cabbage, sausages, and pork products, ranging from *bratwurst* to *boudin noir* (blood sausage), the cumin-flecked Montbéliard sausage, as well as meaty slabs of bacon (what the French call *lard*), *jarret* (pig's knuckle), and *palette* (lean pork shoulder). And I defy you to find a better hot dog in town; this one is juicy, meaty, fresh, and fragrant.

Steger's basic—and my favorite—*choucroute* dish, a simple platter of his sterling sauerkraut and an assortment of four delicious sausages, offers diners one of the city's better bargains. The outgoing, chatty chef's recipe for a great *choucroute* is simple—a great product and a little bit of love—and his seems to have a good dose of both. His sauerkraut arrives fresh from the Alsatian village of Krautergersheim, and in the cool months he will serve up to 2,200 pounds in a given week.

But if sauerkraut is not your cup of tea, you can always vie for a platter of grilled *cervelas* (pork sausages) or a warming dish of potatoes topped with melted Alsatian Munster, served with a side dish of beautifully grilled bacon. There's also *backaofa* (a hefty braise of meat and potatoes), the oversized braised pork knuckle, and *schiffala,* or smoked shoulder.

My favorite starters here include the traditional Alsatian "pizza"—really a flatbread tart topped with strips of delicious bacon, cream, and onions, and the moist and meaty headcheese called *preskopf.* Add to this Steger's cellar of more than 130 different wines (including the full range of Lorenz wines by the pitcher, plus all the famous Alsatian winemakers, from Rolly Gassmann to Trimbach to Ostertag to Domaine Faller). He also offers some 30 Alsatian eaux-de-vie from the prestigious house of J. P. Mette, flavored with everything from coffee to asparagus to black truffle to apple.

My only regret is that the low ceilings, lack of ventilation, and size of the wine bar don't allow for a nonsmoking corner, so come forewarned.

BRASSERIE FLO
7, cour des Petites-Ecuries,
Paris 10.
Tel: 01.47.70.13.59.
Métro: Château-d'Eau.
Service noon to 3:30 P.M. and 7 P.M. to 1:30 A.M.
Open daily.
Credit cards: AE, DC, V.
Air-conditioned.
130- and 179-franc lunch menus; 132- and 179-franc dinner menus.
A la carte, 200 to 250 francs.

SPECIALTIES:
Brasserie: plats du jour (changing daily specials); choucroute garnie (sauerkraut, pork, and sausages); foie gras (fatted duck liver); plateau de fruits de mer (platter of fish and shellfish); poissons et viandes grillés (grilled fish and meats).

This authentic 1900s Alsatian brasserie (reopened the first day of the May 1968 riots) remains a favorite, with a faithful and flashy clientele. Flo is frequently too crowded, too noisy, too hectic, and always a lot of fun. Go with a group, and order up platters of *choucroute,* fish, or shellfish. There are always drinkable Alsatian wines available by the pitcher.

JULIEN
16, rue du Faubourg Saint-Denis,
Paris 10.
Tel: 01.47.70.12.06.
Fax: 01.42.47.00.65.
Métro: Strasbourg-Saint-Denis.
Service noon to 3 P.M. and 7 P.M. to 1:30 A.M.
Open daily.
Credit cards: AE, DC, V.
Air-conditioned.
123-franc weekday lunch menu; 169-franc weekend and holiday lunch menu; 128- and 183-franc dinner menus.
A la carte, 250 francs.

SPECIALTIES:
Brasserie: plats du jour (changing daily specials); cassoulet d'oie (casserole of preserved goose and white beans); foie gras (fatted duck liver); poissons du marché (variety of fresh fish); grillades (grilled meats and fish); homard à la nage (poached lobster).

Despite its rather seedy location, Julien remains one of the city's chic and popular nighttime addresses. One look inside this stunning 1890s dining hall and you understand: Who could not love the mahogany bar, the Art Nouveau mirrors and murals, the noisy brasserie charm? Service can be a bit rushed, depending upon the waiter and the time of day. But the menu offers enough variety to please even the most finicky in the crowd. Try the *foie gras,* the *cassoulet d'oie,* and the fabulous *profiteroles au chocolat,* little rounds of *chou* pastry filled with ice cream and served with a pitcher of steaming-hot chocolate sauce.

CHEZ MICHEL
10, rue Belzunce,
Paris 10.
Tel: 01.44.53.06.20.
Fax: 01.44.53.61.31.
Métro: Poissonnière or Gare du Nord.
Service noon to 2 P.M. and 7 P.M. to midnight.
Closed Sunday, Monday, Christmas week, and August.
Credit card: V.
Sidewalk terrace.
180-franc menu.
A la carte, 200 to 250 francs.

In the 1960s, Chez Michel ranked up there with the best of the city's bistros. Those were the days of oversized portions of steak and fries at L'Ami Louis, hefty sauced pike *quenelles* at Benoit, groaning portions of *brandade de morue* at Chez Cartet, and endless platters of *gigot* and green beans at Chez Georges. At Chez Michel, a cozy, old-fashioned Normandy-inspired restaurant decked out like a village bistro, hungry diners tucked into platters of lobster in puff pastry with a fragrant *sauce Nantua,* plump grilled Belon oysters, sweetbreads sweetened with apples, and grilled turbot with a rich *beurre blanc* sauce.

Times pass, trends change, chefs come and go. Since 1996, young Thierry Breton has been setting trends of his own in this small and still-quaint setting not far from the Gare du Nord. Thierry—a Breton—peppers his menu with regional fish and dessert specialties but also makes use of such modern-day favorites as pasta, fresh tuna, couscous, and goat cheese. Breton has served in the best of kitchens, from the Ritz to the Crillon to the Tour d'Argent, and his food reflects it. He coaxes rich, dense flavors out of his ingredients, and even the simplest of dishes—a tomato stuffed with mushrooms—is made that much more elegant by his careful peeling of the ruby red fruit. You feel he actually sits down and eats the food he serves, an observation that can't be made of many chefs.

A series of visits to Chez Michel has turned up some worthy fare, including a refreshing first course of saladlike room-temperature lasagne filled with artichokes and goat cheese and sauced with a rich garlic and basil *sauce pistou,* and a warming starter of moist, meaty shreds of oxtail paired with a tangle of dressed greens and topped with a giant, succulent wild cèpe mushroom. Other modern fare includes deliciously sweet zucchini steamed and stuffed with golden wild *girolle* mushrooms, accompanied by a warm and creamy shellfish sauce and a few mouthfuls of fresh lobster. The fact that he manages all this on a 180-franc menu is all the more astonishing and welcoming. Thierry's traditional Breton roots come forth in a thick and meaty veal chop pan-fried in fresh Brittany butter, served

SPECIALTIES:
Breton: lasagne de chèvre et artichauts Breton relevée au pistou (layered goat cheese and Brittany artichokes with basil sauce); noix de veau au beurre, fricassée de girolles (veal with chanterelle mushrooms); kouighamann du pays servi tiède (buttery caramelized pastry from Brittany, served warm).

with a piping-hot potato *gratin* soothingly enriched with bits of gelatinous calf's foot. His fish selections are close to flawless, including alabaster-white portions of flaky codfish served on a bed of tomatoes and onions embellished with black olive paste, or *tapenade.* His sparkling fresh turbot is better than you'll find at celebrated fish restaurants, at a quarter the price. Only one day's special—pan-fried monkfish tails—arrived disappointingly soggy and overcooked. Dessert lovers will adore his rich *Kouighamann,* a Breton pastry that oozes with fragrant butter, as well as his cupful of thick *fromage blanc* bedecked with cream and topped with raspberries.

Saumon en Rillettes Julien
JULIEN'S SALMON PATE

Julien is one of Paris's prettiest restaurants (see page 92), and this is one of Julien's most pleasant first courses. The recipe combines smoked and fresh salmon, butter, and Cognac, and it's melt-in-your-mouth delicious, especially served on wedges of toasted homemade rye bread, with a glass of Champagne before a festive meal.

- 4 ounces (125 g) skinned fresh salmon fillet
- ½ cup (12.5 cl) dry white wine
- 1 tablespoon olive oil
- 2 tablespoons Cognac
- Salt and freshly ground black pepper, to taste
- 4 ounces (125 g) smoked salmon
- 6 tablespoons (3 ounces; 90 g) unsalted butter
- Thin slices of warm toast

1. Cut the fresh salmon into bite-size pieces. In a small saucepan, combine the salmon and wine, and bring slowly to a boil over medium heat. Remove from the heat and drain the salmon, discarding the wine.

2. In a small saucepan, heat the olive oil and add the salmon. Cook gently over medium heat for about 5 minutes. Do not let it brown. Add the Cognac, salt, and pepper. Remove from the heat and set aside.

3. Cut the smoked salmon into bite-size pieces. In a small saucepan over medium heat, sauté the smoked salmon in half the butter until it is heated through, 3 to 5 minutes. Remove from the heat, cool the salmon and the butter, then blend in a food processor, adding the remaining butter.

4. Working by hand, combine the fresh salmon and smoked salmon mixtures with a fork in a small bowl until well blended. Check for seasoning. Transfer the *rillettes* to a serving dish or bowl, and carefully smooth the top. Cover with plastic wrap. Refrigerate for at least 12 hours before serving.

5. To serve, remove from the refrigerator about 30 minutes beforehand. Serve with thin slices of warm toast.

Yield: 4 to 6 servings

Bastille, Republique

11th arrondissement

ASTIER
44, rue Jean-Pierre Timbaud,
Paris 11.
Tel: 01.43.57.16.35.
Métro: Parmentier or République.
Service noon to 2 P.M. and 8 to 11 P.M.
Closed Saturday, Sunday, August, one week at Christmas, and two weeks in April.
Credit card: V.
115- and 140-franc lunch menus; 140-franc dinner menu.
A la carte, 200 francs.

SPECIALTIES:
Bistro: terrine de foie de volaille (chicken liver terrine); filets de harengs pommes à l'huile (salad of marinated herring and potatoes bathed in oil); lapin à la moutarde (rabbit with mustard sauce).

When I want an honest, authentic, no-frills bistro meal, Astier is a place that quickly comes to mind. On my last visit I wandered in at lunchtime with a friend, without a reservation, and soon was seated at a small, cozy table, tearing into chunks of delicious country bread as a I contemplated the meal to come. As ever, my first choice was their meaty, well-made *lapin à la moutarde,* good chunks of moist rabbit in a thin but delicious cream and mustard sauce, paired with plenty of fresh pasta for soaking up the sauce. A first-course offering of mixed wild mushrooms—including earthy *girolles* and smooth *trompettes de la mort*—was wholesome and copious and a veritable bargain as part of the 115-franc menu. An unusual terrine of leeks and skate (*raie*) was refreshing and well seasoned. Super-fresh salmon was served atop a bed of seldom-seen nettles (*orties*), a wild herb that's brilliant green and iron-rich. Try the fine Macon Clessé from Jean Thévenet.

AU C'AMELOT
50, rue Amelot,
Paris 11.
Métro: Chemin Vert.
Tel: 01.43.55.54.04.
Fax: 01.43.14.77.05.
Service noon to 2:00 P.M. and 7:00 to 11:00 P.M.
Credit card: V.
Closed Sunday, Monday, and August.
140-franc lunch menu; 160-franc dinner menu.
No à la carte.

SPECIALTIES:
Traditional bistro: bouillon de poule à l'oseille et aux croûtons (chicken bouillon with sorrel and croutons); feuilleté aux pêches et lait d'amandes (peaches in puff pastry with almond cream).

The city's latest crop of bargain bistros has taken on a new look, a décor best dubbed "shabby chic." Gone are the nostalgic brass hat racks, the red-checkered tablecloths, the worn patchwork tile floors, the pert waitresses in frilly white aprons. Enter the leftover look, one that's easy to achieve: Simply take an old neighborhood café and do nothing. Keep the wagon-wheel chandeliers, harsh lighting, and mix-and-match china . . . and cross your fingers. The results are not as dull as one might think. The proof is on the plate, and if C'Amelot, near Place de la Bastille, is any example, I'll look the other way and keep the change. The point is, there's nothing that a packed dining room and a cheery waitress can't fix when you're hungry. There are only ten tables, and there's no written menu—just a list of dishes on the chalkboard, with a dozen or so wines to go with them.

The food is top-quality and bargain-priced. Deliciously crunchy bread, slathered with *pâté* and served with a platter of thinly sliced sausages, arrives almost as soon as you enter. The meal might begin with a rich, filling herbal broth embellished with a dollop of cream and end with a lean lemon tart served with four different flavors of *confiture.* In between, there may be a thick slice of codfish cooked on the bone and served on a bed of well-seasoned cabbage, bacon, and croutons, or a hearty portion of *pintade* (guinea hen) paired with whole roasted potatoes. The cheese (from the best, Alléosse) could be a wedge of perfectly aged Camembert. All straightforward, nothing fancy, and no surprises.

CARTET
62, rue de Malte,
Paris 11.
Tel: 01.48.05.17.65.
Métro: République or Parmentier.
Service noon to 2:00 P.M. and 7:30 to 9:30 P.M.
Closed Saturday, Sunday, and August.
No credit cards.
A la carte, 250 to 300 francs.

SPECIALTIES:
Lyonnaise bistro: choix de charcuteries maison (choice of homemade charcuterie, including parsleyed ham, headcheese, and chicken liver terrine), soufflé de tourteaux (crabmeat soufflé), boeuf à la ficelle (boiled beef and vegetables); saucisson chaud de Lyon (warm pork sausage from Lyons); tarte au citron (lemon tart).

The Cartet slogan might well be *Vive la France,* for almost nothing has changed here since 1932, when Marie-Antoinette Cartet, a farmer's daughter from the Lyonnaise village of Bourg-en-Bresse, opened her tiny eight-table restaurant off the Place de la République. Then, copiousness and bossiness was in fashion, and diners came to be told what they would eat and how much. In the early 1980s Madame Cartet sold her restaurant to Marie-Thérèse Nouaille and her husband, Raymond, who is the chef. The Nouailles have altered little, save for a needed touch-up of the décor. As always, the food remains honest and wholesome—poached Lyonnaise pork sausage or roast leg of lamb with Provençal herbs—and is served without pretension by Madame Nouaille. Why not begin with a quartet of fragrant, impeccably seasoned meat terrines, move on to thick slices of *boeuf à la ficelle* (fillet of beef that's simmered in richly flavored stock, resulting in meat that's perfectly rare and rosy, without a trace of fat), and finish with a nonstop tasting of the house desserts, many of them simple but sublime. Try the buttercup-yellow *crème caramel* (made with eggs the owners bring from their country home in the Loire), the delicate cream puffs dotted with caramel and filled with rum-flavored pastry cream, and the homey-perfect lemon tart, rich with lemon, eggs, cream, and sugar. A pleasant wine to accompany the meal here is the Côtes-du-Rhône from Château St-Estève.

Salade au Lard Cartet
CARTET'S SALAD OF BACON, GREENS, SHALLOTS, AND PARSLEY

*This is the quintessential Parisian bistro salad: bitter winter greens tossed with plenty of hot bacon in a vinegary dressing. This is the version served in copious, all-you-can-eat portions at the tiny historic bistro Cartet (**see facing page**), not far from the Place de la République. In this recipe, the bowl is warmed, along with the shallots and vinegar, a process that not only brings everything to the same temperature but also slightly cooks the shallots, making them more digestible. The parsley and chives add a touch of springtime. Chef Raymond Nouaille serves this with an all-purpose red wine, such as a Beaujolais or a Côtes-du-Rhône.*

2 large shallots, peeled and minced
2 tablespoons best-quality red wine vinegar
2 tablespoons peanut oil
2 ounces (60 g) slab bacon, rind removed, cut into matchstick-size pieces
4 cups (1 liter) dandelion greens, curly endive, or other firm greens, rinsed, dried, and torn into bite-size pieces
Small handful of fresh flat-leaf parsley leaves
Small bunch of fresh chives, minced

1. Preheat the oven to 350°F (175°C).

2. Combine the shallots and vinegar in a large, shallow, ovenproof bowl. Place in the center of the oven and cook just until the mixture is warmed through, about 5 minutes. Remove from the oven, cover with a large plate or lid, and set aside to keep warm.

3. Meanwhile, in a medium-size nonstick skillet, heat the oil over medium-high heat. Add the bacon and cook, stirring frequently, until it is browned and just slightly crisp, 4 to 5 minutes.

4. Place the greens in the warmed bowl with the shallots and vinegar. Pour the bacon and fat over the greens, add the parsley and chives, and toss until thoroughly and evenly coated. Serve immediately.

Yield: 4 servings

DAME JEANNE
60, rue de Charonne,
Paris 11.
Tel: 01.47.00.37.40.
Fax: 01.47.00.37.45.
Métro: Ledru-Rollin.
Service noon to 2:15 P.M. and 7:45 to 11 P.M.
Closed Saturday lunch and Sunday.
Credit card: V.
Sidewalk terrace.
110-, 128-, and 168-franc menus.

Paris diners owe a debt of gratitude to chef Jean-Pierre Vigato. Not only has he wooed us for years with his steady, personalized form of modern cooking at his Michelin two-star restaurant Apicius, but he has influenced a good number of fine young chefs. The newest is Francis Leveque, who plays to a packed dining room at the small bistro-style restaurant Dame Jeanne, not far from the Bastille. Here, in a colorful southern-inspired décor of bold ochers and sunburst reds, scarlet linen napkins, and pristine white china, he offers a model form of updated bistro fare at rock-bottom prices.

There's a deluge of "bargain" restaurants in Paris today. The trick is to find the ones you'll want to

SPECIALTIES: Modern bistro: croustillant de pied de porc, chèvre rôti (crusty pig's trotters with roasted goat cheese); persillade de jarret de veau et foie gras et son mesclun (veal knuckle with foie gras and lamb's lettuce salad); poitrine de veau farcie (stuffed veal breast).

return to. Dame Jeanne's current menu offers some soothing cold-weather favorites, such as falling-off-the-bone braised lamb shanks, known as *souris d'agneau* or *haut de gigot.* Or try the unusual *poitrine de veau,* veal breast stuffed with herbs, then rolled and roasted to perfection. Served in thick slices and bathed in an even-tempered sauce, the steaming veal is surrounded by a pool of mashed potatoes.

For starters, there's a pretty and delicious terrine of tender beef cheeks (they sound better in French, as *joues de boeuf*) and verdant leeks. The terrine is cut in a thick slice, drizzled with a properly vinegary dressing, and served with a small, refreshing mesclun salad. Leveque's starter risotto, flavored with assorted wild mushrooms, is distinctly French and thoroughly delicious. Rather than the creamy, unified *al dente* mass of the Italian version, this risotto is thin, flavored with plenty of cooking juices, and no less appealing.

Just a slight downside, alas: Service in the two small dining rooms is typical of the laid-back Bastille neighborhood. No one here ever seems to be in a hurry. Even wine doesn't come until your first course is on the table. And since Leveque is alone in the kitchen, the wait can seem interminable.

When the wine does arrive, it can be delicious. By all means sample the bargain-priced 120-franc bottle of 1995 Beaujolais Juliénas Côtes du Bessay, from the winemaker Paul Spay, Domaine de la Cave Lamartine. To my palate, it is an ideal rendering of a fine Beaujolais: not overtly fruity, but fun and vigorous, and just serious enough to inhibit you from dancing out the door.

MANSOURIA
11, rue Faidherbe,
Paris 11.
Tel: 01.43.71.00.16.
Fax: 01.40.24.21.97.
Métro: Faidherbe-Chaligny.
Service noon to 2 P.M. and 7:30 to 11:15 P.M.
Closed Monday lunch.
Credit card: V.
99-franc lunch menu; 182-franc dinner menu.
A la carte, 250 to 300 francs.

Fatima Hall is a lively figure, an outgoing hostess who has brought the best of Morocco to Paris. This pleasant restaurant in the Bastille area is not small, but dining here is like eating in someone's home. The food has its own fine personality, with such appealing starters as delightfully smoky grilled red peppers or a chunky purée of eggplant, onions, and tomatoes. The best of the main courses include a fabulous chicken couscous in which moist bits of chicken are hidden beneath a fragrant, steaming mound of couscous. The accompanying broth is as gentle as the dish—slightly sweet, slightly salty.

SPECIALTIES:
Moroccan: couscous aux cinq viandes (couscous with beef, lamb, chicken, sausages, and vegetables); couscous au poulet (fine couscous with chicken, almonds, and broth); tajine d'agneau aux raz al hanout (stew of lamb shanks with sweet sauce of raisins and almonds).

If you have a big appetite, order the meaty *couscous aux cinq viandes,* a traditional version laden with beef, chicken, lamb, and sausages, its broth filled with chickpeas, carrots, and zucchini. *Tagine*-lovers should try the braised lamb shank bathed in a thick, rather sweet, fragrant sauce.

The service at Mansouria is ultra-casual but sincere and friendly.

AUBERGE PYRENEES-CEVENNES
106, rue de la Folie-Méricourt,
Paris 11.
Tel: 01.43.57.33.78.
Métro: République.
Service noon to 2:30 P.M. and 7 to 11 P.M.
Closed Saturday lunch and Sunday.
Air-conditioned.
Credit card: V.
148-franc menu.
A la carte, 160 to 210 francs.

SPECIALTIES:
Southwestern and Lyonnaise: salade lyonnais (curly endive salad with chunks of bacon); cochonnailles de l'Auberge (platter of sausages and cured meats); pipérade (scrambled eggs with tomatoes, peppers, ham, and chorizo sausage); caviar du Puy (green lentils in vinaigrette); cassoulet (casserole of beans and preserved duck); tarte Tatin (upside-down apple tart); fromage blanc à la crème (soft white cheese with cream).

Françoise Petit promised herself four things: She would never marry a chef. She would never own a restaurant. She would never live in Paris. And she would never have a daughter who was a Virgo. Well, Françoise Petit Constantin has all four, and she's as giddy as a schoolgirl. At the age of seventeen the bubbly, animated blonde began working as a waitress at the quintessential Lyons bistro Café des Fédérations. During her thirteen years there, she and her *patron,* Raymond Fulchiron, became minor celebrities in the food world, as gastronomes came from far and near to hear their banter and chow down on *saucissons chauds, andouillettes, blanquette de veau,* and platters of weeping Saint-Marcellin cheese, all washed down with tumblers filled with sturdy Morgon.

In 1994 Françoise left Lyons for Paris and promptly broke her other three promises. Since April 1998, she and chef-husband Daniel Constantin have been happily installed at the Auberge Pyrénées-Cévennes, the classic Parisian bistro, also known as Chez Philippe, that was run by Philippe Serbource until his death in 1997. The bistro, with hams and sausages hanging from the rafters, colorful old tile floors, and rustic stone walls, remains happily unchanged. And while the Constantins have maintained many of the old standbys—platters of sausages and cured meats and *cassoulet*—they have also added such Lyonnaise classics as a green salad loaded with top-quality cured bacon; the rich and densely flavored *sabodet* pork sausage; and those Saint-Marcellin cow's milk cheeses from Mère Richard in Lyons.

Chef Constantin (who has been at the stove since the age of fourteen) is a classic French cook, one of the dying breed that have French cooking in their very veins, and it shows in everything that comes from his spotless kitchen. The food has soul, character, and an honesty one rarely sees today in simple bistro fare. The chef's battery of sturdy copper pots—which he bought from the Eiffel Tower after working there for a decade—attest to his determination and respect for French cuisine. "You can't make a béarnaise in stainless steel," he likes to say. Daily specials here might include thick slices of exquisitely flavorful saddle of lamb seared on an ancient gas grill, a rich and creamy potato *gratin,* and an impeccably prepared plateful of sautéed *girolles* mushrooms. The chef's motto is "It is simple to do, but difficult to succeed."

The wines, all from small producers, have been selected by Françoise. Do try the silky Chiroubles cru Beaujolais Domaine du Clocher from winemaker Jean-Noël Melinand, or the fresh and fruity Coteaux de Lyonnais, available by the glass or the traditional *"pot" lyonnais.*

A SOUSCEYRAC
35, rue Faidherbe,
Paris 11.
Tel: 01.43.71.65.30.
Fax: 01.40.09.79.75.
Métro: Faidherbe-Chaligny or Charonne.
Service noon to 2 P.M. and 7:30 to 10:15 P.M.
Closed Saturday lunch, Sunday, and August.
Credit cards: DC, V.
Private dining room for 12 to 20.
Air-conditioned.
185-franc menu.
A la carte, 220 to 280 francs.

SPECIALTIES:
Bistro: foie gras frais (fresh foie gras); cassoulet (casserole of white beans with various combinations of sausages, duck, pork, lamb, mutton, and goose); lièvre à la royale (wild hare stew).

If one were building a stage set for a Parisian neighborhood bistro, A Sousceyrac would make a terrific model. For more than forty-five years, Luc Asfaux has held court in the warren of rooms that make up his restaurant not far from the Bastille. He is now seconded by his son, Patrick, and together they continue a long tradition of serving their rich, nourishing portions of *lièvre à la royale* each Friday and Saturday from October to January. Here you will be offered the most classic version, a two-days-of-cooking affair, which arrives in a pool of chocolate colored sauce, rich with *foie gras,* served with tiny toast points dipped in minced parsley and a pair of boiled potatoes. Sousceyrac's fare is earthy and prepared with love. You finally realize that some flavors, such as this wild hare stew, are the result of a chef's constant tinkering and fiddling.

Don't leave without sampling their rustic terrine of wild duck and *foie gras*, where a thick slice of *foie gras* becomes "sandwich filling" for two layers of flawlessly seasoned terrine. A bitter green salad is a perfect foil for the rich, meaty fare. Grouse-lovers will enjoy the Asfaux's *mousse* of grouse and *foie gras,* an almost frothy whipped mixture served in small ramekins with grilled bread. Outside of game season, look for their *cassoulet,* veal kidneys, pigeon,

Bresse chicken, quail, and sweetbreads, all earthy bistro classics. The wine list offers numerous treasures, from a simple Beaujolais Moulin à Vent to a well-stocked *cave* of Bordeaux and Burgundies. The bread comes from the best, Lionel Poilâne and Michel Moisan.

SALADE VERTE AUX ECHALOTES ET AUX CIBOULETTES L'OULETTE

L'OULETTE'S FIELD SALAD WITH SHALLOTS AND CHIVES

Give me salad, salad, and more salad! This simple variation on a very familiar theme comes from Marcel Baudis, chef at L'Oulette, the restaurant he runs with his wife, Marie-Noëlle (see page 102). One evening I asked if Chef Baudis would prepare us a simple green salad, and this is what he came up with. The combination of shallots and chives is used often in Baudis' native town of Montauban, in France's southwest. Marinating the shallots in oil softens their often harsh flavor.

Dressing:

1 shallot, minced
¼ cup (6 cl) extra-virgin olive oil
2 teaspoons best-quality red wine vinegar
2 teaspoons sherry wine vinegar
Sea salt to taste

Salad:

6 cups (1.5 l) loosely packed bite-size pieces of mixed greens, rinsed and dried (such as a mixture of curly endive, radicchio, watercress, lamb's lettuce, dandelion greens, and arugula)
1 shallot, minced
⅓ cup chopped fresh chives
Sea salt and freshly ground black pepper, to taste

1. Prepare the dressing: In a small bowl, combine the shallot and oil, and stir to blend. Set aside at room temperature for at least 1 hour and up to 24 hours.

2. In another small bowl combine the vinegars and salt, and stir to blend. Add the shallot and oil mixture, and stir to blend. Taste for seasoning.

3. In a large, shallow salad bowl, combine the salad greens, shallot, and chives, and toss with your hands. Pour the vinaigrette over the salad and toss gently and thoroughly until the greens are evenly coated. Season to taste and serve immediately.

Yield: 4 to 6 servings

LA ZYGOTISSOIRE
101, rue de Charonne,
Paris 11.
Tel: 01.40.09.93.05.
Fax: 01.44.73.46.63.
Métro: Charonne.
Service noon to 2:30 P.M. and 7 to 11:30 P.M.
Closed Saturday lunch and Sunday.
Credit card: V.
80-franc menu.
A la carte, 130 to 160 francs.

SPECIALTIES: Rotisserie-bistro: brochettes de légumes aux anchoïade (grilled brochette of vegetables with anchovy sauce); lapereau farci rôti à la broche (stuffed roasted rabbit on the rotisserie); faux filet échalotes confites (rotisserie-grilled beef with shallot confit).

La Zygotissoire, a small rotisserie restaurant at the edge of the trendy Bastille neighborhood, is perhaps the city's best buy today. Where else can you have a delicious, can't-finish-it-all, three-course meal, with coffee, for 80 francs? And the food is not just okay, it is memorable and inventive.

On the 80-franc menu, one might begin with a chicken wing salad, made up of a quartet of moist, beautifully roasted chicken wings set on a bed of greens; move on to a *faux filet* cooked on the rotisserie and sauced with shallots; and finish with a dessert of homemade ice cream and sorbet. A la carte, the *brochettes de légumes aux anchoïade* include zucchini, tomatoes, and eggplant, sauced with a very delicately flavored anchovy sauce, and is served with a small green salad alongside. Good main courses include a rotisserie-grilled fillet of sea bass, or *bar,* on a bed of Swiss chard greens, served with a round *gratin* of the celery-like whites of chard. The wine list offers some offbeat surprises, such as the rarely seen Ladoix, a worthy red from the northernmost village of the Côte de Beaune, and almost always a bargain.

GARE DE LYON, BASTILLE, NATION, PLACE D'ITALIE

12th and 13th arrondissements

L'OULETTE
15, place Lechambeaudie,
Paris 12.
Tel: 01.40.02.02.12.
Fax: 01.40.02.02.13.
Métro: Dugommier or Cours Saint-Emilion.
Service noon to 2:15 P.M. and 8 to 10:15 P.M.
Closed Saturday lunch and Sunday.
Credit cards: AE, DC, V.
Terrace.
165-franc menu; 250-franc menu, including wine
A la carte, 225 to 350 francs.

As soon as I first sampled Marcel Baudis' authentic, honest, and full-flavored food in 1987, I realized that he was a chef I would want to know for a long, long time. Beginning in a handkerchief-size dining room in the Marais and moving to the "new world" of the Bercy in 1991, he has never faltered or left us with anything but food filled with character and modern sensibility. His road has not been easy, for the Bercy neighborhood has taken a long time to develop, but today his patience and talents are being rewarded by a mostly full dining room at lunch and dinner. Baudis, a native of Montauban in the southwest, draws deeply on his culinary roots with a menu that never neglects tiny *calamars* (squid), generous mounds of fresh white beans (*haricots blancs frais*), duck and *foie gras,* local goat cheese, and all the wonderful little-

SPECIALTIES: Contemporary southwestern: escabèche de calamars aux pommes de terre tièdes (baby squid cooked with onions, peppers, with a warm potato salad); queue de boeuf braisée au foie gras, et tomate farcie (braised oxtail with foie gras and stuffed tomato); pain d'épice perdu "à la coque," crème canelle (French toast with cinnamon ice cream).

known wines of that region. Do go, and do order his now-classic *escabèche de calamars,* the tiniest, tenderest squid cut into fine threads, sizzled in olive oil, deglazed with white wine, then infused with a whole pantry of spices, including both anise and curry. Equally memorable is his *millefeuille de sardines,* a warm and welcoming layered affair made up of raw marinated sardine fillets, Moroccan phyllo-like brick pastry, tomatoes, and Parmesan. Good main courses include a variation on a Morrocan tagine of lamb with olives and lemon *confit*; and a lovely *aïoli,* with poached cod and an array of steamed vegetables ready for seasoning with the golden, garlic-rich mayonnaise.

On my last visit, I added three new wines to my love-list: a dry and refreshing *vin de pays* of Saint-Sardos; a floral, dry Jurançon sec Domaine Bellegarde; and a sweet Sainte-Croix du Mont Château du Pavillion, a neighbor of Sauternes and bargain-priced.

Dessert-lovers should not miss the chef's spicy fingers of French toast, served with a cooling cinnamon ice cream. In good weather, reserve a table on the terrace and listen as the chimes of Notre Dame de la Nativité de Bercy serenade your meal. And if you can't figure out what to order, the dining room's able director, Alain Fontaine, will be sure to steer you in the right direction.

LE PETIT MARGUERY
9, boulevard du Port-Royal, Paris 13.
Tel: 01.43.31.58.59.
Métro: Les Gobelins.
Service noon to 2:15 P.M. and 7:30 to 10:15 P.M.
Closed Sunday, Monday, August, and Christmas week.
Credit cards: AE, DC, V.
Private dining room for 15 to 20.
165-franc lunch menu; 215-franc lunch and dinner menu.
A la carte, 280 to 320 francs.

The cuisine of the Cousin brothers—Alain in the dining room and Michel and Jacques in the kitchen—is directly inspired by their grandmother's kitchen near Poitiers, where, as children, mushroom hunting and cooking were favorite pastimes. They seem to have learned their lessons well, for Le Petit Marguery, a brasserie-like 1930s bistro, remains one of the city's citadels of game cuisine. Game begins appearing on the menu in late September, when the first-of-the-season wild duck makes its appearance on a bed of cabbage laced with tiny cubes of *foie gras.* A cold-weather dish if there ever was one, the wild duck is presented in thin slices that combine well with the crunchy texture of the cabbage and the rich taste of the *foie gras.*

Through much of the season the Cousin brothers try to have available their famous mixture of

SPECIALTIES:
Seasonal: champignons de cueillette (wild mushrooms, in season); gibier (game, in season); coquilles Saint-Jacques (fresh scallops, October to May); lièvre à la royale (wild hare stew; winter months only).

wild *cèpes* and *lactaire* mushrooms, sautéed with a generous touch of garlic. Their extravagant collection of game pâtés includes pairings of wild hare and *foie gras* and pheasant and *foie gras*, a purée of partridge seasoned with juniper berries, and a lush wild boar terrine. Generally, one also finds roast wild partridge, along with the Cousins' variation on *lièvre à la royale,* the famous wild hare stew with *foie gras.*

The Cousin brothers' fare is both traditional and inventive, and though the menu changes wisely with the seasons, one can always be assured of fresh *coquilles Saint-Jacques* from October to May; often a green salad that's showered with thin slices of pork sausage conserved in walnut oil; *pintadeau fermier* smothered with wild *cèpe* mushrooms; and the marvelous *petit salé de canard,* duck that is cured in salt brine for a full week, then poached and served with butter-rich cabbage.

Go to Le Petit Marguery when you are in a mood for a boisterous, gay, thoroughly carefree evening. Jovial and mustachioed young Alain handles the front of the house, bustling about, adding a sense of theater and drama and, yes, a pleasant coziness. This is a model turn-of-the-century family-run bistro, one of the last of a small 1920s "chain" of eighteen Petit Marguery's that were all over Paris. The décor here has changed little over the years, with old-fashioned chandeliers, beautiful tile floors, mirrored walls, and a barely legible handwritten menu. The brilliant blue and rose walls are a bit offbeat, but they do add a festive air.

Readying the next mouthful.

LAPIN A LA MOUTARDE
RABBIT WITH MUSTARD

Rabbit with mustard sauce is a classic bistro dish and a year-round favorite. Traditionally lapin à la moutarde *is served with rice, but I love it with fresh homemade pasta, which absorbs the wonderfully delicious sauce. Do use top-quality French whole-grain mustard; fresh, not frozen, rabbit; and a solid, full-bodied white wine. An Alsatian Riesling is an excellent wine for this dish, but I've also prepared it with Gewürztraminer, as well as with a white Hermitage. You can also experiment by adding various herbs to the sauce just before serving: Fresh rosemary, summer savory, or thyme would be lovely. If you can't find fresh rabbit, chicken makes an excellent substitute.*

⅓ cup (8 cl) peanut oil
1 tablespoon (½ oz; 15 g) unsalted butter
1 fresh rabbit (or chicken), 2½ to 3 pounds (1.25 to 1.5 kg), cut into serving pieces
½ cup (12.5 cl) whole-grain mustard
3 cups (75 cl) dry white wine
1 cup (25 cl) *crème fraîche* (see recipe, page 290) or sour cream
Salt to taste
Small handful of minced fresh parsley

1. Preheat the oven to 350°F (175°C).

2. In a Dutch oven or large ovenproof skillet, heat the oil and butter over medium-high heat. When hot, quickly brown the rabbit. Do not crowd the pan, and turn the pieces, making sure that each is thoroughly browned. Discard the excess oil.

3. Brush the rabbit pieces evenly with mustard, reserving 3 tablespoons for the sauce. Place the rabbit in the oven, covered, and bake for 20 minutes. Pour the wine over the rabbit, making sure all pieces are moistened, and continue cooking, covered, another 25 minutes.

4. Remove from the oven, and reserving the cooking liquid, place the rabbit pieces on an ovenproof dish. Lower the oven heat to 200°F (90°C). Cover the rabbit with foil and keep warm in the very low oven.

5. Prepare the sauce: Over high heat reduce the reserved cooking liquid by half. This should take 8 to 10 minutes. Whisk in the *crème fraîche* or sour cream, the reserved 3 tablespoons mustard, and salt. Reduce the heat and continue cooking for 3 to 4 minutes.

6. To serve, arrange the rabbit pieces on a platter, and cover with the sauce. (Or fill a platter with fresh cooked pasta, toss with the sauce, and arrange the rabbit pieces on top of the pasta.) Sprinkle with the minced parsley.

Yield: 4 to 6 servings

Pot-au-Feu

BEEF SIMMERED WITH VEGETABLES

"Eating pot-au-feu *is an act that gives significance to life," wrote one French critic. A bit precious, to be sure, but few peasant dishes are as healthfully nourishing, fragrant, or satisfying as a superb* pot-au-feu. *In its most classic form, the dish begins with a shallow, steaming bowl of* bouillon, *ladled from the pot in which the meat, marrow, and vegetables have been slowly simmering. To the bowl one might add garlic-touched croutons, freshly grated Parmesan or Gruyère cheese, a few grains of coarsely ground black pepper. The second course is made up of the meat, vegetables, and accompaniments, a procession of condiments that might include fiery horseradish, three or four varieties of mustard, coarse salt, puckery* cornichons, *and tiny white pickled onions.*

2 pounds (1 kg) short ribs of beef
2 pounds (1 kg) boned beef shank
2 pounds (1 kg) oxtail, cut into 2-inch (5-cm) lengths
Coarse (kosher) salt and freshly ground black pepper, to taste
6 small onions, each peeled and studded with a clove
4 leeks, cleaned of sand
1 fennel bulb, trimmed, washed, and quartered
6 whole carrots, peeled
4 cloves garlic, unpeeled
Bouquet garni: 2 bay leaves, 2 sprigs fresh parsley, and 1 teaspoon dried thyme, tied in a piece of cheesecloth
1 whole apple, washed
Approximately 1½ pounds (750 g) beef marrow bones, cut into 2-inch (5-cm) lengths, and each length wrapped in green portion of leek (to seal in the marrow)

1. Using household string, tie in two separate bundles the ribs of beef and the boned shank, so they retain their shape and fit compactly into a large stockpot. Place the oxtail on top of the other meat. Cover the meat completely with cold water and cook, uncovered, over medium-high heat. The water should barely simmer, never boil.

2. After about 20 minutes, carefully skim all traces of foam (which is impurities) and grease from the surface of the stock. Careful skimming is necessary to producing a fine *pot-au-feu.*

3. Move the pot halfway off the heat so that the foam rises on one side of the stock only, making it easier to skim. Return the pot to the heat and continue cooking for another 20 minutes.

4. Season the liquid lightly with coarse salt (about 1 tablespoon should finely season this dish) and pepper. Add the vegetables, using only the white portions of the leeks; the garlic; the bouquet garni; and the apple, which will help absorb some of the fat. Skim again and cook another 30 minutes, skimming frequently. Test the vegetables to see if they are cooked; if not, cook another 10 minutes.

5. Once the vegetables have cooked, transfer them to a heatproof dish and moisten with the broth. Cover with aluminum foil and keep warm in a low oven.

6. Continue cooking the meat, skimming if necessary, for 1 hour more. About 15 minutes before serving, add the marrow bones, submerging them in the broth.

7. To serve the first course, place a slice of toast rubbed with garlic in a warmed soup bowl, cover with broth, and sprinkle with freshly grated Parmesan cheese.

Garnishes and condiments:
Toast rubbed with garlic
Freshly grated Parmesan cheese
Horseradish
Several mustards
Cornichons

8. To serve the second course, remove the twine from the meat and cut it into chunks. Place it on a warmed platter, surrounded by the marrow bones and the vegetables, discarding the bouquet garni and the apple. Serve with the horseradish, a variety of mustards, cornichons, coarse salt, and pepper. The dish can easily be reheated.

Yield: 4 to 6 servings

LE SQUARE TROUSSEAU
1, rue Antoine-Vollon, Paris 12.
Tel: 01.43.43.06.00.
Fax: 01.43.43.00.66.
Métro: Ledru-Rollin.
Service noon to 2:30 P.M. and 7:30 to 11:30 P.M.; Sunday brunch offered.
Open daily.
Credit card: AE, V.
Sidewalk terrace.
100- and 135-franc lunch menus.
A la carte, 200 to 230 francs.

SPECIALTIES:
Bistro: terrine de campagne maison (homemade pork terrine); bavette d'aloyau poêlée sauce choron, gratin dauphinois (pan-fried flank steak with tomato béarnaise and potato gratin); travers de porc au miel et soja, courgettes sautées au thym (spare ribs with a honey-soy sauce, with zucchini sautéed with thyme); tarte feuilletée aux deux pommes, crème anglaise (puff pastry apple tart with crème anglaise).

This archetypal 1900s bistro overlooks one of the city's most charming squares, a pocket park filled with greenery and surrounded by stone Hausmann-style apartment buildings. The lace curtains, moleskin banquettes, high ceilings, and good-times ambience put us all in a good mood, ready to tuck into portions of sturdy bistro fare, from steaks to spare ribs to thick slices of a country terrine. Le Square Trousseau is in the center of the hip Bastille neighborhood, so you are sure to feel you are in the right place at the right time. Wash everything down with Philippe and Michelle Laurent's robust, character-filled Rhône red, Domaine Gramenon. (If you go at lunchtime, visit the lively Place d'Aligre food and flea market nearby.)

POMMES PONT-NEUF

At the end of the 19th century, merchants with deep-fat fryers on rolling carts lined the Pont-Neuf bridge. They cut potatoes into slender sticks, fried them, and bundled them into paper cones. The French food writer Curnonsky exclaimed: "Fried potatoes are one of the most spiritual creations of the Parisian genius." But potatoes were not always so well loved: In 1787 Antoine Parmentier introduced the potato to France, with great hopes that this curious tuber would become so popular they would call it a *parmentier.* To promote the potato, he offered a dinner for one hundred at the Hôtel des Invalides. The menu included potato soup, potato salad, potato fritters, a *brioche* made with potato flour, and to end the meal, potato liqueur.

Soupe de Peches
SUMMER PEACH SOUP

Prepare this delightfully summery dessert when peaches and nectarines are at their height of flavor. It's a simple make-ahead dessert, leaving you free for the rest of the day. The recipe comes from David Van Laer, whose newest restaurant, Maxence, was just about to open as we went to press with this edition. Here is what I had to say about him just before his move:

Would that today's Paris spawned dozens of chefs as talented, sensible, and realistic as David Van Laer. He has been flying solo since 1995, when he opened the thirty-two seat Le Bambouche (French for a spree or a lark). Van Laer, who worked for years with Jean-Pierre Vigato and then later at Le Manufacture outside Paris, has always had a welcome style. His menu remains brief and to the point, his cooking respects the old classics, and yet he is mindful of a modern dining trend that values, above all, lightness and freshness.

Look for Maxence at 9, boulevard du Montparnasse, Paris 14; tel: 01.45.67.11.98; fax: 01.45.67.10.22; Métro: Montparnasse–Bienvenüe. Service will be from noon to 2:30 P.M. and 7:30 to 11 P.M.; closed Saturday, Sunday, and August 15. There will be a 190-franc lunch and dinner menues and 300- and 350-franc tasting menues; AE and V cards accepted.

6 ripe peaches
6 ripe nectarines
1 cup (120 g) confectioners' sugar
2 cups (50 cl) Chardonnay
1 tablespoon orange-flower water, or grated zest of 1 orange
30 fresh mint leaves

Peel and quarter the peaches and nectarines. Sprinkle with sugar (the amount will vary according to taste and the sweetness of the fruit). Add the wine, orange-flower water, and mint leaves. Cover and refrigerate for 2 hours. Serve cold, in individual champagne *coupes.*

Yield: 6 to 8 servings

AU TROU GASCON
40, rue Taine,
Paris 12.
Tel: 01.43.44.34.26.
Fax: 01.43.07.80.55.
Métro: Daumesnil.
Service noon to 2 P.M. and 7:30 to 10 P.M.
Closed Saturday lunch, Sunday, August, and one week at Christmas.
Credit cards: AE, V.
Air-conditioned.
200-franc lunch menu; 320-franc lunch and dinner menus, including wine.
A la carte, 290 to 300 francs.

While many of France's top-ranking chefs continue to bicker about the future of their industry—shall we or shall we not remain traditional French?—Alain Dutournier continues on his own well-chosen way. Along with his wife, Nicole, Dutournier runs two of the city's steadiest establishments, always creating trends rather than slavishly following them. Perhaps it's because more than many other well-known French chefs, Dutournier has true roots in the country, in the southwest of France, that continue to nourish his mind and his soul. He's also a serious eater and a lover of good times, and that passion shows in his food and on his table.

SPECIALTIES:
Updated southwestern: huîtres à la bordelaise (oysters on the half shell, served with warm, spicy sausages); petit pâté chaud de cèpes au jus de persil (warm pastry filled with wild mushrooms, topped with parsley sauce); le vieux jambon de Chalosse "au couteau" (slices of aged ham from the southwest); cassoulet maison (casserole of white beans, homemade sausages, mutton, pork, duck, and tomatoes, September to February); agneau de lait des Pyrénées rôti sur l'os, pour deux (roasted baby lamb from the Pyrénées, for two); tourtière landaise (layers of flaky pastry filled with apples).

That's not to say he's not affected by France's tough economic times. I remember the days when a two-week wait was standard for a table at the cozy Belle Epoque Au Trou Gascon, just off Place Félix Eboué. Now the restaurant may be only one-third full on many nights, despite the well-priced menus. Diners in search of honest value and serious food could do much worse than to dig into Au Trou Gascon's classic *pâté chaude,* a warm and soothing *foie gras* and potato terrine. Or better yet, a platter of sparkling fresh oysters accompanied by grilled homemade sausages. Main-course offerings include an astonishing platter of roasted *brebis* (tender lamb from the southwest), with a rich, robust flavor not soon to be forgotten. As ever, the intensely flavored sheep's-milk cheese served with a tiny salad forms a perfect close. Accompanying the well-priced menu are the Tursan blanc and the dark, vigorous Madiran, the red from Domaine Capmartin, just part of the always exceptional wine list.

LES ZYGOMATES
7, rue de Capri,
Paris 12.
Tel: 01.40.19.93.04.
Fax: 01.44.73.46.63.
Métro: Daumesnil or Michel-Bizot.
Service noon to 2 P.M. and 7:15 to 10:45 P.M.
Closed Saturday lunch, Sunday, August.
Credit card: V.
80-franc lunch menu; 130-franc lunch and dinner menu.
A la carte, 160 to 210 francs.

SPECIALTIES:
Contemporary bistro: compote de lapereau à l'estragon (compote of rabbit with tarragon); rognons à l'aigre doux (kidneys in sweet and sour sauce); volaille à la crème de ciboulette (chicken with cream and chives); fondant au chocolat (chocolate mousse cake).

This truly charming neighborhood restaurant (fashioned out of a 1930s *charcuterie*), with its expansive mirrors, marble counters, and walls of etched glass, is enough to satisfy anyone's nostalgic longings. The cuisine is simple, a perfect balance of traditional and contemporary bistro fare. Les Zygomate's bargain-priced menus offer plenty of choice, from a fine goat cheese *cannelloni* to a *pot-au-feu* of *foie gras* seasoned with *sel de Guérande,* and on to duck with lemon and a *confit* of carrots. "*Les zygomatiques,*" by the way, is French for the facial muscles used to smile.

An enclosed terrace allows plenty of natural lighting.

DENFERT-ROCHEREAU, PORTE D'ORLÉANS, MONTPARNASSE

14th arrondissement

L'ASSIETTE
181, rue du Château,
Paris 14.
Tel: 01.43.22.64.86.
Métro: Pernéty or Mouton-Duvernet.
Service noon to 2:30 P.M. and 8 to 10:30 P.M.
Closed Monday, Tuesday, August, and Christmas week.
Credit cards: AE, V.
200-franc lunch menu.
A la carte, 300 to 400 francs.

SPECIALTIES: *Seasonal, southwestern: gibier, en saison (game, in season); champignons sauvages, en saison (wild mushrooms, in season); saumon rôti au sel de Guérande (roast salmon seasoned with Brittany sea salt); petit salé de canard (poached salt-cured duck with buttery cabbage).*

Lucette Rousseau, chef and owner of L'Assiette, is my kind of chef. She knows what she's after, has a keen eye for quality and freshness, and has managed to attract a loyal and consistent following. L'Assiette is loud, elbow-to-elbow, and casual to excess. Yet if it's top-quality ingredients prepared with remarkable simplicity and great attention to detail you're after, this bistro should fill the bill—assuming you are willing to pay the price.

Today's best chefs let great ingredients shine, and that's where Lucette—better known as Lulu—comes into the picture. L'Assiette's décor is no-frills (bare wooden tables and bare wooden chairs), and

Lucette Rousseau, organized and passionate.

many diners are affronted by the incongruity of minimal comfort with maximal prices. Well, my response to that is, just go dine elsewhere. For nowhere in Paris are you likely to find more fragrant, more succulent, or fresher wild morel mushrooms, thicker fillets of perfectly cooked salmon from the Loire, or such delicious platters of the tiny, spaghetti-like eels known as *pibales*, tossed with fresh parsley and a joyous hit of garlic. In the spring, you'll also find first-of-the-season green asparagus from the Vaucluse and baby lamb from the Pauillac region, and much of the year, a gargantuan lobster salad, moist, glistening, and garden-fresh. With all that comes good bread from Moulin de la Vierge (page 265). So sample a simple Saumur-Champigny and make a toast to tradition, as well as staying power. One caveat: Service can be amateurish and lackadaisical, not up to the quality of the food.

LA CAGOUILLE
10-12, place Brancusi
(across from 23,
rue de l'Ouest),
Paris 14.
Tel: 01.43.22.09.01.
Fax: 01.45.38.57.29.
Métro: Gaîté.
Service noon to 2 P.M. and 7:30 to 10:30 P.M.
Open daily.
Terrace.
Credit cards: AE, V.
Private dining room for 18.
150- and 250-franc menus.
A la carte, 280 to 340 francs.

SPECIALTIES:
Fish and shellfish: petites lottes frites, sauce anchois (tiny fried monkfish with anchovy sauce); moules de bouchot "brûle-doigts" ("burn your fingers" mussels); coquilles Saint-Jacques poêlées et vinaigrette tiède (pan-seared scallops with warm vinaigrette); pavé de thon rouge et ratatouille (tuna steak with ratatouille, June to September).

When the burly Gérard Allemandou opened his tiny fish bistro on the Rue Daguerre in 1980, it was one of the hottest tickets in town. Much like the famed Minchelli brothers of Le Duc and the brother-sister team of Gilbert and Maguy Le Coze of Le Bernardin, Allemandou wowed us with fish and shellfish so sparkling fresh we believed we were at ocean's edge, not steps from a Left Bank métro. What's more, his dogmatic "do the least possible" style of cuisine pulled us out of the *hollandaise/meunière/friture* syndrome. Soon La Cagouille, which resembled a seedy corner café, had a Michelin star and diners were fighting for each table.

La Cagouille moved on to modern quarters in 1988 and for several years held its own, still astonishing us with modesty and simplicity as we burned our fingers on the chef's *moules brûle-doigts* (mussels grilled directly on the stovetop). We devoured fried whole anchovies, raved over the grilled mackerel with mustard sauce and the pan-seared scallops bathed in a warm vinaigrette. Then the decline began: Service became nonexistent, the owner was often absent, prices soared, and the restaurant's freshness seemed to have withered. Even Michelin had had enough and yanked the star.

Several recent visits suggest that Allemandou and his staff are back in form, serving delicately smoked eel from France's southwest, giant fresh *gambas* from Africa, and tiny Breton turbot grilled with aplomb. Allemandou's appetite for wine is as serious as his passion for food, and so you're likely to find selections such as the seldom-seen white Chignin Bergeron from Raymond Quenard in the Savoie, well priced at 100 francs. Today's meal prices also are easier to digest: The 250-franc menu includes half a bottle of wine. The bistro's sterile interior remains as simple and unadorned (and frankly unappealing) as ever. Keep your mind on the food and you shouldn't be disappointed.

Salade de Lardons de Thon La Cagouille
LA CAGOUILLE'S SALAD OF TUNA AND CURLY ENDIVE

This wonderfully modern bistro dish is an updated version of the classic frisée aux lardons, *or curly endive salad with bacon. I sampled it during one of my frequent visits to the popular fish bistro La Cagouille (see page 111), where the menu seems to change moment by moment, depending upon what bargains chef Gérard Allemandou has found in the wholesale market that morning. It's a fine main-course salad for serving with a chilled red Chinon or Beaujolais and crusty grilled bread.*

1 head curly endive, rinsed and dried
1 large bunch fresh chives
4 small white onions, shallots, or scallions, cut into thin rings
1 thick slice fresh tuna steak (about 1 pound; 500 g, untrimmed)
Salt and freshly ground black pepper, to taste
⅓ cup (8 cl) extra-virgin olive oil
⅓ cup (8 cl) best-quality red wine vinegar

1. Tear the leaves of curly endive into bite-size pieces. Combine the endive, chives, and onions in a large, shallow salad bowl, and toss.

2. Cut the tuna into 1-inch (2.5-cm) cubes.

3. Place the tuna in a nonstick frying pan, and, over medium-high heat, quickly brown the cubes. They will cook in just a minute or two and should remain rather rare on the inside. Season generously with salt and plenty of freshly ground black pepper.

4. Add the oil to the tuna in the pan and heat until it sizzles. Then very slowly add the red wine vinegar, stirring to coat the tuna with the oil and vinegar.

5. Quickly spoon the tuna, oil, and vinegar on top of the greens, toss thoroughly, and serve immediately.

Yield: 4 servings

LA COUPOLE
102, boulevard du Montparnasse,
Paris 14.
Tel: 01.43.20.14.20.
Fax: 01.43.35.46.14.
Métro: Vavin.
Service noon to 1:30 P.M. and 7 P.M. to midnight.
Open daily except Christmas Eve dinner.
Credit cards: AE, DC, V.
Private dining room for 200.
Air-conditioned.
89-franc weekday lunch menu; 123-franc lunch menu; 128-franc dinner menu, after 10 P.M.
A la carte, 250 francs.

SPECIALTIES: Brasserie: plats du jour (changing daily specials); banc d'huîtres (fresh oyster selection); plateau de fruits de mer (platter of fish and shellfish); poissons et viandes grillés (grilled fish and meats).

Some traditional brasseries will never go out of fashion, and La Coupole, on the Left Bank's boulevard du Montparnasse, is one of them. I love to go on a Sunday afternoon, when entire multi-generation families, single diners, couples, and groups of a dozen or more gather to fill the vast auditorium-like dining hall created in 1927, at the height of Paris's jazz age. Today the ever-popular institution—completely renovated in 1989—is pleasantly beginning to show signs of wear. La Coupole is part of the Flo chain of brasseries (Flo, Julien, Bofinger, etc.), and the 600-seat restaurant remains the group's crown jewel. While such volume feeding generally gives short shrift to anything one might classify as gastronomy, La Coupole still does an above-average job with some dishes. Their *choucroute,* for instance, arrives sizzling hot, with copious rations of sausages and nicely acidic (but sometimes watery) sauerkraut. And of course one never goes wrong with half a dozen oysters, grilled fish, and a touch of chilled Alsatian white wine.

LE DOME
108, boulevard du Montparnasse,
Paris 14.
Tel: 01.43.35.25.81.
Fax: 01.42.79.01.19.
Métro: Vavin.
Service noon to 2:15 P.M. and 7:30 to 11:30 P.M.
Open daily.
Credit cards: AE, DC, V.
Enclosed terrace.
Private dining room for 10.
Air-conditioned.
A la carte, 400 to 450 francs.

If you can secure the freshest of fresh ingredients, your work as cook is half done. And when the ingredients are fish and shellfish, one might even say, 75 percent done. Then the cook's job becomes one of a minimalist: The less done the better. At historic, ever-popular Le Dôme, they understand fish and shellfish and they understand freshness. The price of your meal may not always be to your liking, you may find that some dishes lack a touch of sophistication, and the service may lag at times. But you will not find fault with the freshness.

Order a plate full of *bouquets bretons,* the tiny salmon-pink shrimp that taste almost nutty and of the sea, and you'll see what I mean. These full-flavored, fresh little shrimp have no relationship to 99 percent of the shrimp commonly found in French markets. They arrive still vibrantly alive, rather than cooked days in advance and perhaps frozen. Sample these Brittany *crevettes* with a bit of the Dôme's crusty bread spread with a healthy dose of salty Breton butter, and you're on your way to heaven.

SPECIALTIES:
Fish and shellfish: plateau de fruits de mer (platters of fresh fish and shellfish); soupe de poissons (fish soup); bouillabaisse (Mediterranean fish soup); turbot rôti, sauce hollandaise (roast turbot with hollandaise sauce).

Delicious as well—though designed for those with a touch of patience—is the *friture de céteaux,* tiny sole the size of a child's hand. Gently fried and served whole, the delicate little Atlantic fish are accompanied with deep-fried celery leaves and a fine *sauce tartare.* (No matter that you may have to carefully remove some of the tiny bones. Whenever fish is cooked whole and on the bone, you're always rewarded with greater flavor.)

On a sunny Saturday afternoon, I love nothing better than to secure a table on the lively Dôme terrace and order up a dozen briny oysters to enjoy with a glass of Didier Dagueneau's rich, golden Pouilly Fumé or André Bonhomme's almondlike Macon Viré. Another favorite is their grilled fish of the day: The waiter parades to your table with an entire platter of bright, firm, glossy fish. One day you may choose a bright-eyed *bar*, on another a glistening *Saint-Pierre.* Once cooked, the fish is filleted tableside and served with nothing more than a sprinkling of fragrant extra-virgin olive oil and a few drops of freshly squeezed lemon juice. And Le Dôme's *sole meunière* is perhaps the best in town. Desserts are quite fine, especially the perfect *tarte aux framboises* and a pleasing offering of fresh fruits and *sorbets.*

LE BISTROT DU DOME
1, rue Delambre,
Paris 14.
Tel: 01.43.35.32.00.
Métro: Vavin.
Service noon to 2:30 P.M. and 7:30 to 11 P.M.
Open daily.
Credit cards: AE, V.
Sidewalk terrace in summer.
Air-conditioned.
A la carte, 250 francs.

SPECIALTIES:
Fish and shellfish: friture de céteaux (pan-fried whole baby sole); raie en vinaigrette (poached skate in vinaigrette); turbotin béarnaise (whole turbot with tarragon sauce).

Give me fish, fish, and more fish. When I am in the mood—any time of the day or year—it's the Bistrot du Dôme that I think of when time is short and the pocketbook is in crisis stage. This bright dining room, with a few tables that stretch out onto the sidewalk in fair weather, offers one of the city's best bargains for fish and shellfish. Prices have hardly budged during the past five years, and wines are still all equally priced at 99 francs, yet another bargain. Since the restaurant is run by the Bras family, who own the excellent Dôme restaurant as well as the Poissonerie du Dôme across the street, one is assured of the freshest fish. There is no written menu, just a blackboard of four or five starters and the same number of main courses.

On my last visit, I loved the first course of *céteaux,* whole baby sole that had been delicately deep-fried. All one needed was a touch of Brittany sea salt, provided right there on the table, and a dab or two of the *sauce tartare.* Pan-grilled squid, or *calamars à la plancha,* were tooth-tender and sweet. This is one place that properly values fish that is cooked whole, such as an entire *turbotin,* simply roasted. If it's on the blackboard that day, try the poached *raie* (skate) *en vinaigrette.*

The small yellow, blue, and white dining room allows barely enough elbow room between tables and is generally packed at lunch and dinner, so reservations are advised. The brief wine list is lovely. Do try the Vouvray *sec* from Gaston Huet, a white that marries perfectly with the Bistrot du Dôme's simple seafood preparations. For dessert, sample a selection of fruit *sorbets* or a fresh fruit salad.

Saumon Nature Sauce Basilic Le Duc
LE DUC'S SALMON WITH BASIL SAUCE

There are many versions of fish cooked on a plate, and this is one of my favorites. It is such a simple, natural, uncomplicated method of steaming fish that I wonder why it isn't more popular. At Le Duc, a Left Bank restaurant devoted to fish (see page 116), this version appears on the menu from time to time. When preparing it, I use two large Pyrex pie plates—so that I can keep track of the salmon steaks as they cook—placed on top of a couscous cooker. At Le Duc, the salmon is served quite rare; it is considered done when the base of the fish turns white. Those who prefer their salmon fully cooked can just continue cooking until the fish is opaque throughout, about 20 minutes.

¼ cup (6 cl) firmly packed fresh basil leaves
½ cup (12.5 cl) extra-virgin olive oil
3 medium tomatoes, cored, peeled, seeded, and chopped
Salt and freshly ground black pepper to taste
1 tablespoon (½ ounce; 15 g) unsalted butter
4 salmon steaks (each weighing 6 to 8 ounces; 180 to 250 g)

1. Prepare the sauce: Wash and dry the basil leaves and snip into shreds, or a *chiffonnade,* with scissors. Combine the basil, oil, tomatoes, salt, and pepper in a small bowl. Cover, and set aside to marinate for 1 hour.

2. Place the salmon steaks in a single layer on the bottom of a large buttered pie plate, preferably glass. Invert a second buttered pie plate, also preferably glass, over the first plate. Place the plates on top of a large pot of boiling water and cook to desired doneness. It will take about 10 minutes for rare salmon, 20 minutes for the salmon to be cooked through.

3. To serve, place each steak in the center of a warmed dinner plate, and spoon the basil sauce all over.

Yield: 4 servings

LE DUC
243, boulevard Raspail,
Paris 14.
Tel: 01.43.20.96.30.
Fax: 01.43.20.46.73.
Métro: Raspail.
Service noon to 2:30 P.M. and 8 to 10:30 P.M.
Closed Saturday lunch, Sunday, and Monday.
Credit cards: AE, DC, V.
Air-conditioned.
260-franc lunch menu.
A la carte, 400 to 600 francs.

SPECIALTIES:
Fish and shellfish: dorade grillée nature (grilled porgy); loup grillé nature (grilled sea bass); salade de crabe frais (fresh crab salad).

If you love your fish ultra-fresh, sparingly prepared, and barely cooked, then Le Duc is for you. Former chef Paul Minchelli moved to his own restaurant in 1994 (see page 74), but the once ultra-trendy Le Duc is still very much worth the detour. The menu has changed not at all since the Minchelli days; it still includes a selection of seasoned raw fish, fish soup, *friture*, and simple *sautés*. A favorite here is *escalopes de lotte à l'huile d'olive et citron vert*, finely sliced monkfish that is doused with oil and lime juice and placed under the grill for just a few seconds until it turns a sweet, milky white. Warm oysters in the style of the Ile de Ré are sauced with a fragrant blend of cream, curry, cayenne, saffron, and butter and gratinéed for just 10 seconds, making for a fresh, rich, mouth-filling starter. Turbot is grilled to perfection, and the *millefeuille* makes a fine, classic closer. The sedate dining room—with wood paneling, leather chairs, and plain white tables—is cozy and comfortable, and the service is generally warm.

MONSIEUR LAPIN
11, rue Raymond-Losserand,
Paris 14.
Tel: 01.43.20 21.39.
Fax: 01.43.21.84.86.
Métro: Gaîté.
Service noon to 2 P.M. and 7:30 to 11 P.M.
Closed Saturday lunch, Monday, and August.
Credit card: V.
Air-conditioned.
170- and 300-franc menus.
A la carte, 250 to 300 francs.

For the past ten years or so, I've received regular telephone calls from the owner of a small Montparnasse restaurant called Monsieur Lapin, pleading for me to make a visit. For no specific reason, the restaurant always seemed to end up at the tail end of my "to try" list. In recent years, the calls became a bit of a joke between myself and co-owner and chef François Ract, who needed only to utter the words "Monsieur Lapin" and I would blurt out a promise to come "one day soon."

My only regret is that I didn't heed his calls earlier, for chef Ract and partner Yves Plantard have one of the more solid and satisfying little restaurants in the area. Some twenty years ago they took over a small neighborhood bistro, complete with a zinc bar with a fine patina of age. They needed to change the restaurant's name quickly, and since they had a pet rabbit at the time, chose to call the restaurant Monsieur Lapin. There is, of course, more than rabbit on the menu, but the lean, moist, and tender farm-raised rabbits that come to them direct from

SPECIALTIES:
Terrine de lapin en gelée (rabbit terrine); râble de lapereau aux champignons des bois (saddle of rabbit with wild mushrooms); lapin sauté aux citrons confits (sauté of rabbit with preserved lemons); carré d'agneau rôti à la broche (rotisserie-grilled rack of lamb); délice de chocolat amer (rich chocolate cake).

the Gatinais are unquestionably their specialty. Here you'll find rabbit in well-seasoned terrines served with a bright and zingy *sauce verte,* a rich green herb-filled mayonnaise, or roasted with a coating of coarse-grained mustard. In one preparation, rabbit arrives in the form of jewel-like nuggets of *râble* (saddle) stuffed with sausage and herbs and paired with a meaty mound of wild mushrooms. Or, as I enjoyed on my recent visit, as an aromatic rabbit *fricassée* teamed up with domestic mushrooms and a glossy, substantial, pleasingly balanced sauce of honey and cider vinegar. The dish was served on a bed of ultra-crisp paper-thin slices of potato, and chef Ract carefully balanced the tenderness of the rabbit with the crunch of the potatoes. It's clear that Ract knows what he's doing and obvious that he loves it, for the food has the polish and studied classic perfection that are France's trademark. Only a mildly excessive presence of salt in many of the dishes marred the meal.

Monsieur Lapin's lightly cooked terrine of *foie gras* is served with deliciously rich slices of toasted *brioche;* and daily specials such as *crêpes* stuffed with salmon and bathed in *beurre blanc* make you eager to launch a campaign to bring back butter. Beyond the rabbit offerings, Monsieur Lapin features a full selection of fish and shellfish (with turbot a specialty), as well as beef, lamb, and organ meats. The inviting, well-priced menu includes at least eight starters and an equal number of main courses, including copious salads, Lyonnaise pork sausage with polenta, varied rabbit selections, and fish and meat. The dessert menu lists a selection of *sorbets* and ice creams from the famed Berthillon family, as well as such traditional favorites as *pot de crème* and *oeufs à la neige.*

The wine list offers some selections ideal for pairing with rabbit, including a lovely golden Rully Mont-Palais from the house of Olivier Leflaive, a wine without a big name or reputation but one that here, at least, has a faint touch of acidity with that golden sweetness of Chardonnay, pairing beautifully with the delicately flavored rabbit. Other good choices come from a full range of Duboeuf Beaujolais, other pricier Leflaive offerings, and Olga Raffault's appealing red Chinon.

Grenelle, Convention

15th arrondissement

LE CLOS MORILLONS
50, rue des Morillons,
Paris 15.
Tel: 01.48.28.04.37.
Fax: 01.48.28.70.77.
Métro: Convention or Porte de Vanves.
Service noon to 2 P.M. and 8 to 10 P.M.
Closed Saturday lunch and Sunday.
Credit cards: AE, V.
175- to 295-franc menus.
A la carte, 250 to 280 francs.

SPECIALTIES: Modern: terrine pressée de pommes de terre et de foie gras à fleur de sel (foie gras and potato terrine); la morue rôtie au bois de casse avec purée de pomme de terre fumée (roasted cod with cassia cinnamon and smoked potato purée); cochon de lait fondant et bouillon d'épices (tender suckling pig with spicy bouillon).

While "fusion" cuisine may be making waves in other parts of the world, the French raise their eyebrows rather quizzically at the thought of tampering with the sacrosanct qualities of codified, traditional French cooking. Yes, one does find an occasional Asian-inspired dose of lime, a pinch of curry, a leaf of cilantro here and there, but it comes on like a gentle breeze, not a gusty storm.

One French chef who does manage to fuse classic French food with a touch of the Far East is Philippe Delacourcelle, chef-owner of Le Clos Morillons, a pleasant little restaurant not far from the beautifully restored Parc Georges Brassens. Delacourcelle spent five years running various French restaurants in Asia, and returned to Paris with a changed palate as well as a new palette of herbs and spices with which to create his gentle alchemy. His fresh lobster salad—sweet and flavorful morsels of lobster tossed with artichokes, a generous sprinkling of fresh basil, greens, and tomatoes—is a delight. I love as well his generous fillet of turbot set on a thick bed of wilted spinach, all seasoned with a sweet, appealing lemongrass-flavored butter, or *citronelle.* Chocolate-lovers will adore his all-chocolate desserts, including dark chocolate infused with jasmine. As a lemon-lover, I favor his *quenelles fondantes de citron,* a lemon custard shaped like scoops of sorbet, served with juniper-infused strawberries.

ERAWAN
76, rue de la Fédération,
Paris 15.
Tel: 01.47.83.55.67.
Métro: La Motte-Picquet–Grenelle.
Service noon to 3 P.M. and 7 to 10:30 P.M.
Closed Sunday and August.
Credit cards: AE, V.
Air-conditioned.
120- to 175-franc menus.
A la carte, 150 to 250 francs.

This lovely, lively, elegant restaurant, not far from Unesco and the Eiffel Tower, offers some of Paris's best and most accessible Thai food. There are two small dining rooms, nicely decorated in pastel colors, with lovely blue and white china used throughout. You'll leave feeling healthy, not heavy, after feasting on salads, fish simmered in a refreshing coconut milk sauce, fabulous rice cooked with snippets of sausage, shrimp and crab, and all manner of dishes filled with the flavor and fragrance of basil, lemongrass (*citronelle*), mint, and spices. If you

SPECIALTIES:
Thai: yam hoy men phou (spicy salad of mussels, basil, and lemongrass); hor mok kuon (spicy shrimp steamed in banana leaves); khao phat ruam mit (rice sautéed with shrimp, crab, and Thai sausages).

adore spicy-hot food, you'll find it here in the salads of spicy shrimp and lemongrass, the classic beef with peppers and lemongrass, or the *moules* stuffed with herbs and spices. If you want a sampling of Thai food, there is a variety of inexpensive fixed menus. With the meal, sample a chilled Bandol rosé.

KIM-ANH
15, rue de l'Eglise,
Paris 15.
Tel: 01.45.79.40.96.
Fax: 01.40.59.49.78.
Métro: Charles Michels.
Open for dinner only.
Service 7:30 to 10:30 P.M.
Open daily except the first three weeks of August.
Credit card: V.
Air-conditioned.
220-franc menu.
A la carte, 200 to 300 francs.

SPECIALTIES:
Vietnamese: langoustines caramelisées (caramelized prawns with Thai rice); coquelet farci (chicken stuffed with spices); lamelles de boeuf sautées aux vermicelles (strips of beef sautéed with noodles and spices).

For refined and traditional Vietnamese fare, head over to the 15th *arrondissement* and rue de l'Eglise, where (evenings only) Caroline Kim-Anh and her husband entertain a select twenty or so diners in their tiny dining room, charmingly decorated with bamboo and wicker. Before moving to France, Mr. Kim-Anh sold American cars in Saigon, while his wife perfected her own brand of home cooking.

Here you'll find all the best elements of Vietnamese cuisine: The food is light, refreshing, full of fresh herbs, light sauces, and gentle spicing. Begin with the *émincé de boeuf à la citronnelle,* a wholesome, evenly spiced salad of strips of beef, greens, and sprouts ready for dousing with their delicate sauce. As a main course, order the elegant *crabe farci,* crabmeat that is pounded and seasoned and put back into the shell, making for a beautifully seasoned crab *pâté.* But my favorite of all is the *marinade de crevettes au curry,* giant shrimp in a soothing curry sauce, all served with saffron-flavored rice. The service here is as friendly and as gentle as the fine fare.

LE PETIT PLAT
49, avenue Emile-Zola,
Paris 15.
Tel: 01.45.78.24.20.
Métro: Charles Michels.
Service noon to 2 P.M. and 8 to 10:45 P.M.
Closed Sunday, Monday, two weeks in August, and ten days in December.
Credit card: V.
Sidewalk terrace.
Air-conditioned.
135-franc menu.
A la carte, 180 to 220 francs.

Le Petit Plat is a unique restaurant situated along the lovely acacia tree–lined avenue Emile Zola. The food here is always creatively composed and carefully prepared, the service is casual but efficient, and the wine list will likely offer some pleasant surprises. Jean and Victor Lampreia have been here since 1994, when they moved from their tiny restaurant in the 5th *arrondissement.* Highlights of my last visit include a refreshing summer salad of thinly sliced artichoke hearts layered with slender French green beans; perfectly cooked pigeon on a bed of couscous; a whole porgy (*dorade*) beautifully prepared with generous portions of sweet fresh fava beans; and warm pound cake, or *quatre quart,* sliced

Marinade de Thon Tiede et Fenouil, Vinaigrette aux Agrumes

WARM FRESH TUNA WITH FENNEL AND SPICY CITRUS VINAIGRETTE

Chef William Ledeuil of Bistro de l'Etoile/Lauriston (see page 124), one of Guy Savoy's "satellite" bistros, is one of Paris's most creative chefs. Each time I dine there, which is often, I'm stunned by the clever culinary ideas that spring from his tiny kitchen. This is one creation that can easily be created at home, to the oohs and aahs of all attending. I love the idea of gently marinating the tuna first, so it is already infused with a piquant vinaigrette. *The marinade also begins to "cook" the tuna slightly and ensures that the fish does not dry out during its brief time in the oven. Note that the tuna is not really cooked, just warmed. Make sure everything is super-fresh, and your taste buds will be rewarded.*

Marinade and Tuna:
2 tablespoons freshly squeezed lemon juice
6 tablespoons extra-virgin olive oil
2 to 3 drops Tabasco sauce
1 thick slice fresh tuna steak (1 pound; 500 g), cut ¾ inch (2 cm) thick

Vinaigrette:
1 lime
1 orange
2 tablespoons balsamic vinegar
1 whole star anise
⅛ teaspoon curry powder
⅛ teaspoon paprika
⅛ teaspoon ground cardamom
5 tablespoons extra-virgin olive oil

Fennel:
2 pounds (1 kg) fresh fennel bulbs, rinsed and trimmed
3 tablespoons extra-virgin olive oil
Several sprigs of fresh thyme
Sea salt, to taste

1. About 5 hours before preparing the dish, marinate the tuna: In a shallow glass dish, combine the lemon juice, oil, and Tabasco. Place the tuna in the dish. Cover with plastic wrap and refrigerate, turning the tuna from time to time. Remove the tuna from the refrigerator 1 hour before cooking. (The tuna can be marinated up to 24 hours, but I prefer a shorter marinade.)

2. Prepare the *vinaigrette:* Zest the lime and orange, then blanch the zest in boiling water for 1 minute. Drain and set aside. Juice the lime and orange and place the juice in a small saucepan along with the vinegar, star anise, and spices. Over high heat, reduce to a thick syrup, about 5 minutes. While still warm, add the oil. Taste for seasoning. Set aside.

3. Preheat the broiler.

4. Prepare the fennel: Place the fennel in a large saucepan, cover with water, and add the oil, thyme, and salt to taste. Bring to a simmer over moderate heat, and simmer gently until the fennel is tender, about 20 minutes. Drain. Cut each bulb lengthwise into thin slices. Transfer the fennel—overlapping the slices—to a warmed serving platter. Moisten with some of the warm *vinaigrette,* cover, and keep warm in a low oven.

5. Remove the tuna from the marinade and place on a broiling pan. Broil 4 inches (10 cm) from the heat to lightly warm the tuna, not cook it, about 1 minute, heating one side only.

6. Transfer the tuna to the serving platter, moisten with the remaining *vinaigrette,* and serve immediately.

Yield: 4 servings

SPECIALTIES:
Modern and seasonal: joues de boeuf en daube (beef cheek stew); tajine de lapin au citron vert (Moroccan-inspired rabbit stew with lime); lotte à la vapeur, légumes du midi rôtis (steamed monkfish with roasted Provençal vegetables).

and layered with fresh strawberries. Wines to sample here include the rich and lush red Côtes-du-Rhône Domaine Saint Claude from Vaison-la-Romaine, and the superlative Gran Corona from the Torres family in Spain. (This wine, from the Penedès, is made of 85 percent Cabernet and 15 percent Tempranillo, a grape that adds extraordinary fragrance and depth to a wine well worth seeking out.) In good weather, reserve a table on the tiny sidewalk terrace.

TROCADERO, VICTOR-HUGO, BOIS DE BOULOGNE

16th arrondissement

LA BUTTE CHAILLOT
112, avenue Kléber,
Paris 16.
Tel: 01.47.27.88.88.
Fax: 01.47.04.85.70.
Internet: http://www.guysavoy.com
Métro: Trocadéro.
Service noon to 2:30 P.M. and 7 P.M. to midnight.
Open daily.
Credit cards: AE, DC, V.
Sidewalk terrace.
Private dining room for 20.
Air-conditioned.
150- and 195-franc menus.
A la carte, 180 to 230 francs.

SPECIALTIES:
Bistro: viandes grillées et rôties (roasted and grilled meats); huîtres en nage glacée (oysters on a bed of cream, topped with jellied oyster liquor); ravioles de Royans au persil simple (tiny cheese ravioli tossed with parsley); poitrine de veau au romarin à la broche (rotisserie-roasted veal breast with rosemary); volaille fermière rôtie à la broche, pommes de terre purées (rotisserie-roasted farm chicken with potato purée); tarte fine aux pommes (apple tart).

Guy Savoy has been an aggressive bistro-maker; he has numerous satellites to his name, with La Butte Chaillot one of the most consistently pleasing. Located just steps from the Trocadéro in the 16th *arrondissement,* La Butte Chaillot attracts a well-heeled, frankly bourgeois clientele. The two-story restaurant is starkly modern, with bright aqua leather chairs and lots of glass. But the menu is vintage Guy Savoy, meaning there's lots that's familiar (rotisserie chicken with a smooth potato purée, roasted breast of veal, Charolais beef with *sauce Béarnaise* and shoestring potatoes) and plenty of Savoy signature dishes. My recent favorites include the salad of giant *gambas* in tempura batter served with matchsticks of beets, cubes of lemon, and a bed of dressed greens; and the fabulous *dorade en écailles,* crunchy, crisp, fresh porgy fillets set on a bed of creamy risotto in a pool of pungent *pistou.* You will also generally find sparkling fresh *huîtres en nage glacée,* soft and fragrant oysters resting on a bed of tangy cream and topped with jellied oyster liquor; and his "rustic-modern" soup of creamy lentils paired with a touch of luxury-priced *langoustines.* The wine list is brief, with some wines by the glass. For a special treat, try André Ostertag's Alsatian Pinot Noir. La Butte Chaillot is open seven days a week, serves until midnight, and also offers a quick-service *plat du jour* at lunchtime.

Paleron Braise a la Bourgeoise
BENOIT'S BRAISED BEEF SHOULDER

Benoit Guichard, chef-owner of Paris's Jamin (see page 125), is the king of braising. He loves long, slow cooking of beef, lamb, duck—you name it. The kitchen is so fragrant when I cook this, I all but want to jump into the pot with the meat! This wintry dish is equally delicious prepared with white or red wine.

2 tablespoons olive oil
2 tablespoons (1 ounce; 30 g) unsalted butter
2 pounds (1 kg) beef shoulder, cut into 8-ounce (250-g) portions
Sea salt and freshly ground black pepper, to taste
2 large onions, peeled and quartered
24 shallots, peeled and quartered
4 carrots, peeled and quartered
Bouquet garni: a large bunch of fresh parsley and several fresh bay leaves tied in a bundle with household string
2 whole star anise
½ teaspoon black peppercorns
About 2 bottles red or white wine (for red, use a wine made with the Syrah grape; for white, a Muscadet or California Pinot Blanc)

1. Preheat the oven to 175°F (135°C).

2. In a large flameproof casserole or Dutch oven, heat the oil and butter over moderate heat. When the fats are hot, begin to brown the beef, carefully regulating the heat to avoid scorching the meat. Do not crowd the pan and be patient: Good browning is essential for the meat to retain its flavor and moistness. Thoroughly brown the meat on all sides in several batches, about 10 minutes per batch. As each batch is browned, use tongs (to avoid piercing the meat) to transfer the beef to a platter. Immediately season generously with salt and pepper. Leave the fat in the casserole.

3. Using a metal spatula, scrape up any browned bits that are sticking to the bottom of the casserole (this will help enrich the final sauce). Return the seasoned meat to the casserole. Add the onions, shallots, carrots, bouquet garni, and spices. Add enough wine to fully cover the meat and vegetables. (This is important: If the meat is not fully covered, it will dry out as it cooks.) Bring just to a simmer over moderate heat. Place a sheet of buttered wax paper over the mixture (this will keep the meat moist and well submerged in the liquid), and cover the casserole with its lid.

4. Place in the center of the oven and cook until the meat is ultra-tender, 3 to 4 hours. Check from time to time to make sure the liquid is at a very gentle simmer. Do not allow it to boil or the meat will become tough. (There is no need to baste, for the fats and wine will automatically baste the meat.)

5. Remove the casserole from the oven. Using tongs, carefully transfer the pieces of beef to a large plate. Set a strainer over a large bowl, and line the strainer with a piece of moistened cheesecloth. Ladle the liquid from the casserole into the strainer, discarding the vegetables, spices, and bouquet garni. Rinse out the casserole, and return the meat and strained liquid to the pan. Refrigerate overnight.

6. At serving time, skim off and discard the layer of fat that has risen to the top. Place the casserole over low heat and warm gently. With tongs, carefully remove the pieces of beef and transfer them to a plate. Over moderately high heat, reduce the liquid by about one-third, about 5 minutes. Return the meat to the liquid and heat through over high heat for 10 minutes more.

7. To serve, place a piece of beef on a warmed dinner plate and spoon the liquid over the meat.

Yield: 6 to 8 servings

ALAIN DUCASSE
59, avenue Raymond Poincaré,
Paris 16.
Tel: 01.47.27.12.27.
Fax: 01.47.27.81.22
E-mail: adplolotte@aol.com (reservations accepted by e-mail).
Internet: http://www.alain-ducasse.com
Métro: Trocadéro or Victor Hugo.
Service noon to 2 P.M. and 7:45 to 10 P.M.
Closed Saturday, Sunday, mid-July to mid-August, and Christmas week.
Credit cards: AE, DC, V.
Air-conditioned.
Valet parking.
490-franc lunch menu; 1,490-franc tasting and 920-franc dinner menus.
A la carte, 800 to 1,400 francs.

SPECIALTIES:
Seasonal: pâtes mi-séchées crèmées et truffes au ris de veau (homemade pasta with cream, truffles, and sweetbreads); lard paysan croustillant aux pommes de terre caramélisées (country bacon with crusty potatoes); tête de porc en salade d'herbes amères et truffes (pig's head with salad of bitter greens and truffles).

Alain Ducasse is still very young, but he has the wisdom, experience, and character of a man twice his age. Add to that the fearlessness of a sixteen-year-old and the ambition and stamina of someone in his twenties. If it sounds pretty astonishing, it's because we're talking about the chef with the brashness to take over the landmark restaurant made famous by chef Joël Robuchon. In the beginning (the summer of 1996), comparisons to Robuchon were obvious, with even Ducasse admitting that he lacked the technical prowess that astonished and pleased Robuchon diners for nearly two decades. But Ducasse, whose other grand restaurant is at the Hôtel de Paris in Monaco, has his own ways of wooing us. His menus offer something for everyone, with dishes geared to appeal to every flavor of gastronome. For the classicist, there are *écrevisses* (crayfish) in a creamy *velouté* of wild *cèpe* mushrooms, a dish that might have come straight from Escoffier. For the modern diner harboring a passion for anything remotely Italian, there is a marvelous, complicated, and delicious creation consisting of discs of partially dried homemade pasta bathed in cream, truffles, sweetbreads, cockscombs, and cock's kidneys. Truffles, *foie gras,* and Bresse chicken was a classic Robuchon combination; if you sample Ducasse's version, you'll see the difference between the two men. Robuchon's was densely flavored; Ducasse's is a tad lighter, simpler, but no less pleasurable.

Ducasse's menu is scattered with references to such historic names as Escoffier and Brillat-Savarin.

But what would they think of his penchant for *lard*—thick, fatty, oozingly delicious slabs of pork, grilled to a crisp and served with thick potato wedges browned in an avalanche of butter? Signs of his Monaco menu appear in such dishes as the rich *légumes des jardins de Provence,* a vegetable *ragoût* enriched with black truffles, Ligurian olive oil, and a touch of coarse Brittany sea salt. Ducasse has a passion for grilling, and so from his newly installed high-tech grill we have delicate roast lamb fillets, Bresse chicken, and Breton lobster. The Mediterranean influence is seen in his fragrant duckling roasted in fig leaves, garnished with fresh purple figs in butter, while Brittany plays a starring role with meaty fillets of turbot steamed in seaweed. Desserts are lively and refreshing, and include such marvels as a blend of apricot tart, marmalade, and vanilla ice cream garnished with lace-thin *tuiles* flavored with apricots and almonds.

BISTRO DE L'ETOILE/LAURISTON
19, rue Lauriston, Paris 16.
Tel: 01.40.67.11.16.
Fax: 01.45.00.99.87.
Internet: http://www.guysavoy.com
Métro: Kléber or Charles de Gaulle–Etoile.
Service noon to 2:30 P.M. and 7 P.M. to midnight.
Closed Saturday lunch and Sunday.
Credit cards: AE, DC, V.
Air-conditioned.
135- and 165-franc lunch menus.
A la carte, 220 to 250 francs.

SPECIALTIES:
Modern bistro: ravioles de Royans aux champignons et parmesan (miniature cheese ravioli with mushrooms and Parmesan); tendrons de veau de lait, macaronis au jus de pistou au jambon fumé (breast of veal with pasta, basil and garlic sauce, and smoked ham); tarte tiède aux pommes (warm apple tart).

Chef Guy Savoy's firmament shines bright, and a favorite star is Le Bistro de l'Etoile on rue Lauriston, just off the Etoile. With room for about fifty diners, this modern mirrored bistro is decorated in a clean bottle green—Savoy's signature color—with touches of daffodil. The supervising chef, William Ledeuil, spent several years under Savoy's tutelage and seems to have a good head on his shoulders. All those common bistro ingredients are here—beets and Bordeaux, *tendrons de veau* and *gratin dauphinois, crème brûlée* and *tarte aux pommes*—except in modern costume.

Chef Ledeuil will take tiny white asparagus, and rather than a traditional (and most times banal) *sauce mousseline* or *vinaigrette,* he sauces it with a perky *sauce ravigote,* a *vinaigrette* spiced with capers, herbs, and shallots. As a starter one evening, he offered an unusual terrine of beets with avocado purée: perfectly cooked beets, sliced oh so thin, stacked in layers with a smooth avocado filling. The *sauce ravigote* had another chance to shine, serving here as a bright flavor accent, turning the dish into a fine palate teaser. During the course of many visits, I've loved his meltingly moist and copious portions of rabbit in a delicately flavored ginger sauce; properly cooked tuna steaks served on a bed of fennel; and pleasantly lean slices of *tendrons de veau* (veal breast), served with macaroni, basil and garlic sauce, and smoked ham.

I particularly applaud chef Ledeuil's approach to tuna. So many chefs sear the life out of tuna, leaving the interior raw and making for an often soggy, unpalatable mess. Here the tuna steak is pan-fried like a beef steak, then set to rest, giving the juices time to flow back into the fish, producing fish that is moist and well cooked.

Desserts can be hit-or-miss. I don't quite get the point of his soggy *pain perdu au praliné* with a sauce that tastes like evaporated milk. But he wins my heart with the warm and crackling *tarte aux pommes,* that perfect combination of apples, butter, and sugar—the sort of dish that will have me coming back for more. The brief wine list offers some real stars, including the unfiltered Alsatian Pinot Noir from Ostertag and a meaty Saumur from Château Langlois in the Loire.

JAMIN
32, rue de Longchamp, Paris 16.
Tel: 01.45.53.00.07.
Fax: 01.45.53.00.15.
Métro: Trocadéro.
Service 12:30 to 2 P.M. and 7:30 to 10 P.M.
Closed Saturday, Sunday, and three weeks in August.
Credit cards: AE, DC, V.
Private dining room for 8 to 16.
Air-conditioned.
280-franc lunch menu; 375-franc dinner menu.
A la carte, 450 to 650 francs.

In nearly two decades of visiting Paris kitchens I've probably spent more time in the presence of Benoit Guichard than of any other chef. It's no surprise that he is not a household name, for he spent fifteen years in the shadow of his master, Joël Robuchon. Beginning his work as an underling with Robuchon in 1980 at the Hotel Nikko, Guichard witnessed the complete Robuchon ascension. For a decade he served as Robuchon's *chef de cuisine,* the good and obedient colonel who carried out the general's orders. Whether he passed his sixteen-hour workdays in the 16th-*arrondissement* kitchens of Jamin or Restaurant Joël Robuchon, or trained the troops in the kitchens of a Tokyo *château,* his was not to reason why but to flawlessly interpret culinary genius. It's a miracle that he ever found time for a private life or, what's more, time to think about a culinary style of his own. But style he has, and since the winter of 1996 Benoit Guichard has been back at the stoves he knows best, in the kitchen of Jamin, where Joël Robuchon rose to fame during the 1980s.

Guichard is a modest, sensible, no-nonsense man, a man of honor and high moral integrity. And his cuisine follows suit: no fanfare, no breast-beating,

SPECIALTIES:
Modern and seasonal: crème légère aux langoustines de petite pêche (light Dublin Bay prawn soup); filet épais de bar aux pistaches, sauce légère au fenouil (thick fillet of sea bass with pistachios and a light fennel sauce); quasi de veau doré, girolles, carottes et oignons nouveaux mitonnés au jus (golden rump of veal with wild mushrooms, carrots, and baby onions in meat juices).

no ultra-sophistication, no self-indulgence. Just plainly delicious food, prepared with the best ingredients that France can offer. His menu is brief and to the point, but punctuated with original flavors and new taste sensations. There are of course those signature Robuchon ingredients—plump alabaster *langoustines* and fat Breton scallops, veal kidneys and the much-revered pig—but they are treated with the straightforward Guichard style. Ultra-fresh *langoustines* are paired with spaghetti-size strips of tender squid with a delicate touch of ginger to make a first-course salad that's ethereally light and refreshing. Perfectly grilled scallops arrive flanked by a crunchy, invigorating salad of black radish, fennel bulb, red onions, and apple. Beef shoulder is braised for hours on end in a black cast-iron casserole, then paired with a sprightly rendition of cooked carrots, deglazed with orange juice and infused with cumin. And his love poem to the pig is irresistibly rich and earthy, arriving in the form of braised, then roasted, cheeks and tail, redolent of marjoram.

Guichard understands the balance of flavors, the essential role of acids in a dish, and intelligently doses each preparation. For years I've harbored a dream of what classic *goujonnettes de sole* should taste like: golden, crisp fried fingerlings of snowy white sole ready to be dipped into a state-of-the art *sauce tartare,* pungent with mustard, pickles, and herbs. I'd forgotten I'd given up hope of ever sampling the perfect version until Guichard offered it up on one of my visits.

The dining room is under the careful direction of André Wawrzyniak, a longtime Robuchon *maître d'hôtel.* Robuchon faithfuls will recognize the crusty miniature loaves of sourdough bread, the giant brick of sweet butter, the cheese tray from Marie-Anne Cantin, and the rolling dessert cart. After all, some traditions need to remain just that—traditions.

LAC HONG
67, rue Lauriston,
Paris 16.
Tel: 01.47.55.87.17.
Métro: Boissière or Victor Hugo.
Service noon to 2:45 P.M. and 7 to 10:45 P.M.
Closed Sunday and August.
Credit card: V.
Air-conditioned.
Non-smoking section.
89-franc lunch menu.
A la carte, 250 to 300 francs.

SPECIALTIES:
Vietnamese: salade de papaya verte aux gambas grillées (salad of unripe papaya with grilled giant shrimp); coquelet désossé grillé aux sept parfums (grilled boned baby chicken with seven spices); moules au tamarin et au basilic (mussels with tamarind and basil).

At the end of a strangely boring street in the 16th, Lac Hong looks like one of thousands of Asian restaurants scattered in every nook and cranny of Paris. But step inside this always busy, always popular Vietnamese restaurant and you will find some very special dishes: mounds of steamed mussels seasoned with tamarind and basil; steamed turbot bathed in ginger; morsels of rich duck seasoned with orange and ginger; and my favorite of all, their famous salad of green (unripe) papaya paired with giant grilled *gambas.* Their Vietnamese spring rolls (*rouleaux de printemps*) are soft and light, like pillows; and the crusty, crunchy boned chicken, grilled and sprinkled with a mix of seven spices, is dreamy in flavor and texture. In short, inspired, inventive, and refined. Service can be slow, so bring along a dose of patience.

PORT ALMA
10, avenue de New York,
Paris 16.
Tel: 01.47.23.75.11.
Fax: 01.47.20.42.92.
Métro: Alma-Marceau.
Service 12:30 to 2:30 P.M. and 7:30 to 10:30 P.M..
Closed Sunday and August.
Credit cards: AE, DC, V.
Private dining room for 14.
Air-conditioned.
200-franc lunch menu.
A la carte, 400 to 500 francs.

SPECIALTIES:
Fish and shellfish: friture d'éperlans (deep-fried smelt); tartare de thon (salad of minced raw tuna); bar cuit dans sa croûte de sel (sea bass cooked in a salt crust); côte de boeuf de Salers poêlée au sel de Guérande (pan-fried rib of beef from Salers); crème brûlée aux noix (caramel cream with walnuts); soufflé au chocolat (chocolate soufflé).

Port Alma, the bright and elegant quayside restaurant overlooking the Eiffel Tower, is unquestionably one of the best fish restaurants in Paris. Several years ago, chef Paul Canal left Le Dôme in Montparnasse to make it on his own, and though there are still some rough edges, Port Alma is the kind of place where one can joyfully consider becoming a regular.

When it comes to freshness, creativity, and surprises, Canal is unbeatable. In summertime he offers tender fried zucchini blossoms, gently filled with a fresh-flavored "salad" of herbs and tiny scallops. Or consider a refreshing crabmeat gazpacho, filled not with meager snippets but with generous mounds of sweet, tender crabmeat.

I applaud any restaurant that makes the effort to display platters of fresh whole fish to help you make a selection (as well as determine freshness for yourself). Port Alma always offers such a choice, and on nearly every visit I opt for a whole *bar en croûte de sel,* sea bass cooked in a crust of sea salt, certainly the finest and most miraculous method for cooking whole fish. It's also the trickiest, for once that fish is hidden in a bed of sea salt (a process in which the salt serves as a tightly sealed baking vessel), you simply have to trust your oven and your own judgment to know when the fish is properly cooked. Here it's filleted tableside and served with a rich and creamy fennel *gratin.* Other excellent choices include a light salad of mixed greens and baby clams, or *coques;* a warm, beautifully seasoned salad of *langoustines;* and *Saint-Pierre* served on a bed of zesty *ratatouille.*

The menu changes according to the market, and prices are well within reason, considering the high cost of fresh fish and shellfish. Canal generally offers an assortment of grilled fish of the day, such as *dorade* (porgy) or sole, served with a light *beurre blanc.* There's a modern rendition of *goujonnettes de sole* (here served with a tossed salad and a curry-flecked sauce); giant *coquilles Saint-Jacques* served on a bed of leeks or braised with a touch of saffron; and a welcoming *friture* of the freshest of anchovies from the port village of Collioure.

The wine list is brief but offers Didier Dagueneau's excellent Pouilly Fumé, Bernard Gripa's pleasing Saint-Joseph *blanc,* and a fine Macon Viré "Vieilles Vignes" from André Bonhomme. Service, as directed by Canal's outgoing wife, Sonya, is discreet yet attentive. And the tables are well arranged, so you don't feel as though your neighbors are overhearing your private conversation.

BRASSERIE DE LA POSTE
54, rue de Longchamp,
Paris 16.
Tel: 01.47.55.01.31.
Métro: Trocadéro.
Open daily noon to 3 P.M. and 7 P.M. to midnight.
Credit cards: AE, V.
Air-conditioned.
125- and 185-franc lunch and dinner menus.
A la carte, 200 francs.

Diners in search of an authentic brasserie meal in the 16th should reserve a table at La Brasserie de la Poste, a mini–Brasserie Lipp on the rue de Longchamp off avenue Kléber. The welcome is warm and professional, the menu traditional, and the quality just what we've all learned to expect in Paris. The décor is right out of a stage set—cute as can be, with golden ocher walls, tile floors, and gigantic mirrors. Each week the brasserie features the cuisine of a different region of France, and on my last visit it was the sunny cuisine of Provence. An excellent version of the fragrant *soupe au pistou* was served out of a giant tureen, while a generous sweet pepper and anchovy salad consisted of a mix of dressed greens accompanied by beautifully cooked red, yellow, and green peppers and both fresh and marinated anchovies. The *gigotin d'agneau*—a portion of leg of lamb—would have been perfect had

SPECIALTIES:
Brasserie: choucroute garnie (sauerkraut and various sausages, bacon, and pork, served with potatoes); oeufs à la neige (stiffly whisked egg whites poached in milk and served in a thin caramelized vanilla sauce); vacherin (meringue filled with ice cream).

it arrived hot and been served on a warm plate. As it was, the meat came swimming in a warm liquid, making for a less than palatable dish. If the weather is wintry and you are in the mood, tuck into La Poste's gargantuan *choucroute garnie,* served piping-hot with delicious sausages, properly puckery sauerkraut seasoned with a generous hit of black peppercorns, and large portions of roast and steamed pork.

Desserts here taste as though they came right out of grandmother's kitchen: a textbook-perfect *oeufs à la neige* with an edge of meringue in an ultra-creamy *crème anglaise;* giant *profiteroles* paired with vanilla ice cream and tons of hot chocolate sauce; and a divine *vacherin,* a basket of crunchy meringue filled with vanilla ice cream and strawberry sauce.

LE PRE CATELAN
Route de Suresnes,
Bois de Boulogne,
Paris 16.
Tel: 01.44.14.41.41.
Fax: 01.45.24.43.25.
Métro: Porte Dauphine.
Service noon to 2:30 P.M. and 7 to 10:30 P.M.
Closed Sunday evening, Monday, and two weeks in February.
Credit cards: AE, DC, V.
Private dining room for 8 to 20.
Garden terrace.
Valet parking.
295-franc lunch menu (355 including wine); 550- and 690-franc dinner menus.
A la carte, 515 to 915 francs.

Mark my words: This may be the first, but it will not be the last, time you'll read the name Frédéric Anton. One of a group of modest, hardworking, exceptionally well trained chefs unleashed when Joël Robuchon closed his restaurant in 1996, Anton took over the helm of the illustrious Pré Catelan in the Bois de Boulogne in 1997 and has been playing to pleased crowds ever since. As a Robuchon acolyte, Anton was responsible for ordering—then accepting or rejecting—every leaf of lettuce, every grain of caviar, every squiggling *langoustine* that entered the kitchen. A perfect dish, as any cook knows, begins with absolutely fresh, flawless ingredients. At the Pré Catelan, Anton illustrates all he learned, then adds his own uncanny ability to create combinations that sing on the palate and, most of all, satisfy.

Anton's solid culinary foundation serves simply as a backdrop. He stays within very traditional classical parameters, all the while playing his own distinct tune. Rarely does a French chef get the point of risotto, but Anton understands it in the way only a pro can: One bite of his smooth, alabaster creamy risotto layered with parchment-thin slices of fresh white summer truffles, Parmesan, and powerfully intense tiny fresh *girolle* mushrooms and you almost do not want to continue. For a second bite means you'll be on your way to finishing this ingenious, ephemeral dish.

SPECIALTIES:
Modern: risotto crémeux aux truffes, feuilles de sauge, et copeaux de parmesan (creamy risotto with truffles, sage, and Parmesan); fricassée de grosses langoustines aux pommes de terre moelleuses et croustillantes (fricassee of large Dublin Bay prawns with both moist and crusty potatoes); petits farcis du "Pré," fondant d'agneau au curry, courgette à la croque (varied stuffed vegetables with tender lamb curry and crunchy zucchini); poire rôtie, petite gaufre caramélisée, crème glace à la bergamote (roasted pear with caramelized waffles and bergamot ice cream).

Every dish follows a repeated theme: The star ingredient is flanked by an enhancing vegetable and herb. So sparkling fresh sea bass is teamed up with a fennel *mousse* and a *vinaigrette* perfumed with anise. Fresh farm pigeon finds a home with creamy fava beans and artichokes stewed in herbs and fruity olive oil. A palette of miniature summer vegetables—tomatoes, zucchini, onions, and eggplant—are stuffed with a mixture of minced lamb, curry, and cumin, making for a dish in which the fat fixes the flavor but does not leave one logy or laden.

Admittedly, desserts rarely send me into fits of ecstasy, but Anton manages to charm once again with such brilliant combinations as warm fruits, tiny caramelized waffles, and bergamot ice cream; caramelized pears, fresh figs, and cinnamon-rich fig compote; and crusty *galettes,* rhubarb marmalade, and chicory ice cream.

Dining indoors or out, this grand turn-of-the-century restaurant is meant to offer a great experience, French-style. Prices follow suit, though the well-priced weekday lunch menu allows diners to get a glimpse of the young chef's genius. The wine list is long and elaborate, and there is a bevy of enthusiastic wine stewards to steer you toward a selection to fit your pocketbook.

CLICHY, TERNES, WAGRAM, ETOILE

17th arrondissement and Clichy

CAFE D'ANGEL
16, rue Brey,
Paris 17.
Tel/Fax: 01.47.54.03.33.
Métro: Charles de Gaulle–Etoile.
Service noon to 2:30 P.M. and 7:30 to 11:00 P.M.
Closed Saturday, Sunday, and August.
Credit card: V.
80- and 95-franc lunch menus; 145- and 170-franc dinner menus.
A la carte, 150 to 200 francs.

Café d'Angel, not far from the Arc de Triomphe, is a trendy spot these days. The food here is neither sophisticated nor as sure-footed as it might be, but the ambience is appealing, the service is rapid and efficient, and diners are sure to find something to please. With angel-motif tablecloths, a classic bistro red-and-white décor, marble tiled floors, red plastic banquettes, sprays of flowers, an assortment of mirrors, and 1930s bistro chairs, Café d'Angel is right out of a stage set. From the *ardoise* (blackboard—all the rage now in Paris) diners can choose *à la carte* or from the bargain menus.

SPECIALTIES:
Bistro: compote de lapin au romarin, salade de petits radis rose (compote of rabbit with rosemary, with radish salad); morceau d'onglet de boeuf aux échalotes, aux pommes de terre (beef flank steak with shallots and potatoes); pot de crème brûlée au chocolat (chocolate crème brûlée).

I relished the refreshing "*carpaccio*" of tomatoes and zucchini, simply alternating rounds of the two vegetables bathed in a lemon-rich *vinaigrette*, with lots of cracked white pepper and a shower of chives. A *carpaccio* of tuna was conceived along the same vein, with a dressing of oil and lemon, the same coarse cracked white pepper and chives, and a welcoming mound of Provençal mixed greens in the center. Main courses were less appealing: The *osso buco* of *lotte*—center-cut portions of monkfish quickly pan-fried—was edible but boring, set on a bed of underseasoned summer vegetables. Ditto for the bland rabbit paired with a delicious serving of wheat berries cooked like risotto.

APICIUS
122, avenue de Villiers, Paris 17.
Tel: 01.43.80.19.66.
Fax: 01.44.40.09.57.
Métro: Péreire or Porte de Champerret.
Service 12:15 to 2 P.M. and 7:45 to 10 P.M.
Closed Saturday, Sunday, and August.
Credit cards: AE, DC, V.
Private dining room for 25.
Air-conditioned.
620-franc tasting menu.
A la carte, 750 francs, including wine.

SPECIALTIES:
Modern and seasonal: foie gras de canard poêlé en aigre doux (pan-fried duck liver with sweet and sour sauce); canette et foie gras rôtis au poivre noir (roasted duck and foie gras with black pepper); pieds de porc rôtis en crépinette (pig's feet wrapped in caul fat).

Jean-Pierre Vigato, one of the darlings of the 1980s, has shown that he has staying power. His food always wins me over with its depth, range, and originality. My last meal was a winner, with giant *langoustines* (Dublin Bay prawns) cooked tempura-style, so the moist, sweet, cloudlike crustaceans could take center stage. Any day he can serve me his soothing cold *terrine* of cucumbers, giant grains of caviar, and whiskers of chives in a stunning horseradish cream. Wild morel mushrooms are turned into a simple, sublime *fricassée,* and both lamb and veal arrive as tender as butter. Dessert-lovers will adore his all-chocolate or all-caramel sweets.

Beginning dinner with a toast.

ROMANTICA
73, boulevard Jean Jaurès, Clichy 92110.
Tel: 01.47.37.29.71.
Métro: Mairie de Clichy.
Service noon to 2:30 P.M. and 7 to 10:30 P.M.
Closed Saturday lunch and Sunday.
Credit cards: AE, V.
Terrace.
Private dining room for 20 to 25.
215- and 295-franc lunch menus; 250- and 395-franc dinner menus.
A la carte, 350 to 400 francs.

SPECIALTIES:
Italian: scampi al pane e prezzemolo (breaded Dublin Bay prawns); leggera di tagliolini "Romantica" (pasta in sage cream flamed—honestly!—in a wheel of Parmesan); tagliolini alla "Claudio" pugliesi (pasta with garlic, olive oil, hot pepper, zucchini, and sun-dried tomatoes).

Neapolitan Claudio Puglia is an energetic, egotistic, talented, never-say-die chef who holds court in this courtyard restaurant just steps from the border of Paris proper. He's a showman, like all proper southern Italians. He's explosive, highly opinionated, and perhaps just a wee bit exaggerated. And he's talented. In an elegant yet unstuffy dining room decorated in rose tones, amid the shiny silver and elegant glassware, he fights an uphill battle to separate his *cuisine* from the world of mom-and-pop pizzerias and red-checkered tablecloths. And the food fits his showman personality: Who else could serve *tagliolini Romantica*—fresh pasta, first sauced in a blend of bouillon, cream, and sage, then tossed tableside in a carved-out half-wheel of Parmesan cheese until it drools with creamy tenderness?

In his state-of-the-art kitchen, Puglia turns out some true culinary wonders, showing us, once again, that the Italians are masters at simplicity, ultra-sensitive to ingredients and their rightful seasons. His *tagliolini Claudio* is no more and no less than fresh homemade pasta tossed with strips of home-dried tomato, strips of zucchini, and a touch of hot pepper—an ethereal, barely sauced dish. Puglia imports tiny fresh balls of mozzarella from Italy and sets them in a pool of homemade tomato sauce, making for a thoroughly simple and sublime first course. Or he'll marinate sparkling fresh sardines in coarse salt, then sauce them with a balsamic *vinaigrette*, all set on a bed of greens. Fresh

langoustines are moistened with a delicate bread-crumb and parsley dip, then quickly deep-fried and paired with a tangle of pasta blackened and flavored by pungent squid ink. Fish are given tender care here, with superbly fresh *rouget* fillets set on a bed of leeks and peas, surrounded with a delicate emulsion of *limoncello* (homemade lemon liqueur), thickened with lemon juice and olive oil. An expert at marinades and infusions, he loves to take his sweet Marzemino wine, boil it off with an avalanche of sugar and a touch of cinnamon, then toss peach slices into the liquid, allowing them to cool until their flavor is rich and infused.

Pasta Romantica

CLAUDIO'S QUICK FRESH TOMATO AND BASIL PASTA

One of the city's best Italian restaurants (see facing page) can be found in Clichy, a working-class suburb just a block over the city line. Here, in his flower-filled garden restaurant, Claudio Puglia holds court, offering a very personal and vibrant version of Italian fare. This recipe is a personal standby throughout the summer, when fresh basil and tomatoes are there for the asking.

2 tablespoons extra-virgin olive oil
2 pounds (1 kg) fresh tomatoes, cored, peeled, seeded, and chopped
About 2 tablespoons tomato paste
2 cups loosely packed (50 cl) fresh basil leaves, coarsely chopped
6 tablespoons coarse sea salt
12 ounces (375 g) fresh fettuccine (do not use dried pasta)
Fine sea salt, to taste
Freshly grated Parmigiano-Reggiano cheese, for serving (optional)

1. In a large pot, bring 6 quarts (6 liters) of water to a rolling boil.

2. While you are waiting for the water to boil, prepare the sauce. Heat the oil in a large skillet over moderately high heat until it is hot but not smoking. Add the tomatoes all at once, stirring to cook evenly and quickly, about 1 minute. Add just enough tomato paste to form a thick, colorful, chunky sauce, and cook about 1 minute more. Add the basil leaves and stir to blend evenly. Cover, remove from the heat, and set aside.

3. Add the coarse sea salt to the boiling water. Add the pasta, stirring to prevent it from sticking. Cook until tender, about 1 minute. Remove the pan from the heat and thoroughly drain the pasta, removing as much water as possible. Immediately transfer the drained pasta to the tomato and basil sauce, and toss to coat evenly. Cover and let rest to allow the pasta to thoroughly absorb the sauce, 1 to 2 minutes. Taste for salt. Transfer to warmed shallow soup bowls and serve immediately. Pass freshly grated cheese if desired.

Yield: 4 servings

MICHEL ROSTANG
20, rue Rennequin,
Paris 17.
Tel: 01.47.63.40.77.
Fax: 01.47.63.82.75.
E-mail: rostang
@relaischateaux.fr
Internet: http://www.
michelrostang.com
Métro: Ternes.
Service 12:30 to 2:30 P.M.
and 7:30 to 10:30 P.M.
Closed Saturday lunch,
Sunday, and the first
two weeks of August.
Credit cards: AE, DC, V.
Air-conditioned.
350-, 650-, and
870-franc menus.
A la carte, 650 to
750 francs.

SPECIALTIES:
Contemporary: les brochettes de langoustines au romarin, grappes de tomates farcies, vinaigrette de crustacés (Dublin Bay prawns with rosemary, with stuffed tomatoes in shellfish vinaigrette); le carré et selle d'agneau des pré-Alpes du Sud rôtis, jus d'olives (rack and saddle of lamb from Provence with olive-based juices); la tarte chaude au chocolat amer, crème pistachée (warm bittersweet chocolate tart with pistachio ice cream).

I'll be honest from the start. I am an asparagus addict. From the first sighting of those slender spears during the doldrums of February until their traditional disappearance from the markets on the feast of St Jean in mid-June, I could savor their dense, mineral-rich flavor morning, noon, and night. So when I discovered that Michelin two-star chef Michel Rostang was offering an all-asparagus menu, I beat a path to the door of his elegant restaurant. I admit to falling out of love with Rostang some years back, after a few meals that seemed to reflect a man on a road to nowhere. He has awakened, big-time, and is now a passionate chef whose table reflects a curious mind and an intensely intellectual approach to food. The asparagus meal was full of surprises, void of clichés, and a veritable paean to that admirable vegetable. I was mildly disappointed that nowhere in the various courses did asparagus play a starring role, but by the end of the meal I realized the wisdom of assigning it a supporting role in a number of dishes. The first-course *soupe claire d'asperges vertes de Provence* was an eye-opener: With Asian overtones, this complex blend of asparagus, cilantro, faintly puckery fresh *épines vinettes* (highbush cranberries), and cubes of fresh tuna bathed in a clear broth was a perfect tonic. No surprise, in fact, to know that asparagus was once revered for its health-giving properties and used as a medicine. The star of the evening was a simple soft-cooked egg nested in tulip of crisp phyllo, topped with a generous spoonful of sevruga caviar. Flanked by pan-seared violet-tipped asparagus from the farm of Jean-Charles Orso in the hills of Cannes, the soothing dish was offset by a rich, heavily reduced, almost caramelized sweet sherry sauce.

Off the special menu, diners can also treat their palates to roasted green asparagus with spiced crabmeat in a reduced shellfish sauce; rich nuggets of lobster meat paired with asparagus and baby violet artichokes in a delicate anchovy sauce; and farm-fresh guinea hen accompanied with risotto with asparagus butter.

The wine list offered a fine new discovery, a finely flinty white 1995 Coteaux d'Aix en Provence, from the Domaine Hauvette, where winemaker

Dominique Hauvette crafts a well-made organic wine on the plains of St Rémy de Provence. And come winter, Rostang regales us with an all-truffle feast.

GUY SAVOY
18, rue Troyon,
Paris 17.
Tel: 01.43.80.40.61.
Fax: 01.46.22.43.09.
E-mail: reserv@guysavoy.com (Reservations accepted by e-mail)
Internet: http://www.guysavoy.com
Métro: Charles de Gaulle–Etoile.
Service noon to 2:30 P.M. and 7:30 to 10:30 P.M.
Closed Saturday lunch and Sunday.
Credit cards: AE, DC, V.
Private dining rooms for 12 and 35.
Air-conditioned.
Valet parking.
950-franc tasting menu.
A la carte, 800 to 1,000 francs.

SPECIALTIES:
Modern and seasonal: huîtres en nage glacée (oysters on a bed of cream, topped with jellied oyster liquor); soupe d'artichauts à la truffe (artichoke soup with truffles); bar en écailles grillés aux épices douces (sea bass grilled with its scales and skin, served with a sweet, spicy sauce of ginger, vanilla, pepper, and cream); bricelets de grué de cacao et sorbet chocolat amer (caramelized cocoa bean shells layered with bittersweet chocolate sorbet in a mocha crème anglaise).

I am in love with Guy Savoy. Is it just that we have a passion for the same foods—artichokes, oysters, sparkling fresh fish, and chocolate? Or that we approach life and our passions as a delicious challenge to be met each and every day? At any rate, he and I are on the same wavelength, and I always leave his cheery green and white dining room feeling as though I have had the best meal in a very long time. If you have not tasted his classics—a perfectly orchestrated soup of artichokes, Parmesan, and truffles, or his cool *nage* of oysters (soft, fragrant mouthfuls of sea-rich oysters set upon a bed of tangy sour cream)—then run, don't walk, to rue Troyon on your next visit. Savoy's cooking is defined by spirit, creativity, and exactitude. He is like a perfumer who knows exactly which fragrance will turn your head. I could close my eyes and identify his signature food without missing a beat. On my last visit, I loved his *feuilleté* of sweet, tasty dried beets layered with fragrant black truffles, set in a bed of vinegary *vinaigrette;* his braised veal with baby vegetables and an avalanche of truffles; and his warm apple tart. As ever, wine choices perfectly fit the meal at hand.

A classic Parisian waiter's pose.

Buttes-Chaumont, Nation

19th and 20th arrondissements

LES ALLOBROGES
71, rue des Grands-Champs, Paris 20.
Tel: 01.43.73.40.00.
Métro: Maraîchers.
Service 12:30 to 2 P.M. and 8 to 10 P.M.
Closed Sunday, Monday, holidays, two weeks in April, and August.
Credit cards: AE, V.
97- and 174-franc menus.
A la carte, 250 francs.
SPECIALTIES:
Modern bistro: salade mêlée aux herbes "Gérard Vié" au vinaigre de Banyuls (tossed green salad with herbs, dressed with Banyuls vinegar vinaigrette); souris d'agneau braisée et ail confit (braised lamb shank with garlic); poulet de Bresse rôti, gâteau de pommes de terre, sur commande (roasted Bresse chicken with potato cake, by advance order only).

It's a Parisian fashion trend that's grown steadily but surely over the past few years: casual restaurants designed and decorated to make you feel as though you are enjoying the meal in your own dining room. The latest in the crop is Les Allobroges, a truly charming, elegantly comfortable spot near Nation. Here Olivier Pateyron and his wife, Annette, entertain a totally mixed group of diners, offering homey, straightforward modern bistro fare. With room for just thirty, the two small rooms are decorated with tweedy green carpets, milky-white light fixtures, and nicely framed prints of fish, vegetables, and fruits.

The menu offers veritable bargains, with such starters as a soup or a meat terrine, and a main-course salt cod *brandade* or beef with carrots. On my last visit, I feasted on the immense green salad, a tumble of greens that included radicchio, lamb's lettuce, curly endive, chervil, tarragon, and dill all masterfully tossed with a Banyuls vinegar *vinaigrette.* Just as memorable is the *souris d'agneau,* which Pateyron braises for a full four hours until it's pleasantly tender and the thin layer of fat surrounding the muscle has turned a deep, rich mahogany. (I only wish he would be a bit less timid with his seasoning.) One could make a meal of their crisp and chewy rolls, and while the wine list is tiny, it often includes some good buys.

LE RESTAURANT D'ERIC FRECHON
10, rue General-Brunet, Paris 19.
Tel/Fax: 01.40.40.03.30.
Métro: Botzaris or Danube.
Service noon to 2:30 P.M. and 7 to 10:30 P.M.
Closed Sunday, Monday, and August.
Credit card: V.
Air-conditioned.
200-franc menu.
A la carte, 250 to 300 francs.

Figure out what the public wants, then deliver—it's the secret to success in any business. Chef Eric Frechon, of the restaurant that bears his name, has found the key. While most restaurateurs groan about tough economic times, Frechon and his youthful crew turn away people night after night. At first glance, you wouldn't think the odds would be with him: The restaurant is in a lackluster café in northeastern Paris, near the Buttes-Chaumont park. But what keeps the place packed is Frechon's attractive menu, his solid and generous cuisine, and the cheery staff that makes you feel instantly at home. The 200-

SPECIALTIES:
Modern seasonal: crème de haricot coco froide aux croutons dorés (cold white bean soup with golden croûtons); pintade fermière rôtie à l'ail, Charlotte fondante au laurier (roast farm-raised guinea hen with garlic, with tender potatoes with bay leaf); croustillant de pain aux épices, glace à la réglisse (crispy gingerbread with licorice ice cream).

franc menu is a bargain, with food that's up-to-date and prepared with attention and authority.

If it's on the menu, begin with the exquisitely fresh seafood *tartare,* a mix of salmon and oysters finely chopped and evenly blended, served in a pool of mild horseradish cream. Topped with a tiny salad of sparkling fresh chervil and parsley, it's an ideal starter, one that perks up the palate and puts you in the mood for more to come. For a meatier starter, begin with delicate ravioli filled with *foie gras* and served in a rich chicken *bouillon.* The *bouillon* arrives in a giant white soup tureen, allowing you to help yourself to as many servings as your appetite allows. Frechon also prepares a pleasant eggplant *confit* topped with fresh tomato sauce and lightly marinated sardines, as well as generous servings of giant *langoustine* ravioli bathed in a sweet honey sauce.

Hearty main courses include *pigeon en crapaudine,* fowl that's split down the back and flattened, then roasted to a moist perfection and served on a bed of lentils bathed in the cooking juices. Bounteous portions of nuggets of lamb—*noisettes d'agneau*—are bathed in an updated version of the rich *sauce grand veneur* (a traditional reduction of meat juices, currant jelly, and cream) and paired with a smooth, soul-satisfying celery root *mousseline.* Delicate veal is roasted ever so simply, with a touch of salted butter, and served with a robust *gratin* of macaroni topped with a glaze of Parmesan cheese.

Fish is not ignored, and offerings include a huge portion of roasted sea bass, or *bar,* set on a bed of tomato *coulis.* The crusty bread here is delicious. Desserts include a fine, light *mendiant de semoule* (mixed dried fruits and nuts topped with a thick wafer prepared from the crunchy grains of wheat) and a less successful mango tart prepared with underripe fruit.

The wine list includes some decent buys, such as the all-purpose, ever-satisfying Saumur-Champigny Domaine Sébastien Haerty and Coteaux du Languedoc Domaine de l'Hortus "Grande Cuvée."

Restaurants: An Alphabetical Listing (with arrondissements)

A

L'Affriolé, 7th

Alcazar, 6th

Allard, 6th

Les Allobroges, 20th

L'Alsaco, 9th

Ambassade d'Auvergne, 3rd

Les Ambassadeurs, 8th

L'Ambroisie, 4th

L'Ami Louis, 3rd

Café d'Angel, 17th

Apicius, 17th

L'Appart', 8th

L'Ardoise, 1st

Arpège, 7th

L'Assiette, 14th

Astier, 11th

Le Restaurant de l'Astor, 8th

B

Balzar, 5th

Baracane–Bistrot de l'Oulette, 4th

Le Bar au Sel, 7th

Au Bascou, 3rd

La Bastide d'Odéon, 6th

Benoit, 4th

Bofinger, 4th

Au Bon Accueil, 7th

Au Bon Saint-Pourçain, 6th

Les Bookinistes, 6th

Les Bouchons de François Clerc, 5th

Bouillon Racine, 6th

La Butte Chaillot, 16th

C

La Cagouille, 14th

Le Caméléon, 6th

Au C'Amelot, 11th

Cap Vernet, 8th

Carré des Feuillants, 1st

Cartet, 11th

Aux Charpentiers, 6th

Le Clos Morillons, 15th

La Closerie des Lilas, 6th

Il Cortile, 1st

La Coupole, 14th

D

Dame Jeanne, 11th

Le Dôme, 14th

Bistrot du Dôme, 14th

Bistrot du Dôme Bastille, 4th

Le Duc, 14th

Alain Ducasse, 16th

E

Les Elysées du Vernet, 8th

L'Epi Dupin, 6th

Erawan, 15th

Bistro de l'Etoile/ Lauriston, 16th

F

Brasserie Flo, 10th

La Fontaine de Mars, 7th

Brasserie les Fontaines, 5th

Restaurant d'Eric Frechon, 19th

G

Pierre Gagnaire, 8th

Chez Georges, 2nd

Les Gourmets des Ternes, 8th

Chez Gramond, 6th

Le Grand Véfour, 1st

Le Grizzli, 4th

I

Brasserie de l'Ile Saint-Louis, 4th

Issé, 2nd

J

Jamin, 16th

Julien, 10th

K

Kim-Anh, 15th

L

Lac Hong, 16th

Laurent, 8th

Lescure, 1st

Brasserie Lipp, 6th

M

Maceo, 1st

Chez Maître Paul, 6th

Mansouria, 11th

Mavrommatis, 5th

Chez Michel, 10th

Paul Minchelli, 7th

Miravile, 4th

Moissonnier, 5th

Monsieur Lapin, 14th

Au Moulin à Vent (Chez Henri), 5th

O

L'O à la Bouche, 6th

Les Olivades, 7th

L'Oulette, 12th

P

Restaurant du Palais Royal, 1st

Le Palanquin, 6th

Le Petit Marguery, 13th

Le Petit Plat, 15th

Au Pied de Cochon, 1st

Pierre au Palais Royal, 1st

Pile ou Face, 2nd

Port Alma, 16th

Brasserie de la Poste, 16th

Le Pré Catelan, 16th

Auberge Pyrénées-Cévennes, 11th

R

Chez René, 5th

Romantica, Clichy

Michel Rostang, 17th

Café Runtz, 2n

S

Guy Savoy, 17th

A Sousceyrac, 11th

Le Square Trousseau, 12th

T

La Table d'Aude, 6th

La Table de Fès, 6th

Taillevent, 8th

Tan Dinh, 7th

La Tour de Montlhéry (Chez Denise), 1st

Au Trou Gascon, 12th

V

Vaudeville, 2nd

Jules Verne, 7th

Chez la Vieille (Chez Adrienne), 1st

Le Violin d'Ingres, 7th

Z

Les Zygomates, 12th

La Zygotissoire, 11th

Restaurants Listed by Arrondissements

Palais-Royal, Les Halles, Tuileries
1st arrondissement

L'Ardoise

Carré des Feuillants

Il Cortile

Le Grand Véfour

Lescure

Maceo

Restaurant du Palais-Royal

Au Pied de Cochon

Pierre au Palais Royal

La Tour de Montlhéry (Chez Denise)

Chez La Vieille (Chez Adrienne)

Opéra, Bourse
2nd arrondissement

Chez Georges

Issé

Pile ou Face

Café Runtz

Vaudeville

Rambuteau, Temple, Arts et Métiers
3rd arrondissement

Ambassade d'Auvergne

L'Ami Louis

Au Bascou

Le Marais, Hôtel de Ville, Ile Saint-Louis
4th arrondissement

L'Ambroisie

Baracane–Bistrot de l'Oulette

Benoit

Bofinger

Bistrot du Dôme Bastille

Le Grizzli

Brasserie de l'Ile Saint-Louis

Miravile

Latin Quarter
5th arrondissement

Balzar

Les Bouchons de François Clerc

Brasserie les Fontaines

Mavrommatis

Moissonnier

Au Moulin à Vent (Chez Henri)

Chez René

Saint-Germain des Prés, Luxembourg, Odéon, Montparnasse
6th arrondissement

Alcazar

Allard

La Bastide d'Odéon

Au Bon Saint-Pourçain

Les Bookinistes

Bouillon Racine

Le Caméléon

Aux Charpentiers

La Closerie des Lilas

L'Epi Dupin

Chez Gramond

Brasserie Lipp

Chez Maître Paul

L'O à la Bouche

Le Palanquin

La Table d'Aude

La Table de Fès

Faubourg Saint-Germain, Invalides, Ecole Militaire
7th arrondissement

L'Affriolé

Arpège

Le Bar au Sel

Au Bon Accueil

La Fontaine de Mars

Paul Minchelli

Les Olivades

Tan Dinh

Jules Verne

Le Violin d'Ingres

Madeleine, Saint-Lazare, Champs-Elysées, Place des Ternes
8th arrondissement

Les Ambassadeurs

L'Appart'

Le Restaurant de l'Astor

Cap Vernet

Les Elysées du Vernet

Pierre Gagnaire

Les Gourmets des Ternes

Laurent

Taillevent

Gare de l'Est, Gare du Nord, République
9th and 10th arrondissements

L'Alsaco

Brasserie Flo

Julien

Chez Michel

Bastille, République
11th arrondissement

Astier

Au C'Amelot

Cartet

Dame Jeanne

Mansouria

Auberge Pyrénées–Cévennes

A Sousceyrac

La Zygotissoire

Gare de Lyon, Bastille, Nation, Place d'Italie
12th and 13th arrondissements

L'Oulette

Le Petit Marguery

Le Square Trousseau

Au Trou Gascon

Les Zygomates

Denfert-Rochereau, Porte d'Orléans, Montparnasse
14th arrondissement

L'Assiette

La Cagouille

La Coupole

Le Dôme

Bistrot du Dôme

Le Duc

Monsieur Lapin

Grenelle, Convention
15th arrondissement

Le Clos Morillons

Erawan

Kim-Anh

Le Petit Plat

Trocadéro, Victor-Hugo, Bois de Boulogne
16th arrondissement

La Butte Chaillot

Alain Ducasse

Bistro de l'Etoile/ Lauriston

Jamin

Lac Hong

Port Alma

Brasserie de la Poste

Le Pré Catelan

Clichy, Ternes, Wagram, Etoile
17th arrondissement and Clichy

Café d'Angel

Apicius

Romantica

Michel Rostang

Guy Savoy

Buttes-Chaumont, Nation
19th and 20th arrondissements

Les Allobroges

Restaurant d'Eric Frechon

Cafés
CAFES

Au Petit Fer à Cheval (*see entry, page 149*).

It is impossible to imagine Paris without its cafés. Parisians are sun worshippers, and the attraction of an outdoor sidewalk stopping place perfectly suits their inclination. Sometime around the first week of February, sunshine or not, café doors open wide, chairs and tables tumble out, and the season begins. The city has some 12,000 cafés varying in size, grandeur, and significance. As diverse as Parisians themselves, the cafés serve as an extension of the French living room, a place to start and end the day, to gossip and debate, a place for seeing and being seen.

No book on Paris literary, artistic, or social life is complete without details of café life, noting who sat where, when, and with whom—and what they drank. One wonders how writers and artists accomplished as much as they did if they really whiled away all those hours at sidewalk tables sipping *café au lait,* Vichy water, and *ballons* of Beaujolais.

When did it start? The café billed as the oldest in Paris is Le Procope, opened in 1686 by a Sicilian, Francesco Procopio dei Coltelli, the man credited with turning France into a coffee-drinking society. He was one of the first men granted the privilege of distilling and selling wines, liqueurs, *eaux-de-vie,* coffee, tea, and chocolate, with a status equal to a baker or butcher. Le Procope attracted Paris's political and literary elite, and its past is filled with history. It has been reported that it was there that Voltaire drank forty cups of his favorite brew each day: a blend of coffee and chocolate, which some credit with inspiring his spontaneous wit. When Benjamin Franklin died in 1790 and the French assembly went into mourning for three days, Le Procope was entirely draped in black in honor of France's favorite American. Even the young Napoleon Bonaparte spent time at Le Procope: When still an artillery officer, he was forced to leave his hat as security while he went out in search of money to pay for his coffee. Le Procope still exists at the original address, 13, rue de l'Ancienne Comédie, but as a restaurant, not a café.

By the end of the 18th century, all of Paris was intoxicated with coffee and the city supported some 700 cafés. These were like all-male clubs, with many serving as centers of political life and discussion. It is no surprise to find that one of the speeches that precipitated the fall of the Bastille took place outside the Café Foy at the Palais-Royal.

By the 1840s the number of Paris cafés had grown to 3,000. The men who congregated and set the tenor of the times included journalists, playwrights, and writers who became known as *boulevardiers.* Certain cafés did have special rooms reserved for women, but in 1916 a law was passed that prohibited serving women sitting alone on the terraces of those along the boulevards.

Around the turn of the century, the sidewalk cafés along boulevard du Montparnasse—Le Dôme, La Rotonde, and later, La Coupole—became the stronghold of artists; those along boulevard Saint-Germain—Les Deux Magots, Flore, and Lipp—were the watering holes and meeting halls for the literary. When the "lost generation" of expatriates arrived in Paris after World War I, they established themselves along both boulevards, drinking, talking, arguing, and writing.

Cafés still serve as picture windows for observing contemporary life. The people you see today at Les Deux Magots, Café de Flore, and Lipp may not be the great artists of the past, but faces worth watching just the same. Linger a bit and you will see that the Paris stereotypes are alive and well: the surly waiters and red-eyed Frenchmen inhaling Gitanes; old men in navy berets; *clochardes* (bag ladies) hauling Monoprix shopping bags holding all their earthly possessions; ultra-thin, bronzed women with hair dyed bright orange; and schoolchildren decked out in blue and white seersucker, sharing an afternoon chocolate with mother.

If you know how to nurse a beer or coffee for hours, café-sitting can be one of the city's best buys. No matter how crowded a café may be, waiters will respect your graceful loafing and won't insist that you order another round just to hold the table. Drinks are usually less expensive if you are willing to stand at the bar. At mealtime, if you see a table covered with a cloth or even a little paper placemat, that means the table is reserved for dining. If it is bare, you are welcome to sit and just have a drink. Note that the service charge is automatically added to all café bills, so you are required to pay only the final total and need not leave an additional tip, although most people leave any loose change.

Les Halles, Pont Neuf, Tuileries, Louvre

1st arrondissement

LE COCHON A L'OREILLE
15, rue Montmartre,
Paris 1.
Tel: 01.42.36.07.56.
Métro: Les Halles.
Open 7 A.M. to 5 P.M. (8 A.M. to 7 P.M. Saturday).
Hot meals at lunch only.
Closed Sunday.

This is the most beautiful workingman's bar in Paris. It houses great murals, fresh flowers on the tiny bistro tables, workers in blue overalls five deep at the zinc bar, and peanut shells on the floor. If you happen to be up and about at 7 A.M., you may want to toss back a few drinks with the local merchants, who still keep this end of Les Halles busy in the early morning hours.

COLETTE
213, rue Saint-Honoré,
Paris 1.
Tel: 01.55.35.33.90.
Métro: Tuileries.
Open 10:30 A.M. to 7:30 P.M.
Closed Sunday.
Credit cards: AE, DC, V.

Colette is a stark, modern, multifaceted shop devoted to style, design, art, and food—carrying everything from digital cameras to Philippe Starck sunglasses to electric bicycles. The downstairs café is a model of purity, all in crisp white and deep blue, and features quick snacks, great bread, a good wine list, and a water bar that features some sixty-nine bottled waters, including *la plus kitsch* Italian Aqua della Madonna as well as the ultra-pure French Chateldon. (Even the café's refined modern glassware and plates, from the contemporary Parisian design company Tse & Tse, are for sale.)

LE FUMOIR
Place du Louvre
6, rue de l'Amiral-Coligny,
Paris 1.
Tel: 01.42.92.00.24.
Métro: Louvre-Rivoli.
Open daily, 11 A.M. to 2 A.M.
Hot meals served all day.

This modern, hip, you-could-be-anywhere café—Eastern Europe, Indochina, America in the 1930s—is the kind of place you are happy to be in while reading the paper early in the morning or enjoying a light and imaginative lunch at midday. With its vast picture windows overlooking the Louvre and the gardens of the Eglise Saint Germain l'Auxerrois, the place is airy, beautifully lit, and just a bit funky. The staff is largely Asian, there are cozy leather chairs for lounging or chatting, and the food is an eclectic mix with a bent toward the modern, sometimes strange. On my last visit on a cold summer's day, the warm salad of sliced grilled potatoes layered with a ton of parsley and chunks of good, earthy beets hit the spot. Also excellent was the goat cheese *lasagne*—a layered mix of sliced warm potatoes, rounds of pasta, goat cheese, and chopped greens. I didn't have the courage or the desire to try the mashed potatoes mixed with avocado and watercress, which is served with the daily chicken special.

LE CAFE MARLY
Palais du Louvre
93, rue de Rivoli,
Paris 1.
Tel: 01.49.26.06.60.
Métro: Palais Royal–Musée du Louvre.
Open daily, 9 A.M. to 2 A.M.
Terrace.
Air-conditioned.

Grand cafés remain Paris's forte, and as soon as it opened in 1994, Parisians made Café Marly the meeting spot of the city center. It doesn't hurt that this homey-elegant Napoleon III café looks out on both I. M. Pei's glass pyramid in the Louvre's main courtyard and the stunning skylit interior Cour Richelieu, part of the massive renovation of the museum. Almost all year round there are tables that spill out onto the Louvre terrace. Come for a single cup of bracing espresso, a platter of roast chicken, or a wedge of Camembert, enjoy the soft classical music, and take in the clever blend of old and new architecture. The bathrooms rate an architectural award of their own.

The Café Marly, in the shadow of I. M. Pei's glass pyramid.

"I was often alone, but seldom lonely: I enjoyed the newspapers and books that were my usual companions at table, the exchanges with waiters, barmen, booksellers, street vendors . . . the sounds of the conversations of others around me, and finally, the talk of the girls I ended some evenings by picking up."
—*A. J. Liebling*

Cafés—home to conversation and romance.

UN CAFE, S'IL VOUS PLAIT

Cafés are, of course, for more than just coffee. Although café fare has not changed drastically since the early days, food, like fashion, goes in and out of style. During the 19th century, one popular drink was *fond de culotte* ("seat of your pants"), so named since supposedly it could be drunk only while sitting down. It was a mixture of gentian liqueur and *crème de Cassis.* During the same period, other popular drinks included the *mêle-Cassis,* half Cassis and half Cognac; the *bicyclette,* a blend of Champagne and vermouth; and the *pompier,* or "fireman," a blend of vermouth and Cassis.

Today, coffee, beer, and anise-flavored *pastis* are the staple drinks, along with various fruit juices sweetened with sugar. The *croque-monsieur*—a ham sandwich topped with grated cheese, then grilled—and the *sandwich mixte*—a thickly buttered baguette filled with Gruyère cheese and thin slices of *jambon de Paris*—are favorite café snacks. For larger meals, there are often meaty *plats du jour,* pork *rillettes,* pâtés, platters of raw vegetables known as *crudités, salade niçoise,* and even hot dogs.

Coffee and other hot drinks come in many forms. This small glossary should help you order what you want.

Café noir or *café express:* plain black espresso

Double express: a double espresso

Café serré: extra-strong espresso, made with half the normal amount of water

Café allongé: weak espresso, often served with a small pitcher of hot water so clients may thin the coffee themselves

Café au lait or *café crème:* espresso with warmed or lightly steamed milk

Grand crème: large or double espresso with milk

Décaféiné or *déca:* decaffeinated espresso

Café filtre: filtered American-style coffee (not available at all cafés)

Chocolat chaud: hot chocolate

Infusion: herb tea

Thé nature, thé citron, thé au lait: plain tea, tea with lemon, tea with milk

LE PAIN QUOTIDIEN
18, place du Marché Saint Honoré,
Paris 1.
Tel: 01.42.96.31.70.
Métro: Tuileries.
Open daily, 7 A.M. to 8 P.M.

How many ways are there to eat breakfast? Le Pain Quotidien—"Daily Bread"—shows you how many. This Belgian import, with its clean wooden tables, ivory bowls for coffee and chocolate, and fabulous assortment of fresh breads and rolls, offers a stunning view of the new Marché Saint Honoré, with its all-glass building reflecting the charming old structures that surround the square. Try their substantive, wheaty *baguettes à l'ancienne,* great rounds of country bread, and tiny rye and raisin rolls served with a huge tray filled with honeys, jams, and jellies to sweeten the day. Newspapers are there for the asking. Service is friendly if a bit distracted. As the day wears on, the menu also moves on, to a selection of *tartines,* or open-face sandwiches, such as mountain ham; beef, basil, and Parmesan; country *terrine;* a mix of goat cheese and honey; or delicate *fromage blanc,* radishes, and onions. Of course Le Pain Quotidien is also a full-fledged bakery, so stop in for a loaf any time of the day.

ALCOHOLIC DRINKS

Calvados: apple brandy

Marc de Bourgogne: pronounced "mar," an *eau-de-vie* distilled from pressed grape skins and seeds

Pippermint Get: bright green alcoholic mint drink

Cidre: hard apple cider

TOUPARY
La Samaritaine department store
2, quai du Louvre,
Paris 1.
Tel: 01.40.41.29.29.
Métro: Pont Neuf.
Café open 9:30 A.M. to 7 P.M. (to 10 P.M. Tuesday).
Restaurant open 11:45 A.M. to 3 P.M. and 7:30 to 11:30 P.M.
Tea salon open 3:30 to 6 P.M.
Closed Sunday.

The popular slogan of this well-known department store is *"On Trouve Tout à La Samaritaine."* That "everything" includes one of the most spectacular views of the Paris cityscape from its combination café, restaurant, and *salon de thé.* Visit on a sunny afternoon, order up a *citron pressé* (lemonade) or a beer, and relax before or after a visit to this mammoth, and confusing, department store. The welcome here is nonexistent and the food not much, but the view is well worth the price of admission. To find Toupary (get it?), go to the fifth floor of Magasin 2 and follow the signs.

Chatelet, Marais, Ile Saint-Louis

4th arrondissement

CAFE BEAUBOURG
100, rue Saint-Martin,
Paris 4.
Tel: 01.48.87.63.96
Métro: Châtelet.
Open daily, 8 A.M. to 1 A.M. (to 2 A.M. Friday and Saturday).
Credit cards: AE, DC, V.

The modern double-decker Café Beaubourg overlooks the circus-like atmosphere of the Centre Pompidou museum plaza, which year-round is filled with bagpipe players, guitarists, actors, and fat men who sit on beds of nails. Yet if you spend a few moments at one of the upstairs tables, you'll realize that the ultra-modern Café Beaubourg fills an age-old Parisian need, for cafés are places where you can be alone in public. Look around and you'll see table after table filled with lone individuals—puffing on a cigarette, drinking a beer, writing, reading, or carefully perfecting the art of doing nothing. And while at first glance the Café Beaubourg's décor is jarring—the adjectives that come to mind are giant, cold, overmodern—the place works. The huge metal armchairs are surprisingly comfortable, the double-decker setting offers room to breathe in a neighborhood that can be utterly stifling, and the train-station voluminosity serves to shelter us, and separate us, from the world just outside the door. Food here is an afterthought: The generous *crudités* platter is fine, but sandwiches tend to be dreadfully dry. This can be remedied if you order a tomato salad on the side and create your own sort of city picnic, a great choice on a rainy day when the colors of the brightly clothed crowd below jump out at you beneath the sobering gray sky.

LA BELLE HORTENSE
31, rue Vieille du Temple,
Paris 4.
Tel: 01.48.04.71.60.
Fax: 01.42.74.59.70.
Métro: Saint-Paul or Hôtel de Ville.
Open daily 5 P.M. to 2 A.M. (1 P.M. to 2 A.M. Saturday and Sunday).

This charming spot—with a beautiful front bar and cozy little rooms in the back—is one of the new wave of "literary" cafés, or spots that double as bookstores, with soft and cushy places to sit while you sip a glass of wine or an apéritif. Right across the street from Au Petit Fer à Cheval (page 149), this spot is open only in late afternoons and evenings. It's a great place to meet friends for a drink and a bit of ambience before dinner.

A BIT OF PARISIAN COFFEE HISTORY

When Louix XIV first tasted coffee in 1664, he was not impressed. But Parisian high society fell in love with the intoxicating brew, enjoying it at lavish and exotic private parties arranged by the Turkish ambassador, who arrived in 1669.

By 1670, the general public got a taste of the rich caffeinated drink when an Armenian named Pascal hawked it at the Saint-Germain fair in the spring. He hired formally dressed waiters to go out among the crowds and through the streets, crying as they went, *"Café. Café."* Later Pascal opened a little coffee boutique like those he had seen in Constantinople. It was not a smashing success, but he survived with the help of his wandering waiters, who even went door to door with jugs of the thick black brew. Their only competition was *"le Candiot,"* a cripple who sold coffee in the streets of Paris for a meager two *sous,* sugar included.

Then, as now, doctors discussed the merits and drawbacks of coffee. Those who favored the drink argued that it cured scurvy, relieved smallpox and gout, and was even recommended for gargling, to improve the voice. *Café au lait* was lauded for its medicinal qualities, and in 1688, Madame de Sévigné, whose letters record the life of the period, noted it as a remedy for colds and chest illness.

By the time the city's first café, Le Procope, opened in 1686, coffee was well on its way to winning the Parisian palate.

Au Petit Fer à Cheval (see entry, facing page), a place for coffee and classical music.

MA BOURGOGNE
19, place des Vosges,
Paris 4.
Tel: 01.42.78.44.64.
Métro: Saint-Paul.
Open daily, 8 A.M. to 1 A.M.
Closed February and the first week of March.
No credit cards.

The most active café/wine bar in the Marais, Ma Bourgogne is set under the arcades of the oldest square in the city. Sit outdoors on the traditional beige and red rattan chairs, absorbing the beauty of the architecture dating back to 1407. The café is calm in the morning and packed with local office workers at lunchtime. The *pommes frites* are not bad—just ask for them *bien cuites* (well cooked). Come for simple café standbys like salads, a glass of wine, or a bowl of Berthillon ice cream; the more complicated restaurant fare is expensive and unexceptional. Writer Georges Simenon's inspector

Maigret spent a lot of time here, perhaps inspecting the varied clientèle, which ranges from old locals to tourists to the chic young residents of one of Paris's most sought-after addresses.

LE FLORE EN L'ILE
42, quai d'Orléans,
Paris 4.
Tel: 01.43.29.88.27.
Métro: Pont Marie.
Open daily, 8 A.M. to 2 A.M.
Hot meals served continuously until 1 A.M.
Credit card: V.

This combination café/restaurant/tea salon on the Ile Saint-Louis has expanded to offer a sidewalk terrace, where they serve extravagant Berthillon ice cream sundaes along with the original café menu. Le Flore en l'Ile offers fun and easy food to snack: good but not great salads, *crêpes,* sandwiches, and tarts. But who can complain about the breathtaking view of Notre Dame? Inside, settle in at one of the marble-topped tables and enjoy the good *café crème* served in silver pitchers. Le Flore en l'Ile is cozy in blustery weather, when you can gaze out the window at the willow trees swaying around Notre Dame and warm yourself with a pot of freshly brewed hot tea. On weekends it's packed with tourists and Parisians who go for a Parisian-style brunch: *croissants, café au lait,* fresh-squeezed orange juice, *oeufs brouillés* (scrambled eggs), and, unfortunately, cold toast. Ask for a *baguette* instead.

AU PETIT FER A CHEVAL
30, rue Vieille du Temple,
Paris 4.
Tel: 01.42.72.47.47.
Métro: Hôtel de Ville.
Open daily 7 A.M. to 2 A.M.
Hot meals served all day.
Credit card: V.

This tiny, popular, and super-trendy neighborhood café dates back to 1903, when the Combes family opened it as the Café de Brésil. Today the café still boasts a fabulous marble-topped horseshoe (*fer à cheval*) bar, mirrored walls, and the original patchwork tile floor. The *patron* has embellished the room a bit but retained a feeling of authenticity by adding another mirror, a giant chandelier, and shelves of glass and brick. The coffee here is delicious, and this is one rare café that serves up a glass of ice water to go with it. The back room, always packed at lunchtime, boasts a giant Métro map and booths made up of old wooden Métro seats.

It's better to come during the day to enjoy the old-fashioned ambience, the eccentric waiters, and the good café fare. Blackboards indicate the daily specials, including the delicious *fer à cheval* salad of warm goat's milk cheese drizzled with olive oil on Poilâne toast with fresh salad greens. In the evening, the crowd is three-deep at the bar and there's a free table once in a blue moon.

Latin Quarter, Luxembourg, Saint-Germain, Sevres-Babylone, Quai d'Orsay

5th, 6th, and 7th arrondissements

LES DEUX MAGOTS
170, boulevard Saint-Germain,
Paris 6.
Tel: 01.45.48.55.25.
Métro: Saint-Germain des Prés.
Open daily, 7:30 A.M. to 2 A.M. (Last orders taken at 1:30 A.M.)
Closed the second week in January.
Credit cards: AE, V.

Les Deux Magots.

At least two mornings a week and many times at lunch, I stop either here or at the next-door rival, Café de Flore. I have developed my own habits, much like other habitués of these two landmark cafés. I leave it to you to visit and decide. I prefer the wide expansive terrace of Les Deux Magots, where one can sit in the shadow of Paris's oldest church, Saint-Germain des Prés. I also think that, outdoors at least, the waiters are just a little friendlier than those at Flore. Also—I know this is a small thing to some but it's big to me—the waiters at Flore carry plastic trays while the waiters at Deux Magots carry metal ones. It is, after all, a question of aesthetics. The food is also a bit better here. If you go for lunch or a snack, order the hearty *crottin chaud pain Poilâne,* which is weirdly listed in the cheese section on the menu. You will find a giant center slice of toasted Poilâne bread topped with two ready-to-melt halves of goat cheese that you spread all the way out to the edges of the bread when it arrives. All is set on a bed of often too-oily salad greens. But it's a meal all on its own.

Any time of day, this is the ultimate Paris café, great for observing the current fashion scene and restoring yourself with a steaming cup of good hot chocolate on a chilly afternoon. The menu boasts more than twenty-five different whiskies, and coffee is still served in thick white cups. In spring and summer, Les Deux Magots offers one of Saint-Germain des Prés' most appealing and expansive terraces, while the interior is calm and appealing, with its mahogany-red banquettes and brass-edged tables, walls of mirrors, and waiters attired in long aprons and neat black vests. You can sit under the famous wooden statues of the two Chinese dignitaries—the *deux magots* who gave their name to the café. (The café's name does not, as some writers have suggested, translate as "two maggots"!)

CAFE DE FLORE
172, boulevard Saint-Germain, Paris 6.
Tel: 01.45.48.55.26.
Métro: Saint-Germain des Prés.
Open daily, 7 A.M. to 1:30 A.M.
Credit cards: AE, V.

I prefer the Café de Flore indoors (I find the outdoor terrace too constricting, with all the traffic noise of the boulevard), where one can sit unbothered all afternoon long with a single cup of coffee, reading a fine novel or catching up on the news. It of course rivals Les Deux Magots next door and was always the more literary hangout, popular with Sartre, Simone de Beauvoir, and Albert Camus. During the Occupation, many of the cafés in the Montparnasse area were full of German soldiers, so the Parisians preferred the cafés along the boulevard Saint-Germain. They also liked Café de Flore because it had a small stove to keep them warm. After the war many artists returned to the Montparnasse cafés, but Picasso came to Flore every night, where he sat at the second table in front of the main door, sipping a glass of mineral water and chatting with his Spanish friends. Little has changed since, except the clientèle, which is very high class and Left Bank, making this fertile people-watching ground. There's still the simple, classic Art Deco interior: red banquettes, walls of mahogany and mirrors, and

Café de Flore.

a large sign suggesting that while pipe smoking is not forbidden, *"l'odeur de certains tabacs de pipe parfumés incommode la plupart de nos clients."* In other words, "courteous clients don't smoke pipes here." The Flore serves excellent coffee and good pastries.

CAFE DES HAUTEURS
Musée d'Orsay
1, rue de Bellechasse,
Paris 7.
Tel: 01.45.49.42.33.
Métro: Solférino or RER Musée d'Orsay.
Open 10 A.M. to 5 P.M.
Closed Monday.

How many cafés—anywhere in the world—can boast of Toulouse-Lautrec murals on the wall and a view of the white domes of Sacré-Coeur in the distance? The rooftop café of the Musée d'Orsay (a lively museum fashioned out of a 19th-century railroad station) is one of the finest spots for viewing the city. The café is situated right next to the museum's famed Impressionist collection, and through chunks of glass cut around a mammoth railway clock, one views a vast expanse of the cityscape, looking out over the slow-moving Seine, across to the Tuileries Gardens, and on beyond to the hills of Montmartre. In good weather one can relax on the small outdoor terrace. Well worth the museum entry fee (about 40 francs).

POPULAR APERITIFS

Absinthe, the highly alcoholic anise-flavored drink invented by a Frenchman in 1797, was banned in 1915 because of its harmful effects on the nerves. It was quickly replaced by another popular though less dangerous drink, *pastis,* which has much in common with absinthe but is lower in alcohol. Wormwood, the ingredient that caused absinthe to be banned, is omitted.

Pastis: anise-seed-flavored aperitif that becomes cloudy when water is added (the most famous brands are Pernod and Ricard)

Suze: bitter liqueur distilled from the root of the yellow mountain gentian

Picon and *Mandarin:* bitter orange-flavored drinks

Pineau des Charentes: sweet fortified wine from the Cognac region

Kir: dry white wine mixed with *crème de Cassis* (black currant liqueur)

Kir royal: Champagne mixed with *crème de Cassis*

BRASSERIE LIPP
151, boulevard Saint-Germain,
Paris 6.
Tel: 01.45.48.53.91.
Métro: Saint-Germain des Prés.
Open daily, 8 A.M. to 2 A.M. Restaurant service from noon to 1 A.M.
Closed mid-July to mid-August.

The terrace of this Left Bank institution is a bit airless, but if you need a Lipp fix, stop in any time of day for a coffee or a snack of ham or cheese, and read your well-thumbed Hemingway. (See also Restaurants.)

CAFE DE LA MAIRIE
8, place Saint-Sulpice,
Paris 6.
Tel: 01.43.26.67.82
Métro: Saint-Sulpice.
Open 7 A.M. to 2 A.M.
Closed Sunday.
No credit cards.

An all-time favorite Parisian café terrace, this rambling expanse of wicker chairs and marble-topped tables faces the shady trees and roaring-lion fountain of the pretty Place Saint-Sulpice. The interior of the Café de la Mairie is nothing special, but on lazy summer afternoons, just settle into one of the chairs, sip a *citron pressé,* and watch *le tout* Rive Gauche walk by: mothers rolling their silver-wheeled navy prams to the nearby Luxembourg Gardens, chic women decked out in the latest Left Bank fashions, editors from the neighboring publishing houses, and a lively mix of students. Come early in the morning after picking up a *croissant* or a *pain au chocolat* from nearby Gérard Mulot (76, rue de Seine) to enjoy a frothy *café crème* and the calm of the city as it wrestles from its slumber. If you're lucky, you might catch a glimpse of Catherine Deneuve, who lives on the *place.* For a quick lunch, order up a *croque monsieur Provençal* (toasted ham, cheese, and a slice of tomato). Slather it with spicy mustard, and enjoy the shade of the plane trees. (In cooler weather, tuck into the tiny upstairs dining room, where smoking is truly forbidden and the view just as spectacular.)

CAFE MOUFFETARD
116, rue Mouffetard,
Paris 5.
Tel: 01.43.31.42.50.
Métro: Censier Daubenton.
Open 7 A.M. to 8:30 P.M.
Closed Sunday afternoon and Monday.

Nothing has changed here in twenty years. The big sign outside reads *"Brasserie"* in bold burgundy lettering, but this rather earthy little spot set right in the middle of the busy rue Mouffetard market is actually one of the homier cafés in Paris. A smoky little workers' hangout, it was brought to my attention by my friend Martha Rose Shulman, who was lured here by the homemade pastries, dense and buttery *croissants,* and delicious, almost creamy *brioches.* This is a rare café where the *patron* and his wife make their own *croissants* and *brioches,* as well as delicious whole-wheat half-*baguettes,* working through the night so the market workers will have something fresh and warm to sustain them through a long morning's labor. In wintertime, they also make little *chaussons aux pommes* and hot apple tarts, perfect for eating with a giant *café crème.*

LE NEMROD
51, rue du Cherche-Midi,
Paris 6.
Tel: 01.45.48.17.05.
Métro: Sèvres-Babylone.
Open 6:30 A.M. to 11 P.M. (to 8:30 P.M. Saturday).
Closed Sunday and three weeks in August.

Le Nemrod is a rambling corner café not far from the Bon Marché department store and serves as a *cantine,* or mealtime meeting spot, for the neighborhood. Food, service, and wine are above par here, for owners Richard and Michel Bonal are more attentive than most café owners. Their morning *croissants* come from Peltier around the corner (see Pastry Shops), they offer an assortment of cold sandwiches on Poilâne bread, and the ice cream comes from famed Berthillon (see Ice Cream Worth Waiting For, page 228). Best of all, you'll find wines selected with care, such as Thevenet's Morgon, *cru* Beaujolais, served out of clear glass *carafes.* Salads are good and copious, including a fine *salade Auvergnate,* chock-full of walnuts, Cantal cheese, country ham, and greens.

LA PALETTE
43, rue de Seine,
Paris 6.
Tel: 01.43.26.68.15.
Métro: Mabillon, Odéon, or Saint-Germain des Prés.
Open 8 A.M. to 2 A.M. Hot meals served at lunch until 3:30 P.M.
Closed Sunday, one week in February, and three weeks in August.
No credit cards.

Before or after a visit to this landmark café, wander up and down the rue de Seine to admire the art galleries that line this famous street: It is as good as a museum visit, with many works by Picasso, Braque, Miró, Giacometti, Bacon, Balthus, and Hockney on view. La Palette remains a picturesque hangout. Even though it is a stone's throw from Les Deux Magots and Café Flore, the clientèle is totally different: fewer tourists, more locals. The food is not worth mentioning, and service varies from "happy to see you today" to nonexistent. But go in the springtime when the cherry trees are in bloom, and you will feel as though you are in the center of the world. Don't forget to take a look inside to admire the brightly painted murals.

Champs-Elysees

8th arrondissement

LE FOUQUET'S
99, avenue des Champs-Elysées,
Paris 8.
Tel: 01.47.23.70.60.
Métro: George V.
Open daily, 8 A.M. to 2 A.M.
Credit cards: AE, DC, V.

This is one of the most popular Right Bank cafés, perfect for observing the ever-changing scene on the Champs-Elysées. Le Fouquet's is always making society news, as starlets and journalists talk and write about their rendezvous here. James Joyce used to dine at Le Fouquet's almost every night, and today well-known French chef Paul Bocuse stops in whenever he's in town. Most people don't come for the scene or the food, but to grab a snack before or after viewing one of the dozens of films playing at movie houses along the avenue. Sexism lives at Le Fouquet's, where a sign warns, *"Les dames seules ne sont pas admises au bar"* ("Women who are alone are not allowed at the bar"). The management insists that the sign, which has been up at the seven-stool bar since the restaurant opened at the turn of the century, was put there to protect women, not insult them. Most women see it otherwise. Incidentally, Le Fouquet's is pronounced to rhyme with "bets" not "bays," a remnant of the fashionable fascination with English early in the century.

BAR DES THEATRES
6, avenue Montaigne,
Paris 8.
Tel: 01.47.23.34.63.
Métro: Alma-Marceau.
Open daily, 6 A.M. to 2 A.M.
Credit cards: AE, V.

Bar des Théâtres is one of those all-purpose cafés where one could take breakfast, lunch, and dinner, should one desire. With its paper tablecloths and friendly waiters, this is a rare no-frills oasis in the highest-rent district in Paris. If you do too much people watching—overly slim and beautiful models are always prancing past on their way to and from the fashion houses—you may lose your appetite for the simple, solid café fare, including sandwiches and salads served in an atmosphere that's pure bustle, pure Paris. At various times I've feasted on platters of fresh oysters, sizzling snails, a giant *salade niçoise,* thick slabs of rosy lamb with mounds of white beans, and fruity *sorbets.* A place that's been around since 1948: in other words, tried and true.

BASTILLE, OBERKAMPF

11th arrondissement

CAFE BA-TA-CLAN
50, boulevard Voltaire,
Paris 11.
Tel: 01.49.23.96.33.
Métro: Saint-Ambroise.
Open daily, 7 A.M. to 2 A.M.
Credit card: V.

Sitting on the terrace or seated inside this bright, cheery café, you feel as though you are in the right place. The Ba-Ta-Clan overlooks a sea of greenery along the boulevard Voltaire, and whether you are sipping a coffee on one of the cream wicker café chairs on the terrace or curled up reading a can't-put-it-down novel in one of the old leather chairs inside, you will feel instantly at home. The food here is good, too: Try the copious *croque montagnarde,* a thin slice of toasted Poilâne bread layered with country ham, chunks of potato, melted Cantal cheese from the Auvergne, and melted Reblochon from the Savoie. The sandwich comes with a green salad and tomatoes. On Sunday, there is a "musical brunch" from 2 to 5 P.M.

Ba-Ta-Clan—one of the newest and most vibrant cafés on the Paris scene.

BEER

Beer *(bière)* comes in many sizes and can be ordered by the bottle, *bouteille,* or on tap, *à la pression.*

Demi—8 ounces (25 centiliters)

Sérieux—16 ounces (50 centiliters)

Formidable—1 quart (1 liter)

CAFE CHARBON
109, rue Oberkampf,
Paris 11.
Tel: 01.43.57.55.13.
Métro: Oberkampf.
Open daily, 9 A.M. to 2 A.M.
No credit cards.

The super-trendy Café Charbon has seen some action over the years. Until 1914 the theater hidden behind the café was known as Le Nouveau Casino, and later it was the site of café-concerts with Edith Piaf. Today it is one of thirty cafés, bars, restaurants, galleries, and shops that have been revived by the success of the *quartier* of the hour, the Oberkampf–Saint Maur neighborhood near Place de la République. Day or night, the Café Charbon feels like the center of modern Parisian life, a watering hole for the young, *branché,* and artistic. On a recent visit, a young Frenchman on my right was smoking Gauloises and reading Emily

The offerings at Café Charbon.

Dickinson in translation, while on my left a gentleman in a gray business suit was working on his laptop computer. The music was jazzy, the crowd eclectic, the air redolent of stale *frites,* and amid the patchwork tile floors and 1930s oak tables, one felt one was fulfilling a romantic dream of experiencing the Paris of the moment. The café sponsors concerts, disc jockeys, and photo exhibits as well.

The neighborhood—named after German industrialist Oberkampf, the inventor of the famed French fabric *toile de Jouy*—was the center of the city's metalworking industry at the turn of the century. In the early 1960s artists, painters, photographers, architects, and film production studios moved into the empty factories, and the neighborhood was revived. Other spots to look at along the route include the Mécano Bar (No. 99), Le Scherkhan (No. 144), and L'Electron Libre (103, rue Saint-Maur).

Montparnasse, Grenelle

14th and 15th arrondissements

LA COUPOLE
102, boulevard du Montparnasse,
Paris 14.
Tel: 01.43.20.14.20.
Métro: Vavin.
Open daily, 7:30 A.M. to 2 A.M.
Credit cards: AE, DC, V.

This Montparnasse café/restaurant (see also Restaurants) is still a favorite meeting place for artists, models, and tourists, and the haunt of young Americans since its opening in 1927. Although today few artists can afford to live in this popular district and the famous *coupole* (glass dome) has been covered over by a five-story building built above the café, this Paris institution still retains some of the Art Deco glitz and glamour of its heyday. The enclosed terrace café serves a daunting array of Hemingway-era cocktails as well as rich dark espresso. It's a good place to stop before or after seeing a movie on boulevard Montparnasse, but aside from pastries and *baguette* sandwiches, no food is served in the café. However, one could make a meal of the enormous *tarte aux framboises,* a shortbread crown topped abundantly with jewel-like fresh raspberries.

LE DOME
108, boulevard du Montparnasse,
Paris 14.
Tel: 01.43.35.34.82.
Métro: Vavin.
Open 8 A.M. to 1 A.M.
Closed Monday.

When Le Dôme first opened at the turn of the century, it was just a drinking shack and Montparnasse was a suburb of the Latin Quarter. Life changes, and so do we. And though Le Dôme has also become a top-rate fish restaurant (see Restaurants), the rather elegant fern-filled terrace is still a nice spot for lingering over coffee, a *ballon de rouge,* or a *croque-monsieur* or a *sandwich mixte,* both available on Poilâne's country bread.

AU ROI DU CAFE
59, rue Lecourbe,
Paris 15.
Tel: 01.47.34.48.50.
Métro: Sèvres-Lecourbe.
Open daily, 7 A.M. to 10 P.M.

If you find yourself in the 15th and in need of a caffeine fix, this adorable corner café—bustling with locals at lunchtime—is a lovely spot. Sit outside on the wicker chairs beneath the bright red awning or indoors, admiring the giant *fin de siècle* oak café doors with beveled glass. Here you can even name your coffee, choosing from arabica, robusta, and Colombia.

SALADE NICOISE
SUMMER SALAD FROM NICE

Few dishes in Paris cafés are as ubiquitous as salade niçoise, *that familiar salad from the Mediterranean. Versions vary from the sad and limp to the refreshing and restorative. Here is my* niçoise—*it brings with it the smile of the southern sun.*

8 ounces (250 g) green beans, trimmed
10 plump ripe tomatoes, peeled and thinly sliced
Fine sea salt, to taste
1 plump, fresh garlic clove, peeled
Handful of fresh arugula leaves, rinsed and dried
1 red bell pepper, trimmed and sliced into thin rounds
1 green bell pepper, trimmed and sliced into thin rounds
6 scallions, trimmed and sliced into thin rounds
3 hard-cooked eggs, peeled and cut lengthwise into quarters
20 best-quality brine-cured black olives, pitted but left whole
12 anchovy fillets, rinsed, soaked in milk for 15 minutes, and drained
1 can (6½ ounces; 190 g) French or Italian tuna packed in olive oil, drained
Handful of fresh basil leaves
Extra-virgin olive oil, to taste

1. Arrange the sliced tomatoes on a large platter, sprinkle them with salt, and set aside to drain.

2. Bring a saucepan of water to a boil and add the beans. Simmer until just tender, about 5 minutes. Then drain and rinse under cold water to stop the cooking. Drain again and pat dry.

3. Spear the garlic clove with a fork and forcefully rub it all over the surface of another large platter.

4. Drain the tomatoes. Arrange on the garlic-rubbed platter, in this order, the arugula, tomatoes, green beans, bell peppers, scallions, tuna, eggs, olives, and anchovies. Scatter the basil leaves on top of the salad. Drizzle generously with extra-virgin olive oil. Serve, passing a cruet of oil, a bowl of fine sea salt, and a peppermill for guests to season the salad to taste.

Yield: 6 servings

VICTOR-HUGO, ARC DE TRIOMPHE

16th arrondissement

LE COPERNIC
54, avenue Kléber,
Paris 16.
Tel: 01.47.27.87.65.
Métro: Kléber.
Open 7 A.M. to 11 P.M. (to 4 P.M. Saturday).
Closed Saturday afternoon, Sunday, and August.
Credit card: V.

Few French customs offer greater satisfaction than the ritual of sitting down in a nice wicker café chair early in the morning and ordering up a great cup of coffee and a buttery croissant to savor with your morning paper. At that hour your palate is clean, highly receptive, and yet highly critical, so it will "just say no" to junk. At Le Copernic—an everyday café along avenue Kléber, a five-minute walk from the Arc de Triomphe—your taste buds should be happy to wake up to the flat, crusty, chewy, *brioche*-like *croissants* made daily by the owner. If you're still not satisfied, walk across to the Lamborghini showroom to window-shop. Note that at lunchtime Le Copernic offers a great selection of sandwiches on Poilâne bread.

A daily Parisian ritual.

SNACKS

The most popular café snacks are sandwiches, made on the long and narrow *baguette*; on *pain de mie*, the square white bread; or on *pain Poilâne*, Paris's most popular country-style loaf.

Here are some of the most popular sandwich ingredients, followed by other popular snacking items.

Jambon de Paris: cooked ham

Jambon de pays: country ham, usually salt-cured

Saucisson sec or *saucisson à l'ail:* dried sausage, plain or with garlic

Rillettes: soft, spreadable pork or goose *pâté*

Pâté de campagne: pork *pâté*

Sandwich mixte: Gruyère cheese and ham on a *baguette*

Cornichons: small French pickles or gherkins

Oeuf dur: hard-cooked egg

Carottes rapées: grated carrot salad, usually with vinaigrette dressing

Crudités: variety of raw vegetables in a salad, usually including grated carrots, beets, and tomatoes

Assiette de charcuterie: a combination plate of dried sausage, *pâté,* and *rillettes*

LE VICTOR HUGO
4, place Victor-Hugo,
Paris 16.
Tel: 01.45.00.87.55.
Métro: Victor Hugo.
Open 7:30 A.M. to 8 P.M.
Closed Sunday.
Credit cards: AE, DC, V.

Le Victor Hugo is not mentioned because of its ambience, its history, or the people who have sipped here. Rather, it's noted for its location and its pleasant terrace, overlooking the fountains of the classic and well-heeled Place Victor-Hugo. I have to admit that I love to position myself at a table on a Saturday, sort of trying to read the paper but all the while noticing the beautiful and fashionable folk who wander past. In the heart of what journalist Richard Bernstein termed the "Deep Sixteenth," this is one of the city's best seats for watching bourgeois Parisians stroll by in all of their cold, chic, and blasé glory. The *garçons* couldn't be more typical: They'll forget what you've ordered and are sure to disappear after you request the check. But wait it out—they serve frothy *café crème* and delicious, buttery *croissant* twists in the morning.

Croque-Monsieur
Grilled Ham and Cheese Sandwich

The croque-monsieur *is the most Parisian of sandwiches. It's really no more than a grilled ham sandwich topped with grated cheese, but it appears in many different guises. One could spend weeks hopping from café to café, taking notes on variations and favorites. Sometimes a* croque-monsieur *is topped with a thick cheese* béchamel *sauce, or transformed into a* croque-madame *with the addition of an egg, but frankly, few Parisian cafés do justice to the sandwich. All too often, a* croque-monsieur *is made with airy, factory-made white bread, second-rate ham, and the cheese, well, it's not always Gruyère. (Parisian supermarkets even sell frozen* croque-monsieurs, *ready for popping in the oven or the microwave!) If you want a great* croque-monsieur, *make it yourself, with exceptional homemade* pain de mie, *the slightly buttery white bread that's been unjustly distorted by industrialization.*

- 3 tablespoons (1½ ounces; 45 g) unsalted butter
- 12 thin slices homemade *pain de mie* (see recipe, page 245)
- 6 thin slices (7 ounces; 200 g) best-quality ham, cut to fit bread
- 4½ ounces (140 g) Gruyère cheese, grated

1. Preheat the broiler.

2. Butter the slices of bread on one side. Place 1 slice of ham on 6 of the buttered sides, and cover with the remaining bread slices, buttered side out.

3. Place the sandwiches under the broiler, buttered side up, and grill until golden. Remove the sandwiches, turn, and cover each with grated Gruyère. Return to the broiler and grill until the cheese is bubbling and golden.

Yield: 6 sandwiches

Note: To transform a *croque-monsieur* into a *croque-madame,* grill a *croque-monsieur* until it is almost bubbling and golden, then cut a small round out of the top piece of cheese-covered bread, exposing the ham. Reserve the round. Break a small egg into the hole and place under the broiler for 2 or 3 more minutes. To serve, top the egg with the cheese-covered round.

One French cookbook even offers a recipe for a sandwich named after the food critic Curnonsky. To prepare a *croque-Curnonsky,* blend equal amounts of butter and Roquefort cheese, spread on thin slices of *pain de mie,* top with ham and another slice of bread, and grill on both sides.

Pere Lachaise

20th arrondissement

LE SAINT-AMOUR
2, avenue Gambetta/ 32, boulevard Ménilmontant, Paris 20.
Tel: 01.47.97.20.15.
Métro: Père Lachaise.
Open daily, 7 A.M. to midnight. Meals served until 10 P.M.
Closed three weeks in August.

This sprawling café situated right on the edge of Père Lachaise makes a wonderful stop for a snack or a meal after a visit to the famous cemetery. In the morning, baskets of *croissants* sit on the bar, accompanied by pretty pots of jam. But Le Saint-Amour's claim to fame rests on its hearty and happy selection of wines by the glass, mostly *crus de Beaujolais,* including the namesake Saint-Amour. You can sample them at the long bar with *pain Poilâne casse-croûtes* (small open-face sandwiches) and Auvergnat specialties such as *saucisson sec* and cheese plates of Cantal, Saint-Nectaire, and Bleu d'Auvergne. Otherwise settle into one of the wicker chairs on the rambling terrace overlooking the busy boulevard and watch the interesting multiethnic mix of old Paris and new immigrants.

The friendly waiters love to play the guessing game of figuring out whose grave people have come to visit. Most of the time it's not too difficult, given the swarm of retroactive hippies making a pilgrimage to the grave of Jim Morrison, the rock singer, who died of a drug overdose in 1970. For ladies of a certain age, they'll suggest: "You aren't here to see Jim Morrison's grave, are you? No, you must be here to see Piaf." The way to a lady's heart . . .

Tête-à-tête at Ma Bourgogne (see entry, page 148).

Salons de Thé
TEA SALONS

Gathering with friends at teatime.

Golden *pains au chocolat,* lush, ruby red strawberry tarts, and moist, dark chocolate cakes form a multicolored still life in the sparkling window. When gazing through, one senses an air of calm, repose, contentment. The door opens, revealing a mysterious blend of jasmine tea, vanilla-scented apple tart, and Haydn. At a far table, elderly women in veiled hats sit tête-à-tête, immersed in gossip and frothy hot chocolate, while nearby a well-dressed businessman flirts with a slender, chic Parisian, who seems more involved in her *tarte abricot* than in his advances. This is the daily life of the Parisian *salon de thé*—cozy, intimate affairs designed to indulge France's insatiable sweet tooth and its flair for guiltlessly whiling away hours at the table.

Though teatime is associated more closely with London, Paris supports dozens of full-fledged *salons de thé,* most of them distinctly French. Parisians don't fool around with frail cucumber sandwiches and dry currant buns—they get right to the heart of the matter, dessert.

In Paris, as in London, tea salons reached the height of popularity at the turn of the century, providing matrons of standing with well-appointed surroundings for entertaining guests outside the home, and offering women a respectable career opportunity. During the 1920s, tea and dance salons became popular along the

Champs-Elysées and in restaurants in the Bois de Boulogne: Here aging *grandes dames* came alone, as did young men. They met, they danced, they drank tea, then went their separate ways.

Thanks to a renaissance during the 1970s, Paris now offers an unlimited variety of tea salons, each with a distinctive décor, menu, and ambience that follow the whim and passion of the owner. A cup of coffee or pot of tea will be more expensive here than in a run-of-the-mill café, but the atmosphere is usually calmer (no noisy pinball machines) and the food generally superior. Lunch, and sometimes dinner, is available at most *salons de thé,* but more often than not, the food is an afterthought. An early morning or late afternoon visit for tea and pastry will, in the end, be more rewarding. Tea salons are, by the way, places where one feels perfectly comfortable alone.

PALAIS-ROYAL, LOUVRE, TUILERIES

1st arrondissement

ANGELINA
226, rue de Rivoli,
Paris 1.
Tel: 01.42.60.82.00.
Métro: Tuileries.
Open daily, 9 A.M. to 7 P.M.
Closed Tuesday and from July to mid-August.
Credit cards: AE, V.

One almost expects a troupe of Proustian characters to wander into this turn-of-the-century *salon* just across the street from the Jardin des Tuileries. Up until 1948, this was the old and celebrated Rumpelmayers, where as a child A. J. Liebling downed ersatz American ice cream sodas and began his love affair with Paris. Today—with its green-veined marble-topped tables and walls embellished with murals and mirrors—it's still snobbish, expensive, and so popular that on weekends one often has to wait at least half an hour to secure a table. If you are willing to brave the crowds and the prices, this is one of the few places in town where they melt real chocolate bars for their *Africain*—a lethally rich, delicious hot chocolate.

Other address:
Galleries Lafayette, 3d floor
40, boulevard Haussmann,
Paris 9.
Tel: 01.42.82.30.32.
Métro: Havre-Caumartin.
Open 9:30 A.M. to 7 P.M. (to 9 P.M. Thursday)
Closed Sunday.

MUSCADE
36, rue de Montpensier,
Paris 1.
Tel: 01.42.97.51.36.
Métro: Palais Royal–Musée du Louvre.
Open daily, noon to midnight. Tea, coffee, and desserts only from 3:30 to 7 P.M.
Credit cards: AE, DC, V.

You don't have to book a table at the Grand Véfour to enjoy the flower garden of the Palais-Royal. From May to September, Muscade expands to the garden terrace, one of the city's most tranquil, elegant outdoor spots for people watching or just resting a weary body. It's a wonderful place to sip tea and watch the world go by. The Palais-Royal garden is an honest neighborhood park as well, filled with old ladies sharing their *baguettes* with the pigeons, maids and mothers pushing infants in old-fashioned prams, and children at play in the sandbox. Stop off before or after a visit to the Louvre or the Comédie Française, ignore the indifferent pastries, and enjoy a *café crème* or a pot of tea under the elegant gray-and-white-striped awnings.

SABLES A LA LAVANDE TEA FOLLIES
TEA FOLLIES' LAVENDER SHORTBREAD COOKIES

Fragrant, delicate, and delicious, these shortbread cookies are great to have around for snacking, for serving with ice cream, or for enjoying at teatime, which is what they do at Tea Follies *(see page 174)**, a very popular tea salon in the city's 9th arrondissement. If you don't have access to dried lavender flowers (look for them at shops that sell* herbes de Provence*), fresh chopped rosemary leaves are a very worthy substitute.*

1¾ cups (250 g) unbleached all-purpose flour
½ cup (100 g) sugar
8 tablespoons (4 ounces; 120 g) unsalted butter, at room temperature
1 egg
1 tablespoon dried lavender flowers or fresh rosemary leaves
Pinch of salt

1. Preheat the oven to 400°F (200°C). Line two baking sheets with cooking parchment.

2. In a large bowl, combine the flour and sugar. Then, using a fork, slowly incorporate the butter, egg, lavender, and salt, working the mixture into a soft dough. Transfer it to a floured work surface and knead into a ball. Roll the cookie dough to a ¼-inch (7-mm) thickness; then cut it into about thirty-six ½-inch (6-cm) cookies.

3. Transfer the rounds to the prepared baking sheets, place the baking sheets in the oven, and bake until evenly brown, 10 to 15 minutes. Transfer the cookies to a baking rack to cool.

Yield: About 36 cookies

Sometimes only café crème *will do.*

TORAYA
10, rue Saint-Florentin, Paris 1.
Tel: 01.42.60.13.00.
Métro: Concorde.
Open 10 A.M. to 7 P.M.
Closed Sunday.
Credit cards: AE, DC, V.

The miniature pastries and handmade ceramics are displayed like diamonds in a jeweler's window; the spotless décor is a sober, modern blend of black, gray, and white. Toraya is an authentic contemporary Japanese tea salon, complete with white ceramic cups used for *matcha* (the ceremonial Japanese green tea), which is frothy, almost bitter, and whisked to a foam. To most Western palates the pastries look much better than they taste, but the adventuresome will want to try the tiny multicolored variations made of adzuki bean purée, or the little leaf-wrapped balls of sticky rice. It's a lot cheaper than a trip to Tokyo, and a nice exotic touch for those with little enthusiasm for pastries laden with cream and sugar.

VERLET
256, rue Saint-Honoré, Paris 1.
Tel: 01.42.60.67.39.
Métro: Louvre-Rivoli or Palais Royal–Musée du Louvre.
Open 9 A.M. to 6:30 P.M.
Closed Saturday from May to October, Sunday, Monday, and August.
Credit card: V.

The rich aroma of freshly roasted coffee mingling with teas from China, Ceylon, India, and Japan draws passersby to the door of Verlet, one of the most reputable and helpful coffee and tea merchants in Paris. Here, not far from the Place du Palais-Royal and the Louvre's Musée des Arts Décoratifs, you enter a casual, cosmopolitan world, crammed with open sacks of coffee beans from all corners of the globe, mounds of dried fruits and nuts, and colorful tins of tea blended to your liking on the spot. There's almost always a line stretching outside the door for Verlet's products, but if there is some table space, settle down for a few minutes in this unadorned 1930s setting for the famous coffee, or for tea served from silver-plated teapots with handles covered by bright felt mittens. There are always four or five rich cakes and pastries made on the premises, including a luscious apricot tart (see recipe, page 170) that goes so well with a warming cup of jasmine tea.

Marais

4th arrondissement

MARIAGE FRERES
30–32, rue du Bourg-Tibourg,
Paris 4.
Tel: 01.42.72.28.11.
Métro: Hôtel de Ville.
Open daily noon to 7 P.M.
(Boutique open 10:30 A.M. to 7:30 P.M.)
Credit cards: AE, V.
Nonsmoking section.

In the trendy yet still very old-fashioned Marais, one of France's oldest and most respected tea importers boasts a combination tea boutique and tasting salon. As you wander down the slightly scruffy Rue du Bourg-Tibourg, you have no idea what is in store. But as soon as you approach Mariage Frères, your senses are transported to an appealing, pleasurable world. The aroma of a mingling of exotic teas from China, Taiwan, Japan, India, and Brazil invades the senses, sounds of classical music fill the air, and your eyes focus on a plant- and wicker-filled neoclassical space bathed in delicate light and decorated in pale ocher and white.

There are some three hundred varieties of teas from twenty countries, as well as an astonishingly complete selection of tea paraphernalia, including about two hundred teapots, charming individual tea services, even a series of wicker picnic sets that will make you want to pack up and take off at the next opportunity. Smokers and nonsmokers are discreetly segregated, as smokers are directed to a second room upstairs. All the available teas are described in painstaking detail in the dictionary-like menu, and even tea experts are likely to feel overwhelmed. But one can always cop out and order one of the more familiar teas, among them a delicately perfumed Darjeeling, a penetrating, flinty Keemun, a rich and pungent Assam, or the house specialty, a spicy, fruity blend called Christmas tea.

With such pleasant surroundings, it's a shame the food is a bit overpriced and not up to par. The salad combinations are simply silly, and the tea-infused specialties barely have the taste of tea. Better to come at breakfast or teatime for the flaky currant-filled scones, served with a variety of tea jellies, or the soothing *tarte aux fraises des bois* in season—an excellent *pâte sablée* smothered with a blend of pastry cream and wild strawberries, all topped with a crackling caramel crust.

Other addresses:
13, rue des Grands-Augustins,
Paris 6.
Tel: 01.40.51.82.50.
Fax: 01.40.09.88.15 (for sales)
Métro: Saint-Michel.
Open daily noon to 6:30 P.M.
(Boutique open
10:30 A.M. to 7:30 P.M.)

260, rue de Faubourg Saint-Honoré
Paris 8.
Tel: 01.46.22.18.54.
Fax: 01.40.09.88.15 (for sales)
Métro: Ternes.
Open daily noon to 7 P.M.
(Boutique open
10:30 A.M. to 7:30 P.M.)

LUXEMBOURG, RUE DU BAC, ASSEMBLEE NATIONALE

6th and 7th arrondissements

DALLOYAU
2, place Edmond-Rostand,
Paris 6.
Tel: 01.43.29.31.10.
Métro: Cluny–La Sorbonne
or RER Luxembourg.
Open 8:30 A.M. to 8:30 P.M.
Closed Saturday and
Sunday.

After a walk through the Luxembourg Gardens, settle in at Dalloyau, formerly Dalloyau-Pons, an aristocratic, Old World tea salon with a pleasant terrace facing the park greenery and the stunning fountain at Place Edmond-Rostand. The snooty young waitresses act as though they'd rather be elsewhere, but overlook that, because in the summertime this is one of the classiest people-watching spots in town. In winter, go at about 10 A.M., climb the curving stairway to the tearoom, take a table overlooking the gardens, order up a steaming cup of smoky Chinese tea or a *café crème* with a pitcher of frothy steamed milk on the side, and enjoy a yeasty little *brioche* in stately silence. (See also Pastry Shops.)

TARTE ABRICOT VERLET
VERLET'S APRICOT TART

Verlet is a tiny tea and coffee shop that also serves good homemade pastries (see page 167). Anyone who loves apricots will love this simple, homey pie. Be sure to use fresh, not canned, apricots. This recipe, revised and updated from earlier editions, is a personal favorite.

Pastry:
8 tablespoons (4 ounces; 12 g) unsalted butter, melted and cooled
½ cup (100 g) sugar
¼ teaspoon pure almond extract
¼ teaspoon pure vanilla extract
½ teaspoon fine sea salt
1¼ cups plus 1 tablespoon (180 g) unbleached all-purpose flour
2 tablespoons finely ground unblanched almonds

Filling:
½ cup (25 cl) *crème fraîche* (see recipe, page 290) or heavy (whipping) cream
1 large egg, lightly beaten
½ teaspoon pure almond extract
½ teaspoon pure vanilla extract
2 tablespoons full-flavored honey, such as lavender
1 tablespoon superfine flour, such as Wondra

About 1½ pounds (750 g) fresh apricots, pitted and halved (do not peel)
Confectioners' sugar, for garnish

1. Preheat the oven to 350°F (175°C).

2. Butter the bottom and sides of a 9-inch (23-cm) fluted tart pan with removable bottom. Set aside.

3. Prepare the pastry: In a large bowl, combine the melted butter and the sugar, and using a wooden spoon, stir to blend. Add the remaining ingredients and stir to form a soft, cookie-like dough. Transfer the dough to the center of the buttered pan. Using the tips of your fingers, evenly press the pastry along the bottom and up the sides of the pan. The pastry will be quite thin.

4. Place the pan in the center of the oven and bake until the dough is slightly puffy and set, 12 to 15 minutes. Sprinkle the ground almonds over the bottom of the crust. (This will prevent the crust from becoming soggy.)

5. Meanwhile, in a medium-size bowl, combine the *crème fraîche,* egg, extracts, and honey and whisk to blend. Whisk in the flour. Pour the filling evenly over the pastry. Starting just inside the edge of the pan, neatly overlap the halved apricots, cut side up, at an angle. Arrange in two or three concentric circles, working toward the center. Fill in the center with the remaining apricots.

6. Place the tart pan on a baking sheet. Place the baking sheet in the center of the oven and bake until the filling is firm and the pastry is a deep golden brown, 55 to 60 minutes. The apricots will shrivel slightly. Remove from the oven and immediately sprinkle with confectioners' sugar. Place the tart on a rack to cool. Sprinkle again with confectioners' sugar just before serving.

Yield: 8 servings

LA NUIT DES THES
22, rue de Beaune,
Paris 7.
Tel: 01.47.03.92.07.
Métro: Rue du Bac.
Open daily 11:30 A.M. to 7 P.M.
Closed in August.

La Nuit des Thés is for those who love Paris in all its gilt-trimmed, frilly formality. The Louis XVI-style décor, the mirrors and marble floors, lend this tea salon a "let-them-eat-cake" ambience. Like Versailles, it's regal but not particularly comfortable. The succulent tarts, however, measure up to their sumptuous surroundings, and good tea is served steaming-hot in metal Art Deco teapots. The birdlike *propriétaire* looks as though she's never poked her head into the kitchen nor tasted her own delicacies (when asked if she made the desserts herself, she looked horrified and replied that she hired a chef to do all the cooking). But like any good ruler, she knows how to delegate: Worth a detour is the *tarte au fromage blanc caramélisée,* an ethereal, creamy cloud of Parisian-style cheesecake with a crackling caramel crust. And for chocolate-lovers, the *dacquoise au chocolat* offers an elegant excuse to sample silky rich, sweet chocolate *mousse* in an edible meringue shell.

ROLLET-PRADIER
6, rue de Bourgogne,
Paris 7.
Tel: 01.45.51.78.36 .
Métro: Assemblée Nationale.
Open daily 8 A.M. to 8 P.M. (to 7 P.M. Sunday).
Closed three weeks in August.
Credit card: V.

Stroll into this posh *pâtisserie* and tea salon in the heart of the 7th arrondissement for a close-up look at *"la vieille France,"* with its emphasis on high quality, tradition, and aristocratic reserve. The curt waitresses in their frilly white aprons are of the old school and are likely to look you over before deigning to give you a seat. But the dainty and delicious

Mariage Frères (see entry, page 168), a tea-lover's paradise.

pastries and the *café crème,* served in a silver pitcher, will win you over. For those who want to take a piece of *"la vieille France"* home with them, stop into the Marie-Pierre Boitard shop across the street to admire the opulent array of tableware (see Kitchen and Tableware Shops, page 366.)

CONCORDE, MADELEINE, CHAMPS-ELYSEES, PIGALLE

8th and 9th arrondissements

BERNARDAUD
11, rue Royale,
Paris 8.
Tel: 01.42.66.22.55.
Métro: Madeleine.
Open 8:30 A.M. to 7 P.M.
Closed Sunday.

The Bernardaud family from Limoges is the china maker to the stars. Turn over the china at any of the world's best restaurants and you will see the Bernardaud name. The Bernardaud shop is located along the ritzy rue Royale, and they now have a small tea salon (audaciously right across from the landmark Ladurée) adjacent to their shop. The place is sweet, all blue and white décor, with cozy armchairs placed beneath a colorful blue and white winter garden. A great place to rest your feet after shopping and sip tea or coffee from Bernardaud china (which you can purchase on the spot). The lemon tart is delicious; the apple strudel could be a touch sweeter.

CAFE JACQUEMART-ANDRE
Musée Jacquemart-André
158, boulevard Haussmann,
Paris 8.
Tel: 01.45.62.04.44.
Métro: Saint-Philippe du Roule or Miromesnil.
Open daily 11:30 A.M. to 6 P.M. (last orders taken at 5:30 P.M.).
Credit cards: AE, V.

Where else in the world could you sip tea beneath a sumptuous *trompe l'oeil* ceiling by Giambattista Tiepolo? A rare place to rest before or after visiting the museum's fine collection of Italian Renaissance and French 18th-century works of art.

Tea anyone?

LADUREE
75, avenue Champs-Elysées,
Paris 8.
Tel: 01.40.75.08.75.
Métro: Georges V.
Open daily, 8 A.M. to 1 A.M.
Hot meals served
at lunch only.
Credit card: V.

This huge and gorgeous tea salon/restaurant is *the* meeting place for chic Parisians in love with Ladurée's incomparable macaroons, great *croissants,* classic *brioche,* and *financiers* with the lovely flavor of *beurre noisettes.* The classicists are still staunch regulars at the original shop on rue Royale (see below). I am not choosy: It's so nice to know we now have two addresses to choose from, should we crave a sugar surge.

LADUREE
16, rue Royale,
Paris 8.
Tel: 01.42.60.21.79.
Métro: Madeleine.
Open 8:30 A.M. to 7 P.M.
(Sunday 10 A.M.
to 7 P.M.). Hot meals
served at lunch only.
Closed holidays.
Credit cards: AE, V.

Until I discovered the delights of Ladurée one day at ten in the morning, I could not have cared less about morning *croissants.* But after visiting some sixty *salons de thé* throughout Paris, it's the frothy cup of *café au lait* and the flaky, yeasty *croissants* of Ladurée, near the Place de la Madeleine, that return in my dreams.

Can there be any early morning atmosphere more elegantly Parisian? There's the hushed and intimate turn-of-the-century décor, with pale olive wood-paneled walls, *trompe l'oeil* ceilings, straight-back chairs, tiny marble-topped tables, curt waitresses in frilly white aprons, and a clientèle that's equally at home at Cartier and the Ritz. The air is not snobbish, just a bit blasé, and while the sandwiches wouldn't keep a bird alive, this most Parisian of tea salons is the place to rediscover what truly perfect *croissants* taste like. And I've never found a better cup of *café au lait* in Paris, served in silver pitchers with a bite of bittersweet chocolate on the side. The pastries, like the meltingly rich *croissant aux noix* and the *Kramich* (a puff-pastry raisin twist), are deliciously fresh. The chewy, almondy, almost marzipan *financiers* (almond cakes) are a little taste of heaven, as are the famous macaroons: vanilla, chocolate, caramel, pistachio, praline, and rose.

TEA FOLLIES
6, place Gustave-Toudouze, Paris 9.
Tel: 01.42.80.08.44.
Métro: Saint-Georges.
Open daily noon to 7 P.M. (to 10:30 P.M. mid-May to mid-September).
Closed one week at Christmas.

Bright, friendly, casual, a stop at Tea Follies is like having afternoon tea on a front porch, strewn with stacks of local newspapers and magazines and fresh flowers. The contemporary red, white, and gray tea salon opens out onto the tree-filled Place Gustave-Toudouze in the 9th arrondissement, and in good weather tables spread out onto the sidewalk for sunning and gossip over a cozy pot of tea. With such a lovely location and such good tea, what a pity that the scones and desserts are so disappointing.

The tea boutique at Mariage Frères (see entry, page 168).

TROCADERO, TERNES, VILLIERS

16th and 17th arrondissements

CARETTE
4, place du Trocadéro,
Paris 16.
Tel: 01.47.27.88.56.
Métro: Trocadéro.
Open 8 A.M. to 7 P.M.
Hot meals served until 4 P.M. only.
Closed Tuesday and August.

By nine in the morning this spacious terraced tea salon facing the Trocadéro swarms with handsome male joggers who come for a little after-run nourishment. It's not unusual to see a trim, well-muscled Frenchman down two *pains au chocolat,* a couple of glasses of freshly squeezed orange juice, and a *café au lait* in record time, as he buries his nose in the French sporting journal *l'Equipe.* The *pain au chocolat* is yeasty and fresh and the smoky Chinese tea is first-rate, but the *financier* is better left to someone else. Ignore the snooty service, and don't bother coming in the afternoon unless you enjoy being asphyxiated by a cigarette-induced haze.

CHOCOLAT VIENNOIS
118, rue des Dames,
Paris 17.
Tel: 01.42.93.34.40.
Métro: Villiers.
Open noon to midnight (Saturday noon to 7 P.M.) Hot meals served noon to 3 P.M. and 7 to 10:30 P.M.
Closed Sunday.
Credit cards: AE, DC, V.

This adorable tea salon not far from the rue de Lévis market is worth a detour for anyone who loves great Viennese coffee (half whipped cream, half bracing black coffee), rich and beautiful *linzertorte,* and warm and fragrant apple strudel. The waitresses are charming, speaking French with a lovely Austrian accent, and the *salon* itself is out of a fairy tale. It's especially beautiful at Christmastime, when the entire building is covered with lights and greenery.

LE STUBLI: LA PATISSERIE VIENNOISE
11, rue Poncelet,
Paris 17.
Tel: 01.42.27.81.86.
Métro: Ternes.
Open 10 A.M. to 6:30 P.M. (to 12:30 P.M. Sunday).
Closed Monday and August.
Credit card: V.

Many a morning I take my newspaper and my string bag to the rue Poncelet, head for this quiet, very private tea salon overlooking the bustling street market below, and grab a few moments to myself. The coffee here is exceptional—always served with a miniature pitcher of cream—and the pastries are the sort that even the strongest among us must struggle to resist. I am in love with their mile-high cheesecake and the flaky, fruit-filled strudels. Diet watchers: Don't let the creamy desserts scare you away. La Pâtisserie Viennoise's brochure proudly notes that they are made with reduced-fat (30 percent) cream and a minimum of butter and sugar. (See also Pastry Shops.)

Bistros et Bars à Vin
WINE BARS

A toast to good times.

Enter into the land of bread and Beaujolais, cheese and *charcuterie.* Known as *bistros à vin* (wine bars), most of these cozy neighborhood spots open about the time much of Paris is rising for breakfast. From the exterior many resemble ordinary cafés, yet once you've entered and sipped a glass of silky, scented Fleurie or fresh and fragrant Sancerre, and sampled an open-face sandwich of garlic-and-thyme-flecked *rillettes* (spreadable pork or goose *pâté*) on thick sourdough bread, you understand the difference.

There is always food and conviviality, but more important, there is wine—by the glass, the *carafe*, the bottle. Light and fruity Beaujolais is king, but one also finds delicate Bourgueil from Touraine; young wines from Bordeaux, Chinon, and Côtes-du-Rhône; the Atlantic Coast's delicious Muscadet; the Jura's white and pleasant Arbois; and Provence's heady, vigorous Gigondas. Obviously, not every wine bar stocks every wine, but most offer from a dozen to thirty wines at from about 20 to 50 francs a glass, along with—at the very least—cold platters of cheese or *charcuterie* designed to complement the house selection. Most are casual affairs with no printed menu, but wine selections and daily specials are usually handwritten on blackboards set behind the bar.

Is there any reason to go to a wine bar rather than a café for a glass of wine? Categorically, yes. The wine sold in most cafés is mass-produced and banal, and much of it watery and undrinkable. The wine sold in wine bars is usually carefully chosen by the *bistrotiers* (owners), most often dedicated men who are passionate about wine. When not behind the bar, many of them are traveling the country in search of good little wines. Often their selections are shipped directly to the wine bar in barrels (it's cheaper that way) and the *bistrotier* bottles them himself, storing the excess in basementlike *caves* beneath the bar.

The food—simple and unpretentious as it may be—is chosen with the same care. Most offer platters of French cheese, several kinds of hams, sausages, *pâtés*, and bread, often either Lionel or Max Poilâne's famous country loaf (see recipe, page 253), redolent of sourdough and fresh from their huge wood-fired ovens. Sometimes homey *pâtés*, *quiches,* or dessert tarts—all dishes chosen to go perfectly with the house wines—are prepared by the owner's wife. Some wine bars offer even heartier fare, such as wintry *daubes* (stews), platters of cooked sausages, and *confit d'oie* (preserved goose). As one *bistrotier* put it, "Wine is made to go with food. Tasting wine alone should be left to the experts."

Best of all, wine bars serve as a tasting and testing ground for wines yet to be discovered, as well as for familiar favorites. Since many wine bars offer little-known, small-production wines by the glass, this is the time to acquaint oneself with those such as Montlouis or Quarts de Chaume, both whites from the Loire; or to sample several of the ten Beaujolais *crus*, perhaps a Moulin-à-Vent, a Juliénas, and a Chiroubles, side by side.

While years ago most wine bars specialized in the young, inexpensive quaffing wines, today the trendier, more formal "English-style" wine bars—such as Willi's and L'Ecluse—offer a wider selection, including older vintages and those from more noble vineyards.

Dozens of wine bars pepper the streets of Paris. Here are a few special ones, a choice selection for a quick lunch, a pleasant afternoon interlude, or a late-night snack. They present a good alternative to a full-fledged meal. One should lunch well for 150 to 175 francs, depending on selections. The most popular spots are crowded at lunchtime, but if you go early (at noon) or late (at 2:30), you're likely to get a seat and still enjoy the atmosphere.

Les Halles, Palais-Royal

1st and 2nd arrondissements

L'ANGE-VIN
168, rue Montmartre,
Paris 2.
Tel: 01.42.36.20.20.
Métro: Rue Montmartre.
Open 10 A.M. to 2 A.M. (noon to 2:30 P.M. and 7 to 11:30 P.M. for meals). Closed Sunday and Monday.
Credit card: V.

Jean-Pierre Robinot was last seen at his heartwarming bistro on the rue Richard-Lenoir in the 11th. In this modern (and cold) wine bar, he continues to share his passions for wine, particularly those long-life, sweet, and surprising white *vins liquoreux* from the Loire, and simple fare, such as *charcuterie*, good farm cheeses, and Marcel Lapierre's fruity and welcoming Beaujolais.

A LA CLOCHE DES HALLES
28, rue Coquillière,
Paris 1.
Tel: 01.42.36.93.89.
Métro: Les Halles.
Open 8 A.M. to 10 P.M. (10 A.M. to 5 P.M. Saturday).
Closed Sunday and two weeks in mid-August.

This well-known wine bar takes its name from the wooden bell that once rang out across Les Halles to signal the beginning and the end of the day's commerce in the old wholesale food market. The market has been gone since 1970, but the wine bar remains. Here, owner Serge Lesage (who won the Meilleur Pot award in 1986) offers delicious cold platters—such as ham cooked on the bone, a *quiche lorraine* that clients cross the city to sample, and a good *tarte Tatin* in the winter months. The specialty here is Beaujolais, Côtes-du-Brouilly, Moulin à Vent, and Fleurie. A major spot for celebrating the arrival of Beaujolais *nouveau,* the third Thursday in November.

JUVENILES
47, rue de Richelieu,
Paris 1.
Tel: 01.42.97.46.49.
Métro: Palais Royal–Musée du Louvre.
Open noon to 11 P.M.
Closed Sunday.
Credit card: V.
Wine may be purchased to take home.

Serious wine bar enthusiasts will not want to miss Tim Johnston and Mark Williamson's fine endeavor, Juveniles, the little brother of Willi's Wine Bar, just off the fashionable Place des Victoires. Juveniles is an unadorned café turned wine bar, and it has rapidly become a great place to get a quick bite to accompany sips of an astonishingly good selection of wines. Their *tapas*—little snacks served at wine bars in Spain—may be a bit unorthodox, but they're delicious nonetheless. There's always a good selection of wines by the glass, as well as a variety of good lesser-known wines at very good prices. One of the rare spots in France to sample good wines from Spain and Australia, plus a fabulous selection of sherries.

LE RUBIS
10, rue du Marché-Saint-Honoré, Paris 1.
Tel: 01.42.61.03.34.
Métro: Tuileries.
Open 7 A.M. to 10 P.M. (9 A.M. to 4 P.M. Saturday).
Closed Sunday, the first three weeks in August, and two weeks at Christmas.

A classic, happy sort of bustling wine bar, where lunch is a free-for-all as clients stand five and six deep at the bar, dodging waiters and nudging neighbors. In good weather you can lunch outside, standing at the huge wine barrels that serve as makeshift tables. Meilleur Pot winner in 1963. Hot meals served at lunch only.

TAVERNE HENRI IV
13, place du Pont-Neuf, Paris 1.
Tel: 01.43.54.27.90.
Métro: Pont Neuf.
Open noon to 10 P.M. (to 4 P.M. Saturday).
Closed Sunday and two weeks in mid-August.
Closed Saturday in July and August.
Wines may be purchased to take home.

Opposite the statue of its namesake, Henri IV, this tobacco shop offers a certain grubby, old-fashioned Parisian charm, where men sit reading *Figaro* or *France-Soir* as they munch on *tartines* of goose *rillettes* between sips and swallows of fruity Morgon, or stand at the bar to chat with beefy, outgoing *patron,* Robert Cointepas. The menu here includes *tartines,* or open-face sandwiches, topped with such variations as warm goat cheese with herbs, ham and Comté, or platters of *foie gras* and toast. Wines available by the glass include Beaujolais-Villages, Morgon, and Fleurie, as well as Médoc, Pomerol, and Sauternes from Bordeaux, Gewürztraminer from Alsace, Sancerre *blanc* and *rosé,* Chinon and Bourgeuil from the Loire, and a fine Muscadet-sur-Lie. Meilleur Pot winner in 1960.

WILLI'S WINE BAR
13, rue des Petits-Champs, Paris 1.
Tel: 01.42.61.05.09.
Métro: Pyramides or Palais Royal–Musée du Louvre.
Open 11 A.M. to midnight.
Closed Sunday.
Credit card: V.

Perhaps the most popular and most respected wine bar in Paris, Willi's is bright, airy, and pleasantly decorated with a highly polished wood bar and an always chic clientèle. This is the place to come for an introduction to the wines of the Côtes-du-Rhône, including the bold, rich, and well-balanced Hermitage of Gérard Chave, or Georges Bernard's fruity Tavel, the *rosé* many consider to be the best in the world. Food here varies, with a changing selection of hot daily specials, a good variety of salads, and delicious bread from one of Paris's best bakers, Jean-Luc Poujauran.

MARAIS, ILE DE LA CITE

4th arrondissement

LA TARTINE
24, rue de Rivoli, Paris 4.
Tel: 01.42.72.76.85.
Métro: Saint-Paul.
Open 8:30 A.M. to 10 P.M. (noon to 10 P.M. on Wednesday).
Closed Tuesday and the first two weeks of August.

If La Tartine were situated in the United States, you might call it a luncheonette. But this is Paris and La Tartine (meaning an open-face sandwich) is a wine bar in the oldest sense of the word. In fact, it's been called a café for wine drinkers, for the place is often filled with regulars. (I have a friend who knocks back a glass or two here with the local mail carrier on a regular basis.) At lunchtime, this downtrodden bar, which has not seen a coat of paint or a redecoration in decades, is home to the crowds that come to share modest platters of paper-thin slices of *jambon de Paris,* the pale-colored ham that's cured in salt brine, then cooked. La Tartine offers a broad range of wines, with some thirty available by the glass, and a cave of some

Raising a glass with a friend.

"It's a naive wine, without any breeding, but I think you'll be amused by its presumption."
—James Thurber

MEILLEUR POT

The annual "Meilleur Pot" award designates the élite in Parisian wine bars. The traveling trophy—named after the traditional half-liter (about 17-ounce) Beaujolais *pot,* or jug—is awarded to *bistrotiers* who carry on the tradition of searching out and buying good French wines direct from the producers. The *bistrotier* then bottles the wines himself and serves them over the counter, by the glass or by the bottle.

The award, begun in Paris in 1957, is given to the *bistrotier* himself, not his establishment. If he sells or moves on, the title goes with him, right into retirement. Only one award is given each year.

Judging takes place from April to December, when a jury of ten makes anonymous visits to various Parisian wine bars. At the end of December or beginning of January, a formal award ceremony is held and the current title holder relinquishes the trophy, handing it to the new season's winner.

You'll note that many wine bars received the awards decades ago, yet they continue to thrive, a testament to the award, the wine bars, and Parisian traditions.

3,000 bottles. Worth sampling here: firm and fragrant *crottin de Chavignol,* the famed goat cheese from the Loire Valley, best enjoyed with owner Jean Bouscarel's crisp white Sancerre.

La Tartine is a nice place to visit before or after a tour of the Marais. This is the neighborhood once frequented by Eastern European refugees, and Trotsky, who supposedly visited La Tartine in its café days, lived right around the corner, on rue Ferdinand Duval. Meilleur Pot winner in 1965.

LE VALENCAY
11, boulevard du Palais, Paris 4.
Tel: 01.43.54.64.67.
Métro: Cité or Saint-Michel.
Open 11 A.M. to 10 P.M.
Closed Saturday, Sunday, and August.
Credit card: V.

A calm oasis in the neighborhood of Notre-Dame and the Place Saint-Michel, Le Valençay is the perfect spot to come to for a quick—and well-chosen—glass of wine, a huge green salad tossed with walnuts, and a platter of lovely cheese, all served with freshly toasted *pain Poilâne.* At lunch time, local businessmen come in their shirtsleeves for the *plat du jour,* at 67 to 75 francs. On one visit, this was a copious meal that included green salad, pan-fried steak smothered with shallots, and delicious potatoes cooked in goose fat. One good daily special to try is the plate of soft, young *crottin,* or goat cheese, sprinkled with white wine and heated, making for a hit-the-spot lunch. A good selection of wines from throughout France is available by the glass, *carafe,* or bottle. Service is swift, professional, and friendly.

Luxembourg, Saint-Michel, Sevres-Babylone, Ecole Militaire

5th, 6th, and 7th arrondissements

BISTROT DES AUGUSTINS
39, quai des Grands-Augustins,
Paris 6.
Tel: 01.43.54.04.41.
Métro: Saint-Michel.
Open daily 11 A.M. to 2 A.M.

Wander into this minuscule wine bar right across from the book stalls on the *quai,* and you feel as though you've walked into a village bistro. The carved Art Deco oak bar is pure 1930s; the owner, Noëlle Oily, sports a well-worn apron from Chiroubles, a village in the Beaujolais; and the aroma of the *plat du jour* fills the air. If it is on the menu, try the succulent platter of sautéed chicken, served with sautéed potatoes. Other good bets include a simple tossed green salad topped with either grilled *crottin* goat cheese or the marvelous cow's milk cheese Saint Marcellin. Around two in the afternoon, just as your thoughts turn to dessert, she sets down a hot-from-the-oven homemade apple

tart, allowing it to cool near the window as you plan your future. The bread's Poilâne, and there are at least a dozen wines available by the glass, including selections from René Sinard's Côtes-du-Rhône and a fine Saint-Amour, *cru* Beaujolais, from the Domaines des Ducs. A great spot to know about when you need to get away from the throngs of tourists that inhabit this popular *quartier*.

LE MAUZAC
7, rue de l'Abbé-de-l'Epée, Paris 5.
Tel: 01.46.33.75.22.
Métro: RER Luxembourg.
Open 7:30 A.M. to 10 P.M. Open for dinner Thursday and Friday until 1 A.M. (reservations required).
Closed Saturday evening, Sunday, the first three weeks of August, one week at Christmas, and one week at Easter.
Credit card: V.

Come to Le Mauzac when you are really hungry, and order up a delicious *onglet* (pan-fried hanger steak), served with excellent fries. Owners Michel and Christien Delhoume formerly owned the popular wine bar Les Pipos, and they have made this café-like spot on the lovely tree-lined rue de l'Abée-de-l'Epée one of the neighborhood's most popular hangouts. Their Beaujolais is delicious and unfiltered, and the Saint Marcellin cow's milk cheese is as runny and creamy as can be.

Le Rubis (see entry, page 179), a lunchtime portrait.

Flognarde aux Framboises Caves Petrissans
CAVES PETRISSANS' RASPBERRY FRUIT FLAN

A flognarde *(also spelled* flaugnarde, flangnarde, *and* flougnarde*) is a traditional French fruit flan, similar to the better-known* clafoutis. *This recipe was shared with me by Marie-Christine and Jean-Marie Allemoz, owners of the outstanding Caves Petrissans (see page 192), where this dessert is made with raspberries, cherries, or pears, depending upon the season.*

1 teaspoon unsalted butter, for buttering the pan
5 eggs
¾ cup (150 g) granulated sugar
⅓ cup (45 g) unbleached all-purpose flour
Pinch of salt
1 tablespoon Cognac
2 cups (50 cl) heavy (whipping) cream
1 teaspoon vanilla extract
1 pound (500 g) fresh raspberries (about 4 cups)
Confectioners' sugar, for garnish

1. Preheat the oven to 400°F (200°C).

2. Generously butter a straight-sided 10½-inch round baking dish.

3. In the bowl of an electric mixer, combine the eggs, granulated sugar, and flour, and mix at low speed until thoroughly blended. Add the salt, Cognac, cream, and vanilla extract; mix again. Pour the batter through a fine-mesh sieve into the prepared baking dish. Arrange the raspberries in a single layer over the batter.

4. Place in the center of the oven and bake until golden brown on top (the batter puffs up around the fruit, enveloping it like a cloud), with the center custard-like and still trembling, 45 to 50 minutes. Transfer to a rack to cool. Serve at room temperature, sprinkling generously with confectioners' sugar just before serving. Cut into pie-shaped wedges, using a spatula to transfer the wedges to dessert plates.

Yield: 8 servings

CAFE DE LA NOUVELLE MAIRIE
19, rue des Fossés-Saint-Jacques,
Paris 5.
Tel: 01.44.07.04.41.
Métro: RER Luxembourg.
Open 9 A.M. to 8 P.M. (to midnight Tuesday and Thursday).
Closed Saturday, Sunday, and the first two weeks of August.
No credit cards.

There are few prettier or more typically Left Bank squares than the tiny Place de l'Estrapade, just steps from the Panthéon and the Luxembourg Gardens. Reserve a table at lunch on a sunny day to look out on the tree-covered square with a lovely view of the fine turn-of-the-century façade of La Boulangerie Moderne. Service here is hurried and the staff may appear aloof and sleepy-eyed, but turn the other cheek, order up a nice glass of Saumur-Champigny, a platter of *crudités* (varied raw vegetables), and a plate of *carpaccio de canard* (thinly sliced raw duck breast), and simply enjoy. The wine list offers just twelve wines, most of them choices from reliable vineyards in Chinon, Saumur-Champigny, Bourgueil, or Sancerre, and there is a single hot *plat du jour* offered daily. The bread's Poilâne, and the neighborhood's the tops.

SANCERRE
22, avenue Rapp,
Paris 7.
Tel: 01.45.51.75.91.
Métro: Ecole Militaire or Alma-Marceau.
Open 8:30 A.M. to 9:30 P.M. (to 4:30 P.M. Saturday).
Closed Sunday and the first three weeks of August.
Credit card: V.
Wine may be purchased to take home.

This is a low-key, casual little wine bar with the folkloric décor of the pleasant wine village of Sancerre, about 125 miles from Paris. The dry, flinty white Sancerre from the Domaine la Moussière is featured here, along with its perfect mate, the dry, almost chalky *crottin de Chavignol* goat cheese. The wine bar is popular with workers from the French television studios located nearby and features a quiet (if citylike) sidewalk terrace. (Architecture buffs should be sure to walk across the street to look at the fantastic 1905 Art Nouveau apartment building at 29, avenue Rapp.)

AU SAUVIGNON
80, rue des Saint-Pères,
Paris 7.
Tel: 01.45.48.49.02.
Métro: Sèvres-Babylone.
Open 8:30 A.M. to 10 P.M.
Closed Sunday, two weeks in February, and August.

Au Sauvignon certainly takes the award for the chicest wine bar in Paris, right in the center of the city's affluent neighborhood inhabited by the B.C.B.G. (*bon chic, bon genre*) crowd. If you're into people watching (and who isn't?), love a good *tartine* on Poilâne country bread and a glass or two of Bourgueil, Muscadet, or Puligny-Montrachet, then stop in while you're in the neighborhood. Au Sauvignon offers no hot food, only assorted platters and sandwiches of cheese and meats, particularly great when time is limited and your stomach is empty. Meilleur Pot winner in 1961.

HEART OF THE MATTER

Most Paris bars open early not just to brew espresso, but also to accommodate the nearly 5 percent of the population who indulge in a spiritous breakfast, a practice known as *tuer le ver,* or "killing the worm."

According to legend, a certain madame, the wife of Monsieur de la Varende, died suddenly as a result of a worm gnawing away at her heart. An autopsy was performed, the worm was still alive, and all attempts to kill the creature failed. Finally, someone doused the worm with white wine, bringing about its quick demise. Quite logically, the moral of the story is: A glass of wine early in the day will keep the worms at bay.

"Wine is one of the most civilized things in the world and one of the natural things of the world that has been brought to the greatest perfection, and it offers a greater range of enjoyment and appreciation than possibly any other purely sensory thing which may be purchased."

—Ernest Hemingway

L'ECLUSE

If you've ever wondered whether members of food chains of any sort can remain charming and chic and retain at least a semblance of authenticity, the answer is yes. Over the past several years, little L'Ecluse wine bars have popped up all over Paris, following the same formula that made the first L'Ecluse, on the Quai des Grands-Augustins, a success. The décor, menu, and style are the same in each, appealing to a largely well-heeled business clientèle. Belle Epoque posters, converted gas lamps, a long wooden bar, and mirrored walls give L'Ecluse a turn-of-the-century atmosphere, though the food and wine are totally up-to-date. Note, however, that a meal here will not be cheap.

Service tends to be slow, perhaps intentionally. The first glass of wine comes quickly, and it's likely to be consumed by the time your snack or meal arrives. So if you think you might want more than one glass, order a bottle—it will likely be less expensive in the long run. Don't come here looking for Beaujolais; this is Bordeaux country. You may choose from more than seventy *château*-bottled Bordeaux, with some eighteen of these offered by the glass on a list that changes every three weeks. Good bets: a slice of *foie gras* and a glass of either Sauternes or Barsac; a plate of *carpaccio* with a young red Bordeaux; and then a slice of fudgy *gâteau au chocolat* with a cup of thick, black *express*.

Open into the early morning hours, L'Ecluse is a good choice for late-night snacks, especially after the theater, opera, or a film. Each L'Ecluse is open from 11:30 A.M. to 1:30 A.M. daily. Credit cards: AE, V.

L'ECLUSE GRANDS-AUGUSTINS
15, quai des Grands-Augustins,
Paris 6.
Tel: 01.46.33.58.74.
Métro: Saint-Michel.

L'ECLUSE FRANCOIS 1ER
64, rue François 1er,
Paris 8.
Tel: 01.47.20.77.09.
Métro: Franklin D. Roosevelt.

L'ECLUSE MADELEINE
15, place de la Madeleine,
Paris 8.
Tel: 01.42.65.34.69.
Métro: Madeleine.

L'ECLUSE BASTILLE
13, rue de la Roquette,
Paris 11.
Tel: 01.48.05.19.12.
Métro: Bastille.

L'ECLUSE CARNOT
1, rue d'Armaillé,
Paris 17.
Tel: 01.47.63.88.29
Métro: Charles de Gaulle–Etoile

A LA TOUR DE PIERRE
53, rue Dauphine,
Paris 6.
Tel: 01.43.26.08.93.
Métro: Odéon or Pont Neuf.
Open 8 A.M. to 9 P.M.
Closed Sunday, two weeks in July, and one week in winter.
Credit cards: DC, V.

I love wine bars that open at 8 A.M. for those who prefer a *coup de rouge* over coffee at that hour. This is an authentic neighborhood spot, where everyone seems to know one another, with locals wandering in and out at all hours of the day. Owner Michel Guenet (Meilleur Pot 1992) offers Beaujolais; twenty different *vins de terroirs* from Alsace, the Loire, Burgundy, Bordeaux, and Lirac; Alsatian *vendanges tardives*; and Champagne. Specialities include *foie gras, terrines, saumon fumé de St-Sever, charcuteries* from Savoie, and *plats du jour* such as *blanquette de veau*.

Sampling the new Beaujolais at Au Sauvignon (see entry, page 185).

BEAUJOLAIS

In Paris, the third Thursday of November—the first day of sale of Beaujolais *primeur,* the new Beaujolais—signals the beginning of a season-long *fête* that doesn't cease until after the holiday revelry has cleared sometime in January.

It really doesn't matter if the year's crop happens to be overabundant, short on acidity, or even lacking in that special fruitiness associated with Beaujolais. It doesn't matter that almost everyone in Paris agrees that the publicity surrounding the wine is out of proportion with its real worth. The fact is that Beaujolais is a "happy" wine, one that is there to enjoy; you don't have to take it too seriously.

In the wine bars that sell Beaujolais, it is available by the glass, year-round. Although the terms *primeur* and *nouveau* are used interchangeably, technically *primeur* is served only from the third Thursday of November to December 15. The term *nouveau* is technically reserved for the wines released for sale December 15, to be drunk through the next November.

Les Grands Boulevards

8th arrondissement

MA BOURGOGNE
133, boulevard Haussmann, Paris 8.
Tel: 01.45.63.50.61.
Fax: 01.42.56.33.71.
Métro: Miromesnil.
Open 7 A.M. to 10 P.M. Hot meals served noon to 2:30 P.M. and 7 to 10 P.M.
Closed Saturday, Sunday, holidays, and mid-July to mid-August.
Credit cards: AE, V.
Wines may be purchased to take home.

Well-dressed businessmen and -women stand elbow to elbow at the bar at lunchtime, when you won't be able to sit down without a reservation. This is a solid, serious wine bar. Serious, that is, about wine, but not about daily cares; the atmosphere is comfortable and happy, just the way you ought to feel when you're standing in a room filled with sausages and hams dangling from the rafters. The friendly, chatty *patron,* one Louis Prin, was winner of the Meilleur Pot in 1962. Wines worth sampling here include Beaujolais, Mâcon, Sancerre, Pouilly-Fumé, and a small assortment of Bordeaux. There's always a warm *plat du jour,* such as *coq au vin* (chicken in red wine), *boeuf bourguignon* (beef in red wine), or *andouillette au Pouilly* (chitterling sausage in white wine).

BASTILLE, NATION

11th arrondissement

CLOWN BAR
114, rue Amelot,
Paris 11.
Tel: 01.43.55.87.35.
Métro: Filles du Calvaire.
Open 11 A.M. to 1:30 A.M. Closed Saturday lunch, Sunday, and August.
Credit card: V.

The Clown Bar—just a few steps from Paris's giant Cirque d'Hiver (indoor circus)—is a turn-of-the-century café turned wine bar that's worth a detour on décor alone. The walls are covered with cute, kitschy, and beautiful tiles based on a circus theme, while circus posters and other related memorabilia form a stage set for a pleasant mealtime interlude. The food here is above average for wine bar fare and includes salads of thinly sliced ham layered with pears cooked in red wine and spices (a great play of sweet and sour); platters of poached, lightly smoked sausages from the Jura village of Morteau; and nicely grilled lamb chops. Clown Bar also offers traditional wine bar platters of sausages, *charcuterie,* or cheese. The wine list is decent, offering some good wines from the Loire, Burgundy, Rhône, the southwest, and Corsica. I'm particularly fond of Alain Graillot's sturdy, finely balanced Crozes-Hermitage.

JACQUES MELAC
42, rue Léon-Frot,
Paris 11.
Tel: 01.43.70.59.27.
Métro: Charonne.
Open 9 A.M. to 10:30 P.M. (to 5 P.M. Monday).
Closed Sunday and two weeks in August.
Credit card: V.
Wines may be purchased to take home.

One of the most authentic and liveliest wine bars in Paris. Situated just west of the Place de la Bastille, this bar is run by Jacques Mélac, an outgoing, energetic *patron* devoted to wine and good times. With his handlebar mustache, this proud Auvergnat looks as though he walked right out of central casting. If there's any question about what you're to do here, there's a sign on the wall that tells you clearly: "If you want water, you must place

Jacques Mélac takes a break with the crew (see entry, above).

your order the day before." Another reminds clients that "water is reserved for cooking potatoes." Coffee is served reluctantly, and lemonade is reserved for children under eleven years of age.

At lunchtime, the wine bar takes on the frenzy of the stock exchange at the height of trading as workers, businessmen, and secretaries crowd about the bar or vie for a rickety stool around one of the tables to take part in the day's meaty specials as well as the fine selection of regional cheeses, including Bleu des Causses, Saint-Nectaire, and Laguiole. Wine selections include Beaujolais, Chinon, Saint-Joseph, Muscat de Beaumes de Venise, Lirac, Vouvray, and Monsieur Mélac's own Lirac, Domaines des Trois Filles. Jacques Mélac's is the only wine bar in Paris with its own "vineyard"—vines rise along the exterior walls of the bar—and a celebratory harvest is held each fall. A hot meal is served at lunch, and at dinner Tuesday through Saturday. Meilleur Pot winner in 1982.

LE PASSAGE
18, passage de la Bonne-Graine, Paris 11.
Tel: 01.47.00.73.30.
Métro: Ledru-Rollin.
Open 8 A.M. to 2 A.M.
Closed Saturday lunch and Sunday.
Credit card: V.
Wines may be purchased to take home.

Here it is, the wine bar of my dreams: Charles Jouget's Chinon; Alain Graillot's Crozes-Hermitage; Eloi Durrbach's Domaine de Trevallon; Burgundy from Domaine Rion; salads tossed with my favorite olive oil (from Mausanne-les-Alpilles in Provence); bouncy jazz music; and a staff that's cheery, helpful, and efficient. Add to that a thor-

Jacque Mélac, a proud, outgoing patron *(see entry, page 189).*

oughly varied menu—everything from a good *steak tartare* to a selection of pasta dishes to sample with Italian wines—great country bread from Boulangerie Féret around the corner, and respectable homemade desserts, such as a trio of *pots de crème* or a rich chocolate tart.

Hidden at the end of a rather dingy alley that connects rue du Faubourg-Saint-Antoine and avenue Ledru-Rollin, Le Passage bustles day and night, offering a pleasant refuge from traffic and the urban roar. The wine bar offers a list of more than seventy wines, Champagnes, *eaux-de-vie,* and sweet *vins liquoreux* to take home with you. Owner Soizik de Lorgeril, from Brittany, should be proud indeed.

Denfert-Rochereau

14th arrondissement

L'ECHANSON
89, rue Daguerre,
Paris 14.
Tel: 01.43.22.20.00.
Métro: Denfert-Rochereau.
Open noon to 2 P.M. and 7:30 P.M. to 11 P.M.
Closed Sunday, Monday lunch, and August.
Credit card: V.

If you're looking for a spot for a good glass of wine and a quick lunch or dinner near the Gare Montparnasse, L'Echanson is it. The welcome here is almost nonexistent, and be sure to double-check the addition on your bill—but aside from that, the food is delicious and light, and the wine selection is enormous, focusing on the Rhône and Loire valleys. Some of the fine dishes include well-seasoned salads topped with perfectly cooked artichokes or with a tender *confit* of duck gizzards; a refreshing *gaspacho;* and thick slabs of beautifully cooked and expertly seasoned salmon.

LE RALLYE–PERET
6, rue Daguerre,
Paris 14.
Tel: 01.43.22.57.05.
Métro: Denfert-Rochereau.
Open 8 A.M. to 11:30 P.M. (9 A.M. to 6 P.M. Sunday and Monday).
Closed Saturday.
Wines may be purchased at adjacent boutique to take home.

Stop in around 12:30 on a nice day, and settle in on the terrace to watch the activity of the merchants along the bustling, neighborhood-like market street, rue Daguerre. The Péret family runs a serious wine shop next door, so be advised to take time to sample a few different wines by the glass (more than forty are available); then later select a few bottles to take home. Le Rallye offers classic wine bar fare: platters of cheese or sausage, to go with their fine selections of wine, including well-priced Beaujolais, wines from the Loire valley, and small *châteaux* of Bordeaux.

ARC DE TRIOMPHE

17th arrondissement

CAVES PETRISSANS
30 bis, avenue Niel,
Paris 17.
Tel: 01.42.27.83.84.
Métro: Ternes or Péreire.
Open noon to 2:30 P.M. and 8 to 10:30 P.M.
Closed Saturday, Sunday, and the first three weeks of August.
Credit cards: AE, V.
Wines may be purchased to take home.

Now in their fourth generation—the Petrissans have sold wine here since 1895—the Caves Petrissans has expanded into a fine neighborhood wine bar/restaurant where you will always be assured of very drinkable wines by the glass or bottle, plus a menu that changes every few weeks. At lunch, service is à la carte, with lovely main courses such as *lapin en gelée au basilic* (jellied rabbit terrine) served with *ratatouille,* as well as *steak tartare* and daily specials such as *navarin d'agneau* (lamb stew) or *lapin à la moutarde* (rabbit with mustard). The 170-franc dinner menu includes a first course, main course, cheese, and dessert. The décor is pure 1930s —lots of glass, wood, and nostalgia—and the owners, Marie-Christine and Jean-Marie Allemoz, are proud of their little establishment, as they should be. One of the best bets in the neighborhood.

MONTMARTRE, BELLEVILLE

18th and 20th arrondissements

BISTRO-CAVE DES ENVIERGES
11, rue des Envierges,
Paris 20.
Métro: Pyrénées.
Tel: 01.46.36.47.84.
Open noon to 1 A.M. Hot meals until 2 P.M. and Wednesday through Saturday nights.
Closed Monday, Tuesday, and the third week of August.
Wines may be purchased at adjacent boutique to take home.

Authentic Paris! A glass of fruity red Chinon, a wicker basket of golden *baguette de campagne,* a plate of creamy blue-veined Fourme d'Ambert and fresh *chèvre,* and a look-out on the lively street life and the treetops of the Parc de Belleville beyond. Around 7:30 on a Sunday evening, the wicker chairs of the Bistro-Cave des Envierges terrace fill up with locals returning from a stroll through the neighboring park. The men at the next table are embroiled in their chess game and glasses of Gamay de Touraine, while an artist at the corner table sketches his mistress smiling at him over her *café.* Meanwhile on the sidewalk, little boys patrol the street on bicycles, North African immigrant families stroll by in bright-colored robes, old ladies walk their dogs, laundry hangs out to dry. One has the feeling that this is what the Latin Quarter and Montmartre must have looked like once.

> *"They drank with unbuttoned bellies."*
> —*Rabelais*

Pass under the rose-colored awning into this simple turn-of-the-century wine bar–café. No frills or fanfare here, just reasonably priced, good-quality wine, cheese (perfectly fresh *chèvre* in season), and *charcuterie* for a happy local clientèle with not too many francs to spare. The chewy, dense country *baguettes* come from the bakery down the street, so they're always fresh. The adjoining *cave* sells carefully selected and reasonably priced wines, mostly *vins de pays* and *crus bourgeois*.

A wine bar lunch.

AUX NEGOCIANTS
27, rue Lambert,
Paris 18.
Tel: 01.46.06.15.11.
Métro: Lamarck-Caulincourt.
Open noon to 10:30 P.M. (to 8 P.M. Monday and Friday).
Closed Saturday, Sunday, and three weeks in August.
Credit card: V.
Wines may be purchased to take home.

At the foot of Montmartre, across from 48, rue Castine, this unpretentious and inexpensive neighborhood wine bar seems to have been spared the ravages of time and tourism that have attacked the Place du Tertre neighborhood farther up the hill. Waiting for a table at the old-fashioned zinc bar of Aux Négociants, observing the rowdy regulars walking up to the bar to refill their wineglasses and yelling for *le patron* like children crying for their mother, one could imagine Toulouse-Lautrec coming in for a *ballon de rouge. Le patron,* Jean Navier, who doubles as the chef and the waiter, quiets them with simple French home cooking while Madame tends the bar. Every day they offer a different *plat du jour* on the chalkboard, such as *gigot* with white *haricot* beans simmered in cider on

At Au Sauvignon, it's smiles and toasts when the new Beaujolais arrives (see entry, page 185).

Friday and *poulet fermier rôti "au diable"* on Thursday, with crocks of *terrine* and *cornichons* and hearty *pain de campagne* to start. Be forewarned: The only hot meal is the daily special, and it sells out early. But Monsieur Navier will whip up a fluffy omelet and a green salad for latecomers. Do save room for dessert: the *sablée aux framboises* (a buttery, thick short pastry crust overflowing with raspberries) is worth hiking up and down the hills of Montmartre for, and the cherry *clafoutis* is popping with fruit. Wines to look for include the Loire valley's Bourgueil and Jasnières, as well as Cahors, Bordeaux, and a Gaillac *rouge* from the southwest.

Marchés
MARKETS

Rue Mouffetard: a daily ritual (see entry, page 199).

Most mornings after an early jog around Paris's Parc Monceau, I extract a string bag from my pocket and head straight for rue Poncelet, the lively open-air street market. Marketing is best in the morning, when the vegetable man is in good temper (and sober), the crowds thin, and the produce freshest.

The cluttered, colorful market—one of many scattered about Paris—opens precisely at 9 A.M., when most days the sky is thick, somber, and a dozen shades of gray, and the city is just beginning to wake up. A tour of Paris's markets offers a rare glimpse of an immensely important French ritual—one that should be of interest even to those not particularly passionate about food—since it allows one to examine the authentic fabric and texture of contemporary Gallic society.

Parisians devote a good part of their day to marketing, and it's obvious that what many Frenchmen do between meals is make shopping lists, market, and talk about meals past and meals future. Daily marketing is still the rule in Paris, where everything from Camembert to cantaloupe is sold to be eaten that day, preferably within a few hours. I still smile appreciatively when the cheese man asks if the Camembert will be savored that afternoon, or perhaps that evening, then shuffles through his larder, touching and pinching to come up with one that's perfectly ripe and properly creamy.

Most of the merchants are fiercely proud people, and though some may be rough and peasant-like, they display a refined sense of aesthetics. The vegetable man admirably attacks his *métier* like an artist: Each morning, beginning around 7 A.M., he painstakingly arranges the fruits and vegetables in orderly rows, paying careful attention to shapes, textures, and shading. The result is a colorful, vibrant mosaic: fat stalks of celery rest next to snow-white cauliflower, the ruffled green leaves of Swiss chard stand beside them, followed by yellow-white Belgian endive, pale green artichokes, then—zap!—rosy tomatoes or ruby red peppers. Across the aisle, green Granny Smith apples line up alongside the sweet Italian blood oranges called *sanguines* (favored for their juice, which runs the color of a brilliant sunset), while bananas from Martinique and walnuts from Grenoble fill out the palette.

Mastering the intricacies and etiquette of French marketing is no simpler than learning French, and easily as frustrating. And it requires patience. A serious marketing trip—which will only get you through the next meal—can take an hour or more.

The selection at even the smallest markets is amazing. A large *rue commerçante* (merchant street) such as rue Poncelet might include half a dozen *boulangeries* and *pâtisseries;* two supermarkets; a good dozen fruit and vegetable merchants; a coffee, tea, and spice shop; four poultry shops; two *triperies* for tripe, kidneys, sweetbreads, and liver; three *fromageries;* one butcher for horsemeat; five other *boucheries;* four *charcuteries* for cold cuts; two or three regional or foreign specialty shops; and at least half a dozen restaurants and cafés. Depending on the length of the lines and the merchants' chatter, each individual purchase can take five to ten minutes.

French merchants, it must be noted, are not just merchants. They're philosophers, songsters, comics, tutors, and culinary counselors. Parisian housewives don't need cookbooks. The butcher, poultryman, and fishmonger all willingly dispense verbal recipes with each purchase. (Otherwise, merchants are not known for their generosity. The concept of a baker's dozen is not generally put into practice in Paris, though the fishmonger will, on occasion, throw in a bunch of dill with the salmon.)

Booming voices and shrill cries fill the air throughout the day as merchants hawk their finest produce, selling from rickety wooden pushcarts or narrow stalls. One piercing voice boasts of *"la très belle salade"* (very beautiful lettuce), while another shouts, *"Jetez un petit coup d'oeil"* (take a little look) at the *"canette de barbarie extra"* (extra-special duckling). Another ruddy-faced butcher holds out a fresh, plump *boudin* (blood sausage) for a shopper to inhale, announcing that it offers *"une véritable symphonie"* of lively aromas.

Meanwhile, at one corner, you may trip over a donkey tended by a trader selling an exotic array of herbs and essences, while nearby a jazzy brass band plays on.

The chatter is often amusing. One fall, I looked on as a shopper requested a kilo of *raisins de Hambourg,* France's popular muscat grape. Then, by accident, she noticed that the plump purple grapes came from Provence, in the south of France, not Germany. "But Madame," the merchant replied with a serious wink and a broad smile, "you know that in France, agriculture is very, very complicated."

I always begin at one end of the street—flanked by indoor and outdoor stalls—and tour the entire market before buying a thing, making mental notes of what's fresh, stopping to wave at the flower lady (who, due to my affinity for red tulips, calls me "Madame Tulipe"), reading the price and origin of each item, chalked on little blackboards that dangle above the stalls.

Lots of things here work on what one friend calls the *"pas possible"* principle, meaning "it isn't done this way here, so tough luck for you if you want it otherwise." Merchants bristle at any atypical request, particularly from foreigners. One friend worked for weeks to get her pork butcher to cut the *poitrine fumée,* or smoked slab bacon, thin enough to fry American-style. The butcher finally won, insisting that if he sliced the bacon any thinner, she'd end up with lace.

Once I ordered two kilos of fresh jalapeño peppers for pickling, and the vegetable merchant looked as though he'd seen a mirage. He asked, "How do you eat them?" "Just like this," I responded, pretending to bite into a fiery raw pepper. The merchant smiled, turned to a colleague, and playfully whispered, "She comes by every morning, buys two kilos at a time!"

And it took a long time to wean myself of the democratic American form of marketing: self-service. Here, the law is *ne touchez pas*—don't touch—and anyone caught selecting his own pears and peaches is forcefully admonished.

The full flavor of the market varies according to the time of day. It's as much fun to tour markets at morning's close, promptly at 1 P.M., as it is when they first open. One o'clock is the hour when a sudden hush falls over all of Paris. Shoppers scurry home to lunch while merchants sing, chant, and shout like schoolchildren let free for recess.

Sometimes the population density in markets can be just too much. On a rainy Saturday around six in the afternoon, Poncelet is a veritable obstacle course. Families with strollers, slow-moving old ladies pulling metal shopping carts, dogs, and long lines make passage all but impossible. But no matter the time of day, the season, or the market, Paris is ever a moveable feast.

The city's markets, like its neighborhoods, reflect a variety of cultures and classes, and a tour of one or several will tell you much about the daily life of the city, and of the habits of those who live in each neighborhood.

There are three basic sorts of markets: The *rues commerçantes,* or merchant streets, are stationary indoor-outdoor street markets, generally large, rambling, and open six days a week. There are some fifty-seven *marchés volants,* or roving markets, which include more than 5,000 independent merchants moving from neighborhood to neighborhood on given days. The old-fashioned *marchés-couverts,* or covered markets, have basically not been able to withstand modern-day competition from supermarkets and other open-air markets and are far less interesting and vibrant than in the past.

RUES COMMERCANTES

Merchant Streets

Standard hours are 9 A.M. to 1 P.M. and 4 P.M. to 7 P.M. Tuesday through Saturday; 9 A.M. to 1 P.M. Sunday. Most are closed Monday, and the number of merchants is often reduced during the months of July and August.

1st arrondissement

RUE MONTORGUEIL
Beginning at the rue Rambuteau, Paris 1.
Métro: Les Halles.

Les Halles, Paris's most famous market, is no more, but Rue Montorgueil remains. The city has made attempts to spiff up a rather grubby and run-down market by adding a pleasant new cobblestone street, and many of the city's finest chefs still do their marketing here, sharing chores as one chef markets for fish, another goes after the meat, still another for the produce, then all meeting for coffee before heading back to their restaurants. Stop into Stohrer (No. 51; see Pastry Shops) for perfect pastries. While in the neighborhood, walk down the restored Passage du Grand Cerf and visit the majestic 16th-century Saint-Eustache church, where you will find a little chapel dedicated to the fruit and vegetable markets of Les Halles.

5th arrondissement

RUE MOUFFETARD
Beginning at rue de l'Epée-de-Bois, Paris 5.
Métro: Censier Daubenton or Place Monge.

Parisians complain of high prices, poor-quality produce, and too many tourists, but Rue Mouffetard remains one of the city's classic and most popular merchant streets. Begin at the top of the market just before noon to get a feel of the

Taking time for the news between sales.

spirit and texture of the street, which has an honest sort of beaten-down charm. There's a lot of hawking and jostling here as tough merchants sell out of wooden crates balanced on tattered wooden sawhorses. Stop in at Café Mouffetard (No. 116; see Cafés) for the dense and buttery *croissants,* homemade *baguettes,* and rich *brioches.* Also take a quick look at the Facchetti Italian market (No. 134), with its four-story mural of animals wandering through the forest. At the top of rue Mouffetard, at No. 16, stop by Michel Brusa (see Bakeries) for a tangy *baguette au levain.*

6th arrondissement

RUE DE SEINE/BUCI
Beginning at boulevard Saint-Germain, Paris 6.
Métro: Odéon.

This is considered Paris's most expensive market street, and it is certainly one of the most densely populated, but it is not the city's best. Merchants tend to be a bit cranky, and the produce ranges from ordinary to fine. The Hamon Fromagerie (81, rue de Seine) offers some of the best goat cheese in the neighborhood. It's also one of the few Paris *fromageries* to sell *fromage frais bien égoutté,* a fresh curd cheese and key ingredient in American-style cheesecake. Walk a few shops down to Jean-Pierre Carton (6, rue de Buci; see Pastry Shops) for an excellent *tarte rustique* (pizza-like savory tart) and delicious fruit tarts and *viennoiseries.*

7th arrondissement

RUE CLER
Beginning at avenue de la Motte-Piquet, Paris 7.
Métro: Ecole Militaire.

One of Paris's tidiest high-class markets, this broad pedestrian street allows for comfortable browsing. Since many Americans live in the quarter, merchants are used to curious stares and constant questioning about unusual items. Take a look at Charcuterie Gonin (No. 40), a brilliantly spotless corner shop with a huge assortment of carry-out items, including *moussaka, coulibiac* of salmon, and tarts; and Davoli (No. 34), one of the city's few real Italian markets, all mirrors and black marble, with an amusing clutter of hams and sausages. Off Rue Cler, at 12, rue du Champ-de-Mars, Marie-Anne Cantin offers a remarkable selection of cheeses (see Cheese Shops.) Then make a short detour to Jean-Luc Poujauran at 20, rue Jean-Nicot for his fabulous selection of breads and pastries (see Bakeries).

At 16, rue Montmartre, there's a curiously named alley, the Queen of Hungary Passage (Passage Reine de Hongrie). Sometime during the 18th-century reign of Marie Antoinette, the queen was passing through the alley when she was handed a petition by a woman who ran a market stall. The queen commented on the merchant's likeness to the queen of Hungary, and soon the alley was renamed.

TO MARKET, TO MARKET

Paris's first food market was established during the 5th century, on what is now the Ile de la Cité. As the city expanded, other small markets were created, first at the city gates, then, beginning in the 13th century, at the old ironworks between rue Saint-Denis, rue Saint-Honoré, and rue Croix-des-Petits-Champs, the site of the present Forum des Halles shopping mall.

At the time, the big *halles,* or market, was shared by merchants, craftsmen, and peddlers offering an international array of goods. To encourage trade here, other city merchants and craftsmen were ordered to close their shops two days each week. It was not until the 16th century, when Paris had 300,000 inhabitants, that produce and other foodstuffs came to dominate the market.

By 1546 Paris boasted four major bread markets and one live-animal market. In the 17th century, the Quai de la Mégisserie along the Seine's Right Bank—now the site of the live-bird market, then known as the "valley of misery"—was the chicken, wild game, lamb, goat, and milk-fed pig market; rue de la Poissonière was established as the fish market; and the wine market was installed on the Left Bank's Quai Saint-Bernard.

The French Revolution of 1789 put an end to the royal privilege of authorizing markets and transferred the power to the city. By 1860 Paris had fifty-one markets, twenty-one of them covered and the rest open-air affairs.

By the mid-19th century, the central Les Halles was badly in need of repair, so a new hall with iron girders and skylight roofs—reminiscent of the still-existing Gare de l'Est—was built by the architect Baltard between 1854 and 1866. The design, complete with vast underground storehouses and linked by roofed passages and alleys, became a model for markets throughout France and the rest of the world. As the city's population grew, the market space eventually became inadequate, and in 1969 the market was moved to Rungis, south of Paris, near Orly airport. Les Halles was torn down to make way for a major modern shopping complex, now a frenetic neighborhood of shops and restaurants, with gardens at the center.

9th arrondissement

RUE DES MARTYRS
Beginning at rue Notre-Dame de Lorette, Paris 9.
Métro: Notre-Dame de Lorette.

In 1787 this street boasted twenty-five *auberges* for fifty-eight houses—that's about one eatery for every two houses! While this ratio has been substantially reduced, you won't go hungry here, especially if you stop into Terrier Charcuterie Lyonnaise (No. 58) or Fromagerie Molard (No. 48), a century-old *fromagerie* that still retains its original marble counters. It's about a fifteen-minute walk down from the rue Lepic market street, and one could easily visit both in a morning.

12th arrondissement

BEAUVAU
Place d'Aligre, Paris 12.
Métro: Ledru-Rollin.

This is actually three markets in one: an open-air market with 105 merchants, in operation from Tuesday through Sunday from 7:30 A.M. to 1:30 P.M.; a *marché aux puces,* or flea market, Tuesday through Sunday from 10 A.M. to 7:30 P.M.; and a traditional covered market (first built in 1781) Tuesday through Sunday morning. It is one of the city's liveliest, and worth visiting simply for its ambience. There's an old-fashioned feel, and the market serves as the social and commercial hub of this heterogeneous working-class immigrant neighborhood. You can find everything here—French, Kosher, and Halal butchers as well as Asian specialties. While the quality is not always first-rate, the prices are some of the lowest in town. Be sure to visit Le Pain au Naturel, at 5, Place d'Aligre (see Bakeries), for apricot bread and *brioche* prepared with *sucre de canne,* or pure cane sugar.

Marketing advice is ageless.

Espadon aux Capres, Citron, et Coriandre
QUICK SWORDFISH WITH CAPERS, LEMON, AND CILANTRO

There are days when I don't have much time to cook but would rather eat at home than dine out. That's when I pray that my fishmonger at Daguerre Marée on rue Bayen will have silky, glistening sides of swordfish (espadon), *which I have him slice about 1 inch thick for easy searing. The combination of capers and lemon zest satisfies my need for food with a mild acidic tang, and the pungently aromatic cilantro adds its own spicy note.*

Zest of 3 lemons, preferably organic
2 tablespoons oil from Oil-Cured Capers (see below)
4 swordfish steaks, each about 6 ounces (180 g) and cut about 1 inch (2.5 cm) thick
Sea salt and freshly ground black pepper, to taste
6 tablespoons freshly squeezed lemon juice
3 tablespoons Oil-Cured Capers (see below)
Handful fresh cilantro leaves, for garnish

1. Blanch the lemon zest: Place the zest in a medium-size saucepan, add 1 cup (25 cl) cold water, and bring to a rolling boil over high heat. Remove from the heat and drain into a small fine-mesh sieve. Rinse under cold water and drain again. Set aside.

2. In a large nonstick skillet, heat the oil over moderately high heat until it is hot but not smoking. Place the swordfish steaks in the skillet and sear for 3 minutes, or to desired doneness, on one side. Using tongs, turn the fish. Season the cooked side well with salt and pepper. Cook for 3 minutes more, or to desired doneness. Transfer the fish to a warmed platter and season the second side. Cover with foil and set aside.

3. Off the heat, immediately deglaze the pan with the lemon juice, scraping up any browned bits. Stir in the capers and lemon zest. Pour the sauce over the steaks, garnish with cilantro, and serve immediately.

Yield: 4 servings

Capres a l'Huile d'Olive
OIL-CURED CAPERS

Years ago, while researching trattoria dining in Italy, I came across some delicious capers preserved in oil. I loved using the slightly salty, tangy oil when searing fish but guarded my stock fiercely. The capers were hard to find, since most capers are cured in vinegar or in salt. Finally I decided to experiment and make my own with common vinegar-cured capers from the supermarket, and the results were fantastic. Try it—you'll be a convert for life.

1 jar (3 ounces; 90 g) capers in brine
About 2 tablespoons olive oil, or enough to cover the capers

Drain the capers into a small sieve and rinse well under cold running water. Return them to the jar and cover with olive oil. Refrigerate for about 2 weeks to allow the flavors to mellow and blend. Use the oil to sear fish or meat, and the capers to season salads.

Yield: One 3-ounce (90 g) jar capers (about ½ cup)

16th arrondissement

RUE DE L'ANNONCIATION
Beginning at place de Passy and rue de l'Annonciation, Paris 16.
Métro: La Muette.

This cobblestoned street has a pristine village-like character and caters to well-heeled Passy residents. Shops to look into include Le Palais des Thés tea merchants (No. 21), with an encyclopedic selection of teas and pretty teapots and accessories; and Beurre et Cacao *pâtisserie* (No. 35) for homey old-fashioned pastries. Walk through a quaint courtyard to Caves Châteauneuf (No. 23), a neighborhood wine shop with a good selection of Bordeaux.

17th arrondissement

RUE DE LEVIS
Beginning at boulevard des Batignolles, Paris 17.
Métro: Villiers.

A lively market street not far from the tiny, elegant Parc Monceau, where you can picnic on the market's offerings. Pick up a *pain paillasse,* a rustic sourdough loaf, at the Cousanon *boulangerie* (No. 21; see Bakeries). Farther along, the Jean Carmès et Fils *fromagerie* (No. 24; see Cheese Shops) offers more than a hundred varieties of French cheeses, all aged in its own cellars.

RUE PONCELET–RUE BAYEN
Beginning at avenue des Ternes, Paris 17.
Métro: Ternes.

Highlights of this high-quality market street include Alléosse (No. 13; see Cheese Shops), for its impeccable assortment of cheeses; Brûlerie des Ternes (No. 10; see Specialty Shops), for coffee and tea; Le Stübli (No. 11; see Pastry Shops), with fairy-tale sweets that make you dream of the Danube; Boulangerie Paul (No. 4; see Bakeries); and the fresh and astonishing assortment of fish and shellfish at Daguerre Marée (4, rue Bayen). Stop into L'Epicerie Verte, a health food store at 5, rue Saussier-Leroy, for a tangy, dense, organic sourdough *baguette.* Around the corner on avenue des Ternes (No. 16), the glass front of the Maison Pou shields one of the neatest neighborhood *charcuteries.*

18th arrondissement

RUE LEPIC
Beginning at place Blanche, Paris 18.
Métro: Abbesses or Blanche.

This somewhat grubby street, which winds up the hill from Place Blanche to Place des Abbesses, still retains an old-fashioned Montmartre charm, especially if you stop into the Lux Bar (No. 12), a neighborhood café with original tile murals and Art Nouveau woodwork from 1910. Les Petits Mitrons (No. 26) artisanal *pâtisserie* bakes some of the most beautiful homemade fruit tarts to be found in Paris. At the top of the hill, stop into J. Perrat at 36, rue des Abbesses, for fabulous *pain de seigle* made with chestnuts and almonds. Le Sancerre (35, rue des Abbesses), a lively wine bar/café, is a fun spot for a *tartine* and a glass of wine on the terrace.

RUE DU POTEAU
Beginning at place Jules-Joffrin, Paris 18.
Metro: Jules Joffrin.

A pretty market street set high above Paris on the *butte,* or hill, of Montmartre along several winding streets. The market's worth a detour simply to get an idea of what a real Paris neighborhood might have looked like a few decades ago. Take your time peeking into the shops along rue du Poteau, where the spotless turn-of-the-century storefronts will amaze you. A real find is Fromagerie de Montmartre (No. 9; see Cheese Shops), where you'll be certain to find something appealing among the forty varieties of goat cheese and a hundred other cow's and sheep's milk varieties. Just across the street Maistre Rôtisserie (No. 10), filled with churning rotisseries, offers unusual roasted meat specialties, such as quail, rabbit in mustard, pork with prunes, farm-raised chicken, and spit-roasted lamb—all warm and ready to take home for dinner or a picnic.

An irresistible selection.

"The air was laden with the various smells of the city and its markets: The strong smell of leeks mingled with the faint but persistent scent of lilacs, all carried along by the pungent breeze which is truly the air of Paris."
—*Jean Renoir*

RUNGIS WHOLESALE MARKET

France's largest food market—south of Paris, near the Orly airport—covers some 440 acres of blacktopped surface, with 864 wholesalers and 1,050 producers selling everything from fresh fruits and vegetables, to whole sides of rosy beef, to basket upon basket of fresh Brittany oysters. To feed the city's 10 million inhabitants, the Rungis wholesale market annually processes some 700,000 tons of potatoes, 500 million eggs, 560,000 tons of meat, and 750 million liters of wine.

There's no question that Rungis, open since 1969, lacks the romantic, grubby charm of the old Les Halles market it replaced. The modern-day wholesale market is spacious and sanitary, with hangar upon hangar of sober gray buildings. Specialty markets open and close throughout the day and night, with fishmongers opening the market at 3 A.M. and flower merchants opening their stalls at 11 A.M.

Rungis is open only to professionals, and casual onlookers are not welcomed openly. There are, however, two public tours daily, Monday through Friday. One is offered by the Rungis market in French or in English, and must be arranged in advance. Groups must number at least fifteen, arriving in a tour bus or mini-van. This tour begins at 6:30 A.M., lasts at least two hours, and costs 35 francs per person. For reservations (two months in advance for July and August), contact Madame Gillot, Société Semmaris, 1, rue de la Tour, 94152 Rungis Cedex. Tel: 01.46.87.35.35. Fax: 01.46.87.56.77.

The second public tour is conducted by American Stephanie Curtis. Tours are conducted in English, beginning at 5:30 A.M. and ending around 9 A.M. The tour takes visitors through all of the major markets. Tel: 01.40.15.04.57. Fax: 01.40.15.04.58.

MARCHES VOLANTS

Roving Markets

Note that these markets are open from around 8 A.M. to just past noon, and only on the days listed. These tend to be less expensive than the other markets, and you'll find fresher, more unusual produce here, but sometimes less variety. They are usually set up on sidewalks or along the islands of major boulevards and offer a full range of products, including fruits and vegetables, meats, poultry, fish, cheese, and fresh flowers. These markets often have a good deal of neighborhood character, and you'll also find a fine assortment of *maraîchers,* or market gardeners, who bring their produce in from farms in the Paris region. The following is a selection of the most interesting markets.

Look but don't touch.

5th arrondissement

CARMES
Place Maubert,
Paris 5.
Métro: Maubert-Mutualité.
Tuesday, Thursday, and Saturday.

This small, animated market square is best on Saturdays, when you'll find Claude and Chantal Conard's biodynamic produce displayed in attractive wicker baskets, as well as Le Soleil Provençal, with its authentic selection of meaty black *tanche* olives from Nyons (the first olive in France to receive its A.O.C.), tangy green *picholine* and *lucques* olives, and the extraordinary olive oil from the cooperative in Mausanne-les-Alpilles. They also sell other oils,

A bounty of freshness at an outdoor market.

tapenade, pistou, rouille, aïoli, artisanal jams, and blocks of *savon de Marseille* sold by weight—all great for gifts. There are several market gardeners with beautiful wild mushrooms, fresh herbs, and unusual salad greens. Across the street, the Brûlerie de Maubert (3, rue Monge) sells excellent fresh-roasted coffee and artisanal jams and has a coffee-tasting bar. La Pirée (at 47, boulevard Saint-Germain) is a family-run Greek deli offering fresh high-quality salads, including excellent *tarama* and roasted red pepper and garlic dip, as well as garlic-flecked olives.

A bit of Paris history: The square has been home to a produce market only since 1923, when it had some 125 merchants, compared to about 45 today. In the 19th century it was known as the *Marché aux Mégôts: clochards,* or bums, would wander the streets of Paris collecting cigarette butts (*mégôts*), and would gather in the market square in the morning to resell the butts to industrialists who recycled the tobacco.

MONGE
Place Monge, Paris 5.
Métro: Place Monge.
Wednesday, Friday, and Sunday.

In place since 1921, this lively, tree-lined market square features several excellent market gardeners. The *"Roi des Patates"* boasts about potato varieties you never knew existed. Pick up an excellent *baguette au levain* at S. Hervet (69, rue Monge; see Bakeries). Céline Poppeville offers beautiful wild mushrooms, fresh herbs, and unusual salad greens.

Look for Patrick Casson's fruits and vegetables (superb cherries in the spring, golden mirabelle plums in the fall) and Marc Mascetti's tender green beans and succulent baby peas. Before or after the market, pause for a cup of coffee at the lively café Rendez-Vous du Marché.

6th arrondissement

RASPAIL
Boulevard Raspail, between rue du Cherche-Midi and rue de Rennes, Paris 6.
Métro: Rennes or Sèvres-Babylone.
Tuesday and Friday. On Sunday this is an organic market.

The only street market in the neighborhood, with several market gardeners. Best on Sundays, when it becomes Paris's only organic market. The produce is generally top-rate, and you'll find a great selection of grains, such items as homemade sauerkraut, organic wines, sea salt, cultivated mushrooms, and organic wines. On Tuesday and Friday look for Noé Producteur's beautiful salads. From December through February, be sure to visit Dominique Martino's stand for home-grown fresh black truffles from Provence; and all year round, check out the organic meats from Catherine and Jean-Pierre Salmon, who have a shop at Au Bon Gout Retrouvé (83, rue Daguerre, Paris 14). Try their Limousin beef, poultry from the Vendée and the Gers, pork from Brittany, and chemical-free *charcuterie.*

7th arrondissement

BRETEUIL
Avenue de Saxe, from avenue de Ségur to place de Breteuil, Paris 7.
Métro: Ségur.
Thursday and Saturday.

With some 184 stands, this market, in operation since 1873, is one of the city's largest and best. Buy a pound of coveted potatoes from Noirmoutier and you'll be given a little sachet of *fleur de sel* to season them. Get to La Boulange des Marchés stand early for their *pain pepitas* (see recipe, page 211), studded with *grains de courges,* or pumpkin seeds. But my favorite is Le Nouveau Verger, with thirty-eight varieties of apples. Try the Chantecler, a great variety with nice acidity, one that won't fall apart in your *tarte Tatin.* Some other varieties to look for include Gala, Reinettes de Mans, Sainte Germaine, Canada Golden Doré, and Court Pendu "Suntan," a tiny late-season apple that is tart and delicious; also Fuji, Rubinette, Braeburn, Bertanne, Jubile, and Reinette d'Amorique. There is a stand with a great selection of olives and olive oil; Evelyne Bernard brings geese from the Périgord; Patrick Buisson brings his potato specialties; Charcuterie Leconte offers a flavorful *terrine de cabil-*

laud aux fines herbes (cod terrine with *fines herbes*); and Madame Verbel makes delicious homemade jams. Father and daughter Stéphane and Dominique Frémont, known for their milk-fed veal from the Périgord, lamb from Charentes, ducks, *pintades,* and sausages, are right across from the famous fishmonger Lorenzo. Also try the Lebanese "pizza" cooked on the spot. Before or after the market, visit one of the city's last artisanal wells at the tiny Place de Breteuil.

11th arrondissement

BELLEVILLE-MENILMONTANT
Beginning at boulevard de Belleville and continuing to boulevard de Ménilmontant, Paris 11.
Métro: Belleville or Ménilmontant.
Tuesday and Friday.

One of the city's best-priced markets, and one of the largest with some 340 stands, all in operation since 1858. Make a special trip to this souk-like market near Père Lachaise to find Madame Saint-Ellier, an *apicultrice* (beekeeper) who sells slices of acacia honeycomb fresh from her hives outside Paris. She's at the corner of boulevard de Belleville and rue de Ménilmontant, next to Métro Ménilmontant. (Her husband sells honey at the Richard-Lenoir market.) Many stands selling African herbs, spices, and couscous ingredients.

RICHARD-LENOIR
Boulevard Richard-Lenoir, beginning at rue Amelot, Paris 11.
Métro: Bastille or Richard Lenoir.
Thursday and Sunday.

In the shadow of the Bastille Opera, this is one of Paris's best, biggest (some 200 merchants), and most heterogeneous markets, especially on Sundays. Jackie Lorenzo is here with his fabulous fish; Chez Ceccaldi offers dozens of beautiful potatoes, noting how to cook each variety. Madame Annie Boulanger presides over one of Paris's best market stands: a fantasy *charcuterie* with fresh salads such as *ratatouille* and *pipérade* and first-rate specialties including grilled peppers, cooked sea snails served with homemade mayonnaise, grilled sardines, fresh pasta, smoked herring, *tarte provençale, pâté de foie au porto,* and much more. Pierre Lucien et Fils creamery stocks rounds of rich, low-fat, and nonfat raw-milk *fromage blanc*—better than any American cream cheese and perfect for cheesecake—including a variation that's filled with garlic and *fines herbes,* as well as creamy Fontainebleau (see recipe, page 284).

Pain Pepitas

AVENUE DE SAXE PUMPKIN SEED BREAD

Each Thursday and Saturday morning at the Breteuil market (see page 209), one can find gorgeous fresh breads at the Boulange des Marchés stand. This is one of the city's finest markets and not to be missed for freshness and exuberance.

1 teaspoon active dry yeast
1 teaspoon sugar
1⅓ cups (33 cl) lukewarm water
2 teaspoons fine sea salt
About 3¾ cups (500 g) bread flour
1 cup (4 ounces; 125 g) pumpkin seeds
1 large egg beaten with 1 tablespoon cold water

1. In the bowl of a heavy-duty electric mixer fitted with a dough hook, combine the yeast, sugar, and ⅓ cup (8 cl) of the lukewarm water, and stir to blend. Let stand until foamy, about 5 minutes. Stir in the remaining 1 cup (25 cl) water and the salt.

2. Add the flour all at once, mixing at medium speed until most of the flour has been absorbed and the dough forms a ball. Add the pumpkin seeds and continue to knead until soft and satiny but still firm, adding additional flour to keep the dough from sticking, 4 to 5 minutes. Transfer to a clean floured work surface, and continue to knead by hand for 1 minute to help distribute the pumpkin seeds.

3. Place the dough in a clean bowl, cover it securely with plastic wrap, and refrigerate. Let the dough rise until doubled or tripled in bulk, 8 to 12 hours.

4. Remove the dough from the refrigerator. Punch down the dough, cover it securely with plastic wrap, and let it rise again, at room temperature, until doubled in bulk, about 1 hour. Punch down the dough and let it rise once more until doubled in bulk, about 1 hour.

5. Punch down again. Form the dough into a tight rectangle. Place the dough in a nonstick 1-quart (1-liter) rectangular bread pan. Cover with a clean cloth and let rise until doubled in bulk, about 1 hour.

6. Meanwhile, preheat the oven to 425°F (220°C).

7. Brush the dough with the egg wash. With a razor blade, slash the top of the dough several times. Place the pan on the bottom shelf of the oven and bake until the bread is lightly browned and nicely risen, about 15 minutes. Reduce the heat to 375°F (190°C), and bake, rotating the loaf so that it browns evenly, until the crust is firm and golden brown and the bread sounds hollow when tapped on the bottom (or until an instant-read thermometer plunged into the center of the bread reads 200°F or 100°C), about 40 minutes more. Remove the loaf from the pan and place it on a rack to cool. Do not slice the bread for at least 1 hour.

Yield: 1 loaf

12th arrondissement

COURS DE VINCENNES
Cours de Vincennes, between avenue du Trône and avenue du Docteur Netter, Paris 12.
Métro: Nation.
Wednesday and Saturday.

Created in the 1850s, this vast 212-stall market is one of the city's most spacious. Look for GAEC du Château-d'Eau for *quetsche* (small Damson plums); Guy Naudin's fruits, including cherries, *quetsche,* prunes, and *mirabelle;* Bernard Groult's strawberries; and flowers from GAEC de Villedieu.

13th arrondissement

GOBELINS
Boulevard Auguste-Blanqui from place d'Italie to rue Barrault, Paris 13.
Métro: Place d'Italie.
Tuesday, Friday, and Sunday.

In place since 1898, this animated market features some 160 merchants, including several organic stands and oyster growers from the Ile d'Oléron. Maison Lorenian creamery stocks fresh goose eggs from February until the beginning of July. While in the neighborhood, walk down the village-like Rue de la Butte aux Cailles.

14th arrondissement

BRUNE
Boulevard Brune, beginning at No. 49, Paris 14
Métro: Porte de Vanves.
Thursday and Sunday.

A lively neighborhood market, open since 1933, with some 100 merchants, including at least half a dozen market gardeners and good rye bread—*pain de seigle*—to be found at L'Epi Gaulois, 23 bis, boulevard Brune. Monsieur and Madame Lanie run an impressive cheese stand, stocking over thirty varieties of fresh *chèvre* (goat cheese) in season, as well as a delicious Chablis-infused Epoisses. On Sundays, visit the nearby flea market at Porte de Vanves (see Kitchen and Tableware Shops).

EDGAR QUINET
Along boulevard Edgar-Quinet, beginning at rue de Départ, Paris 14.
Métro: Edgar Quinet.
Wednesday and Saturday.

A sprawling boulevard market in place since 1883, particularly good on winter Saturdays when Jackie and Marcel Deshaies sell their *Marennes d'Oléron* oysters. Look for good bread from La Mie du Pain; mushrooms from Meyer Champi; fruits and vegetables from Yves Richard; olives and dried fruits from René Mélet. Several market gardeners are here also, with gorgeous salads from Sylvain Hordessaux.

LES MARCHES BIOLOGIQUES ORGANIC MARKETS

These are food markets unlike others in Paris—more like old-fashioned country farmers' markets. On weekends from thirty to fifty independent organic farmers set up stalls on Paris's boulevard Raspail and along one of the main streets of Boulogne and Joinville, two Parisian suburbs. They sell organically grown fruits and vegetables; homemade breads; dried fruits and nuts; *charcuterie;* farm-raised chickens, ducks, and geese; and even wine that's guaranteed to be "natural." The organic, or *biologique,* movement in France is active and well organized, and these markets are shining examples of its success. On a given weekend you might find one stand selling freshly made pizza and another selling rustic whole-wheat breads. There is also homemade apple or pear cider, a huge variety of artisanal goat cheeses, sausages, and beer, and even one merchant offering bright and glorious sprays of dried flowers. For all markets, it is best to go early in the day for a good selection.

Le Marché Boulevard de Raspail
1, boulevard Raspail, Paris 6; beginning at rue de Rennes. Métro: Rennes.
Every Sunday, 8:30 A.M. to 1 P.M.

Le Marché Boulevard de Batignolles
96, rue Lemercier, Paris 17. Métro: Brochant.
Every Saturday, 8:30 A.M. to 1 P.M.

Le Marché Boulogne
140, route de la Reine, 92 Boulogne-sur-Seine.
Métro: Boulogne–Pont de Saint-Cloud, or accessible via Paris's No. 72 bus.
First and third Saturdays of each month, 8 A.M. to 4 P.M.

Le Marché Joinville-le-Pont
Place Mozart, 94 Joinville. Métro: RER Line B to Joinville, then via the suburban No. 106 and 108N buses.
Second and fourth Saturdays of each month, 8:30 A.M. to 1 P.M.

Le Marché Sceaux-Robinson
Rue des Mouille-Boeuf, rue Jules-Guesde, 92 Sceaux. Métro: RER Line B to Robinson.
Every Sunday, 8:30 A.M. to 1 P.M.

Flowers, anyone?

ORGANIC SUPERMARKETS

Organic supermarkets are on the rise. Here are two worth looking into:

Côté Vert
332, rue Lecourbe, Paris 15.
Métro: Lourmel.
Tel: 01.40.60.60.66
Monday through Saturday, 10 A.M. to 8 P.M.
Credit card: V.

Some 300 square meters of space (the size of three two-bedroom apartments), 95 percent organic, with cereal, fully cooked prepared meals, as well as fresh fruits, vegetables, cheeses, etc.

Les Nouveaux Robinson
14, rue des Graviers, 92200 Neuilly-sur-Seine.
Tel: 01.47.47.92.80.
Métro: Pont de Neuilly.
Tuesday through Saturday, 10 A.M. to 2 P.M. and 3:30 to 8 P.M. (Saturday 10 A.M. to 8 P.M.).

More than 400 items, 80 percent of them organic, with famed *pain au camut, pain a l'épautre,* honey and raisin bread, Gouda cheese with nettles (*orties*), and *herbes de Provence.*

MONTROUGE
On the *place* between the rues Brézin, Saillard, Mouton-Duvernet, and Boulard.
Métro: Mouton-Duvernet.
Tuesday and Friday.

On a pretty square in front of the town hall of the 14th *arrondissement,* this 69-stand market has been in operation since 1925. Monsieur and Madame Lanie bring their impressive cheeses to Montrouge as well as to Brune (page 212).

Prime produce from a small cart.

15th arrondissement

CERVANTES
36, rue Bargue, Paris 15.
Métro: Volontaires.
Wednesday and Saturday.

The city's newest market, open only since 1981, boasts just twenty-six *commerçantes.*

Balancing a heavy load.

CONVENTION
Rue de la Convention, between rue Alain-Chartier and rue de l'Abbé Groult, Paris 15.
Métro: Convention.
Tuesday, Thursday, and Sunday.

With 126 stands, this market has been in operation since 1899. Look for fresh herbs from Michel Sort and Sylvain Hordessaux's vibrant green salads.

DUPLEIX/GRENELLE
Boulevard du Grenelle, between rue Lourmel and rue du Commerce, Paris 15.
Métro: Dupleix or La Motte-Picquet–Grenelle.
Wednesday and Sunday.

A picturesque market under the arches of the elevated Métro line, particularly hectic and impressive on Sunday morning, when all 140 merchants are in full operation. Look for Bernard Balmisse, with his spring vegetables and fruits (particularly his sweet-tart oval *garriguette* strawberries from the Dordogne); the family Nochet for their thirty-six varieties of apples from their farm near Montbazon; fresh goat's milk cheese from La

Ferme du Poirier Rong in Saint-Vrain; and Jacques Brockers, with his French olives at Le Soleil de Provence. You'll also find fish from Michel Gaigner, fresh flowers from Bernard Quennejean, and fifteen kinds of salad and exquisite fresh herbs from the Loeb family of *maraîchères.*

16th arrondissement

AUTEUIL
Place Jean-Lorrain, Paris 16.
Métro: Michel-Ange–Auteuil.
Wednesday and Saturday.

An adorable, tiny market square with excellent produce. Several market gardeners, including one (across from Hédiard) with baskets of exotic salad greens and boutique vegetables, such as baby eggplant. Don't think about becoming one of the forty-seven merchants in this ultra-popular market: there is a thirty-six-year waiting list! Paris history buffs will want to visit the rue la Fontaine nearby, to look at architect Hector Guimard's Art Nouveau masterpieces at No. 85 (the famed Castel Béranger, which he built for his family) as well Marcel Proust's home at No. 96.

COURS DE LA REINE/PRESIDENT WILSON
Avenue du Président Wilson, between rue Debrousse and place d'Iéna.
Métro: Alma-Marceau or Iéna, Paris 16.
Wednesday and Saturday.

Since 1873 this market, with some 128 merchants, has enchanted the well-heeled 16th-arrondissement shopper. Wandering along this tree-lined boulevard in the shadow of the Eiffel Tower and in front of the sober Palais d'Art Moderne—built for the 1937 world's fair, or Exposition Universelle—you will find several excellent market gardeners, with some organic produce. Jackie Lorenz is here with his famous fish stand; the Lecluyse family offers their excellent, pristine selection of cheeses, including many fine goat cheeses; Joël Thiebaut offers a beautiful selection of salads; and butcher Jacques Allain brings in a marvelous assortment of meats and poultry. Madame Annie Boulanger offers her fantasy *charcuterie* with fresh salads, including grilled peppers, cooked sea snails served with homemade mayonnaise, grilled sardines, and *tarte provençale.* The best snack to be found is the Lebanese stand offering *manaeesh* (also called *mankouche*), a flatbread sprinkled with *zatar,* a savory powder made with dried thyme, sumac, and raw or toasted sesame seeds, cooked on the spot on a gas cooker that resembles an upside-down wok. Stop in at the nearby *pâtisserie* Malitourne (30, rue de Chaillot; see Pastry Shops) for a delicious *chausson aux pruneaux.*

19th arrondissement

PLACE DES FETES
Place des Fêtes, Paris 19.
Métro: Place des Fêtes.
Tuesday, Friday, and Sunday.

Operating as a market since 1893, this is one of the city's loveliest market squares, tree-shaded, picturesque, and sprawling. *Poissonerie* "Goia des Mers" has an especially good selection Sunday mornings. You'll find a few market gardeners, one who sells nothing but potatoes, another who sells nothing but mushrooms, and another who sells only chicken, and some nice cheese stands where the merchants bring in their own aged cheeses. You'll usually find some spectacular Brie and raw-milk cheeses from just east of Paris. Stop into nearby Pâtisserie de l'Eglise (10, rue du Jourdain, Paris 20; see Pastry Shops) for an after-market treat.

Side mirrors would be helpful.

Markets at a Glance

If this is Tuesday, take me to the Rennes metro stop. Or Convention, or Mouton-Duvernet. Here is a handy Tuesday-through-Sunday guide to the roving markets of Paris.

TUESDAY MARKETS

Paris 5
Carmes
Place Maubert.
Métro: Maubert-Mutualité.

Paris 6
Raspail
Boulevard Raspail, between rue du Cherche-Midi and rue de Rennes.
Métro: Rennes or Sèvres-Babylone.

Paris 11
Belleville-Ménilmontant
Beginning at boulevard de Belleville and continuing to boulevard de Ménilmontant.
Métro: Belleville or Ménilmontant.

Paris 13
Gobelins
Boulevard Auguste-Blanqui, from place d'Italie to rue Barrault.
Métro: Place d'Italie.

Paris 14
Montrouge
On the *place* between the rues Brézin, Saillard, Mouton-Duvernet, and Boulard.
Métro: Mouton-Duvernet.

Paris 15
Convention
Rue de la Convention, between rue Alain-Chartier and rue de l'Abbé Groult.
Métro: Convention.

Paris 19
Place des Fêtes
Place des Fêtes
Métro: Place des Fêtes.

WEDNESDAY MARKETS

Paris 5
Monge
Place Monge.
Métro: Place Monge.

Paris 12
Cours de Vincennes
Cours de Vincennes, between avenue du Trône and avenue du Docteur Netter.
Métro: Nation.

Paris 14
Edgar Quinet
Along boulevard Edgar-Quinet, beginning at rue de Départ.
Métro: Edgar Quinet.

Paris 15
Cervantes
36, rue Bargue.
Métro: Volontaires.

Dupleix/Grenelle
Boulevard du Grenelle, between rue Lourmel and rue du Commerce.
Métro: Dupleix or La Motte-Picquet–Grenelle.

Paris 16
Auteil
Place Jean-Lorrain.
Métro: Michel-Ange–Auteuil.

Cours de la Reine/Président Wilson.
Avenue du Président Wilson, between rue Debrousse and place d'Iéna.
Métro: Alma-Marceau or Iéna.

THURSDAY MARKETS

Paris 5
Carmes
Place Maubert.
Métro: Maubert-Mutualité.

Paris 7
Breteuil
Avenue de Saxe, from avenue de Ségur to place de Breteuil.
Métro: Ségur.

Paris 11
Richard-Lenoir
Boulevard Richard-Lenoir, beginning at rue Amelot.
Métro: Bastille or Richard Lenoir.

Paris 14
Brune
Boulevard Brune, beginning at No. 49.
Métro: Porte de Vanves.

Paris 15
Convention
Rue de la Convention between rue Alain-Chartier and rue de l'Abbé Groult.
Métro: Convention.

FRIDAY MARKETS

Paris 5
Monge
Place Monge.
Métro: Place Monge.

Paris 6
Raspail
Boulevard Raspail, between rue du Cherche-Midi and rue de Rennes.
Métro: Rennes or Sèvres-Babylone.

Paris 11
Belleville-Ménilmontant
Beginning at boulevard de Belleville and continuing to boulevard de Ménilmontant.
Métro: Belleville or Ménilmontant.

Paris 13
Gobelins
Boulevard Auguste-Blanqui from place d'Italie to rue Barrault.
Métro: Place d'Italie.

Paris 14
Montrouge
On the *place* between the rues Brézin, Saillard, Mouton-Duvernet, and Boulard.
Métro: Mouton-Duvernet.

Paris 19
Place des Fêtes
Place des Fêtes
Métro: Place des Fêtes.

SATURDAY MARKETS

Paris 5
Carmes
Place Maubert.
Métro: Maubert-Mutualité.

Paris 7
Breteuil
avenue de Saxe, from avenue de Ségur to place de Breteuil.
Métro: Ségur.

Paris 12
Cours de Vincennes
Cours de Vincennes, between avenue du Trône and avenue du Docteur Netter.
Métro: Nation.

Paris 14
Edgar Quinet
Along boulevard Edgar-Quinet, beginning at rue de Départ.
Métro: Edgar Quinet.

Paris 15
Cervantes
36, rue Bargue.
Métro: Volontaires.

Paris 16
Auteuil
Place Jean-Lorrain.
Métro: Michel-Ange–Auteuil.

Cours de la Reine/Président Wilson.
Avenue du Président Wilson, between rue Debrousse and place d'Iéna.
Métro: Alma Marceau or Iéna.

SUNDAY MARKETS

Paris 5
Monge
Place Monge.
Métro: Place Monge.

Paris 6
Raspail
Boulevard Raspail, between rue du Cherche-Midi and rue de Rennes.
Métro: Rennes or Sèvres-Babylone.

Paris 11
Richard-Lenoir
Boulevard Richard-Lenoir, beginning at rue Amelot.
Métro: Bastille or Richard Lenoir.

Paris 13
Gobelins
Boulevard Auguste-Blanqui, from place d'Italie to rue Barrault.
Métro: Place d'Italie.

Paris 14
Brune
Boulevard Brune, beginning at No. 49.
Métro: Porte de Vanves.

Convention
Rue de la Convention, between rue Alain-Chartier and rue de l'Abbé Groult.
Métro: Convention.

Dupleix/Grenelle
Boulevard du Grenelle, between rue Lourmel and rue du Commerce.
Métro: Dupleix or La Motte-Picquet–Grenelle.

Paris 19
Place des Fêtes
Place des Fêtes.
Métro: Place des Fêtes.

Pâtisseries
Pastry Shops

Demonstrating appropriate madeleine *technique.*

The Parisian pastry chef is truly a man to be admired. Imagine his responsibility. Day in and day out, season after season, he must attend to the care and feeding of the formidable Parisian sweet tooth.

Everywhere you turn in Paris, someone—man, woman, or child—seems to be either munching on a *pain au chocolat,* peering wide-eyed into the window of a pristine, wondrous pastry shop, savoring the last lick on an ice cream cone, or carrying, with admirable agility, a beribboned white box filled with the day's dessert.

Perhaps the city's per capita consumption of butter, sugar, cream, and eggs is not the highest in the world, but if a population won prizes simply on its level of enthusiasm for all things sweet and satisfying, I think that Parisians would win. I have watched reed-thin women heartily down three and four dessert helpings in a row—unashamedly, unabashedly, with no remorse. I have eavesdropped as a pair of businessmen huddled at lunchtime, talking in hushed, animated tones. The subject was not politics, not the European Community, not racing cars, but chocolates. Chocolates! I have listened as one enthusiastic *pâtissier* explained, "I love *éclairs,* but I don't make them in my shop. So when I visit my buddies, I have an *éclair* feast. Seven is my limit. And I usually meet my limit."

French regional and ethnic pastries, of course, are important in Paris. The cheese-filled Alsatian *gâteau au fromage blanc* and the just-sweet-and-buttery-enough *kougelhoph* are everywhere; from Basque country in the southwest comes the cream-filled *gâteau basque;* from Normandy, the simply perfect apple tart. Don't miss at least a visual tour of rue des Rosiers, the main street of the Jewish quarter, where there are almost as many pastry shops as street numbers, or a peek inside one of Gaston Lenôtre's several elegant shops, where a look is just about (but not quite) as good as a taste.

Everywhere one finds *croissants* (along with the chocolate-filled version known as *pain au chocolat*); *brioches* (the *mousseline* variety is more buttery and typically Parisian); the *madeleine* (a lemony tea cake that Proust made famous); and the *financier* (a personal favorite), the almondy rectangle that is part cake, part cookie, and absolutely satisfying when fresh and carefully made.

For many—Parisians as well as those passing through—a day in this town without a pastry is a day not worth living. Why this is so could be the subject of a major treatise, but suffice it to say that they climb the sweet mountain because it is there.

BASTILLE, ILE SAINT-LOUIS, MARAIS, LES HALLES

2nd and 4th arrondissements

PAUL BUGAT
5, boulevard Beaumarchais,
Paris 4.
Tel: 01.48.87.89.88.
Métro: Bastille.
Open 8 A.M. to 8 P.M.
Closed Monday and August.
Credit card: V.

Steps away from the Place de la Bastille, Paul Bugat's modern, spacious pastry shop/tea salon excels at traditional desserts. The *crème brûlée,* with its rich vanilla flavor and caramelized crust, merits a special trip. Don't miss the fruit *clafoutis, gâteau opéra, gâteau Paris-Brest,* delicate *millefeuille,* simple apricot tarts, and excellent *pains au chocolat.* They also serve savory tarts, sandwiches, and salads. In nice weather, Bugat sets out tables on the terrace facing the Bastille, and this is a great place to get a quick bite before a performance at the Opéra de la Bastille. Paul Bugat's pastry cookbook—*Mastering the Art of French Pastry*—is a modern classic.

CALIXTE
64, rue Saint-Louis-en-l'Ile,
Paris 4.
Tel: 01.43.26.42.28.
Métro: Pont Marie.
Open 9:30 A.M. to 1:30 P.M. and 4 to 7:30 P.M. (to 6:30 P.M. Sunday).
Closed Thursday, August, and holidays.

In the heart of the Ile Saint-Louis, Calixte seems strangely hidden from the fray on this well-traveled tourist path. The understated windows would never lead one to believe that here lie some of Paris's most perfect *croissants* and *pains au chocolat,* worth making a special trip to find (they bake only one batch and often run out by 11:30). The shop's small but select pastry display doesn't seduce you with fancy, gilt-covered cakes and mousses, but chef Bernard's creations are the real thing: rich and full of flavor, uncluttered by excess sugar and cream. If you have time to taste only one *millefeuille* (Napoleon) in Paris, come here for one so good that you truly believe it has a thousand layers of buttery puff pastry. Chef Bernard also bakes state-of-the-art renditions of classic desserts, such as the *gâteau opéra,* truffle cake, and *mousse aux cassis.* Calixte is the secret address of a faithful local clientèle, and many of the privileged neighborhood matrons order their entire dinner menu here, starting with the flavorful *terrine de poisson* (either plain or encased in a phyllo dough crust) and continuing straight through dessert.

SACHA FINKELSZTAJN
27, rue des Rosiers,
Paris 4.
Tel: 01.42.72.78.91.
Métro: Saint-Paul.
Open 10 A.M. to 2 P.M. and 3 to 7 P.M.
Closed Monday, Tuesday, and July.

and

FLORENCE FINKELSZTAJN
24, rue des Ecouffes,
Paris 4.
Tel: 01.48.87.92.85.
Métro: Saint-Paul.
Open 10 A.M. to 1 P.M. and 2 to 7 P.M.
Closed Wednesday and August.

Sacha and Florence Finkelsztajn run the best of the many pastry shops that line rue des Rosiers, the heart of Paris's Jewish quarter. Finkelsztajn's cheesecake (better known as *vatrouchka*) rivals anything you'll find in New York, especially when it comes fresh and warm from the oven in the afternoon. Their *gâteau aux figues* helps you understand where the fig Newton began, and the shop's assortment—poppy-seed cakes, hazelnut cakes, and

strudels filled with apples and raisins, honey and citrus peel, even dates—is enough to make one weep real tears. Finkelsztajn also has a deli counter filled with tempting specialties such as *tarama,* chopped herring, smoked fish, *fromage blanc hongrois,* and more. They also bake authentic Jewish rye bread and a rich, spicy onion bread. Throw discipline to the winds for a day, and enjoy.

STOHRER
51, rue Montorgueil,
Paris 2.
Tel: 01.42.33.38.20.
Métro: Les Halles.
Open 7:30 A.M. to 8:30 P.M.
Closed the first two weeks of August.
Credit cards: AE, V.

One of Louis XV's pastry chefs opened this shop in 1730, and it continues to thrill clients with its delicious individual *pithiviers*—cream-filled flaky puff pastry decorated like a crown—little apricot or apple tarts, and superbly fresh *pains au chocolat. Baba au rhum* was invented here, and this is the place to try the sweet sponge cake soaked in rum syrup, along with excellent *chaussons aux pommes fraîches, tartes aux fraises des bois,* and *puits d'amour,* little puff pastry rounds filled with custard. Elderly salesladies seem to swarm about the tiny shop, eager to assist in your selection. Take time to walk through the neighboring rue Montorgueil market, which is slightly seedy but still retains the charm of old Les Halles.

LATIN QUARTER, SAINT-GERMAIN

5th and 6th arrondissements

PATISSERIE BOULANGERIE ALSACIENNE (ANDRE LERCH)
4, rue du Cardinal Lemoine,
Paris 5.
Tel: 01.43.26.15.80.
Métro: Cardinal Lemoine.
Open 7 A.M. to 7 P.M.
Closed Sunday from 1 to 2 P.M., Monday, Tuesday, and August.

A jolly, super-active pastry chef/baker, André Lerch brings the best of Alsace to Paris with his golden *kougelhoph* (see recipe, page 236), twenty different kinds of simple, family-style fruit tarts that vary with the seasons, giant rounds of fresh cheesecake (*tarte au fromage blanc*), along with whatever new creation he dreamed up overnight. (When Monsieur Lerch can't sleep, he picks up a cookbook to inspire himself to try a new recipe the next day in the shop!) He'd like nothing better than to be able to spend four or five hours decorating a single tart, but instead he lives realistically and feeds his creative urges by changing his repertoire with the seasons. He's busiest from November to March, when wintry Alsatian baked goods are most in demand: *springerle, quiche lorraine,* and the delicious spice bread *pain d'épices* are all there. Year-round, he sells *kougelhoph* (along with the folkloric ceramic molds for baking them at home) and the famous plump tea cakes known as *madeleines*. Pâtisserie Lerch is also a *boulangerie* and bakes a dense crusty *baguette* and *pain de campagne* with stone-ground flour.

GERARD BEAUFORT
6, rue Linné,
Paris 5.
Tel: 01.47.07.10.94.
Métro: Jussieu.
Open 7:30 A.M. to 8 P.M.
Closed Saturday, Sunday, and August.
Credit cards: AE, V.

This friendly, welcoming shop near rue des Boulangers offers a marvelous assortment of serious pastries and breads. Try the delicious *mousse caramel poire,* with a lovely mix of flavors; excellent *tarte aux framboises,* with a thick, cookie-like dough topped with whipped cream; and chocolate *mousse* flavored with tea. The breads are equally good, with wonderful *baguettes au levain* and *Benoitons,* rich, moist, rye bread chock-full of honey, raisins, and nuts. These breads are delicious plain or spread with a creamy Camembert or fresh *chèvre*. In addition to classic bakery fare—such as ultra-buttery *croissants* and *pains au chocolat*—Beaufort is always inventing new delicacies. When he offers *pain aux pépites de chocolat* (rich *brioche* spirals filled with chocolate chips), don't pass it up. Also try the *week-end au citron,* a round *financier*-like cake, perfect with coffee in the shop's café or, in nice weather, as a sweet snack in the neighboring Jardin des Plantes.

BON
159, rue Saint-Jacques,
Paris 5.
Tel: 01.43.54.26.44.
Métro: RER Luxembourg.
Open 7:30 A.M. to 8 P.M.
Closed Sunday afternoon, Monday, and August.
Credit cards: AE, V.

Stop by this Left Bank pastry shop for an extraordinary *gâteau fromage blanc 0%,* a no-fat cheesecake that is delicious and lemony. Also a good chocolate cake (*gâteau au chocolat*) and macaroons.

A BAKER'S DOZEN

In the 17th century, butlers were charged with buying the wine and bread for their households. A contract would be signed with the local baker for a year's worth of bread. For every twelve loaves bought for the household, the butler got to keep the thirteenth for himself.

André Lerch and his madeleines. *(see entry, page 223).*

Madeleines
LEMON TEA CAKES

While researching this book, I became fixated, absolutely fanatical, about madeleines, *the plump golden tea cakes shaped like scallop shells. They were something to boost my spirits on the days when I walked for miles sleuthing in search of culinary jewels. I tasted dozens of* madeleines, *but only a few that were "just right." The best, freshest* madeleine *has a dry, almost dusty taste when eaten on its own. One of my favorite versions is made by André Lerch, an Alsatian baker with a bread and pastry shop on the Left Bank (see page 223).*

*To be truly appreciated—to "invade the senses with exquisite pleasure" as they did for Marcel Proust—*madeleines *must be dipped in tea, ideally the slightly lime-flavored* tilleul, *which releases the fragrant, flavorful lemon essence of the little tea cake. Special* madeleine *tins can be found in all the French restaurant supply shops and in the housewares section of department stores. The following is a recipe I developed.*

4 eggs
1 cup (200 g) sugar
Grated zest of 2 lemons
1¾ cups (225 g) all-purpose flour (do not use unbleached flour)
¾ cup (6 ounces; 185 g) unsalted butter, melted and cooled
1 tablespoon (½ ounce; 15 g) unsalted butter, for buttering *madeleine* tins

1. Place the eggs and sugar in a large bowl; then, using a whisk or an electric mixer, beat until lemon colored. Add the zest. Fold in the flour, then the ¾ cup melted butter.

2. Refrigerate the batter, covered, for 1 hour.

3. Preheat the oven to 375°F (190°C).

4. Butter the *madeleine* tins; then spoon in the batter, filling each well about three-fourths full. Bake 10 to 12 minutes, or until the *madeleines* are golden brown.

5. Remove the *madeleines* from their tins as soon as they're baked, and cool them on a wire rack. (*Note:* Wash the tins immediately with a stiff brush and hot water but no detergent so that they retain their seasoning.) The *madeleines* are best eaten as soon as they've cooled. They may, however, be stored for several days in an airtight container.

Yield: Thirty-six 3-inch (8-cm) *madeleines*

Wishful looking.

JEAN-PIERRE CARTON
6, rue de Buci,
Paris 6.
Tel: 01.43.26.04.13.
Métro: Odéon.
Open 7 A.M. to 8:30 P.M.
Closed Monday.
Credit card: V.

It is hard to resist Jean-Pierre Carton's beautifully puckery and perfect *tarte citron,* as well as the *tarte au chocolat,* aided by a rush of fruit on the top. The raspberry *soufflé* is good, though the apple and almond tart (*tarte aux pommes amandes*) is dry. Stop into this tempting modern bakery in the rue de Buci market street to also try the earthy *tarte rustique:* a *fougasse*-like savory tart on a thick whole-grain crust topped with flavorful combinations of leeks and onions with rosemary and *crème fraîche;* chorizo sausage and goat cheese; or olives and anchovies. Many specialties here come in miniature sizes too, so you can sample *petit pains* filled with olives, Gruyère, onions, or bacon, and perhaps take home a bagful of miniature *pains au chocolat* and almond *croissants* without too many guilt pangs. For a special brunch, try the *baguette*-size *pain au lait aux pépites de chocolat,* a rich golden bread bursting with bittersweet chocolate chips. For those with small appetites, they also offer a *demi-baguette.*

CHRISTIAN CONSTANT
37, rue d'Assas,
Paris 6.
Tel: 01.53.63.15.15.
Métro: Rennes or Saint-Placide.
Open daily, 8 A.M. to 8:30 p.m.
Credit Card: V.

Christian Constant is one of the city's better pastry chefs, and his pristine windows are full of modern, simple, straightforward creations. I love his ultra-bitter *tarte au chocolat,* almost black in color, with a rich chocolate *sablet* crust and smooth, mouth-filling interior. A great lemon tart cannot be beat, and Constant's lemon meringue version is all it should be: properly golden and tart, with a firm, crisp crust. All pastries and chocolates can be sampled in the small tea salon in this all white-and-black shop.

J. C. GAULUPEAU
12, rue Mabillon,
Paris 6.
Tel: 01.43.54.16.93.
Métro: Mabillon.
Open 7 A.M. to 7 P.M.
Closed Monday.
Credit cards: AE, V.

Many locals in the neighborhood prefer the breads and pastries at Gaulupeau to those of Mulot across the market square. I love them both, for different reasons. His *Retrodor baguette* is a dream, especially when it's right from the oven in the morning. I also love his *tarte au citron* (a bit rich and buttery and less tart than most) as well as his rich pistachio *croissants,* a perfect morning indulgence.

PAINT YOUR OWN SUNDAE

When the line is longer than your patience at the famed Berthillon ice cream shop, head over to Damman's, a combination tea salon/ice cream parlor that also offers top-quality teas as well as tarts and cakes. The real attraction here is some of best ice cream in Paris—not overly sweet, and filled with pure fruit flavor. Damman's offers an original selection of ice cream and *sorbet* flavors, including bitter tangerine, amaretto, Bulgarian yogurt, even *pastis.* Come especially for the *palettes* of ice cream, an original twist on ice-cream sundaes: They fill palette-shaped plates with scoops of ice cream and wells of sauce and *coulis,* so you can paint your own sundae, allowing your artistic and gastronomic fancies go wild. Surprisingly reasonable prices, five minutes from Berthillon.

Damman's, 20, rue du Cardinal Lemoine, Paris 5. (01.46.33.61.30). Métro: Cardinal Lemoine. Open 11:30 A.M. to 10 P.M. in summer; to 7 P.M. in winter. Closed Sunday in winter.

Always a crowd at Berthillon.

ICE CREAM WORTH WAITING FOR

The line stretches right around the corner, and neither subzero temperatures nor pouring rain can deter the hearty souls who queue up for a taste of Berthillon, Paris's finest ice creams, *sorbets,* and *granités*. There's always a lot of good-natured grumbling about the wait while perfect strangers trade tales of past visits or argue passionately about which of the sixty-plus Berthillon flavors is best, purest, most authentic, most decadent.

There's always a lot of "place saving" as customers race up to the front of the line to check the list of current seasonal offerings. Once you reach the window you'd better have your choice well in mind—there is no time for hemming, hawing, asking advice, or posing questions. Will it be *glace au chocolat amer,* bitter chocolate ice cream rich with cream and eggs, or maybe *nougat au miel,* a crunchy, heavenly blend of nuts and smooth, smooth honey? Or perhaps the glistening black currant *(cassis) sorbet* that tastes so much like the real thing you can't believe you're not nibbling the fruit itself.

Berthillon, 31, rue Saint-Louis-en-l'Ile, Paris 4. (01.43.54.31.61). Métro: Pont Marie. Open 10 A.M. to 8 P.M. Closed Monday, Tuesday, July, August, and Easter break.

If the thought of waiting in line is discouraging, don't despair. Berthillon ice cream and *sorbets* are sold in many Paris cafés.

Le Flore en l'Ile, 42, quai d'Orléans, Paris 4. (01.43.29.88.27).

Le Mandarin, 148, boulevard Saint-Germain, Paris 6. (01.46.33.98.35).

Le Reveil, 29, boulevard Henri IV, Paris 4. (01.42.72.73.26).

La Rotonde, 105, boulevard Montparnasse, Paris 6. (01.43.26.68.84 and 01.43.26.48.26).

Nicolsen, 112, rue Mouffetard, Paris 5. (01.43.36.78.04).

Aux Gourmandises, 97, rue Claude Decaen, Paris 12. (01.43.43.88.61).

L'Hermine Paul, 114, rue de Patay, Paris 13. (01.45.83.80.13).

Colom, 150, avenue Victor Hugo, Paris 16. (01.47.27.90.30).

Régis Chocolatier, 89, rue de Passy, Paris 16. (01.45.27.70.00).

Sometimes one just isn't enough.

Brioche Mousseline Denis Ruffel
DENIS RUFFEL'S MOUSSELINE BRIOCHE

Paris bakeries offer many variations on the classic brioche, *a buttery, egg-rich yeast bread that's enjoyed for luxurious breakfasts or snacks, appearing in various forms and sizes. This* brioche, *known as* brioche mousseline *because it is richer in butter than* brioche ordinaire, *is incredibly golden and delicious.* Brioche mousseline *is typically Parisian, and the light and sticky dough is often baked in tin coffee cans. Denis Ruffel, from the Left Bank pastry shop Pâtisserie Millet (see page 233), offers his personal version, baked in a rectangular loaf pan. Ruffel's special glaze gives all sweet breads a certain glow.*

Brioche:
1 tablespoon or 1 package active dry yeast
¼ cup (6 cl) milk, heated to lukewarm
⅓ cup (65 g) sugar
1 teaspoon salt
4 cups (560 g) unbleached all-purpose flour
8 eggs
1¼ cups (10 ounces; 310 g) unsalted butter at room temperature, plus
2 teaspoons unsalted butter for buttering the loaf pans

Glaze:
1 egg
1 egg yolk
Pinch of salt
Pinch of sugar
1 teaspoon milk

1. In the bowl of an electric mixer, combine the yeast, milk, and sugar. Stir by hand, and set aside for 5 minutes until the yeast has dissolved.

2. Stir in the salt. Then, with the mixer at low speed, add the flour, cup by cup, then the eggs, one by one, mixing well after each addition.

3. Add the 1¼ cups butter, bit by bit, incorporating it smoothly into the dough. The dough will be very soft and sticky. Cover securely with plastic wrap and let rise at room temperature until doubled in bulk, about 1 hour.

4. With a wooden spoon, stir the dough to deflate it. Cover again, refrigerate, and let rise until doubled in bulk, 1½ to 3 hours.

5. Preheat the oven to 350°F (175°C).

6. Stir down the dough again, and pour equal portions of the dough into two well-buttered 6-cup (1.5-liter) loaf pans. The dough will remain very soft and sticky. Cover and let rise at room temperature until almost doubled in bulk, about 1 hour. Don't worry if it doesn't double in bulk; it will rise more during the baking.

7. Combine the ingredients for the glaze, and brush over the top of the *brioches*. Bake until golden brown, about 35 minutes. Unmold immediately and cool on a rack. The *brioches* can easily be frozen.

Yield: 2 loaves

SEVRES-BABYLONE, ECOLE MILITAIRE, LA TOUR MAUBOURG

7th arrondissement

DESGRIPPES
16, avenue Rapp,
Paris 7.
Tel: 01.45.51.66.39.
Métro: Ecole Militaire or Pont de l'Alma.
Open 7:15 A.M. to 8 P.M.
Closed Sunday and August.
Credit card: V.

Make a detour to this *boulangerie-pâtisserie* not far from the Eiffel Tower for the delicious and unusual *raissol aux pruneaux,* a slipper of rich puff pastry filled with prunes, almost like a flat *baguette.* It makes a cozy and comforting breakfast or teatime treat. The breads here are just okay.

Irresistible, buttery croissants.

DUCHESNE
112, rue Saint-Dominique,
Paris 7.
Tel: 01.45.51.31.01.
Métro: Ecole Militaire or Pont de l'Alma.
Open 7:30 A.M. to 8 P.M.
Closed Sunday and either July or August.

Duchesne could be called the "ballroom pastry shop" because of the glittering mosaic walls and the chandeliers hanging from the gilt-painted ceilings. Stop by to admire this pretty boutique near the Eiffel Tower, across the street from the lovely Fontaine de Mars arcade. Then, if you're in the mood for something sinfully rich, try the excellent chocolate *mousse* cake with orange; a lovely *amandine* with orange and chocolate; or the thick and rich almond-flavored *croissants.* On the savory side, there's the deliciously rich *galette aux pommes de terre,* a puff pastry packet stuffed with chunks of potatoes, garlic, *crème fraîche,* and *fines herbes*—it gives new meaning to sour cream and chive potatoes. The breads don't always live up to their surroundings.

Financiers
ALMOND CAKES

The little rectangular almond cakes known as financiers *are sold in many of the best pastry shops in Paris. Perfect* financiers *are about as addictive as chocolate, and I'd walk a mile or two for a good one. The finest have a firm, crusty exterior and a moist, almondy interior, tasting almost as if they were filled with almond paste. Next to the* madeleine, *the* financier *is probably the most popular little French cake, common street food for morning or afternoon snacking. The cake's name probably comes from the fact that a* financier *resembles a solid gold brick. Curiously, as popular as they are,* financiers *seldom appear in recipe books or in French literature.*

The secret to a good financier *is in the baking: For a good crust, they must begin baking in a very hot oven. Then the temperature is reduced to keep the interior moist. Placing the molds on a thick baking sheet while they are in the oven is an important baking hint from the Left Bank pastry chef Jean-Luc Poujauran (see page 261), who worked for months to perfect his* financiers, *which are among the best in Paris. The special tin* financier *molds, each measuring 2 × 4 inches (5 × 10 cm), can be found at restaurant supply shops. Small oval* barquette *molds or even muffin tins could also be used.*

- 2 tablespoon (30 g) unsalted butter, melted, for buttering 21 *financier* molds
- 1 cup (140 g) finely ground almonds
- 1⅔ cups (210 g) confectioners' sugar
- ½ cup (70 g) unbleached all-purpose flour
- Pinch of salt
- ¾ cup (185 g) egg whites (5 to 6)
- ¾ cup (6 ounces; 185 g) unsalted butter, melted and cooled

1. Preheat the oven to 450°F (230°C).

2. With a pastry brush, use the 2 tablespoons melted butter to thoroughly butter the *financier* molds. Arrange them side by side, but not touching, on a baking sheet. Place the baking sheet with the buttered molds in the freezer to resolidify the butter and make the financiers easier to unmold.

3. In a large bowl, combine the almonds, sugar, flour, and salt. Mix to blend. Add the egg whites and mix until thoroughly blended. Add the ¾ cup butter and mix until thoroughly blended. The mixture will be fairly thin and pourable.

4. Spoon the batter into the molds, filling them almost to the rim. Place the baking sheet in the center of the oven. Bake until the *financiers* just begin to rise, about 7 minutes. Reduce the heat to 400°F (205°C). Bake until the *financiers* are a light, delicate brown and begin to firm up, about another 7 minutes. Turn off the oven heat and let the *financiers* rest in the oven until firm, about another 7 minutes.

5. Remove the baking sheet from the oven and let the *financiers* cool in the molds for 10 minutes. Unmold. (Note: Wash molds immediately with a stiff brush in hot water without detergent so that they retain their seasoning.) The financiers may be stored in an airtight container for several days.

Yield: Twenty-one 2 × 4-inch (5 × 10-cm) *financiers*

PATISSERIE MILLET
103, rue Saint-Dominique,
Paris 7.
Tel: 01.45.51.49.80.
Métro: Ecole Militaire or La Tour-Maubourg.
Open 9 A.M. to 7:30 P.M. (8 A.M. to 1 P.M. Sunday).
Closed Monday and August.
Credit card: V.

A classic, spotless pastry shop offering a fabulous *tarte paysanne* (puff pastry leaves with apples, Grand Marnier, and cream). Also good pure honey *madeleines;* almond-flavored *financiers;* buttery, egg-rich *brioche mousseline* (see recipe, page 230); some twenty different varieties of cakes and tarts; and twenty flavors of ice cream. Their *croissants* and *croissants aux amandes* are some of the best in town, and Denis Ruffel, Millet's energetic pastry chef, tucks two delicious sticks of chocolate into his remarkable *pain au chocolat*. Upstairs, behind the scenes, there's a chocolate "factory," while on the main floor a small tea salon provides the perfect spot for sampling everything that tempts the palate.

PELTIER
66, rue de Sèvres,
Paris 7.
Tel: 01.47.34.06.62. or 01.47.83.66.12.
Métro: Vaneau.
Open daily, 9:30 A.M. to 7:45 P.M. (8:30 A.M. to 7 P.M. Sunday).
Credit card: V.

Since 1961, the Peltier name has stood for quality pastry in Paris. Today the family's spacious, pristine shop offers some of the most beautiful tarts and cakes in the city, along with superb *croissants* and lovely frozen fruit soufflés. Sample their special cakes and tarts—one covered with seven different fresh fruits, another a mango-flavored *charlotte*—at the counter in the corner of the shop. Then take home a *princesse*—a meringue cake with almonds, vanilla cream, and grains of *nougatine*.

MADELEINE, CHAMPS-ELYSEES

8th arrondissement

LADUREE
16, rue Royale,
Paris 8.
Tel: 01.42.60.21.79.
Métro: Madeleine.
Open 8:30 A.M. to 7 P.M.
Closed Sunday and August.
Credit cards: AE, V.

Ladurée remains one of Paris's most elegant and traditional shops—a tea salon and pastry shop of note. Press your nose against the window and dream on. The choice is not a simple one. Shall it be a buttery early morning *croissant,* an exquisite lunchtime strawberry or raspberry tart, or a mid-afternoon chocolate macaroon? And this doesn't even take into account some of the best classic cakes in Paris, perfect to order for a birthday or special occasion. If there's time—and a table free—stop for a cup of *café au lait,* one of the best in the city. On your way out, buy a delicate *brioche mousseline* or the raisin-filled *brioche* called *cramique* to lure you out of bed the next morning. (See also Tea Salons.)

LADUREE
75, avenue Champs-Elysées,
Paris 8.
Tel: 01.40.75.08.75.
Métro: Georges V.
Open daily, 8 A.M. to 1 A.M.
Credit cards: AE, V.

Pastry chef Pierre Hermé has left Ladurée to go it on his own, but his mark remains. Here you will find *financiers* and *madeleines,* the famous macaroons of many flavors, and not one but two versions of rich and buttery *croissants* and golden *brioche*. But as well you will find seasonal creations that manage to lure even those who could not care less about sugar. This gigantic café/tea salon/restaurant along one of the city's grandest avenues is *the* meeting place for chic Parisians. Don't miss it. (See also Tea Salons.)

PASSY, AUTEUIL, TERNES

16th and 17th arrondissements

MALITOURNE
30, rue de Chaillot,
Paris 16.
Tel: 01.47.20.52.26.
Métro: Iéna.
Open 7:30 A.M. to 7:30 P.M.
Closed Sunday afternoon and Monday.
Credit card: V.

This shop features original pastries created by Jean-Yves Malitourne, a *pâtissier* from the Sarthes region of France who worked in the kitchens of Roger Vergé at Moulin de Mougins in the south of France before opening his own *pâtisserie* in this posh Paris neighborhood. Try the *téméraire,* an almond biscuit topped with Cointreau-infused *crème pâtissière* and wrapped in hazelnut *nougat;* or the *savoureux,* a chocolate biscuit topped with chocolate *mousse.* His raspberry tarts and prune turnovers are also lovely.

LE STUBLI/LA PATISSERIE VIENNOISE
11, rue Poncelet,
Paris 17.
Tel: 01.42.27.81.86.
Métro: Ternes.
Open 9 A.M. to 7:30 P.M. (to 1 P.M. Sunday).
Closed Monday.
Credit card: V.

If you love classic and beautiful Austrian pastries—ultra-fresh crumb-topped cherry or rhubarb strudels, light cheesecakes—then this is the boutique for you. Note the tea salon upstairs and the delicatessen across the street for a quick bite or carry-out. (See also Tea Salons.)

French fruit tarts: always luscious.

YAMAZAKI
6, chaussée de la Muette,
Paris 16.
Tel: 01.40.50.19.19.
Métro: La Muette.
Open 8 A.M. to 7:30 P.M.
(Sunday 9 A.M. to 7 P.M.)
Closed holidays.
Credit card: V.

With shops in Paris and Tokyo, this Japanese/French pastry shop offers fine examples of some of the country's most classic sweets: excellent *tarte au chocolat,* an oozing and puckery lemon tart, and—my favorite—a rhubarb tart with fresh strawberries and a streusel-like topping. You will want to try everything in the shop, for everything is pretty, pristine, appealing.

GASTON LENOTRE, THE PARIS PASTRY KING

One wonders how Gaston Lenôtre does it. He and his band of pastry chefs are all over the world, turning out cakes and pastries, breads, chocolates and ice creams, four-course meals, and light snacks by the thousands. Yet throughout, everything stamped Lenôtre has that certain quality that's hard to top. His chocolates are still among the best in town, and no one makes a *gâteau opéra* or a meringue and chocolate *mousse*–filled *concorde* like Lenôtre's. Great spots for a snack, a sandwich, or a quick picnic. All shops are open daily, 9 A.M. to 9 P.M.

61, rue Lecourbe, Paris 15.
Tel: 01.42.73.20.97.
Métro: Sèvres-Lecourbe.

193, avenue de Versailles, Paris 16.
Tel: 01.45.25.70.45.
Métro: Mirabeau.

44, rue d'Auteuil, Paris 16.
Tel: 01.45.24.52.52.
Métro: Michel-Ange–Auteuil.

48, avenue Victor-Hugo, Paris 16.
Tel: 01.45.02.21.21.
Métro: Victor Hugo.

15, boulevard de Courcelles, Paris 17.
Tel: 01.45.63.87.63.
Métro: Villiers.

121, avenue de Wagram, Paris 17.
Tel: 01.47.63.70.30.
Métro: Wagram.

KOUGELHOPH ANDRE LERCH
ANDRE LERCH'S ALSATIAN COFFEE CAKE

In Paris, André Lerch, an outgoing Alsatian baker (see page 223), runs a popular bread and pastry shop where he bakes forty to fifty kougelhoph *each day, using well-seasoned molds a half-century old. There's a curious story behind these molds: Apparently before World War II there was an Alsatian bakery where his now is. The baker went off to war, leaving behind his molds, buttered and prepared with whole almonds. He never returned, and when Monsieur Lerch moved in decades later, he found the molds stashed behind the ovens. He insists that well-seasoned molds are the secret to good* kougelhoph. *"The mold isn't good until it's been used two hundred times," he warns. Since most of us won't make two hundred* kougelhoph *in two and a half lifetimes, Monsieur Lerch offers a shortcut: Thoroughly butter a new mold and place it in a low oven for several hours, rebuttering every fifteen minutes or so. The mold will take on a seductive essence of browned butter and will be ready to produce fragrant, golden loaves.*

½ cup (80 g) golden raisins
2 tablespoons kirsch (cherry brandy) or other fruit-based *eau-de-vie*
1 cup (25 cl) milk
1 tablespoon or 1 package active dry yeast
3¾ cups (525 g) unbleached all-purpose flour
2 eggs, beaten
½ cup (100 g) sugar
1 teaspoon salt
¾ cup (6 ounces; 185 g) unsalted butter, at room temperature
1 tablespoon (½ ounce; 15 g) unsalted butter, for buttering the *kougelhoph* mold
½ cup (70 g) whole almonds
1 tablespoon confectioners' sugar

1. In a small bowl, combine the raisins and kirsch.

2. Heat the milk to lukewarm, add the yeast, stir well, and set aside for 5 minutes.

3. Place the flour in a large bowl and make a well in the center. Add the dissolved yeast and milk, the eggs, sugar, and salt, mixing well after each addition. The dough will be quite sticky. Knead by hand for 10 minutes by slapping the dough against the side of the bowl, or knead by machine for 5 minutes. Add the butter, bit by bit, and knead until the dough is smooth or until the dough comes cleanly off the sides of the bowl. Drain the raisins and knead them into the dough.

4. Place the dough in a large clean bowl and cover securely with plastic wrap. Let rise at room temperature, about 1 hour. The dough will rise slightly.

5. Punch down, knead gently, cover, and let rise again, about 1 hour. The dough will rise slightly.

6. Preheat the oven to 350°F (175°C).

7. Heavily butter a 2-quart (2-liter) earthenware *kougelhoph* mold or bundt pan, and place an almond in the well of each of the mold's indentations. Place the dough in the mold and let rise until it reaches the top, about 1 hour.

8. Bake 1 hour, or until the *kougelhoph* is golden brown.

9. Unmold, and when cool, sprinkle with confectioners' sugar. *Kougelhoph* tastes best the day after it's baked, when it's been allowed to "ripen."

Yield: 1 *kougelhoph*, about 20 servings

MENILMONTANT

20th arrondissement

PATISSERIE DE L'EGLISE
10, rue du Jourdain,
Paris 20.
Tel: 01.46.36.66.08.
Métro: Jourdain.
Open 8 A.M. to 8 P.M.
Closed Sunday afternoon and Monday in July and August.
Credit cards: AE, V.

A good place to know while in the neighborhood: Be sure to at least take a look at the beautifully restored ceiling of this 1887 boutique, situated on a quiet, village-like square. If you're in the mood, try a good and flaky *pain au chocolat,* a rectangle of *tarte aux cerises* (watch out for pits!) made with state-of-the-art puff pastry, or the individual *clafoutis aux abricots,* ideal for eating out of hand.

Warm bread at any hour.

DALLOYAU, SINCE 1802

Since 1802, when Napoléon ruled the republic, Dalloyau has done its best to satisfy the Parisian sweet tooth. Today the company has five boutiques in Paris and five in Japan, and its activities are incredibly diverse, offering pastries, chocolates, *charcuterie,* and fully catered meals and banquets. Best bets, though, are the coffee macaroons and the *cake mogador,* composed of chocolate cake, chocolate *mousse,* and a fine layer of raspberry jam. All shops are open daily, 9 A.M. to 9 P.M. Visit the Website: www.dalloyau.fr.

25, boulevard des Capucines, Paris 2.
Tel: 01.47.03.47.00.
Métro: Opéra.

2, place Edmond-Rostand, Paris 6.
Tel: 01.43.29.31.10.
Métro: RER Luxembourg.
(See Tea Salons)

63, rue de Grenelle, Paris 7.
Tel: 01.45.49.95.30.
Métro: Rue du Bac.

99–101, rue du Faubourg-Saint-Honoré, Paris 8.
Tel: 01.43.59.18.10.
Métro: Saint-Philippe du Roule.

69, rue de la Convention, Paris 15.
Tel: 01.45.77.84.27.
Métro: Charles Michels.

André Lerch's kougelhoph *(for recipe, see page 236).*

Boulangeries BAKERIES

Fresh bread daily—in France it's a must.

Of the hundreds of Parisians I've interviewed over the years, I love the bakers best. In days past, they were most often roly-poly men in worn white T-shirts, who came to Paris from little French towns and villages to make their way; they are men who love their wives, who never seem to have enough time to sleep, and who are passionate—almost crazily, over-the-edge, off-the-wall passionate—about bread. So am I.

Today's French baker wears many hats—those of baker, banker, entrepreneur. It could be said that the face of Paris changes with the face of its bread bakers. While historically the price of a *baguette* was controlled by law (generally, a *baguette,* a liter of milk, and the daily newspaper all cost the same), those controls were lifted in 1988, changing forever the way bread is prepared, baked, and sold in Paris.

There are now two kinds of baker. One is the dedicated *boulanger* who cares about the flour, the water, the oven, the bread, and the consumer. The other is the entrepreneur who bakes without passion (often frozen dough that comes from a central factory) and is interested only in the bottom line. (Whenever I am in a neighborhood where I know there's great bread and I see someone walking down the street with a flabby impostor, I am tempted to tap them on the shoulder and offer a bit of unsolicited gastronomic advice.) Here, of course, we're interested in the first kind of baker, the traditional baker, who mixes, kneads, rises, and bakes the bread on the premises. With love.

One of my greatest treats is to walk into a favorite *boulangerie* around noon, my stomach growling with hunger. I order a crusty *baguette "bien cuite,"* and before I've set down my few francs, I've bitten off the heel. Chewy, yeasty ecstasy. Bread is life. It's food that makes you feel good, feel healthy, food that goes with everything, especially the things we love most about France—fine cheese, great wine.

Baking good bread is hard, tedious, lonely work, and unfortunately few young Frenchmen these days aspire to be bakers. Working through the night in suffocatingly hot basements holds little glamour for them. The truth is, the romantic notion of the frail French baker slaving to provide breakfast fare is basically a memory these days, although there still remain a few diligent souls who do labor through the darkest hours.

How does one tell the good loaf from the bad, and what makes the difference? The good French loaf is made with a respect for the simple nature of the ingredients: wholesome stone-milled wheat or rye flour, fresh yeast (*levure*) or a fresh sourdough starter (*levain*), pure water, and a minimum of salt. This is true whether it's a thin, crisp, golden *baguette* or *ficelle;* a plump, round, country-style *pain de campagne;* or a made-to-eat-with-cheese loaf studded with hazelnuts, walnuts, or raisins.

In the best bakeries, ovens are fired all day long, ensuring that customers can purchase loaves just minutes old throughout the day. (French bread often contains no fat and thus quickly goes stale.) Most dough is now kneaded mechanically, but the best is done slowly so the flavor is not killed by overkneading. Good dough is allowed to rise slowly, several times, with plenty of rest between kneadings. At the finest bakeries every loaf is formed by hand. Good bread has a thick crust, a dense and golden interior with lots of irregular air holes, and a fresh wheaty aroma and flavor.

About fifteen years ago, French bakers organized a nationwide "good bread campaign," a loose attempt to bring back the kind of bread made before World War II brought modernization to the corner bakery. Today that campaign seems to have paid off in a renaissance of artisanal breads. Sourdough *baguettes* and crusty ryes now vie for space on some bakery shelves with such novelty breads as *pain à l'emmenthal et noix* (Emmenthal and walnut bread), *fougasse* (ladder-like flat country bread), and *pain aux plantes* (whole-grain bread baked with herbs), not to mention ten-grain loaves baked with everything from flax seeds to pumpkin seeds. This artisanal trend has also spawned a bevy of brand-name breads, made from industrially patented flour. Bakeries buy the flour and the recipe that goes with it and bake loaves with wholesome-sounding names, like Mannedor, Rétrodor, Baguepi, and Pain Passion.

At the same time, the interest in all things natural and *biologique* (organic) is stronger than ever, but no longer new. The terms *"pain de campagne"* and *"paysanne"* (usually crusty white bread made with a portion of whole-wheat or rye flour) have become bakery standards. What's positive is that the growing demand has pushed passionate bakers to create (or re-create) innovative variations on the country theme—*pains campagnotte, triple alliance, vieille France, paillasse, bûcheron,* to name a few. Unfortunately, this is a phenomenon found only at the best bakeries, and it is far from ubiquitous.

While I can't promise you'll find great bread on every corner or even in every neighborhood, I've done my best to scour the city for the best breads that Paris has to offer.

Parisians still thrive on warm and fragrant golden country loaves.

LES HALLES, BOURSE, OPERA

1st and 2nd arrondissements

ANDRE CLERET
4, rue des Lavandières-Sainte-Opportune,
Paris 1.
Tel: 01.42.33.82.68.
Métro: Châtelet.
Open 7 A.M. to 8 P.M.
Closed Sunday, Monday, and July or August.

André Cléret's is a bakery haven hidden on a side street near the frenetic Place du Châtelet, a *boulangerie* that's ideal for escaping from the neighborhood's lineup of fast-food joints. Local workers flock here for the incomparable selection of sandwiches: Westphalian ham and Gruyère on a raisin-rye bun; a chunky purée of radishes and *fromage blanc* on a whole-grain roll; rosemary-flecked goat cheese with tomatoes; feta cheese and salad; *brioche* "pockets" filled with tuna salad and tomatoes; and countless other combinations, all stacked in tidy piles behind the counter. The *boulangerie* is just around the corner from the Châtelet theaters, so stop off for a pre-performance bite, or for fortification before a visit to nearby Notre Dame and the Ile de la Cité. Cléret also offers a solid selection of country breads, such as *baguettes au levain;* flat, golden discs of *pain à l'ancienne* with a slightly sour, fermented taste; and chewy Gruyère and onion *fougasse,* here a filled oval-shaped flatbread.

GOSSELIN
125, rue Saint-Honoré,
Paris 1.
Tel: 01.45.08.03.59.
Métro: Louvre-Rivoli.
Open 7 A.M. to 8 P.M.
Closed Monday.
Credit card: V.

Philippe Gosselin won the best *baguette* award in 1996, and his is definitely worth a detour. It is everything a *baguette* should be: fragrant, golden, firm (not the least bit flabby), with a golden *mie* (interior) and the aroma of freshly milled wheat. The wheaty natural crust has a golden-brown glow with just the right amount of crackling, just lightly dusted with flour. Oh, how I would be pleased to make it my *"baguette quotidienne."* Gosselin is just a few blocks from the Louvre. Other treasures you will find here include good *pain au levain* and *pain de seigle.*

JULIEN
75, rue Saint-Honoré,
Paris 1.
Tel: 01.42.36.24.83.
Métro: Pont Neuf or Les Halles.
Open 6:30 A.M. to 8 P.M.
Closed Sunday.
Credit cards: AE, V.

The first time I sampled Jean-Noël Julien's golden *baguette* in a nearby restaurant, I fell instantly in love with its freshness, its crustiness, its fine handmade quality. He was well rewarded for his work in 1995 when he received first prize for the best *baguette* in Paris.

LE PAIN QUOTIDIEN
18, place du Marché Saint Honoré,
Paris 1.
Tel: 01.42.96.31.70.
Métro: Tuileries.
Open daily, 7 A.M. to 7:30 P.M.
Credit cards: AE, V.

With blond wood tables, ancient parquet floors, and walls with a rich ivory patina, this combination *boulangerie/café/épicerie/* dining room is filled with the aromas of hot chocolate, freshly brewed coffee, and freshly baked rolls. This Belgian import is a hit—I often stop here in the morning on my way to work, just to linger over coffee, bread, and the morning news. Try the rye bread, versions with raisins and hazelnuts, and the orange cake with almonds. (See also Cafés.)

Le Pain Quotidien, at table.

AU PANETIER
10, place des Petits-Pères,
Paris 2.
Tel: 01.42.60.90.23.
Métro: Bourse.
Open 8 A.M. to 7 P.M.
Closed Saturday, Sunday, and July or August.

By 8 A.M. most mornings, there's a line of customers streaming in to buy Bernard Lebon's *baguette au levain* (sourdough *baguette*), still baked in a sturdy wood-fired brick-lined oven built in the 1890s. Up at 5 A.M. each day, he travels just a few floors from his apartment above the shop to a flour-dusted but impeccably tidy cellar, where his assistant has been working since midnight. Monsieur Lebon gets right to work, ready to greet the first crackling batch of bread as it comes from the oven at 6 A.M. Working steadily, he continues to mix, knead, and form additional loaves for later bakings at 9 A.M. and noon. The 250 baguettes they produce each day are crisp and chewy, and like the baker, authentic and honest.

But Monsieur Lebon and his wife, Yvette, don't stop there: They offer some fifty different shapes of bread (not all of them available each day), including giant *couronnes* (rings) of wheat and rye and special *baguettes moulées* baked in molds to yield even crispier crusts—in all preparing eight different kinds of dough. What's the hardest thing about his job? "Getting the various breads to rise evenly, so they're ready for baking at the same time," says the agile, square-jawed baker. Does he love his own bread? He eats it three meals a day. Plus every afternoon he enjoys one of his pastry chef's apple tarts, warm from the oven.

Decorated breads can be made to order. At lunchtime the bakery often offers a wonderful *galette de pommes de terre* (puff pastry tart filled with potatoes, herbs, and *crème fraîche*), and there is always a good variety of sandwiches and savory tarts.

BAGUETTES

The crackling-crisp, slender *baguette*—the name comes from the French for "wand"—is not as old as some people think. And it wasn't born; it evolved essentially out of consumer demand. According to Raymond Calvel, one of France's more respected bread experts, the *baguette* came into being just before World War I, when the classic French loaf had two shapes: the round *miche,* weighing about 5 pounds (2.5 kilos), and the *pain long,* an 8-inch by 30-inch (20.5-cm by 76-cm) loaf of the same weight. The *mie,* or interior, of the *pain long* was dense and heavy, the crust crisp and flavorful. Most consumers preferred the crust and bakers accommodated, making the bread thinner and thinner to obtain maximum crust, reducing the loaf's volume until they came up with the traditional 30-inch (76-cm) *baguette,* weighing 8 ounces (250 grams).

Other historians suggest that the *baguette* evolved from the *viennois,* a long, thin Austrian-type loaf popular around the turn of the century. The loaf has the same form as the *baguette,* but the dough is sweetened with sugar and softened with milk.

PAIN DE MIE DENIS RUFFEL
DENIS RUFFEL'S SANDWICH LOAF

This is France's firm, fine-grained sandwich loaf: milky, just slightly sweet, and delicious when fresh and toasted. Denis Ruffel, from Pâtisserie Millet (see page 233), the Left Bank pastry shop, manages to turn a single loaf of pain de mie *into an entire buffet, making dozens of tiny highly decorated open-face sandwiches. He tops some with caviar or smoked salmon and lemon triangles, others with a blend of Roquefort, walnuts, and butter, and still others with thin slices of sausages topped with piped butter rosettes. The* mie, *by the way, is the crumb, or noncrusty portion, of any bread, and since this bread has virtually no crust, it's called* pain de mie. *Some Paris bakers advertise* pain de mie au beurre, *to distinguish their bread from those made with margarine. The loaf is usually made in a special pan fitted with a sliding cover, which helps mold the bread into a tidy rectangle. The molds are available at many cookware shops, although the bread can be made in any straight-sided loaf pan. To obtain a neat rectangular loaf, cover the dough-filled loaf pan with foil and a baking sheet, then weight the sheet with a brick or other heavy object and bake.*

1 cup (25 cl) milk, heated to lukewarm
3 tablespoons (1½ ounces; 45 g) unsalted butter, melted
1 tablespoon or 1 package active dry yeast
2 tablespoons sugar
2 teaspoons salt
2¾ cups (385 g) unbleached all-purpose flour
1 tablespoon (½ ounce; 15 g) unsalted butter, for buttering the bowl and loaf pan

1. In a large bowl, combine the milk, 3 tablespoons melted butter, yeast, and sugar. Stir, and set aside for 5 minutes to proof the yeast.

2. Once proofed, stir in the salt. Then add the flour, cup by cup, mixing well after each addition. Knead by hand for 2 or 3 minutes, or until the dough forms a smooth ball. Place in a well-buttered large bowl and cover securely with plastic wrap. Let rise in a warm place until double in bulk, 1 to 1½ hours.

3. Butter a 6-cup (1.5-liter) loaf pan, or the mold and cover of a 6-cup (1.5-liter) *pain de mie* pan. If using a loaf pan, butter a piece of aluminum foil to use as a lid. Punch down the dough, knead for 1 minute, then transfer it to the pan or mold. Press down the dough smoothly, being sure it fills the corners, and cover. Let rise at room temperature until double in bulk, another 1 to 1½ hours.

4. About 30 minutes before the dough is ready to be baked, preheat the oven to 375°F (190°C).

5. Bake until the loaf is golden brown, about 45 minutes. (If using a loaf pan, cover with buttered foil and a baking sheet, then weight the sheet with a brick or other heavy object.) Unmold immediately and cool on a rack. The bread will stay fresh for several days, wrapped and stored at room temperature. *Pain de mie* also freezes well.

Yield: 1 loaf

MAX POILANE
42, place du Marché Saint-Honoré,
Paris 1.
Tel: 01.42.61.10.53.
Métro: Tuileries.
Open 8:30 A.M. to 7:30 P.M.
Closed Sunday.

One of Paris's best-kept secrets is that there is more than one Poilâne: famous brother Lionel, and less famous brother Max. Working with the same ingredients and huge wood-fired ovens, they produce essentially the same large, round country loaf, with slight variations: Max's tastes less acidic, and he also bakes breads that can't be found *chez* Lionel, like a white *levain* bread and *petits pains aux noix* and *au seigle et froment* (mini nut breads and rye wheat breads). Lean, intense, and poetic, Max Poilâne is a fanatic about bread: "I love bread, I eat bread with bread. One day I even found myself eating bread with *sorbet*—that was too much." When he goes to restaurants, he brings a little sack of his own bread with him. Like Lionel, he has managed to keep his operation streamlined and homey, despite the fact that five huge wood-fired ovens are kept going twenty-four hours a day. His large personalized *pain décoré* (decorated country loaf) can be ordered several days in advance.

REPUBLIQUE, MARAIS

3rd and 4th arrondissements

DRAHONNET
32, rue Vieille-du-Temple,
Paris 4.
Tel: 01.42.72.78.01.
Métro: Saint-Paul.
Open 7 A.M. to 9:30 P.M. (8 A.M. to 9:30 P.M. Sunday).
Closed Thursday and August.

Right next door to Au Petit Fer à Cheval (see Cafés), this lovely Marais *boulangerie* offers an excellent *pain au levain,* rye and walnut breads, multi-grain *baguettes,* and crusty *boules de campagne.*

Fresh and crusty loaves await at Le Pain Quotidien *(see entry, page 243).*

ESPACE GOURMAND
27, rue des Archives,
Paris 4.
Tel: 01.42.72.93.94.
Métro: Hôtel de Ville or Rambuteau.
Open 7:30 A.M. to 8 P.M.
Closed Sunday and the first three weeks in August.

This airy, modern *boulangerie/pâtisserie/café* is a real find in this neighborhood, where wholesale boutiques and art galleries are squeezing out quality food shops. Come in for the special modern-day thyme-flecked *fougasse,* filled with *béchamel* and combinations such as tomatoes and *herbes de Provence;* or the *campagnarde,* stuffed with bacon, *béchamel,* and potatoes, or with Roquefort, leeks, olives, and anchovies. The *fougasse* also comes in cute cocktail-size versions. For a festive touch to any table or picnic, try the daisy-shaped *marguerite,* a sourdough roll with sesame and poppy seeds sprinkled over the crisp golden crust.

At lunchtime the Espace Gourmande serves sandwiches and fresh salads to take out or to sample at the shop's café. Pick up some bread and then poke your head into the nearby 18th-century Archives Nationales, an impressive mansion just down the street.

AU LEVAIN DU MARAIS
32, rue de Turenne,
Paris 4.
Tel: 01.42.78.07.31.
Métro: Saint-Paul.
Open 7 A.M. to 8 P.M.
Closed Sunday.

This gorgeous turn-of-the-century *boulangerie,* run by the Rabineau family, offers such organic treats as a raisin rye bread, *fougasse* with olives and with nuts, and excellent tart *tartelettes au citron.*

BOULANGERIE MARTIN
40, rue Saint-Louis-en-l'Ile,
Paris 4.
Tel: 01.43.54.69.48.
Métro: Pont Marie.
Open 7 A.M. to 1:30 P.M. and 3:30 to 8 P.M.
Closed Sunday and Monday.

This newly redone 1930s boutique in the heart of the Ile Saint-Louis is now run by Philippe Martin, who studied with bakers Jean-Luc Poujauran and Basile Kamir, two strong proponents of organic breads. In 1992 he took over the family *boulangerie,* and he turns out lovely old-fashioned breads, including organic *baguettes,* whole-wheat breads, and, at the end of the week, dark rye breads.

HERVE MOLINEAU
26, rue Saint-Paul,
Paris 4.
Tel: 01.48.87.64.10.
Métro: Saint-Paul or Bastille.
Open 7 A.M. to 8 P.M.
Closed Wednesday and July or August.

Hervé Molineau transformed himself from industrial to artisanal baker, using top-quality flours with no additives and a slow-rise method that results in full-flavored loaves. He has moved from the 9th to the Marais, and you will be sure to fall in love with his *fougasse aux olives, anchois, et lardons* and his *seigle aux noix et raisins.*

ONFROY
34, rue de Saintonge,
Paris 3.
Tel: 01.42.77.56.46.
Métro: Filles du Calvaire.
Open 8:15 A.M. to 1:30 P.M. and 3 to 8 P.M.
Closed Saturday afternoon, Sunday, and mid-July through August.

This is one baker I almost wish I could keep a secret. The nondescript bakery harbors some of the city's best bread treasures. On my last visit I wandered in at about 10 A.M., ordered a plump round of *pain au Gruyère,* and was transported. The bread was still warm, the cheese was melting, the flavors were rich, authentic, satisfying. I am also wild about the rich sour rye bread, the sort of hearty Eastern European loaf on which you could survive forever. And this is exactly what comes out of Fernand Onfroy's old-fashioned wood-fired oven. This unflappable Normandy baker—whose first childhood memory is of the Americans landing on Omaha Beach—works quietly and diligently, also producing a fine *baguette biologique* from organically grown flour, a whole-wheat *baguette complète,* as well as the everyday *baguette.* The excellent breads here surpass the pastries.

When Monsieur Onfroy opened his modest little shop not far from the Place de la République in 1965, he discovered the remains of an old underground Roman oven, then a more recent, though still ancient, oven at another level. Rue de Saintonge was first created in 1628, and most likely there's been a bakery at No. 34 for several centuries.

RACHINEL
87, rue Saint-Antoine,
Paris 4.
Tel: 01.48.87.87.59.
Métro: Saint-Paul.
Open 6:30 A.M. to 9 P.M. (5 A.M. to 9 P.M. Sunday).
Closed Monday.

This always bustling bakery on the busy corner of rue Saint-Antoine and rue Saint-Paul offers a wonderfully crusty flattened *baguette* called a *"crocus"*—absolutely delicious, with a good crust and nice golden interior. There is also a dazzling assortment of goodies, from *financiers* to spinach tarts to macaroons of all flavors. Rachinel makes *fougasse* with a split top to show off a variety of fillings, from the unusual and delicious combination of salmon and Gruyère, to olives and anchovies, to ham, Gruyère, and mushrooms. Baked four times each day, the *fougasse* is a crowd-pleaser for the hordes of hungry *lycée* (grammar school) students and neighborhood workers who jam into the shop. So if one specialty is sold out, just take a walk through the bric-a-brac shops of the nearby Village St. Paul (closed Tuesday and Wednesday) and come back later.

Pissaladiere
PROVENCAL ONION TART

Nearly every boulangerie *in Paris offers some form of this classic Provençal onion tart. This is my version. Served at room temperature, the crisp and flavorful tart hits the spot on a sweltering summer day, especially when served with a chilled glass of* rosé. *Note that the bread dough is brushed with a salt/oil/water mixture as it rises, resulting in a slightly salty, very crisp dough. The name, by the way, comes from the Provençal word* pissalat, *which was a fish-based condiment used to flavor many preparations. The condiment changed over the centuries, and the term now represents a combination of anchovies and thyme.*

The dough:
1 recipe Basic Bread Dough (see page 250)

The salt wash:
1 tablespoon water
2 teaspoons fine sea salt
1 tablespoon extra-virgin olive oil

The topping:
3 tablespoons extra-virgin olive oil
6 medium onions (about 12 ounces; 750 g), peeled, halved, and cut into thin rings
6 plump, fresh cloves garlic, peeled and halved
Bouquet garni: generous bunch of parsley, celery leaves, fresh bay leaves, and sprigs of thyme tied in a bundle with cotton string
1 teaspoon fine sea salt
2 ounces (60 g) best-quality black olives, pitted and halved
8 anchovy fillets, rinsed, soaked in milk for 15 minutes
½ teaspoon fresh or dried thyme leaves

1. Preheat the oven to 450°F (230°C).

2. Roll the dough out to form a rectangle measuring about 11 inches (28 cm) x 15 inches (38 cm). Place the dough on a lightly oiled baking sheet, and prick it all over with a fork. In a small bowl, combine the water, salt, and oil; brush this over the dough. Set aside to rise for about 30 minutes.

3. Prepare the topping: In a large heavy-duty skillet, combine the oil, onions, garlic, *bouquet garni,* and salt. Sweat, covered, over low heat until soft and cooked through, about 30 minutes. The onions should not brown. Remove and discard the *bouquet garni.*

4. Spread the onion mixture evenly over the bread dough.

5. Place in the center of the oven and bake until the dough is evenly browned and crisp, 25 to 30 minutes. Do not let the onions burn. Remove from the oven and arrange the olives and anchovies in an even pattern over the onions. Sprinkle with the thyme. Serve warm or at room temperature, cut into rectangles.

Yield: 16 servings

Pain

BASIC BREAD DOUGH

Use this dough to make the onion tart on page 249. The refrigerator rise gives it a finer texture and a more developed flavor. With such a long rise, the small amount of yeast is sufficient.

- 1 teaspoon active dry yeast
- 1 teaspoon sugar
- 1½ cups (33 cl) lukewarm water
- 2 tablespoons extra-virgin olive oil
- 2 teaspoons fine sea salt
- About 3¾ cups (1 pound; 500 g) bread flour

1. In the bowl of a heavy-duty electric mixer fitted with a dough hook, combine the yeast, sugar, and ⅓ cup (80 ml) of the lukewarm water, and stir to blend. Let stand until foamy, about 5 minutes. Stir in the remaining 1 cup (250 ml) water, the oil, and the salt.

2. Add the flour all at once, mixing at medium speed until most of the flour has been absorbed and the dough forms a ball. Continue to knead until soft and satiny but still firm, adding additional flour if necessary to keep the dough from sticking, 4 to 5 minutes. Transfer the dough to a clean work surface and knead by hand for 1 minute.

3. Place the dough in a bowl and cover tightly with plastic wrap. Place in the refrigerator. Let the dough rise until doubled or tripled in bulk, 8 to 12 hours. (The dough can be kept for up to 2 days in the refrigerator. Simply punch down the dough as it doubles or triples.)

Yield: Dough for 1 onion tart

Bread by the armful is only a one-day supply for an enthusiastic eater.

Latin Quarter

5th arrondissement

BOULANGERIE BEAUVALLET
6, rue de Poissy,
Paris 5.
Tel: 01.43.26.94.24.
Métro: Maubert-Mutualité.
Open 7:15 A.M. to 8 P.M.
Closed Wednesday and July or August.

A simple, old-fashioned *boulangerie* with a great *baguette* (a classic, with a gentle crust and a delicious interior) and good *pain rustique.* Baker Mohamed Ousbib supplies several neighborhood restaurants. Be sure to get there early in the day—near day's end the *baguettes* are likely to disappoint.

MICHEL BRUSA
16, rue Mouffetard,
Paris 5.
Tel: 01.47.07.06.36.
Métro: Cardinal Lemoine or Place Monge.
Open 7:30 A.M. to 9 P.M.
Closed Sunday and July or August.

A short walk up from the rue Mouffetard market, this tiny bakery on the Place de la Contrescarpe bakes tangy, moist sourdough *baguettes,* the best in the neighborhood. Other breads here are nothing special.

Master bread baker Eric Kayser with his superlative sourdough bread (see entry, page 252).

BOULANGERIE GARCIA
52, boulevard Saint-Germain,
Paris 5.
Tel: 01.43.54.48.72.
Métro: Maubert-Mutualité.
Open 7 A.M. to 8 P.M.
Closed Sunday, February school holidays, and July or August.
Credit card: V.

Boulangerie Garcia offers a dark, crispy, extra-sour *baguette à l'ancienne.* Pick one up to nibble on while strolling through the Carmes market in Place Maubert (Tuesday, Thursday, and Saturday). Be forewarned: they always run out by 6 P.M., earlier on market days. Aside from a delicious lattice-topped mushroom tart, the pastries here are unexceptional.

S. HERVET
69, rue Monge,
Paris 5.
Tel: 01.43.31.27.36.
Métro: Place Monge.
Open 7 A.M. to 8 P.M. (to 7 P.M. Sunday).
Closed Monday.
Credit card: V.

An employee at a nearby bakery once confided that the best *pain au levain*—traditional sourdough bread—could be found *"chez Madame Hervet."* And on market days, the long line streaming out the door of this pretty *boulangerie* attests to the fact. If it is possible for a bakery to be frustrating, this one is, because the assortment of artisanal breads is so vast. To help you with your choice, take a look at the labeled display outside so that when you get in line, your choice will have been made. Try the *baguette au levain* or one of their specialty breads, like the crusty *pain paillasse,* the *pain aux dix céréales,* the *fougasse aux olives,* the *pain au cumin,* or the *flûte à l'ancienne.*

KAYSER
8, rue Monge,
Paris 5.
Tel: 01.44.07.01.42.
Métro: Maubert-Mutualité.
Open 7 A.M. to 8 P.M.
Closed Tuesday.

If you have time for just one or two bakery visits, make sure that Eric Kayser's shop is on your route. You will no doubt stand in line, and while you do you will have time to decide what your order shall be. I adore his open-face sandwiches, topped with such delicious combinations as goat cheese and pear, as well as his old-fashioned quiche-like tarts filled with goat cheese or spinach. Son of a baker, Eric Kayser used to teach baking and in 1996 took over this shop, which opens wide onto the well-trafficked rue Monge. He uses all stone-ground flour and Brittany *sel de Guérande*, making for breads with a nice acidity, almost a fruitiness. His *baguettes* have a beautiful patina, and many of his breads are made with a flavorful combination of whole-wheat and buckwheat flours. (Just up the street, at No. 14, he has taken over a charming old *boulangerie* where he now offers 100 percent organic bakery products.)

Pain Poilane au Levain Naturel
POILANE'S NATURAL SOURDOUGH BREAD

I don't know anything that makes me prouder as a cook than to succeed with a fragrant, densely crusted loaf of sourdough bread, made—miraculously—with nothing but flour, water, and salt.

This is the recipe that Paris's most famous baker, Lionel Poilâne (see page 257), created for the French housewife, and the closest I've come to re-creating his superb and popular loaf at home. I also call it "Patience Bread," because it takes almost a week to make the first batch of this natural, slightly sour loaf.

To bakers accustomed to the fast-acting whoosh one gets from yeast doughs, Poilâne's dough is a real sleeper. This dough really takes its time expanding, but the reward for your patience is a very fine-grained, acidic, gentle loaf. It's the most subtle and delicious bread I know, at once sophisticated and countryish. When you bite into it, you'll say, "Now, this is bread!" A great crust, with a moist, chewy, wheaty-brown interior.

This recipe should offer a consistent loaf, with a vibrantly acidic interior and an irresistibly thick and chewy crust. If you love good bread, invest in a baking stone, and get into the habit of spraying the oven for the first few moments: The added humidity, along with the baking stone, works to create a beautifully dense crust and gives the bread better keeping qualities. Also, do not be fearful of baking in a very hot oven, for it's that initial high heat that helps the bread rise during the first 15 minutes.

Once you become comfortable with the process of sourdough bread, you can improvise, adding whole grains, a bit of whole-wheat flour, or other ground grains and flour, including rye, semolina, or cornmeal. Just be sure not to overdo it, or your starter will become heavy and less active. And no matter how many times you make sourdough bread, remember that no two loaves are ever exactly alike: That's part of their eternal charm.

Sourdough starter:
1 cup (25 cl) water, at room temperature
2 cups (280 g) bread flour

The final loaf:
3 cups (75 cl) water, at room temperature
1 tablespoon fine sea salt
5½ to 6 cups (980 g to 1.12 kg) bread flour

1. Days 1 to 4: Prepare the starter. In a small bowl combine ¼ cup (6.5 cl) of the water and ½ cup (70 g) of the flour and stir until the water absorbs all of the flour and forms a soft dough. Transfer the dough to a lightly floured work surface and knead into a smooth ball. It should be fairly soft and sticky. Return the starter to the bowl, cover with plastic wrap, and set aside at room temperature for 24 hours. The starter should rise slightly and take on a faintly acidic aroma. Repeat this for 3 more days, each day adding another ¼ cup (6.5 cl) water and ½ cup (70 g) flour. Each day the starter should rise slightly and should become more acidic.

2. Day 5: Now you are ready to make the bread. Transfer the starter to a large, shallow bowl. Add the 3 cups (75 cl) water and the 1 tablespoon salt. Using a wire whisk, stir for about 1 minute to thoroughly dissolve the starter. Add the flour, a bit at a time, stirring well after each addition. After you have added about 5 cups (650 g) of flour, the dough should be firm enough to knead. Lightly flour a large, clean work surface, and transfer the dough to the floured surface. (If your bowl

is large and shallow enough, you can knead the bread right in the bowl, reducing cleanup later.) Begin kneading, at first folding the dough over itself to incorporate air (it may actually be too soft to knead), adding additional flour until the dough is nicely elastic and soft, but still firm enough to hold itself in a ball. Knead for a full 10 minutes. (Set a timer, to be sure there's no cheating!)

3. Before you form the loaf, reserve the starter: Pinch off a handful of dough, about 1 cup (250 g), to set aside for the next loaf. Transfer this starter to a medium-size covered container (see Note). Shape the remaining dough into a tight ball by folding it over itself. Place a large floured cloth in a round shallow bowl or basket—one about 10 inches (25.5 cm) wide works well—and place the dough, smooth (top) side down, in the cloth-lined bowl or basket. Loosely fold the cloth over the dough. Set aside at room temperature for 6 to 12 hours. (You have a lot of flexibility here. A 6-hour rise is the minimum, but I often prepare bread in the evening and bake it the next morning, allowing the dough to rise for up to 12 hours. I have even forgotten the bread, baking it 24 hours later, and it was deliciously light and airy.) The dough will rise very slowly, but a good loaf should just about double in size.

4. At least 40 minutes before placing the dough in the oven, preheat it—with a baking stone—to 500°F (260°C).

5. Lightly flour a baking peel or paddle (or a flat baking sheet), invert the loaf onto the peel, and slash the top of the bread several times with a razor blade to a depth of about ¼ inch (7 mm) so that it can expand evenly during baking. With a quick jerk of the wrists, propel the bread onto the baking stone. Spray the bottom and sides of the oven with water. Spray 3 more times during the next 6 minutes. (The spray will help give the loaf a good crust, and will give the dough a boost during rising.) The bread will rise very slowly, reaching its full height during the first 15 minutes of baking. Once the bread begins to brown nicely—after about 15 minutes—reduce the heat to 425°F (220°C) and continue baking until the crust is a deep golden brown and the loaf sounds hollow when tapped, 35 to 40 minutes total. Transfer to a baking rack to cool.

6. Do not slice the bread for at least 1 hour, for it will continue to bake as it rests. For best results, store the bread in a paper or cloth bag once it is thoroughly cool.

Plastic will tend to soften the dense crust you worked so hard to create. The bread should remain deliciously fresh for 3 to 4 days.

Note: After you have made your first loaf and have saved the starter, begin at step 2 for subsequent loaves. Proceed through the rest of the recipe, always remembering to save about 1 cup of the starter. The starter may be stored at room temperature (in a covered plastic container or in a bowl covered with a damp cloth) for 1 or 2 days, or refrigerated for up to 1 week. Reactivate the starter every week by adding ¼ cup (6.5 cl) water and ½ cup (70 g) flour. Do not use more than 1 cup (250 g) of starter per loaf. (If you find you can't bake bread every week and you end up with more than 1 cup starter, offer the excess to a friend, add it to a yeast dough, or—as a last resort—discard it.) If refrigerated, remove the starter from the refrigerator at least 2 hours before preparing the dough. Although starter can be frozen, I find it takes so long to reactivate, one might just as well begin with a new starter.

Yield: 1 loaf

The hearty Poilâne loaf.

BOULANGERIE MODERNE
16, rue des Fossés-Saint-Jacques,
Paris 5.
Tel: 01.42.54.12.22.
Métro: Cluny–La Sorbonne or RER Luxembourg.
Open 7 A.M. to 8 P.M.
Closed Saturday afternoon and Sunday.

There's nothing modern about the Belle Epoque storefront of this tiny neighborhood *boulangerie* set on the active Place de l'Estrapade near the Panthéon. The *baguette* is a neighborhood favorite, with a crisp crust and a denser than average, chewy interior. Just don't expect to find one late in the day; they sell out early.

STEFF LE BOULANGER
123, rue Mouffetard,
Paris 5.
Tel: 01.47.07.35.96.
Métro: Censier Daubenton.
Open 7 A.M. to 8 P.M. (to 2 P.M. Sunday).
Closed Monday.

Steff is Stephane Delaunay, who studied with master baker Bernard Ganachaud and now produces his trademark baguette, *la flûte Gana*—golden, wheaty, and delicious. The breads are made with care: slow fermentation, kneaded at moderate speed, carefully shaped, and baked at just the right temperature to make sure the bread is crusty and full-flavored.

Other address:
54, rue de Sèvres,
Paris 7.
Tel: 01.47.83.97.12.
Métro: Vaneau or Duroc.
Open 7 A.M. to 8:30 P.M. (to 8 P.M. Saturday).
Closed Sunday.

SAINT-GERMAIN, SEVRES-BABYLONE, LA TOUR MAUBOURG

6th and 7th arrondissements

GERARD MULOT
76, rue de Seine,
Paris 6.
Tel: 01.43.26.85.77.
Métro: Odéon.
Open 7 A.M. to 8 P.M.
Closed Wednesday.

Gérard Mulot offers some of the best and most popular breads and pastries in the Saint-Germain neighborhood. (This is a great place for French movie star watching—they all have Mulot sweet tooths.) Here you will find what may be Paris's best *brioche,* almost muffin-like, topped with caramelized brown sugar and popping with raisins. They often run out before noon, so be there early, and take home a crusty loaf of *pain au levain* (sourdough bread made with natural yeast) for later in the day. Unlike many *pains au levain,* this bread has a light, airy texture that doesn't weigh you down. The pretty *baguette rustique,* however, doesn't live up to its earthy exterior. Opt instead for the crusty, moist rye raisin buns. Mulot's buttery *croissants* and *pains au chocolat* are so good that they're the breakfast of senators at the nearby Senate in the Palais du Luxembourg. His carry-out salads (I love the green bean and mushroom combo) and pizza-like breads are also favorites.

Early in the day at Gérard Mulot's shop.

LIONEL POILANE
8, rue du Cherche-Midi, Paris 6.
Tel: 01.45.48.42.59.
Métro: Sèvres-Babylone or Saint-Sulpice.
Open 7:15 A.M. to 8:15 P.M.
Closed Sunday.

Pain Poilâne . . . need one say more? There is no question that Lionel Poilâne makes the most famous bread in France, perhaps in the world. Thousands of Parisians buy his moist sourdough loaf each day. It's sold at hundreds of shops and restaurants in Paris, and Federal Express orders are shipped around the world daily. Each giant, round, wholesome loaf is made with a pungent sourdough starter, all-French flour, and fragrant sea salt. Each is formed by hand, rising in a rustic—yet practical—fabric-lined wicker basket. The loaves are baked in wood-fired ovens, one of which was built by the *patron* himself. But Poilâne bread is far from perfect, as Monsieur Poilâne readily admits. "People complain that it is uneven," he notes, suggesting that "with *levain,* that's the name of the game. No two batches are ever the same; a simple storm can ruin an entire baking." And he's right. There are days Poilâne bread is so dry, so lacking in authority and flavor, you know something's gone

DECORATED BREADS

One of the most beautiful and festive breads in Paris is the *pain décoré,* generally a large, round loaf that is personalized with one's name, a favorite symbol or saying, or most classically, decorated with a bunch of grapes or sheaves of wheat. The following *boulangeries* will prepare decorated breads to order, though all must be ordered in advance. The breads, by the way, are not simply decorative; they are edible when fresh.

LENOTRE
Three days in advance:

61, rue Lecourbe, Paris 15.
Tel: 01.42.73.20.97.
Métro: Sèvres-Lecourbe or Volontaires

44, rue d'Auteuil, Paris 16.
Tel: 01.45.24.52.52.
Métro: Porte d'Auteuil or
Michel-Ange–Auteuil

48, avenue Victor-Hugo, Paris 16.
Tel: 01.45.02.21.21.
Métro: Victor Hugo

15, boulevard de Courcelles, Paris 17.
Tel: 01.45.63.87.63.
Métro: Villiers

121, avenue de Wagram, Paris 17.
Tel: 01.47.63.70.30.
Métro: Wagram

LIONEL POILANE
Two days in advance:

8, rue du Cherche-Midi, Paris 6.
Tel: 01.45.48.42.59.
Métro: Sèvres-Babylone or Saint-Sulpice

MAX POILANE
Two days in advance:

87, rue Brancion, Paris 15.
Tel: 01.48.28.45.90.
Métro: Porte de Vanves

The line flows out the door at Poilâne.

wrong. I've also tasted the bread so rich, dense, so properly acidic and authoritative, that every other loaf, before or after, pales by comparison. Criticism aside, no one has yet attempted to meet the Poilâne challenge. Rarely imitated—and never successfully—he remains *"le roi du pain."* The Poilâne loaf has set the contemporary standard for bread, the loaf against which almost all others are judged (see recipe, page 253).

Other delicacies include some of the best apple tartlets in Paris—caramelized apples in a rich cloud of buttery puff pastry—and buttery baby *sablés* in a basket at the front of the shop. Visitors to the family shop on rue du Cherche-Midi are almost always welcome to visit the wonderfully fragrant, flour-dusted cellar, to watch the famous bread being mixed, kneaded, and baked in the ancient wood-burning oven set beneath the street. Large personalized *pain décoré* can be ordered several days in advance. On busy Saturday afternoons, the proprietors often pass out butter cookies to soothe those waiting in line.

Other address:
49, boulevard de Grenelle,
Paris 15.
Tel: 01.45.79.11.49.
Métro: Bir-Hakeim or
La Motte-Picquet–Grenelle.
Open 7:15 A.M. to 8:15 P.M.
Closed Monday.

A Ganachaud (Jeudon) assortment *(see entry, page 273).*

THE DAILY LOAF

The following are just a few breads—of various sizes, flours, *fantaisie* shapes—found in the Parisian *boulangerie.*

Baguette: In Paris, this is legally a loaf weighing about 8 ounces (250 grams) and made from flour, water, and yeast. It may also contain fava bean flour and ascorbic acid, or vitamin C. *Baguettes* dusted with flour may be sold as *baguette de campagne, baguette à l'ancienne,* or *baguette paysanne.* There are also several "brand name" *baguettes,* the Belle Epoque, Rétrodor, and Banette, sold in various bakeries. The bakers guarantee that these are made without the addition of fava bean flour or ascorbic acid and are made according to old-fashioned methods.

Baguette au levain (also sold by other names, sometimes called *baguette à l'ancienne*): Sourdough baguette.

Boule: Ball, or round loaf, either small or large.

Chapeau: Small round loaf, topped with a little *chapeau,* or hat.

Couronne: Ring-shaped *baguette.*

Le fer à cheval: Horseshoe-shaped *baguette.*

Ficelle: Very thin, crusty *baguette.*

Fougasse: Generally, a crusty, flat rectangular-shaped, lacy bread made of *baguette* dough; can be filled with onions, herbs, spices, or anchovies, or can be made of puff pastry dough.

Miche: Large, round country-style loaf.

Pain de campagne: There is no legal definition for the country loaf, which can vary from a white bread simply dusted with flour to give it a rustic look (and fetch a higher price) to a truly hearty loaf that may be a blend of white, whole-wheat, and perhaps rye flour with added bran. It comes in every shape, from a small round individual roll to a large family loaf.

Pain complet: Bread made partially or entirely from whole-wheat flour, with bakers varying proportions according to their personal tastes.

Pain de fantaisie: Generally, any odd or imaginatively shaped bread. Even *baguette de campagne* falls into the *fantaisie* category.

Pain de mie: Rectangular white sandwich loaf that is nearly all *mie* (interior crumb) and very little crust. It is made for durability, its flavor and texture developed for use in sandwiches. Unlike most French breads, it contains milk, sugar, and butter, and possibly chemical preservatives as well.

Pain aux noix and *pain aux noisettes:* Bread, most often rye or wheat, filled with walnuts or hazelnuts.

Pain polka: Bread that is slashed in a crisscross pattern; usually a large country loaf cut in this manner.

Pain aux raisins: Bread, most often rye or wheat, filled with raisins.

Pain de seigle: Bread made from 60 to 70 percent rye flour and 30 to 40 percent wheat flour.

Pain de son: Legally, a dietetic bread that is quality-controlled, containing 20 percent bran mixed with white flour.

Pain viennois: Shaped like a *baguette,* with regular horizontal slashes, this loaf usually contains white flour, sugar, powdered milk, water, and yeast.

JEAN-LUC POUJAURAN
20, rue Jean Nicot,
Paris 7.
Tel: 01.47.05.80.88.
Métro: La Tour-Maubourg.
Open 8:30 A.M. to 8:30 P.M.
Closed Sunday.

Jean-Luc Poujauran—an energetic, idealistic baker—claims he was the first in Paris to turn out a *baguette biologique,* made with organically grown, stone-ground, all-French flour. That was years ago, and his honey-colored, dense, and chewy *baguette* is unquestionably one of the best in Paris, a standard against which all others can be judged. A native of the rich and rustic southwest, Monsieur Poujauran is always trying new ideas: He once made a *croissant biologique,* using organic eggs, butter, and flour, in memory of his grandmother, who brought him up on pure and healthy foods. He's the sort of young man who inspires confidence: When he was first starting out and had little money, faithful customers chipped in to help him buy his first bread mixer.

Try Poujauran's earthy sourdough *pain de campagne,* along with the delightful and delicious

Jean-Luc Poujauran, all in a day's work.

pastries that fill this charming turn-of-the-century *boulangerie.* His famed *canelés* (sweet, tiny bundt cakes) are the best in town, and his tiny breads and rolls filled with walnuts or a *confit* of shallots, squares studded with anchovies, and sweet pound cake (*quatre quarts*) are all a delight. Today Poujauran supplies nearly two hundred of the city's restaurants with his excellent bread, with ovens working twenty-four hours a day to meet the demand.

Les Grands Boulevards

8th arrondissement

JULIEN
73, avenue Franklin D. Roosevelt,
Paris 8.
Tel: 01.42.56.19.81.
Métro: Saint-Philippe du Roule.
Open 6:30 A.M. to 8 P.M.
Closed Saturday, and Sunday in August.
Credit cards: AE, V.

The last time I strolled into this neighborhood shop I spied what I thought was a great-looking raisin bread, which seemed like the perfect sustenance for the long walk ahead of me. When it turned out to be studded with chocolate, not raisins, my spirits and appetite soared! Half bread, half cake, it was the perfect walking companion.

There is always a line out the door at this popular bakery and pastry shop, where office workers of the *quartier* seem to spend a good portion of their day, lunching in the back room or waiting to sample the breads or pastries. Their superbly classic *baguette* is dense, chewy, properly crisp (one could easily polish off a loaf without noticing it was gone). Stop in for a crisp, buttery *croissant* or *pain au chocolat,* fresh from the oven several times a day—sweets that are delicious with a strong *café crème* at the bar. I'm also a big fan of their delightful lemon tart.

RENE DE SAINT-OUEN
111, boulevard Haussmann, Paris 8.
Tel: 01.42.65.06.25.
Métro: Miromesnil.
Open 7 A.M. to 8 P.M.
Closed Sunday and July or August.

If René Gérard de Saint-Ouen ever decides to stop being a baker, he could be a press agent—for himself. His window is so plastered with awards and prizes and press clippings you can barely see the bread for the bravado. But I will admit his *baguette présidentielle* (he won the prize in 1994 and 1997) is delicious, as is his rye bread with walnuts. And I have to admit that the decorative breads—from owls to snails to birds to cats—make me giggle.

FAUBOURG SAINT-ANTOINE, BASTILLE, REPUBLIQUE, VINCENNES

11th and 12th arrondissements

L'AUTRE BOULANGE
43, rue de Montreuil, Paris 11.
Tel: 01.43.72.86.04.
Métro: Faidherbe-Chaligny.
Open 7:30 A.M. to 1:30 P.M. and 4 to 7:30 P.M.
Closed Saturday afternoon, Sunday, and August.

Take a trek down this dingy side street to *pain au levain* heaven. Monsieur and Madame Michel Cousin offer a mind-boggling array of breads, all *au levain,* fresh from the wood-fired oven in the back of this cozy shop (they'll let you take a look if they're not too busy). In addition to baking crusty, super-sour *pain au levain* and rye bread, they turn out exceptional specialty breads found nowhere else in Paris, like a state-of-the-art sourdough bread with Emmenthal cheese and walnuts: a moist *brioche* egg dough practically melting with an Emmenthal crust and a cheesy, nutty interior—it's amazing toasted. Also sample the whole-wheat prune and raisin bread, a perfect Roquefort *fougasse* (it also comes plain and with olives, onions, bacon, and other whims of the baker), organic whole-wheat bread, or rye with orange zest, to name a few. These hearty breads keep well for several days, so don't worry about buying too much!

At lunchtime you can choose from the list of thirty different sandwiches served on a variety of specialty breads. In the winter you can find chestnut bread (*pain à la châtaigne*) to accompany game, a chorizo and pistachio bread to serve with salads, and an eight-grain *pain des moines.* Many of the breads are made with organic flour, spring water, and *sel de Guérande* from Brittany. An aspiring baker from the United States came here to learn how to use a wood-fired oven, and in return she taught the Cousins how to make delicious not-too-sweet chocolate chip cookies—just in case you're feeling homesick.

BAZIN
85 bis, rue de Charenton,
Paris 12.
Tel: 01.43.07.75.21.
Métro: Reuilly-Diderot.
Open 7 A.M. to 8:30 P.M.
Closed Wednesday, Thursday, one week in February, and July or August.

A ten-minute walk from the ultra-modern Opéra Bastille, this turn-of-the-century bakery reassures you that *"vieux Paris"* is still alive and well. Jacques Bazin bakes a beautiful and unusual medley of breads (all *au levain*), like rye with almonds, hazelnuts, walnuts, and raisins; *petit-pains* filled with apple or *mimolette* cheese; and a moist, crusty whole-grain *pain bûcheron,* baked with a crunchy mix of rye and whole wheat flours and sunflower seeds. Monsieur Bazin also offers a selection of organic breads, including a long-fermented *pain sur poolish* with the flavor of hazelnuts.

The tiny, historic bakery is so beautiful, it has even appeared as a stage set in advertisements. It's a short walk from the lively Beauveau street market in the Place d'Aligre (see Markets).

A welcoming window at Le Moulin de la Vierge (see entry, facing page).

BOULANGERIE FERET
149, rue du Faubourg Saint-Antoine,
Paris 11.
Tel: 01.43.46.02.08.
Métro: Ledru-Rollin.
Open 7 A.M. to 8:15 P.M.
Closed Sunday.

An ordinary bakery offering fabulous crusty and soul-satisfying *pain de campagne,* which I discovered while lunching at Le Passage, a nearby wine bar that's worth the detour. (See Wine Bars.)

LE PAIN AU NATUREL (PAIN MOISAN)
5, place d'Aligre,
Paris 12.
Tel: 01.43.45.46.60.
Fax: 01.43.45.47.50.
Métro: Ledru-Rollin or Faidherbe-Chaligny.
Open 8 A.M. to 1:30 P.M. and 3:30 to 8 P.M. (to 2 P.M. Sunday).
Closed Monday.

Both of Michel Moisan's parents were bakers, so he likes to say that he was *"né dans le pétrain,"* or born in the wooden kneading trough. After years in the restaurant business, he opened this totally organic bakery in the fall of 1997. It is worth a detour to the 12th, especially in the mornings when the covered market and flea market on the place d'Aligre are in full swing. Moisan offers a sparkling selection of unusual breads and bread-based sweets, all prepared with stone-ground flour and certified organic products. Try especially the flatbread *pain au basilic,* a lovely round of golden sourdough bread so loaded with basil it tastes almost Middle Eastern, and the fat round of *pain aux abricots,* studded with moist dried apricots. If you are in the mood for a great cup of coffee, you can bring your purchases to the counter of Café Aouba (30, rue d'Aligre) and sample whichever coffee they are featuring that day; they stock seldom-seen Cuban coffee, as well as a smooth, rich, fragrant house blend from Central America.

BIR HAKEIM, MONTPARNASSE, PLAISANCE

14th arrondissement

AUX DELICES DU PALAIS
60, boulevard Brune,
Paris 14.
Tel: 01.45.39.48.68.
Métro: Porte d'Orléans.
Open 7 A.M. to 7 P.M.
Closed Sunday and August.

One of the most recent winners of Paris's best *baguette* award (1998), Antoine Teixera produces a "brand name" *Bannette baguette* worth sampling if you are in the neighborhood.

LE MOULIN DE LA VIERGE
105, rue Vercingétorix,
Paris 14.
Tel: 01.45.43.09.84.
Métro: Pernéty or Plaisance.
Open 8 A.M. to 8 P.M.
Closed Sunday and August.

A passion for bread is the only explanation for Basile Kamir's extraordinary and creative variety of breads. A bite into one of his sourdough loaves reminds you that this is what bread should taste like: moist and slightly tangy on the inside, surrounded by a thick, earthy crust. Monsieur Kamir's delicious, dense, golden country bread, baked with organically grown wheat, is some of the best in town. Come here also to find a perfect *fougasse*—

crispy and golden on the outside with a rich olive and anchovy interior (it also comes plain and with a variety of other fillings). The moist sourdough rye bread bears a crater-like crust that seems to erupt with walnuts and flour (it also comes plain and with raisins). Do try the simple and unusual provincial pastry specialties, like the *carré dijonnaise,* a sandwich of brown butter *sablés* that resemble rich graham crackers filled with raspberry jam; the *galette charentaise* (an overgrown wheel of melt-in-your-mouth butter *galette* doused with almonds); or the *canelés* (sweet miniature molded butter cakes, a specialty of Bordeaux). There is nothing fancy here, and there doesn't need to be. The old-fashioned 1890s bakery sits as a historical monument in the middle of block after block of impersonal, modern high-rise buildings at the southern edge of town. Don't give up trying to find it!

Lacy fougasse *on display.*

Other addresses:
82, rue Daguerre,
Paris 14.
Tel: 01.43.22.50.55.
Métro: Gaîté.
Open 7:30 A.M. to 8 P.M.
Closed Sunday, Monday, and July or August.

166, avenue de Suffren,
Paris 15.
Tel: 01.47.83.45.55.
Métro: Sèvres-Lecourbe.
Open 7 A.M. to 8 P.M.
Closed Sunday and holidays.

35, rue Violet,
Paris 15.
Tel: 01.45.75.85.85.
Métro: La Motte-Picquet–Grenelle or Avenue Emile Zola.
Open 7:30 A.M. to 8 P.M. (8:30 A.M. to 1:30 P.M. and 4:30 to 7:30 P.M. in August).
Closed Saturday and Sunday.
No credit cards.

19, rue de l'Etoile,
Paris 17.
Tel: 01.44.09.99.90.
Métro: Charles de Gaulle–Etoile or Ternes.
Open daily, 7:30 A.M. to 8 P.M. (8 A.M. to 1:30 P.M. Sunday)

MAX POILANE
29, rue de l'Ouest,
Paris 14.
Tel: 01.43.27.24.91.
Métro: Montparnasse–Bienvenüe or Gaîté.
Open 8:30 A.M. to 7:30 P.M. (10:30 A.M. to 7 P.M. in July and August).
Closed Saturday afternoon and Sunday.

Max Poilâne's branch in the modern Place Constantin Brancusi is a lovely place to come for breakfast before or after seeing someone off at the Gare Montparnasse. Despite the jarringly modern neighborhood, this bakery makes every effort at old-fashioned charm—from the marble tables and good *café crème* served with pitchers of steamed milk to the little gourmet gifts like homemade jams, apple cider, bonbons, and boxes of *madeleines de Commercy.* They also serve sandwiches on *pain Poilâne,* perfect to take for a snack on the train.

CONVENTION, PORTE DE VANVES

15th arrondissement

LA BOULANGERIE ALSACIENNE
129 bis, rue Saint-Charles,
Paris 15.
Tel: 01.45.77.84.61.
Métro: Lourmel or Boucicaut or Charles Michels.
Open 7 A.M. to 8 P.M.
Closed Wednesday and July or August.

Benoit Maeder and his wife, Véronique, offer some top-quality breads, such as the *flûte Gana* with a great, thick crust and an irresistibly fragrant and wheaty interior; a rustic *pain forestier,* packed with grains; a wonderful rhubarb tart; and a rarely seen *tarte à sucre* (a flat round of dough topped with sugar).

L'EPI GAULOIS
23 bis, boulevard Brune,
Paris 15.
Tel: 01.45.39.34.18.
Métro: Porte de Vanves.
Open 8 A.M. to 8:30 P.M. (9 A.M. to 8:30 P.M. Sunday and Monday).
Closed in August.

This funny little modern shop, opening out onto the busy boulevard Brune, offers a great rye bread—dense, crusty, chewy—and a good six-grain bread (*pain aux six céréales*), as well as a golden, substantial *pain de campagne.* Worth a visit on market day, each Thursday and Sunday along the boulevard.

MAX POILANE
87, rue Brancion,
Paris 15.
Tel: 01.48.28.45.90.
Métro: Porte de Vanves.
Open 7:15 A.M. to 8 P.M. (10 A.M. to 2 P.M. and 3 to 7 P.M. Sunday).

Max Poilâne's original 15th-*arrondissement* bakery is worth a detour. The charming 1890s shop—with its marble floors, glistening chandelier, and beautiful crusty loaves arranged like a still life in wicker baskets around the room—is one of the most romantic little *boulangeries* in town. The rye bread is worth a second detour! (See page 246 for more on Poilâne.)

VICTOR-HUGO, AUTEUIL, SAINT CLOUD

16th arrondissement

LAURENT CHAVENET
14, rue de Longchamp,
Paris 16.
Tel: 01.47.27.95.94.
Métro: Boissière.
Open 7:30 A.M. to 7:30 P.M. (8 A.M. to 1 P.M. Sunday).
Closed Monday.

At this nondescript corner bakery, Laurent and Catherine Chavenet offer some extraordinary *Banette* breads, including whole rye bread, organic breads, and varieties flavored with olive oil, basil, or chunks of delicious *lardons* (salty bacon).

Bostock Bernard Ganachaud
BERNARD GANACHAUD'S BOSTOCK

Bostock *is a terrific way to recycle day-old* brioche, *which on its own is already quite marvelous. Bernard Ganachaud, one of my favorite Parisian bakers, now retired, kindly shared the recipe for this kirsch-and-almond-flavored pastry. Superb fresh from the oven,* bostock *is still delicious a few days later. Eat it for breakfast or dessert.*

1¼ cups (170 g) whole blanched almonds
1 cup (25 cl) water
1⅜ cups (275 g) sugar
10 slices day-old *brioche*
2 large eggs
3 tablespoons kirsch *eau-de-vie* (cherry brandy)

1. Preheat the oven to 375°F (190°C).

2. Toast the almonds on a baking sheet until browned, about 5 minutes. Remove but leave the oven on. When cooled (about 10 minutes), grind ¾ cup (100 g) of the almonds to a fine powder in a food processor. Coarsely chop the remaining almonds.

3. In a medium-size saucepan over medium heat, combine the water and ⅝ cup (125 g) sugar, and stir until dissolved. Remove the syrup from the heat.

4. Dip the slices of *brioche* in the syrup and drain them on a wire rack. Once drained, arrange the slices on a baking sheet.

5. In a small mixing bowl, combine the eggs, finely ground almonds, and remaining ¾ cup (150 g) sugar and blend to form a thick paste. Spread the mixture on the *brioche.*

6. Sprinkle the *brioche* with the kirsch, then with the coarsely chopped almonds. Bake until golden brown, 15 minutes.

Yield: 10 servings

ARC DE TRIOMPHE, PORTE MAILLOT, VILLIERS

17th arrondissement

BOULANGERIE COUASNON
21, rue de Lévis,
Paris 17.
Tel: 01.43.87.28.27.
Métro: Villiers.
Open 7 A.M. to 8:45 P.M. (to 7 P.M. Sunday).
Closed Monday.
Credit card: V.

The loaves of incredibly crusty *pain paillasse* (a free-form, stone-shaped country bread) piled high in the front window beckon you inside and don't disappoint—break open the golden crisp shell to reveal a moist, white sourdough interior.

ANTOINE PAPILLON
49 rue Laugier,
Paris 17.
Tel: 01.47.63.95.65.
Métro: Péreire.
Open 6:45 A.M. to 8 P.M. (7 A.M. to 8 P.M. Saturday, 7:30 A.M. to 1 P.M. Sunday).
Closed Monday and July or August.

From this nondescript *boulangerie* Antoine Papillon captured third place in the city-sponsored competition for 1998 *baguette* of the year with his crusty, wonderful *baguette Rétrodor.*

PAUL
4, rue Poncelet,
Paris 17.
Tel: 01.42.27.80.25.
Métro: Ternes.
Open 7:30 A.M. to 7:30 P.M. (to 1:30 P.M. Sunday).

This high-quality bakery chain offers extraordinary breads, baked around the clock, including a simple country loaf with a fine, nutty flavor; a surprising and satisfying *baguette aux sésame,* chockablock with sesame seeds; and a wonderful *ficelle rustique.* I dare you to stop eating it.

Other addresses:
5, rue du Havre,
Paris 8.
Tel: 01.42.93.41.03.
Métro: Saint-Lazare.

12, rue des Belles-Feuilles,
Paris 16.
Tel: 01.47.27.83.92.
Métro: Trocadéro.

MONTMARTRE, BARBES-ROCHECHOUART

18th arrondissement

BLONDEAU
24, rue des Abbesses,
Paris 18.
Tel: 01.46.06.18.77.
Métro: Abbesses.
Open 6:30 A.M. to 8 P.M.
Closed Monday.

At the foot of Montmartre, walk down the bustling street market along rue Lepic to Blondeau for hearty homemade breads that will fill you with enough energy to climb the hill up to Sacré Coeur. Their *pain sportif* mixes at least ten different grains, including soybean flour, pumpkin seed, and linseed, into a whole-wheat base filled with raisins and nuts. They also bake a homey *triple alliance* loaf, a wheat bread mixed with linseed and sesame seeds. On weekends they offer specialties such as olive bread. Blondeau may not bake the best bread in Paris, but this is definitely the best in the neighborhood. The pastries and tea salon fare, however, are soggy and unexceptional.

Do take the time to admire the nearby Place des Abbesses, which boasts one of Paris's last remaining Art Nouveau Métro stations, designed by Hector Guimard. This sunny neighborhood overlooking all of Paris retains an old-fashioned feeling.

AU PAIN D'ANTAN
2, rue Eugène-Sue,
Paris 18.
Tel: 01.42.64.71.78.
Métro: Marcadet-Poissonniers.
Open 7 A.M. to 1 P.M. and 3:30 to 7:45 P.M. (7 A.M. to 7:45 P.M. Friday, to 7 P.M. Saturday).
Closed Sunday and July or August.

Literally "bread from bygone days," this homey *boulangerie* offers some of the best sourdough bread in Paris. The brick-lined oven, dating from the 1920s, turns out a small but delicious selection of fragrant, hearty, old-fashioned breads: dark, crusty loaves of sourdough bread and rye sourdough rounds with or without nuts and raisins. Try their specialty, *fouace aveyronnaise,* a butter-enriched *brioche* dusted with a bit of sugar, from central France.

AU PETRIN D'ANTAN
174, rue Ordener,
Paris 18.
Tel: 01.46.27.01.46.
Métro: Guy Môquet.
Open 7:30 A.M. to 1:30 P.M. and 3:30 to 8 P.M.
Closed Thursday and July or August.

Baker Philippe Viron likes to show off his talents, and why not? The exterior of his bakery has a giant RETRO-DOR sign and he displays *baguettes* sliced in half to show what the *mie,* or interior, of an honest *baguette* should look like. His is just that—golden, with irregular holes in the *mie,* proof that the bread rose slowly and naturally. His *fougasse* and rye bread are also worth sampling

MENILMONTANT

20th arrondissement

AU 140
140, rue de Belleville,
Paris 20.
Tel: 01.46.36.92.47.
Métro: Jourdain.
Open 7 A.M. to 8:30 P.M. (7:30 A.M. to 8 P.M. Saturday; 5 A.M. to 2 P.M. and 4 to 8 P.M. Sunday).
Closed Monday, and Sunday afternoon in July and August.

The wood-fired oven is right there in the center of this tiny *boulangerie* right off the Place des Fêtes, in the kind of bakery I dream of: Everything is fragrant, ripe, wholesome, correct. The slim *baguettes au levain* tempt you on without remorse, so dense, fragrant, and chewy that you think you will never meet another *baguette* you will love as much as this one. The heavy, giant round of *pur seigle au levain* is so moist, dense, and sour you could make a meal of it. Or two. (All I wanted was to stop and buy a slice of aged Cantal to go with it.) And how could one not fall in love with the *pain à l'orange aux amandes,* a long golden whole-wheat loaf studded with candied orange peel and topped with feather-thin slices of almonds. Worth a detour, for sure.

LA FLUTE GANA
226, rue des Pyrénées,
Paris 20.
Tel: 01.43.58.42.62.
Métro: Gambetta.
Open 7:30 A.M. to 8 P.M.
Closed Sunday, Monday, and July or August.

Isabelle and Valérie Ganachaud—daughters of Bernard Ganachaud, one of the city's legendary bakers—offer an incredible assortment of first-class breads. Try the *flûte Gana,* irresistibly crusty, thin *baguettes;* breads stuffed with raisins and hazelnuts;

Poujauran's special boutique (see entry, page 261).

country breads enriched with wheat germ; and an assortment prepared with organic (*biologique*) flours.

Other address:
29–31, rue Raymond du Temple,
Vincennes.
Tel: 01.43.28.00.64.
Métro: Château de Vincennes.
Open 7:30 A.M. to 8 P.M.
Closed Sunday, Monday, and July or August.

GANACHAUD (JEUDON)
150–152, rue Ménilmontant,
Paris 20.
Tel: 01.46.36.13.82.
Métro: Pelleport.
Open 7:30 A.M. to 8 P.M. (2:30 P.M. to 8 P.M. Tuesday; 7:30 A.M. to 1:30 P.M. Sunday).
Closed Monday and July or August.

The great Bernard Ganachaud has retired, but his successor, Monsieur Jeudon, continues in a fine tradition, offering more than thirty different breads. Definitely worth a detour.

Fromageries
CHEESE SHOPS

Fromagerie de Montmartre (see entry, page 291).

If all France had to offer to the world of gastronomy was bread, cheese, and wine, that would be enough for me. Of the trinity, it is cheese that links one to the other. I cannot imagine a more understated, unified French meal than one perfectly fresh *baguette,* a single Camembert, so ripe and velvety it won't last another hour, and a glass or two of young, fruity, well-balanced red wine. And I can't imagine a better place to discover French cheese than in Paris, where dozens of *fromageries* line the streets, each shop as different and distinctive as the personality of its owner, each offering selections that vary with the seasons.

Only the French produce so many varieties of cheese, so graphically reflecting their regional landscape and the many kinds of soil, climate, and vegetation. From the milk of cows, goats, and sheep; from the green, flat lands of Normandy, the steep mountain Alps, and the plains of Champagne east of Paris comes a veritable symphony of aromas, textures, colors, and forms. Cheese fresh from little farms and big cooperatives, cheese to begin the day and to end it. The French consume a great deal of cheese—about forty-two pounds per capita per year, compared to the American's twenty pounds—and of all the varieties, Camembert is the undisputed favorite.

How many varieties of French cheese are there, really? The French are not a people given to simple agreement. When Winston

Churchill said, "A country that produces 325 varieties of cheese can't be governed," he was, undoubtedly, responding to a bit of cheese hype. The real figure, say experts, is more like 150 to 200 serious varieties, with perhaps an additional 100 cheeses that are minor variations.

There's an old *New Yorker* magazine cartoon that describes the confusion perfectly: An elderly woman is sitting on the sofa, poring over maps of France. She looks up at her husband and says: "Has it ever occurred to you, dear, that most of the villages and towns in France seem to have been named after cheeses?"

Don't let anyone convince you that the cheese you eat in France and the French cheese you eat in the United States are necessarily the same. A major reason they don't taste the same has to do with United States Department of Agriculture regulations barring the importation of cheese made from unpasteurized milk that has been aged less than sixty days. Pasteurization may make cheese "safe," but in the process it kills all the microbes that give the cheese its character and flavor, that keep it a live, ever-changing organism. There is no question that pasteurized milk produces uniformly bland, "dead" cheese. The regulation rules out the importation of France's finest fresh young cheese, including raw-milk Camembert and Brie and the dozens of varieties of lively, delicate goat cheese, although on occasion a few may slip through.

Yet even in France, cheese made from pasteurized milk is increasingly common. For instance, less than 5 percent of the 160,000 tons of Camembert produced in France each year is made from raw milk. The advantage, of course, is that cheese made with pasteurized milk can be made available year-round and will have more stable keeping qualities. When in France, take the time to get a true taste of fresh French cheese: Specify raw-milk cheese by asking for *fromage fermier* or *au lait cru*. These cheeses are produced in limited quantities, the result of traditional production methods.

Paris has dozens of *fromageries* that specialize in raw-milk cheese, with some shops offering as many as 200 different varieties. Before living in Paris I thought that cheese merchants only bought and sold cheese. Wrong. The best, most serious cheese people actually age the cheese they sell. That is, they buy the cheese ready-made from the farmer, then, following a sensitive and tricky aging process, they take the cheese from its young, raw state to full maturity, refining the cheese in underground cellars that are usually humid and cold. The process is called *affinage,* and it can last from days to months, depending on the cheese. As each cheese matures, it takes on its own personality, influenced by the person responsible for its development. Maturing cheese needs daily attention: Some varieties are washed with beer, some with a blend of salt and water, some with *eau-de-vie.* Some are turned every day, moved from one cellar to another as the aging process continues. Each merchant has his own style of aging, and there are varying opinions on how cold and how humid the cellar should be; whether the cheese should be aged on clean straw or old straw, paper, or even plastic; or whether the cheese should be turned daily or just every now and then. And each merchant has a different opinion on when a cheese is ripe, and thus ready to be put on sale.

I adore watching the dedicated *fromagers,* whose love for cheese is totally infectious. In their cellars they are in heaven, as they vigorously inhale the heady, pungent aromas that fill the air and give the cheese little "love taps," the same way bakers give their unbaked loaves a tender touch before putting them in the oven. Now, having toured most of the various aging cellars that exist beneath the streets of the city, I see what a single individual can do to change the course of a cheese's life, ultimately determining taste and texture. Henry Voy's cheese, from La Ferme Saint-Hubert, has a lusty, almost over-the-hill quality about it that at times can be quite appealing. Cheeses from Alléosse are refined and elegant, always in perfect, presentable shape.

A few words on selecting cheese: Be sensitive to the seasons. For instance, don't expect to find Vacherin in the middle of summer. Ask to know the seasonal specialties in a given shop. In selecting cheese for a *dégustation* (a sample selection for tasting) either at home or in a restaurant, choose three or four varieties, generally including a semi-soft cheese, a goat cheese, and a blue. Eat the mild cheese first, then move on to the stronger varieties.

Be wary of cheese wrapped in plastic. Like us, cheese has to breathe to maintain life and vigor. Don't be afraid of a bit of mold. Generally the bluish film on goat's milk cheese is a sign that the cheese is made with raw milk and has been ripened on fresh straw. Cheese that won't mold and won't spoil is already too dead to bother about.

Be open-minded and adventurous. The first months I lived in Paris I rarely bought Brie or Camembert—I'd had so many disappointing pasteurized-milk varieties that I had lost my enthusiasm for these wonderful cheeses. Then one day, I happened to sample a perfect Camembert and "click," I instantly understood what the fuss was all about.

OPERA, PALAIS-ROYAL

1st arrondissement

MARCEL LEVERRIER
25, rue Danielle Casanova, Paris 1.
Tel: 01.42.61.30.06.
Métro: Pyramides.
Open 8 A.M. to 1:45 P.M. and 4 to 7:15 P.M. (8 A.M. to 1:45 P.M. Saturday).
Closed Sunday and August.
Credit card: V.

Right around the corner from the jewel-rich Place Vendôme, this landmark Art Deco building boasting *"beurre/oeufs/fromage"* (butter, eggs, cheese) is the site of a delicious cheese shop offering sparkling fresh goat cheese and an abundant assortment of such delights as aged Comté (*vieux Comté*); a state-of-the-art Saint Marcellin cow's milk cheese; a fine sheep's milk *brebis de pyrénées;* and a lovely young farm-fresh goat cheese from the Tarn.

CHEZ TACHON
38, rue de Richelieu, Paris 1.
Tel: 01.42.96.08.66.
Métro: Palais Royal–Musée du Louvre.
Open 9:30 A.M. to 2 P.M. and 4 to 8 P.M.
Closed Sunday, Monday, July, and August.

A truly classic, old-fashioned *fromagerie,* near the Louvre and the Palais-Royal. Little handwritten signs tell you about the origin and history of many cheese varieties, and there is even an advisory list noting which ones are currently at their best. Tachon's owner, Jean-Claude Benoit, presents some wonderful finds, including many small-production farm cheeses: great Burgundian Epoisses from the Laiterie de la Côte in Gevrey-Chambertin; superb Swiss Tête de Moine; an above-average farm-fresh Saint-Nectaire, mild, sweet, tangy, and aged a full two months on beds of rye straw; and Livarot, from Normandy farms, a cheese that's strong, spicy, and elastic, the sort of cheese that sticks agreeably to your teeth. Also try the Roquefort Maria-Grimal, the Camembert from the Coopérative d'Isigny, and the earthy smoked pork sausages from the French Alps.

TEMPLE

3rd arrondissement

FROMAGERS DE FRANCE
39, rue de Bretagne,
Paris 3.
Tel: 01.42.78.52.61.
Métro: Filles du Calvaire.
Open 8 A.M. to 1 P.M. and 4:30 to 8 P.M. (8 A.M. to 1 P.M. Sunday).
Closed Monday.

This fairly new shop, run by owner William Jouanault, offers a truly fine selection of the best cheeses France has to offer, including butter-rich Beaufort *d'alpage;* farm-fresh Livarot; a sweet Saint-Nectaire; and the fine, smooth farmhouse *tomme* d'Abondance from the Haut-Savoie, with a golden, fruity aftertaste; as well as Lezeen, a gentle disc of goat's milk cheese from the Deux-Sèvres.

ILE SAINT-LOUIS

4th arrondissement

LA FERME SAINT AUBIN
76, rue Saint-Louis en l'Ile,
Paris 4.
Tel: 01.43.54.74.54.
Fax: 01.47.97.03.99.
Métro: Sully-Morland or Pont Marie.
Open 8 A.M. to 8 P.M. (8 A.M. to 1 P.M. and 3 to 8 P.M. Sunday).
Closed Monday.

Tidy, spotless, fragrant, and welcoming—what more can one ask of a cheese shop? And it's a rare one, open on Sunday afternoons! The only problem here is limiting one's choice: Will it be a flawless and aromatically spicy Langres cow's milk cheese from the Champagne region, a beautifully aged and pungent Livarot cow's milk cheese from Normandy, or a dry and clean sheep's milk (*brebis*) cheese from the Basque country? The Laguiole and Saint-Nectaire cow's milk cheeses come direct from the Auvergne, the butter is pure farm fare, and in winter months go for the creamy Reblochon.

CHEESE TO GO

If you are planning to tuck a selection of French cheese into your suitcase for your welcome-back meal in the United States, be careful. U.S. Customs observes very strict government rules on foods coming into the country. Technically, no cheese, unless it is commercially sealed, can be brought by tourists into the U.S. This rules out virtually all French cheese.

BAC, SEVRES-BABYLONE, ECOLE MILITAIRE

7th arrondissement

ANDROUET
83, rue Saint-Dominique,
Paris 7.
Tel: 01.45.50.45.75.
Métro: La Tour-Maubourg.
Open 8 A.M. to 8:30 P.M.
Closed Sunday, and
Monday morning.
Credit card: V.

In Paris the name Androuët (pronounced ahn-drew-ETT) has been synonymous with cheese since the original shop on rue d'Amsterdam opened its doors in 1909. The boutique has long since been sold and resold, and there are now three shops, including a restaurant/boutique in the 8th *arrondissement.* The restaurant is not particularly recommended, but the cheese boutiques are appealing, and at least at this left Bank shop, the service is extremely well informed. Androuët still offers some specialties you don't find everywhere, including the triple-cream Lucullus; *fouchtrou,* a delicate cow's milk cheese from the Auvergne; Chevrotin d'Aravis, a smooth goat's milk cheese from the Savoie; and Arôme au Gêne from the region of Lyons, pungent discs washed with *marc de Bourgogne,* an *eau-de-vie* distilled from pressed grape skins and seeds. Also try the Munster, aged for several months at large farms and given a daily splash of white wine; Rove, the delicate golf-ball-size goat's milk cheese infused with the flavor of wild rosemary and thyme; Epoisses, brushed with *marc de Bourgogne* to give it a rare pungency and a rind the color of fall leaves; and Rollot, the smooth and spicy cow's milk cheese from Picardy, aged two months and washed daily with a salty brine.

Other addresses:

6, rue Arsène-Houssaye,
Paris 8.
Tel: 01.42.89.95.00.
Métro: Charles de Gaulle–Etoile.
Open 10 A.M. to 10:30 P.M.
Closed Monday.

19, rue Daguerre,
Paris 14.
Tel: 01.43.21.19.09.
Métro: Denfert-Rochereau.
Open 8 A.M. to 8:30 P.M.
Closed Sunday afternoon and Monday.
Credit card: V.

BARTHELEMY
51, rue de Grenelle,
Paris 7.
Tel: 01.45.48.56.75.
Métro: Rue du Bac.
Open 7:30 A.M. to 7:30 P.M.
Closed Sunday and Monday.
Credit card: V.

The simple, old-fashioned, butter-yellow storefront does not prepare you for the delights inside: Roland Barthélemy is the king of Fontainebleau, Camembert, and Brie, and in the winter months, no 7th-*arrondissement* dinner party would be complete without his rich and earthy rounds of Swiss mountain Vacherin. Everyone from the president of the French Republic to actress Catherine Deneuve shops here, and even without that recommendation, this Paris landmark demands a visit. Barthélemy offers some of the finest Vacherin you're ever likely to find (from October to March only), well-aged Epoisses, Camembert from the Coopérative d'Isigny, and Gabriel Coulet's exceptional Roquefort.

MARIE-ANNE CANTIN
12, rue du Champ-de-Mars,
Paris 7.
Tel: 01.45.50.43.94.
Métro: Ecole Militaire.
Open 8:30 A.M. to 1 P.M. and 4 to 7:30 P.M. (8:30 A.M. to 1 P.M. Sunday).
Closed Monday.
Credit cards: AE, V.

One of Paris's prettiest cheese boutiques, just off the bustling rue Cler open-air market. Marie-Anne is the daughter of Christian Cantin, whose cheese shop at 2, rue de Lourmel, in the 15th *arrondissement,* was long a Paris landmark. She and her husband, Antoine Diaz, offer some eighty to one hundred remarkably well-aged selections, and you'll find their cheese at many illustrious restaurants. The two are passionate about cheese, and that excitement carries over into the neatly organized, appealing little store. They're especially proud of the aging cellars beneath the shop, with one for

Marie-Anne Cantin's perfectly aged selection makes choosing very difficult.

A selection of Cantal.

goat cheese (very dry) and one for cow's milk (very humid). The floor of the cow's milk cellar is lined with pebbles, which are watered regularly to ensure proper humidity. All cheese is aged on straw, and varieties such as Munster and Maroilles get a daily rubdown with beer or saltwater to transform mild, timid little discs into cheese loaded with character.

The true cheese-lover, says Monsieur Diaz, is someone who invariably selects Camembert, Brie, or Livarot as part of his cheese course. The best varieties sampled here include a classic and elegant Camembert; a dusty, creamy little *bouton-de-chèvre* (farm-fresh buttons of goat cheese); and a remarkable Charolais goat cheese—refined, clean, and full-flavored. If you are in the mood for a mercilessly pungent cheese, try the northern Vieux Lille ("old Lille"): Strong and rugged, it's a cheese that almost attacks your palate. More soothing and Cheddar-like are Salers, the mild and nutty cheese from the Auvergne, and Comté, France's version of the well-known Swiss Gruyère. And do not leave without a superbly runny Saint-Marcellin, aged as in Lyons.

THE RIND

The million dollar question: Should you eat the rind or shouldn't you? Even the experts don't agree. According to *Larousse des Fromages,* the French cheese bible, it is all a question of personal taste. Larousse advises, however, not to leave a messy plate full of little bits of crust. Pierre Androuët, the former dean of Paris cheese merchants, is more definite. Never eat the rind, he says, because it harbors all the cheese's developing molds and yeasts and can emit an alkaline odor. The truth? It's really up to you, though let logic rule. The rinds of soft-ripened cheeses such as Brie and Camembert are definitely edible, and when the cheese is perfectly ripe, the thin, bloomy *croûte* adds both flavor and texture. However, with another soft cheese, Vacherin, the rind is always removed, and the creamy cheese is scooped out with a spoon. The rinds of semi-soft cheeses, such as Reblochon, can have a very nutty flavor. The crust is always discarded when eating hard mountain cheese, such as Emmenthal, Gruyère, and *tête-de-moine*.

STREET NAME MENU

It should come as no surprise to find that in Paris, a city so devoted to food, dozens of street names have a food connection. Here are a few, with the *arrondissement,* or neighborhood, in which they are now located:

Rue des Boulangers, 5th *arrondissement:* When the street was named in 1844, it was lined with numerous bakeries. Today there's not a loaf of bread for sale on "Bakers' Street."

Passage de la Brie, 19th *arrondissement:* named for the region east of Paris known for its wheat, pastures, butter, and of course, cheese.

Rue Brillat-Savarin, 13th *arrondissement:* named in honor of the gastronome and author of the famous *Physiology of Taste.*

Rue Brise-Miche, 4th *arrondissement:* During the Middle Ages, it was on this street that clergymen distributed bread to the needy. Brise-miche, named in 1517, literally means "break bread."

Rue Curnonsky, 17th *arrondissement:* named in memory of the gastronome Maurice-Edmond Sailland, who took on the Russian-sounding pseudonym around the turn of the century, when everything Russian was fashionable in Paris. The author of the multi-volume *La France Gastronomique* died in 1956, and the street was later named in his honor.

Rue des Eaux, 16th *arrondissement:* In 1650, when this road was opened in the Passy district, workers had discovered the area's mineral waters. (Passy is now one of the more fashionable Paris neighborhoods.) The source dried up during the 18th century, but the name, "Street of the Waters," remained. Who knows, if the source still existed, we could all be drinking Passy water instead of Perrier.

Rue de la Faisanderie, 16th *arrondissement:* A pheasant preserve, or *faisanderie,* once existed here, near the château of the Muette.

Rue des Fermiers, 17th *arrondissement:* There are no farmers, or *fermiers,* left here today, but in the 1800s there were still a few farms in this nowcitified neighborhood not far from Parc Monceau. The street was named in 1840, when the area became part of Paris.

Rue des Jeûneurs, 2nd *arrondissement:* The name perhaps comes from a sign that hung above one of the houses in 1715, during the reign of Louis XV. It read: "Aux Déjeuners," or "Lunches Here."

Rue des Maraîchers, 20th *arrondissement:* During the 18th century, vegetable garden markets, or *maraîchers,* bordered the region. The street was named in 1869.

Impasse Marché aux Chevaux, 5th *arrondissement:* There are many Paris streets named after past or still-existing markets, but this is one story I particularly enjoy. Beginning in 1687, this was a major market site. Early each Wednesday and Saturday, pigs were brought to market for sale, then later in the day mules, donkeys, and horses (*chevaux*) were sold, giving the street its name. On Sundays, they sold wagons and dogs.

Rue des Meuniers, 12th *arrondissement:* The street of the millers takes its name from the flour mill that existed here during the 18th century. Today there's no sign of a mill.

Rue des Morillons, 15th *arrondissement:* Morillon is the name of a grapevine that flourished in the Parisian climate at a time when Parisians and those living on the outskirts still had room to grow grapes. The path that led from the vineyard was declared a road in 1730 and a street in 1906. Vineyards have once again been planted in the nearby Parc Georges-Brassens, but they're of the Pinot Noir variety, not Morillon.

Impasse de la Poissonnerie, 4th *arrondissement:* This street was built in 1783 when the Sainte-Catherine market first opened. It bordered a fish shop, thus its name.

Boulevard Poissonnière, 2nd and 9th *arrondissements:* Opened at the beginning of the 17th century, this street served as a passage for fish merchants coming direct from the Port of Calais, delivering their fish to the Paris central market, Les Halles. It was named in 1685.

Two types of Emmental, first Savoyard, then Swiss, and two types of Comté cheese from the Jura regsion of France, first aged, next to it, young.

Fontainebleau

This creamy white, succulent dessert cheese is found from time to time in Paris fromageries. *Usually sold in little white containers lined with cheesecloth, the fresh cheese takes its name from the town of Fontainebleau, south of Paris. Although Fontainebleau is far from rare, this elegant cheese is seen less and less frequently: It stays fresh for just twenty-four hours, and it is not economical for most cheese shops to handle. But since this appealing dessert is easy to make, there's no reason not to serve it often.*

In France, Fontainebleau is made at home with fromage blanc, *a sort of a "curdless" cottage cheese, but I found that yogurt is an excellent substitute. This version is similar to* coeur à la crème, *but since it is lightened with egg whites, Fontainebleau is less rich. It is an ideal dessert for a large group because the recipe can easily be doubled or tripled. And since it is made in advance, it takes no last-minute preparation. Fontainebleau is particularly beautiful when made in a white ceramic* coeur à la crème *mold, but it can be formed in a strainer as well. I serve Fontainebleau with a fresh raspberry sauce and the little almond cakes* financiers *(see recipe, page 232). It is also delicious with strawberries, fresh figs, or blueberries.*

- 2 cups (50 cl) whole-milk yogurt
- 1 cup (200 g) sugar
- 2 cups (50 cl) heavy (whipping) cream (preferably not ultrapasteurized) or *crème fraîche* (see recipe, page 290)
- 3 egg whites

1. In a large mixing bowl, combine the yogurt and all but 2 tablespoons of the sugar.

2. In a second bowl, whip the cream or *crème fraîche* until stiff. Fold into the yogurt mixture.

3. In yet another bowl, whip the egg whites until stiff. Add the reserved 2 tablespoons sugar, and whip until glossy, about another 20 seconds. Gently fold the egg whites into the yogurt-cream mixture.

4. Transfer the mixture to a 6-cup (1.5-liter) cheesecloth-lined perforated mold (or use two or more smaller molds). Cover the mold, and place it in a bowl in the refrigerator. Refrigerate for 24 hours, draining off the liquid from time to time. The cheese should become fairly firm and dry, almost like a whipped cream cheese.

5. To serve, unmold the Fontainebleau onto a platter, unwrap, and surround with a colorful fresh fruit sauce or fresh berries. Serve immediately.

Yield: 8 to 10 servings

FROMAGERIE QUATREHOMME
62, rue de Sèvres,
Paris 7.
Tel: 01.47.34.33.45.
Métro: Sèvres-Babylone.
Open 8:45 A.M. to 7:45 P.M.
Closed Sunday and Monday.
Credit card: V.

This popular Left Bank shop supplies some of the better restaurants in town. Look out for superb Beaufort from the Savoie; a Parmesan that's aged two and a half years; the cow's milk Saint-Marcellin, as creamy and runny as you'll find in Lyon. Also try the Swiss Fribourg, a superb cheese to sample with the sweet wines of the Jura; and from November to March, the Swiss Vacherin.

Browsing at Marie-Anne Cantin's (see entry, page 280).

Etoile, Madeleine

8th arrondissement

LA FERME SAINT-HUBERT
21, rue Vignon,
Paris 8.
Tel: 01.47.42.79.20.
Métro: Madeleine.
Open 9 A.M. to 8 P.M.
Closed Sunday.
Credit cards: AE, V.

Just around the corner from Fauchon, this small, compact shop offers a remarkable cheese selection, including what's probably the best and most carefully selected Roquefort in Paris; a spectacular Beaufort, aged at least two years in special cellars; and a vigorous Maroilles from Flanders, aged for four months and bathed daily with a healthy dose of beer. Owner Henry Voy also offers the Swiss *tête-de-moine,* so named because the fruity cylinder resembles the round, bald head of a monk. It's a cheese full of punch, depth, and character, a must for fans of Gruyère. Also worth sampling are the delicate, pale, goat's milk butter and a good goat's milk yogurt. Monsieur Voy's palate goes toward cheeses that are rough and rustic, and sometimes aged just a bit too long, thus losing their charm. On my last visit, the Banon, a delicate goat's milk cheese from

Provence that's wrapped in dried chestnut leaves and tied with raffia, looked great on the outside but its inside had been abandoned and aged badly; it looked (and tasted) like soap covered with bits of mold.

Other address:
14, rue des Sablons/14, rue des Belles Feuilles (Galerie Saint-Didier),
Paris 16.
Tel: 01.45.53.15.77.
Métro: Victor Hugo.
Open 9 A.M. to 7:30 P.M. (8 A.M. to 8 P.M. Friday and Saturday).
Closed Sunday.
Credit cards: AE, DC, V.

DENFERT-ROCHEREAU, PORTE D'ORLEANS, PORTE DE VERSAILLES

14th and 15th arrondissements

LA FERME DU HAMEAU
223, rue de la Croix-Nivert,
Paris 15.
Tel: 01.45.32.88.70.
Métro: Porte de Versailles.
Open 8:30 A.M. to 1:00 P.M. and 3:30 to 7:30 P.M.
Closed Sunday, Monday, and July.
Credit card: V.

A tidy cheese shop that offers a little bit of everything, from delicious-looking *cassoulet* or *poule au riz* in glass jars to lovely packages of macaroons. In the cheese department they offer a superb Coulommiers—a creamy cow's milk cheese that is generally overshadowed by its often-bland neighbor Brie. Here the Coulommiers is a delight: well aged and tasting faintly of almonds. Brie's "little brother," this bloomy, fat disc of cow's milk cheese is worth going out of the way to find. Other cheeses of note: a rare Beaufort *d'alpage,* a nicely aged Saint-Nectaire, and in the fall and winter months, Vacherin Mont d'Or.

FIL O'FROMAGE
4, rue Poirier-de-Narçay,
Paris 14.
Tel: 01.40.44.86.75.
Métro: Porte d'Orléans.
Open 8:30 A.M. to 1:00 P.M. and 4 to 8 P.M. (4 to 8 P.M. Sunday).
Closed Monday and August.
Credit card: V.

This beautifully restored *fromagerie*—with marble counters and bright sprays of flowers—reflects good intentions and a sense of pride. Owners Sylvie and Chérif Bourbrit offer an excellent assortment of goat cheeses and specialties from all over France. Try their well-aged sheep's milk cheese from Corsica—*brebis Corse*—a delicately earthy cheese that's great on toasted rye bread.

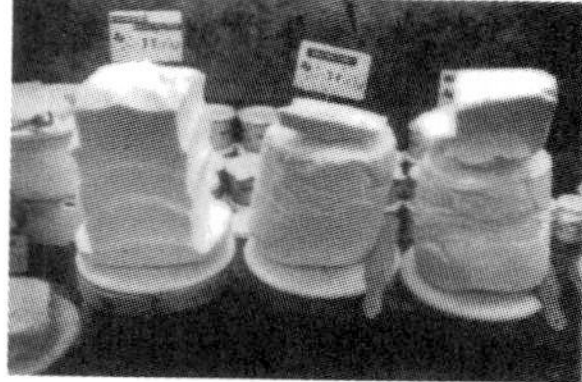

BUTTER

France produces 10 percent of the world's butter, most of it unsalted. Though Normandy, with its shining green pastures and fawn-colored cows, produces a high-quality product, the best butter comes from Charentes, in the southwest of France. Charentes butter, sold in packets under the label *"beurre d'Echiré"* or *"beurre de Ligueil,"* is favored by French pastry chefs because it is firmer and less watery than other varieties and makes superior pastry.

In cheese shops you often see huge creamy blocks of butter behind the counter. They are usually labeled *"beurre des Charentes," "beurre de Normandie,"* or *"beurre demi-sel." Demi-sel* is Brittany's lightly salted butter. Rarely used in cooking, it finds its place on the table. (While the bulk butters look good and fresh, beware: They sit all day absorbing the mingled odors of the cheese and are not always terribly fresh.)

The French don't usually butter their bread, so whether or not the butter appears on the home or restaurant table is really a matter of personal taste. Butter is always served with *charcuterie* (cold cuts), with radishes, anchovies, sardines, and with the rye bread that comes as part of any order of oysters or other shellfish. If you don't see butter on a restaurant table, it is perfectly proper to ask for it, though in more casual restaurants you may be charged a *supplément* of a few francs. Butter is usually included with the cheese course and is used to soften the effect of strong and salty cheeses such as Roquefort.

Cheese from the mountains, an Alléosse assortment (see entry, page 288).

COURCELLES, VILLIERS

17th arrondissement

ALLEOSSE
13, rue Poncelet,
Paris 17.
Tel: 01.46.22.50.45.
Métro: Ternes.
Open 9 A.M. to 1 P.M. and 4 to 7:15 P.M.
Closed Sunday afternoon and Monday.
Credit card: V.

The hardworking, outgoing, and thoroughly professional Alléosse family runs the best cheese shop in Paris. The father, Roger Alléosse, travels throughout France, searching out the best farm cheeses, the best *laiteries* (dairies), the best cheese agers in each region. Their wide selection of cheeses from France, Italy, Greece, and the Netherlands is astonishing and serves as a mini cheese university. I always come home with more cheeses than I'd planned to buy, but somehow every last morsel gets devoured. Some of the Alléosse cheeses are aged in a series of *caves* beneath the store, others in their own private *caves* outside the city. Special cheeses to note include always perfect raw-milk Camembert; beautifully aged Langres, a soft, smooth, pungent cheese from the Champagne area; a smoother and super-rich *brebis fermier,* a farm-made sheep's milk cheese from the Pays Basque; and a supple raw-milk, blue-veined Forme d'Ambert, aged with a dose of sweet Sauternes wine.

There is generally a good selection of very fresh and young goat cheeses from Burgundy; always a well-aged Beaufort; a delicious Coulommiers; and at times a well-aged Saint-Marcellin. If they have it in stock, do try the ugly but delicious *brique de brebis* sheep's milk "brick"; the luscious Rove goat's milk cheese, which tastes of wild rosemary and thyme; and their own creation, a Picodon "sandwich" filled with black olive *tapenade.*

JEAN CARMES ET FILS
24, rue de Lévis,
Paris 17.
Tel: 01.47.63.88.94.
Métro: Villiers.
Open 8 A.M. to 1 P.M. and 4 to 7:30 P.M.
Closed Sunday afternoon, Monday, and August.
Credit card: V.

Situated right in the middle of the hectic rue de Lévis market, Carmès is a big, open, family-run cheese shop with one member behind the cash register while another rushes about, keeping an eye on incoming deliveries and checking on the progress of the two hundred or so varieties of cheese aging in the humid *caves* below the shop. These people are passionate about cheese, taking the care to label each variety, happy to help you select a single cheese or an entire platter. Most varieties spend an average of three to four weeks in the Carmès cellars, aging on fresh, clean straw mats until the cheese is ready to be put on sale. Some specialties here include l'Ecume, a triple-cream cheese so rich it easily replaces butter; Tanatais goat cheese, much like a Charolais, dry and delicious with a bloomy crust; and a Petit-Suisse *"comme autrefois,"* a fragile cheese that stays fresh for just four or five days. Real fresh *crème Chantilly* (sweetened *crème fraîche*) and Fontainebleau (a creamy dessert cheese) are sold here as well.

ALAIN DUBOIS
79, rue de Courcelles,
Paris 17.
Tel: 01.43.80.36.42.
Métro: Courcelles.
Open 8:30 A.M. to 1 P.M. and 4 to 7:30 P.M.
Closed Sunday, Monday morning, and August.
Credit card: V.

and

80, rue de Tocqueville,
Paris 17.
Tel: 01.42.27.11.38.
Métro: Villiers.
Open 7:30 A.M. to 1 P.M. and 3:45 to 8 P.M. (9 A.M. to 1 P.M. Sunday).
Closed Sunday in July and August, and Monday.
Credit card: V.

There's always a line out the door at this tiny, spotless shop, where the raw-milk Camembert, Pyramide goat cheese, and Saint-Marcellin are generally in excellent form. Do take advantage of their blackboard listing of cheeses of the month, hung on the wall behind the cash register: They are usually best bets.

SCENTS OF PARIS

"It was the Camembert above all that they could smell. The Camembert with its gamey scent of venison had conquered the more muffled tones of Maroilles and Limbourg. . . . Into the middle of this vigorous phrase the Parmesan threw its thin note on a country flute, while the Brie added the dull gentleness of damp tambourines. Then came the suffocating reprise of a Livarot. And the symphony was held for a moment on the high, sharp note of an aniseed Gérôme, prolonged like the note of an organ."

—Emile Zola, *Le Ventre de Paris.*

CREME FRAICHE

Where would French cuisine be without crème fraîche, *that thick and slightly tangy cream that lies somewhere between heavy cream and sour cream? Every* crémerie *in France sells* crème fraîche *in bulk, usually ladled out of giant round crockery bowls. It's versatile and nearly indispensable, showing up in both hot and cold sauces, and is perfect for whipping with a touch of sugar to dab on a mound of fresh wild strawberries.*

2 cups (50 cl) heavy (whipping) cream (you cannot use ultrapasteurized)
1 cup (25 cl) sour cream

1. Mix the heavy cream and sour cream together in a medium-size bowl. Cover loosely with plastic wrap and let stand at room temperature overnight, or until fairly thick.

2. Cover tightly and refrigerate for at least 4 hours, to thicken it even more. The *crème fraîche* will keep for up to 1 week in the refrigerator, where the tangy flavor will continue to develop.

Yield: 2 cups (50 cl)

FROMAGE DE CHEVRE MARINE A L'HUILE D'HERBES
GOAT CHEESE MARINATED IN OIL WITH HERBS

This is a traditional method of storing and extending the life of a goat cheese, particularly useful for chèvre *that has become very firm and dry. It's great to have on hand for days when you haven't had time to market. After the cheese has been consumed, you can continue adding more cheese and herbs to the oil, or use it for cooking or for salad dressings.*

6 small goat cheeses (Picodon, Crottin, or Cabécou)
1 clove garlic, peeled
1 teaspoon fresh thyme leaves
1 sprig fresh rosemary
2 bay leaves
12 black peppercorns
12 white peppercorns
12 coriander seeds
2 cups (50 cl) extra-virgin olive oil

1. Cut each cheese in half horizontally. Place the cheese, then the garlic and herbs and spices, in a wide-mouth pint (50-cl) jar. Cover with the oil. Close securely and store in a cool place for at least 1 week but no more than 2 weeks.

2. To serve, remove the cheese from the jar and drain off the oil. Broil the cheese just until warm, and serve with a tossed green salad and slices of fresh bread.

Yield: 12 servings

Montmartre

18th arrondissement

FROMAGERIE DE MONTMARTRE
9, rue du Poteau,
Paris 18.
Tel: 01.46.06.26.03.
Métro: Jules Joffrin.
Open 9 A.M. to 1 P.M. and 4 to 7:30 P.M.
Closed Sunday and Monday.
Credit card: V.

If you just love looking at beautiful cheese displays, don't miss this spacious *fromagerie,* typical of the pretty food shops along the rue du Poteau. Fromagerie de Montmartre offers a sparkling variety of farm-fresh raw-milk cheeses from all over France, and the owner, Edith Delbey, is happy to let you "window-shop" as you wander about the well-organized store, examining the flawless selection of cheeses displayed on trays of straw and aged in her own cellars. Goat cheese is one of their strongest features—they offer more than forty different varieties. Outstanding cheeses sampled here include a beautifully aged Comté from the Jura; Auvergnat Cantal aged more than eighteen months; and their creamy Fontainebleau *"maison."*

Charcuteries
PREPARED FOODS TO GO

Decisions are easy if you know what you want.

To lovers of all things earthy, hearty, rib-sticking, and aromatic, the *charcuterie* is a touch of heaven. Paris has hundreds of these shops where you can buy *chair cuite* (cooked meat). Some are museum-like, with carved marble counters and hanging brass racks, others modern and spotless with products displayed like diamonds in a jeweler's window. Here you can buy fragrant sausages and mosaic *pâtés,* salted and smoked hams, and strange-sounding items such as *grattons, fritons, rillettes,* and *rillons.* Who else but the French could manage to make so much of the lowly pig? And where else but in Paris can you find one shop with endless varieties of *boudin* sausage made right on the premises; another with more than a dozen varieties of ham; still others that sell not only pork products but also caviar, *foie gras,* fresh country breads and smoked salmon, and even the vodka, Champagne, and Sauternes to go with them?

You need not go beyond Paris to sample the wonders of the whole world of French *charcuterie.* My favorite regional shops feature products from the rugged Auvergne region in south-central France and offer farm-fresh goat and sheep's milk cheeses, a heady Bleu d'Auvergne, dozens of kinds of ham, sausages, and *pâtés* with so many different names, colors, and shapes it makes the head spin. There are also Alsatian-owned shops redolent with the pungent warmth of cooked sauerkraut, mounds of pork chops, and colorful assorted sausages, plus some of the finest farm Munster cheese and romantic heart-shaped gingerbread cookies.

Run-of-the-mill *charcuteries* make only a small portion of the products themselves (unfortunately, a large percentage of the products sold in *charcuteries* nationwide are industrially produced), but the finest shops, such as those mentioned here, either produce most of their own sausages and hams, *pâtés,* and *terrines,* or buy them direct from independent farmers in various regions of France.

Many Paris *charcuteries* also offer hot meals at lunch and dinnertime, a carry-out concept that to most of us seems distinctly modern. It's not. Ever since *charcuteries* were established in 1475, their very reason for existence was to sell cooked pork products. In days when a large percentage of Parisians lived without even rudimentary cooking facilities, the *charcuterie* served as a kitchen away from home, ready with hot and cold carry-out meals all week long.

Along with the hundreds of different meat products, most *charcuteries* also sell *escargots* (snails) ready for popping in the oven, a variety of pastry-topped *pâtés* or *terrines* to be eaten warm or at room temperature, pizzas, *quiches,* and dozens of salads, ranging from those of ivory-colored celery root or bright red beets to a julienne of carrots showered with *vinaigrette.* Condiments such as olives, pickles, and *cornichons* can almost always be found, along with many kinds of regional packaged cakes, cookies, and pastries. The modern-day Parisian *charcuterie* also takes note of the modern palate and a desire for lighter fare, and such Asian specialties as the Vietnamese spring roll (*rouleau de printemps*) have become part of the standard repertoire. And should one be too concerned about all that fat, listen to what one French doctor has to say about *boudin,* the savory steaming sausage made with pork blood: "*Boudin* is so full of iron and vitamins, it should be reimbursed by social security!"

Today the Parisian definition of *charcuterie* is a broad one, and major shops such as Fauchon, Lenôtre, Dalloyau, Hédiard, and Flo Prestige (all listed elsewhere in this guide) perform the services of *charcuterie* and caterer, offering, as well, pastries, breads, chocolates, wines, liquors, and condiments. What follows here, then, is a choice selection of the smaller shops, most of them family run, with unique personalities of their own. In each case, a sampling of this, a slice of that, will help make a picnic lunch or snack a true Parisian feast.

Marais, Bastille

4th arrondissement

PRODUITS HONGROIS
11, rue de Sévigné,
Paris 4.
Tel: 01.48.87.46.06.
Métro: Saint-Paul.
Open 9 A.M. to 1 P.M. and 3 to 7 P.M.
Closed Sunday, Monday, and mid-July through August.

A tiny, tidy Eastern European shop not far from the trendy Place des Vosges, where they offer fresh, aromatic, and delicious Hungarian sausages. *Propriétaire* Anna Suba specializes in smoked *charcuterie,* and her beef and pork sausage seasoned with hot peppers is a special treat.

A LA VILLE DE RODEZ
22, rue Vieille-du-Temple,
Paris 4.
Tel: 01.48.87.79.36.
Métro: Saint-Paul or Hôtel de Ville.
Open 8 A.M. to 1 P.M. and 3 to 7:30 P.M.
Closed Sunday, Monday, and mid-July through August.
Credit card: V.

The long, hearty loaves of country bread come up from Aurillac in south-central France four times a week, while the fragrant sausages and hams that hang from the rafters of this spotless shop all have the wholesome Auvergnat stamp. You will also find buckwheat flour for earthy *crêpes; fouace* (an extra-buttery regional *brioche* studded with candied fruits); *boudin noir* (blood sausage); rough red regional wines; that delicate straw-yellow Cantal-like cheese, Laguiole; sweet cow's milk Saint-Nectaire; *tomme fraîche* for making *aligot,* that rich purée of potatoes and melted cheese; country honey and *confitures,* as well as the famous knives from Laguiole. You can select an entire picnic or a simple snack, then buy a handmade wicker basket in which to carry your treasures.

Carefully slicing into a terrine.

ORDERING CHARCUTERIE

The best way to visit a Paris *charcuterie* is armed with a little knowledge and a hearty appetite. The following are some of the most commonly found products:

Andouille: cold smoked chitterling (tripe) sausage.

Andouillette: smaller chitterling (tripe) sausage, usually served grilled.

Ballotine: usually poultry, boned, stuffed, and rolled.

Boudin blanc: white sausage of veal, chicken, or pork.

Boudin noir: pork blood sausage.

Cervelas: garlicky cured pork sausage.

Confit: duck, goose, or pork cooked and preserved in its own fat.

Cou d'oie farci: neck skin of goose, stuffed with meat and spices, much like a sausage.

Crépinette: small sausage patty wrapped in caul fat.

Fritons: coarse pork *rillettes,* or a minced spread, that includes organ meats.

Fromage de tête: headcheese, usually pork.

Galantine: cooked boned poultry or meat, stuffed and rolled, classically glazed with gelatin, and served cold.

Grattons: crisply fried pieces of pork, goose, or duck skin; cracklings.

Hure (de porc or *de marcassin):* a headcheese prepared from the head of a pig or boar.

Jambon (ham)

d'Auvergne: salt-cured ham.

de Bayonne: raw dried, salt-cured ham.

de Bourgogne, also *persillé:* cold cooked ham, cubed and preserved in parsleyed gelatin, usually sliced from a terrine.

cru: any raw cured ham.

cuit: any cooked ham.

fumé: any smoked ham.

de montagne: any mountain ham.

à l'os: ham with the bone in

de Paris: pale, lightly salted, cooked ham.

de Parme: Italian *prosciutto* from Parma.

du pays: any country ham.

persillé, also *de Bourgogne:* cold cooked ham, cubed and preserved in parsleyed gelatin, usually sliced from a terrine.

sec: any dried ham.

de Westphalie: German Westphalian ham, raw-cured and smoked.

de York: smoked English-style ham, usually poached.

Jambonneau: cured ham shank or pork knuckle.

Jésus: smoked pork sausage from the Franche-Comté.

Lard: bacon

Lardons: cubes of bacon.

Merguez: small spicy sausage.

Museau de porc: vinegared pork muzzle.

Oreilles de porc: cooked pig's ears, served grilled, with a coating of egg and bread crumbs.

Pâté (seasoned chopped meats that are molded, baked, and served hot or cold)

de campagne: coarse country-style.

de canard: of duck.

de chevreuil: of venison.

en croûte: baked in pastry.

de foie: of liver.

de grive: of thrush, or songbird.

de lapin: of rabbit.

de lièvre: of wild hare.

maison: in the style of the house or *charcuterie.*

d'oie: of goose.

Pied (foot)

de cochon: pig's foot.

de mouton: sheep's foot.

de porc: pig's foot.

Poitrine fumée: smoked bacon.

Poitrine d'oie fumée: smoked goose breast.

Rillettes (d'oie): minced spread of pork (goose); also can be made with duck, fish, or rabbit.

Rillons: pork belly, cut up and cooked until crisp, then drained of fat; can also be made of duck, goose, or rabbit.

> *"Drink wine when you eat ham.*
> *Soup is for ordinary hunger; roasts make a meal festive.*
> *Venison pâté is too good for disobedient children."*
> *—Lesson from a 17th-century French schoolbook.*

Coils of boudin.

Rosette (de boeuf): dried pork (or beef) sausage, usually from Beaujolais.

Saucisse (most often, small fresh sausage, which is cooked in liquid and/or broiled, and eaten warm)

chaude: warm sausage.

de Francfort: hot dog.

de Morteau: smoked pork sausage from the Franche-Comté.

de Strasbourg: red-skinned hot dog.

de Toulouse: mild country-style pork sausage.

Saucisson (most often, a large air-dried sausage, such as salami, eaten sliced as a cold cut. When fresh, usually called *saucisson chaud*—hot sausage)

à l'ail: garlic sausage, usually to be cooked and served warm.

d'Arles: dried, salami-type sausage.

de campagne: any country-style sausage.

en croûte: sausage cooked in pastry crust.

de Lyon: air-dried pork sausage, flavored with garlic and pepper, and studded with chunks of pork fat, sometimes flavored with pistachio nuts or truffles.

sec: any dried sausage or salami.

Terrine (actually the earthenware container used for cooking meat, game, fish, or vegetable mixtures. It also refers to the *pâté* served in the vessel. It differs from a *pâté* proper in that the *terrine* is actually sliced out of the vessel, while a *pâté* has been removed from the terrine)

d'anguille: eel.

de caille: quail.

de campagne: country-style.

de canard: of duck.

du chef: in the chef's special style.

de faisan: of pheasant.

de foie: of liver.

de foies de volaille: of chicken liver.

de grives: of thrush, or songbird.

maison: in style of the *charcuterie* or house.

de perdreau: of partridge.

de volaille: of chicken.

Oh là là!

SAINT-GERMAIN DES PRES, ODEON, SEVRES-BABYLONE

6th arrondissement

CHARCUTERIE ALSACIENNE
10, rue de Buci,
Paris 6.
Tel: 01.43.54.93.49.
Métro: Saint-Germain des Prés.
Open daily, 8 A.M. to 8:30 P.M.
Credit card: V.

Oh boy, sausage-lovers' heaven! I'm a real fan of Alsatian food, especially the incredible collection of sausages one finds in this charming, fragrant boutique, an offshoot of the company founded in Mulhouse back in 1876. Try the cumin-flecked pork sausages, the *boudin* blood sausages, or the slender smoked Montbéliard sausages from the Jura, to the south of Alsace. The word "cute" must have been coined to describe the interior of this cheery modern shop, its woodwork decorated with bright folkloric floral designs.

Other address:

37, rue de Belles-Feuilles,
Paris 16.
Tel: 01.47.27.33.74.
Métro: Victor-Hugo.
Open 7:30 A.M. to 1 P.M. and 3:30 to 8 P.M. (7:30 A.M. to 1 P.M. Sunday).
Closed Monday.

CHARCUTERIE CHARLES
10, rue Dauphine,
Paris 6.
Tel: 01.43.54.25.19.
Métro: Odéon.
Open 8:30 A.M. to 2 P.M. and 4 to 8 P.M.
Closed Saturday and Sunday.
Credit card: V.

Claude Charles and his son, Philippe, are grand and award-winning specialists of *boudin blanc* (white pork and veal sausage), including those seasoned with truffles, hazelnuts, pistachios, wild *cèpe* mushrooms, prunes, and corn, as well as the "plain" variety. Also good blood sausage *(boudin noir)* and hams.

Other address:
135, rue Saint Dominique,
Paris 7.
Tel: 01.47.05.53.66.
Métro: Ecole Militaire.
Open 8:30 A.M. to 8 P.M.
Closed Saturday and Sunday.

CHARCUTERIE COESNON
30, rue Dauphine,
Paris 6.
Tel: 01.43.54.35.80.
Métro: Odéon.
Open 8:30 A.M. to 7:30 P.M.
Closed Sunday and Monday.
Credit card: V.

This, one of the city's most respected family *charcuteries,* was begun by the friendly Coesnon family, who came to Paris from Normandy during the 1950s. Today Bernard Marchaudon carries on the tradition: Specialties include homemade French sausages, *boudin blanc* and *boudin noir,* fresh *foie gras,* beautiful *terrines,* dried sausages, cured hams, and their famed *andouillettes* (chitterling sausages).

MADELEINE

9th arrondissement

HENRY-CECCALDI
21, rue des Mathurins,
Paris 9.
Tel: 01.47.42.66.52.
Métro: Havre-Caumartin.
Open 8:30 A.M. to 7:30 P.M.
Closed Saturday, Sunday, and August.

A Corsica-lover's paradise, with all the best products of that sun-kissed island, including the local cheesecake *(fiadone),* delicate sheep's milk cheese *(brocciu),* and various dried meats, sausages, and *charcuterie.*

Sausage and frites.

FOIE GRAS

Foie gras—one of the crown jewels of French gastronomy—is the smooth and buttery liver from a fattened duck or goose. Seasoned lightly with salt and pepper, then cooked gently in a white porcelain terrine, this highly perishable delicacy demands no further embellishment than a slice of freshly toasted country bread and a glass of chilled sweet Sauternes. At its best, *foie gras* is one of the world's most satisfying foods. Earthy and elegant, a single morsel of it melts slowly on the palate, invading one's senses with an aroma and flavor that's gracefully soothing, supple, and rich, with a lingering, almost organic aftertaste. Depending on its origin and length of cooking time, the color of *foie gras* ranges from a slightly golden brown to a peach-blushed rose. Rich in calories, *foie gras* is best enjoyed slowly and parsimoniously—it is also expensive.

Which is better, goose or duck liver? It is purely a matter of preference. Fattened goose liver *(foie gras d'oie)* is less common and more expensive than fattened duck liver *(foie gras de canard)* because its production requires more intensive care and feeding. Geese are very susceptible to disease and to perturbation in their daily routine, so the casualty rate is high. Ducks are hardier and less demanding, and during the past twenty years the fattened duck liver has gained popularity as French restaurateurs and consumers have also developed a strong appetite for the breast of the fattened duck, the *magret de canard.* As for taste, goose liver is slightly subtle and mild, duck liver more forward-tasting and a bit more acidic.

What does one look for in *foie gras?* Ideally, a slice of *foie gras* should be the same color throughout, a sign that it is from the same liver and has been carefully and uniformly cooked. It should always have a fresh, appealing, liverlike aroma.

Serve *foie gras* slightly chilled but not too cold. If possible, remove it from the refrigerator fifteen to twenty minutes before serving. When too cold, flavors are masked. When too warm, *foie gras* can turn mushy, losing its seductive charm.

The following are the legal French definitions and preparations for *foie gras*. When purchasing it preserved, look for products packed in terrines or

glass jars, rather than tins, so you can see exactly what you are buying. The best *foie gras* has a fresh color, slices neatly, is generally free of blood vessels, and is not heavily surrounded with fat. Many shops also sell *foie gras* by the slice, cut from a larger terrine. This should be refrigerated and is best eaten within a few hours. *Foie gras* that can legally enter the United States must have been sterilized—cooked at a temperature of 230°F (110°C)—and is generally marked *foie gras de conserve.*

Foie gras cru: Raw liver. If of good quality, this is the ultimate in *foie gras*. Usually found only at select Paris *charcuteries* around the end of the year, it is delicious sliced raw and spread on warm toasted bread; it can also be preserved in a terrine at home. Often sold vacuum-packed. The best are the smallest, a little over 1 pound (500 to 600 grams) for goose, a little under 1 pound (400 grams) for duck. Lobes should be supple, round, smooth rather than granular, and without spots. A good buy when purchased from a reputable merchant.

Foie gras mi-cuit **or** ***nature:*** The lightly cooked preserved *foie gras* of connoisseurs, and the best way to sample *foie gras* for the first time. Ideally, only the highest-quality livers are preserved in this manner. The terms *mi-cuit* and *nature* are used interchangeably with *foie gras frais,* denoting that the livers have been pasteurized at 175° to 200°F (80° to 90°C). Next to raw, this is the best way to enjoy *foie gras,* for it is barely cooked, retaining its pure, agreeably rich flavor. Sold in terrines, vacuum packed, in aluminum foil–wrapped rolls, or in a can or jar, it requires refrigeration. Depending on packaging, it will last several days to several months.

Foie gras entier: Entire lobe of the fattened liver, lightly seasoned and generally cooked in a terrine or glass jar. If the container is large, additional pieces of another liver may be added to fill it. Sold fresh (*frais*), which requires refrigeration and must be consumed within a few weeks or months (depending on length of cooking time); and *en conserve,* which requires no refrigeration and will last several years.

Foie gras en conserve: Fattened livers, whole or in pieces, that have been seasoned, then sterilized in a jar or can at 230° to 240°F (108° to 115°C). Requires no refrigeration. Carefully conserved, high-quality *foie gras* will actually ripen and improve with age. It should be stored in a cool, dry place and turned from time to time, and could be kept for up to ten years. A good buy when purchased from a reputable merchant.

Bloc de foie gras: By law, composed of either 50 percent fattened duck liver or 35 percent goose liver that must be obviously present in chunks, held together by *foie gras* that has been mechanically blended. Not the best buy, for there is also a 10 percent allowance for pork barding fat.

Foie gras truffé: *Foie gras* with at least 3 percent truffles. A bad buy, for the flavor of the expensive truffle is totally lost, the price greatly inflated.

Foie gras parfait: A mechanically mixed blend of usually mediocre-quality *foie gras* surrounded with stuffing of pork, veal, or chicken meat, then wrapped in barding fat. A bad buy.

Foie gras pâté, galantine,* or *purée: Various products with a base of *foie gras*. Usually composed of lowest-quality livers mixed with pork, chicken, or veal, surrounded by barding fat. The word *gras* may be missing, but the mixtures must contain a minimum of 50 percent *foie gras*, with added stuffing mixture and pork barding fat. A bad buy.

Today's specials.

VICTOR-HUGO, ETOILE, VILLIERS

16th and 17th arrondissements

DIVAY
4, rue Bayen,
Paris 17.
Tel: 01.43.80.16.97.
Métro: Ternes.
Open 8 A.M. to 1:30 P.M. and 3:30 to 7 P.M. (8 A.M. to 1:30 P.M. Sunday).
Closed Monday.
Credit card: V.

Divay, a large and dependable *charcuterie,* likes to advertise that it has the cheapest *foie gras* in Paris. It *is* less expensive than others, and both their duck and goose *terrines* are delicious. Also excellent are the hams, sausages, carry-out salads, and raw *foie gras* (much of the year) for preparing one's own homemade *terrines.*

JEAN-CLAUDE ET NANOU
46, rue Legendre,
Paris 17.
Tel: 01.42.27.15.08.
Métro: Malesherbes.
Open 8:30 A.M. to 1 P.M. and 4 to 8 P.M. (8:30 A.M. to 1 P.M. Sunday).
Closed Sunday during summer, Monday, and mid-July through August.

Chic, friendly, and outgoing, Jean-Claude and Nanou Clément run a tidy family *charcuterie,* where they bring in marvelous products from their native Auvergne, including very firm and flavorful hams that have been aged for a full eight months, and many farm cheeses from Laguiole and Saint-Nectaire (look for the sheep's milk cheese from the Benedictine Abbaye de Belloc). Also excellent sausages that have been dried the old-fashioned way, in huge barrels of cinders.

MAISON POU
16, avenue des Ternes,
Paris 17.
Tel: 01.43.80.19.24.
Métro: Ternes.
Open 9:30 A.M. to 1:15 P.M. and 3:30 to 7:15 P.M. (9:30 A.M. to 7:15 P.M. Saturday).
Closed Sunday and Monday.
Credit cards: DC, V.

A "press-your-nose-against-the-window" shop: elegant, upscale, and spotless, filled with fragrant sausages, steaming sauerkraut, and hams, not to mention a wide selection of wines, cheeses, preserved and dried wild mushrooms, fresh truffles in season, and preserved truffles year-round. Also a fabulous selection of beautiful *pâtés.*

SCHMID
36, rue de Lévis,
Paris 17.
Tel: 01.47.63.07.08.
Métro: Villiers.
Open 9 A.M. to 7 P.M.
Closed Sunday.
Credit card: V.

Almost as good as a trip to Alsace: windows filled with heart-shaped Alsatian spice cookies, golden farm-aged Munster, sausages for slicing or poaching, wines, liqueurs, and *foie gras* from the region.

Chocolatiers
CHOCOLATE SHOPS

The allure of chocolate.

The way the French fuss over chocolate, you might think they had invented it. They didn't, but as in so many matters gastronomic, the French inspire envy. They've refined the art of fine chocolate making, coaxing and coddling their sweets into existence, working carefully until they've produced some of the smoothest and strongest, richest, most intoxicating and flavorful candies to be found anywhere in the world.

The French chocolate-buying public is discriminating, and *chocolatiers,* or chocolate makers, are fortunate to have a clientèle willing to pay a premium price for confections prepared with the finest South American cocoa beans, the best Madagascar vanilla, the freshest Sicilian pistachios, the most expensive Dutch cocoa butter.

But chocolate is not without its trends. Today the French palate has gone crazy for *"le gout amer,"* the bittersweet taste of chocolate high in cocoa butter and low in sugar. But beware: A low sugar content is not necessarily a sign of quality. The best bet is to buy in small quantities and judge for yourself.

Before there was chocolate as we know it today—in bars and in flavored squares and rounds, enjoyed as a snack or dessert—chocolate was prepared as a drink. As the brew became popular in Europe during the 17th century, it also became the subject of discord. Was chocolate healthy? Was it lethal? Was it a dangerous aphrodisiac? The famous 17th-century letter writer Madame de Sévigné wrote to her daughter: "It flatters you for a while, it warms you for an instant; then it kindles a mortal fever in you." But when her daugher moved from Paris, she worried how she could get along without a *chocolatière,* or chocolate pot.

Paris's first chocolate shop—situated on the rue de l'Arbre Sec in what is now the 1st *arrondissement*—was opened in 1659, when Louis XIV gave one of Queen Anne's officers the exclusive privilege to sell chocolate.

Chocolate soon became the rage of the French courts. It was served at least three times a week at Versailles, and it is said that Napoleon preferred chocolate to coffee as a morning pick-me-up. In Voltaire's later years, he consumed twelve cups a day, always between five in the morning and three in the afternoon. (He lived to be eighty-four years old.) Brillat-Savarin, the 18th-century gastronome, put it concisely: "Chocolate is health."

In the early 1800s, two very clever Parisians figured a way around the still-raging dispute over the merits of chocolate: They sold it as medicine. A certain Monsieur Debauve, a *chocolatier,* and a Monsieur Gallais, a pharmacist, teamed up and opened an elegant shop at 30, rue des Saints-Pères, just off the boulevard Saint-Germain. Soon the nervous, the sickly, the thin, the obese, were going to Debauve and Gallais for "the chocolate cure." It's no surprise to learn that the chocolate preparations became a bigger business than the other pharmaceuticals, and Debauve & Gallais—where chocolates are still sold in the same shop today—soon became the most important chocolate shop in Paris.

Today in France, chocolate remains synonymous with *gourmandise* and comfort. There is even a Club des Croqueurs de Chocolat, a private group of chocolate-loving Parisian connoisseurs that meets regularly to taste and judge the latest chocolate creations. Still, the French display a great deal of discipline when it comes to their beloved chocolate. They actually eat less chocolate than their neighbors—the French consume about fifteen pounds of chocolate per person annually, compared to twenty-three for the Swiss and nineteen for the Belgians (the Americans consume about twelve pounds). But when they eat chocolate, they want plenty of it, and fast: 80 percent of all the chocolate sold in Paris is sold during the final three weeks of December!

BOURSE

2nd arrondissement

DEBAUVE & GALLAIS
33, rue Vivienne,
Paris 2.
Tel: 01.40.39.05.50.
Métro: Bourse.
Open 9 A.M. to 7 P.M.
Closed Saturday in the summer, and Sunday.
Credit card: V.

Formerly a *confiserie* called Duc de Praslin, this shop has been transformed into an annex of the famed Left Bank establishment. The same ravishing chocolates, without crossing the river. (See 6th and 7th *arrondissements*).

SAINT-GERMAIN DES PRES, SEVRES-BABYLONE, ECOLE MILITAIRE

6th and 7th arrondissements

MICHEL CHAUDUN
149, rue de l'Université,
Paris 7.
Tel: 01.47.53.74.40.
Métro: Invalides.
Open 9:30 A.M. to 7:30 P.M.
Closed Sunday, Monday, and August.
Credit card: V.

Michel Chaudun's fragrant little shop offers some truly spectacular chocolates. I'm particularly in love with his super bittersweet *tablettes* (chocolate bars). He's also famous for his *esmeralda* (bittersweet truffles), *veragua* (chocolates filled with praline and caramel), and dark, rich chocolate cakes. The windows are often decorated with chocolates in the form of big capital letters, perfect gifts for the person who has everything.

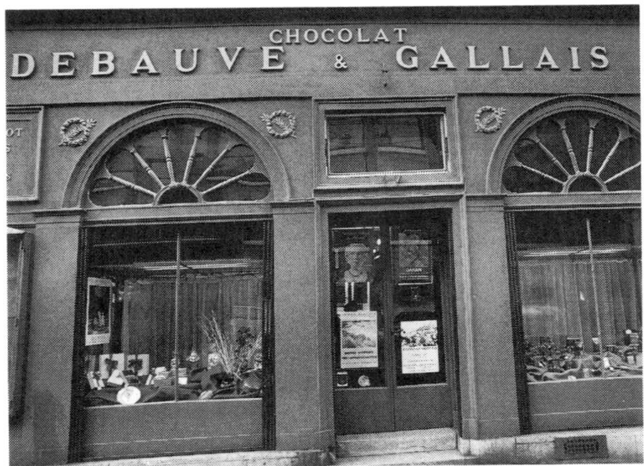

CHOCOTRUFFE
38, rue du Cherche-Midi,
Paris 6.
Tel: 01.42.22.49.99.
Fax: 01.42.84.12.26.
Métro: Sèvres-Babylone.
Open 10 A.M. to 7 P.M.
Closed Sunday,
Monday, and August.

A lovely boutique offering a variety of homemade chocolates (excellent thin discs of chocolate, called *palats,* are their specialty), top-quality chocolate bars from the chocolate-maker Voisin in the Isère, and sweets from all over France.

DEBAUVE & GALLAIS
30, rue de Saint-Pères,
Paris 7.
Tel: 01.45.48.54.67.
Métro: Saint-Germain
des Pres.
Open 10 A.M. to 7 P.M.
Closed Sunday and Monday
in July and August.
Credit cards: DC, V.

An old shop with a bright new interior, this little jewel began life in 1800 as a pharmacy that dispensed chocolate. The counter is now covered with glass amphoras filled with hazelnut pralines and chocolate truffles dusted with cocoa. Chocolates are handled as though they were precious jewels, and no matter how small your order, it will be wrapped, ribboned, and decorated with a lovely gold seal. The chocolates here are dark, intense, and masculine. On a sunny day, the sun shines through the shop's elegant *cosse d'orange* windows, arranged to form an elegant orange wedge. They will ship internationally.

JEAN-PAUL HEVIN
3, rue Vavin,
Paris 6.
Tel: 01.43.54.09.85.
Métro: Vavin or Notre-
Dame des Champs.
Open 10 A.M. to 7:30 P.M.
(to 6:30 P.M. Sunday).
Closed Sunday in
July and August.
Credit card: V.

and

16, avenue de la
Motte Picquet,
Paris 7.
Tel: 01.45.51.77.48.
Métro: La Tour-Maubourg.
Open 10 A.M. to 7:30 P.M.
Closed Sunday, Monday,
and three weeks
in August.
Credit card: V.

Jean-Paul Hévin is one of the new generation of chocolate makers who specialize in modern shops that resemble jewelry stores, where the saleswoman acts as though you're about to steal the family jewels and also wishes you wouldn't bother her with your presence. But if you're a chocolate maven, by all means go, for the assortment is beautiful and varied. I find his chocolates just so-so. In fact, the *florentines* I sampled on the last visit resembled squares of chocolate topped with stale Rice Krispies. A better bet are the *palets amers,* tiny squares of bittersweet chocolat that melt oh, so soothingly. But chocolate-lovers, go see for yourselves. He's young and perhaps just needs to mature. You can also purchase tea, coffee, sandwiches, croissants, cakes, and chocolate bars (*tablettes*) here.

PUYRICARD
27, avenue Rapp,
Paris 7.
Tel: 01.47.05.59.47.
Métro: Ecole Militaire or Alma-Marceau.
Open 9:30 A.M. to 7:30 P.M. (2 to 7 P.M. Monday).
Closed Sunday and mid-July through August.
Credit cards: AE, V.

A sober, old-fashioned shop selling handmade chocolates from Aix-en-Provence—rich and creamy, with the intensity of good South American chocolate. Try as well the famed *calissons d'Aix* and the *nougatine* filled with pine nuts (*pignons*).

RICHART
258, boulevard Saint-Germain,
Paris 7.
Tel: 01.45.55.66.00.
Métro: Solférino.
Open 10 A.M. to 7 P.M. (11 A.M. to 7 P.M. Saturday and Monday).
Closed Sunday.
Credit card: V.

A lovely modern, elegant chocolate shop, featuring delicious *tablettes* (chocolate bars) made with Venezuelan chocolate, as well as an exceptional *sorbet* of chocolate and cinnamon, *chocolat-cannelle*. Their sampling collection, *"grignotage,"* features some twenty different handmade chocolates, flavored with everything from Alsatian *marc de Gewürztraminer* to a *coulis* of pineapple.

MADELEINE, ROND-POINT, ARC DE TRIOMPHE, GRANDS BOULEVARDS, TRINITE, LE PELETIER, GARE SAINT-LAZARE

8th and 9th arrondissements

DENISE ACABO/ A L'ETOILE D'OR
30, rue Fontaine,
Paris 9.
Tel: 01.48.74.59.55.
Métro: Blanche.
Open 10:30 A.M. to 8 P.M.
Closed Sunday and August.
Credit cards: AE, V.

How does a chocolate-lover visit Paris and yet manage to sample all the best homemade chocolates from all over France? The answer is a simple Métro ride to the Blanche station, then a swift anticipatory walk down rue Fontaine until you reach the charming old-fashioned storefront of Denise Acabo. She's round and pig-tailed, with an obvious passion for chocolate. Show a little interest and, no questions asked, she'll take you on a guided tour of her fragrant boutique, as you travel to Lyon with the Bernachons, to Nice with the Auer family, to La Clayette with Bernard Dufoux, and to Monsieur Bonnat's in Voiron. Her selections are pure, honest, invigorating. If you have time for only one chocolate shop in Paris, make it this one. I assure you, it won't disappoint.

BOISSIER
46, avenue Marceau,
Paris 8.
Tel: 01.47.20.31.31.
Métro: Alma-Marceau or Charles de Gaulle–Etoile.
Open 10 A.M. to 5 P.M.
Closed Saturday, Sunday, and August.
Credit card: V.

Boissier always make me think that someone is having a very exclusive bake sale, with its little trays of perfect cakes and chocolates all lined up for inspection. Even though the wealthy families in the neighborhood may have full-time cooks, the lady of the house still comes in to select the evening's dessert.

Other address:

184, avenue Victor-Hugo,
Paris 16.
Tel: 01.45.04.87.88.
Métro: Victor Hugo or Rue de la Pompe.
Open 10 A.M. to 7 P.M.
Closed Sunday and August.
Credit card: V.

CANDIED CHESTNUTS

Candied chestnuts—*marrons glacés*—are fall and winter specialties that are sold at most of the better chocolate shops in town. They appear around the beginning of November, when the first fresh chestnuts start to arrive from the Ardèche, in southeastern France. They generally disappear at the close of the season, around the middle of January. The process of turning fresh raw chestnuts into little candied jewels is painstakingly slow and requires immense patience.

The fresh chestnuts are first boiled several times to free them from their shells and skins. If any bits of skin remain, they are removed by hand. The chestnuts are then wrapped in cheesecloth to prevent them from falling apart during the next process—a three- to seven-hour stint in a pressure cooker. Next they are cooked again, this time for forty-eight hours in a vanilla sugar syrup over very low heat. The chestnuts are often delivered to shops in this form, conserved in syrup. They are then glazed in small quantities by sprinkling them with water and baking them, a process that gives the chestnuts their characteristic sugary appearance. Finally they are wrapped in the traditional shiny gold foil paper.

LA BONBONNIERE DE LA TRINITE
4, place d'Estienne d'Orves,
Paris 9.
Tel: 01.48.74.23.38.
Métro: Trinité.
Open 9 A.M. to 7 P.M.
Closed Sunday, and Saturday in July and August.
Credit card: V.

See La Bonbonnière Saint-Honoré below.

LA BONBONNIERE SAINT-HONORE
28, rue de Miromesnil,
Paris 8.
Tel: 01.42.65.02.39.
Métro: Miromesnil.
Open 10 A.M. to 7 P.M.
Closed Saturday and Sunday.
Credit card: V.

This pristine family-run shop is the sister of the charming and fragrant Bonbonnière de la Trinité (above). They both offer deep, dark, fresh-tasting chocolates, as well as a healthy assortment of packaged regional candies (*bonbons*), cakes, and cookies. I'm partial to their fragile discs of bittersweet chocolate for serving with coffee. There are also pretty rows of artisanal jams and jellies.

LA MAISON DU CHOCOLAT
225, rue du Faubourg Saint-Honoré
Paris 8.
Tel: 01.42.27.39.44.
Métro: Ternes.
Open 9:30 A.M. to 7 P.M.
Closed Sunday, Monday, and the last week of July through the third week of August.
Credit cards: AE, V.

and

52, rue François 1er,
Paris 8.
Tel: 01.47.23.38.25.
Métro: Franklin D. Roosevelt.
Open 9:30 A.M. to 7 P.M.
Closed Sunday.
Credit cards: AE, V.

and

A chocolate-lover's dream: chocolate-colored façade, chocolate-colored blinds, even the *chocolatier,* Robert Linxe, in a chocolate-colored apron. You feel as though you'll gain a pound or two just breathing, in his marvelous quintet of shops. Monsieur Linxe is the undisputed king of chocolate in Paris, selling a sophisticated handmade assortment of delights prepared in the neat little basement workshop on the rue du Faubourg Saint-Honoré. He's rightly proud of his *framboise* (raspberry-flavored chocolate), and his creamy *palets d'or* melt in your mouth. Other excellent creations include *rigoletto* (filled with a caramel butter), *la bohème* (milk chocolate), and *roméo,* with an interior of fresh-brewed arabica coffee.

At the cool, pristine, chocolate-hued boutique on rue François 1er, you can sit at the marble-topped bar or around low round tables and indulge in one of the world's greatest passions. One scorching summer's day I was miraculously invigorated by a *Guayaquil frappé,* a tall glass of perfect iced chocolate—a whipped blend of bitter chocolate ice cream and rich melted chocolate. The menu here offers no fewer than five variously flavored hot chocolates, as well as chocolate *mousses, sorbets,* and ice creams. Chocolates, pastries, and cakes can be

8, boulevard de la Madeleine,
Paris 9.
Tel: 01.47.42.86.52.
Métro: Madeleine.
Open 9:30 A.M. to 7 P.M.
Closed Sunday.
Credit cards: AE, V.

purchased to sample in the shop or to take home. The diminutive menu offers a sampling of appropriate gastronomic sayings, including a pertinent warning from Saint Ignatius of Loyola, founder of the Jesuit order: "Gourmandise is a capital sin. So therefore, my brothers, let us guard against being gourmands. Let's be gourmets."

Other addresses:

19, rue de Sèvres,
Paris 6.
Tel: 01.45.44.20.40.
Métro: Sèvres-Babylone.
Open 9:30 A.M. to 7 P.M.
Closed Sunday.
Credit cards: AE, V.

89, avenue Raymond Poincaré,
Paris 16.
Tel: 01.40.67.77.88.
Métro: Victor Hugo.
Open 9:30 A.M. to 7 P.M.
Closed Sunday.
Credit cards: AE, V.

Robert Linxe, chocolatier at La Maison du Chocolat.

MACARONS CREOLES
CHOCOLATE MACAROONS

One day I was exhausted and a friend suggested that what I needed was chocolate. Not just any chocolate, but something special from La Maison du Chocolat, one of the best chocolate shops in Paris (see page 310). Fortunately, it just happens to be at the end of my street. I bought a chocolate-filled chocolate macaroon and was instantly cured. In gratitude and greed, I created this recipe the very next day, and have never found anyone who'd turn them down.

Macaroons:
1 cup (140 g) almonds
3½ ounces (110 g) bittersweet chocolate (preferably Valrhona or Lindt)
1 teaspoon vanilla extract
2 large egg whites (2½ ounces; 80 g)
¾ cup (150 g) sugar
1 tablespoon (½ ounce; 15g) unsalted butter, for buttering the baking sheet

Filling:
1¾ ounces (50 g) bittersweet chocolate
2 tablespoons *crème fraîche* (see recipe, page 290) or heavy (whipping) cream (preferably not ultra-pasteurized)

1. Preheat the oven to 275°F (135°C).

2. Toast the almonds on a baking sheet until browned, about 5 minutes. Remove, but leave the oven on. When cool (about 10 minutes), grind the almonds to a fine powder in a food processor.

3. In a small saucepan over very low heat, melt the 3½ ounces (110 g) chocolate with the vanilla.

4. In the bowl of an electric mixer on slow speed, mix the egg whites, almonds, and sugar until well blended. With the machine still running, add the melted chocolate mixture, and continue beating until thoroughly blended.

5. Butter a baking sheet (or line it with cooking parchment paper, then butter the paper). Spoon the batter onto the baking sheet, allowing 1 heaping tablespoon of batter for each macaroon.

6. Bake just until the macaroons are set, 15 to 18 minutes. They should be slightly firm but not dry. Transfer the macaroons to a rack to cool.

7. Meanwhile, prepare the filling: In a small saucepan over very low heat, melt the 1¾ ounces (50 g) chocolate. Add the *crème fraîche* or heavy cream and stir until well blended. Set aside to cool.

8. When the macaroons and the filling have cooled, spread a heaping tablespoon of the filling on half the macaroons, and cover each with a second macaroon, making a sort of sandwich. The macaroons may be served immediately, though they are best if they sit for a few hours.

Yield: 10 to 12 filled macaroons

A LA MERE DE FAMILLE
35, rue du Faubourg
Montmartre,
Paris 9.
Tel: 01.47.70.83.69.
Métro: Le Peletier
or Rue Montmartre.
Open 8:30 A.M. to 1:30 P.M.
and 3 to 7 P.M.
Closed Sunday, Monday,
and August.
Credit card: V.

This shop comes right out of a fairy tale. Stop in late in the afternoon, when the children are getting out of school, and watch the owners spoil the entire neighborhood with their incredible variety of sweets from all over France. In the chocolate department, sample the little *barquettes* of dark chocolate filled with *cassis* (black currants) or *framboise* (raspberry).

BASTILLE

11th arrondissement

A LA PETITE FABRIQUE
12, rue Saint-Sabin,
Paris 11.
Tel: 01.48.05.82.02.
Métro: Bastille.
Open 10:30 A.M. to 7:30 P.M.
Closed Sunday and Monday.
Credit card: V.

Wandering into La Petite Fabrique from the exhaust-fumed streets of Paris is like falling right into chocolate heaven. The aromas that envelop you are intoxicating. If you have ever wondered how people really make their own chocolates, you can see it all right here: The glass windows open out onto the tiny workshop, where workers temper their chocolates, mold specialties, make your day a little happier and just that much more sane. I wouldn't judge these the best-tasting chocolates in Paris, but they're delicious, and the boutique is worth a trip if you're in the neighborhood.

An exquisite display.

CHOCOLATE FOR ALL SEASONS

In Paris, chocolate is always in fashion. Throughout the year, the sparkling windows of the city's shops serve as a calendar, announcing each holiday, beginning with Valentine's Day, when thousands of chocolate hearts are broken.

Spring is ushered in as shop windows are aswim with chocolate fish in anticipation of Poisson d'Avril, April Fool's Day. Large fish with bows around their tails are filled with schools of *fritures,* tiny chocolate minnows. And little boxes filled with milk chocolate "sardines" appear everwhere.

At Easter time chocolate bunnies, chicks, ducks, and puppies frolic in displays. They are surrounded by chocolate eggs wrapped with silvery, glittery, magical paper. On the Place de la Madeleine, Fauchon's huge, lacy chocolate egg sits in regal splendor, stopping pedestrian traffic for weeks.

Easter has hardly passed when tiny chocolate pots of *muguets* (lilies of the valley) appear as the traditional French symbol for the first of May. They keep company with the hearts and flowers that burst forth for the Fête des Mères, Mother's Day.

Although the summer heat signals a slowdown for chocolates in Paris, chocolate shops refuse to give up. Windows are full of summer symbols, all nicely molded in chocolate—pails and shovels for playing in the sand, starfish, and shells.

Fall comes in with blustery days that announce the season for chocolate mushrooms and luscious, creamy truffles. All of this is a fanfare to Christmas, when chocolate shops split their attention between the candied chestnuts known as *marrons glacés* and *bûches de Noël,* or Christmas log cakes, homey reminders of times past, when guests offered their hosts a real log to keep the fire burning.

Spécialités Gastronomiques
SPECIALTY SHOPS

The exotic world of Izraël (see entry, page 320).

The specialty shops of Paris, ranging from old-fashioned family-owned candy and spice shops to slick, rambling food emporiums, offer a potpourri of good things at your fingertips. Whether you're looking for the freshest black truffle; whether you plan to indulge in thirty different kinds of honey, want to sample *foie gras,* or would like to taste mustard made with Saint Pourçain wine; or whether you just want to purchase a little sack of licorice to enjoy as you wander about Paris, the following should offer some guidance. From the exotic to the commonplace, here is a hint of the things of which dreams are made.

PALAIS-ROYAL, OPERA, TUILERIES, LES HALLES

1st and 2nd arrondissements

G. DETOU
58, rue Tiquetonne,
Paris 2.
Tel: 01.42.36.54.67.
Fax: 01.42.39.08.04.
Métro: Etienne Marcel or Les Halles.
Open 8:30 A.M. to 6 P.M. (8:15 A.M. to 12:15 P.M. Saturday).
Closed Sunday.

Do as Parisian pastry chefs do: They come to Détou for some of the finest ingredients—Valrhona chocolate (sold in 3-kilo bars), almonds from Spain, pure cocoa butter, and dried fruits. Also dried mushrooms, nut oils, salmon, and *foie gras.* Baker Gérard Mulot is one of the shop's better customers; this is where he buys chocolates for his lovely chocolate-chip *pains au chocolat.*

GARGANTUA
284, rue Saint-Honoré,
Paris 1.
Tel: 01.42.60.63.38.
Fax: 01.42.61.49.81.
Métro: Tuileries.
Open daily 8 A.M. to 9:00 P.M. (to 8 P.M. Sunday).
Credit cards: AE, V.

As the name suggests, everything here is king-size. Enjoy quality *croissants, pains au chocolat,* and oversize puff pastry *palmiers,* all big enough to feed a family of four, at the small counter tucked in back of the shop. The place is casual and colorful, with a wide selection of *charcuterie,* wines, liquors, and salads, ready to take home, on a picnic, or on a plane.

TETREL EPICERIE/ CONFISERIE
44, rue des Petits-Champs,
Paris 2.
Tel: 01.42.96.59.58.
Métro: Pyramides.
Open 9 A.M. to 5:30 P.M.
Closed Sunday.

A pristine (but not very friendly) little shop for fine foodstuffs, the polished wood counters and sparkling windows are crowded with tins of candies, *confit,* and sardines. This is a good place to experience old Paris and pick up some old-fashioned sweets or a small gift reminiscent of the 19th century.

VERLET
256, rue Saint-Honoré,
Paris 1.
Tel: 01.42.60.67.39.
Métro: Palais Royal–Musée du Louvre.
Open 9 A.M. to 7 P.M.
Closed Saturday and Sunday from May to October, Sunday and Monday from October to May.
Credit card: V.

A block away from the elegant Palais Royal, this is one of Paris's most famous coffee shops, known for common and uncommon coffees and teas from the world over. Stop into this cozy shop filled with open sacks of coffee for a pick-me-up in the homey, aromatic tearoom. The friendly proprietors love to discuss the merits and differences of each coffee variety. They also serve a good *croque-monsieur* and fine fresh desserts, including a delectable apricot tart (see recipe, page 170).

HEDIARD

Tea, spice, and everything nice, Hédiard is one of the more stylish groups of gourmet shops in town, with one-stop shopping for everything from their famous spices to exotic blends of vinegar or oil, great canned tuna and sardines, as well as chocolates, carry-out deli items, and exotic fruits and vegetables. Many visitors make annual visits simply to stock up on a few of Hédiard's thirty varieties of tea. Their freshly roasted coffee beans (I love the Colombian Maragogype) are also top-quality. Hédiard's wine cellars offer an extensive selection of Bordeaux at high prices. Good to know on off-hours when you want a quick pastry, *charcuterie,* a house gift. All shops are open from 9:15 A.M. to 11 P.M. Closed Sunday. Credit cards: AE, DC, V.

1, rue Pierre-Lescot, Paris 1.
Tel: 01.40.39.98.04.
Métro: Les Halles.

126, rue du Bac, Paris 7.
Tel: 01.45.44.01.98
Métro: Rue du Bac.

21, place de la Madeleine, Paris 8.
Tel: 01.42.66.44.36.
Métro: Madeleine.

Centre Beaugrenelle, Paris 15.
Tel: 01.45.75.57.50.
Métro: Charles Michels.

70, avenue Paul-Doumer, Paris 16.
Tel: 01.45.04.51.92.
Métro: Trocadéro or La Muette.

6, rue Donizetti, Paris 16.
Tel: 01.40.50.71.94.
Métro: Michel-Ange–Auteuil.

106, boulevard de Courcelles, Paris 17.
Tel: 01.47.63.32.14.
Métro: Courcelles.

FLO PRESTIGE

One of Paris's more trustworthy carry-out food shops, Flo Prestige offers a bright and fresh selection of raw-milk cheeses, beautiful smoked salmon, assorted *charcuterie, foie gras,* sushi, salads, and full meals. Everything can be purchased in individual portions, so put together a picnic and head for the Tuileries gardens (or the nearest useful picnicking spot). Wine and pastries are also available. Flo delivers (for a healthy price), and these are useful addresses to keep in mind for late-night hunger pangs. The shops are open from 8 A.M. to 10 P.M. Credit cards: AE, DC, V.

42, place du Marché Saint-Honoré, Paris 1.
Tel: 01.42.61.45.46.
Métro: Pyramides.

10, rue Saint-Antoine, Paris 4.
Tel: 01.53.01.91.91.
Métro: Bastille or Saint-Paul.

69, rue de Rennes, Paris 6.
Tel: 01.53.63.40.20.
Métro: Saint-Sulpice.

36, avenue de La Motte-Picquet, Paris 7.
Tel: 01.45.55.71.25.
Métro: La Tour-Maubourg.

211, avenue Daumesnil, Paris 12.
Tel: 01.43.44.86.36.
Métro: Daumesnil.

22, avenue de la Porte de Vincennes, Paris 12.
Tel: 01.43.74.54.32.
Métro: Porte de Vincennes.

41, avenue des Gobelins, Paris 13.
Tel: 01.55.43.52.30.
Métro: Les Gobelins or Place d'Italie.

91, avenue du General-Leclerc, Paris 14.
Tel: 01.53.90.24.50.
Métro: Alésia.

352, rue Lecourbe, Paris 15.
Tel: 01.45.54.76.94.
Métro: Balard.

61, avenue de la Grande-Armée, Paris 16.
Tel: 01.45.00.12.10.
Métro: Argentine.

102, avenue du Président-Kennedy, Paris 16.
Tel: 01.55.74.44.44.
Métro: Passy.

Temple

3rd arrondissement

TANTIFLA
Poissonnerie Epicerie Provençale
7, rue de Bretagne, Paris 3.
Métro: Filles du Calvaire.
Tel: 01.42.78.38.18.
Fax: 01.42.78.38.38.
Open 9:30 A.M. to 1 P.M. and 3:30 to 8 P.M.
Closed Sunday afternoon and Monday.
Credit card: V.

A spotless, sparkling little shop in the midst of a wealth of food shops along the Rue de Bretagne. You will rarely find fresher or more beautiful fish anywhere: On my last visit they had buckets full of squiggling baby crabs (*étrilles*); gorgeous sea bass (*bar*); tuna and salmon with that right-from-the-sea shimmer. There's also a fine selection of wines from Provence, *fleur de sel* (rare fine raw sea salt) from the Camargue, pastas, oils, honeys, unusual mustards (try the saffron-flavored one, great for pairing with fish), and a delicious *tartare d'algue* (seaweed *tartare*) for spreading on toasted country bread. Of course they also sell *tantifla,* a Provençal potato purée prepared with olive oil.

Chock-full at Izraël.

MARAIS

4th arrondissement

IZRAEL EPICERIE DU MONDE
30, rue François-Miron,
Paris 4.
Tel: 01.42.72.66.23.
Métro: Saint-Paul.
Open 9:30 A.M. to 1 P.M. and 2:30 to 7 P.M. (9:30 A.M. to 7 P.M. Saturday).
Closed Sunday, Monday, two weeks in February, and August.
Credit cards: V.

Many of the city's chefs depend upon Izrael, "Spice Shop to the World." The Ali Baba–type shop opened more than sixty-five years ago, specializing in North African products. Today the cluttered, delicious-smelling store features more than 3,000 products from all over the world, and current owners Monsieur and Madame Szolski offer everything from guava paste to Fritos, delicious Polish buckwheat to woven African baskets. There's a marvelous assortment of grains, rices, flours, dried fruits, and nuts, all sold out of giant sacks.

A L'OLIVIER
23, rue de Rivoli,
Paris 4.
Tel: 01.48.04.86.59.
Métro: Saint-Paul or Hôtel de Ville.
Open 9:30 A.M. to 1 P.M. and 2 to 7 P.M.
Closed Sunday, Monday, and the week of August 15.
Credit card: V.

Olivier has been supplying the Parisian palate with oils since the 19th century. This bright, updated shop offers every kind of oil imaginable, from olive, walnut, and hazelnut for the table to palm oil for frying and almond oil for massages. Although the quality of the oil is not extraordinary, the nicely packaged products make fine gifts.

THANKSGIVING
13, rue Charles V,
Paris 4.
Tel: 01.42.77.68.29.
Fax: 01.42.77.70.83.
Métro: Saint-Paul.
Open 10 A.M. to 7 P.M. (to 6 P.M. Sunday).
Closed Monday, three weeks in August, and one week after Christmas.

Anyone in search of dark brown sugar for chocolate chip cookies, or for pancake mix, baking soda, or bagels and cream cheese in Paris will truly give thanks for this tiny American food shop in the Marais. As the name suggests, the shop will cater Thanksgiving meals.

CORNICHONS
TINY TART PICKLES

The cornichon, *a tiny tart pickle, is ubiquitous in France.* Cornichons *arrive at the table in squat white crocks, ready to be served with* pâtés, rillettes, *slices of salty country ham, or with* pot-au-feu. *The first time I made* cornichons *was in New York City. Picking through a bin full of garden-fresh cucumbers at the farmer's market in Union Square, I was able to come up with enough tiny cucumbers to make one precious quart. Now, frankly, I'm spoiled, for each August, the fresh cucumbers appear in abundance in Paris's open-air markets, ready for "putting up" with tiny white onions and plenty of fresh tarragon. I like them spicy and hot, so I add plenty of garlic and hot peppers.*

60 to 70 2-inch (5-cm) pickling cucumbers (about 2 pounds; 1 kg)
¼ cup (65 g) coarse (kosher) salt
1 quart (1 liter) cold water, plus an additional 1½ cups (375 ml)
3 cups (75 cl) best-quality white wine vinegar
1 tablespoon sugar
12 small white pickling onions, peeled but with ends intact
4 large sprigs fresh tarragon
6 cloves garlic, peeled
8 small hot red peppers (fresh or dried)
½ teaspoon black peppercorns
2 bay leaves

1. Trim off the stem ends of the cucumbers; then rinse and drain. In a large bowl combine the salt with the 1 quart (1 liter) water. Stir until the salt is dissolved. Add the cucumbers, and let stand in a cool place for 6 hours.

2. Scald two 1-quart (1-liter) canning jars, lids, and rings with boiling water and drain well.

3. Drain the cucumbers, discarding the salted water.

4. In a medium-size saucepan over medium heat, combine the vinegar, 1½ cups (37.5 cl) water, and the sugar, and bring to a boil.

5. Fill the jars with layers of the drained cucumbers, the onions, herbs, and spices, making sure to divide the ingredients evenly between the jars.

6. Pour the boiling vinegar mixture into the jars, letting a bit of the liquid overflow the jars; this helps seal the lids well. Wipe the rim of each jar and seal. Let stand until cool. Store in a cool place for at least 3 weeks before serving. Refrigerate after opening.

Yield: 2 quarts (2 liters) cornichons

TRUFFLES

Delicate, earthy, and increasingly rare, the prized black Périgord truffle symbolizes the grand gastronomic life of Paris, past and present. The writer Colette, who devoted one day each year to eating truffles, said it best: "If I can't have too many truffles, I'll do without truffles."

The Périgord truffle—in appearance a rather inelegant, wrinkled black nugget generally the size of a walnut, although it can be as small as a pea or as large as an orange—is perhaps the world's most mysterious food. A fungus with a capricious personality, it stubbornly refuses to be cultivated. (As one Frenchman observed, "Growing truffles is not farming; it's luck.") And its flavor is just as elusive. No one has succeeded in adequately describing the taste of a truffle. Some say it's licorice-like, others find a hint of black pepper. As with many highly aromatic foods, it is the truffle's rich, pungent, and pervasive aroma that makes its flavor so singular. Eating fresh truffles makes me think of a quiet walk in the autumn woods under a slow drizzle, of freshly upturned black earth, of hazelnuts, of luxury, and of pleasure.

The traditional truffle used to come primarily from the southwest of France, in the Quercy and Périgord regions east of Bordeaux; in recent years the crop has been slowly moving to the southeast. Today the majority of French truffles are found in the Tricastin area of the Rhône Valley, and in the French *départements* of the Vaucluse, the Gard, and Haute Provence.

Truffles grow three inches to a foot underground, in stony, porous soil near the roots of scrub-oak trees. Gathered from November to March by farmers using dogs or pigs trained to scent out and unearth the elusive tuber, the truffle reaches its peak of flavor after the winter's first freeze, toward the month of January. Truffles thrive on a rainy summer and autumn, and their presence sometimes can be spotted by the burned-looking patch around the base of the tree—the truffle's way of ensuring enough air for itself is by killing the undergrowth—or by the presence of a swarm of truffle flies hovering above the tuber's hiding place.

Someone who's tall and lanky is known as a "bean pole" in English, "une asperge" or asparagus in French.

Fresh truffles (*truffes fraîches*) are sold in Parisian specialty shops from mid-November through March. An average-size fresh truffle weighs about 3 ounces, or about 100 grams, and though one truffle can't be considered an avalanche, it's enough for a gastronomic adventure.

At La Maison de la Truffe, which sells more than 600 pounds (about 300 kilos) of fresh and preserved truffles each year, fresh truffles arrive every two or three days from November to March direct from Provence or the Périgord. Still encrusted with soil, the fragrant gems are placed, unwrapped, in small wicker baskets so that they can breathe during the four- to five-hour train ride. A fresh truffle will last only three or four days, losing about one twentieth of its weight by evaporation each day after it is unearthed. At the same time, its flavor fades rapidly. Guy Monier, owner of La Maison de la Truffe, suggests that if a fresh truffle must be kept longer than three or four days, it should be gently washed, then buried in goose or duck fat and refrigerated; otherwise it is likely to mildew. It may be stored in fat for up to six months. A fresh truffle can also be refrigerated for two or three days, locked tight in a glass jar with several raw eggs in their shells. The pungent truffle aroma will permeate the eggs, which can then be used to prepare a truffle-laced omelet, perhaps the best way to first experience a truffle.

For most of the world, the only known truffle is a preserved one. Although fresh is best, well-preserved truffles are better than no truffles at all. What does one look for in buying a preserved truffle? First, buy only truffles in a glass container so that you can see what you're getting, and buy only:

Truffes brossées au naturel: truffles that have been sterilized in water and salt with no alcohol or spices used to mask or heighten their flavor. For the closest thing to a fresh truffle, try the whole preserved *truffe extra,* the top-grade truffle that is uniformly black and firm. If available, ask for a truffle of *première ébullition,* that is, a truffle that has been brushed, salted, placed in its container, then sterilized. Since a truffle loses 25 percent of its weight during cooking, the weight of the *première ébullition* truffle cannot be verified on the label. Thus, processors are required to underestimate the true weight of the truffle. Most common are truffles of *deuxième ébullition.* In this process, the truffle is sterilized, removed from its container to verify its weight, then sterilized. All preserved truffles should be consumed within three years of being processed.

The following are other truffle gradings and other truffle preparations found on the market:

Truffes premier choix: small, irregularly shaped truffles that are more like pieces than whole truffles, and are more or less black.

Truffes en morceaux: broken pieces of truffle that must be at least ¼ inch (5 mm) thick. Considered equal in quality to *premier choix,* and generally lower in price.

Truffes en pelures: truffle peelings or shavings. Generally not worth the price.

Truffes préparées: truffles sterilized in water and salt, with liquor, alcohol, or wine added. A bad buy.

Jus de truffe: truffle juice. Not worth the price.

SAINT-GERMAIN, INVALIDES, EIFFEL TOWER

6th and 7th arrondissements

L'AMBASSADE DU SUD-OUEST
46, avenue de la Bourdonnais,
Paris 7.
Tel: 01.45.55.59.59.
Métro: Ecole Militaire.
Open daily, 10 A.M. to 11 P.M.
Closed one week in August.
Credit card: V.

Foie gras frais, mi-cuit, and *cuit* (fresh, semi-cooked, and cooked), *pâté, rillettes, terrines, tourte Landaise* (apple tart with strudel-like dough), *eaux-de-vie,* and all the earthy bounty of the French southwest can be found a couple of blocks from the Eiffel Tower. Open daily until late, l'Ambassade du Sud-Ouest makes a convenient stop for last-minute gifts or picnic provisions for a feast in the Champs de Mars. You can sample *foie gras* sandwiches, *brouillade aux cèpes* (scrambled eggs with *cèpes*), *cassoulet,* and other specialties in their café.

THE GENERAL STORE
82, rue de Grenelle,
Paris 7.
Tel: 01.45.48.63.16.
Métro: Rue du Bac.
Open 10:30 A.M. to 7:30 P.M.
Closed Sunday.
Credit cards: AE, V.

After sampling your fill of caviar, *foie gras, croissants,* and chocolate truffles, if what you're really craving is Hershey bars and corn chips, homemade brownies, muffins, and chocolate chips, this shop is the ticket to your dreams. Jean-Pierre Boubillon's General Store is a sparkling boutique full of star-spangled goodies, all cheaper than a one-way ticket to the States.

Other address:

30, rue de Longchamp,
Paris 16.
Tel: 01.47.55.41.14.
Métro: Trocadéro.
Open 10 A.M. to 7:30 P.M.
Closed Sunday.
Credit cards: AE, DC, V.

LES HERBES DU LUXEMBOURG
3, rue des Médicis,
Paris 6.
Tel: 01.43.26.91.53.
Métro: Odéon or RER Luxembourg.
Open 10 A.M. to 7:30 P.M. (11 A.M. to 7 P.M. in summer).
Closed Sunday and one week in August.
Credit card: V.

This delightful shop is like a health food general store. It offers everything from dried herbs and oils, fruits and nuts, honeys, jams, and fresh whole-grain breads (each Wednesday), to organic baby foods and teas, all with an eye toward health and well-being. Some special items of note: the line of l'Olivier oils; sea salt from Brittany; an assortment of miniature soaps, shampoos, and toiletries for travel; and lily- or cedar-scented paper for lining drawers.

HUILERIE J. LEBLANC
6, rue Jacob,
Paris 6.
Tel: 01.46.34.61.55.
Métro: Saint-Germain des Prés.
Open 10:30 A.M. to 7 P.M. (2:30 to 7:00 P.M. Monday).
Closed Sunday.

Some of the finest oils in France come from the artisanal mills of the Leblanc family. I feel my cupboard is bare if it doesn't hold bottles of walnut and hazelnut oil, ready for preparing a nutty *vinaigrette* for tossing into salads, for drizzling on warm *foie gras,* or for sprinkling on freshly cooked white beans. Their nuts are deliciously fresh, and there is also a good selection of other oils, including olive, pistachio, and the rare grilled *colza* (rapeseed) oil, which was traditionally made as a substitute for olive oil when the olive harvest was bad. It is delicious drizzled on fresh goat cheese.

VIVE LES SUPERMARCHES!

You've had a hard day, didn't have time to go to the market, and are expecting guests for dinner. Don't despair! Parisian department stores are home to some of the world's most luxurious and well-stocked supermarkets. Spacious and open late, many even deliver. Finicky Parisians can stop by after work and fill their shopping cart with *foie gras,* ripe cheese and produce, smoked salmon, even a bottle of Pétrus. Here are some of the best addresses.

LA GRANDE EPICERIE DE PARIS
Bon Marché
38, rue de Sèvres (Magasin 2, main floor), Paris 7.
Tel: 01.44.39.81.00.
Métro: Sèvres-Babylone.
Open 8:30 A.M. to 9 P.M.
Closed Sunday.
Credit card: V.

It's the Left Bank Fauchon, and though this fairly new supermarket lacks the tradition and history of the classic establishment on the Place de la Madeleine, La Grande Epicerie de Paris is a dream of a modern supermarket: every packaged good you can imagine (from the most ordinary to the most exotic); a good choice of Italian cheeses, sausages, and carry-out items; a wine shop, a bread shop, an extensive frozen food department; and a special delivery service for those who live in the neighborhood.

LAFAYETTE GOURMET
Galeries Lafayette
48, boulevard Haussmann, Paris 8.
Tel: 01.48.74.46.06.
Métro: Chausée-d'Antin–La Fayette or Havre-Caumartin.
Open 9 A.M. to 8 P.M. (until 9 P.M. Thursday).
Closed Sunday.
Credit cards: AE, V.

A supermarket to rival the food halls of London, with special butcher shops; wine, fish, and cheese shops; counters for sitting and sipping a glass

of Champagne, a coffee, or an aquavit with your caviar or smoked salmon; plus a great selection of fresh produce and packaged items from around the world. Also special departments run by such names as Lenôtre and Petrossian.

MARKS & SPENCER
35, boulevard Haussmann, Paris 8.
Tel: 01.44.61.08.00.
Fax: 01.47.42.42.91.
Métro: Chausée-d'Antin–La Fayette or Havre-Caumartin.
Open 9 A.M. to 8 P.M. (9:30 A.M. to 9 P.M. Tuesday).
Closed Sunday.
Credit card: V.

88, rue de Rivoli,
Paris.
Tel: (same as above)
Métro: Châtelet or Châtelet–Les Halles.
Open: 9 A.M. to 8 P.M. (9:30 A.M. to 9 P.M. Tuesday).
Closed Sunday.
Credit card: V.

British jams, smoked fish from Scotland and Ireland, an astonishingly good (and expensive) assortment of hard-to-find fresh baby vegetables, great apples from England, cottage cheese, typically British biscuits, crackers, and cookies, English muffins, and a fine assortment of top-quality sandwiches make this a favorite stop among Parisians, French and otherwise.

PETROSSIAN
18, boulevard de La Tour-Maubourg,
Paris 7.
Tel: 01.44.11.32.22.
Métro: La Tour-Maubourg or Invalides.
Open 9 A.M. to 8 P.M. (9:30 A.M. to 8 P.M. Monday and Saturday).
Closed Sunday, and Mondays in August.
Credit cards: V, AE

As the Petrossians like to say, "We sell dreams." And dreams are made of Russian caviar, smoked salmon, *foie gras,* truffles, and Sauternes. Everything here is of high quality, but the prices are competitive. I rarely buy caviar anywhere else in Paris—the Petrossians make regular trips to the Caspian Sea to monitor its processing. Other specialties in this well-appointed shop include Russian pastries, fresh blinis, assorted herring, vodka, and delicious black Georgian tea.

Madeleine, Le Peletier, Gare du Nord

8th and 9th arrondissements

BETJEMAN AND BARTON
23, boulevard Malesherbes, Paris 8.
Tel: 01.42.65.86.17.
Métro: Madeleine.
Open 9:30 A.M. to 7 P.M.
Closed Sunday, and Saturdays in August.
Credit cards: AE, V.

A shop for Anglophiles almost across the street from Burberrys. You can stock up for afternoon tea here: They offer an excellent selection of teas—some one hundred ninety—both classic varieties and seldom-seen flower and herbal mixtures, as well as old-fashioned biscuits and even scones (be forewarned, they often run out by the afternoon). To accompany all this, you may be tempted to buy one of the whimsical teapots shaped like animals and houses, among other things. Their extra-sour lemon drops can't be beat.

CAVIAR KASPIA
17, place de la Madeleine, Paris 8.
Tel: 01.42.65.33.32.
Métro: Madeleine.
Open 10 A.M. to 1 A.M.
Closed Sunday.
Credit cards: AE, DC, V.

This neat, uncluttered boutique on the Place de la Madeleine offers an excellent assortment of quality caviar, wonderfully delicate smoked eel, superb smoked salmon, and delightfully fresh blinis to take with you. The selection of caviar paraphernalia—special spoons and crystal "vases" to keep your caviar chilled—is also appealing. There is a cozy restaurant upstairs, where you can sample the house specialties on the spot.

FAUCHON
26, place de la Madeleine, Paris 8.
Tel: 01.47.42.60.11
Métro: Madeleine.
Open 9:40 A.M. to 7 P.M.
Closed Sunday.
Credit cards: AE, DC, V.

A visit to Fauchon is better than going to the theater. Many people find their several shops on the Place de la Madeleine even more fascinating than the Louvre. Fauchon's pristine glass windows, filled with expensive and exotic fruits and vegetables from every corner of the world, still stop traffic. Even the most jaded palates are tempted by the sheer quantity of food: more than 20,000 products, including extraordinary chocolates and exquisite pastries, wonderful breads, a mammoth international selection of fresh and packaged goods, coffee, tea, spices, a complete *charcuterie,* and a fine cheese selection. This is the best-known food shop in town, but not always the friendliest and not always the best. On the lower level there is a café and a self-service cafeteria for sampling some of the goods they sell above.

BOUTIQUE MAILLE
6, place de la Madeleine,
Paris 8.
Tel: 01.40.15.06.00.
Métro: Madeleine.
Open 10 A.M. to 7 P.M.
Closed Sunday.
Credit card: V.

Nothing makes me feel more romantic and in touch with the past than to stroll into this beautifully lit, warm white oak boutique and order a small jar of fresh mustard. Fresh, you say? None of us remember, and most of us never knew, that at one time housewives bought mustard the way we buy bread today: for that meal. The mustard was not pasteurized and, once exposed to heat and air, quickly lost its zest, flavor, and heady hotness. The Maille company brought back the custom, now offering mustard "on tap," pumped out of giant containers and poured into tiny gray crockery jars. The shop also features Maille's entire line of flavored mustards, vinegars, and condiments such as *cornichons* (pickles) and capers. Many of the selections can be found only in this shop. The array of collectors' hand-painted mustard jars—designs dating back to the company's founding in 1747—is vast and very tempting.

LA MAISON DU MIEL
24, rue Vignon,
Paris 9.
Tel: 01.47.42.26.70.
Métro: Madeleine.
Open 9 A.M. to 7 P.M.
Closed Sunday.
Credit card: V.

Even if you're not passionate about honey, put this shop on your list. The "House of Honey" is one of the few stores in the world devoted totally to honey and honey products, and it's been at rue Vignon since 1908. The fantasy-like tile décor—buzzing with bees and colorful hives—has not changed since then, nor has the founding family, the Gallands. They tend their own hives throughout France and buy selectively around the world. Personal favorites include the hearty, rust-toned heather (*bruyère*) and the delicate, mellow linden-tree blossom (*tilleul*), and lavender honey from Provence. Sample tastings are offered in the shop, and most varieties are available in miniature jars, allowing one to sample several. Honey-based soaps, wonderfully fragrant candles, and health products are also sold.

SARDINES

A Breton, Pierre-Joseph Colin, invented the tinned sardine in 1810. The first tins—well soldered and opened with a hammer—left with Napoléon on his Russian campaign. Today many French *gourmands* tuck tins of fine, delicate Brittany sardines away in their *caves* (cellars), sometimes aging the tender little fish for a decade or more. Vintage, or *millésime,* sardines are the rage in Paris, where most fine specialty shops offer a mixed assortment, tinned and carefully dated. Once they're taken home, the tins must be stored in a cool spot and turned every three or four months. As the unctuous, chewy sardines age, they become softer, more refined and delicate, ready to be consumed with a slice of crusty bread.

Sardines destined for *millésime* stardom bear no resemblance to the cheap garden-variety canned fish. Vintage sardines are always preserved fresh, whereas most ordinary sardines are frozen, then fried and processed. To prepare vintage sardines for processing, the fish are usually washed, grilled, and quickly deep-fried (traditionally, the time it takes to say a Hail Mary) before being packed, by hand, into small oval tins. Generally the head, skin, and central backbone are removed by hand from sardines packed for aging. Oil—usually the finest virgin olive oil—is added, perhaps a touch of spice or simply salt; then the tins are sealed and stored. They are turned regularly to ensure even aging, then put on the market one or two years after processing. While many companies make vintage sardines, only three—La Quibéronnaise, Gonidec, and La Belle Illoise—work exclusively with fresh sardines. Other brands to look for include Connétable (they change the design on the tin with each vintage!), Rodel, Albert Ménès, Les Mouettes d'Avor, Capitaine Cook, and Hédiard.

Many tins of vintage sardines display the words *première catégorie* or *extra* on the label, assuring that the sardines were prepared fresh, not frozen. Check for the processing date stamped into the bottom of the tin so that you know how long to keep them. Experts recommend the sardines be kept no more than four years, but some sardine lovers hold them up to ten years, being sure to turn the tins regularly.

The following are just a few of the shops offering vintage sardines. The tin or wrapper will bear the processing date.

HEDIARD
21, place de la Madeleine, Paris 8.
Tel: 01.42.66.44.36.
Métro: Madeleine.

FAUCHON
26, place de la Madeleine, Paris 8.
Tel: 01.47.42.60.11.
Métro: Madeleine.

AU VERGER DE LA MADELEINE
4, boulevard Malesherbes, Paris 8.
Tel: 01.42.65.51.99.
Métro: Madeleine.

ALBERT MENES
41, boulevard Malesherbes, Paris 8.
Tel: 01.42.66.95.63.
Métro: Saint-Augustin.
Open 10 A.M. to 7 P.M. (2 P.M. to 7 P.M. Monday).
Closed Sunday, and from mid-July to mid-August.
Credit cards: AE, DC, V.

The high-gloss red exterior of this lovely shop beckons you inside. There you will find a pretty wood-paneled boutique that looks like a room in a doll's house. Albert Ménès specializes in old-fashioned items, such as its famous *galettes Bretonnes* (rich butter cookies), jams, conserved flower petals, and an extensive selection of oils and vinegars—all great for gifts. Try the *vinaigre de xérès* (sherry vinegar) and exotic condiments, such as garlic *confit,* curry sauces, and a super-hot pimiento purée. At Christmastime the shop sells pretty gingerbread ornaments (better for hanging on the tree than for eating).

A LA MERE DE FAMILLE
35, rue du Faubourg Montmartre,
Paris 9.
Tel: 01.47.70.83.69
Métro: Le Peletier or Rue Montmartre.
Open 8:30 A.M. to 1:30 P.M. and 3 to 7 P.M.
Closed Sunday, Monday, and August
Credit cards: AE, V.

Walking into this spotless, sparkling candy shop—which dates back to 1791—is like wandering into a naïve painting. The window display and exterior are worth a trip on their own: the colorful, decorative boxes of sugar candies, biscuits, and artisanal jams change with the seasons, but there's always a sense of organized clutter inside and out. You'll find products from all over France, including boxes of Madeleines de Commercy (perfect for gifts) and caramel-coated Pralines de Montargis.

BOUCHERIE NIVERNAISES
99, rue du Faubourg Saint-Honoré,
Paris 8.
Tel: 01.43.59.11.02.
Fax: 01.42.25.92.32.
Métro: Saint-Phillipe du Roule.
Open 8:30 A.M. to 12:30 P.M. and 3:30 to 7 P.M. (8:30 A.M. to 12:30 P.M. Sunday).
Closed Monday.
Credit cards: AE, DC, V.

Guy Bissonnet is the butcher to the stars—Michelin stars, that is. When you dine in the city's finest establishments, that *agneau de Pauillac, boeuf de Normandie, poulet de Bresse,* or *canard de Challans* probably passed through the Bissonnet family's hands. What better reference can there be?

A la Mere de Famille's exterior is as much fun as its interior (see entry, page 331).

LA MAISON DE LA TRUFFE
19, place de la Madeleine,
Paris 8.
Tel: 01.42.65.53.22.
Métro: Madeleine.
Open 9 A.M. to 9 P.M. (to 8 P.M. Monday).
Closed Sunday.
Credit cards: AE, DC, V.

From November to March, come for the fresh (and expensive) black French truffles. Owner Guy Monier made a splash in December 1997 when he purchased the largest truffle ever found in France, weighing in at some 1.140 kilos. The truffle can be seen preserved in a jar in his shop window. Year-round, there are preserved truffles, goose and duck *foie gras,* exotic fruits, smoked salmon, a variety of *charcuterie,* and a respectable assortment of wines and liqueurs.

Gare de l'Est, Oberkampf

10th and 11th arrondissements

LE FURET-TANRADE
63, rue de Chabrol,
Paris 10.
Tel: 01.47.70.48.34.
Métro: Poissonnière or Gare de l'Est.
Open 8 A.M. to 8 P.M.
Closed Sunday.
Credit cards: AE, V.

For those who miss the *confitures* of Tanrade, that extraordinary shop that once graced rue Vignon in the 8th *arrondissement,* here you can find the old-fashioned smooth *confitures* (jams)—such as the intensely pear-flavored *confiture de poires passées*—truly honey-like, liquidy, but smooth and spreadable, designed for sweetening your morning bowl of thick, creamy yogurt. Try the *confiture*-yogurt combination, and you'll be hooked for life! Also artisanal pastries, chocolates, and honey, all prepared by Alain Furet.

LE PETIT BLEU
21, rue Jean-Pierre Timbaud,
Paris 11.
Tel: 01.47.00.90.73.
Métro: Oberkampf.
Open 10:30 A.M. to 8 P.M. (noon to 8 P.M. Monday).
Closed Sunday and two weeks in August.
Credit card: V.

This brightly colored corner shop will lure you inside to marvel at the lovely selection of ocher pottery from Provence, oils from all over the Mediterranean, wines from the south of France, as well as artisanal *confitures* and the famed caramels from Le Havre.

Pasteur

15th arrondissement

LE COMPTOIR CORREZIEN
8, rue Volontaires,
Paris 15.
Tel: 01.47.83.52.97.
Métro: Volontaires.
Open 10 A.M. to 1:30 P.M. and 3 to 8 P.M.
Closed Sunday and three weeks in August.
Credit cards: AE, V.

Take a trip to the Volontaires Métro stop and it's almost as good as a trip to the southwest: fresh wild mushrooms most of the year, top-quality hazelnut and walnut oils (from the Moulin de la Tour in Sainte-Nathalène, near Sarlat), delicate *cabécous* goat cheese, plus a huge variety of wine and packaged goods. Don't miss it, especially for the hard-to-find, ultra-fresh nut oils.

TROCADERO, TERNES

16th and 17th arrondissements

BRULERIE DES TERNES
10, rue Poncelet,
Paris 17.
Tel: 01.46.22.52.79.
Métro: Ternes.
Open 9 A.M. to 2 P.M. and 3:30 to 7:30 P.M. (9 A.M. to 7:30 P.M. Saturday, 9 A.M. to 1 P.M. Sunday).
Closed Monday.
Credit card: V.

and

28, rue de l'Annonciation,
Paris 16.
Tel: 01.42.88.89.90.
Métro: Passy.
Open 9 A.M. to 7:30 P.M. (to 1 P.M. Sunday).
Closed Monday.
Credit card: V.

With more than twenty-four different varieties of coffee beans freshly roasted right in the shop, Rémy Romieu's Brûlerie des Ternes is the Cartier of coffee roasters in Paris. I'm a diehard fan of any of their coffees from Costa Rica, Nicaragua, or Guatemala. Tea drinkers are not ignored here, either, with more than seventy varieties of teas and herbs for brewing, plus all the tea- and coffee-drinking paraphernalia one might desire.

They will happily prepare a gift box of selected 125-gram (4-ounce) bags of coffee, sold either as beans or ground to your specification. You might want to mix two for the morning (their Goût Viennois, Java-Timor, or Mélange San Pedro), two coffees for the afternoon, with a coarser and more persistent flavor (the Goût Italien Tostado, Moka Harrar, Antigua du Guatemala, or Papouasie Nouvelle-Guinée), and for the evening, two that are less rich in caffeine (Tarrazu du Costa Rica or Maragogype) or their exquisitely fragrant, flavorful decaffeinated coffee.

GANDOM
16, rue Franklin,
Paris 16.
Tel: 01.45.20.56.51.
Métro: Trocadéro or Passy.
Open 10 A.M. to 1 P.M. and 2 to 8 P.M. (10 A.M. to 1 P.M. and 3 to 7 P.M. Saturday).
Closed Sunday, Monday, and five weeks in July and August.
Credit card: V.

If you've ever dreamed of creating a banquet out of "A Thousand and One Nights," stop into Gandom, near Place du Trocadéro. You can feast on rose petal *gelée* with delicate and seldom-seen Persian pastries made from rice, almond, and chick-

pea flour. They stock Iranian caviar and fresh and packaged specialties, including basmati rice, saffron, and Turkish delight. Gandom also serves as Paris's Maison de la Pistache, offering the finest roasted nuts in the capital.

SERVANT LE CONFISERIE D'AUTEUIL
30, rue d'Auteuil,
Paris 16.
Tel: 01.42.88.49.82.
Métro: Michel-Ange–Auteuil.
Open 9 A.M. to 7:30 P.M.
Closed Sunday.
Credit card: V.

This lovely old-fashioned boutique features some eighty varieties of *bonbons* stored in antique widemouthed jars. Try the *ardoise d'Angers, nougamandines de Saint-Etienne, caramels au beurre salé de Bretagne, concon de Lyon.* Travel the sugar road of France without leaving Paris.

Vins et Alcools
WINE AND LIQUOR SHOPS

Wine, an indispensable part of a meal.

In Paris, wine and liquor shops are not designed for popping in and out of quickly. Like almost everything gastronomic in France, wine is selected with great care, after conversation and contemplation. Wine shop owners are much like restaurant *sommeliers.* Passionate about their chosen field, they love to discuss, to advise, to help clients select just the right wine for a perfect little meal. Many of the shops listed here are small and specialized, reflecting the personal tastes of their owners. They are not wine supermarkets, so don't expect to find an infinite selection. Rather, think of each visit as a step toward a greater understanding, and appreciation, of wines and spirits.

CONCORDE, BOURSE

1st and 2nd arrondissements

CARRE DES FEUILLANTES
14, rue de Castiglione,
Paris 1.
Tel: 01.42.86.82.82.
Fax: 01.42.86.07.71.
Métro: Concorde or Opéra.
Open 10:30 A.M. to 6:30 P.M.
Closed Sunday, Monday, and August.
Credit cards: AE, V.

Few Parisian chefs are as passionate about wine as Alain Dutournier, who recently opened a stunning cellar beneath his elegant restaurant off the Place Vendôme (see Restaurants). You can certainly trust his selections of fine Bordeaux, as well as his special finds from his native southwest.

JEAN DANFLOU
36, rue du Mont-Thabor (at the back of the courtyard, second floor)
Paris 1.
Tel: 01.42.61.51.09.
Fax: 01.42.61.31.62.
Métro: Concorde.
Open by appointment, 9 A.M. to 1 P.M. and 2 to 5 P.M.
Closed Saturday (except in December), Sunday, and August.
Credit cards: AE, V.

Set aside a long and languid afternoon for sampling the wide assortment of Jean Danflou's fine fruit-based liqueurs, Calvados, Armagnac, and Cognac. This is a wine and spirits shop, yes, but also an elegant, friendly tasting salon set in a tiny apartment just off the rue de Rivoli. Here you are invited to sample some of the exquisite clear *eaux-de-vie,* including a fine Poire William, made only from the freshest Rhône Valley pears (more than 16 pounds of fruit go into preparing each bottle of Danflou's Poire William). Sample, too, the raspberry (*framboise*), cherry (*kirsch*), yellow plum (*mirabelle*), and purple plum (*quetsche*) liqueurs, all distilled in the Vosges, east of Paris. Along with the tasting, you will learn some history and take a lesson in *eau-de-vie* etiquette (drink it at room temperature, not chilled, but from a chilled glass). Call or stop by for an appointment. Their motto, taken from Jean Cocteau, is *"La tradition c'est une statue qui marche"*—"Tradition is a statue that walks."

LEGRAND FILLE & FILS
1, rue de la Banque,
Paris 2.
Tel: 01.42.60.07.12.
Métro: Bourse or Palais Royal–Musée du Louvre.
Open 9 A.M. to 7:30 P.M. (8:30 A.M. to 1 P.M. and 3 to 7 P.M. Saturday).
Closed Sunday and Monday.
Credit cards: AE, V.

There are at least two reasons to go out of your way to visit this lovely, well-stocked wine shop. One reason, of course, is the carefully chosen selection of French wines (many from small independent growers in little-known wine-growing regions, such as the Savoie and the Languedoc-Roussillon) and spirits. The other is to examine the perfectly retained décor of this 19th-century *épicerie fine,* dating from 1890 and packed to the ceiling with candies, coffees, teas, and chocolates. Despite its renown, Legrand lacks pretension; the friendly *patronne* Francine Legrand-Richard, daughter of the original *patron* Lucien Legrand, will just as happily sell you a few chocolates as a vintage Bordeaux.

THE QUINTESSENTIAL WINEGLASS

Getting the most out of a good wine involves more than just uncorking the bottle and pouring it into a glass. If the wine is good enough to merit attention, it merits a special wineglass for tasting. The Institut National des Appellations d'Origine (I.N.A.O.) in Paris responded to this need by designing what it considers the perfect tasting glass, as complementary to the wine as it is agreeable to the taster.

The glass has a wide base, a short stem, and an elongated egg-shaped cup that embraces the wine, carefully guarding its bouquet. Made of lead crystal, it is simple and undecorated, holding 1 cup (25 cl).

What are the qualities of a good wineglass? It should allow the wine to breathe without losing its strength, to develop without becoming faint; and it must permit the wine to show its deep, rich colors with no cuttings or etchings to interfere. The stem should be long enough to allow the wine to be swirled without being warmed by one's hand, and the bowl itself should be longer than it is wide so that the bouquet is gently contained.

The I.N.A.O. glass is available in Paris at L'Esprit et le Vin, 81, avenue des Ternes, Paris 17 (01.45.74.80.99), and at Simon, 36, rue Etienne-Marcel, Paris 2 (01.42.33.71.65).

ODEON, SAINT-GERMAIN DES PRES, RUE DU BAC

6th and 7th arrondissements

LA DERNIERE GOUTTE
6, rue Bourbon-le-Château, Paris 6.
Tel: 01.43.29.11.62.
Fax: 01.40.46.84.47.
Métro: Saint-Germain des Prés or Odéon.
Open daily, 9:30 A.M. to 1:30 P.M. and 4 to 9 P.M. (9:30 A.M. to 9 P.M. Saturday, 10:30 A.M. to 2 P.M. and 3 to 6:30 P.M. Sunday, 4 to 8 P.M. Monday).
Credit card: V.

American Juan Sanchez runs a charming little wine shop right off the well-trafficked rue de Buci market. His selection is well chosen, with new finds from every region of France and with all the great names, from Ostertag to Chapoutier. Whether it's a special bottle to take home or a simple picnic wine, he is there to help with the selection.

A thoughtful selection.

CAVES MIARD
9, rue des Quatre Vents, Paris 6.
Tel: 01.43.54.99.30.
Fax: 01.44.07.27.73.
Open 10:30 A.M. to 8:30 P.M.
Closed Sunday and August.
Métro: Odéon.
Credit card: V.

This stunning 1880s *crémerie* is home to Marielle Guinot and Fabrice Billou's lovely wine shop. This place is a real find for good bargain wines, including the reds from Ludovic Cornillon, with his stunning and well-priced pure Syrah Coteaux du Tricastan; Côtes-du-Rhône; the lively *vin de pays* of l'Hérault Figaro; and the vigorous red and *gris de gris* Corbières, Château La Baronne. This is a stunning, well-preserved former cheese and dairy shop.

RYST-DUPEYRON
79, rue du Bac, Paris 7.
Tel: 01.45.48.80.93.
Métro: Rue du Bac.
Open 10:30 A.M. to 7:30 P.M. (12:30 to 7:30 P.M. Monday).
Closed Sunday and the week of August 15.
Credit card: V.

This fine, classic old wine shop on the well-traveled rue du Bac makes a good Left Bank spot for searching out vintage Armagnac, whiskey, and port, as well as fine Bordeaux or great Champagne. The owners will even personalize bottles for special occasions—to celebrate a birthday, anniversary, wedding, or birth. Gift certificates are also available.

PARISIAN VINEYARDS

Vineyards in Paris? Their history dates back to the Middle Ages, when abbey vineyards dotted the city and the wines they produced found their way to the noblest tables. (It was, in fact, the white claret from the suburb of Suresnes that François I said was "as light as a tear in the eye.")

Today the tradition continues as each year a little more than 1,000 bottles of authentic Parisian wines are carefully, ceremoniously bottled.

Tucked away in the hills of Montmartre, hidden among the narrow houses and car-filled sidewalks, there is a minuscule vineyard that annually produces just 500 bottles of a red wine simply labeled "Clos Montmartre." The harvest *fête,* a traditional celebration full of pageantry, takes place the first Saturday of October. For the harvest itself, the basement of the 18th-*arrondissement mairie* (town hall) is turned into a wine cellar, and later some 300 bottles are sold there, with the remainder sold at auction. The wine does not lay any claims to greatness: It is more of a historical amusement than a gustatory treasure.

A second vineyard lies in the suburban community of Suresnes, west of Paris. Once considered the best in the Ile-de-France, the Suresnes vineyard was replanted in 1965. Now the local rugby team turns out to harvest the grapes, and the community celebrates the event on the first Sunday in October. Most of the 2,000 or so bottles of Clos du Pas-Saint-Maurice are sold on the last Saturday of September and the first Sunday of October at the Suresnes *cave municipale.* (It is also sold at Lucien Legrand and Au Verger de la Madeleine wine shops in Paris.)

In 1983, in an apparent effort to revive its illustrious wine heritage, the city of Paris planted another 700 vines of Pinot Noir grapes on the south side of Georges-Brassens Square, in the 15th-*arrondissement* park built on the site of the former stockyards. In 1985 neighborhood children, members of the Lions Club, and the elderly helped pick the first Clos des Morillons harvest, which produced a total of 300 bottles of red wine, carefully aged in oak casks. The wine is sold at auction each December 15 at the 15th-*arrondissement mairie.*

For more information about the harvests and wine sales, contact:

Montmartre: *Mairie* of the 18th *arrondissement,*
1, rue Jules-Joffrin, Paris 18.
Tel: 01.42.52.42.00.
Métro: Jules Joffrin.

Suresnes: *Cave Municipale,*
28, rue Merlin-de-Thionville, 92150 Suresnes.
Tel: 01.45.06.32.10.

Accessible via the No. 244 bus from Porte Maillot, the No. 144 bus from Pont de Neuilly, or the suburban train from Gare Saint-Lazare. The stop is Suresnes–Mont Valérin.

Clos de Morillons: *Mairie* of the 15th *arrondissement*,
31, rue Péclet, Paris 15.
Tel: 01.48.28.40.12.
Métro: Vaugirard.

VINS RARES ET DE COLLECTION
(Peter Thurstrup)
20, rue Serpente,
Paris 6.
Tel: 01.44.41.42.43.
Fax: 01.46.34.01.71.
Métro: Odéon or Saint-Michel.
By appointment only, 9 A.M. to 8 P.M.
Closed Saturday and Sunday.
Credit cards: AE, V.

A wine merchant who deals in antiques? That's it. Swedish wine expert Peter Thurstrup's passion for rare vintage wines has grown into a business, and now he offers more than 5,000 bottles—what he calls *"les introuvables,"* or wines that are virtually impossible to find. If you're searching for a special bottle of Romanée Conti, Mouton Rothschild, Yquem, or a vintage Champagne, this is the place to look. His growing stock also includes younger wines, including American vintages.

Champs-Elysees, Madeleine, Grands Boulevards

8th and 17th arrondissements

CAVES AUGE
116, boulevard Haussmann, Paris 8.
Tel: 01.45.22.16.97.
Métro: Miromesnil or Saint-Augustin.
Open 9 A.M. to 7:30 P.M. (1 to 7:30 P.M. Monday).
Closed Sunday.
Credit cards: AE, V.

With its black marble front and antique gold lettering, this elegant, classic wine shop—perhaps the oldest wine shop in Paris—offers not just a carefully chosen selection of wines but also a fine assortment of vintage and nonvintage port, Cognac, Armagnac, and Champagne. This old-fashioned, wood-paneled shop has a gentleman's club air about it, but despite the formality, Augé offers many reasonably priced wines and the salespeople dispense useful advice when helping you make a selection for that evening's dinner.

FAUCHON
26–28, place de la Madeleine,
Paris 8.
Tel: 01.47.42.60.11.
Métro: Madeleine.
Open 9:40 A.M. to 7 P.M.
Closed Sunday.
Credit cards: AE, DC, V.

While pressing your nose against the glass at this landmark shop, take time to wander in to at least examine the well-stocked *cave,* particularly if you're shopping for a truly special bottle of Armagnac or Cognac. Prices are on the high side, but I like to save up my *centimes* for an occasional bottle of their fabulous wild raspberry brandy, *eau-de-vie de framboise sauvage.* (See also Specialty Shops.)

LA CAVE D'HEDIARD
21, place de la Madeleine,
Paris 8.
Tel: 01.43.12.88.88.
Métro: Madeleine.
Open 8 A.M. to 11 P.M.
Closed Sunday.
Credit cards: AE, DC, V.

This expansive *cave* offers one the largest selections of Bordeaux wines in Paris. Also a large selection of Armagnac, Calvados, and Cognac. Prices are on the high side. (See also Specialty Shops.)

Caves Auge offers a classic selection (see entry, page 341).

CAVES PETRISSANS
30 bis, avenue Niel,
Paris 17.
Tel: 01.42.27.83.84.
Métro: Ternes or Péreire.
Open 9:00 A.M. to 8:30 P.M. (10 A.M. to 1 P.M. Saturday).
Closed Sunday and the first three weeks of August.
Credit cards: AE, V.

A small, old-fashioned family operation, offering excellent selections of Burgundy and Bordeaux as well as their fine house Champagne. A wine bar/restaurant adjoins the shop, if you should decide to sample on the spot. (See also Wine Bars.)

LES CAVES TAILLEVENT
199, rue du Faubourg Saint-Honoré,
Paris 8.
Tel: 01.45.61.14.09.
Fax: 01.45.61.19.68.
Métro: Charles de Gaulle–Etoile or Ternes.
Open 9 A.M. to 8 P.M. (to 7:30 P.M. Saturday, 2 to 8 P.M. Monday).
Closed Sunday and the first two weeks of August.
Credit cards: AE, DC, V.

Without batting an eye, I would stand behind anything that Jean-Claude Vrinat supported. He's a remarkable man, and everything he touches has the mark of perfection and authenticity. Since the wine list at his family's restaurant, Taillevent, is one of the finest and most fairly priced in town, it comes as no surprise to find that his wine shop has at its disposition some 450,000 bottles of 350 different wines, as well as 150 different *eaux-de-vie,* liqueurs, excellent house Cognac, port, and sherry, dating back to 1848. Note that all of his wines are stored in a *cave* kept at—what else—perfect temperature and humidity. Monsieur Vrinat's daughter, Valérie, runs the shop along with several wine experts, who are always helpful and informative. Their motto: "A client is first of all a friend." When you stop in, ask about the regularly scheduled wine tastings. From time to time the shop also offers a list of food-friendly wines, such as a selection of wines to drink with asparagus or other seasonal ingredients.

When someone has had too much to drink, we say they're plastered, while the French are "beurré," or buttered.

CURNONSKY

Curnonsky, the French food critic named "prince of gastronomes" by his peers, designated the five best white wines in France, perhaps the world:

Château d'Yquem: "The matchless sweet wine: true liquid gold."

Château-Chalon: "The prince of the Jura yellow wines, full-bodied, with the penetrating bouquet of walnuts."

Château-Grillet: "The legendary wine of the Côtes-du-Rhône, with a stunning aroma of violets and wildflowers; as changing as a pretty woman."

Montrachet: "The splendid lord of Burgundy, which Alexander Dumas counseled to drink, bareheaded, while kneeling."

Savennières Coulées de Serrant: "The dazzling dry wine from the vineyards of the Loire."

AU VERGER DE LA MADELEINE
4, boulevard Malesherbes, Paris 8.
Tel: 01.42.65.51.99.
Fax: 01.49.24.05.22.
Métro: Madeleine.
Open 10 A.M. to 8 P.M. (to 7:30 P.M. Saturday, 10 A.M. to 1 P.M. and 3:30 to 8 P.M. Monday).
Closed Sunday.
Credit card: V.

Need a 1788 Madeira, an 1820 Cognac, an 1893 Sauternes, or a 1922 Lafite-Rothschild? Jean-Pierre Legras will be happy to oblige. Since 1937 the Legras family has operated one of Paris's grand *épiceries fines,* and today they specialize in old bottles, odd bottles, new bottles, miniature bottles. Just give them a special date—birthday, anniversary, wedding—from within the last hundred years and they should come up with an appropriate bottle to help you celebrate. Jean-Pierre is crazy about wine and loves digging up dust-covered relics from the spacious underground *caves*. They offer more than ninety vintages of Armagnac, twenty-five of Calvados, and more than forty of Madeira. He's proud of their collection of Sauternes old and new and of the straw-colored *vin de paille* of the Jura, not to mention his exclusive right to sell wine from Liechtenstein. His stock also features the famous Paris wines from the vineyards at Montmartre and Suresnes, as well as a dry and fruity wine from the Netherlands, Louwber/Maastricht, to commemorate meetings of the European union.

Librairies Spécialisées: Gastronomie
FOOD AND WINE BOOKSHOPS

Paris bookstores are havens for books on food and wine. The following are just a few suggestions for finding old and new cookbooks, guidebooks, and historical food-related volumes.

LES HALLES, CONCORDE, OPERA

1st arrondissement

GALIGNANI
224, rue de Rivoli,
Paris 1.
Tel: 01.42.60.76.07.
Métro: Tuileries or Concorde.
Open 10 A.M. to 7 P.M.
Closed Sunday.
Credit card: V.

Since 1802 this neat-as-a-pin, old-fashioned, professional shop along the arcades of the rue de Rivoli has fascinated and pleased bibliophiles from around the world. Courteous service and a fabulous selection of English, American, and French tomes make this a must stop for book-lovers.

M.O.R.A.
13, rue Montmartre,
Paris 1.
Tel: 01.45.08.19.24.
Métro: Les Halles.
Open 8:30 A.M. to 6:15 P.M. (to noon Saturday).
Closed Sunday.
Credit cards: AE, V.

A professional cookware shop that features a small but complete assortment of professional books devoted to breads, pastries, general cooking, and hotel and restaurant cooking. (See also Kitchen and Tableware Shops.)

W. H. SMITH
248, rue de Rivoli,
Paris 1.
Tel: 01.44.77.88.99.
Métro: Concorde.
Open 9:30 A.M. to 7 P.M.
Closed Sunday.
Credit cards: AE, V.

W.H. Smith offers a small selection of English-language books on food, wine, and travel, most of them British. Also a good selection of current British and American magazines.

PYRAMIDES

2nd arrondissement

BRENTANO'S
37, avenue de l'Opéra,
Paris 2.
Tel: 01.42.61.52.50.
Métro: Opéra or Pyramides.
Open 10 A.M. to 7:30 P.M.
Closed Sunday.
Credit card: V.

This English-language bookshop offers a huge selection of cookbooks, in both American and British editions. A good place to go for food- and wine-related guidebooks in both English and French. Also a good spot to find current American or British magazines on food and the home.

BOOKS AND MORE: FNAC

FNAC is a mammoth stereo/record/camera/book emporium that always includes extensive selections of French books on food, wine, and travel. Prices are competitive. General hours are 10 A.M. to 7:30 P.M. Closed Sunday. Credit cards: AE, V. Web site: www.frac.fr

FNAC-FORUM LES HALLES
1, rue Pierre Lescot,
Paris 1.
Tel: 01.40.41.40.00.
Métro: Les Halles.

FNAC-RENNES
136, rue de Rennes,
Paris 6.
Tel: 01.49.54.30.00.
Métro: Montparnasse–Bienvenüe.

FNAC-ETOILE
26–30, avenue des Ternes,
Paris 17.
Tel: 01.44.09.18.00.
Métro: Charles de Gaulle–Etoile or Ternes.

SAINT-MICHEL, MONGE

5th arrondissement

GIBERT JEUNE
5, place Saint-Michel,
Paris 5.
Tel: 01.43.25.70.07.
Métro: Saint-Michel.
Open 9:30 A.M. to 7:30 P.M.
Closed Sunday.
Credit cards: AE, V.

Gibert Jeune is one of the city's largest bookstores, specializing in both new and used books, mostly in French but also in English. Food and wine books are scattered about on the ground floor.

LIBRAIRIE GOURMANDE
4, rue Dante,
Paris 5.
Tel: 01.43.54.37.27.
Internet: http//www.librairie-gourmande.fr
Métro: Saint-Michel.
Open daily, 10 A.M. to 7 P.M.
Credit card: V.

This is a very pleasant shop on a charming Left Bank street, where one can spend hours browsing amidst the collection of cookbooks, tomes recounting the history of the table, and assorted food-related antiques, posters, lithographs, and drawings.

LA LIBRAIRIE DES GOURMETS
98, rue Monge,
Paris 5.
Tel: 01.43.31.16.42.
Métro: Censier Daubenton.
Open 10:30 A.M. to 7 P.M.
Closed Sunday, and Monday in August.
Credit cards: AE, V.

Walk across the threshold of this cheery ocher-colored storefront and you open the door to literary-gastronomic heaven: a bookstore devoted exclusively to food and wine, with more than 2,500 titles, mostly in French, but some in English, as well. Owner Anne Brunneau used to run a hotel in the Auvergne but decided to try her hand at this for a change of pace. A must for bibliophiles.

We say "the good old days," while the French call those lovely times of days past "les temps des cerises," the days of cherries.

COOKING SCHOOLS

The following are the most popular cooking and wine schools in Paris. If you plan to visit any of the schools, write or call for a brochure first, so you know what to expect. In many cases, custom-tailored courses can be arranged for groups of ten or more.

LE CORDON BLEU
8, rue Léon Delhomme, Paris 15.
Tel: 01.53.68.22.50.
Fax: 01.48.56.03.96.
Métro: Vaugirard.

This famous school has been instructing students in French cooking and pastry since 1895. Visitors may reserve a few days ahead for a single afternoon demonstration, and menus are available in advance for each month's program. Courses are ongoing, in French (with English translations), and the number of students varies according to the program.

ECOLE DE GASTRONOMIE RITZ-ESCOFFIER
30, rue Cambon, Paris 1.
Tel: 01.42.60.38.30.
Fax: 01.40.15.07.65.
Métro: Concorde.

The famed Ritz Hotel and restaurant opens its kitchens and shares its chefs' expertise with students interested in French cuisine. The school offers a multifaceted cooking course, offering everything from weekday afternoon demonstration classes to twelve-week diploma courses. For many of its classes, the school draws upon the talents of Ritz executive chef Guy Legay and its master bakers, chefs, and *sommeliers.* The spotless kitchens are outfitted with the best in professional cookware and equipment. For groups, courses can be custom-tailored to fit requests.

ECOLE LENOTRE
40, rue Pierre-Curie, 78370 Plaisir.
Tel: 01.30.81.46.46.
Fax: 01.30.55.96.14.

Accessible by train from the Montparnasse station or by car.

This is where the best pastry chefs of France go for refresher courses. Gaston Lenôtre is one of the most respected and successful pastry chefs in France, and his school in the suburbs of Paris is open to professionals only. Ongoing full-participation courses are offered in pastry, chocolate, breadbaking, ice cream, *charcuterie,* and catering. A knowledge of French is essential.

PATRICIA WELLS AT HOME IN PARIS
10, rue Jacob, Paris 6.
Métro: Saint-Germain des Prés.
Fax in the U.S.: (214) 343-1227.
Email: cookingclasses@patriciawells.com
Internet: www.patriciawells.com

For several weeks each year I offer English-language cooking classes in my Parisian artist's studio. The weeklong spring and fall classes are limited to a maximum of five students. Cooking is hands on, and the week includes visits to markets and various merchants, wine tastings, and selected meals in some of the city's best restaurants.

ODEON, SAINT-GERMAIN, DUROC

6th arrondissement

LIBRAIRIE GUENEGAUD
10, rue de l'Odéon,
Paris 6.
Tel: 01.43.26.07.91.
Métro: Odéon.
Open 9:30 A.M. to 6:30 P.M.
Closed Sunday.
Credit card: V.

Owners Jean-Etienne and Edmonde Huret specialize in antiquarian books about the French provinces and have an abundant collection of hard-to-find books about French regional cooking and wine, as well as cookbooks. Each month they concentrate on a different region, so their selection is always changing.

LIBRAIRIE JACQUES LANORE
4, rue de Tournon,
Paris 6.
Tel: 01.43.29.43.50.
Fax: 01.43.54.97.81.
Métro: Odéon.
Open 10 A.M. to 1 P.M. and 2 to 7 P.M. (to 6 P.M. Saturday).
Closed Sunday and Monday.

A tiny shop that caters to the French hotel and restaurant trade, with a delightful, broad selection of books devoted to every aspect of cooking. The offerings include many seldom-found tomes, such as professional works on French baking, pastry, *charcuterie,* and catering. Worth a detour for those hard-to-find books.

LA MAISON RUSTIQUE
26, rue Jacob,
Paris 6.
Tel: 01.42.34.96.60.
Métro: Saint-Germain des Prés or Mabillon.
Open 10 A.M. to 7 P.M.
Closed Sunday.
Credit cards: AE, DC, V.

This forest-green bookstore provides a bucolic haven in the heart of Saint-Germain des Prés. Maison Rustique, with more than 18,000 books in stock, specializes in all things related to the countryside—in particular, gardening, design, and *art de vivre.* In addition to a good cookbook collection (with some English titles), they stock how-to books on everything from beekeeping to raising dairy cows and sheep, jam-making, organic gardening, and wine-making. I'm a particular fan of the La Rustica series, which includes tomes on home preserving, cooking with herbs, and cooking with edibles found in the wilds. Ignore the cool service.

TEA AND TATTERED PAGES
24, rue Mayet,
Paris 6.
Métro: Duroc.
Tel: 01.40.65.94.35.
Generally open 11 A.M. to 7 P.M. (Hours are flexible.)
Closed Sunday.

More than 10,000 books in English, including many new and used cookbooks, are to be found in this combination tea salon/bookstore run by American Christy Chavane. Also brownies, fudge cookies, snacks, quilts, mugs, and teapots.

MUSEE D'ORSAY

7th arrondissement

REMI FLACHARD
9, rue du Bac,
Paris 7.
Tel: 01.42.86.86.87.
Métro: Rue du Bac.
Open 10 A.M. to noon and 2 to 6:30 P.M.
Closed Saturday, Sunday, and August.

A small, tranquilizing shop devoted to old and rare books on the subject of gastronomy. Rémi Flachard's collection includes books dating back to the 15th century, with prices ranging from 100 to 30,000 francs. I wouldn't mind being locked in this shop for hours, examining books on making honey, old tomes on how to care for your sensitive stomach, ancient and beautifully illustrated books on wine-making. You'll find a bit of everything here, from a 1946 edition of the *Better Homes and Gardens Cookbook* and a biography of Madame Veuve Clicquot-Ponsardin of Champagne fame to original editions of Brillat-Savarin's *Physiologie du Goût* and an 1840 manual for bread bakers. If he hasn't yet sold it, take a look at the magnificent oil portrait of one of France's great chefs, Alexandre Dumaine, dating from about 1935. A must, too, for menu collectors.

Pour la Maison KITCHEN AND TABLEWARE SHOPS

Papeterie Moderne for any sign you desire *(see entry, page 355).*

If you have been searching for long-lasting cotton chefs' uniforms, odd-size baking tins, antique Champagne glasses, or that extra gadget to make cooking more efficient and fun, you need look no more. These items, plus lovely pastel-toned turn-of-the-century oyster or asparagus plates, sparkling contemporary glassware, antique silver *porte-couteaux* (knife rests), and sturdy copper pots are just a few of the hundreds of particularly French kitchen and table items found in the following shops. Note that some are small and sometimes casually run, so that opening and closing hours may not always be followed to the letter.

Les Halles, Chatelet, Palais-Royal, Place des Victoires

1st and 2nd arrondissements

LA BOVIDA
36, rue Montmartre,
Paris 1.
Tel: 01.42.36.09.99.
Métro: Les Halles.
Open 9 A.M. to 12:30 P.M. and 2 to 5:30 P.M. (8 to 11:45 A.M. Saturday).
Closed Sunday, and Saturdays in August.

Professional equipment: A kitchen equipment shop for professionals, La Bovida has an impressive inventory of stainless steel, copper, porcelain, and earthenware, as well as serving platters, a variety of spices in bulk, and paper doilies in more than a dozen shapes and sizes. Service can be cool indeed.

LE CEDRE ROUGE
22, avenue Victoria,
Paris 1.
Tel: 01.42.33.71.05.
Métro: Châtelet.
Open 10:30 A.M. to 7 P.M. (12:30 to 7 P.M. Monday).
From April to June open Sunday from 11 A.M. to 6 P.M.; otherwise, closed Sunday. Closed for two weeks in August.
Credit cards: AE, V.

House and garden: A fabulous fantasy shop for home and garden. Most of the items here—garden furniture and umbrellas, gigantic bowls and pots—will be too big to fit into your suitcase, but this is a lovely shop for dreamers. You're certain to go home with at least an idea or two.

E. DEHILLERIN
18–20, rue Coquillière,
Paris 1.
Tel: 01.42.36.53.13.
Fax: 01.45.08.96.83.
Internet: http:www.e-dehillerin.fr
Métro: Les Halles.
Open 8 A.M. to 6 P.M. (8 A.M. to 12:30 P.M. and 2 to 6 P.M. Monday). In August, open 10 A.M. to 6 P.M. Monday through Saturday.
Closed Sunday.
Credit card: V.

Professional equipment: A fascinating, though often overwhelming, clutter of professional cookware, covering every inch of available wall, floor, and ceiling space. The remarkable selection of copper cookware, baking pans, and unusual kitchen tools includes items such as copper tabletop potato warmers for *raclette* and *crémaillères* (hanging pots) to hang from the hearth. Some English is spoken by the helpful, if gruff, salespeople, and merchandise catalogs are available. They're experts at retinning copper, but plan on waiting two to three weeks.

DUTHILLEUL ET MINART
14, rue de Turbigo,
Paris 1.
Tel: 01.42.33.44.36.
Métro: Etienne Marcel.
Open 10 A.M. to 6:30 P.M.
Closed Sunday.

Professional uniforms: Artisans' uniforms designed around 1850; natural-fiber work clothes; café waiters' vests, shirts, and ties; jewelers' smocks; meat deliverers' hooded robes; animal purveyors' blouses in red, black, and tan; and professional chef outfits, tailored to fit. They also have an extensive selection of professional-quality cotton and linen dish towels.

MURIEL GRATEAU BOUTIQUE
132, galerie de Valois, Palais-Royal,
Paris 1.
Tel: 01.40.20.90.30.
Métro: Palais Royal–Musée du Louvre.
Open 11 A.M. to 7 P.M. (2 to 7 P.M. Monday).
Closed Sunday and three to four weeks in August.
Credit card: V.

Linens: Under the arches of the Palais-Royal, Muriel Grateau has created a shop for dreamers. Her opulent, richly colored (and priced) brocade table linens look as if they're part of a banquet scene in a Veronese painting. She designs them herself and has them made for her in Venice. She also sells at least a dozen shades of simple linen table sets, as well as fine hand-painted reproduction and antique porcelain in rarely seen designs.

KITCHEN BAZAAR
Galerie des 3 Quartiers
23, boulevard de la Madeleine,
Paris 1.
Tel: 01.42.60.50.30.
Fax: 01.42.60.07.55.
Métro: Madeleine.
Open 10 A.M. to 7 P.M.
Closed Sunday.
Credit cards: AE, DC, V.

Kitchen: Name a kitchen gadget and they have it here—especially if it's in stainless steel or sleek white. For decades, Kitchen Bazaar has been in the forefront of kitchen design, offering items that are not only beautiful but functional. You'll find all sort of items that are "Made in USA," such as those fabulous Rubbermaid spatulas, measuring cups, all sorts of metal polishes and polishing gloves, and the ever-worthy Kitchen Aid mixer, as well as a host of items from Japan, such as slicers, graters, and knives. They also stock larger items, such as elegant shopping carts, garbage cans, and espresso makers. I never leave here without finding something I *have* to have. (Note their sister store, Bath Bazaar, right across the hall.)

BOUTIQUE LAGUIOLE
1, place Saint-Opportune,
Paris 1.
Tel: 01.40.28.09.42.
Fax: 01.40.39.03.89.
Métro: Châtelet–Les Halles.
Open 10:30 A.M. to 7:30 P.M.
Closed Sunday and Monday. Closed from 1 to 2 P.M. in August.
Credit card: V.

Knives: French designer Philippe Starck created this spare, gray, knife-blade-colored shop to go with his updated design for the classic Laguiole knives of the Auvergne, in central France. Although the knife was intended for cattle farmers in the 19th century, the sleek Laguiole pocketknife has become a must for the modern Frenchman. Here you can find it with both the traditional metal blade (it oxidizes with wear) and a modern stainless steel version. Different sizes and models of this foldable knife come with an assortment of blades and corkscrews. The ecology-minded can breathe easily: The hand-crafted horn handles that mold perfectly to the shape of the hand come from cattle (the horns are cut in a procedure that does not harm the animal). If you have the patience to wait the three or four weeks it will take, monogrammed Laguiole knives make a fabulous gift.

M.O.R.A.
13, rue Montmartre,
Paris 1.
Tel: 01.45.08.19.24.
Fax: 01.45.08.49.05.
Métro: Les Halles.
Open 8:30 A.M. to 6:15 P.M. (to noon on Saturday).
Closed Sunday.
Credit cards: AE, V.

Professional equipment: Another in the group of cookware shops near Les Halles, still frequented by professionals. M.O.R.A. has a large assortment of tools, baking tins (including several sizes of *pain de mie* molds), large *baguette* pans, cake molds, ice cube trays shaped like chocolates, and linen-lined wicker bread-rising baskets. They also stock the rectangular *baguette* baskets one often sees on the arms of waiters carrying fresh bread back to their restaurants. (Be sure to come with the dimensions of your oven: Many objects are oversize, made to fit large professional ovens.) They also have a good professional cookbook selection (see Food and Wine Bookshops).

LA BOUTIQUE DU MUSEE DES ARTS DECORATIFS
Palais du Louvre
107, rue de Rivoli,
Paris 1.
Tel: 01.42.61.04.20.
Métro: Palais Royal–Musée du Louvre.
Open daily 10:30 A.M. to 6:30 P.M.

Design: Imagine such creations as Biedermeier drinking glasses—or, pardon me, *verres de nuit*—to place at your bedside, all manner of reproductions of crystal, china, and glassware, and exquisite sets of *pots de crème,* silver, and table linens. This is one of Paris's finest shops for great design.

PAPETERIE MODERNE
12, rue de la Ferronnerie,
Paris 1.
Tel: 01.42.36.21.72.
Métro: Châtelet–Les Halles.
Open 9 A.M. to noon and 1:30 to 6:30 P.M. (10:30 A.M. to noon and 1:30 to 6:30 P.M. Friday).
Closed Sunday and the week of August 15.
Will ship in France.

Signs: When you see this simple shop, unchanged for decades, you'll know the source of the city's myriad signs. They're everywhere—all the signs you have ever dreamed of—stashed into corners, piled on counters, hanging from the wall and the ceiling, on nails and thumbtacks. There are street signs for cheese, butter, sausages, beef tongue, or headcheese, along with café menus, bakery price lists, requests for people to stop smoking or spitting, even French "Beware of Dog" and "Post No Bills" warnings. Custom-made signs take about ten days.

A. SIMON
36, rue Etienne Marcel and 48, rue Montmartre,
Paris 2.
Tel: 01.42.33.71.65.
Métro: Les Halles.
Open 8:30 A.M. to 6:30 P.M.
Closed Sunday, holidays, and Monday in August.
Credit cards: AE, V.

Professional equipment: This sedate establishment has professional serving dishes, porcelain, crystal, china, salt and pepper grinders, mustard jars, lovely white terrines, a wide variety of paper doilies, wicker cheese trays, and bread baskets. At their annex across the street, there's professional cookware, from copper pots to baking molds, from scales to cookie cutters, along with the attractive marble-base Roquefort cheese cutters used in the best restaurants.

MARAIS, REPUBLIQUE

3rd and 4th arrondissements

ARGENTERIE DES FRANCS-BOURGEOIS/ JEAN-PIERRE DE CASTRO
17, rue des Francs-Bourgeois,
Paris 4.
Tel: 01.42.72.04.00
Métro: Saint-Paul.
Open 10:30 A.M. to 1 P.M. and 2 to 7 P.M. (10:30 A.M. to 7 P.M. Saturday, 11 A.M. to 7 P.M. Sunday, 2 to 7 P.M. Monday).
Closed from 1 to 2 P.M. on Sunday in August.
Credit card: V.

Silver: A great shop for silver-lovers, where antique silver knives, forks, spoons—you name it—are sold by weight. Selecting from a stack of wicker baskets, you can put together your own place settings. There's an abundant selection, and prices are generally reasonable. Also silver candlesticks, teapots, and so on.

POUR LA CUISINE MODERNE

Offering the usual and unusual for the kitchen and the table, these shops mix modern and traditional tableware at reasonable prices and have become favorites among young French women—and men. The Conran Shop offers good design, and one is always sure to find something worthwhile. At Culinarion you'll find *madeleine* tins, *financier* molds, a small roaster for home-roasted coffee beans, egg-shaped timers, and colorful cast-iron cookware. Habitat—a candy store for anyone setting up house—designs state-of-the-art kitchenware but also stocks traditional crockery, marble cheese boards, and picnic baskets. Quatre Saisons and Geneviève Lethu have more of a country style, with a huge selection of handmade baskets, brightly striped cotton and cotton/linen fabric for making tea towels, Alsatian cookie stamps, white porcelain *chocolatières,* painted pottery dishes, and pretty wicker shopping carts to take to the market.

THE CONRAN SHOP
117, rue du Bac,
Paris 7.
Tel: 01.42.84.10.01.
Fax: 01.42.84.29.75.
Métro: Sèvres-Babylone.
Open 10 A.M. to 7 P.M.
(noon to 7 P.M. Monday).
Closed Sunday.
Credit card: V.

CULINARION
99, rue de Rennes,
Paris 6.
Tel: 01.45.48.94.76.
Métro: Saint-Placide.
Open 10:15 A.M. to 7 P.M.
Closed Sunday. Closed Monday
and from 1:00 to 2:00 P.M.
in August.
Credit cards: AE, V.

75, rue de Commerce,
Paris 15.
Tel: 01.42.50.37.50.
Métro: Commerce or Avenue Emile Zola.

Open 10 A.M. to 9:15 P.M.
(2 P.M. to 9:15 P.M. Monday).
Closed Sunday.
Credit cards: AE, V.

83 bis, rue de Courcelles,
Paris 17.
Tel: 01.42.27.63.32.
Métro: Courcelles.
Open 10:15 A.M. to 7 P.M.
(10:45 A.M. to 6 P.M. in August).
Closed Sunday.
Credit cards: AE, V.

HABITAT
202, porte de Rambuteau,
Forum des Halles,
Paris 1.
Tel: 01.40.39.91.06.
Métro: Châtelet–Les Halles.
Open 10 A.M. to 7:30 P.M.
Closed Sunday.
Credit cards: AE, V.

12, boulevard de la Madeleine,
Paris 9.
Tel: 01.42.68.12.76.
Métro: Madeleine.
Open 10 A.M. to 7:30 P.M.
Closed Sunday.
Credit cards: AE, V.

10, place de la République,
Paris 11.
Tel: 01.48.07.13.14.
Métro: République.
Open 10 A.M. to 7:30 P.M.
Closed Sunday.
Credit cards: AE, V.

17, rue de l'Arrivé,
Tour Montparnasse,
Paris 15.
Tel: 01.45.38.69.90.
Métro: Montparnasse–Bienvenüe.
Open 10 A.M. to 7:30 P.M.
Closed Sunday.
Credit cards: AE, V.

35, avenue de Wagram,
Paris 17.
Tel: 01.47.66.25.52.
Métro: Charles de Gaulle–Etoile or Ternes.
Open 10 A.M. to 7:30 P.M.
Closed Sunday.
Credit cards: AE, V.

GENEVIEVE LETHU
91, rue de Rivoli,
Paris 1.
Tel: 01.42.60.14.90.
Métro: Châtelet.
Open 10 A.M. to 7 P.M. (1 to 7 P.M. Monday, 10:30 A.M. to 6:30 P.M. in August).
Closed Sunday. Closed 2 to 3 P.M. in August.
Credit cards: AE, V.

28, rue St. Antoine,
Paris 4.
Tel: 01.42.74.21.25.
Métro: Bastille.
Open 10:30 A.M. to 7:30 P.M. (2 to 7:30 P.M. Monday in August).
Closed Sunday. Closed 1:30 to 2:30 P.M. in August.
Credit cards: AE, V.

95, rue de Rennes,
Paris 6.
Tel: 01.45.44.40.35.
Métro: Rennes.
Open 10:15 A.M. to 7 P.M.
Closed Sunday. Closed Monday in July and August, and from noon to 1:30 P.M. in August.
Credit cards: AE, V.

25, avenue du Général Leclerc,
Paris 14.
Tel: 01.45.38.71.30.
Métro: Denfert-Rochereau.
Open 10:15 A.M. to 7 P.M. (2 to 7 P.M. Monday).
Closed Sunday.
Credit cards: AE, V, MC.

1, avenue Niel,
Paris 17.
Tel: 01.45.72.03.47.
Métro: Ternes.
Open 10 A.M. to 7:30 P.M.
Closed Sunday. Closed Monday in August.
Credit cards: AE, V.

QUATRE SAISONS
203, porte de Rambuteau,
Forum des Halles,
Paris 1.
Tel: 01.40.39.98.21.
Métro: Châtelet–Les Halles
Open 10 A.M. to 7:30 P.M.
Closed Sunday.
Credit card: V.

88, avenue du Maine,
Paris 14.
Tel: 01.43.21.28.99.
Métro: Gaîté.
Open 10 A.M. to 7:30 P.M.
Closed Sunday.
Credit card: V.

53, rue de Passy,
Paris 16.
Tel: 01.45.25.17.22.
Métro: La Muette.
Open 10 A.M. to 7:30 P.M.
Closed Sunday.
Credit card: V.

L'ARLEQUIN
19, rue de Turenne,
Paris 4.
Tel: 01.42.78.77.00.
Métro: Saint-Paul.
Open 11:30 A.M. to 7 P.M.
Closed Sunday, Monday, and August.

Antiques: Ancient and beautiful glassware on dusty shelves that reach from floor to ceiling. Liqueur glasses, Champagne *coupes,* wineglasses, juice glasses. The perfect place to compose your own mixed or matched set. A few vases as well.

LES CARRELAGES DU MARAIS
46, rue Vieille du Temple,
Paris 4.
Tel: 01.42.78.17.43.
Métro: Hôtel de Ville.
Open 10 A.M. to 6:30 P.M. (2 to 6:30 P.M. Monday).
Closed Sunday and the first three weeks of August.
Credit card: V.

Tiles: Lovely, workable, timeless square glazed tiles in every shade of nearly every color make this a personal favorite. (My kitchen counters in Provence are covered with their tiles in varied shades of ocher, in Paris with a blend of off-white and lavender blue). Also a fine selection of traditional handmade floor tiles. Service can be cool or even downright rude, so come with a dose of patience and stamina.

COUP DE TORCHON
15, rue de Turenne,
Paris 4.
Tel: 01.42.74.39.26
Métro: Saint-Paul.
Open 11 A.M. to 7 P.M. (2 to 7 P.M. Monday).
Closed Sunday and the second and third weeks of August.
Credit cards: AE, DC, V.

Linens: Tea-towel-lovers unite! This tidy modern shop near the Bastille is a French linen paradise. The selection is modest yet complete, with a variety of solid and multicolored all-cotton or cotton/linen dish towels (*torchons* in French), tablecloths and napkins, and bed linens, as well as a small selection of charming country pottery bowls. Everything is made in France, largely in the Basque country or in the Vosges, to the west. They often have a selection of single-monogram dish towels, and if it's your lucky day, they may have yours. Service is pleasant and efficient.

CUISINEOPHILIE
28, rue du Bourg-Tibourg,
Paris 4.
Tel: 01.40.29.07.32.
Métro: Hôtel de Ville.
Open 2 P.M. to 7 P.M.
Closed Sunday, Monday, and August.
Credit cards: AE, V.

Kitchen gadgets: This tiny shop is worth a look when in the neighborhood. The selection is as small as the shop, but there is always something to want, from kitchen utensils of the 1950s and enamel coffee pots and pans to faïence and old milk bottles—you name it.

Beautiful kitchenware beautifully displayed is always tempting.

D.O.T.
47, rue de Saintonge,
Paris 3.
Tel: 01.40.29.90.34.
Fax: 01.42.74.76.22.
Métro: Filles du Calvaire or République.
Open: 9 A.M. to 1 P.M. and 2 to 6 P.M.
Closed Saturday, Sunday, and three weeks in August.

Eclectic mix: This charming, old-fashioned-looking shop hidden away in the back of the Marais is a must for those who love the odd, the unusual kitchen gadget. On my last visit I found an antique spoon for scoring a decorative row of lines on a pat of butter (doesn't everyone need one?); a reproduction of the individual asparagus tongs used at the Ritz; an attractive silver paddle for scooping up a bunch of asparagus; and a thick-bottomed glass bottle, or *pot,* used for Beaujolais in the old cafés. For those of us who miss the now-defunct Au Bain Marie, this is the next best thing. In fact D.O.T. used to manufacture some of Au Bain Marie's store-label products.

They also carry an eclectic array of bric-a-brac and antiques. You won't find rare antique silver and porcelain here. Rather, the windows boast cozier items, including an enormous collection of *café au lait* bowls, egg cups, and pots for making hot chocolate, as well as knickknacks such as whiskey flasks and antique picnic sets. While you're in the neighborhood, stop by Onfroy *boulangerie* for a perfect *pain de seigle* (see Bakeries).

LESCENE-DURA
63, rue de la Verrerie,
Paris 4.
Tel: 01.42.72.08.74.
Métro: Hôtel de Ville.
Open 10 A.M. to 7 P.M.
Closed Sunday, Monday, and the first three weeks of August.
Credit card: V.

Glassware, wine-making supplies: The city's best supply of absolutely everything for the wine maker and wine drinker—bottles and corks, small grape presses, beautiful preprinted wine labels along with those to inscribe yourself for your own house vintage. There are brass-bound wooden measuring containers and casks for aging wine (or making vinegar), along with a variety of corkscrews, tasting cups, and other table accessories.

The shop offers a large selection of glassware, from a special French wine-tasting glass (ask for the one approved by I.N.A.O.) to small Riesling glasses with deep green stems. You can also find espresso coffee machines and pocketknives of every price and description.

LES GRANDS MAGASINS

The *grands magasins* (department stores) have been a Parisian tradition since Galeries Lafayette invented the concept in the late 19th century. While shopping at the original Galeries Lafayette store in the 9th *arrondissement,* do take a moment to admire the painted cupola and circular *rotonde* design. La Samaritaine's original building, facing the Pont Neuf, also merits a visit for its Art Deco design and for the superb view of Paris from the café at the top.

Department stores offer large selections, convenience, and efficiency that smaller boutiques often lack, and their housewares departments are loaded with can't-live-without gadgets. If you want to buy jacquard table linens, a set of Lunéville *faïence,* or Havilland porcelain, for example, it will probably be simplest to make your purchase here. A few stay open late at least one night per week, and most have excellent sales in July. Shop around before making a large purchase—not all stores offer competitive prices.

B.H.V. (BAZAAR DE L'HOTEL DE VILLE)
52, rue de Rivoli,
Paris 4.
Tel: 01.42.74.90.00
Métro: Hôtel de Ville.
Open 9:30 A.M. to 7 P.M. (until 10 P.M. Wednesday).
Closed Sunday.
Credit cards: AE, V.
Art de la table department on third floor.

Almost every contemporary kitchen tool or piece of equipment ever invented is available on the third floor of this enormous catch-all department store, as are china and crystal, baskets, table linens, and everyday kitchen products.

AU BON MARCHE
22, rue de Sèvres,
Paris 7.
Tel: 01.44.39.80.00.
Métro: Sèvres-Babylone.
Open 9:30 A.M. to 6:30 P.M.
Closed Sunday.
Credit cards: AE, V.
Art de la table department on second floor.

Au Bon Marché prides itself on its slogan—*l'Esprit Rive Gauche*—and to its credit stocks an original, boutique-like selection of tableware. Also an excellent selection of linens for the kitchen and table.

GALERIES LAFAYETTE
40, boulevard Haussmann,
Paris 9.
Tel: 01.42.82.34.56.
Métro: Chausée d'Antin–La Fayette.
Open 9:30 A.M. to 6:45 P.M. (to 9 P.M. Thursday)
Closed Sunday.
Credit cards: AE, V.
Art de la table department in basement.

The *doyenne* of department stores stocks a classic selection of kitchen and table wares that no proper French home should be without. Porcelain, crystal, crockery, and to sustain you, a Mariage Frères tea counter.

AU PRINTEMPS
64, boulevard Haussmann,
Paris 9.
Tel: 01.42.82.50.00.
Métro: Chaussée d'Antin–La Fayette.
Open: 9:35 A.M. to 7 P.M.
(to 10 P.M. Thursday).
Closed Sunday.
Credit cards: AE, V.
Art de la table department on second floor of the "Magasin de la Maison."

Au Printemps' convenient and spacious housewares/tableware department offers no surprises, but I always love wandering through for that extra hot pad, the latest gadgets in grating or slicing, and an always appealing selection of tableware and glassware.

LA SAMARITAINE
19, rue de la Monnaie,
Paris 1.
Tel: 01.40.41.20.20.
Métro: Pont Neuf.
Open 9:30 A.M. to 7 P.M. (to 10 P.M. Thursday).
Closed Sunday.
Credit cards: AE, V.
Art de la table department
on third floor of building 2.

One of my favorite spots for that hard-to-find kitchen gadget, whether it's a state-of-the-art timer, a bundt cake pan, knives, unique coffeemakers, graters, or canning supplies.

MONASTICA
12, rue du Pont
Louis-Philippe,
Paris 4.
Tel: 01.48.87.85.13.
Métro: Pont Marie.
Open 10 A.M. to 12:15 P.M.
and 1 to 7 P.M. (12:30 to
1:30 P.M. Sunday).
Closed Monday and August.
Credit card: V.

Eclectic mix: What a lovely idea! All those beautiful linens, delicious honeys, jams, and cookies, excellent shampoos, bath oils, and herbs, not to mention the handmade pottery, found in monasteries all over France, can now be found in a lovely boutique on the colorful rue du Pont Louis-Philippe. I love my pure linen drying towels that read *Verre* ("Glass") as well as the fragrant beeswax candles found in many forms and sizes. Prices are extremely reasonable and service comes with a smile.

QUIMPER FAIENCE
84, rue Saint-Martin,
Paris 4.
Tel: 01.42.71.93.03.
Métro: Hôtel de Ville.
Open 11 A.M. to 7 P.M.
Closed Sunday.
Credit card: V.

Pottery: This folkloric shop features the popular, ultra-expensive, brilliantly colored pottery from Brittany known as Quimper *faïence*. There's a good selection, and whether you're picking up a teacup or an entire place setting, they'll be happy to ship the pottery home for you. It's the next best thing to a trip to Brittany!

ESPACE LA ROCHERE
41, rue des Francs-Bourgeois,
Paris 4.
Tel/Fax: 01.42.72.08.07.
Métro: Saint-Paul.
Open daily, 10 A.M. to 7 P.M.
(11 A.M. to 7 P.M. Sunday,
1 to 7 P.M. Monday).
Credit card: V.

Glassware: This bright, welcoming shop features handmade glass objects—glassware, plates, lamps—that are well designed, well priced, and functional. And they are all made in France, largely in the village of Passavant, located in the eastern part of the country, where the glassblowing tradition dates back to 1475.

LAURENCE ROQUE—LE COMPTOIR DES OUVRAGES
69, rue Saint-Martin, Paris 4.
Tel: 01.42.72.22.12.
Métro: Hôtel de Ville.
Open 10:30 A.M. to 6:30 P.M.
Closed Sunday and Monday morning (all day Monday in August).
Credit card: V.

Embroidery: A charming shop for do-it-yourself decorators: beautiful embroidery and needlepoint patterns, tablecloths and napkins, lace, jaunty-patterned fabrics for edging kitchen shelves, upholstery patterns and fabrics.

LATIN QUARTER, SAINT-GERMAIN, SEVRES-BABYLONE, MONTPARNASSE

5th, 6th, and 7th arrondissements

BISTROTS D'AUTREFOIS
135 bis, boulevard du Montparnasse, Paris 6.
Tel: 01.43.35.54.17.
Fax: 01.42.79.97.51.
Métro: Montparnasse–Bienvenüe
Open 2 to 7 P.M. (open mornings by appointment).
Closed Sunday.
Credit card: V.

Antique bistro paraphernalia: Those who love the traditional old bistro chairs, tables, and hat-racks, zinc or copper bars, glasses, ashtrays, and oak doors with Art Nouveau etched glass will love this charming shop along the busy boulevard du Montparnasse. You name it—Suze or Ricard pitchers, absinthe glasses, sturdy bentwood bar stools—they have it, at a price. If you are looking for something special and don't see it, just ask and they will research it for you.

BLANC D'IVOIRE
104, rue du Bac, Paris 7.
Tel: 01.45.44.41.17.
Métro: Rue du Bac.
Open 10:30 A.M. to 7 P.M. (2 to 7 P.M. Monday).
Closed Sunday.
Credit cards: AE, V.

Pottery: The *fin-de-siècle*—the 20th *siècle,* that is—colors are, without doubt, those lovely natural shades of eggshell, ivory, linen, creamy beige, set off from time to time by pale celadon and with a touch of natural wicker to bring it all together. This combination well describes Blanc d'Ivoire, where your house can be decorated in a second with the lovely items displayed in this elegant/rustic boutique. For good luck, there's also a touch of Provence, with lovely quilts, or *boutis,* for covering the table, the bed, or using as a comfy throw while lounging in front of the fire.

MARIE-PIERRE BOITARD
Galerie de l'Assemblée,
9 and 11, place du
Palais Bourbon,
Paris 7.
Tel: 01.47.05.13.30.
Métro: Invalides or
Assemblée Nationale.
Open 10 A.M. to 7 P.M.
Closed Sunday. August
hours vary, so call ahead.
Credit cards: AE, V.

The home: This shop would be a good source for decorating the dining room of a *château.* Parisian socialites and old-guard matrons come here to buy wedding presents or to find that extra knickknack for their *hôtel particulier.* Marie-Pierre Boitard displays one-of-a-kind antiques as well as limited-series porcelain patterns, hand-painted crystal, and silk brocade table linens. Her specialty is thick stained-glass-like Bohemian crystal goblets and crystal edged in gold leaf. Boitard, a porcelain designer for Havilland, designs many of the items here. Lower priced but equally appealing gifts include chic *passementerie* key chains and reproduction 19th-century potpourri diffusers. The prices are as opulent as the merchandise, and service here can be snooty indeed.

TIANY CHAMBARD
32, rue Jacob,
Paris 6.
Tel: 01.43.29.73.15.
Métro: Saint-Germain
des Prés.
Open 2 to 7 P.M.
Closed Sunday, Monday,
and August.
No credit cards.

Antique labels: A tiny shop with tiny things like wonderful chef's salt and pepper shakers from the 1950s and old, colorful, beautifully designed fruit and liqueur labels from obsolete canneries and distilleries, perfect for framing and hanging in the kitchen or in the bar.

COMOGLIO
22, rue Jacob,
Paris 6.
Tel: 01.43.54.65.86.
Métro: Saint-Germain
des Prés.
Open 10:30 A.M. to 7 P.M.
(2:30 to 7 P.M. Monday).
Closed Sunday.
Credit card: V.

The home: This is the kind of store I would love to be locked into overnight, to wander, dream, imagine my living room or dining room filled with Comoglio's wonderful antique finds. Everything here—from the fine reproduction of 18th- and 19th-century fabrics to the country antiques to the one-of-a-kind folkloric items for the kitchen or table— simply reeks of good taste and style. I want it all.

GALLERIE LA CORNUE
18, rue Mabillon,
Paris 6.
Tel: 01.46.33.84.74.
Métro: Mabillon.
Open 10 A.M. to 1 P.M. and
2 to 6:30 P.M.
Closed Sunday and two
weeks in August.
Credit cards: AE, DC, V.

Stoves and kitchenware: If you love beautiful, sturdy, last-a-lifetime stoves, then take a look at the restaurant-style collection displayed here. Each and every one is individually made to order, using thick metal, quality enamels, bronze, copper, and cast iron. They're available in both gas and electric. (If your visit inspires you, La Cornue stoves can be purchased in the U.S. from Purcell-Murray Co., 113 Park Lane, Brisbane, CA 94005. Tel: 800-892-4040. Fax: 415-468-0667. Web site: www.purcellmurray.com)

DINERS EN VILLE
27, rue de Varenne,
Paris 7.
Tel: 01.42.22.78.33.
Métro: Rue du Bac.
Open 11 A.M. to 7 P.M.
Closed Sunday and Monday.
Credit card: V.

The home: An elegant shop that specializes in both useful and frivolous accessories and objects for home and table, stocking a wide variety of 19th- and 20th-century silver, sets of dishes, coffee pots, teapots and cups, serving dishes, and some fabrics.

ETAMINE
63, rue du Bac,
Paris 7.
Tel: 01.42.22.03.16.
Fax: 01.42.84.12.47.
Métro: Rue du Bac.
Open 11 A.M. to 7 P.M.
Closed Sunday, Monday, and August.
Credit card: V.

The home: Everything in this store seems to say, "Don't take life so seriously!" Each item is close to unique, whimsical, not too expensive, and puts a smile on your face. The stock here is ever-changing, and there is also a selection of inexpensive imported pottery, including a fish and shellfish set with a scallop-shell shape and all-white oyster plates.

MAISON DE FAMILLE
29, rue Saint-Sulpice,
Paris 6.
Tel: 01.40.46.97.47.
Métro: Odéon.
Open 10:30 A.M. to 7 P.M.
Closed Sunday, and Monday in August.
Credit cards: AE, V.

The home: There is a little bit of everything in this homey shop, with china, table linens, some kitchen gadgets, and tableware, as well as items for the bath, bedroom, and even some clothing and furniture. It's hard to leave without something in your shopping bag.

BOUTIQUE LE FLORE
26, rue Saint-Benoit,
Paris 6.
Tel: 01.45.44.33.40.
Métro: Saint-Germain des Prés.
Open 11 A.M. to 1 P.M. and 2 to 8 P.M. (2 to 8 P.M. Monday).
Closed Sunday and three weeks in August.
Credit cards: AE, DC, V.

Café items: If you've ever been tempted to steal the pretty silver coffee pitchers or trays from a café, this boutique could be a dream come true. Boutique Le Flore sells the table service and café accoutrements from the famous Café Flore next door: white porcelain coffee cups, floor-length waiters' aprons, and café memorabilia that will put Saint-Germain des Prés on your table long after you return home—at a price.

LA MAISON IVRE
38, rue Jacob,
Paris 6.
Tel: 01.42.60.01.85.
Métro: Saint-Germain des Prés.
Open 10:30 A.M. to 7 P.M.
Closed Sunday, Monday, and two weeks in August.
Credit card: V.

Pottery: Young, friendly Sophie Nobécourt has filled her shop with bright hand-painted *faïence.* Her collection of artisanal pottery and hand-blown glass comes from all over France, as well as England, Germany, and Portugal. Come here to find traditional floral-design *faïence* from Provence, including lovely *café au lait* cups; plant-shaped ceramic knife rests; ceramic platters and salad bowls in abstract designs; and wicker cups lined with resin—great for a picnic.

Marchés aux Puces
FLEA MARKETS

The quality of a flea or antiques market depends on the last good buy you found. I have unearthed a treasured 5-franc *OLIVES DE NICE* crock at the Puces de Vanves, snatched up irreplaceable 35-franc *FRITES A TOUTE HEURE* signs at the Clignacourt market, and paid 60 francs for a charming blue and white porcelain *CAFE* canister at the Place d'Aligre. You know the drill: Go often, keep your eyes open, and don't be disappointed if you don't spend a *centime*. Think of it as exercise and a nice walk in the city.

PUCES SAINT-OUEN
Avenue Michelet and rue de Rosiers,
Paris 18.
Métro: Porte de Clignacourt.
Saturday and Sunday 8 A.M. to 6 P.M.;
Monday 10 A.M. to 5 P.M.

Enter at the crossroads of the avenue Michelet and rue de Rosiers at the Marché Vernaison, and let your eyes and nose lead you through the more than 75 acres of flea market, with hundreds of stalls. My favorite market is Paul Bert, where I always find something. Other good bets include Marché Biron and Marché Vernaison.

VILLAGE SAINT-PAUL
Rue Saint-Paul,
Paris 4.
Métro: Saint-Paul.
Thursday through Monday,
11 A.M. to 7 P.M.

Don't miss a visit to the dozens of little shops harboring treasures, from entire collections of old baskets to a shop with hundreds of corkscrews. Shops are open and closed at the owners' whims but are always shut tight on Tuesday and Wednesday.

PUCES VANVES
Avenue de la Porte de Vanves, avenue Georges Lafenestre, and avenue Marc Sangnier,
Paris 14.
Métro: Porte de Vanves.
Saturday and Sunday,
7 A.M. to 7:30 P.M. second-hand items;
2 P.M. to 7:30 P.M. new items.

Like a garage sale that goes on forever. Sometimes you strike it rich, other times you just take a stroll.

MARCHE D'ALIGRE
Beauvau Saint-Antoine, Place d'Aligre,
Paris 12.
Métro: Ledru-Rollin.
Tuesday through Sunday,
7:30 A.M. to 12:30 P.M.

No one is likely to be super-impressed with this garage-sale-style market, but when one does find a treasure, one's not disappointed. A good collection of old tools, some decent *brocante* (second-hand furniture).

E. Dehillerin, filled to overflowing with professional cookware *(see entry, page 352).*

LAURE JAPY
34, rue du Bac,
Paris 7.
Tel: 01.42.86.96.97.
Fax: 01.42.97.40.10.
Métro: Rue du Bac.
Open 10:30 A.M. to 7 P.M.
Closed Sunday, and Monday in August. (August hours vary, so call ahead.)
Credit card: V.

The table: If you like a lot of color in your life, this is the place for you. In fact, you can coordinate your kitchen and your dining room in bright, primary yellows, blues, and oranges. There are modern, inexpensive matching plates, place mats, tablecloths, cookware, lamps, even tableware.

CATHERINE MEMMI
32–34, rue Saint-Sulpice,
Paris 6.
Tel: 01.44.07.22.28.
Métro: Saint-Sulpice.
Open 10:30 A.M. to 7:30 P.M. (12:30 to 3:30 P.M. Monday).
Closed Sunday and the third week of August.
Credit cards: AE, V.

Linens: If you love beige and ivory, this beautifully monotone shop is for you. There is a lovely selection of linens in a subtle range from beige to white, as well as elegant modern pottery to match. There are also items for the home and bath.

The making of a dream kitchen.

QUARTZ
12, rue des Quatres-Vents,
Paris 6.
Tel: 01.43.54.03.00.
Métro: Odéon.
Open 10:30 A.M. to 7 P.M. (2:30 to 7 P.M. Monday).
Closed Sunday.
Credit card: V.

Glassware: Glass, glass, and more glass. Vases, pitchers, glass trays, glass plates and platters in all forms and sizes, can be found in this long, narrow shop. Whether it's clear glass, chunky or fine, or in a rainbow of colors, you are sure to find your heart's desire. The eternal problem is, of course, how to get the treasures home...

LE RIDEAU DE PARIS
32, rue du Bac,
Paris 7.
Tel: 01.42.61.18.56.
Metro: Rue du Bac.
Open 11 A.M. to 7 P.M.
Closed Sunday.

The home: This minuscule boutique is one of my dreams, filled with everything from lovely embroidered linen tablecloths to lamps, picture frames, napkin rings, and lovely Provençal *boutis,* or quilts. A sure win.

FLORENCE ROUSSEAU
9, rue de Luynes,
Paris 7.
Tel: 01.45.48.04.71.
Métro: Rue du Bac.
Open 2 to 6:30 P.M.
Closed Sunday, Monday, and August.

The table: A limited but very high quality selection of tabletop furnishings, including *barbotines* (artichoke, oyster, and asparagus plates and serving dishes), turn-of-the-century vases with grandiose patterns, unusual serving platters, and silver sugar tongs and spoons. The door of this small shop is often locked, so be sure to knock.

SALON B
86, rue du Cherche-Midi,
Paris 6.
Tel: 01.42.22.52.58.
Métro: Sèvres-Babylone.
Open 11 A.M. to 6 P.M.
Closed Sunday, July, and August.

Fireplace: An entire shop devoted the art of the fireplace. This wonderful boutique always has a gas fire going and is full of fireplace screens, a few grills, a huge selection of fantasy andirons, and other gadgets that relate to the fireplace.

SENTOU GALERIE
26 bis, boulevard Raspail,
Paris 7.
Tel: 01.45.49.00.05.
Fax: 01.45.49.98.05.
Métro: Sèvres-Babylone or Rue du Bac.
Open 11 A.M. to 7 P.M.
Closed Sunday and August.
Credit card: V.

The home: The reason to wander over to this modern, hip, up-to-date design shop is to pick up a few creations of Tse & Tse Associées, the company name for two young French designers, Catherine Levy and Sigolène Prébois. Each day I drink my coffee out of the lovely, almost monastic white cups from the tableware collection called *"affamée & assoifée"* ("starving and parched"). I love their offbeat sense of humor and always find a reason to giggle when I wander in.

ESPACE SHORE
16, rue de Lille,
Paris 7.
Tel: 01.49.27.90.00.
Métro: Rue du Bac or RER Muséed'Orsay.
Open 10 A.M. to 1 P.M. and 2 to 7 P.M.
Closed Sunday.
Credit card: V.

Kitchen: The *grand maison* of La Cornue (see page 366) has created a new, less expensive line of kitchenware for the home cook who has little space. Another fantasy shop designed for dreaming, with a small but nice selection of kitchen items, cabinets, and of course stoves.

SIECLE
24, rue du Bac,
Paris 7.
Tel: 01.47.03.48.03.
Fax: 01.47.03.48.01.
Métro: Saint-Germain des Prés.
Open 11 A.M. to 7 P.M. (noon to 7 P.M. Tuesday)
Closed Sunday and Monday.
Credit card: V.

The home: Benedictine Geevers has a great eye, and is kind enough to share it with us. It's hard to leave this elegant boutique without something, or at least a deep longing for that special item to make your day. She specializes in what the French call *"insolite,"* a sort of unique specialness. It's here, from the gold and white Limoges espresso cups to the one-of-a-kind nutcrackers, glass plates, caviar spoons, smooth eggshell-toned china, drawer pulls, unusual tableware, even special keyhole escutcheons. The welcome is always friendly, and you're encouraged to browse or ask questions. Prices are not outrageous.

LE SOMMEIL D'ORPHEE
93, rue du Bac,
Paris 7.
Tel: 01.42.22.80.22.
Métro: Rue du Bac.
Open 10 A.M. to 7:30 P.M.
Closed Sunday and Monday.
Credit card: V.

Linens: For some thirty-five years, this minuscule shop has catered to locals for their linens—kitchen, table, bed, and bath. This is where I order all my monogrammed aprons for the kitchen, as well as pure linen "cheesecloth" for straining stocks. I also love to browse through their collection of linen or linen/cotton tea towels, tablecloths, and bed linens. It's a one-of-a-kind shop in one of the city's most stimulating neighborhoods.

GALERIE MICHEL SONKIN
10, rue de Beaune,
Paris 7.
Tel: 01.42.61.27.87.
Métro: Rue du Bac.
Open 2:30 to 7 P.M.
Closed Sunday and August.
Credit cards: AE, DC, V.

Antiques: As much cozy museum as antique shop, Galerie Michel Sonkin is filled with lovingly restored folk objects, most of them in golden, gleaming wood. Monsieur and Madame Sonkin have searched throughout Europe to find their treasures and are particularly proud of their intricately carved, initialed bread stamps, dating from the days when villagers depended on communal ovens for baking. Each loaf was stamped with the family seal or initials so the baker could tell the loaves apart. Also wooden butter molds, milk filters and carved spoons, porcelain cheese molds, some solid antique chests and pieces of furniture.

LA TUILE A LOUP
35, rue Daubenton,
Paris 5.
Tel/Fax: 01.47.07.28.90.
Métro: Censier Daubenton.
Open 10:30 A.M. to 1 P.M. and 3 to 7:30 P.M. (10:30 A.M. to 1 P.M. Sunday).
Closed Monday.
Credit cards: AE, DC, V.

Regional crafts: A rustic little shop specializing in French regional arts and crafts, with pottery dishes in rich green and blue glazes, beautiful handmade wooden bowls, baskets, and candles, and a wide selection of books on the folklore and customs of different areas of France.

VERRERIE DES ECOLES ET DU PANTHEON
14, rue des Ecoles,
Paris 5.
Tel: 01.43.54.15.55.
Métro: Maubert-Mutualité or Cardinal Lemoine.
Open 10 A.M. to 7 P.M.
Closed Sunday and Monday.
Credit card: V.

Professional kitchenware: If you don't want to make the trip to Les Halles for kitchen and restaurant supplies, this lovely Left Bank shop will do. An excellent selection of knives, professional kitchen gadgets, and inexpensive glassware and tableware can be found in this sunny, friendly store.

XANADOU
10, rue Saint-Sulpice,
Paris 6.
Tel: 01.43.26.73.43.
Métro: Odéon.
Open 11 A.M. to 1 P.M. and 2 to 7 P.M.
Closed Sunday, Monday, and August.
Credit cards: AE, DC, V.

Design: Those who love fine design shouldn't miss this eclectic shop. Unfortunately, "form follows function" is not always the rule here: Many objects are beautiful to look at but awkward to use. What I do love is the purely aesthetic look of the items by such designers as Joseph Hoffman from the 1930s, reeditions of 20th-century designer Charles Rennie Mackintosh's tableware dating back to the beginning of the 1900s, and of course all of Philippe Starck's wacky—and largely unfunctional—designs for those who love to look at the beautiful objects in their kitchen but rarely cook.

MADELEINE, COURCELLES, FRANKLIN ROOSEVELT

8th arrondissement

LA CARPE
14, rue Tronchet,
Paris 8.
Tel: 01.47.42.73.25.
Métro: Madeleine or Havre-Caumartin.
Open 9:30 A.M. to 6:45 P.M.
Closed Sunday, Monday morning, and August.
Credit card: V.

Kitchen: Located just off the Place de la Madeleine, this is the place to find items you didn't know you needed: different kinds of oyster knives, cherry and peach pitters, an espresso machine that works off a car battery, and much more. The staff is very friendly and helpful.

CHASTEL COUTELIER
190, boulevard Haussmann,
Paris 8.
Tel: 01.45.63.20.59.
Métro: Courcelles or Saint-Philippe du Roule.
Open 10 A.M. to 7 P.M.
Closed Saturday afternoon, Sunday, and August.

Knives, sharpening, resilvering: Should you purchase knives in need of a new coat of silver or new blades, stop in to see Alain Chastel, who works out of a tiny boutique on the corner of Rue des Courcelles and Boulevard Haussmann. He's been my "knife doctor" for years, adding new old-fashioned stainless steel blades to favorite antique knives (which also makes them dishwasher-proof) and resilvering beat-up silverplate cutlery with which I hate to part. Although it takes three weeks for resilvering and two weeks for new blades, Monsieur Chastel will be happy to arrange international delivery. His professional knife-sharpening service is of top quality.

LA BOUTIQUE DE LA MAISON DE L'ALSACE
10, rue de Colisée,
Paris 8.
Tel: 01.56.59.04.84.
Métro: Franklin D. Roosevelt.
Open 10:30 A.M. to 7 P.M. (10:30 A.M. to 5 P.M. Saturday).
Closed Saturday in summer, and Sunday.
Credit card: V.

Regional crafts: This newly enlarged shop is home to an Alsatian carry-out shop (including sauerkraut, *quiche,* you name it), but our reason for going is the fine selection of colorful *kougelhoph* molds and terrines from the Alsatian village of Soufflenheim.

PUIFORCAT ORFEVRE
22, rue François 1er,
Paris 8.
Tel: 01.47.20.74.27.
Métro: Franklin D. Roosevelt
Open 9:30 to 1 p.m. and 2:15 to 6:30 p.m.
Closed Sunday, and Monday in July and August.
Credit cards: AE, DC, V.

Silver, crystal, and china: My favorite Paris shop for superbly designed silver cups—*timbales* (monogrammed, they make perfect baby gifts, ready for use much later in life as brandy or Cognac snifters)—elegant silver wine and Champagne buckets, fine reproductions of antique china, and exquisite Puiforcat silver patterns from the 1920s and 1930s.

TERRITOIRE
30, rue Boissy d'Anglas,
Paris 8.
Tel: 01.42.66.22.13.
Métro: Concorde.
Open 10:30 A.M. to 7 P.M. (11 A.M. to 7 P.M. Saturday).
Closed Sunday, and Saturday in August.
Credit cards: AE, DC, V.

Eclectic mix: A really wonderful idea for a shop: celebrating *les fêtes et les vacances!* Would that we could spend our lives making use of all the goodies found within. There are objects for picnics and gardening, a good selection of food and garden cookbooks, as well as all sorts of paraphernalia for parties, including menu cards, invitations, fireworks, and a great assortment of fantasy birthday candles.

Bastille

12th arrondissement

LA PINCE A BUCHES
251, rue de Bercy,
Paris 12.
Tel: 01.43.42.10.25.
Fax: 01.43.42.90.26.
Métro: Bastille.
Open 11 A.M. to 7 P.M.
Closed Saturday, Sunday, and August.
Credit card: V.

Fireplace: Anyone who loves grilling in the fireplace (indoors or out) should make a beeline to this shop, where they sell a sturdy black cast-iron grilling system that can be purchased in component parts; it includes a marvelous vertical grill that easily doubles as a radiator on chilly days, a handy horizontal grill, and an electric rotisserie. Not something to slip inside your carry-on luggage, but transportable nonetheless.

A wonderful but difficult choice.

Montparnasse, Grenelle

15th arrondissement

DEVINE QUI VIENT DINER CE SOIR
83, avenue Emile-Zola,
Paris 15.
Tel: 01.40.59.41.14.
Métro: Charles Michels.
Open 10:30 A.M. to 7:30 P.M.
Closed Sunday, Monday, and August.
Credit card: V.

The table: This lovely haven for Art Deco fans is a find. On my last visit to "Guess Who's Coming to Dinner" I found adorable glasses, and napkin rings labeled "*Toi*" and "*Moi*" ("You" and "Me") caught my eye, as did 1930s Limoges dessert plates adorned with bright red cherries. Service is pleasant and informative, and the selection is of high quality, whether it is Champagne glasses, teapots, odd services of china, or silver napkin rings for Monsieur and Madame.

FANETTE
1, rue d'Alençon,
Paris 15.
Tel: 01.42.22.21.73.
Métro: Montparnasse–Bienvenüe.
Open 1 to 7 P.M.
Closed Sunday.
No credit cards.

The table: Owner Magali Desclozeaux spends her mornings searching auctions, *brocantes* (secondhand shops), and flea markets for the treasures you find in her adorable shop: beautiful collections of pottery, china, glassware, table linens, turn-of-the-century Limoges, decorative *barbotine* (such as asparagus plates), and anything her or your heart desires.

KITCHEN BAZAAR
11, avenue du Maine,
Paris 15.
Tel: 01.42.22.91.17.
Métro: Montparnasse–Bienvenüe.
Open 10 A.M. to 7 P.M.
Closed Sunday.
Credit cards: AE, V.

Kitchen: Everything for the kitchen, from timers on strings to Italian-designed balancing scales, tiny chocolate molds, and citrus peelers, zesters, curlers—all of good quality. Some baking dishes and a small collection of cookbooks.

Arc de Triomphe

16th arrondissement

VERRERIE CRISTALLERIE D'ARQUES
6, place des Etats-Unis,
Paris 16.
Tel: 01.47.23.31.34.
Métro: Boissière.
Open 9:30 A.M. to 6 P.M.
Closed Saturday and Sunday.
Credit card: V.

Glassware: A factory outlet in this chic tree-filled square in the 16th? This cheery shop (with excellent service) serves both as a showroom and as a factory outlet for a vast assortment of French everyday and Sunday crystal, glassware, tableware, and cookware. The shop has a huge selection, including elegant silver holders to cradle your bottle of mineral water, and nice gift items, such as metal clips to hold your picnic tablecloth down in a windstorm!

French/English FOOD GLOSSARY

Ask for your perfect peach in perfect French.

For many diners, a restaurant menu can present a confusing and intimidating barrier to the pleasure of dining out. The French language, of course, is no help with so many sound-alike words. It is easy to confuse *tourteau* (crab) with *tortue* (turtle), *ail* (garlic) with *aile* (a poultry wing), *chevreau* (young goat) with *chevreuil* (venison).

The variety of fish and shellfish found in France's waters can be equally confusing, particularly when one is faced with a multitude of regional or local names given to each species. The large, meaty monkfish, for example, might be called *baudroie, lotte,* or *gigot de mer,* depending upon the region or the whim of the chef.

In preparing this glossary, I have tried to limit the list to contemporary terms, making this a practical guide for today's traveler in France. Translations are generally offered for those dishes, foods, and phrases one is most likely to encounter on menus, in markets, and in shops. I have also added regional expressions or terms one might not find explained elsewhere.

A

Abat(s): organ meat(s).
Abati(s): giblet(s) of poultry or game fowl.
Abbacchio: young lamb, specialty of Corsica.
Abondance: firm thick wheel of cow's milk cheese from the Savoie, a *département* in the Alps.
Abricot: apricot.
Acacia: the acacia tree, the blossoms of which are used for making fritters; also honey made from the blossom.
Acajou: cashew nut.
Achatine: land snail, or *escargot,* imported from China and Indonesia; less prized than other varieties.
Addition: bill.
Affamé: starving.
Affinage: process of aging cheese.
Affiné: aged, as with cheese.
Agneau (de lait): lamb (young, milk-fed).
chilindron: sauté of lamb with potatoes and garlic, specialty of the Basque country.
de Pauillac: breed of lamb from the southwest.
pré-salé: delicately salted lamb raised on the salt marshes of Normandy and the Atlantic coast.
Agnelet: baby milk-fed lamb.
Agnelle: ewe lamb.
Agrume(s): citrus fruit(s).
Aïado: roast lamb shoulder stuffed with parsley, chervil, and garlic.
Aiglefin, aigrefin, églefin: small fresh haddock, a type of cod.
Aïgo bouido: garlic soup, served with oil, over slices of bread; specialty of Provence.
Aïgo saou: "water-salt" in Provençal; a fish soup that includes, of course, water and salt, plus a mixture of small whitefish, onions, potatoes, tomatoes, garlic, herbs, and olive oil; specialty of Provence.
Aigre: bitter; sour.
Aigre-doux: sweet and sour.
Aigrelette, sauce: a sort of tart sauce.
Aiguillette: a long, thin slice of poultry, meat, or fish. Also, top part of beef rump.
Ail: garlic.
Aile: wing of poultry or game bird.
Aile et cuisse: used to describe white breast meat (*aile*) and dark thigh meat (*cuisse*), usually of chicken.
Aillade: garlic sauce; also, dishes based on garlic.
Aillé: with garlic.
Aillet: shoot of mild winter baby garlic, a specialty of the Poitou-Charentes region along the Atlantic coast.
Aïoli, ailloli: garlic mayonnaise. Also, a dish of salt cod, hard-cooked eggs, boiled snails, and vegetables served with garlic mayonnaise; specialty of Provence.
Airelle: wild cranberry
Aisy cendré: thick disc of cow's-milk cheese, washed with *eau-de-vie* and patted with wood ashes; also called *cendre d'aisy;* specialty of Burgundy
Albuféra: *béchamel* sauce with sweet peppers, prepared with chicken stock instead of milk; classic sauce for poultry.
Algue(s): edible seaweed.
Aligot: mashed potatoes with *tomme* (the fresh curds used in making Cantal cheese) and garlic; specialty of the Auvergne.
Alisier, alizier: *eau-de-vie* with the taste of bitter almonds, made with the wild red serviceberries that grow in the forests of Alsace.
Allumette: "match"; puff pastry strips; also fried matchstick potatoes.
Alose: shad, a spring river fish plentiful in the Loire and Gironde rivers.
Alouette: lark.
Aloyau: loin area of beef; beef sirloin, butcher's cut that includes the rump and *contre-filet.*
Alpage, d': from mountain pastures.
Alsacienne, à l': in the style of Alsace, often including sauerkraut, sausage, or *foie gras.*
Amande: almond.
Amande de mer: smooth-shelled shellfish, like a small clam, with a sweet, almost almond flavor.
Amandine: with almonds.
Ambroisie: ambrosia.
Amer: bitter; as in unsweetened chocolate.
Américaine, Amoricaine: sauce of white wine, Cognac, tomatoes, and butter.
Ami du Chambertin: "friend of Chambertin wine"; moist and buttery short cylinder of cow's milk cheese with a rust-colored rind, made near the village of Gevrey-Chambertin in

Burgundy. Similar to Epoisses cheese.

Amourette(s): spinal bone marrow of calf or ox.

Amuse-bouche or ***amusegueule:*** "amuse the mouth"; appetizer.

Ananas: pineapple.

Anchoïade: sauce that is a blend of olive oil, anchovies, and garlic, usually served with raw vegetables; specialty of Provence; also, paste of anchovies and garlic, spread on toast.

Anchois (de Collioure): anchovy (prized salt-cured anchovy from Collioure, a port town near the Spanish border of the Languedoc), fished in the Atlantic and the Mediterranean.

Ancienne, à l': in the old style.

Andouille: large smoked chitterling (tripe) sausage, usually served cold.

Andouillette: small chitterling (tripe) sausage, usually served grilled.

Aneth: dill.

Ange à cheval: "angel on horseback"; grilled bacon-wrapped oyster.

Anglaise, à l': English style, plainly cooked.

Anguille (au vert): eel (poached in herb sauce).

Anis: anise or aniseed.

Anis étoilé: star anise; also called *badiane*.

AOC: see *Appellation d'origine contrôlée*.

Apéritif: a before-dinner drink that stimulates the appetite, usually somewhat sweet or mildly bitter.

Appellation d'origine contrôlée (AOC): specific definition of a particular cheese, butter, fruit, wine, or poultry—once passed down from generation to generation, now recognized by law—regulating the animal breed or variety of fruit, the zone of production, production techniques, composition of the product, its physical characteristics, and its specific attributes.

Arachide (huile d'; pâté d'): peanut (oil; butter).

Araignée de mer: spider crab.

Arbousier (miel d'): trailing arbutus, small evergreen shrubby tree of the heather family, also called strawberry tree, ground laurel, and madrona tree, with strawberry-like fruit dotted with tiny bumps; (honey of). Used for making liqueurs, jellies, and jams.

Arc en ciel (truite): rainbow (trout).

Ardennaise, à l': in the style of the Ardennes, a *département* in northern France; generally a dish with juniper berries.

Ardi gasna: Basque name for sheep's milk cheese.

Ardoise: blackboard; bistros often use a blackboard to list specialties in place of a printed menu.

Arête: fish bone.

Arlésienne, à l': in the style of Arles, a town in Provence; with tomatoes, onions, eggplant, potatoes, rice, and sometimes olives.

Armagnac: brandy from the Armagnac area of southwestern France.

Aromate: aromatic herb, vegetable, or flavoring.

Arômes à la gêne: generic name for a variety of tangy, lactic cheeses of the Lyon area that have been steeped in *gêne,* or dry *marc,* the dried grape skins left after grapes are pressed for wine. Can be of cow's milk, goat's milk, or a mixture.

Arosé: sprinkled, basted, moistened with liquid.

Arpajon: a town in the Ile-de-France, the dried-bean capital of France; a dish containing dried beans.

Artichaut (violet) (camus): artichoke (small purple).

à la Barigoule: in original form, artichokes cooked with mushrooms and oil; also, artichoke stuffed with ham, onion, and garlic, browned in oil with onions and bacon, then cooked in water or white wine; specialty of Provence.

Asperge (violette): asparagus (purple-tipped asparagus, a specialty of the Côte-d'Azur).

Assaisonné: seasoned; seasoned with.

Assiette anglaise: assorted cold meats, usually served as a first course.

Assiette de pêcheur: assorted fish platter.

Assoifé: parched, thirsty.

Assorti: assorted.

Auberge: inn; small hotel.

Aubergine: eggplant.

Aulx: plural of *ail* (garlic).

Aumônière: "beggar's purse"; thin *crêpe,* filled and tied like a bundle.

Aurore: tomato and cream sauce.

Auvergnat: in the style of the Auvergne; often with cabbage, sausage, and bacon.

Aveline: hazelnut or filbert, better known as *noisette*.
Avocat: avocado.
Avoine: oat.
Axoa: a dish of ground veal, onions, and the local fresh chiles, *piment d'Espelette;* specialty of the Basque region.
Azyme, pain: unleavened bread; matzo.

B

Baba au rhum: sponge cake soaked in rum syrup.
Badiane: star anise.
Baeckeoffe, baekaoffa, backofa, backenoff: "baker's oven"; stew of wine, beef, lamb, pork, potatoes, and onions; specialty of Alsace.
Bagna caudà: sauce of anchovies, olive oil, and garlic, for dipping raw vegetables; specialty of Nice.
Baguette: "wand"; classic long, thin loaf of bread.
au levain or ***à l'ancienne:*** sourdough *baguette*.
Baie: berry.
Baie rose: pink peppercorn.
Baigné: bathed.
Ballotine: usually poultry boned, stuffed, and rolled.
Banane: banana.
Banon: village in the Alps of Provence, source of dried chestnut leaves traditionally used to wrap goat cheese that was washed with *eau-de-vie* and aged for several months; today refers to various goat's milk cheeses or mixed goat and cow's milk cheeses from the region, sometimes wrapped in fresh green or dried brown chestnut leaves and tied with raffia.
Bar: ocean fish, known as *loup* on the Mediterranean coast, *louvine* or *loubine* in the southwest, and *barreau* in Brittany; similar to sea bass.
Barbouillade: stuffed eggplant, or an eggplant stew; also, a combination of beans and artichokes.
Barbue: brill, a flatfish related to turbot, found in the Atlantic and the Mediterranean.
Barder: to cover poultry or meat with strips of uncured bacon in order to add moisture while cooking.
Baron: hindquarters of lamb, including both legs.
Barquette: "small boat"; pastry shaped like a small boat.
Basilic: basil.
Basquaise, à la: Basque style; usually with ham or tomatoes or red peppers.
Bâtard, pain: "bastard bread"; traditional long, thin white loaf, larger than a *baguette*.
Batavia: salad green, a broad, flat-leafed lettuce.
Bâton: small white wand of bread, smaller than a *baguette*.
Bâtonnet: garnish of vegetables cut into small sticks.
Baudroie: in Provence, the name for monkfish or anglerfish, the large, firm-fleshed ocean fish also known as *lotte* and *gigot de mer*; also a specialty of Provence, a fish soup that includes potatoes, onions, fresh mushrooms, garlic, fresh or dried orange zest, artichokes, tomatoes, and herbs.
Bavaroise: cold dessert, a rich custard made with cream and gelatin.
Bavette: skirt steak.
Baveuse: "drooling"; method of cooking an omelet so that it remains moist and juicy.
Béarnaise: tarragon-flavored sauce of egg yolks, butter, shallots, white wine, vinegar, and herbs.
Béatille: "tidbit"; dish combining various organ meats.
Bécasse: small bird, a woodcock.
Bécassine: small bird, a snipe.
Béchamel: white sauce made with butter, flour, and milk, usually flavored with onion, bay leaf, pepper, and nutmeg.
Beignet: fritter or doughnut.
de fleur de courgette: batter-fried zucchini blossom; native to Provence and the Mediterranean, now popular all over France.
Belle Hélène (poire): classic dessert of chilled poached fruit (pear) served on ice cream and topped with hot chocolate sauce.
Bellevue, en: classic presentation of whole fish, usually in aspic on a platter.
Belon: river in Brittany identified with a prized flat-shelled (*plate*) oyster.
Belondines: Brittany *creuses*, or crinkle-shelled

oysters, that are finished off in the Belon river.

Berawecka, bierewecke, bireweck, birewecka: dense, moist Christmas fruit bread stuffed with dried pears, figs, and nuts; specialty of Kaysersberg, a village in Alsace.

Bercy: fish stock–based sauce thickened with flour and butter and flavored with white wine and shallots.

Bergamot: name for both a variety of orange and a variety of pear. *Thé à la bergamote* is Earl Grey tea.

Berrichonne: garnish of bruised cabbage, glazed baby onions, chestnuts, and lean bacon named for the old province of Berry.

Betterave: beet.

Beurre: butter.

blanc: classic reduced sauce of vinegar, white wine, shallots, and butter

des Charentes: finest French butter, from the region of Poitou-Charentes along the Atlantic coast.

cru: raw cream butter.

du cru: butter given the *appellation d'origine contrôlée* pedigree.

demi-sel: lightly salted.

Echiré: brand of the finest French butter, preferred by French chefs, with an AOC pedigree, from the region of Poitou-Charentes along the Atlantic coast.

de Montpellier: classic butter sauce seasoned with olive oil, herbs, garlic, and anchovies.

noir: sauce of browned butter, lemon juice or vinegar, parsley, and sometimes capers; traditionally served with *raie,* or skate.

noisette: lightly browned butter.

vierge: whipped butter sauce with salt, pepper, and lemon juice.

Bibelskäs, bibbelskäse: fresh cheese seasoned with horseradish, herbs, and spices; specialty of Alsace.

Biche: female deer.

Bien cuit: cooked well done.

Bière: beer.

blonde: lager, light ale.

en bouteille: bottled.

à la pression: on tap.

Bifteck: steak.

Bigarade: orange sauce.

Biggareau: red firm-fleshed variety of cherry.

Bigorneau: periwinkle, tiny sea snail.

Bigoudène, à la: in the style of Bigouden, a province in Brittany; (*pommes*) baked slices of unpeeled potato; (*ragôut*) sausage stewed with bacon and potato.

Billy Bi, Billy By: cream of mussel soup, specialty of the Atlantic coast.

Biologique: organic.

Biscuit à la cuillère: ladyfinger.

Bistro: originally a café-bar serving a limited selection of simple meals in an informal setting. It is suggested that the name dates back to 1814 when occupying Russian Cossacks in Paris would demand quick service by shouting *"Bistro,"* the Russian word for "quick."

Bistrotier: bistro owner.

Blanc (de poireau): white portion (of leek).

Blanc (de volaille): usually breast (of chicken).

Blanc-manger: chilled pudding of almond milk with gelatin.

Blanquette: classic mild stew of poached veal, lamb, chicken, or seafood, enriched with an egg and cream white sauce; supposedly a dish for convalescents.

Blé (noir): wheat (buckwheat).

Blette, bette: Swiss chard.

Bleu: "blue"; cooked rare, usually for steak. See also *Truite au bleu.*

Bleu d'Auvergne: a strong, firm, moist, flattened cylinder of blue-veined cheese made from cow's milk in the Auvergne, sold wrapped in foil; still made on some farms.

Bleu de Bresse: a cylinder of mild blue-veined cow's milk cheese from the Bresse area in the Rhône-Alps region; industrially made.

Bleu de Gex: thick, savory blue-veined disc of cow's milk cheese from the Jura; made in only a handful of small dairies in the *département* of the Ain.

Bleu des Causses: a firm, pungent, flat cylinder of blue-veined cow's milk cheese, cured in cellars similar to those used in making Roquefort.

Blini: small thick pancake, usually eaten with caviar.

Boeuf: beef.

à la ficelle: beef tied with string and poached in broth.

gros sel: boiled beef, served with vegetables and coarse salt.

à la mode: beef marinated and braised in red wine, served with carrots, mushrooms, onions, and turnips.

Bohémienne, à la: gypsy style; with rice, tomatoes, onions, sweet peppers, and paprika, in various combinations.

Boisson (non) comprise: drink (not) included.

Bolet: type of wild boletus mushroom. See *Cèpe.*

Bombe: molded, layered ice cream dessert.

Bonbon: candy or sweet.

Bon-chrétien: "good Christian"; a variety of pear, also known as *poire William.*

Bondon: small cylinder of delicately flavored, mushroomy cow's milk cheese made in the Neufchâtel area in Normandy.

Bonite: a tuna, or oceanic bonito.

Bonne femme (cuisine): meat garnish of bacon, potatoes, mushrooms, and onions; fish garnish of shallots, parsley, mushrooms, and potatoes; or white wine sauce with shallots, mushrooms, and lemon juice; (home-style cooking).

Bordelaise: Bordeaux style; also refers to a brown sauce of shallots, red wine, and bone marrow.

Bouchée: "tiny mouthful"; may refer to a bite-size pastry or to a *vol-au-vent.*

Boucherie: butcher shop.

Bouchoteur: mussel fisherman; a dish containing mussels.

Boudeuses: literally, pouting; tiny oysters from Brittany that refuse to grow to normal size, iodine-rich and prized.

Boudin: technically a meat sausage, but generically any sausage-shaped mixture.

blanc: white sausage of veal, chicken, or pork.

noir: pork blood sausage.

Bouillabaisse: popular Mediterranean fish soup, most closely identified with Marseilles, ideally prepared with the freshest local fish, preferably rockfish. Traditionally might include dozens of different fish, but today generally includes the specifically local *rascasse* (scorpion fish), *Saint-Pierre* (John Dory), *fiéla* (conger eel), *galinette* (gurnard or grondin), *vive* (weever), and *baudroie* (monkfish) cooked in a broth of water, olive oil, onions, garlic, tomatoes, parsley, and saffron. The fish is served separately from the broth, which is poured over garlic-rubbed toast, and seasoned with *rouille,* which is stirred into the broth. Varied additions include boiled potatoes, orange peel, fennel, and shellfish. Expensive shellfish are often added in restaurant versions, but this practice is considered inauthentic.

Bouilli: boiled.

Bouilliture: eel stew with red wine and prunes, specialty of the Poitou-Charentes on the Atlantic coast.

Bouillon: stock or broth.

Boulangère, à la: in the style of the "baker's wife"; meat or poultry baked or braised with onions and potatoes.

Boulangerie: bakery, bread shop.

Boule: "ball"; a large round loaf of white bread, also known as a *miche.*

Boule de Picoulat: meatball from Languedoc, combining beef, pork, garlic, and eggs, traditionally served with cooked white beans.

Boulette d'Avesnes: pepper-and-tarragon-flavored cheese, made from visually defective Maroilles, formed into a cone, and colored red with paprika; named for Avesnes, a village in the north.

Bouquet: large reddish shrimp. See also *Crevette rose.*

Bouquet garni: typically fresh whole parsley, bay leaf, and thyme tied together with string and tucked into stews; the package is removed prior to serving.

Bouquetière: garnished with bouquets of vegetables.

Bourdaloue: hot poached fruit (often pear), sometimes wrapped in pastry, often served with vanilla custard.

Bourgeoise, à la: with carrots, onions, braised lettuce, celery, and bacon.

Bourguignonne, à la: Burgundy style; often with red wine, onions, mushrooms, and bacon.

Bouribot: spicy red-wine duck stew.

Bourride: a Mediterranean fish soup that generally includes a mixture of small whitefish, onions, tomatoes, garlic, herbs, and olive oil, thickened with egg yolks and *aïoli* (garlic mayonnaise); there are many variations.

Bourriole: rye flour pancake, both sweet and savory; specialty of the Auvergne.

Boutargue, poutargue: salty paste prepared from dried mullet or tuna roe, mashed with oil; specialty of Provence.

Bouton de culotte: "trouser button"; tiny buttons of goat cheese from the Lyon area; traditionally made on farms, aged until rock hard and pungent; today found in many forms, from soft and young to hard and brittle.

Braiser: to braise; to cook meat by browning in fat, then simmering in covered dish with small amount of liquid.

Branche, en: refers to whole vegetables or herbs.

Brandade (de morue): a warm garlicky purée (of salt cod) with milk or cream or oil, and sometimes mashed potatoes; specialty of Provence; currently used to denote a variety of flavored mashed potato dishes.

Brassado: a doughnut that is boiled, then baked, much like a bagel; specialty of Provence.

Brasserie: literally, a brewery; initially beer saloons which later also provided traditional Alsatian dishes. Today's brasseries are large, decorative, generally offer platters of shellfish, and remain open late.

Brayaude, gigot: leg of lamb studded with garlic, cooked in white wine, and served with red beans, braised cabbage, or chestnuts.

Brebis (fromage de): sheep (sheep's milk cheese).

Brési, Breuzi: smoked, salted, dried beef from the Jura.

Bretonne, à la: in the style of Brittany; a dish served with white beans; or may refer to a white wine sauce with carrots, leeks, and celery.

Bretzel: a pretzel; specialty of Alsace.

Brie de Meaux: "king of cheese," the flat wheel of cheese made only with raw cow's milk and aged at least four weeks; from Meaux, just east of Paris; *brie* made with pasteurized milk does not have the right to be called *brie de Meaux*.

Brie de Melun: smaller than *brie de Meaux*, another raw cow's milk cheese, aged at least one month, with a crackly rust-colored rind.

Brillat-Savarin: famed gastronome (1755-1826), coiner of food aphorisms, and author of *The Physiology of Taste;* the high-fat, supple cow's milk cheese from Normandy is named for him.

Brioche: buttery egg-enriched yeast bread.

mousseline: large, cylindrical, lighter-than-normal *brioche*.

Brocciu: soft, young, sheep's milk cheese from Corsica.

Broche, à la: spit-roasted.

Brochet(on): freshwater pike (small pike).

Brochette: cubes of meat or fish and vegetables on a skewer.

Brocoli: broccoli.

Brouet: old term for soup.

Brouillade: a mixture of ingredients as in a stew or soup; also, scrambled eggs.

Brouillé(s): scrambled, usually eggs.

Brousse: a very fresh and unsalted (thus bland) sheep's or goat's milk cheese, not unlike Italian ricotta; specialty of Nice and Marseilles.

Broutard: young goat.

Brugnon: nectarine.

Brûlé(e): "burned"; usually refers to caramelization.

Brunoise: tiny diced vegetables.

Brut: very dry or sugarless, particularly in reference to Champagne.

Buccin: large sea snail or whelk, also called *bulot*.

Bûche de Noël: Christmas cake shaped like a log (*bûche*), a sponge cake often flavored with chestnuts and chocolate.

Buffet froid: variety of dishes served cold, sometimes from a buffet.

Bugne: deep-fried yeast-dough fritter or doughnut dusted with confectioner's sugar; popular in and around Lyon at Easter.

Buisson: "bush"; generally a dish including vegetables arranged like a bush; classically a crayfish presentation.

Bulot: large sea snail or whelk, also called *buccin*.

Buron: traditional hut where cheese is made in the Auvergne mountains.

C

Cabécou(s): small, round goat's milk cheese from the southwest, sometimes made with a mix of goat's and cow's milk.

Cabillaud: fresh codfish, also currently called *morue,* known as *doguette* in the north, *bakalau* in the Basque region, *eglefin* in Provence.

Cabri: young goat.

Cacahouète, cacahouette, cacachuète: prepared peanut—roasted, dry roasted, or salted. A raw peanut is *arachide.*

Cacao: cocoa; powdered cocoa.

Cachat: a very strong goat cheese; generally a blend of various ends of leftover cheese, mixed with seasonings that might include salt, pepper, brandy, and garlic, and aged in a crock; specialty of Provence.

Caen, à la mode de: in the style of Caen, a town in Normandy; a dish cooked in Calvados and white wine and/or cider.

Café: coffee; also a bar; casual spot for simple meals and snacks.

allongé: weakened espresso, often served with a small pitcher of hot water so clients may thin the coffee themselves.

déca or ***décaféiné:*** decaffeinated coffee.

express: plain black espresso.

faux: decaffeinated coffee.

filtre: filtered American-style coffee (not available at all cafés).

glacé: iced coffee.

au lait or ***crème:*** espresso with warmed or steamed milk.

liègeois: iced coffee served with ice cream (optional) and whipped cream; also coffee ice cream with whipped cream.

noir: plain black espresso.

noisette: espresso with a tiny amount of milk.

serré: extra-strong espresso, made with half the normal amount of water.

Caféine: caffeine.

Cagouille: on the Atlantic coast, name for small *petit gris* land snail, or *escargot.*

Caille: quail.

Caillé: clotted or curdled; curds of milk.

Caillette: round pork sausage containing chopped spinach or Swiss chard, garlic, onions, parsley, bread, and egg and wrapped in *crépine* (caul fat); served hot or cold; specialty of northern Provence.

Caisse: cash register or cash desk.

Caissette: literally, "small box"; bread, *brioche,* or chocolate shaped like a small box.

Cajasse: a sort of *clafoutis* from the Dordogne, made with black cherries.

Cajou: cashew nut.

Calisson d'Aix: small, diamond-shaped iced confection of fruity almond paste on a thin film of *azyme* (unleavened bread), specialty of Aix-en-Provence.

Calmar: small squid, similar to *encornet*; with interior transparent cartilage instead of a bone. Also called *chipiron* in the southwest.

Calvados: a *département* in Normandy known for the famed apple brandy.

Camembert (de Normandie): village in Normandy that gives its name to a supple, fragrant cheese made of cow's milk.

Camomille: camomile, herb tea.

Campagnard(e) (assiette): country-style, rustic; (an informal buffet of cold meats, terrines, etc.).

Campagne, à la: country-style.

Canada: cooking apple.

Canapé: originally a slice of crustless bread; now also used to refer to a variety of hors d'oeuvre consisting of toasted or fried bread spread with forcemeat, cheese, and other flavorings.

Canard: duck.

à la presse: roast duck served with a sauce of juices obtained from pressing the carcass, combined with red wine and Cognac.

sauvage: wild duck, usually mallard.

Cancoillotte: spreadable cheese from the Jura; usually blended with milk, spices, or white wine when served.

Canelé: popular confection from Bordeaux, crenelated small cake with soft interior and crisp, dark brown exterior, often flavored with rum.

Caneton: young male duck.

Canette: young female duck.

Cannelle: cinnamon.

Cannoise, à la: in the style of Cannes.
Canon: the marrow bone.
Cantal: large cylindrical cheese made in the Auvergne from shredded and pressed curds of cow's milk.
Cantalon: smaller version of *Cantal*.
Cantaloup: cantaloupe melon.
Cantine: restaurant, cafeteria.
Capilotade: basically any leftover meat or poultry cooked to tenderness in a well-reduced sauce.
Capre: caper.
Capucine: nasturtium; the leaves and flowers are used in salads.
Carafe (d'eau): pitcher (of tap water). House wine is often offered in a *carafe*. A full *carafe* contains one liter; a *demi-carafe* contains half a liter; a *quart* contains one-fourth of a liter.
Caraïbes: Caribbean, usually denotes chocolate from the Caribbean.
Caramélisé: cooked with high heat to brown the sugar and heighten flavor.
Carbonnade: braised beef stew prepared with beer and onions; specialty of the north; also refers to a cut of beef.
Cardamome: cardamom.
Carde: white rib, or stalk, portion of Swiss chard.
Cardon: cardoon; large celery-like vegetable in the artichoke family, popular in Lyon, Provence, and the Mediterranean area.
Cargolade: a copious mixed grill of snails, lamb, pork sausage, and sometimes blood sausage, cooked over vine clippings; specialty of Catalan, an area of southern Languedoc.
Carotte: carrot.
Carpe: carp.
à la juive: braised marinated carp in aspic.
Carré d'agneau: rack (ribs) or loin of lamb; also crown roast.
Carré de porc: rack (ribs) or loin of pork; also crown roast.
Carré de veau: rack (ribs) or loin of veal; also crown roast.
Carrelet: see *Plaice*.
Carte, (à la): menu; (dishes, which are charged for individually, selected from a restaurant's full list of offerings).
Carte promotionelle or ***conseillée:*** a simple and inexpensive fixed-price meal.
Carvi (grain de): caraway (seed).
Cary: curry.
Casher: kosher.
Casse-croûte: "break bread"; slang for snack.
Casseron: cuttlefish.
Cassis (crème de): black currant (black currant liqueur).
Cassolette: usually a dish presented in a small casserole.
Cassonade: soft brown sugar; Demerara sugar.
Cassoulet: popular southwestern casserole of white beans with various combinations of sausages, duck, pork, lamb, mutton, and goose.
Cavaillon: a town in Provence, known for its small, flavorful orange-fleshed melons.
Cave (à vin): cellar (wine).
Caviar d'aubergine: cold seasoned eggplant purée.
Caviar du Puy: green lentils from Le Puy, in the Auvergne.
Cébette: a mild, leeklike vegetable, sliced and eaten raw in salads; native to Provence, but seen occasionally outside the region.
Cebiche: seviche; generally raw fish marinated in lime juice and other seasonings.
Cédrat: a variety of Mediterranean lemon.
Céleri (en branche): celery (stalk).
Céleri-rave: celeriac, celery root.
Céleri remoulade: popular first-course bistro dish of shredded celery root with tangy mayonnaise.
Cendre (sous la): ash (cooked by being buried in embers); some cheeses made in wine-producing regions are aged in the ash of burned rootstocks.
Cèpe: large, meaty wild boletus mushroom.
Céréale: grain.
Cerf: stag, or male deer.
Cerfeuil: chervil.
Cerise: cherry.
noire: black cherry.
Cerneau: walnut meat.
Cervelas: garlicky cured pork sausage; now also refers to fish and seafood sausage.
Cervelle(s): brain(s), of calf or lamb.
Cervelle de canut: a soft, fresh herbed cheese known as "silkworker's brains"; specialty of Lyon.
Céteau(x): small ocean fish, *solette* or baby sole, found in the gulf of Gascony and along the Atlantic coast.

Cévenole, à la: Cevennes style; garnished with chestnuts or mushrooms.

Chalutier: trawler; any flatfish caught with a trawl.

Champêtre: rustic; describes a simple presentation of a variety of ingredients.

Champignon: mushroom.

à la bague: parasol mushroom with a delicate flavor; also called *coulemelle*, *cocherelle*, and *grisotte*.

de bois: wild mushroom, from the woods.

de Paris: most common cultivated mushroom.

sauvage: wild mushroom.

Champvallon, côtelette d'agneau: traditional dish of lamb chops baked in alternating layers of potatoes and onions; named for a village in northern Burgundy.

Chanterelle: prized pale orange wild mushroom; also called *girolle*.

Chantilly: sweetened whipped cream.

Chaource: soft and fruity cylindrical cow's milk cheese, with a 50 percent fat content; takes its name from a village in Champagne.

Chapeau: "hat"; small round loaf of bread, topped with a little dough hat.

Chapelure: bread crumbs.

Chapon: capon, or castrated chicken.

Chapon de mer: Mediterranean fish, in the *rascasse* (scorpion-fish) family.

Charbon de bois, au: charcoal-grilled.

Charcuterie: cooked or cured meats, sausages, pâtés; also a shop where the meats are sold. From the words *chair* (meat) and *cuit* (cooked).

Charentais: variety of sweet cantaloupe, originally from the Charentes, on the Atlantic coast.

Charlotte: classic dessert in which a dish is lined with ladyfingers, filled with custard or other filling, and served cold; in the hot version, the dish is lined with crustless white bread sautéed in butter, filled with fruit compote, and baked. Also a potato.

Charolais: area of Burgundy; light-colored cattle producing high-quality beef; also, firm white cylinder of cheese made with goat's or cow's milk, or a mixture of the two.

Chartreuse: dish of braised partridge and cabbage; also herb- and spice-based liqueur made by the Chartreuse monks in the Savoie.

Chasseur: hunter; also, sauce with white wine, mushrooms, shallots, tomatoes, and herbs.

Châtaigne: chestnut, smaller than *marron*, with multiple nut meats.

Chateaubriand: thick fillet steak, traditionally served with sautéed potatoes and a sauce of white wine, dark beef stock, butter, shallots, and herbs, or with a *béarnaise* sauce.

Châtelaine, à la: elaborate garnish of artichoke hearts and chestnut purée, braised lettuce, and sautéed potatoes.

Chaud: hot or warm.

Chaud-froid: "hot-cold"; cooked poultry dish served cold, usually covered with a cooked sauce, then with aspic.

Chaudrée: Atlantic fish stew, often including sole, skate, small eels, potatoes, butter, white wine, and seasoning.

Chausson: a filled pastry turnover, sweet or savory.

Chemise, en: wrapped with pastry.

Cheval: horse, horse meat.

Cheveux d'ange: "angel's hair"; thin vermicelli pasta.

Chèvre (fromage de): goat (goat's milk cheese).

Chevreau: young goat.

Chevreuil: young roe buck or roe deer; venison.

Chevrier: small, pale green, dried kidney-shaped bean, a type of *flageolet*.

Chichi: doughnut-like deep-fried bread spirals sprinkled with sugar; often sold from trucks at open-air markets; specialty of Provence and the Mediterranean.

Chicons du Nord: Belgian endive.

Chicorée (frisée): a bitter salad green (curly endive); also chicory, a coffee substitute.

de Bruxelles: Belgian endive.

Chiffonnade: shredded herbs and vegetables, usually green.

Chinchard: also called *saurel*, scad or horse mackerel; Atlantic and Mediterranean fish similar to mackerel.

Chipiron (à l'encre): southwestern name for

small squid, or *encornet* (in its own ink).

Chipolata: small sausage.

Chips, pommes: potato chips.

Chocolat: chocolate.

amer: bittersweet chocolate, with very little sugar.

chaud: hot chocolate.

au lait: milk chocolate.

mi-amer: bittersweet chocolate, with more sugar than *chocolat amer.*

noir: used interchangeably with *chocolat amer*.

Chocolatier: chocolate maker.

Choix, au: a choice; usually meaning one may choose from several offerings.

Chorizo: highly spiced Spanish sausage.

Choron, sauce: *béarnaise* sauce with tomatoes.

Chou: cabbage.

de Bruxelles: brussels sprout.

de Milan: Savoy cabbage.

rouge: red cabbage.

vert: curly green Savoy cabbage.

Chou de mer: sea kale.

Chou-fleur: cauliflower.

Chou frisé: kale.

Chou-navet: rutabaga.

Chou-rave: kohlrabi.

Choucas: jackdaw; European blackbird, like a crow, but smaller.

Choucroute (nouvelle): sauerkraut (the season's first batch of sauerkraut, still crunchy and slightly acidic); also main dish of sauerkraut, various sausages, bacon, and pork, served with potatoes; specialty of Alsace and served in *brasseries* all over France.

Choux, pâte à: cream pastry dough.

Ciboule: spring onion, or scallion.

Ciboulette: chives.

Cidre: bottled, mildly alcoholic cider, either apple or pear.

Cigale de mer: "sea cricket"; tender, crayfish-like, blunt-nosed rock lobster.

Cîteaux: creamy, ample disc of cow's milk cheese with a rust-colored rind made by the Cistercian monks at the Abbaye de Cîteaux in Burgundy.

Citron: lemon.

Citron pressé: lemon juice served with a *carafe* of tap water and sugar, for sweetening to taste.

Citron vert: lime.

Citronnelle: lemongrass, an Asian herb.

Citrouille: pumpkin, gourd. Also called *courge, potiron, potimarron*.

Cive: spring onion.

Civelle: spaghetti-like baby eel, also called *pibale.*

Civet: stew, usually of game traditionally thickened with blood.

de lièvre: jugged hare, or wild rabbit stew.

de tripes d'oies: a stew of goose innards, sautéed in fat with onions, shallots, and garlic, then cooked in wine vinegar and diluted with water, and thickened with goose blood; from Gascony.

Clafoutis: traditional custard tart, usually made with black cherries; specialty of the southwest.

Claire: oyster; also a designation given to certain oysters to indicate they have been put in *claires*, or oyster beds in salt marshes, where they are fattened up for several months before going to market.

Clamart: Paris suburb once famous for its green peas; today a garnish of peas.

Clémentine: small tangerine, from Morocco or Spain.

Clouté: studded with.

Clovisse: variety of very tiny clam, generally from the Mediterranean.

Cocherelle: parasol mushroom with a delicate flavor; also called *champignon à la bague, coulemelle,* and *grisotte.*

Cochon (de lait): pig (suckling).

Cochonnaille(s): pork product(s); usually an assortment of sausages and/or pâtés served as a first course.

Coco blanc (rouge): type of small white (red) shell bean, both fresh and dried, popular in Provence, where it is a traditional ingredient of the vegetable *soupe au pistou*; also, coconut.

Coco de Paimpol: Cream-colored shell bean striated with purple, from Brittany, in season from July to November; the first bean in France to receive the AOC.

Cocotte: a high-sided cooking pot (casserole) with a lid; a small ramekin dish for baking and serving eggs and other preparations.

Coeur: heart.

de filet: thickest (and best) part of beef fillet, usually cut into chateaubriand steaks.

de palmier: delicate shoots of the palm tree, generally served with a *vinaigrette* as an hors d'oeuvre.

Coffre: "chest"; refers to the body of a lobster or other crustacean, or of a butchered animal.

Coiffe: traditional lacy hat; sausage patty wrapped in caul fat.

Coing: quince.

Col vert: wild ("green-collared") mallard duck.

Colbert: method of preparing fish by coating it with egg and bread crumbs and then frying.

Colère, en: "anger"; method of presenting fish in which the tail is inserted in the mouth, so it appears agitated.

Colin: hake, ocean fish related to cod; known as *merluche* in the North, *merluchon* in Brittany, *bardot* or *merlan* along the Mediterranean.

Colombe: dove.

Colza: rape, a plant of the mustard family, colorful yellow field crop grown throughout France, usually pressed into vegetable (rapeseed) oil.

Commander avant le repas, à: a selection of desserts that should be ordered when selecting first and main courses, as they require longer cooking.

Complet: filled up, with no more room for customers.

Compote: stewed fresh or dried fruit.

Compotier: fruit bowl; also stewed ftuit.

Compris: see *Service (non) compris*.

Comté: large wheel of cheese of cooked and pressed cow's milk; the best is made of raw milk and aged for six months, still made by independent cheesemakers in the Jura mountains.

Concassé: coarsely chopped.

Concombre: cucumber.

Conférence: a variety of pear.

Confiserie: candy, sweet, or confection; a candy shop.

Confit: a preserve, generally pieces of duck, goose, or pork cooked and preserved in their own fat; also fruit or vegetables preserved in sugar, alcohol, or vinegar.

Confiture: jam.

Confiture de vieux garçon: varied fresh fruits macerated in alcohol.

Congeler: to freeze.

Congre: conger eel, a large ocean fish resembling a freshwater eel (*anguille*); often used in fish stews.

Conseillé: advised, recommended.

Consommation(s): "consumption"; drinks, meals, and snacks available in a café or bar.

Consommé: clear soup.

Contre-filet: cut of sirloin taken above the loin on either side of the backbone, tied for roasting or braising (can also be cut for grilling).

Conversation: puff pastry tart with sugar glazing and an almond or cream filling.

Copeau(x): shaving(s), such as from chocolate, cheese, or vegetables.

Coq (au vin): mature male chicken (stewed in wine sauce).

au vin jaune: chicken cooked in the sherry-like *vin jaune* of the region, with cream, butter, and tarragon, often garnished with morels; specialty of the Jura.

Coq de bruyère: wood grouse.

Coque: cockle, a tiny, mild-flavored, clamlike shellfish.

Coque, à la: served in a shell. See *Oeuf à la coque*.

Coquelet: young male chicken.

Coquillage(s): shellfish.

Coquille: shell.

Coquille Saint-Jacques: sea scallop.

Corail: coral-colored egg sac, found in scallops, spiny lobster, and crayfish.

Corb: a Mediterranean bluefish.

Coriandre: coriander; either the fresh herb (cilantro) or dried seeds.

Corne d'abondance: "horn of plenty"; dark brown wild mushroom, also called *trompette de la mort*.

Cornet: cornet-shaped; usually refers to foods rolled conically; also an ice cream cone, and a conical pastry filled with cream.

Cornichon: gherkin; tiny tart cucumber pickle.

Côte d'agneau: lamb chop.

Côte de boeuf: beef blade or rib steak.

Côte de veau: veal chop.

Côtelette: thin chop or cutlet.

Cotriade: a fish stew, usually including mackerel, whiting, conger eel, sorrel, butter, potatoes, and vinegar; specialty of Brittany.

Cou d'oie (de canard) farci: neck skin of goose (or duck), stuffed with meat and spices, much like sausage.

Coulant: refers to runny cheese.

Coulemelle: parasol mushroom with a delicate flavor; also called *champignon à la bague, cocherelle,* and *grisotte.*

Coulibiac: classic, elaborate, hot Russian pâté, usually layers of salmon, rice, hard-cooked eggs, mushrooms, and onions, wrapped in *brioche.*

Coulis: purée of raw or cooked vegetables or fruit.

Coulommiers: town in the Ile-de-France that gives its name to a supple, fragrant disc of cow's milk cheese, slightly larger than Camembert.

Courge (muscade): generic term for squash or gourd (bright orange pumpkin).

Courgette: zucchini.

Couronne: "crown"; ring or circle, usually of bread.

Court-bouillon: broth, or aromatic poaching liquid.

Couscous: granules of semolina, or hard wheat flour; also refers to a hearty North African dish that includes the steamed grain, broth, vegetables, meats, hot sauce, and sometimes chickpeas and raisins.

Couteau: razor clam.

Couvert: a place setting, including dishes, silver, glassware, and linen.

Couverture: bittersweet chocolate high in cocoa butter; used for making the shiniest chocolates.

Crabe: crab.

Crambe: sea kale, or *chou de mer.*

Cramique: *brioche* with raisins or currants; specialty of the north.

Crapaudine: preparation of grilled poultry or game bird with backbone removed.

Craquant: crunchy.

Craquelot: smoked herring.

Crécy: a dish garnished with carrots.

Crémant: sparkling wine.

Crème: cream.

aigre: sour cream.

anglaise: light egg-custard cream.

brûlée: rich custard dessert with a top of caramelized sugar.

caramel: vanilla custard with caramel sauce.

catalane: creamy anise-flavored custard from the southern Languedoc.

chantilly: sweetened whipped cream.

épaisse: thick cream.

fleurette: liquid heavy cream.

fouettée: whipped cream.

fraîche: thick sour, heavy cream.

pâtissière: custard filling for pastries and cakes.

plombières: custard filled with fresh fruits and egg whites.

Crémerie: creamery; a dairy products store, stall, or counter.

Crêpe: thin pancake.

Crêpes Suzette: hot *crêpe* dessert flamed with orange liqueur.

Crépine: caul fat.

Crépinette: traditionally, a small sausage patty wrapped in caul fat; today boned poultry wrapped in caul fat.

Cresson(ade): watercress (watercress sauce).

Crête (de coq): (cock's) comb.

Creuse: elongated, crinkle-shelled oyster.

Crevette: shrimp.

grise: tiny soft-fleshed shrimp that turns gray when cooked.

rose: small firm-fleshed shrimp that turns red when cooked; when large, called *bouquet.*

Crique: potato pancake from the Auvergne.

Criste marine: edible algae.

Croque au sel, à la: served raw, with a small bowl of coarse salt for seasoning; tiny purple artichokes and cherry tomatoes are served this way.

Croque-madame: open-face sandwich of ham and cheese with an egg grilled on top.

Croque-monsieur: toasted ham and cheese sandwich.

Croquembouche: *choux* pastry rounds filled with cream and coated with a sugar glaze, often served in a conical tower at special events.

Croquette: ground meat, fish, fowl, or vegetables bound with eggs or sauce, shaped into various forms, usually coated in bread crumbs and deep fried.

Crosne: small, unusual tuber with a subtle artichoke-like flavor; known as a Chinese or Japanese artichoke.

Crottin de Chavignol: small flattened ball of goat's milk cheese from the Loire valley.

Croustade: usually small pastry-wrapped dish; also regional southwestern pastry filled with prunes and/or apples.

Croûte (en): crust; (in) pastry.

Croûte de sel (en): (in) a salt crust.
Croûtons: small cubes of toasted or fried bread.
Cru: raw.
Crudité: raw vegetable.
Crustacé(s): crustacean(s).
Cuillière (à la): (to be eaten with a) spoon.
Cuisse (de poulet): leg or thigh (chicken drumstick).
Cuissot, cuisseau: haunch of veal, venison, or wild boar.
Cuit: cooked.
Cul: haunch or rear, usually of red meat.
Culotte: rump, usually of beef.
Cultivateur: "truck farmer"; fresh vegetable soup.
Curcuma: turmeric.
Cure-dent: toothpick.

D

Damier: "checkerboard"; arrangement of vegetables or other ingredients in alternating colors like a checkerboard; also, a cake with such a pattern of light and dark pieces.
Dariole: truncated cone- or oval-shaped baking mold.
Darne: a rectangular portion of fish fillet; also a fish steak, usually of salmon.
Dartois: puff pastry rectangles layered with an almond cream filling as a dessert, or stuffed with meat or fish as an hors-d'oeuvre.
Datte (de mer): date (date-shaped prized wild Mediterranean mussel).
Daube: a stew, usually of beef, lamb, or mutton, with red wine, onions, and/or tomatoes; specialty of many regions, particularly Provence and the Atlantic coast.
Dauphin: cow's milk cheese shaped like a *dauphin*, or dolphin; from the north.
Daurade: sea bream, similar to porgy, the most prized of a group of ocean fish known as *dorade.*
Décaféiné or ***déca:*** decaffeinated coffee.
Décortiqué(e): shelled or peeled.
Dégustation: tasting or sampling.
Déjeuner: lunch.
Demi: half; also, an 8-ounce (25-cl) glass of beer; also, a half-bottle of wine.
Demi-baguette: half a *baguette.*
Demi-deuil: "in half mourning"; poached (usually chicken) with sliced truffles inserted under the skin; also, sweetbreads with a truffled white sauce.
Demi-glace: concentrated beef-based sauce lightened with *consommé,* or a lighter brown sauce.
Demi-sec: usually refers to goat cheese that is in the intermediate aging stage between one extreme of soft and fresh and the other extreme of hard and aged.
Demi-sel (beurre): lightly salted (butter).
Demi-tasse: small cup; after-dinner coffee cup.
Demoiselle de canard: marinated raw duck tenderloin; also called *mignon de canard.*
Demoiselles de Cherbourg: small lobsters from the town of Cherbourg in Normandy, cooked in a *court-bouillon* and served in cooking juices. Also, restaurant term for Breton lobsters weighing 300 to 400 grams (10 to 13 ounces).
Dent, denté: one of a generic group of Mediterranean fish known as *dorade,* similar to porgy.
Dentelle: "lace"; a portion of meat or fish so thinly sliced as to suggest a resemblance. Also, large lace-thin sweet *crêpe.*
Dents-de-lion: dandelion salad green; also called *pissenlit.*
Dés: diced pieces.
Désossé: boned.
Diable: "devil"; method of preparing poultry with a peppery sauce, often mustard-based. Also, a round pottery casserole.
Dieppoise: Dieppe style; usually with white wine, mussels, shrimp, mushrooms, and cream.
Digestif: general term for spirits served after dinner; such as Armagnac, Cognac, *marc, eau-de-vie.*
Dijonnaise: Dijon style; usually with mustard.
Dinde: turkey hen.
Dindon(neau): turkey (young turkey).
Dîner: dinner; to dine.
Diot: pork sausage cooked in wine, often served with a potato gratin; specialty of the Savoie.
Discrétion, à: on menus usually refers to wine, which may be consumed—without limit—at the customer's discretion.
Dodine: cold stuffed boned poultry.

Dorade: generic name for group of ocean fish, the most prized of which is *daurade,* similar to porgy.
Doré: browned until golden.
Dos: back; also the meatiest portion of fish.
Doucette: see *Mâche.*
Douceur: sweet or dessert.
Douillon, duillon: a whole pear wrapped and cooked in pastry; specialty of Normandy.
Doux, douce: sweet.
Doyenné de Comice: a variety of pear.
Dugléré: white flour-based sauce with shallots, white wine, tomatoes, and parsley.
Dur (oeuf): hard (hard-cooked egg).
Duxelles: minced mushrooms and shallots sautéed in butter, then mixed with cream.

E

Eau: water
gazeuse: carbonated water.
minérale: mineral water.
du robinet: tap water.
de source: spring water.
Eau-de-vie: literally, "water of life"; brandy, usually fruit-based.
Ecaille (d'huître): scale, shell (oyster).
Echalote (gris): shallot (prized purplish shallot).
Echalote banane: banana-shaped onion.
Echine: sparerib.
Eclade de moules: mussels roasted beneath a fire of pine needles; specialty of the Atlantic coast.
Ecrasé: crushed; with fruit, pressed to release juice.
Ecrevisse: freshwater crayfish.
Effiloché: frayed, shredded.
Eglantine: wild rose jam; specialty of Alsace.
Eglefin, égrefin, aiglefin: small fresh haddock, a type of cod.
Elzekaria: soup made with green beans, cabbage, and garlic; specialty of the Basque region.
Embeurré de chou: buttery cooked cabbage.
Emincé: thin slice, usually of meat.
Emmental: large wheel of cooked and pressed cow's milk cheese, very mild in flavor, with large interior holes; made in large commercial dairies in the Jura.
Emondé: skinned by blanching, such as almonds, tomatoes.
En sus: see *Service en sus.*
Enchaud: pork fillet with garlic; specialty of Dordogne.
Encornet: small squid, also called *calmar*; in Basque region called *chipiron.*
Encre: squid ink.
Endive: Belgian endive; also chicory salad green.
Entier, entière: whole, entire.
Entrecôte: beef rib steak.
maître d'hôtel: beef rib steak with sauce of red wine and shallots.
Entrée: first course.
Entremets: dessert.
Epais(se): thick.
Epaule: shoulder (of veal, lamb, mutton, or pork).
Epeautre: poor man's wheat from Provence; spelt.
Eperlan: smelt or whitebait, usually fried, often imported but still found in the estuaries of the Loire.
Epi de maïs: ear of sweet corn.
Epice: spice.
Epigramme: classic dish of grilled breaded lamb chop and a piece of braised lamb breast shaped like a chop, breaded, and grilled; crops up on modern menus as an elegant dish of breaded and fried baby lamb chops paired with lamb sweetbreads and tongue.
Epinard: spinach.
Epine vinette: highbush cranberry.
Epoisses: village in Burgundy that gives its name to a buttery disc of cow's milk cheese with a strong, smooth taste and rust-colored rind.
blanc: fresh white Epoisses cheese.
Equille: sand eel, a long silvery fish that buries itself in the sand; eaten fried on the Atlantic coast.
Escabèche: a Provençal and southwestern preparation of small fish, usually sardines or *rouget,* in which the fish are browned in oil, then marinated in vinegar and herbs and served very cold. Also, raw fish marinated in lemon or lime juice and herbs.
Escalope: thin slice of meat or fish.
Escargot: land snail.
de Bourgogne: land snail prepared with butter, garlic, and parsley.
petit-gris: small land snail.
Escarole: bitter salad green of the chicory family with thick broad-lobed leaves, found in both flat and round heads; also called *scarole.*
Espadon: swordfish found in the gulf of Gascony, the Atlantic, and the Mediterranean.

Espagnole, à l': Spanish style; with tomatoes, peppers, onions, and garlic.

Estival: summer, used to denote seasonality of ingredients.

Estoficado: a purée-like blend of dried codfish, olive oil, tomatoes, sweet peppers, black olives, potatoes, garlic, onions, and herbs; also called *stockfish niçoise*; specialty of Nice.

Estofinado: a purée-like blend of dried codfish, potatoes, garlic, parsley, eggs, walnut oil, and milk, served with triangles of toast; specialty of the Auvergne.

Estouffade à la provençale: beef stew with onions, garlic, carrots, and orange zest.

Estragon: tarragon.

Etoile: star; star-shaped.

Etouffé, étuvé: literally "smothered"; method of cooking very slowly in a tightly covered pan with almost no liquid.

Etrille: small swimming crab.

Express: espresso coffee.

F

Façon (à ma): (my) way of preparing a dish.

Fagot: "bundle"; meat shaped into a small ball.

Faisan: pheasant.

Faisandé: game that has been hung to age.

Fait: usually refers to a cheese that has been well aged and has character—runny if it's a Camembert, hard and dry if it's a goat cheese; also means ready to eat.

Fait, pas trop: refers to a cheese that has been aged for a shorter time and is blander; also for a cheese that will ripen at home.

Falette: veal breast stuffed with bacon and vegetables, browned, and poached in broth; specialty of the Auvergne.

Fanes: green tops of root vegetables such as carrots, radishes, turnips.

Far: Breton sweet or savory pudding-cakes; the most common, similar to *clafoutis* from the Dordogne, is made with prunes.

Farci: stuffed.

Farigoule(tte): Provençal name for wild thyme.

Farine: flour.

d'avoine: oat flour.

de blé: wheat flour; white flour.

complète: whole-wheat flour.

de maïs: corn flour.

de sarrasin: buckwheat flour.

de seigle: rye flour.

de son: bran flour.

Faux filet: sirloin steak.

Favorite d'artichaut: classic vegetable dish of artichoke stuffed with asparagus, covered with a cheese sauce, and browned.

Favou(ille): in Provence, tiny male (female) crab often used in soups.

Fenouil: fennel.

Fer à cheval: "horseshoe"; a *baguette* that has that shape.

Féra, feret: salmon-like lake fish, found in Lac Léman, in the Morvan, in Burgundy, and in the Auvergne.

Ferme (fermier, fermière): farm (farmer); in cheese, refers to farm-made cheese, often used to mean raw-milk cheese; in chickens, refers to free-range chickens.

Fermé: closed.

Fernkase: young cheese shaped like a flying saucer and sprinkled with coarsely ground pepper; specialty of Alsace.

Feu de bois, au: cooked over a wood fire.

Feuille de chêne: oak-leaf lettuce.

Feuille de vigne: vine leaf.

Feuilletage (en): (in) puff pastry.

Feuilletée: puff pastry.

Fève (févette): broad, fava, coffee, or cocoa bean; also, the porcelain favor baked into the *galette des rois*.

Fiadone: Corsican flan made from cheese and oranges.

Ficelle (boeuf à la): "string"; (beef suspended on a string and poached in broth). Also, small thin *baguette*. Also, a small bottle of wine, as in *ficelle* of Beaujolais.

Ficelle picarde: thin *crêpe* wrapped around a slice of ham and topped with a cheesy cream sauce; specialty of Picardy, in the north.

Figue: fig.

Filet (de hareng): fillet (of herring).

Financier: small rectangular almond cake.

Financière: Madeira sauce with truffle juice.

Fine de claire: elongated crinkle-shelled oyster

that stays in fattening beds (*claires*) a minimum of two months.

Fines herbes: mixture of herbs, usually chervil, parsley, chives, tarragon.

Flageolet: small white or pale green kidney-shaped dried bean.

Flagnarde, flaugnarde, flognarde: hot, fruit-filled batter cake made with eggs, flour, milk, and butter, and sprinkled with sugar before serving; specialty of the southwest.

Flamande, à la: Flemish style; usually with stuffed cabbage leaves, carrots, turnips, potatoes, and bacon.

Flamber: to burn off the alcohol by igniting. Usually the brandies or other liqueurs to be flambéed are warmed first, then lit as they are poured into the dish.

Flamiche (au Maroilles): a vegetable tart with rich bread dough crust, commonly filled with leeks, cream, and cheese; specialty of Picardy, in the north; (filled with cream, egg, butter, and Maroilles cheese).

Flammekueche: thin-crusted savory tart, much like a rectangular pizza, covered with cream, onions, and bacon; also called *tarte flambée*; specialty of Alsace.

Flan: sweet or savory tart. Also, a crustless custard pie.

Flanchet: flank of beef or veal, used generally in stews.

Flétan: halibut, found in the English Channel and North Sea.

Fleur: flower.

de courgette: zucchini blossom.

Fleur de sel: fine, delicate sea salt, from Brittany or the Camargue.

Fleuron: puff pastry crescent.

Florentine: with spinach. Also, a cookie of *nougatine* and candied fruit brushed with a layer of chocolate.

Flûte: "flute"; usually a very thin *baguette;* also, form of champagne glass.

Foie: liver.

blond de volaille: chicken liver; also sometimes a chicken-liver *mousse.*

de veau: calf's liver.

Foie gras d'oie (de canard): liver of fattened goose (duck).

Foin (dans le): (cooked in) hay.

Fond: cooking juices from meat, used to make sauces. Also bottom, base.

Fond d'artichaut: heart and base of an artichoke.

Fondant: "melting"; refers to cooked, worked sugar that is flavored, then used for icing cakes. Also, the bittersweet chocolate high in cocoa butter used for making the shiniest chocolates. Also, puréed meat, fish, or vegetables shaped in *croquettes.*

Fondu: melted.

Fontainebleau: creamy white fresh dessert cheese from the Ile-de-France.

Forestière: garnish of wild mushrooms, bacon, and potatoes.

Fouace: a kind of *brioche;* specialty of the Auvergne.

Fouchtrou: cow's milk cheese from the Auvergne, made when there is not enough milk to make an entire wheel of Cantal.

Foudjou: a pungent goat cheese spread, a blend of fresh and aged grated cheese mixed with salt, pepper, brandy, and garlic and cured in a crock; specialty of northern Provence.

Fougasse: a crusty lattice-like bread made of *baguette* dough or puff pastry, often flavored with anchovies, black olives, herbs, spices, or onions; specialty of Provence and the Mediterranean. Also, a sweet bread of Provence flavored with orange-flower water, oil, and sometimes almonds.

Four (au): (baked in an) oven.

Fourme d'Ambert: cylindrical blue-veined cow's milk cheese, made in dairies around the town of Ambert in the Auvergne.

Fourré: stuffed or filled.

Foyot: classic sauce made of *béarnaise* with meat glaze.

Frais, fraîche: fresh or chilled.

Fraise: strawberry.

des bois: wild strawberry.

Framboise: raspberry.

Française, à la: classic garnish of peas with lettuce, small white onions, and parsley.

Frangipane: almond custard filling.

Frappé: usually refers to a drink served very cold or with ice, often shaken.

Frémi: "quivering"; often refers to barely cooked oysters.

Friandise: sweetmeat, petit four.

Fricadelle: fried minced meat patty.

Fricandeau: thinly sliced veal or a rump roast, braised with vegetables and white wine.

Fricassée: classically, ingredients braised in wine sauce or butter with cream added; currently denotes any mixture of ingredients—fish or meat—stewed or sautéed.

Fricot (de veau): veal shoulder simmered in white wine with vegetables.

Frisé: "curly"; usually curly endive, the bitter salad green of the chicory family sold in enormous round heads.

Frit: fried.

Frite: French fry.

Fritons: coarse pork *rillettes* or a minced spread which includes organ meats.

Fritot: small organ meat fritter, where meat is partially cooked, then marinated in oil, lemon juice, and herbs, dipped in batter and fried just before serving; also can refer to any small fried piece of meat or fish.

Friture: fried food; also a preparation of small fried fish, usually white-bait or smelt.

Froid(e): cold.

Fromage: cheese.

d'alpage: cheese made in mountain pastures during the prime summer milking period.

blanc: a smooth low-fat cheese similar to cottage cheese.

Echourgnac: delicately flavored, ocher-skinned cheese made of cow's milk by the monks at the Echourgnac monastery in the Dordogne.

fort: pungent cheese.

frais: smooth, runny, fresh cheese, like a cottage cheese.

frais, bien égouté: well-drained fresh cheese.

maigre: low-fat cheese.

Fromage de tête: headcheese, usually pork.

Fromagerie: cheese shop.

Fruit confit: whole fruit preserved in sugar.

Fruits de mer: seafood.

Fumé: smoked.

Fumet: fish stock.

G

GAEC (groupement agricole d'exploitation en commun): a farm run as a partnership by two to ten farmers.

Galantine: classic preparation of boned meat or whole poultry that is stuffed or rolled, cooked, then glazed with gelatin and served cold.

Galette: round flat pastry, pancake, or cake; can also refer to pancake-like savory preparations; in Brittany usually a savory buckwheat *crêpe*, known as *blé noir*.

bressane or ***de Pérouges:*** cream and sugar tart from the Bresse area of the Rhône-Alpes.

des rois: puff pastry filled with almond pastry cream, traditional Twelfth Night celebration cake.

Galinette: tub gurnard, Mediterranean fish of the mullet family.

Gamba: large prawn.

Ganache: classically a rich mixture of chocolate and *crème fraîche* used as a filling for cakes and chocolate truffles; currently may also include such flavorings as wild strawberries and cinnamon.

Garbure: a hearty stew that includes cabbage, beans, and salted or preserved duck, goose, turkey or pork; specialty of the southwest.

Gardiane: stew of beef or bull (*toro*) meat with bacon, onions, garlic, and black olives; served with rice; specialty of the Camargue, in Provence.

Gargouillau: pear cake or tart; specialty of northern Auvergne.

Garni: garnished.

Garniture: garnish.

Garriguette: elongated, pale red, slightly acidic variety of strawberry.

Gasconnade: roast leg of lamb with garlic and anchovies; specialty of the southwest.

Gaspacho: a cold soup, usually containing tomatoes, cucumber, onions, and sweet peppers; originally of Spanish origin.

Gâteau: cake.

basque: a chewy sweet cake filled with pastry cream or, historically, with black cherry jam; also called *pastiza*; specialty of the Basque region.

breton: a rich round pound cake; specialty of Brittany.

opéra: classic almond sponge cake layered with coffee and chocolate butter cream and covered with a sheet of chocolate; seen in every pastry shop window.

Paris-Brest: a ring-shaped cake made from cream puff (*chou*) pastry, filled with praline cream and coated with flaked almonds. Said to have been created in the late 19th century to mark the first bicycle race from Paris to Brest, the ring shape evoking the bicycle wheel.

Saint-Honoré: classic cake of *choux* puffs dipped in caramel and set atop a cream-filled *choux* crown on a pastry base.

Gaude: thick corn-flour porridge served hot, or cold and sliced, with cream.

Gaufre: waffle.

Gave: southwestern term for mountain stream; indicates fish from the streams of the area.

Gayette: small sausage patty made with pork liver and bacon, wrapped in caul fat and bacon.

Gelée: aspic.

Gendarme: salted and smoked herring.

Genièvre: juniper berry.

Génoise: sponge cake.

Gentiane: gentian; a liqueur made from this mountain flower.

Germiny: garnish of sorrel. Also, sorrel and cream soup.

Germon: albacore or long-fin tuna.

Gésier: gizzard.

Gibassier: round sweet bread from Provence, often flavored with lemon or orange zest, orange-flower water, and/or almonds. Also sometimes called *fougasse* or *pompe à l'huile*.

Gibelotte: *fricassée* of rabbit in red or white wine.

Gibier: game, sometimes designated as *gibier à plume* (feathered) or *gibier à poil* (furry).

Gigot (de pré salé): usually a leg of lamb (lamb grazed on the salt meadows along the Atlantic and Normandy coasts).

Gigot de mer: a preparation, usually of large pieces of monkfish (*lotte*) oven-roasted like a leg of lamb.

Gigue (de): haunch (of) certain game meats.

Gillardeau: prized oyster raised in Normandy and finished in *claires*, or fattening beds, on the Atlantic coast.

Gingembre: ginger.

Girofle: clove.

Girolle: prized pale orange wild mushroom; also called *chanterelle*.

Givré; orange givré: frosted; orange sherbet served in orange shell.

Glace: ice cream.

Glacé: iced, crystallized, or glazed.

Gnocchi: dumplings made of *choux* paste, potatoes, or semolina.

Goret: young pig.

Gougère: cheese-flavored *choux* pastry.

Goujon: small catfish; generic name for a number of small fish. Also, preparation in which the central part of a larger fish is coated with bread crumbs, then deep-fried.

Goujonnette: generally used to describe a small piece of fish, such as sole, usually fried.

Gourmandise(s): weakness for sweet things; (sweetmeats or candies).

Gousse d'ail: clove of garlic.

Gousse de vanille: vanilla bean.

Goût: taste.

Goûter (le): to taste, to try; (children's afternoon snack).

Graine de moutarde: mustard seed.

Graisse: fat.

Graisserons: crisply fried pieces of duck or goose skin; cracklings.

Grand crème: large or double espresso with milk.

Grand cru: top-ranking wine.

Grand veneur: "chief huntsman"; usually a brown sauce for game, with red currant jelly.

Granité: a type of sherbet; a sweetened, flavored ice.

Grappe (de raisins): cluster; bunch (of grapes).

Gras (marché au): fatty (market of fattened poultry and their livers).

Gras-double: tripe baked with onions and white wine.

Gratin: crust formed on top of a dish when browned in broiler or oven; also the dish in which such food is cooked.

dauphinoise: baked casserole of sliced potatoes, usually with cream, milk, and sometimes cheese and/or eggs.

savoyarde: baked casserole of sliced potatoes, usually with *bouillon*, cheese, and butter.

Gratiné: having a crusty, browned top.

Gratinée lyonnaise: *bouillon* flavored with port, garnished with beaten egg, topped with cheese, and browned under a broiler.

Grattons, grattelons: crisply fried pieces of pork, goose, or duck skin; cracklings.

Gratuit: free.

Grecque, à la: cooked in seasoned mixture of oil, lemon juice, and water; refers to cold vegetables, usually mushrooms.

Grelette, sauce: cold sauce with a base of whipped cream.

Grelot: small white bulb onion.

Grenade: pomegranate.

Grenadin: small veal scallop.

Grenaille: refers to small, bite-size new potato of any variety.

Grenouille (cuisse de): frog (leg).

Gressini: breadsticks, seen along the Côte-d'Azur.

Gribiche, sauce: mayonnaise with capers, cornichons, hard-cooked eggs, and herbs.

Grillade: grilled meat.

Grillé: grilled.

Griotte: shiny, slightly acidic, reddish black cherry.

Gris de gris: literally, "gray from gray." Term applied to pale-colored rosé wine generally obtained by following the white wine method using red grapes, that is, pressed before fermentation begins (unlike rosé, which ferments briefly before pressing).

Grisotte: parasol mushroom with a delicate flavor; also called *champignon à la bague, cocherelle,* and *coulemelle*.

Grive: thrush.

Groin d'ane: "donkey's snout"; Lyonnaise name for a bitter winter salad green similar to dandelion greens.

Grondin: red gurnard, a bony ocean fish, a member of the mullet family, used in fish stews such as *bouillabaisse*.

Gros sel: coarse salt.

Groseille: red currant.

Gruyère: strictly speaking, cheese from the Gruyère area of Switzerland; in France, generic name for a number of hard, mild, cooked cheeses from the Jura, including Comté, Beaufort, and Emmental.

Gyromite: group of wild mushrooms, or gyromitra, known as false morels.

H

Hachis: minced or chopped meat or fish preparation.

Haddock: small fresh cod that have been salted and smoked.

Hareng: herring, found in the Atlantic, the English Channel (the best between Dunkerque and Fécamp), and the mouth of the Gironde river.

baltique, bismark: marinated herring.

bouffi: herring that is salted, then smoked.

à l'huile: herring cured in oil, usually served with a salad of warm sliced potatoes.

pec: freshly salted young herring.

roll-mop: marinated herring rolled around a small pickle.

saur: smoked herring.

Haricot: bean.

beurre: yellow bean.

blancs (à la Bretonne): white beans, usually dried; (white beans in a sauce of onions, tomatoes, garlic, and herbs).

gris: green string bean mottled with purplish black; also called *pélandron;* a specialty of the Côte-d'Azur.

de mouton: stew of mutton and white beans (also called *halicots*).

rouge: red kidney bean; also, preparation of red beans in red wine.

sec: dried bean.

vert: green bean, usually fresh.

Hâtelet, attelet: decorative skewer; currently used to mean meat or fish cooked on a skewer.

Haut de gigot: upper portion of a leg of lamb, near the saddle.

Herbes de Provence: mixture of thyme, rosemary, summer savory, and bay leaf, often dried and blended.

Hirondelle: swallow.

Hochepot: a thick stew, usually of oxtail; specialty of Flanders, in the north.

Hollandaise: sauce of butter, egg yolks, and lemon juice.

Homard (à l'Amoricaine, à l'Américaine): lobster (a classic dish of many variations, in which lobster is cut into sections and browned, then simmered with shallots, minced onions, tomatoes, Cognac, and white wine; served with a sauce of the reduced cooking liquid, enriched with butter).

Hongroise, à la: Hungarian style; usually with paprika and cream.

Hors-d'oeuvre: appetizer; can also refer to a first course.

Hortillon: picturesque market garden plot built between crisscrossed canals on the outskirts of Amiens, a city in the north.

Huile: oil.

d'arachide: peanut oil.

de colza: rapeseed oil.

de maïs: corn oil.

de noisette: hazelnut oil.

de noix: walnut oil.

d'olive (extra vierge): olive oil (extra virgin, or the first cold pressing).

de pépins de raisins: grapeseed oil.

de sésame: sesame oil.

de tournesol: sunflower oil.

Huître: oyster.

Hure de porc or ***de marcassin:*** head of pig or boar; usually refers to headcheese preparation.

Hure de saumon: a salmon "headcheese," or pâté, prepared with salmon meat, not actually the head.

Hysope: hyssop; fragrant, mintlike thistle found in Provence, used in salads and in cooking.

I

Ile flottante: "floating island"; most commonly used interchangeably with *oeufs à la neige,* poached meringue floating in *crème anglaise;* classically, a layered cake covered with whipped cream and served with custard sauce.

Impératrice, l': usually a rice pudding dessert with candied fruit.

Imperiale: variety of plum. Also, a large bottle for wine, holding about 4 quarts (4 liters).

Impériale, à l': classic haute cuisine garnish of mussels, cockscombs, crayfish, and other extravagant ingredients.

Indienne, à l': East Indian style, usually with curry powder.

Infusion: herb tea.

Isman bayaldi, imam bayaldi: "the priest fainted" in Turkish; a dish of eggplant stuffed with sautéed onions, tomatoes, and spices; served cold.

J

Jalousie: "venetian blind"; classic small, latticed, flaky pastry filled with almond paste and spread with jam.

Jambon: ham; also refers to the leg, usually of pork, but also of poultry.

d'Auvergne: raw, dry, salt-cured smoked ham.

de Bayonne: raw, dry salt-cured ham, very pale in color.

blanc: lightly salted unsmoked, or very lightly smoked ham, served cooked; sold, cold, in *charcuteries* as *jambon de Paris, glacé,* or *demi-sel.*

de Bourgogne: See *Jambon persillé.*

cru: salted or smoked ham that has been cured but not cooked.

cuit: cooked ham.

fumé: smoked ham.

de montagne: any mountain ham, cured according to local custom.

à l'os: ham with the bone in.

de Paris: pale, lightly salted, cooked ham.

de Parme: Italian prosciutto from Parma, air-dried and salt-cured ham, sliced thin and served raw.

pata négra: (literally black-feet ham) prized ham from Spain.

de pays: any country ham, cured according to local custom.

persillé: cold cooked ham, cubed and preserved in parsleyed gelatin, usually sliced from a terrine; a specialty of Burgundy.

salé: salt-cured ham.

sec: dried ham.

de Westphalie: German Westphalian ham, raw, cured, and smoked.

de York: smoked English-style ham, usually poached.

Jambon de poulet: boned stuffed chicken leg.

Jambon d'oie (or ***de canard):*** breast of fattened goose (or duck), smoked, salted, or sugar cured, somewhat resembling ham in flavor.

Jambonneau: cured ham shank or pork knuckle.

Jambonnette: boned and stuffed knuckle of ham or poultry.

Jardinière: refers to a garnish of fresh cooked vegetables.

Jarret (de veau, de porc, de boeuf): knuckle (of veal or pork), shin (of beef).

Jerez: refers to sherry; also spelled *Xérès*.

Jésus de Morteau: plump smoked pork sausage that takes its name from the town of Morteau in the Jura; distinctive because a wooden peg is tied in the sausage casing on one end; traditionally, the sausages eaten at Christmas, hence its name; also called *saucisson de Morteau*.

Jeune: young.

Jonchée: rush basket in which certain fresh sheep's or goat's milk cheeses of Poitou (along the Atlantic coast) are contained; thus, by extension, the cheese itself.

Joue: cheek.

Julienne: cut into slivers, usually vegetables or meat.

Jurançon: district in the Béarn, the area around Pau in southwestern France, known for its sweet and spicy white wine.

Jus: juice.

K

Kaki: persimmon.

Kari: variant spelling of *cary*.

Kiev: deep-fried breast of chicken stuffed with herb and garlic butter.

Kir: an *apéritif* made with *crème de cassis* (black currant liqueur) and most commonly dry white wine, but sometimes red wine.

royal: a Kir made with Champagne.

Kirsch: *eau-de-vie* of wild black cherries.

Knepfla: Alsatian dumpling, sometimes fried.

Kougelhoph, hougelhof, kouglof, kugelhoph: sweet crown-shaped yeast cake, with almonds and raisins; specialty of Alsace.

Kouigh-amann: sweet, buttery pastry from Brittany.

Kummel: caraway seed liqueur.

L

Lactaire: the edible *lactaire pallidus* mushroom, also called *sanguine*. Apricot-colored, with red, blood-colored juices when raw.

Laguiole: Cantal cheese from the area around the village of Laguiole, in southern Auvergne, still made in rustic huts.

Lait: milk.

demi-écremé: semi-skimmed milk.

écremé: skimmed milk.

entier: whole milk.

ribot: from Brittany, buttermilk, served with *crêpes*.

stérilizé: milk heated to a higher temperature than pasteurized milk, so that it stays fresh for several weeks.

Laitance: soft roe (often of herring), or eggs.

Laitier: made of or with milk; also denotes a commercially made product as opposed to *fermier*, meaning farm-made.

Laitue: lettuce.

Lamelle: very thin strip.

Lamproie (à la bordelaise): lamprey eel, ocean fish that swim into rivers along the Atlantic in springtime (hearty stew of lamprey eel and leeks in red wine).

Lançon: tiny fish, served fried.

Landaise, à la: from the Landes in southwestern France; classically a garnish of garlic, pine nuts, and goose fat.

Langouste: clawless spiny lobster or rock lobster; sometimes called crawfish, and mistakenly crayfish.

Langoustine: clawed crustacean, smaller than either *homard* or *langouste*, with very delicate meat. Known in British waters as Dublin Bay prawn.

Langres: supple, tangy cylindrical cow's milk cheese with a rust-colored rind; named for village in Champagne.

Langue (de chat): tongue ("cat's tongue"; thin, narrow, delicate cookie often served with sherbet or ice).

Languedocienne: garnish, usually of tomatoes, eggplant, and wild *cèpe* mushrooms.

Lapereau: young rabbit.

Lapin: rabbit.

de garenne: wild rabbit.

Lard: bacon.

Larder: to thread meat, fish, or liver with strips of fat for added moisture.

Lardon: cube of bacon.

Larme: "teardrop"; a very small portion of liquid.

Laurier: bay laurel or bay leaf.

Lavaret: lake fish of the Savoie, similar to salmon.

Léger, légère: light.

Légume: vegetable.

Lentilles (du Puy): lentils (prized green lentils from the village of Le Puy in the Auvergne).

Levain: lactic, natural sourdough starter; without commercial yeast.

Levure (chimique): commercial yeast (baking powder).

Lieu jaune: green pollack, in the cod family, a pleasant, inexpensive small yellow fish; often sold under name *colin;* found in the Atlantic.

Lieu noir: pollack, also called black cod; in the cod family, a pleasant, inexpensive fish found in the English Channel and the Atlantic.

Lièvre (à la royale): hare (cooked with red wine, shallots, onions, and cinnamon, then rolled and stuffed with *foie gras* and truffles).

Limaces à la suçarelle: snails cooked with onions, garlic, tomatoes, and sausage; specialty of Provence.

Limaçon: land snail.

Limande: lemon sole, also called dab or sand dab, not as firm or prized as sole, found in the English Channel, the Atlantic, and, rarely, in the Mediterranean.

Lingot: type of kidney-shaped dry white bean.

Lisette: small *maquereau,* or mackerel.

Livarot: village in Normandy that gives its name to an elastic and pungent thick disc of cow's milk cheese with reddish golden stripes around the edge.

Lotte: monkfish or angler fish, a large firm-fleshed ocean fish.

Lotte de rivière (or ***de lac):*** fine-fleshed river (or lake) fish, prized for its large and flavorful liver. Not related to the ocean fish *lotte.*

Lou magret: breast of fattened duck.

Loup de mer: wolf fish or ocean catfish; name for sea bass in the Mediterranean.

Louvine: Basque name for striped bass, fished in the Bay of Gascony.

Lucullus: a classic, elaborate garnish of truffles cooked in Madeira and stuffed with chicken forcemeat.

Lumas: name for land snail in the Poitou-Charentes region along the Atlantic coast.

Luzienne, à la: prepared in the manner popular in Saint-Jean-de-Luz, a Basque fishing port.

Lyonnaise, à la: in the style of Lyon; often garnished with onions.

M

Macaron: macaroon, small cookie of almonds, egg whites, and sugar.

Macaronade: a rich blend of wild and domestic mushrooms and chunks of *foie gras*, smothered in fresh pasta; specialty of the southwest. Also, macaroni with mushrooms, bacon, white wine, and Parmesan cheese; an accompaniment to a beef stew, or *daube;* specialty of Provence.

Macédoine: diced mixed fruit or vegetables.

Mâche: dark small-leafed salad green known as lamb's lettuce or corn salad. Also called *doucette.*

Mâchon: early morning snack of sausage, wine, cheese, and bread; also, the café that offers the snack; particular to Lyon.

Macis: mace, the spice.

Madeleine (de Commercy): small scalloped-shaped tea cake made famous by Marcel Proust; (the town in the Lorraine where the tea cakes are commercialized).

Madère: Madeira.

Madrilène, à la: in the style of Madrid; with tomatoes. Classically a garnish of peeled chopped tomatoes for *consommé.*

Magret de canard (or ***d'oie):*** breast of fattened duck (or goose).

Maigre: thin, non-fatty.

Maïs: corn.

Maison, de la: of the house, or restaurant.

Maître d'hôtel: headwaiter. Also, sauce of butter, parsley, and lemon.

Maltaise: orange-flavored *hollandaise* sauce.

Malvoisie, vinaigre de: vinegar made from the malvasia grape, used for the sweet, heavy Malmsey wine.

Mandarine: tangerine.

Mange-tout: "eat it all"; a podless green runner bean; a sweet pea; a snow pea. Also, a variety of apple.

Mangue: mango.

Manière, de: in the style of.

Maquereau: mackerel; *lisette* is a small mackerel.

Mara de bois: small fragrant strawberry, like a cross between a domestic and wild strawberry.

Maraîcher (à la maraîchière): market gardener or truck farmer (market-garden style; usually refers to a dish or salad that includes various greens).

Marbré: striped sea bream, Mediterranean fish that is excellent grilled.

Marc: *eau-de-vie* distilled from pressed grape skins and seeds or other fruits.

Marcassin: young wild boar.

Marchand de vin: wine merchant. Also, sauce made with red wine, meat stock, and chopped shallots.

Marée, la: literally "the tide"; usually used to indicate seafood that is fresh.

Marennes: flat-shelled green-tinged *plate* oyster. Also, the French coastal village where flat-shelled oysters are raised.

Marinade: seasoned liquid in which food, usually meat, is soaked for several hours. The liquid seasons and tenderizes at the same time.

Mariné: marinated.

Marjolaine: marjoram. Also, multilayered chocolate and nut cake.

Marmelade: traditionally a thick purée of fruit, or sweet stewed fruit; today purée of vegetable, or stewed vegetables.

Marmite: small covered pot; also a dish cooked in a small casserole.

Maroilles: village in the north that gives its name to a strong-tasting, thick, square cow's milk cheese with a pale brick-red rind.

Marquise (au chocolat): mousse-like (chocolate) cake.

Marron (glacé): large (candied) chestnut.

Matelote (d'anguilles): freshwater fish (or eel) stew.

Matignon: a garnish of mixed stewed vegetables.

Mauviette: wild meadow lark or skylark.

Médaillon: round piece or slice, usually of fish or meat.

Mélange: mixture or blend.

Méli-mélo: an assortment of fish and/or seafood.

Melon de Cavaillon: small cantaloupe-like melon from Cavaillon, a town in Provence known for its wholesale produce market.

Ménagère, à la: "in the style of the housewife"; usually a simple preparation including onions, potatoes, and carrots.

Mendiant, fruits du: traditional mixture of figs, almonds, hazelnuts, and raisins, whose colors suggest the robes of the mendicant friars it is named after.

Menthe: mint.

Merguez: small spicy sausage.

Merlan: whiting.

Merle: blackbird.

Merlu: hake, a member of the codfish family often sold improperly in Paris markets as *colin;* found in the English Channel, Atlantic, and Mediterranean.

Mérou: a large grouper, an excellent tropical or near-tropical fish, generally imported from North Africa but sometimes found in the Atlantic and Mediterranean.

Merveille: hot sugared doughnut.

Mesclum, mesclun: a mixture of at least seven multishaded salad greens from Provence.

Mets: dish or preparation.
selon la saison: seasonal preparation; according to the season.

Méture: corn bread from the Basque region.

Meule: "millstone"; name for wheel of cheese in the Jura.

Meunière, à la: "in the style of the miller's wife"; refers to a fish that is seasoned, rolled in flour, fried in butter, and served with lemon, parsley, and hot melted butter.

Meurette: in, or with, a red wine sauce. Also, a Burgundian fish stew.

Mi-cru: half raw.

Mi-cuit: half cooked.

Miche: a large round country-style loaf of bread. Also, Basque name for aniseed cakelike bread.

Mie: interior, or crumb, of the bread (see *Pain de mie*).

Miel: honey

Mignardise: see *Petit-four*.

Mignon de canard: see *Demoiselle de canard.*

Mignonette: small cubes, usually of beef. Also refers to coarsely ground black or white pepper.

Mijoté (plat): simmered (dish or preparation).

Millefeuille: refers to puff pastry with many thin layers; usually a cream-filled rectangle of puff pastry, or a Napoléon.

Mimosa: garnish of chopped hard-cooked egg yolks.

Minute (à la): "minute"; something quickly grilled or fried in butter with lemon juice and parsley (prepared at the last minute).

Mique: generally a large breaded dumpling, poached and served with stews and meats; specialty of the southwest.

Mirabeau: garnish of anchovies, pitted olives, tarragon, and anchovy butter.

Mirabelle: small sweet yellow plum. Also, colorless *eau-de-vie* made from yellow plums.

Mirepoix: cubes of carrots and onions or mixed vegetables, usually used in braising to boost the flavor of a meat dish.

Miroir: "mirror"; a dish that has a smooth glaze; currently a fruit mousse cake with a layer of fruit glaze on top.

Miroton (de): slice (of). Also, stew of meats flavored with onions.

Mitonnée: a simmered souplike dish.

Mode de, à la: in the style of.

Moëlle: beef bone marrow.

Mogette, mojette, mougette: a kind of dried white bean from the Atlantic coast.

Moka: refers to coffee; coffee-flavored dish.

Mollusque: mollusk.

Mont blanc: classic rich pastry of baked meringue, chestnut purée, and whipped cream.

Montagne, de la: from the mountains.

Montmorency: garnished with cherries; historically a village known for its cherries, now a suburb of Paris.

Morbier: supple cow's milk cheese from the Jura; a thin sprinkling of ashes in the center gives it its distinctive black stripe and light smoky flavor.

Morceau: piece or small portion.

Morille: wild morel mushroom, dark brown and conical.

Mornay: classic cream sauce enriched with egg yolks and cheese.

Morue: salt cod; also currently used to mean fresh cod, which is *cabillaud*.

Morvandelle, jambon à la: in the style of the Morvan (ham in a piquant creamy sauce made with white wine, vinegar, juniper berries, shallots, and cream).

Morvandelle, râpée: grated potato mixed with eggs, cream, and cheese, baked until golden.

Mosaïque: "mosaic;" a presentation of mixed ingredients.

Mostèle: forkbeard mostelle; small Mediterranean fish of the cod family.

Mouclade: creamy mussel stew from the Poitou-Charentes on the Atlantic coast, generally flavored with curry or saffron.

Moufflon: wild sheep.

Moule: mussel. Also a mold.

de bouchot: small, highly prized cultivated mussel, raised on stakes driven into the sediment of shallow coastal beds.

de Bouzigues: iodine-strong mussel from the village of Bouzigues, on the Mediterranean coast.

d'Espagne: large, sharp-shelled mussel, often served raw as part of a seafood platter.

de parques: Dutch cultivated mussel, usually raised in fattening beds or diverted ponds.

Moulé: molded, baked in a shaped pan.

Moules marinière: mussels cooked in white wine with onions, shallots, butter, and herbs.

Moulin (à poivre): mill (peppermill); also used for oil and flour mills.

Mourone: Basque name for red bell pepper.

Mourtayrol, mourtaïrol: a *pot-au-feu* of boiled beef, chicken, ham, and vegetables, flavored with saffron and served over slices of bread; specialty of the Auvergne.

Mousse: light, airy mixture usually containing eggs and cream, either sweet or savory.

Mousseline: refers to ingredients that are usually lightened with whipped cream or egg whites, as in sauces, or with butter, as in *brioche mousseline*.

Mousseron: tiny, delicate, wild mushroom.

Moutarde (à l'ancienne, en graines): mustard (old-style, coarse-grained).

Mouton: mutton.
Muge: grey mullet.
Mulard: breed of duck common to the southwest, fattened for its delicate liver, for *foie gras*.
Mulet: the generic group of mullet, found in the English Channel, Atlantic, and Mediterranean.
Munster: village in Alsace that gives its name to a disc of soft, tangy cow's milk cheese with a brick-red rind and a penetrating aroma; the cheese is also sometimes cured with cumin seeds.
Mûre (de ronces): blackberry (bush).
Muscade: nutmeg.
Muscat de Hambourg: variety of popular purple table grape, grown in Provence.
Museau de porc (or ***de boeuf***)***:*** vinegared pork (or beef) muzzle.
Myrtille: bilberry (bluish black European blueberry).
Mystère: truncated cone-shaped ice cream dessert. Also, dessert of cooked meringue with ice cream and chocolate cake.

N

Nage (à la): "swimming"; aromatic poaching liquid (served in).
Nantua: sauce of crayfish, butter, cream, and, traditionally, truffles; also garnish of crayfish.
Nappé: covered, as with a sauce.
Natte: woven loaf of bread.
Nature: refers to simple, unadorned preparations.
Navarin: lamb or mutton stew.
Navarraise, à la: Navarre-style, with sweet peppers, onions, and garlic.
Navet: turnip.
Navette: "little boat"; small pastry boats.
Nèfle: medlar; also called Japanese loquat; tart fruit that resembles an apricot and tastes like a mango.
Neufchâtel: white, creamy, delicate (and often heart-shaped) cow's milk cheese, named for village in Normandy where it is made.
Newburg: lobster preparation with Madeira, egg yolks, and cream.
Nivernaise, à la: in the style of Nevers; with carrots and onions.
Noilly: a vermouth-based sauce.
Noisette: hazelnut; also refers to small round piece (such as from a potato), generally the size of a hazelnut, lightly browned in butter. Also, center cut of lamb chop. Also, dessert flavored with hazelnuts.
Noix: general term for nut; also, walnut. Also, nut-size, typically *une noix de beurre,* or lump of butter.
Non compris: see *Service (non) compris*.
Nonat: small river fish in Provence, usually fried. Also known as *poutine*.
Normande: in the style of Normandy; sauce of seafood, cream, and mushrooms. Also refers to fish or meat cooked with apple cider or Calvados; or dessert with apples, usually served with cream.
Note: another word for *addition* (bill or tab).
Nougat: candy of roasted almonds, egg whites, and honey; specialty of Montélimar.
Nougat glacé: frozen dessert of whipped cream and candied fruit.
Nougatine: a confectionary preparation of caramel, chopped almonds, and hazelnuts.
Nouilles: noodles.
Nouveau, nouvelle: new or young.
Nouveauté: a new offering.

Oeuf: egg.
brouillé: scrambled egg.
à la coque: soft-cooked egg.
dur: hard-cooked egg.
en meurette: poached egg in red wine sauce.
mollet: egg simmered in water for 6 minutes.
poché: poached egg.
sauté à la poêle or ***sur le plat:*** fried egg.
Oeufs à la neige: "eggs in the snow"; sweetened whipped egg whites poached in milk and served with vanilla custard sauce; see also *Ile flottante*.
Offert: offered; free or given.
Oie: goose.
Oignon: onion.
Olive: olive.
Also used for oil.
lucques: elongated variety of olive, usually preserved in a salt brine.
noire: black olive.

de Nyons: wrinkled black olive, first olive in France to receive the AOC.
tanche: variety of olive from the region of Nyons in Provence; always picked ripe and black, and preserved in salt brine. Also pressed for oil.
verte: green olive.
Olives cassées: fresh green olives cured in a rich fennel-infused brine; specialty of Provence.
Omble (ombre) chevalier: lake fish, similar to salmon trout, with firm, flaky flesh varying from white to deep red. Found in lakes in the Savoie.
Omelette norvégienne: French version of Baked Alaska; a concoction of sponge cake covered with ice cream and a layer of sweetened, stiffly beaten egg whites, then browned quickly in the oven.
Onglet: cut similar to beef flank steak; also cut of beef sold as *biftek* and *entrecôte,* usually a tough cut, but better than flank steak.
Orange pressé: orange juice served with a *carafe* of tap water and sugar, for sweetening to taste.
Oreille de porc: cooked pig's ear; served grilled, with a coating of egg and bread crumb.
Oreillette: thin, crisp rectangular dessert fritters, flavored with orange-flower water; specialty of Provence.
Orge (perlé): barley (pearl barley).
Orientale, à l': general name for vaguely Eastern dishes cooked with saffron, tomatoes, and sweet red peppers.
Origan: oregano.
Ortie: nettle.
Oseille: sorrel.
Osso bucco à la niçoise: sautéed veal braised with tomatoes, garlic, onions, and orange zest; specialty of the Mediterranean.
Ostréiculteur: oyster grower.
Oursin: sea urchin.
Oursinade: creamy sea urchin soup.
Ouvert: open.

P

Pageot: a type of sea bream or porgy. The finest is *pageot rouge*, wonderful grilled. *Pageot blanc* is drier and needs to be marinated in oil before cooking.
Paillarde (de veau): thick slice (of veal); also, piece of meat pounded flat and sautéed.
Pailles (pommes): fried potato sticks.
Paillette: cheese straw, usually made with puff pastry and Parmesan cheese.
Pain: bread. Also, loaf of any kind.
d'Aix: variously shaped sourdough loaves, sometimes like a sunflower, other times a chain-like loaf of four linked rounds.
à l'ancienne: in the old style, often bread simply dusted with flour to appear more rustic.
azyme: unleavened bread, matzo.
bis: brown bread.
brié: very dense, elongated loaf of unsalted white bread; specialty of Normandy.
de campagne: country loaf; can vary from a white bread simply dusted with flour to give it a rustic look (and fetch a higher price) to a truly hearty loaf that may be a blend of white, whole-wheat, and perhaps rye flour with bran added. Comes in every shape.
au chocolat: an oblong milk pastry with a strip of chocolate filling.
aux cinq céréales: five-grain bread.
complet: bread made partially or entirely from whole-wheat flour, with bakers varying proportions according to their personal tastes.
cordon: seldom-found regional country loaf decorated with a strip of dough.
décoré: decorated.
d'épices: spice bread, a specialty of Dijon.
de fantaisie: generally any odd or imaginatively shaped bread. Even *baguette de campagne* falls into this category.
forestier: with mushrooms.
de Gênes: classic almond sponge cake.
grillé: toast.
levain: with natural sourdough yeast.
de mie: rectangular white sandwich loaf that is nearly all *mie* (interior crumb) and very little crust. It is made for durability, its flavor and texture developed for use in sandwiches. Unlike most French breads, it contains milk, sugar, and butter, and

may contain chemical preservatives.

aux noix (aux noisettes): bread, most often rye or wheat, filled with walnuts (hazelnuts).

paillaisse: literally, mattress; usually a flat, rectangular rustic loaf.

paillé: country loaf from the Basque region.

petit: small loaf.

polka: white sourdough bread from central France, usually round and scored.

aux raisins: bread, most often rye or wheat, filled with raisins.

rustique: rustic, usually hand-formed, sometimes containing ingredients such as cheese, ham, bacon, etc.

de seigle: bread made from 60 to 70 percent rye flour and 30 to 40 percent wheat flour.

sans sel: salt-free bread.

de son: legally a dietetic bread that is quality controlled, containing 20 percent bran mixed with white flour.

viennois: bread shaped like a *baguette,* with regular horizontal slashes, usually containing white flour, sugar, powdered milk, water, and yeast.

Paleron: shoulder of beef.

Palestine: classically a garnish of Jerusalem artichokes.

Palette (de porc): shoulder (of pork).

Palmier: palm leaf–shaped cookie made of sugared puff pastry.

Palmier, coeur de: heart of palm.

Palombe: wood or wild pigeon, or dove.

Palourde: prized medium-size clam.

Pamplemousse: grapefruit.

pressé: grapefruit juice served with a *carafe* of tap water and sugar, for sweetening to taste.

Pan bagna: large round bread roll, split, brushed with olive oil, and filled with a variable mixture including anchovies, onions, black olives, green peppers, tomatoes, and celery; café specialty from Nice.

Panaché: mixed; now liberally used menu term to denote any mixture.

Panade, panada: a thick mixture used to bind forcemeats and *quenelles,* usually flour and butter based, but can also contain fresh or toasted bread crumbs, rice, or potatoes. Also refers to soup of bread, milk, and sometimes cheese.

Panais: parsnip.

Pané: breaded.

Panisse: a thick fried pancake of chickpea flour, served as accompaniment to meat; specialty of Provence.

Pannequet: rolled *crêpe,* filled and/or covered with sweet or savory mixture.

Panoufle: Generally discarded belly flap from saddle of lamb, veal, and beef; sometimes grilled.

Pantin: small pork pastry.

Papeton: eggplant, fried, puréed, and cooked in a ring mold; specialty of Provence.

Papillon: "butterfly"; small crinkle-shelled *creuse* oyster from the Atlantic coast.

Papillote, en: cooked in parchment paper or foil wrapping.

Paquet (en): (in) a package or parcel.

Parfait: a dessert *mousse.* Also, *mousse*-like mixture of chicken, duck, or goose liver.

Parfum: flavor.

Paris-Brest, gâteau: classic large, crown-shaped *choux* pastry filled with praline buttercream and topped with chopped almonds.

Parisienne, à la: varied vegetable garnish that generally includes potato balls that have been fried and tossed in a meat glaze.

Parmentier: dish with potatoes.

Pas trop fait: refers to a cheese that has been aged for a shorter time and is blander; also for a cheese that will ripen at home.

Passe Crassane: flavorful variety of winter pear.

Passe-Pierre: edible seaweed.

Pastèque: watermelon.

Pastilla: Moroccan puff pastry pie, usually filled with pigeon or chicken.

Pastis: anise-flavored alcohol that becomes cloudy when water is added (the most famous brands are Pernod and Ricard). Also, name for *tourtière,* the flaky prune pastry from the southwest.

Pastiza: see *Gâteau basque.*

Pata Négra (jambon): literally "black-feet"; prized ham from Spain.

Patagos: clam.

Pâte: pastry or dough.

d'amande: almond paste.

brisée: pie pastry.
sablée: sweeter, richer, and more crumbly pie dough than *pâte sucrée,* sometimes leavened.
sucrée: sweet pie pastry.
Pâté: minced meat that is molded, spiced, baked, and served hot or cold.
Pâtes (fraîches): pasta (fresh).
Pâtisserie: pastry shop.
Patron: owner of an establishment.
Patte blanche: small crayfish no larger than 2½ ounces (75 g).
Patte rouge: large crayfish.
Pauchouse, pochouse: stew of river fish that generally includes tench, perch, pike, and eel; specialty of Burgundy.
Paupiette: slice of meat or fish, filled, rolled, then wrapped; served warm.
Pavé: "paving stone"; usually a thick slice of boned beef or calf's liver. Also, a kind of pastry.
Pavé d'Auge: thick ocher-colored square of cow's milk cheese that comes from the Auge area of Normandy.
Pavot (graine de): poppy (seed).
Paysan (à la paysanne): country style; (garnish of carrots, turnips, onions, celery and bacon).
Peau: skin.
Pèbre d'ail: see *Poivre d'âne.*
Pêche: peach. Also, fishing.
Pêche Alexandra: cold dessert of poached peaches with ice cream and puréed strawberries.
Pêche Melba: poached peach with vanilla ice cream and raspberry sauce.
Pêcheur: "fisherman"; usually refers to fish preparations.
Pélandron: see *Haricot gris.*
Pélardon: small flat, dried, pungent disc of goat's milk cheese; specialty of the Languedoc.
Pèlerine: another name for scallop or *coquille Saint-Jacques.*
Pépite (au chocolat): nugget; (chocolate chip).
Pequillo: small red Spanish pepper, usually stuffed with salt cod purée.
Perce-pierre: samphire, an edible seaweed.
Perche: perch.
Perdreau: young partridge.
Perdrix: partridge.
Périgourdine, à la, or ***Périgueux:*** sauce, usually with truffles and *foie gras,* named for the Périgord in southwestern France.
Persil (simple): parsley (flat-leaf).
Persillade: blend of chopped parsley and garlic.
Persillé: "parsleyed"; describes certain blue-veined cheeses. See also *Jambon persillé.*
Pet de nonne: "nun's fart"; small, dainty *beignets,* or fried pastry.
Pétale: "petal"; very thin slice.
Petit-beurre: popular tea cookie made with butter.
Petit déjeuner: breakfast.
Petit-four (sucré or salé): tiny cake or pastry (sweet or savory); in elegant restaurants, served with cocktails before dinner or with coffee afterward; also called *mignardise.*
Petit-gris: small land snail.
Petit-pois: small green pea.
Petit salé: salt-cured portions of lean pork belly, often served with lentils.
Petite marmite: earthenware casserole; the broth served from it.
Pétoncle: tiny scallop, similar to American bay scallop.
Pibale: tiny eel, also called *civelle.*
Picholine, pitchouline: a variety of green olive, generally used to prepare *olives cassées*; specialty of Provence.
Picodon (méthode Dieulefit): small disc of goat's milk cheese, the best of which (qualified as *méthode Dieulefit*) is hard, piquant, and pungent from having soaked in brandy and aged a month in earthenware jars; specialty of northern Provence.
Pièce: portion, piece.
Piech: poached veal brisket stuffed with vegetables, herbs, and sometimes rice, ham, eggs, or cheese; specialty of the Mediterranean.
Pied de cheval: "horse's foot"; giant Atlantic coast oyster.
Pied de mouton: meaty cream-colored wild mushroom. Also, sheep's foot.
Pied de veau: calf's foot, used for its gelatin in stocks; also poached or braised and served with lemon sauce.
Pieds et paquets: "feet and packages"; mutton tripe rolled and cooked with sheep's feet, white wine, and tomatoes; specialty of Provence and the Mediterranean.
Pierre-Qui-Vire: "stone that moves"; a supple, tangy, flat disc of cow's

milk cheese with a reddish rind, made by the Benedictine monks at the Abbaye de la Pierre-Qui-Vire in Burgundy.

Pigeon (neau): pigeon or squab (young pigeon or squab).

Pignons: pine nuts, found in the cones of pine trees growing in Provence and along the southwestern Atlantic coast.

Pilau, pilaf: rice sautéed with onion and simmered in broth.

Pilchard: name for sardines on the Atlantic coast.

Piment: red pepper or pimiento.

doux: sweet pepper.

d'Espelette: slender, mildly hot chile pepper from Espelette, a village in the Basque region.

Piment (or ***poivre) de Jamaïque:*** allspice.

Pimenté: hot, peppery, spicy.

Pimpernelle: salad burnet, a salad green with a somewhat bitter taste.

Pince: claw. Also, tongs used when eating snails or seafood.

Pineau des Charentes: sweet fortified wine from the Cognac region on the Atlantic coast, served as an *apéritif*.

Pintade(au): (young) guinea fowl.

Pipérade: a dish of bell peppers, onions, tomatoes, and often ham and scrambled eggs; specialty of the Basque region.

Piquant: sharp or spicy tasting.

Piqué: larded; studded.

Piquenchagne, picanchagne: a pear tart with walnut or *brioche* crust; specialty of the Bourbonnais, a province in Auvergne.

Pissaladière: a flat open-face tart like a pizza, garnished with onions, olives, and anchovies; specialty of Nice.

Pissenlit: dandelion green.

Pistache: pistachio nut.

Pistil de safran: thread of saffron.

Pistou: sauce of basil, garlic, and olive oil; specialty of Provence. Also a rich vegetable, bean, and pasta soup flavored with *pistou* sauce.

Pithiviers: a town in the Loire valley that gives its name to a classic large puff pastry round filled with almond cream. Also, lark pâté.

Plaice: a small, orange-spotted flounder or fluke, a flat ocean fish; also known as *plie franch* or *carrelet*. Found in the English Channel.

Plat: dish.

cuisiné: dish containing ingredients that have cooked together, usually in a sauce.

du jour: today's special.

principal: main dish.

Plate: flat-shelled oyster.

Plateau: platter.

de fruits de mer: seafood platter combining raw and cooked shellfish; usually includes oysters, clams, mussels, *langoustines,* periwinkles, whelks, crabs, and tiny shrimp.

Plates côtes: part of beef ribs usually used in *pot-au-feu*.

Pleurote: very soft fleshed, feather-edged wild mushrooms; also now being cultivated commercially in several regions of France.

Plie: see *Plaice*.

Plombière: classic dessert of vanilla ice cream, candied fruit, kirsch, and apricot jam.

Pluche: small sprig of herbs or plants, generally used for garnish.

Poché: poached.

Pochouse: see *Pauchouse*.

Poêlé: pan-fried.

Pogne: *brioche* flavored with orange-flower water and filled with fruits; specialty of Romans-sur-Isère, in the Rhône-Alpes.

Point (à): ripe or ready to eat, the perfect moment for eating a cheese or fruit. Also, cooked medium rare.

Pointe (d'asperge): tip (of asparagus).

Poire: pear.

Poire William: variety of pear; colorless fruit brandy, or *eau-de-vie*, often made from this variety of pear.

Poireau: leek.

Pois (chiche): pea (chickpea).

Poisson: fish.

d'eau douce: freshwater fish.

fumé: smoked fish.

de lac: lake fish.

de mer: ocean fish.

noble: refers to prized, thus expensive, variety of fish.

de rivière: river fish.

de roche: rockfish.

Poissonerie: fish shop.

Poitrine: breast (of meat or poultry).

d'oie fumée: smoked goose breast.

Poitrine demi-sel: unsmoked slab bacon.

Poitrine fumée: smoked slab bacon.
Poivrade: a peppery brown sauce made with wine, vinegar, and cooked vegetables and strained before serving.
Poivre: pepper.
d'ain: Provençal name for wild savory. Also, small goat cheese covered with sprigs of savory. Also known as *pèbre d'ail* and *pèbre d'ase*.
frais de Madagascar: green peppercorn.
en grain: peppercorn.
gris: black peppercorn.
moulu: ground pepper.
noir: black peppercorn.
rose: pink peppercorn.
vert: green peppercorn.
Poivron (doux): (sweet bell) pepper.
Pojarski: finely chopped meat or fish shaped like a cutlet and fried.
Polenta: cooked dish of cornmeal and water, usually with added butter and cheese; also, cornmeal.
Pommade (beurre en): usually refers to a thick, smooth paste; (creamed butter).
Pomme: apple.
Pommes de terre: potatoes.
allumettes: "matchsticks"; fries cut into very thin julienne.
à l'anglaise: boiled.
à la Bigoudène: baked slices of unpeeled potato.
boulangère: potatoes cooked with the meat they accompany. Also, a gratin of sliced potatoes, baked with milk or stock and sometimes flavored with onions, bacon, and tomatoes.
sous la cendre: baked under cinders in a fireplace.
darphin: grated potatoes shaped into a cake.
dauphine: mashed potatoes mixed with *choux* pastry, shaped into small balls and fried.
dauphinoise: a gratin of sliced potatoes, baked with milk and/or cream, garlic, cheese, and eggs.
duchesse: mashed potatoes with butter, egg yolks, and nutmeg, used for garnish.
frites: French fries.
gratinées: browned potatoes, often with cheese.
lyonnaises: potatoes sautéed with onions.
macaire: classic side dish of puréed potatoes shaped into small balls and fried, or baked in a flat cake.
mousseline: potato purée enriched with butter, egg yolks, and whipped cream.
paillasson: fried pancake of grated potatoes.
pailles: potatoes cut into julienne strips, then fried.
Pont-Neuf: classic fries.
en robe des champs, en robe de chambre: potatoes boiled or baked in their skin; potatoes in their jackets.
sarladaise: sliced potatoes cooked with goose fat and (optionally) truffles.
soufflées: small, thin slices of potatoes fried twice, causing them to inflate so they resemble little pillows.
vapeur: steamed or boiled potatoes.
Pommes en l'air: caramelized apple slices, usually served with *boudin noir* (blood sausage).
Pompe à l'huile, pompe de Noël: see *Gibassier*.
Pompe aux grattons: bread containing cracklings.
Pont l'Evêque: village in Normandy that gives its name to a very tender, fragrant square of cow's milk cheese.
Porc (carré de): pork (loin).
Porc (côte de): pork (chop).
Porcelet: young suckling pig.
Porchetta: young pig stuffed with offal, herbs, and garlic, and roasted; seen in *charcuteries* in Nice.
Porto (au): (with) port.
Portugaise: elongated, crinkle-shell oyster.
Pot-au-feu: traditional dish of beef simmered with vegetables, often served in two or more courses; today chefs often use it to mean fish poached in fish stock with vegetables.
Pot bouilli: another name for *pot-au-feu*.
Pot-de-crème: individual classic custard dessert, often chocolate.
Pot Lyonnais: bottle from the region of Lyon with the capacity of three-quarters of an ordinary bottle.
Potage: soup.
Potée: traditional hearty meat soup, usually containing pork, cabbage, and potatoes.
Potimarron: see *Citrouille*.
Potiron: see *Citrouille*.
Potjevleisch: a mixed-meat *terrine*, usually of veal, pork, and rabbit; specialty of the north.

Poularde: fatted hen.
Poule au pot: boiled stuffed chicken with vegetables; specialty of the city of Béarn in the southwest.
Poule d'Inde: turkey hen.
Poule faisane: female pheasant.
Poulet (rôti): chicken (roast).
basquaise: Basque-style chicken, with tomatoes and sweet peppers.
de Bresse: high-quality chicken raised on farms to exacting specifications, from the Rhône-Alpes.
fermier: free-range chicken.
de grain: corn-fed chicken.
Pouligny-Saint-Pierre: village in the Loire valley that gives its name to a goat's milk cheese shaped like a truncated pyramid with a mottled, grayish rind and a smooth-grained, ivory-white interior.
Poulpe: octopus.
Pounti: also spelled *pounty*; a pork meat loaf that generally includes Swiss chard or spinach, eggs, milk, herbs, onions, and prunes; specialty of the Auvergne.
Pousse-en-claire: oysters that have been aged and fattened in *claires,* or oyster beds, for four to eight months.
Pousse-pierre: edible seaweed; also called sea beans.
Poussin: baby chicken.
Poutargue, boutargue: salted, pressed, and flattened mullet roe, generally spread on toast as an appetizer; specialty of Provence and the Mediterranean.
Poutine: see *Nonat.*
Praire: small clam.
Pralin: ground caramelized almonds.
Praline: caramelized almonds.
Preskoph: pork headcheese, often served with a *vinaigrette*; specialty of Alsace.
Primeur: refers to early fresh fruits and vegetables, also to new wine.
Printanière: garnish of a variety of spring vegetables cut into dice or balls.
Prix fixe: fixed-price menu.
Prix net: service included.
Profiterole(s): classic *choux* pastry dessert, usually puffs of pastry filled with vanilla ice cream and topped with hot chocolate sauce.
Provençale: in the style of Provence; usually includes garlic, tomatoes, and/or olive oil.
Prune (d'ente): fresh plum; (variety of plum grown in the famed Agen region of the southwest).
Pruneau: prune.
Puits d'amour: "wells of love"; classic small pastry crowns filled with pastry cream.

Q

Quasi (de veau): standing rump (of veal).
Quatre épices: spice blend of ground ginger, nutmeg, white pepper, and cloves.
Quatre-quarts: "four quarters"; pound cake made with equal weights of eggs, flour, butter, and sugar.
Quenelle: dumpling, usually of veal, fish, or poultry.
Quetsche: small purple Damson plum.
Queue (de boeuf): tail (of beef; oxtail).
Quiche lorraine: savory custard tart made with bacon, eggs, and cream.

R

Râble de lièvre (lapin): saddle of hare (rabbit).
Raclette: rustic dish, from Switzerland and the Savoie, of melted cheese served with boiled potatoes, tiny pickled cucumbers, and onions; also, the cheese used in the dish.
Radis: small red radish.
noir: large black radish, often served with cream, as a salad.
Rafraîchi: cool, chilled, or fresh.
Ragoût: stew, usually of meat.
à la Bigoudène: sausage stewed with bacon and potato.
Raie: skate or ray, found in the English Channel, Atlantic, and Mediterranean.
Raifort: horseradish.
Raisin: grape; raisin.
de Corinthe: currant.
sec: raisin.
de Smyrne: sultana.
Raïto: red wine sauce that generally includes onions, tomatoes, garlic, herbs, olives, and capers, usually served warm over grilled fish; specialty of Provence.
Ramequin: small individual casserole. Also, a small tart. Also, a small goat's milk cheese from the

Bugey, an area in the northern Rhône valley.

Ramier: wood or wild pigeon.

Râpé: grated or shredded.

Rascasse: gurnard, or scorpion fish, in the rockfish family; an essential ingredient of *bouillabaisse,* the fish stew of the Mediterranean.

Ratafia: liqueur made by infusing nuts or fruit in brandy.

Ratatouille: a cooked dish of eggplant, zucchini, onions, tomatoes, peppers, garlic, and olive oil, served hot or cold; specialty of Provence.

Ratte: small, bite-size potatoes, often used for purées.

Ravigote: classic thick *vinaigrette* sauce with vinegar, white wine, shallots, and herbs. Also, cold mayonnaise with capers, onions, and herbs.

Raviole: small squares of ravioli with cheese or vegetable filling.

de Royans: tiny ravioli pasta filled with goat cheese, from the Rhône-Alpes.

Ravioli à la niçoise: square or round pasta filled with meat and/or Swiss chard and baked with grated cheese.

Reblochon: smooth, supple, creamy cow's milk cheese from the Savoie, in the Alps.

Réglisse: licorice.

Reine-Claude: greengage plum.

Reinette, reine de: fall and winter variety of apple, deep yellow with a red blush.

Religieuse, petite: "nun"; a small version of a classic pastry consisting of two *choux* puffs filled with chocolate, coffee, or vanilla pastry cream, placed one on top of another, and frosted with chocolate or coffee icing to resemble a nun in her habit.

Rémoulade (céleri): sauce of mayonnaise, capers, mustard, herbs, anchovies, and gherkins; (dish of shredded celery root with mayonnaise).

Repas: meal.

Rhubarbe: rhubarb.

Rhum: rum.

Rigotte: small cow's milk cheese from the Lyon region.

Rillettes (d'oie): minced spread of pork (goose); can also be made with duck, fish, or rabbit.

Rillons: usually pork belly, cut up and cooked until crisp, then drained of fat; also made of duck, goose, or rabbit.

Ris d'agneau (de veau): lamb (veal) sweetbreads.

Rissolé: browned by frying, usually potatoes.

Riz: rice.

de Camargue: nutty, fragrant rice grown in the Camargue, the swampy area just south of Arles in Provence.

complet: brown rice.

à l'impératrice: cold rice pudding with candied fruit.

sauvage: wild rice.

Rizotto, risotto: creamy rice made by stirring rice constantly in stock as it cooks, then mixing in other ingredients such as cheese or mushrooms.

Robe des champs, robe de chambre (pommes en): potatoes boiled or baked in their skin; potatoes in their jackets.

Rocamadour: village in southwestern France that gives its name to a tiny disc of cheese, once made of pure goat's or sheep's milk, now generally either goat's milk or a blend of goat's and cow's milk. Also called *cabécou.*

Rognonnade: veal loin with kidneys attached.

Rognons: kidneys.

Rollot: spicy cow's milk cheese with a washed ocher-colored rind, in small cylinder or heart shape; from the north.

Romanoff: fruit, often strawberries, macerated in liqueur and topped with whipped cream.

Romarin: rosemary.

Rondelle: round slice—of lemon, for example.

Roquefort: disc of blue-veined cheese of raw sheep's milk from southwestern France, aged in the village of Roquefort-sur-Soulzon.

Roquette: rocket or arugula, a spicy salad green.

Rosé: rare; used for veal, duck, or liver. Also, rose-colored wine.

Rosette (de boeuf): large dried pork (beef) sausage, from area around Lyon.

Rôti: roast; meat roast.

Rouelle: slice of meat or vegetable cut at an angle.

Rouennaise (canard à la): in the style of Rouen; (classic dish of duck stuffed with its liver in a blood-thickened sauce).

Rouget barbet, rouget de roche: red mullet, a prized, expensive rockfish, with sweet flesh and red skin; its flavorful liver is reserved for sauces.

Rouget grondin: red gurnard, a large, common rockfish, less prized than *rouget barbet*. A variety of *galinette*. An ingredient in *bouillabaisse*.

Rougette: a small red-leafed butterhead lettuce, specialty of Provence.

Rouille: mayonnaise of olive oil, garlic, chile peppers, bread, and fish broth; usually served with fish soups, such as *bouillabaisse*.

Roulade: meat or fish roll, or rolled-up vegetable soufflé; larger than a *paupiette*, and often stuffed.

Roulé: rolled.

Roussette: dogfish, also called *salmonette* because of its pinkish skin; found on the Atlantic coast. Good when very fresh.

Roux: sauce base or thickening of flour and butter.

Rove: breed of goat; also small round of Provençal soft goat's milk cheese, fragrant with wild herbs.

Royale, à la: "royal-style"; rich classic preparation, usually with truffles and a cream sauce.

Rumsteck: rump steak.

Russe, salade à la: cold mixed salad of peas, diced carrots, and turnips in mayonnaise.

S

Sabayon, zabaglione: frothy sweet sauce of egg yolks, sugar, wine, and flavoring that is whipped while being cooked in a water bath.

Sablé: literally, sandy; round sweet biscuit or cookie with crenelated edges.

Sabodet: strong, earthy pork sausage of pig's head and skin, served hot; specialty of Lyon.

Safran: saffron.

Saignant: cooked rare, for meat, usually beef.

Saindoux: lard or pork fat.

Saint-Germain: with peas.

Saint-Hubert: *poivrade* sauce with chestnuts and bacon added.

Saint Jacques, coquille: sea scallop.

Saint-Marcellin: small flat disc of cow's milk cheese (once made of goat's milk) made in dairies in the Isère, outside Lyon. The best is well aged and runny. Found only in Paris, the Lyon area, and northern Provence.

Saint-Nectaire: village in the Auvergne that gives its name to a supple, thick disc of cow's milk cheese with a mottled gray rind.

Saint-Pierre: John Dory, a prized mild, flat, white ocean fish. Known as *soleil* and *Jean Doré* in the north, and *poule de mer* along the Atlantic coast.

Saint-Vincent: moist, buttery, thick cylinder of cow's milk cheese from Burgundy with a rust-colored rind; similar to Epoisses, but aged a bit longer, therefore stronger.

Sainte-Maure: village in the Loire valley that gives its name to a soft, elongated cylinder of goat's milk cheese with a distinctive straw in the middle and a mottled, natural blue rind.

Salade: salad; also, a head of lettuce.

folle: mixed salad, usually including green beans and *foie gras*.

lyonnaise: green salad with cubed bacon and soft-cooked eggs, often served with herring and anchovies, and/or sheep's feet and chicken livers; specialty of Lyon; also called *saladier lyonnais*.

niçoise: salad with many variations, but usually with tomatoes, green beans, anchovies, tuna, potatoes, black olives, capers, and artichokes.

panachée: mixed salad.

russe: mixed diced vegetables in mayonnaise.

verte: green salad.

Saladier (lyonnais): see *Salade lyonnaise*.

Salé: salted.

Salers: Cantal-type cheese, made in rustic cheese-making houses only when the cows are in the Auvergne's mountain pastures, from May to September.

Salicorne: edible seaweed, sea string bean; often pickled and served as a condiment.

Salmis: classic preparation of roasted game birds or poultry, with sauce made from the pressed carcass.

Salon de thé: tearoom, tea salon.

Salpicon: diced vegetables, meat, and/or fish in a sauce, used as a stuffing, garnish, or spread.

Salsifis: salsify, oyster plant.

Sandre: pickerel, a perchlike river fish, found in the Saône and Rhine.
Sang: blood.
Sanglier: wild boar.
Sangue: Corsican black pudding, usually made with grapes or herbs.
Sanguine: "blood" orange, so named for its red juice.
Sansonnet: starling or thrush.
Sar, sargue: blacktail, a tiny flat fish of the sea bream family, best grilled or baked.
Sarcelle: teal, a species of wild duck.
Sardine: small sardine. Large sardines are called *pilchards*. Found year-round in the Mediterranean, from May to October in the Atlantic.
Sarladaise: as prepared in Sarlat in the Dordogne; with truffles.
Sarrasin: buckwheat.
Sarriette: summer savory. See *Poivre d'ain.*
Saucisse: small fresh sausage.
chaude: warm sausage.
de Francfort: hot dog.
de Strasbourg: red-skinned hot dog.
de Toulouse: mild country-style pork sausage.
Saucisson: most often, a large air-dried sausage, such as salami, eaten sliced as a cold cut; when fresh, usually called *saucisson chaud,* or hot sausage.
à l'ail: garlic sausage, usually to be cooked and served warm.
d'Arles: dried salami-style sausage that blends pork, beef, and gentle seasoning; a specialty of Arles, in Provence.
de campagne: any country-style sausage.
en croûte: sausage cooked in a pastry crust.
de Lyon: air-dried pork sausage, flavored with garlic and pepper and studded with chunks of pork fat.
de Morteau: see *Jésus de Morteau.*
sec: any dried sausage, or salami.
Sauge: sage.
Saumon (sauvage): salmon ("wild," to differentiate from commercially raised salmon).
d'Ecosse: Scottish salmon.
de fontaine: small, commercially raised salmon.
fumé: smoked salmon.
norvégien: Norwegian salmon.
Saumonette: see *Roussette.*
Saupiquet: classic aromatic wine sauce thickened with bread.
Sauté: browned in fat.
Sauvage: wild.
Savarin: yeast-leavened cake shaped like a ring, soaked in sweet syrup.
Savoie (biscuit de): sponge cake.
Savoyarde: in the style of Savoy, usually flavored with Gruyère cheese.
Scarole: escarole; see *Escarole.*
Schieffele, schieffala, schifela: smoked pork shoulder, served hot and garnished with pickled turnips or a potato and onion salad.
Sec (sèche): dry or dried.
Seiche: cuttlefish.
Seigle (pain de): rye (bread).
Sel: salt
gris: unbleached sea salt.
gros: coarse salt.
(fin) de Guérande: unrefined (fine) salt from Brittany.
marin: sea salt.
Selle: saddle (of meat).
Selles-sur-Cher: village in the Loire valley identified with a small, flat, truncated cylinder of goat's milk cheese with a mottled bluish gray rind (sometimes patted with powdered charcoal) and a pure white interior.
Selon grosseur (S.G.): according to size, usually said of lobster or other seafood.
Selon le marché: according to what is in season or available.
Selon poid (S.P.): according to weight, usually said of seafood.
Semoule: semolina or crushed wheat. Also used in France as a savory garnish, particularly in North African dishes such as *couscous.*
Serpolet: wild thyme.
Service: meal, mealtime, the serving of the meal. A restaurant has two *services* if it serves lunch and dinner; a dish *en deux services,* like *canard pressé,* is served in two courses.
Service (non) compris: service charge (not) included in the listed menu prices (but invariably included on the bill).
Service en sus: service charge to be made in addition to menu prices. Same as *service non compris.*

Simple: simple, plain, unmixed. Also, a single scoop of ice cream.

Smitane: sauce of cream, onions, white wine, and lemon juice.

Socca: a very thin, round *crêpe* made with chickpea flour, sold on the streets of Nice and eaten as a snack.

Soissons: dried or fresh white beans, from the area around Soissons, northeast of Paris.

Soja (pousse de): soybean (soybean sprout).

Soja, sauce de: soy sauce.

Solette: small sole.

Sommelier: wine waiter.

Sorbet: sherbet.

Soubise: onion sauce.

Soufflé: light mixture of puréed ingredients, egg yolks, and whipped egg whites, which puffs up when baked; sweet or savory, hot or cold.

Soumaintrain: a spicy, supple flat disc of cow's milk cheese with a red-brown rind; from Burgundy.

Soupir de nonne: "nun's sighs"; fried *choux* pastry dusted with confectioners' sugar. Created by a nun in an Alsatian abbey. Also called *pet de nonne.*

Souris (d'agneau): "mouse"; muscle that holds the leg of lamb to the bone; lamb shanks.

Spätzel, spaetzle, spetzli: noodle-like Alsatian egg and flour dumpling, served poached or fried.

Spoom: wine or fruit juice mixed with egg whites, whipped, and frozen to create a frothy iced dessert.

Steak-frites: classic French dish of grilled steak served with French-fried potatoes.

Stockfish, stocaficada, estoficada, estoficado, morue plate: flattened, dried cod found in southern France. Also, a purée-like blend of dried codfish, olive oil, tomatoes, sweet peppers, black olives, potatoes, garlic, onions, and herbs; specialty of Nice. Sometimes served with *pistou.*

Strasbourgeoise, à la: ingredients typical of Strasbourg, including sauerkraut, *foie gras,* and salt pork.

Succès à la praline: cake made with praline meringue layers, frosted with meringue and buttercream.

Sucre: sugar.

Supion, supioun, suppion: cuttlefish.

Suprême: a veal- or chicken-based white sauce thickened with flour and cream. Also, a boneless breast of poultry or a fillet of fish.

T

Table d'hôte: open table or board. Often found in the countryside, these are private homes that serve fixed meals and often have one or two guest rooms as well.

Tablette (de chocolat): bar (of chocolate).

Tablier de sapeur: "fireman's apron"; tripe that is marinated, breaded, and grilled; specialty of Lyon.

Tacaud: whiting pour, a marine fish related to cod. Found in the English Channel and Bay of Gascony, it is somewhat lean and bony.

Tagine: spicy North African stew of veal, lamb, chicken, or pigeon, and vegetables.

Talmouse: savory pastry triangle of cheese-flavored *choux* dough baked in puff pastry.

Tamié: Flat disc of cow's milk cheese, made at the Trappist monastery in the Savoie village of Tamié. Similar to Reblochon.

Tanche: tench, a river fish with a mild, delicate flavor; often an ingredient in *matelote* and *pauchouse,* freshwater fish stews.

Tapenade: a blend of black olives, anchovies, capers, olive oil, and lemon juice, sometimes with rum or canned tuna added; specialty of Provence.

Tarama: carp roe, often made into a spread of the same name.

Tarbas: variety of large white bean, usually dried.

Tartare (de poisson): traditionally chopped raw beef, seasoned and garnished with raw egg, capers, chopped onion, and parsley; (today, a popular highly seasoned raw fish dish).

Tarte: tart; open-face pie or flan, usually sweet.

encalat: name for cheesecake in the Auvergne.

flambée: thin-crusted savory tart, much like a

rectangular pizza, covered with cream, onions, and bacon; specialty of Alsace; also called *Flamekueche*.

à sucre: sugared bread tart.

Tatin: caramelized upside-down apple pie, made famous by the Tatin sisters in their hotel in Lamotte-Beuvron, in the Sologne; a popular dessert, seen on menus all over France.

Tartine: open-face sandwich; buttered bread.

Tasse: cup; a coffee or tea cup.

Telline: a tiny violet-streaked clam, the size of a fingernail, seen in Provence and the Camargue; generally seared with a bit of oil in a hot pan to open the shells and seasoned with parsley and garlic.

Tendre: tender.

Tendron: cartilaginous meat cut from beef or veal ribs.

Terrine: earthenware container used for cooking meat, game, fish, or vegetable mixtures; also the pâté cooked and served in such a container. It differs from a pâté proper in that the *terrine* is actually sliced in the container, while a pâté has been removed from its mold.

Tête de veau (porc): head of veal (pork), usually used in headcheese.

Tétragone: spinach-like green, found in Provence.

Teurgoule: a sweet rice pudding with cinnamon; specialty of Normandy.

Thé: tea.

Thermidor, homard: classic lobster dish in which lobster is split lengthwise, grilled, and served in the shell with a cream sauce.

Thon (blanc) (germon): tuna (white albacore).

rouge: bluefin tuna.

Thym: thyme.

Tian: an earthenware gratin dish; also vegetable gratins baked in such a dish; from Provence.

Tiède: lukewarm.

Tilleul: linden tree; linden-blossom herb tea.

Timbale: small round mold with straight or sloping slides; also, a mixture prepared in such a mold.

Torréfiée: roasted, as in coffee beans or chocolate.

Tomate: tomato.

Tomates à la provençale: baked tomato halves sprinkled with garlic, parsley, and bread crumbs.

Tomme: generic name for cheese; usually refers to a variety of cheeses in the Savoie; also, the fresh cheese used to make Cantal in the Auvergne.

arlésienne: rectangular cheese made with a blend of goat's and cow's milk and sprinkled with summer savory; also called *tomme de Camargue*; a specialty of the Languedoc and Arles, in Provence.

fraîche: pressed cake of fresh milk curds, used in the regional dishes of the Auvergne.

Topinambour: Jerusalem artichoke.

Toro (taureau): bull; meat found in butcher shops in the Languedoc and Pays Basque, and sometimes on restaurant menus.

Torteau au fromage: goat cheese cheesecake from the Poitou-Charentes along the Atlantic coast; a blackened, spherical loaf found at cheese shops throughout France; once a homemade delicacy, today prepared industrially.

Tortue: turtle.

Toucy: village in Burgundy that gives its name to a local fresh goat cheese.

Tourain, tourin, tourrin: generally a peasant soup of garlic, onions (and sometimes tomatoes), and broth or water, thickened with egg yolks and seasoned with vinegar; specialty of the southwest.

Tournedos: center portion of beef fillet, usually grilled or sautéed.

Rossini: sautéed *tournedos* garnished with *foie gras* and truffles.

Touron: marzipan loaf, or a cake of almond paste, often layered and flavored with nuts or candied fruits and sold by the slice; specialty of the Basque region.

Tourte (aux blettes): pie (common Niçoise dessert pie filled with Swiss chard, eggs, cheese, raisins, and pine nuts). Also, name for giant rounds of country bread found in the Auvergne and the southwest.

Tourteau: large crab.

Tourtière: shallow three-legged cooking vessel, set over hot coals for baking. Also, southwestern pastry dish filled with apples and/or prunes and sprinkled with Armagnac.

Train de côtes: rib of beef.

Traiteur: caterer; delicatessen.

Tranche: slice.

Trappiste: name given to the mild, lactic cow's milk cheese made in a Trappist monastery in Echourgnac, in the southwest.

Travers de porc: spareribs.

Trévise: radicchio, a bitter red salad green of the chicory family.

Triperie: shop selling innards or organ meats; the collective name for such meats.

Tripes à la mode de Caen: beef tripe, carrots, onions, leeks, and spices, cooked in water, cider, and Calvados (apple brandy); specialty of Normandy.

Triple crème: legal name for cheese containing more than 75 percent butterfat, such as Brillat-Savarin.

Tripoux: mutton tripe.

Tripoxa: Basque name for sheep's or calf's blood sausage served with spicy red Espelette peppers.

Trompettes de la mort: dark brown wild mushroom, also known as "horn of plenty."

Tronçon: cut of meat or fish resulting in a piece that is longer than it is wide; generally refers to slices from the largest part of a fish.

Trouchia: flat omelet filled with spinach or Swiss chard; specialty of Provence.

Truffade: a large layered and fried potato pancake made with bacon and fresh Cantal cheese; specialty of the Auvergne.

Truffe (truffé): truffle (with truffles).

Truffes sous la cendre: truffles wrapped in pastry or foil and warmed in a bed of ashes.

Truite (au bleu): trout (a preferred method of cooking trout, not live, as often assumed, but rather in a "live condition." The trout is gutted just moments prior to cooking, but neither washed nor scaled. It is then plunged into a hot mixture of vinegar and water, and the slimy lubricant that protects the skin of the fish appears to turn the trout a bluish color. The fish is then removed to a broth to finish its cooking.)

de lac: lake trout.

de mer: sea trout or brown trout.

de rivière: river trout.

saumonée: salmon trout.

Ttoro: fish soup from the Basque region. Historically, the liquid that remained after poaching cod was seasoned with herbs and used to cook vegetables and potatoes. Today, a more elaborate version includes the addition of *lotte,* mullet, mussels, conger eel, *langoustines,* and wine.

Tuile: literally, "curved roofing tile"; delicate almond-flavored cookie.

Tulipe: tulip-shaped cookie for serving ice cream or *sorbet.*

Turban: usually a mixture or combination of ingredients cooked in a ring mold.

Turbot(in): turbot (small turbot); prized flatfish found in the Atlantic and Mediterranean.

V

Vache: cow.

Vacherin: dessert of baked meringue, with ice cream and whipped cream. Also a strong, supple winter cheese encircled by a band of spruce, from the Jura.

Vallée d'Auge: area of Normandy. Also, garnish of cooked apples and cream or Calvados and cream.

Vanille: vanilla.

Vapeur, à la: steamed.

Varech: seaweed.

Veau: veal.

Velouté: classic sauce based on veal, chicken, or fish stock, thickened with a *roux* of butter and flour; also, variously seasoned classic soups thickened with cream and egg yolks.

Ventre: belly or stomach.

Ventrèche: bacon.

Vénus: American clam.

Verdure (en): garnish of green vegetables.

Verdurette: herb *vinaigrette.*

Verjus: juice of unripe grapes, used to make a condiment that is used like vinegar in sauces.

Vernis: large fleshy clam with small red tongue and shiny "varnished" shell.

Véronique, à la: garnish of peeled white grapes.

Vert-pré: a watercress garnish, sometimes including potatoes.

Verveine: lemon verbena herb tea.

Vessie, en: cooked in a pig's bladder (usually chicken).

Viande: meat.

Vichy: with glazed carrots. Also, a brand of mineral water.

Vichyssoise: creamy leek and potato soup, served cold.

Viennoise: coated in egg, breaded, and fried.

Vierge (sauce): "virgin"; term for the best-quality olive oil, from the first pressing of the olives; (sauce of olive oil, lemon juice, garlic, tomatoes, and fresh herbs).

Vieux (vielle): old.

Vieux Lille: thick, square cheese named for the old part of the north's largest city, made in the same way as Maroilles, with cow's milk, only salted more, then aged six months until stinking ripe. Also called *vieux puant,* or "old stinker."

Vin: wine.

jaune: specialty of Arbois in the Jura, yellow wine like *fino* sherry, made with late-harvested grapes.

de paille: speciality of Arbois in the Jura, wine from grapes dried on straw mats, consequently very sweet.

de pays: literally, country wine. There are more than 140 active *vin de pays* names, mainly in the Midi or Languedoc region.

de table: standard everyday table wine, not subject to particular regulations about grapes or origin. Generally less good than *vin de pays.*

Vinaigre (vieux): vinegar (aged).

de xérès: sherry vinegar.

Vinaigrette: oil and vinegar dressing.

Viognier: increasingly popular white grape of the Rhône, used for the famed Condrieu wine.

Violet or ***figue de mer:*** unusual iodine-strong, soft-shelled edible sea creature, with a yellowish interior. A delicacy along the Mediterranean, particularly in Marseilles.

Violet de Provence: braid of plump garlic, a specialty of Provence and the Côte d'Azur.

Violette: violet; its crystallized petals are a specialty of Toulouse.

Viroflay: classic garnish of spinach for poached or soft-cooked eggs.

Vive or ***vipère de mer:*** weever; a small firm-fleshed ocean fish used in soups, such as *bouillabaisse,* or grilled. The venomous spine is removed before cooking.

Vol-au-vent: puff pastry shell.

Volonté (à): at the customer's discretion.

Vonnaissienne, à la: in the style of Vonnas, a village in the Rhône-Alpes. Also, *crêpes* made with potatoes.

Waterzooi: Flemish chicken stew cooked with aromatic herbs and vegetables in a sauce of cream and chicken broth.

Winstub: wine bar in the style of Alsace, usually offering such specialties as sauerkraut and sausages, and Riesling and Gewürztraminer wines.

Xérès (vinaigre de): sherry (vinegar).

Yaourt: yogurt.

Z

Zeste: zest (citrus peel with white pith removed).

Zewelmai, zewelwai: Alsatian onion tart.

Zingara, à la: gypsy style; with tomato sauce. Also classically, a garnish of ham, tongue, mushrooms, and truffles.

Food Lover's Ready Reference

Restaurants: Bistros

L'Affriolé, Paris 7
Allard, Paris 6
L'Alsaco, Paris 9
L'Ami Louis, Paris 3
Café d'Angel, Paris 12
L'Ardoise, Paris 1
L'Assiette, Paris 14
Astier, Paris 11
Balzar, Paris 5
Baracane–Bistrot de l'Oulette, Paris 4
Au Bascou, Paris 2
La Bastide d'Odéon, Paris 6
Benoit, Paris 4
Les Bookinistes, Paris 6
Au Bon Acceuil, Paris 7
Au Bon Saint-Pourçain, Paris 6
La Butte Chaillot, Paris 16
Bistrot du Dôme, Paris 14
Bistrot du Dôme Bastille, Paris 4
La Cagouille, Paris 14
Le Caméléon, Paris 6
Au C'Amelot, Paris 11
Cartet, Paris 11
Aux Charpentiers, Paris 6
Dame Jeanne, Paris 11
L'Epi Dupin, Paris 6
Le Bistro de l'Etoile/ Lauriston, Paris 16
La Fontaine de Mars, Paris 7
Brasserie Les Fontaines, Paris 5
Restaurant d'Eric Frechon, Paris 12
Chez Georges, Paris 2
Les Gourmets des Ternes, Paris 8
Le Grizzli, Paris 4
Lescure, Paris 1
Chez Maître Paul, Paris 6
Chez Michel, Paris 10
Moissonnier, Paris 5
Au Moulin à Vent (Chez Henri), Paris 5
L'O à la Bouche, Paris 6
Les Olivades, Paris 7
L'Oulette, Paris 12
Restaurant du Palais Royal, Paris 1
Pierre au Palais Royal, Paris 1
Chez René, Paris 5
Café Runtz, Paris 1
A Sousceyrac, Paris 11
Le Square Trousseau, Paris 12
La Table d'Aude, Paris 6
La Tour de Montlhéry (Chez Denise), Paris 1
Chez La Vieille, Paris 1
Les Zygomates , Paris 12
La Zygotissoire, Paris 11

Restaurants: Brasseries

Alcazar, Paris 6
Bofinger, Paris 4
Bouillon Racine, Paris 6
La Coupole, Paris 14
Brasserie Flo, Paris 10
Brasserie de l'Ile Saint-Louis, Paris 3
Julien, Paris 10
Brasserie Lipp, Paris 6
Au Pied de Cochon, Paris 1
Vaudeville, Paris 2

Restaurants Costing 200 Francs or Less (not including wine)

Note that many restaurants offer reduced-price menus at lunchtime.

L'Affriolé, Paris 7
Allard, Paris 6
Les Allobroges, Paris 20
L'Alsaco, Paris 9
Ambassade d'Auvergne, Paris 3
Cafe d'Angel, Paris 17
L'Appart', Paris 8
L'Ardoise, Paris 1
Astier, Paris 11
Balzar, Paris 5
Le Bar au Sel, Paris 7
Baracane–Bistrot de l'Oulette, Paris 4
Au Bascou, Paris 3
La Bastide d'Odéon, Paris 6
Bofinger, Paris 4
Au Bon Acceuil, Paris 7
Au Bon Saint-Pourçain, Paris 6
Les Bookinistes, Paris 6
Bouillon Racine, Paris 6
La Butte Chaillot, Paris 16
La Cagouille, Paris 14
Le Caméléon, Paris 6
Au C'Amelot, Paris 11
Aux Charpentiers, Paris 6
Le Clos Morillons, Paris 15
Dame Jeanne, Paris 11
Bistrot du Dôme Bastille, Paris 4
L'Epi Dupin, Paris 6
Erawan, Paris 15
Brasserie Flo, Paris 10
Brasserie Les Fontaines, Paris 5
Restaurant d'Eric Frechon, Paris 19
Les Gourmets des Ternes, Paris 8
Le Grizzli, Paris 4
Brasserie de l'Ile Saint-Louis, Paris 4
Julien, Paris 10
Lescure, Paris 1
Brasserie Lipp, Paris 6
Chez Maître Paul, Paris 6
Mansouria, Paris 11
Mavrommatis, Paris 5
Chez Michel, Paris 10
Moissonnier, Paris 5
Monsieur Lapin, Paris 14
Au Moulin à Vent, Paris 5
L'O à la Bouche, Paris 6
Les Olivades, Paris 7
L'Oulette, Paris 12
Le Palanquin, Paris 6
Le Petit Plat, Paris 15
Au Pied de Cochon, Paris 1
Brasserie de la Poste, Paris 16
Auberge Pyrénées-Cévennes, Paris 11
Chez René, Paris 5
Café Runtz, Paris 2
A Sousceyrac, Paris 11
Le Square Trousseau, Paris 12
La Table d'Aude, Paris 6
Vaudeville, Paris 2
Chez la Vieille, Paris 1
Les Zygomates, Paris 12
La Zygotissoire, Paris 11

Restaurants Accepting Dinner Reservations at 7 p.m.

Alcazar, Paris 6
L'Alsaco, Paris 9
Balzar, Paris 5
Le Bar au Sel, Paris 7
Baracane–Bistrot de l'Oulette, Paris 4
Bofinger, Paris 4
Les Bookinistes, Paris 6
Bouillon Racine, Paris 6
La Butte Chaillot, Paris 16
Au C'Amelot, Paris 11
Cap Vernet, Paris 8
La Coupole, Paris 14
Erawan, Paris 15
Le Bistro de l'Etoile/Lauriston, Paris 16
Brasserie Flo, Paris 10
Brasserie Les Fontaines, Paris 5
Restaurant d'Eric Frechon, Paris 19
Les Gourmets des Ternes, Paris 8
Chez Gramond, Paris 6
Issé, Paris 2
Julien, Paris 10
Lac Hong, Paris 16
Brasserie Lipp, Paris 6
Maceo, Paris 1
Mavrommatis, Paris 5
Chez Michel, Paris 10
Au Pied de Cochon, Paris 1
Brasserie de la Poste, Paris 16
Le Pré Catelan, Paris 16
Auberge Pyrénées-Cévennes, Paris 11
Romantica, Clichy
Café Runtz, Paris 2
La Table d'Aude, Paris 6
Taillevent, Paris 8
La Tour de Montlhéry (Chez Denise), Paris 1
Vaudeville, Paris 2
La Zygotissoire, Paris 11

Restaurants Accepting Reservations after 11 p.m.

Alcazar, Paris 6
L'Appart', Paris 8
Balzar, Paris 5
Baracane–Bistrot de l'Oulette, Paris 4
Bofinger, Paris 4
Les Bookinistes, Paris 6
Bouillon Racine, Paris 6
La Butte Chaillot, Paris 16
Cap Vernet, Paris 8
Aux Charpentiers, Paris 6
La Coupole, Paris 14
Le Dôme, Paris 14
Bistrot du Dôme Bastille, Paris 4
Le Bistot de l'Etoile/ Lauriston, Paris 16
Brasserie Flo, Paris 10
Julien, Paris 10
Brasserie Lipp, Paris 6
Chez Michel, Paris 10
Au Pied de Cochon, Paris 1
Pierre au Palais Royal, Paris 1
Brasserie de la Poste, Paris 16
Café Runtz, Paris 2
Le Square Trousseau, Paris 12
La Tour de Montlhéry (Chez Denise), Paris 1
Vaudeville, Paris 2
La Zygotissoire, Paris 11

Restaurants Open on Saturday

L'Affriolé (dinner only), Paris 7
Alcazar, Paris 6
Allard, Paris 6
Les Allobroges, Paris 20
L'Alsaco (dinner only), Paris 9
Ambassade d'Auvergne, Paris 3
Les Ambassadeurs, Paris 8
L'Ambroisie, Paris 4
L'Ami Louis, Paris 3
L'Appart', Paris 8
L'Ardoise, Paris 1
L'Assiette, Paris 14
Balzar, Paris 5
Le Bar au Sel, Paris 7
Baracane–Bistrot de l'Oulette (dinner only), Paris 4
Au Bascou (dinner only), Paris 3
La Bastide d'Odéon, Paris 6
Benoit, Paris 4
Bofinger, Paris 4
Au Bon Saint-Pourçain, Paris 6
Les Bookinistes (dinner only), Paris 6
Les Bouchons de François Clerc (dinner only), Paris 5
Bouillon Racine, Paris 6
La Butte Chaillot, Paris 16
La Cagouille, Paris 14
Le Caméléon (dinner only), Paris 6
Au C'Amelot, Paris 11
Cap Vernet, Paris 8
Carré des Feuillants (dinner only), Paris 1
Aux Charpentiers, Paris 6
Le Clos Morillons (dinner only), Paris 15
La Closerie des Lilas, Paris 6
La Coupole, Paris 14
Dame Jeanne (dinner only), Paris 11
Le Dôme, Paris 14
Bistrot du Dôme, Paris 14
Bistrot du Dôme Bastille, Paris 4
Le Duc (dinner only), Paris 14
Erawan, Paris 15
Le Bistro de l'Etoile/ Lauriston (dinner only), Paris 16
Brasserie Flo, Paris 10
La Fontaine de Mars, Paris 7
Brasserie Les Fontaines, Paris 5
Restaurant d'Eric Frechon, Paris 19
Pierre Gagnaire (dinner only), Paris 8
Chez Georges, Paris 2
Chez Gramond, Paris 6
Le Grizzli, Paris 4
Brasserie de l'Ile Saint-Louis, Paris 4
Issé (dinner only), Paris 2
Julien, Paris 10
Kim-Anh, Paris 15
Lac Hong, Paris 16
Laurent, Paris 8
Lescure (lunch only), Paris 1
Brasserie Lipp, Paris 6
Maceo, Paris 1
Chez Maître Paul, Paris 6
Mansouria, Paris 11
Mavrommatis, Paris 5
Chez Michel, Paris 10
Paul Minchelli, Paris 7
Miravile (dinner only), Paris 4
Moissonnier, Paris 5
Monsieur Lapin (dinner only), Paris 14
Au Moulin à Vent (Chez Henri), Paris 5
L'O à la Bouche, Paris 6
Les Olivades (dinner only), Paris 7
L'Oulette (in summer; otherwise dinner only), Paris 12
Restaurant du Palais Royal (dinner only), Paris 1

Le Palanquin, Paris 6
Le Petit Marguery, Paris 13
Le Petit Plat, Paris 15
Au Pied de Cochon, Paris 1
Pierre au Palais Royal, Paris 1
Pile ou Face (dinner only), Paris 2
Port Alma, Paris 16
Brasserie de la Poste, Paris 16
Le Pré Catelan, Paris 16
Auberge Pyrénées-Cévennes (dinner only), Paris 11
Chez René (dinner only), Paris 5
Romantica (dinner only), Clichy
Michel Rostang (dinner only), Paris 17
Café Runtz (dinner only), Paris 2
Guy Savoy (dinner only), Paris 17
A Sousceyrac (dinner only), Paris 11
Le Square Trousseau, Paris 12
La Table d'Aude, Paris 6
La Table des Fès, Paris 6
Tan Dinh, Paris 7
Au Trou Gascon (dinner only), Paris 12
Vaudeville, Paris 2
Jules Verne, Paris 7
Le Violin d'Ingres, Paris 7
Les Zygomates (dinner only), Paris 12
La Zygotissoire (dinner only), Paris 11

Restaurants Open on Sunday

Alcazar, Paris 6
Ambassade d'Auvergne, Paris 3
Les Ambassadeurs, Paris 8
L'Ami Louis, Paris 3
L'Appart', Paris 8
L'Ardoise, Paris 1
L'Assiette, Paris 14
Balzar, Paris 5
Le Bar au Sel, Paris 7
Benoit, Paris 4
Bofinger, Paris 4
Les Bookinistes (dinner only), Paris 6
Bouillon Racine, Paris 6
La Butte Chaillot, Paris 16
La Cagouille, Paris 14
Cap Vernet, Paris 8
Aux Charpentiers, Paris 6
La Closerie des Lilas, Paris 6
La Coupole, Paris 14
Le Dôme, Paris 14
Bistrot du Dôme, Paris 14
Bistrot du Dôme Bastille, Paris 4
Brasserie Flo, Paris 10
La Fontaine de Mars, Paris 7
Brasserie de l'Ile Saint-Louis, Paris 4
Julien, Paris 10
Kim-Anh, Paris 15
Laurent, Paris 8
Brasserie Lipp, Paris 6
Chez Maître Paul (except July and August), Paris 6
Mansouria, Paris 11
Mavrommatis, Paris 5
Moissonnier (lunch only), Paris 5
Monsieur Lapin, Paris 14
Restaurant du Palais Royal (summer only), Paris 1
Au Pied de Cochon, Paris 1
Brasserie de la Poste, Paris 16
Le Pré Catelan (lunch only), Paris 16
Le Square Trousseau, Paris 12
Vaudeville, Paris 2
Jules Verne, Paris 7

Restaurants Open in August

L'Affriolé, Paris 7
Alcazar, Paris 6
Ambassade d'Auvergne, Paris 3
Les Ambassadeurs, Paris 8
L'Appart', Paris 8
Arpège, Paris 7
Balzar, Paris 5
Le Bar au Sel, Paris 7
Baracane–Bistrot de l'Oulette, Paris 3
Bofinger, Paris 3
Au Bon Acceuil, Paris 7
Les Bookinistes, Paris 6
Les Bouchons de François Clerc, Paris 5
Bouillon Racine, Paris 6
La Butte Chaillot, Paris 16
La Cagouille, Paris 14
Cap Vernet, Paris 8
Aux Charpentiers, Paris 6
Le Clos Morillons, Paris 15
La Closerie des Lilas, Paris 6
Il Cortile, Paris 1
La Coupole, Paris 14
Dame Jeanne, Paris 11
Le Dôme, Paris 14

Bistrot du Dôme, Paris 14
Bistrot du Dôme Bastille, Paris 4
Le Duc, Paris 14
Alain Ducasse (two weeks), Paris 16
L'Epi Dupin, Paris 6
Le Bistro de l'Etoile/ Lauriston, Paris 16
Brasserie Flo, Paris 10
La Fontaine de Mars, Paris 7
Brasserie Les Fontaines, Paris 5
Pierre Gagnaire (two weeks), Paris 8
Le Grizzli, Paris 4
Issé (two weeks), Paris 2
Julien, Paris 10
Laurent, Paris 8
Brasserie Lipp, Paris 6
Maceo, Paris 1
Chez Maitre Paul, Paris 6
Mansouria, Paris 11
Mavrommatis, Paris 5
Miravile (two weeks), Paris 4
L'Oulette, Paris 12
Restaurant du Palais Royal, Paris 1
Le Palanquin, Paris 6
Le Petit Plat (two weeks), Paris 15
Au Pied de Cochon, Paris 1
Pierre au Palais Royal, Paris 1
Brasserie de la Poste, Paris 16
Le Pré Catelan, Paris 16
Auberge Pyrénées-Cévennes, Paris 11
Romantica, Clichy
Michel Rostang (two weeks), Paris 17
Guy Savoy, Paris 17
Le Square Trousseau, Paris 12
La Tour de Montlhéry (Chez Denise) (two weeks), Paris 1
Vaudeville, Paris 2
Jules Verne, Paris 7
La Zygotissoire, Paris 11

Restaurants with Sidewalk Tables or Open Terrace

Balzar, Paris 5
Le Bar au Sel, Paris 7
Au Bon Acceuil, Paris 7
La Butte Chaillot, Paris 16
La Cagouille, Paris 14
Cap Vernet, Paris 8
Aux Charpentiers, Paris 6
Il Cortile, Paris 1
Dame Jeanne, Paris 11
Le Dôme, Paris 14
Bistrot du Dôme, Paris 14
L'Epi Dupin (lunch only), Paris 6
La Fontaine de Mars, Paris 7
Brasserie Les Fontaines, Paris 5
Les Gourmets des Ternes, Paris 8
Le Grizzli, Paris 4
Brasserie de l'Ile Saint-Louis, Paris 4
Laurent, Paris 8
Lescure, Paris 1
Brasserie Lipp, Paris 6
Mavrommatis, Paris 5
Chez Michel, Paris 10
Miravile, Paris 4
Les Olivades, Paris 7
L'Oulette, Paris 12
Restaurant du Palais Royal, Paris 1
Le Petit Plat, Paris 15
Au Pied de Cochon, Paris 1
Le Pré Catelan, Paris 16
Chez René, Paris 5
Romantica, Clichy
Le Square Trousseau, Paris 12
Vaudeville, Paris 2

Air-Conditioned Restaurants

L'Affriolé, Paris 7
Alcazar, Paris 6
Allard, Paris 6
Ambassade d'Auvergne, Paris 3
Les Ambassadeurs, Paris 8
L'Ambroisie, Paris 4
Apicius, Paris 17
L'Appart', Paris 8
Arpège, Paris 7
Le Restaurant de l'Astor, Paris 8
Balzar, Paris 5
La Bastide d'Odéon, Paris 6
Benoit, Paris 4
Les Bookinistes, Paris 6
Bouillon Racine, Paris 6
La Butte Chaillot, Paris 16
Cap Vernet, Paris 8
Carré des Feuillants, Paris 1
Il Cortile, Paris 1
La Coupole, Paris 14
Le Dôme, Paris 14
Bistrot du Dôme, Paris 14
Bistrot du Dôme Bastille, Paris 4

Le Duc, Paris 14
Alain Ducasse, Paris 16
Bistro de l'Etoile/Lauriston, Paris 16
Les Elysées du Vernet, Paris 8
Erawan, Paris 15
Brasserie Flo, Paris 10
Restaurant d'Eric Frechon, Paris 19
Pierre Gagnaire, Paris 8
Chez Georges, Paris 2
Le Grand Véfour, Paris 1
Jamin, Paris 16
Julien, Paris 10
Kim-Anh, Paris 15
Lac Hong, Paris 16
Lescure, Paris 1
Brasserie Lipp, Paris 6
Chez Maître Paul, Paris 6
Mavrommatis, Paris 5
Paul Minchelli, Paris 7
Miravile, Paris 4
Monsieur Lapin, Paris 14
Les Olivades, Paris 7
Le Petit Plat, Paris 15
Au Pied de Cochon, Paris 1
Pierre au Palais Royal, Paris 1
Pile ou Face, Paris 2
Port Alma, Paris 16
Brasserie de la Poste, Paris 16
Auberge Pyrénées-Cévennes, Paris 11
Michel Rostang, Paris 17
Café Runtz, Paris 2
Guy Savoy, Paris 17
A Sousceyrac, Paris 11
La Table d'Aude, Paris 6
Taillevent, Paris 8
Au Trou Gascon, Paris 12
Vaudeville, Paris 2
Jules Verne, Paris 7
Le Violin d'Ingres, Paris 7

Restaurants with Private Dining Rooms or Dining Areas

Alcazar, Paris 6 (15 to 30)
Ambassade d'Auvergne, Paris 3 (10 to 40)
L'Ambroisie, Paris 4 (10 to 12)
Apicius, Paris 17 (25)
L'Ardoise, Paris 1 (15 to 17)
Arpège, Paris 7 (14)
Le Restaurant de l'Astor, Paris 8 (10 to 20)
La Bastide d'Odéon, Paris 6 (12 to 15)
Bofinger, Paris 4 (30 to 80 at lunch; 10 at dinner)
Bouillon Racine, Paris 6 (22)
La Butte Chaillot, Paris 16 (20)
La Cagouille, Paris 14 (18)
Cap Vernet, Paris 8 (20)
Carre des Feuillants, Paris 1 (7 to 35)
La Closerie des Lilas, Paris 6 (20)
La Coupole, Paris 14 (200)
Le Dôme, Paris 14 (10)
Les Elysées du Vernet, Paris 8 (2 to 17)
La Fontaine de Mars, Paris 7 (16 to 20)
Pierre Gagnaire, Paris 8 (15)
Le Grand Véfour, Paris 1 (8 to 22)
Le Grizzli, Paris 4 (30 to 35)
Issé, Paris 2 (8)
Jamin, Paris 16 (8 to 16)
Laurent, Paris 8 (4 to 70)
Lescure, Paris 1 (12)
Brasserie Lipp, Paris 6 (45)
Maceo, Paris 1 (10 to 50)
Chez Maître Paul, Paris 6 (20)
Paul Minchelli, Paris 7 (8 to 10)
Miravile, Paris 4 (10 to 30)
Les Olivades, Paris 7 (20)
Restaurant du Palais Royal, Paris 1 (15)
Le Palanquin, Paris 6 (16)
Le Petit Marguery, Paris 13 (15 to 20)
Au Pied de Cochon, Paris 1 (20 to 40)
Pile ou Face, Paris 2 (8 to 20)
Port Alma, Paris 16 (14)
Le Pré Catelan, Paris 16 (8 to 20)
Romantica, Clichy (20 to 25)
Cafe Runtz, Paris 2 (40)
Guy Savoy, Paris 17 (10 to 35)
A Sousceyrac, Paris 11 (10 to 20)
La Table d'Aude, Paris 6 (12 Or 50)
Taillevent, Paris 8 (12 to 32)
Tan Dinh, Paris 7 (20 to 30)
Chez la Vieille, Paris 1 (28)

Index

Following French style, any articles such as *au, la,* or *le* and the words *bar, bistro, boulangerie, brasserie, café, cave, charcuterie, chez, fromagerie,* or *pâtisserie* appearing before the proper name of the establishment are ignored in the alphabetizing. For example, Au Pied de Cochon is listed as "Pied de Cochon, Au" and Chez Pauline is listed as "Pauline, Chez," both under the letter *P.* Likewise, when the name of an establishment is also the full name of a person, such as Guy Savoy, the entry appears under the last name (Savoy).

A

Absinthe, 152
Acabo, Denise (A l'Etoile d'Or), 308
Adrienne, Chez (Chez la Vielle), 24
Affinage, 276
Affriolé, L', 68–69
Air-conditioned restaurants, 420
A la carte, 5
Alcazar, 51
Alcoholic drinks:
  aperitifs, 152
  beer, 157
  in cafés, 146
  see also Wines
Aligre, Marché d', 369
Allard, 52
Alléosse, 276, 288
Allobroges, Les, 136
Alsacienne, Boulangerie, 268
Alsacienne, Charcuterie, 298
Alsacienne, Pâtisserie Boulangerie (André Lerch), 223–24
Alsaco, L', 90–91
Alsatian products, specialty shop for, 374
Ambassade d'Auvergne, 32
Ambassade du Sud-Ouest, L', 324
Ambassadeurs, Les, 79
Ambroisie, L', 36
American foods, specialty shops for, 320, 325
Ami Louis, L', 33
Androuët (6, rue Arsène-Houssaye), 285
Androuët (83, rue Saint-Dominque), 279
Angel, Café d', 130–31
Angelina, 165
Ange-Vin, L', 178
Antique (flea) markets, 368–69
Antiques, specialty shops for, 372
  bistro paraphernalia, 365
  glassware, 359
  labels, 366
Aperitifs, 152
Apicius, 131
Appart', L', 80
Ardoise, L', 11–12
Argenterie des Franc-Bourgeois (Jean-Pierre de Castro), 355
Arlequin, L', 359
Arpège, 70–71
Art Deco, specialty shop for, 376
Assiette, L', 110–11
Astier, 95
Astor, Le Restaurant de l', 81–82
Auge, Caves, 341–42
August, restaurants open in, 419
Augustins, Bistrot des, 182–83
Auteuil, 216
Autre Boulange, L', 263–64

B

Baguettes, 244
Bakeries, 239–73
Bakeries, listed by neighborhoods and arrondissements:
  Arc de Triomphe, Porte Maillot, Villiers (17th arrondissement), 270
  Bir Hakeim, Montparnasse, Plaisance (14th arrondissement), 265–67
  Convention, Porte de Vanves (15th arrondissement), 268
  Faubourg Saint-Antoine, Bastille, République, Vincennes (11th and 12th arrondissements), 263–65
  Les Grands Boulevards (8th arrondissement), 262–63
  Les Halles, Bourse, Opéra (1st and 2nd arrondissements), 242–46
  Ménilmontant (20th arrondissement), 272–73
  Montmartre, Barbes-Rochechouart (18th arrondissement), 271
  République, Marais (3rd and 4th arrondissements), 246–48
  Saint-Germain, Sèvres-Babylone, La Tour-Maubourg (6th and 7th arrondissements), 256–62
  Victor Hugo, Auteuil, Saint Cloud (16th arrondissement), 268
Baker's dozen, 224
Balzar, 45
Baracane-Bistrot de l'Oulette, 36–37
Bar au Sel, Le, 72
Bars à vin, 176–94
  see also Wine bars
Barthélemy, 280
Bascou, Au, 33–34
Bastide d'Odéon, La, 52
Ba-Ta-Clan, Café, 156
Batignolles, 213
Bazaar de l'Hôtel de Ville (B.H.V.), 362
Bazin, 264

Beaubourg, Café, 147
Beaufort, Gérard, 224
Beaujolais, 188
Beauvallet, Boulagerie, 251
Beauvau, 202
Beer, 157
Belle Hortense, La, 147
Belleville-Ménilmontant, 210
Benoit, 37
Bernardaud, 172
Berthillon, 228
Betjeman and Barton, 328
Beverages:
  hot, glossary of, 145
  see also Alcoholic drinks; Coffee; Wines
B.H.V. (Bazaar de l'Hôtel de Ville), 362
Bill paying, in restaurants, 5–6
Bistro paraphernalia, specialty shop for, 365
Bistros, 3
  list of, 416
  see also Restaurants
Bistros à vin, 176–94
  see also Wine bars
Bistrots d'Autrefois, 365
Blanc d'Ivoire, 365
Blondeau, 271
Bofinger, 38–40
Boissier, 309
Boitard, Marie-Pierre, 366
Bon, 224
Bon Accueil, Au, 72–73
Bonbonnière Saint-Honoré, La, 310
Bonbonnière de la Trinité, La, 310
Bon Marché, Au, 363
Bon Saint-Pourçain, Au, 53
Bookinistes, Les, 53–54
Bookshops, food and wine, 345–50
Bouchons de François Clerc, Les, 45
Bouillon Racine, 54–55
Boulangeries, 239–73
  see also Bakeries
Boulevard Poissonière, 283
Boulogne, Le Marché, 213
Bovida, La, 352
Brasseries, 3–4
  list of, 416
  see also Restaurants
Breads:
  baguettes, 244
  decorated, 258
  glossary of, 260–61
  see also Bakeries
Breakfast, spiritous (*tuer le ver*), 185
Brentano's, 346
Breteuil, 209–10
Brûlerie des Ternes, 334
Brune, 212
Brusa, Michel, 251
Bugat, Paul, 221
Butcher shop, 332
Butte Chaillot, La, 121
Butter, 287
  in restaurants, 7–8

C

Café items, specialty shop for, 367
Cafés, 141–63
  alcoholic drinks in, 146
  aperitifs in, 152
  beer in, 157
  coffee and other hot drinks in, 145
  history of, 141–42
  snacks in, 161
  tipping in, 143
  wine in, 176–77
Cafés, listed by neighborhoods and arrondissements:
  Bastille, Oberkampf (11th arrondissement), 156–57
  Champs Elysées (8th arrondissement), 155
  Châtelet, Marais, Ile Saint-Louis (4th arrondissement), 147–49
  Les Halles, Pont Neuf, Tuileries, Louvre (1st arrondissement), 143–46
  Latin Quarter, Luxembourg, Saint-Germain, Sèvres-Babylone, Quai d'Orsay (5th, 6th, and 7th arrondissements), 150–54
  Montparnasse, Grenelle (14th and 15th arrondissements), 158
  Père Lachaise (20th arrondissement), 163
  Victor Hugo, Arc de Triomphe (16th arrondissement), 160–61
Cagouille, La, 111–12
Calixte, 222
Calvados, 146
Caméléon, Le, 55–56
C'Amelot, Au, 95–96
Candy shops, 332, 335
  see also Chocolate shops
Cantin, Marie-Anne, 280–81
Cap Vernet, 82–83
Carette, 175
Carmes (Place Maubert market), 207–8
Carmès, Jean, et Fils (cheese shop), 289
Carpe, La, 373
Carré des Feuillants (Alain Dutournier), 12–13
  wine shop at, 337
Carrelages du Marais, Les, 359
Cartet, 96
Carton, Jean-Pierre, 226
Castro, Jean-Pierre de (Argenterie des Franc-Bourgeois), 355
Caviar Kaspia, 328
Caviar shops, 327, 328
Cèdre Rouge, Le, 352
140, Au, 272
Cervantes, 215
Chambard, Tiany, 366
Charbon, Café, 156–57
Charcuteries, 292–303
  foie gras in, 300–302
  glossary of products found in, 295–97
Charcuteries, listed by neighborhoods and arrondissements:
  Madeleine (9th arrondissement), 299
  Marais, Bastille (4th arrondissement), 294
  Saint-Germain, Odéon, Sèvres-Babylone (6th arrondissement), 298–99
  Victor-Hugo, Etoile, Villiers (16th and 17th arrondissements), 302–3
Charles, Charcuterie, 299
Charpentiers, Aux, 57
Chastel Coutelier, 374
Chaudun, Michel, 306

Chavenet, Laurent, 268
Cheese:
aging of, 275–76
eating rind of, 281
French, imported to U.S., 275
scents of, 289
selecting, 276
U.S. Customs and, 278
Cheese shops, 274–91
butter sold in, 287
Cheese shops, listed by neighborhoods and arrondissements:
Bac, Sèvres-Babylone, Ecole-Militaire (7th arrondissement), 279–81
Courcelles, Villiers (17th arrondissement), 288–89
Denfert-Rochereau, Porte d'Orléans, Porte de Versailles (14th and 15th arrondissements), 286
Etoile, Madeleine (8th arrondissement), 285–86
Ile Saint-Louis (4th arrondissement), 278
Montmartre (18th arrondissement), 291
Opéra, Palais-Royal (1st arrondissement), 277
Temple (3rd arrondissement), 278
Chestnuts, candied, 309
Chocolate, dispute over merits of, 304–5
Chocolate shops, 304–14
candied chestnuts in, 309
seasonal specialties in, 314
Chocolate shops, listed by neighborhoods and arrondissements:
Bastille (11th arrondissement), 313
Bourse (2nd arrondissement), 306
Madeleine, Rond-Point, Arc de Triomphe, Grands Boulevards, Trinité, Le Peletier, Gare Saint-Lazare (8th and 9th arrondissements), 308–13
Saint Germain, Sèvres-Babylone, Ecole Militaire, 306–8
Chocolat Viennois, 175
Chocotruffe, 307
Cidre, 146
Cléret, André, 242
Cloche des Halles, A la, 178
Closerie des Lilas, La, 58
Clos Montmartre, 340, 341
Clos Morillons, Le (restaurant), 118
Clos des Morillons (vineyard), 340, 341
Clos du Pas-Saint-Maurice, 340
Clown Bar, 189
Cochon à l'Oreille, Le, 143
Coesnon, Charcuterie, 299
Coffee:
glossary of, 145
history of, 148
in restaurants, 8
specialty shops for, 316, 334
see also Cafés
Colette, 143
Colom, 229
Comoglio, 366
Comptoir Correzien, Le, 333
Comptoir des Ouvrages, Le (Laurence Roque), 365
Condiments, specialty shops for, 329, 333
Conran Shop, The, 356
Constant, Christian, 227
Convention, 215
Cooking schools, 348–49
Copernic, Le, 160
Cordon Bleu, Le, 348
Cornue, Gallerie La, 366
Cortile, Il, 13–15
Côté Vert, 214
Couasnon, Boulangerie, 270
Coupole, La, 113, 142, 158
Coup de Torchon, 360
Cours de la Reine/Président Wilson, 216
Cours de Vincennes, 212
Crafts, regional, specialty shops for, 373, 374
Credit cards, 6
Cuisineophilie, 360
Culinarion, 356–57
Curnonsky (Maurice-Edmond Sailland), 19, 343

D

Dalloyau, 169, 237
Dame Jeanne, 97–98
Damman's, 227
Danflou, Jean, 337
Debauve & Gallais (30, rue des Saint-Pères), 305, 307
Debauve & Gallais (35, rue Vivienne), 306
Dégustations:
of cheese, 276
menu (tasting menu), 7
Dehillerin, E., 352
Délices du Palais, Aux, 265
Denise, Chez (La Tour de Montlhéry), 23
Department stores, 362–64
Dernière Goutte, La, 339
Desgrippes, 231
Design, specialty shops for, 354, 373
Détou, G., 316
Deux Magots, Les, 142, 150–51
Devine Qui Vient Dîner ce Soir, 376
Dîners en Ville, 367
Dining hours, in restaurants, 4–5
Divay, 302
Dôme, Le:
restaurant, 113–14
terrace café, 142, 158
Dôme, Le Bistrot du, 114–15
Dôme Bastille, Bistrot du, 40
D.O.T., 361
Drahonnet, 246
Dubois, Alain, 289
Duc, Le, 116
Ducasse, Alain, 123–24
Duchesne, 231
Dupleix/Grenelle, 215–16
Duthilleul et Minart, 353
Dutournier, Alain (Carré des Feuillants), 12–13
wine shop at, 337

E

Echanson, L', 191
Ecluse, L' (chain), 186–87
Ecole de Gastronomie Ritz-Escoffier, 348
Ecole Lenôtre, 348–49
Edgar Quinet, 212
Eglise, Pâtisserie de l', 238
Elysées du Vernet, Les, 83–84
Embroidery, specialty shop for, 365

English foods, specialty shop for, 328
Envierges, Bistro-Cave des, 192–93
Epi Dupin, L', 58–60
Epi Gaulois, L', 268
Equipment:
professional, specialty shops for, 352, 354, 355, 373
see also Kitchen and tableware shops
Erawan, 118–19
Espace Gourmand, 247
Espace la Rochère, 364
Espace Shore, 372
Etamine, 367
Etoile/Lauriston, Bistro de l', 4–25
Etoile d'Or, A l' (Denise Acabo), 308

F

Fanette, 376
Fauchon, 328, 331
wines and liquors at, 342
Feret, Boulangerie, 264
Fil O'Fromage, 286
Finkelsztajn, Florence, 222–23
Finkelsztajn, Sacha, 222–23
Fireplace, specialty shops for, 371, 375
Fish:
oysters, 42–43
in restaurants, 8
sardines, 330–31
Fish shop, 319
Flachard, Rémi, 350
Flea markets, 368–69
Flo, Brasserie, 92
Flore, Boutique le, 367
Flore, Café de, 142, 151–52
Flore en l'Ile, Le, 149, 228
Flute Gana, La, 272–73
FNAC, 346
Foie gras, 300–302
Fontaine de Mars, La, 73–74
Fontaines, Brasserie Les, 46
Food bookshops. *See* Bookshops, food and wine
Fouquet's, Le, 155
France, Fromagers de, 278
Frechon, Eric, Le Restaurant d', 136–37
Fromageries, 274–91
see also Cheese shops
Fumoir, Le, 144
Furet-Tanrade, Le, 333

G

Gagnaire, Pierre, 85–86
Galerie Michel Sonkin, 372
Galeries Lafayette, 363
supermarket at (Lafayette Gourmet), 326–27
Galignani, 345
Gallerie la Cornue, 366
Ganachuad (Jeudon), 273
Gandom, 334–35
Garcia, Boulangerie, 252
Garden items, specialty shop for, 352
Gargantua, 316
Gaulupeau, J. C., 227
General Store, The, 325
Georges, Chez, 27–28
Gibert Jeune, 347
Glassware:
specialty shops for, 359, 361, 364, 371, 374, 376
wineglasses, 338
Glossaries:
of alcoholic drinks, 146
of aperitifs, 152
of breads, 260–61
of *charcuterie,* 295–97
of food, 377
of hot beverages, 145
of snacks, 161
Gobelins, 212
Gosselin, 242
Gourmandises, Aux, 229
Gourmet shops, 315–35
see also Specialty shops
Gourmets des Ternes, Les, 86–87
Gramond, Chez, 60–61
Grande Epicerie de Paris, La, 326
Grands magasins, 362–64
Grand Véfour, Le, 15–17
Grateau, Muriel, Boutique, 353
Grizzli, Le, 40–41

H

Habitat, 357
Les Halles, 201
Hameau, La Ferme du, 286
Hauteurs, Café des, 152
Health food shop, 325
Hédiard (specialty shop), 317, 331
Hédiard, La Cave d' (wine and liquor shop), 342
Hemingway, Ernest, 186
Henri, Chez (Au Moulin à Vent), 48
Henri IV, Taverne, 179
Henry-Ceccaldi, 299
Herbes du Luxembourg, Les, 325
Hermine Paul, L', 229
Hervet, S., 252
Hévin, Jean-Paul, 307
Honey, specialty shop for, 329
Hugo, Le Victor, 161
Huilerie J. Leblanc, 325

I

Ice cream shops, 227–29
Ile Saint Louis, Brasserie de l', 41
Impasse Marché aux Chevaux, 283
Impasse de la Poissonnerie, 283
Institut National des Appellations d'Origine (I.N.A.O.), 338
Issé, 28
Izrael Epicerie du Monde, 320

J

Jacquemart-André, Café, 172
Jamin, 125–26
Japy, Laure, 370
Jean-Claude et Nanou, 303
Jeudon (Ganachaud), 273
Joinville-Le-Pont, 213
Julien (bakery) (73, avenue Franklin D. Roosevelt), 262–63
Julien (bakery) (75, rue Saint-Honoré), 242
Julien, Brasserie, 92
Juveniles, 178

K

Kayser, 252
"Killing the worm" (*tuer le ver*), 185

Kim-Anh, 119
Kir, 152
Kir royal, 152
Kitchen Bazaar, 353, 376
Kitchen and tableware shops, 351–76
with both modern and traditional items, 356–59
department stores with houseware departments, 362–64
Kitchen and tableware shops, listed by neighborhoods and arrondissements:
Arc de Triomphe (16th arrondissement), 376
Bastille (12th arrondissement), 375, 375
Les Halles, Châtelet, Palais-Royal, Place des Victoires (1st and 2nd arrondissements), 352–55
Latin Quarter, Saint-Germain, Sèvres-Babylone, Montparnasse (5th, 6th, and 7th arrondissements), 365–73
Madeleine, Courcelles, Franklin Roosevelt (8th arrondissement), 373–74
Marais, République (3rd and 4th arrondissements), 355–65
Montparnasse, Grenelle (14th and 15th arrondissements), 376
Knives, specialty shops for, 354, 374

L

Labels, antique, specialty shop for, 366
Lac Hong, 127
Ladurée (16, rue Royale), 233
tea salon at, 173–74
Ladurée (75, avenue Champs-Elysées), 234
tea salon at, 173–74
Lafayette, Galeries, 363
supermarket at (Lafayette Gourmet), 326–27
Laguiole, Boutique, 354
Lapin, Monsieur, 116–17
Laurent, 87
Leblanc, Huilerie J., 325
Legrand Fille & Fils, 338, 340
Lenôtre, Gaston, 235, 258
Lerch, André (Pâtisserie Boulangerie Alsacienne), 223–24
Lescene-Dura, 361
Lescure, 17
Lethu, Geneviève, 358
Levain du Marais, Au, 247
Leverrier, Marcel, 277
Librairie Gourmande, 347
Librairie des Gourmets, La, 347
Librairie Guenegaud, 349
Librairie Jacques Lanore, 349
Librairies spécialisées: gastronomie, 345–50
Liebling, A. J., 145
Linens, specialty shops for, 353, 360, 370, 372
Lipp, Brasserie, 61–62, 142
café terrace at, 153
Liquor:
in restaurants, 9
see also Alcoholic drinks; Wines
Liquor shops. *See* Wine and liquor shops

M

Ma Bourgogne (19, place des Vosges), 148–49
Ma Bourgogne (133, boulevard Haussmann), 188
Maceo, 18–19
Maille, Boutique, 329
Mairie, Café de la, 153
Maison de l'Alsace, La Boutique de la, 374
Maison du Chocolat, La, 310–11
Maison de Famille, 367
Maison Ivre, La, 367
Maison du Miel, La, 329
Maison Pou, 303
Maison Rustique, La, 349–50
Maison de la Truffe, La, 323, 332
Maître Paul, Chez, 62
Malitourne, 234
Mandarin (aperitif), 152
Mandarin, Le (ice cream shop), 229
Mansouria, 98–99
Marc de bourgogne, 146
Marchés, 195–219
see also Markets
Marchés aux puces, 368–69
Marchés volants (roving markets), 198, 207–17
Mariage Frères, 168–69
Markets, 195–219
covered (*marchés-couverts*), 198
flea, 368–69
at a glance, 218–19
history of, 201
merchant streets (*rue commerçantes*), 198, 199–205
organic (*marchés biologiques*), 213
roving (*marchés volants*), 198, 207–17
Rungis wholesale, 201, 206
Marks & Spencer, 327
Marly, Le Café, 144
Marrons glacés, 309
Martin, Boulangerie, 247
Mauzac, Le, 183
Mavrommatis, 46
Meat:
in restaurants, 8
see also Charcuteries
"Meilleur Pot" award, 181
Mélac, Jacques, 189–90
Memmi, Catherine, 370
Ménès, Albert, 331
Menu dégustation, 7
Merchant streets (*rue commerçantes*), 199–205
Mère de Famille, A la, 313, 331
Miard, Caves, 339
Michel, Chez, 93–94
Millet, Pâtisserie, 233
Minchelli, Paul, 74
Miravile, 44
Moderne, Boulangerie, 256
Moissonnier, 47–48
Molineau, Hervé, 247
Monastica, 364
Monge, 208–9
Montmartre, Fromagerie de, 291
Montmartre, Queen of Hungary Passage in, 201
Montrouge, 214
M.O.R.A.:
books on food at, 345

professional equipment at, 354
Mouffetard, Café, 153–54
Moulin à Vent, Au (Chez Henri), 48
Moulin de la Vièrge, Le, 265–67
Mulot, Gérard, 256–57
Muscade, 166
Musée des Arts Décoratifs, La Boutique du, 354

N

Near Eastern foods, specialty shop for, 334–35
Négociants, Aux, 193–94
Nemrod, Le, 154
Nicolsen, 229
Nivernaises, Boucherie, 332
North African foods, specialty shop for, 320
Nouveaux Robinson, Les, 214
Nouvelle Mairie, Café de la, 184
Nuit des Thés, La, 171

O

O à la Bouche, L', 63
Oils, specialty shops for, 320, 325
Old-fashioned items, specialty shop for, 331
Olivades, Les, 75–76
Olivier, A l', 320
Onfroy, 248
Ordering:
in restaurants, 7
wine, 9–10
Organic markets (*marchés biologiques*), 213
Organic supermarkets, 214
Oulette, L', 102–3
Outdoor terrace, restaurants with, 420
Oysters, 42–43

P

Pain d'Antan, Au, 271
Pain au Naturel, Le (Pain Moisan), 265
Pain Quotidien, Le, 146, 243
Palais-Royal, Restaurant du, 19–20
Palanquin, Le, 65
Palette, La, 154
Panetier, Au, 243–44
Papeterie Moderne, 355
Papillon, Antoine, 270
Parmentier, Antoine, 19
Passage, Le, 190–91
Passage de la Brie, 282
Pastis, 152
Pastry ingredients, specialty shop for, 316
Pastry shops, 220–38
Pastry shops, listed by neighborhoods and arrondissements:
Bastille, Ile Saint Louis, Marais, Les Halles (2nd and 4th arrondissements), 221–23
Latin Quarter, Saint-German (5th and 6th arrondissements), 223–27
Madeleine, Champs-Elysées (8th arrondissement), 233–34
Ménilmontant (20th arrondissement), 238
Passy, Auteuil, Ternes (16th and 17th arrondissements), 234–35
Sèvres-Babylone, Ecole Militaire, La Tour-Maubourg (7th arrondissement), 231–33
Pâtisseries, 220–38
see also Pastry shops
Paul (bakery chain), 270
Peas, 41
Peltier, 233
Pepper, in restaurants, 8
Petit Bleu, Le, 333
Petite Fabrique, A la, 313
Petit Fer à Cheval, Au, 149
Petit Marguery, Le, 103–4
Petit Plat, Le, 119–21
Petrin d'Antan, Au, 271
Petrissans, Caves, 192, 342
Petrossian, 327
Picon, 152
Pied du Cochon, Au, 20–21
Pierre au Palais Royal, 21–23
Pile ou Face, 29–30
Pince à Buches, La, 375
Pineau des Charentes, 152
Pippermint Get, 146
Place des Fêtes, 217
Plat du jour, 7
Poilâne, Lionel, 257–59
Poilâne, Max (29, rue de l'Ouest), 267
Poilâne, Max (42, place du Marché Saint-Honoré), 246
Poilâne, Max (87, rue Brancion), 258, 268
Port Alma, 127–28
Poste, Brasserie de la, 128–29
Potatoes, 19
Pottery, specialty shops for, 364, 365, 367
Poujauran, Jean-Luc, 261–62
Poultry, in restaurants, 8
Pré Catelan, 129–30
Prepared foods to go, 292–303
see also Charcuteries
Prestige, Flo, 318–19
Prices, in restaurants, 5
Printemps, Au, 363
Private dining rooms or dining areas, 6
restaurants with, 421
Procope, Le, 141–42, 148
Produits Hongrois, 294
Professional equipment, specialty shops for, 352, 354, 355, 373
Puces, marchés aux, 368–69
Puiforcat Orfèvre, 374
Puyricard, 308
Pyrénées-Cévennes, Auberge, 99–100

Q

Quartz, 371
Quatrehomme, Fromagerie, 285
Quatre Saisons, 359
Queen of Hungary Passage, 201
Quimper Faience, 364

R

Rabelais, 194
Rachinel, 248
Rallye-Péret, Le, 191
Raspail, 209, 213
Régis Chocolatier, 229
René, Chez, 49–51
Renoir, Jean, 206
Reservations, 4

Restaurants, 2–140
- air-conditioned, 420
- alphabetical listing of (with arrondissements), 138–39
- bistros, 3, 416
- brasseries, 3–4, 416
- butter in, 7–8
- coffee in, 8
- credit cards in, 6
- dining hours in, 4–5
- fish, meat, and poultry in, 8
- less expensive, 417
- listed by arrondissements, 139–40
- open in August, 419
- open on Saturday, 418
- open on Sunday, 419
- ordering in, 7
- paying bill and tipping in, 5–6
- prices of, 5
- with private dining rooms or areas, 6, 421
- reservations for, 4
- salt and pepper in, 8
- with sidewalk tables or outdoor terrace, 420
- taking orders until 11 p.m. or later, 418
- water in, 8–9
- wines and liquor in, 9–10

Restaurants, listed by neighborhoods and arrondissements:
- Bastille, République (11th arrondissement), 95–102
- Buttes-Chaumont, Nation (19th and 20th arrondissements), 136–37
- Clichy, Ternes, Wagram, Etoile (17th arrondissement and Clichy), 130–35
- Denfert-Rochereau, Porte d'Orléans, Montparnasse (14th arrondissement), 110–17
- Faubourg, Saint-Germain, Invalides, Ecole Militaire (7th arrondissement), 68–78
- Gare del'Est, Gare du Nord, République (9th and 10th arrondissements), 90–94
- Gare de Lyon, Bastille, Nation, Place d'Italic (12th and 13th arrondissements), 102–9
- Grenelle, Convention (15th arrondissement), 118–21
- Latin Quarter (5th arrondissement), 45–51
- Madeleine, Saint-Lazare, Champs-Elysées, Place dês Ternes (8th arrondissement), 79–90
- Le Marais, Hôtel de Ville, Ile Saint-Louis (4th arrondissement), 36–44
- Opéra, Bourse (2nd arrondissement), 27–31
- Palais-Royal, Les Halles, Tuileries (1st arrondissement), 11–24
- Rambuteau, Temple, Arts et Métiers (3rd arrondissement), 32–34
- Saint-Germain, Luxembourg, Odéon, Montparnasse (6th arrondissement), 51–67
- Trocadéro, Victor-Hugo, Bois de Boulogne (16th arrondissement), 121–30

Reveille, Le, 229
Richard-Lenoir, 210
Richart, 308
Rideau de Paris, Le, 371
Roi du Café, Au, 158
Rollet-Pradier, 171–72
Romantica, 132–33
Roque, Laurence (Le Comptoir des Ouvrages), 365
Rostang, Michel, 134–35
Rotonde, La, 142, 229
Rousseau, Florence, 371
Rubis, Le, 179
Rue de l'Annonciation, 204
Rue des Boulangers, 282
Rue Brillat-Savarin, 282
Rue Brise-Miche, 282
Rue Cler, 200
Rue Curnonsky, 282
Rue des Eaux, 282
Rue de la Faisanderie, 282
Rue des Fermiers, 282–83
Rue des Jeûneurs, 283
Rue Lépic, 204–5
Rue de Levis, 204
Rue des Maraîchers, 283
Rue des Martyrs, 202
Rue des Meuniers, 283
Rue Montorgeuil, 199
Rue des Morillons, 283
Rue Mouffetard, 199–200
Rue Poncelet-Rue Bayen, 204
Rue du Poteau, 205
Rues commerçantes (merchant streets), 198, 199–205
Rue de Seine/Buci, 200
Rungis wholesale market, 201, 206
Runtz, Café, 30–31
Russian foods, specialty shop for, 327
Ryst-Dupeyron, 339

S

Saint-Amour, Le, 163
Saint-Aubin, Le Ferme, 278
Saint-Hubert, La Ferme, 276, 285–86
Saint-Ouen, Puces, 368
Saint-Ouen, René de, 263
Salon B, 371
Salons de thé, 164–75
- *see also* Tea salons

Salt, in restaurants, 8
Samaritaine, La, 364
- Toupary at, 146

Sancerre, 185
Sardines, 330–31
Saturday, restaurants open on, 418
Sauvignon, Au, 185
Savoy, Guy, 135
Sceaux-Robinson, 213
Schmid, 303
Sentou Galerie, 371
Servant le Confiserie d'Auteuil 335
Sidewalk tables, restaurants with, 420
Siècle, 372
Signs, specialty shop for, 355
Silver, specialty shops for, 355, 374
Simon, A., 355
Smith, W. H., 346
Snacks, glossary of, 161
Sommeil d'Orphée, Le, 372
Sonkin, Michel, Galerie, 372
Sousceyrac, A, 100–101

Southwestern foods, specialty shops for, 324, 333
Specialty shops, 315–35
sardines in, 330–31
truffles in, 322–24
see also Kitchen and tableware shops
Specialty shops, listed by neighborhoods and arrondissements:
Gare de l'Est, Oberkampf (10th and 11th arrondissements), 333
Madeleine, le Peletier, Gare du Nord (8th and 9th arrondissements), 328–32
Marais (4th arrondissement), 320
Palais-Royal, Opéra, Tuileries, Les Halles (1st and 2nd arrondissements), 316–19
Pasteur (15th arrondissement), 333
Saint-Germain, Invalides, Eiffel Tower (6th and 7th arrondissement), 324–27
Temple (3rd arrondissement), 319
Trocadéro, Ternes (16th and 17th arrondissements), 334–35
Spices, specialty shop for, 320
Square Trousseau, Le, 107
Steff le Boulanger, 256
Stohrer, 223
Stoves, specialty shop for, 366
Street names with food connections, 282–83
Stübli, Le (La Pâtisserie Viennoise), 234
tea salon at, 175
Sunday, restaurants open on, 419
Supermarkets, 326–27
organic, 214
Suresnes, 340–41
Suze, 152

T

Table d'Aude, La, 66–67
Table de Fès, La, 67
Tableware. *See* Kitchen and tableware shops
Tachon, Chez, 277
Taillevent (restaurant), 90
Taillevent, Les Caves (wine shop), 343
Tan Dinh, 76–77
Tantifla, 319
Tartine, La, 180–81
Tasting menus, 7
Tea Follies, 174
Tea salons, 164–75
Tea salons, listed by neighborhoods and arrondissements:
Concorde, Madeleine, Champs-Elysées, Pigalle (8th and 9th arrondissements), 172–74
Luxembourg, Rue du Bac, Assemblée Nationale (6th and 7th arrondissements), 169–72
Marais (4th arrondissement), 168–69
Palais-Royal, Louvre, Tuileries (1st arrondissement), 165–68
Trocadéro, Ternes, Villers (16th and 17th arrondissements), 175
Tea and Tattered Pages, 350
Territoire, 374
Tetrel Epicerie/Confiserie, 316
Thanksgiving, 320
Théâtres, Bar des, 155
Thurber, James, 181
Thurstrup, Peter (Vins Rares et de Collection), 341
Tiles, specialty shop for, 359
Tipping, 5–6, 143
Toraya, 167
Toupary, 146
Tour de Montlhéry, La (Chez Denise), 23
Tour de Pierre, A la, 187
Trou Gascon, Au, 108–9
Truffles, 322–24
Truffles, specialty shop for, 331
Tuer le ver ("killing the worm"), 185
Tuile à Loup, La, 373

U, V

Uniforms, professional, specialty shop for, 353
U.S. Customs, 278
Valençay, Le, 181–82
Vanves, Puces, 369
Vaudeville, 31
Verger de la Madeleine, Au, 331, 340, 344
Verlet, 167, 316
Verne, Jules, 77
Verrerie Cristallerie d'Arques, 376
Verrerie des Ecoles et du Panthéon, 373
Vieille, Chez la (Chez Adrienne), 24
Viennoise, La Pâtisserie (Le Stübli), 175, 234
Village Saint-Paul, 368
Ville de Rodez, A la, 294
Vineyards, Parisian, 340–41
Vins Rares et de Collection (Peter Thurstrup), 341
Violin d'Ingres, Le, 78

W

Water, in restaurants, 8–9
Willi's Wine Bar, 180
Wine bars, 176–94
L'Ecluse chain, 186–87
Les Grands Boulevards (8th arrondissement), 188
"Meilleur Pot" award and, 181
spiritous breakfasts in, 185
Wine bars, listed by neighborhoods and arrondissements:
Arc de Triomphe (17th arrondissement), 192
Bastille, Nation (11th arrondissement), 189–91
Denfert-Rochereau (14th arrondissement), 191
Les Halles, Palais-Royal (1st and 2nd arrondissements), 178–80
Luxembourg, Saint-Michel, Sèvres-Babylone, Ecole Militaire (5th, 6th, and 7th arrondissements), 182–85
Marais, Ile de la Cité (4th arrondissement), 180–82

Montmartre, Belleville (18th and 20th arrondissements), 192–94
Wine bookshops. *See* Bookshops, food and wine
Wineglasses, 338
Wine and liquor shops, 336–44
Wine-making supplies, specialty shop for, 361
Wines:
Beaujolais, 188
best white, Curnonsky's rating of, 343
at breakfast, 185
from Parisian vineyards, 340–41
in restaurants, 9–10
in wine bars vs. cafés, 176–77

X, Y, Z

Xanadou, 373

Yamazaki, 235

Zola, Emile, 289
Zygomates, Les, 109
Zygotissoire, La, 102

Recipe Index

Following French style, any articles such as *au, la,* or *le* and the words *Chez* and *Caves* appearing before the proper name of an establishment are ignored in the alphabetizing. For example, Le Duc is listed under *D* and Chez René is listed under *R.* Likewise, when the name of an establishment is also the full name of a person, such as André Lerch, the last name (Lerch) is used for alphabetizing.

A

Almond:
bostock, Bernard Ganachaud's, 269
cakes, 232
Alsatian coffee cake, André Lerch's, 236
Ambassade d'Auvergne's stuffed cabbage, 35
Appetizers, *see* First courses
Apples, escarole salad with ham and, 49
Apricot tart, Verlet's, 170
Avenue de Saxe pumpkin seed bread, 211

B

Bacon:
salad of greens, shallots, parsley and, Cartet's, 97
sausages, sauerkraut and, 71
Basil and fresh tomato pasta, Claudio's quick, 133
Beans, white, mutton with, Chez René's, 50
Beef:
rib steak with salt and pepper, Chez la Vieille's, 26
shoulder, braised, Benoit's, 122–23
simmered with vegetables, 106–7
Benoit's braised beef shoulder, 122–23
Benoit's marinated smoked salmon with herbs, 38
Bistro fare:
mutton with white beans, Chez René's, 50
rabbit with mustard, 105
salad of bacon, greens, shallots, and parsley, Cartet's, 97
salad of tuna and curly endive, La Cagouille's, 112
sauerkraut, sausages, and bacon, 71
Bostock Bernard Ganachaud, 269
Bread(s):
brioche, mousseline, Denis Ruffel's, 230
dough, basic, 250
pumpkin seed, Avenue de Saxe, 211
sandwich loaf, Denis Ruffel's, 245
sourdough, Poilâne's natural, 253–55
Brioche:
bostock, Bernard Ganachaud's, 269
mousseline, Denis Ruffel's, 230

C

Cabbage, stuffed, Ambassade d'Auvergne's, 35
La Cagouille's salad of tuna and curly endive, 112
Cakes:
almond, 232
chocolate, Taillevent's, 88
coffee, André Lerch's Alsatian, 236
lemon tea, 225
pear, golden, Le Caméléon's, 56
Le Caméléon's golden pear, 56
Cannelloni, spinach and cheese, Chez la Vieille's Corsican, 25
Cannelloni Chez la Vieille, 25
Capers, oil-cured, 203
Capres à l'huile d'olive, 203
Cartet's salad of bacon, greens, shallots, and parsley, 97
Cheese:
Fontainebleau, 284
goat, marinated in oil with herbs, 290
Gruyère, tossed green salad with, Moissonier's 47
and ham sandwich, grilled, 162
and spinach cannelloni, Chez la Vieille's, 25
Chicken, broiled gratinéed, Chez Maître Paul's, 64–65
Chocolate:
cake, Taillevent's, 88
macaroons, 312
Choucroute, 71
Chou farci Ambassade d'Auvergne, 35

Coffee cake, André Lerch's Alsatian, 236
Cookies:
chocolate macaroons, 312
lavender shortbread, Tea Follies', 166
Cornichons, 321
Corsican spinach and cheese cannelloni, Chez la Vieille's, 25
Il Cortile's fresh fennel with tuna sauce, 14
Côte de boeuf en croûte de sel La Vieille, 26
Crème fraîche, 290
Croque-monsieur, 162

D

Desserts:
almond cakes, 232
apricot tart, Verlet's, 170
bostock, Bernard Ganachaud's, 269
chocolate cake, Taillevent's, 88
chocolate macaroons, 312
Fontainebleau, 284
lavender shortbread cookies, Tea Follies', 166
lemon tea cakes, 225
peach soup, summer, 108
pear cake, golden, Le Caméléon's, 56
raspberry fruit flan, Caves Pétrissans', 184
Le Duc's salmon with basil sauce, 115

E

Endive, curly, salad of tuna and, La Cagouille's, 112
Entrées:
beef shoulder, braised, Benoit's, 122–23
beef simmered with vegetables, 106–7
chicken, broiled gratinéed, Chez Maître Paul's, 64–65
mutton with white beans, Chez René's, 50
rabbit with mustard, 105
rib steak with salt and pepper, Chez la Vieille's, 26
salad of tuna and curly endive, La Cagouille's, 112
salmon with basil sauce, Le Duc's, 115
sauerkraut, sausages, and bacon, 71
spinach and cheese cannelloni, Chez la Vieille's Corsican, 25
stuffed cabbage, Ambassade d'Auvergne's, 35
summer salad from Nice, 159
swordfish with capers, lemon, and cilantro, quick, 203
tuna, warm fresh, with fennel and spicy citrus vinaigrette, 120
Escarole salad with ham and apples, 49
Espadon aux capres, citron et coriandre, 203

F

Fennel:
fresh, with tuna sauce, Il Cortile's, 14
warm fresh tuna with spicy citrus vinaigrette and, 120
Fenouil Il Cortile, sauce au thon, 14
Financiers, 232
First courses:
escarole salad with ham and apples, 49
fennel, fresh, with tuna sauce, Il Cortile's, 14
onion tart, Provençal, 250
salad of bacon, greens, shallots, and parsley, Cartet's, 97
salmon pâté, Julien's, 94
tomato, fresh, and basil pasta, Claudio's quick, 133
tossed green salad with Gruyère, Moissonnier's, 47
Fish:
salmon, marinated smoked, with herbs, Benoit's, 38
salmon with basil sauce, Le Duc's, 115
salmon pâté, Julien's, 94
swordfish with capers, lemon, and cilantro, quick, 203
tuna, salad of curly endive and, La Cagouille's, 112
tuna, in summer salad from Nice, 159
tuna, warm fresh, with fennel and spicy citrus vinaigrette, 120
tuna sauce, fresh fennel with, Il Cortile's, 14
Flan, raspberry fruit, Caves Pétrissans', 184
Flognarde aux framboises Caves Pétrissans, 184
Fondant aux poires Le Caméléon, 56
Fontainebleau, 284
Fromage de chèvre mariné à l'huile d'herbes, 290

G

Bernard Ganachaud's *bostock,* 269
Goat cheese marinated in oil with herbs, 290
Grilled ham and cheese sandwich, 162
Gruyère, tossed green salad with, Moissonier's, 47

H

Ham:
and cheese sandwich, grilled, 162
escarole salad with apples and, 49
Haricot de mouton Chez René, 50

J, K, L

Julien's salmon pâté, 94

Kougelhopf André Lerch, 236

Lapin à la moutarde, 105
Lavender shortbread cookies, Tea Follies', 166
Lemon tea cakes, 225
André Lerch's Alsatian coffee cake, 236

M

Macarons créoles, 312
Macaroons, chocolate, 312
Madeleines, 225

Chez Maître Paul's broiled gratinéed chicken, 64–65
Marinade de thon tiède et fenouil, vinaigrette aux agrumes, 120
Marquise au chocolat Taillevent, 88
Moissonnier's tossed green salad with Gruyère, 47
Mutton with white beans, Chez René's, 50

O, P

Onion tart, Provençal, 249
L'Oulette's field salad with shallots and chives, 101

Pain (basic bread dough), 250
Pain de mie Denis Ruffel, 245
Pain pepitas, 24
Pain Poilâne au levain naturel, 253–55
Paleron braisé à la bourgeoise, 122–23
Pasta, fresh tomato and basil, Claudio's quick, 133
Pasta Romantica, 133
Pâté, Julien's salmon, 94
Pâte de pistache, 89
Peach soup, summer, 108
Pear cake, golden, Le Caméléon's, 56
Caves Pétrissans' raspberry fruit flan, 184
Pickles, tiny tart, 321
Pissaladière, 249
Pistachio:
 paste, 89
 sauce, 89
Poilâne's natural sourdough bread, 253–55
Pot-au-feu, 106–7
Poulette à la crème gratinée Chez Maître Paul, 64–65
Provençal onion tart, 250
Pumpkin seed bread, Avenue de Save, 211

R

Rabbit with mustard, 105
Raspberry fruit flan, Caves Pétrissans', 184
Chez René's mutton with white beans, 50
Rib steak with salt and pepper, Chez la Vieille's, 26
Denis Ruffel's mousseline *brioche,* 230
Denis Ruffel's sandwich loaf, 245

S

Sables à la lavande Tea Follies, 166
Salade au lard Cartet, 97
Salade de lardons de thon La Cagouille, 112
Salade niçoise, 159
Salade verte au Comté Moissonnier, 47
Salade verte aux échalotes et aux ciboulettes L'Oulette, 101
Salads:
 of bacon, greens, shallots, and parsley, Cartet's, 97
 escarole, with ham and apples, 49
 field, with shallots and chives, L'Oulette's, 101
 summer, from Nice, 159
 tossed green, with Gruyère, Moissonnier's, 47
 of tuna and curly endive, La Cagouille's, 112
Salmon:
 with basil sauce, Le Duc's, 115
 marinated smoked, with herbs, Benoit's, 38
 pâté, Julien's, 94
Sandwiches, grilled ham and cheese, 162
Sandwich loaf, Denis Ruffel's, 245
Sauce à la pistache, 89
Sauerkraut, sausages, and bacon, 71
Saumon fumé mariné aux aromates Benoit, 38
Saumon nature sauce basilic Le Duc, 115
Saumon en rillettes Julien, 94
Sausages, sauerkraut, and bacon, 71
Scarole à la julienne de jambon et aux pommes, 49
Shortbread cookies, lavender, Tea Follies', 166
Soup, summer peach, 108
Soupe de peches, 108
Sourdough bread, Poilâne's natural, 253–55
Spinach and cheese cannelloni, Chez La Vieille's Corsican, 25
Stuffed cabbage, Ambassade d'Auvergne's, 35
Summer peach soup, 108
Summer salad from Nice, 159
Swordfish with capers, lemon, and cilantro, quick, 203

T

Taillevent's chocolate cake, 88
Tarte abricot Verlet, 170
Tarts:
 apricot, Verlet's, 170
 onion, Provençal, 250
Tea Follies' lavender shortbread cookies, 166
Tomato, fresh, and basil pasta, Claudio's quick, 133
Tuna:
 salad of curly endive and, La Cagouille's, 112
 sauce, Il Cortile's fresh fennel with, 14
 summer salad from Nice, 159
 warm fresh, with fennel and spicy citrus vinaigrette, 120

V, W

Verlet's apricot tart, 170
Chez la Vieille's Corsican spinach and cheese cannelloni, 25
Chez la Vieille's rib steak with salt and pepper, 26
Vinaigrette, spicy citrus, 120

White beans, mutton with, Chez René's, 50